Lecture Notes in Computer Science   3707

Commenced Publication in 1973
Founding and Former Series Editors:
Gerhard Goos, Juris Hartmanis, and Jan van Leeuwen

Doron A. Peled   Yih-Kuen Tsay (Eds.)

Automated Technology for Verification and Analysis

Third International Symposium, ATVA 2005
Taipei, Taiwan, October 4-7, 2005
Proceedings

 Springer

Volume Editors

Doron A. Peled
University of Warwick
Department of Computer Science
Coventry, CV4 7AL, UK
E-mail: doron@dcs.warwick.ac.uk

Yih-Kuen Tsay
National Taiwan University
Department of Information Management
No. 1, Sec. 4, Roosevelt Rd., Taipei 106, Taiwan (ROC)
E-mail: tsay@im.ntu.edu.tw

Library of Congress Control Number: 2005932760

CR Subject Classification (1998): B.1.2, B.2.2, B.5.2, B.6, B.7.2, C.2, C.3, D.2, D.3, F.3

ISSN   0302-9743
ISBN-10   3-540-29209-8 Springer Berlin Heidelberg New York
ISBN-13   978-3-540-29209-8 Springer Berlin Heidelberg New York

Springer is a part of Springer Science+Business Media

springeronline.com

© Springer-Verlag Berlin Heidelberg 2005
Printed in Germany

Typesetting: Camera-ready by author, data conversion by Scientific Publishing Services, Chennai, India
Printed on acid-free paper   SPIN: 11562948   06/3142   5 4 3 2 1 0

Preface

The Automated Technology for Verification and Analysis (ATVA) international symposium series was initiated in 2003, responding to a growing interest in formal verification spurred by the booming IT industry, particularly hardware design and manufacturing in East Asia. Its purpose is to promote research on automated verification and analysis in the region by providing a forum for interaction between the regional and the international research/industrial communities of the field. ATVA 2005, the third of the ATVA series, was held in Taipei, Taiwan, October 4–7, 2005. The main theme of the symposium encompasses design, complexities, tools, and applications of automated methods for verification and analysis. The symposium was co-located and had a two-day overlap with FORTE 2005, which was held October 2–5, 2005.

We received a total of 95 submissions from 17 countries. Each submission was assigned to three Program Committee members, who were helped by their subreviewers, for rigorous and fair evaluation. The final deliberation by the Program Committee was conducted over email for a duration of about 10 days after nearly all review reports had been collected. In the end, 33 papers were selected for inclusion in the program. ATVA 2005 had three keynote speeches given respectively by Amir Pnueli (joint with FORTE 2005), Zohar Manna, and Wolfgang Thomas. The main symposium was preceded by a tutorial day, consisting of three two-hour lectures given also by the keynote speakers.

ATVA 2005 was supported by National Science Council, Ministry of Education, and Academia Sinica of Taiwan and also by the Center for Information and Electronics Technologies at National Taiwan University and Cadence Design Systems. Their generous sponsorships are gratefully acknowledged. We would like to thank the Program Committee members and their subreviewers for the hard work in evaluating the submissions and selecting the program. We thank the keynote speakers for their extra effort in delivering the tutorials. We thank the Steering Committee for their advice, particularly Farn Wang, who also served as program chair of the two previous ATVA symposia and of FORTE 2005, for providing many valuable suggestions and for being very cooperative with the joint events of ATVA 2005 and FORTE 2005.

For administrative support, we thank the Department of Information Management and the Department of Electrical Engineering at National Taiwan University. In particular, we thank Mr. Yu-Fang Chen for maintaining the conference Web site among many other administrative chores. We thank also the MyReview team for making available a free and convenient submission system.

October 2005   Doron A. Peled and Yih-Kuen Tsay

Organization

Steering Committee

E. Allen Emerson	University of Texas at Austin, USA
Oscar H. Ibarra	University of California, Santa Barbara, USA
Insup Lee	University of Pennsylvania, USA
Doron A. Peled	University of Warwick, UK
Farn Wang	National Taiwan University, Taiwan
Hsu-Chun Yen	National Taiwan University, Taiwan

General Chair

Insup Lee	University of Pennsylvania, USA

Program Committee

Parosh Aziz Abdulla	Uppsala University, Sweden
Rajeev Alur	University of Pennsylvania, USA
Christel Baier	University of Bonn, Germany
Tevfik Bultan	University of California, Santa Barbara, USA
Yung-Pin Cheng	National Taiwan Normal University, Taiwan
Ching-Tsun Chou	Intel, USA
Jin Song Dong	National University of Singapore, Singapore
Susanne Graf	VERIMAG, France
Teruo Higashino	Osaka University, Japan
Pei-Hsin Ho	Synopsys, USA
Gerard J. Holzmann	NASA/JPL, USA
Pao-Ann Hsiung	National Chung Cheng University, Taiwan
Chung-Yang Huang	National Taiwan University, Taiwan
Oscar H. Ibarra	University of California, Santa Barbara, USA
Bengt Jonsson	Uppsala University, Sweden
Orna Kupferman	Hebrew University, Israel
Robert P. Kurshan	Cadence, USA
Shaoying Liu	Hosei University, Japan
Doron A. Peled	University of Warwick, UK (Co-chair)
Scott Smolka	SUNY, Stony Brook, USA
Yih-Kuen Tsay	National Taiwan University, Taiwan (Co-chair)
Moshe Y. Vardi	Rice University, USA
Bow-Yaw Wang	Academia Sinica, Taiwan
Hsu-Chun Yen	National Taiwan University, Taiwan
Tomohiro Yoneda	Tokyo Institute of Technology, Japan
Lenore Zuck	University of Illinois, Chicago, USA

Local Arrangements

Chung-Yang Huang   National Taiwan University, Taiwan
Bow-Yaw Wang   Academia Sinica, Taiwan

Reviewers

Zaher S. Andraus
Ittai Balaban
Constantinos Bartzis
Samik Basu
Frederic Beal
Aysu Betin-Can
Per Bjesse
Bernhard Boigelot
Chunqing Chen
Yean-Ru Chen
Yu-Fang Chen
Johann Deneux
Yifei Dong
Julien Dorso
Ashvin Dsouza
Lars-Henrik Eriksson
Yi Fang
Yuzheng Feng
Martin Fränzle
Xiang Fu
Noriyuki Fujimoto
Jim Grundy
Anubhav Gupta

Kiyoharu Hamaguchi
Ziyad Hanna
Kunihiko Hiraishi
Chun-Hsian Huang
Geng-Dian Huang
Marcin Jurdzinski
Andreas Kassler
Tomoya Kitani
Barbara König
Gregor von Laszewksi
Martin Leucker
Yuan Fang Li
Shang-Wei Lin
Annie Liu
Shiyong Lu
Rupak Majumdar
Oded Maler
In-Ho Moon
Akio Nakata
Andrei Paun
Andreas Podelski
Hongyang Qu
Jakob Rehof

Kai Salomaa
Pierluigi San Pietro
Hiroyuki Seki
Oleg Sokolsky
Martin Steffen
Scott Stoller
Jun Sun
Ashutosh Trivedi
Ming-Hsien Tsai
Tatsuhiro Tsuchiya
Takaaki Umedu
Björn Victor
Dirk Walther
Dong Wang
Heike Wehrheim
Frank Wolter
Keh-Ren Wu
Ping Yang
Pei Ye
Wang Yi
Fang Yu
Gaoyan Xie

Sponsoring Institutions

National Science Council, Taiwan (ROC)
Ministry of Education, Taiwan
Institute of Information Science, Academia Sinica, Taiwan
National Taiwan University (NTU), Taiwan
Center for Information and Electronics Technologies, NTU, Taiwan
Department of Information Management, NTU, Taiwan
Department of Electrical Engineering, NTU, Taiwan
Cadence Design Systems

Table of Contents

Keynote Speeches

Model Checking

Combined Methods

Timed, Embedded, and Hybrid Systems (I)

Abstraction and Reduction Techniques

Decidability and Complexity

Established Formalisms and Standards

Compositional Verification and Games

Timed, Embedded, and Hybrid Systems (II)

Protocols Analysis, Case Studies, and Tools

Infinite-State and Parameterized Systems

Ranking Abstraction as a Companion to Predicate Abstraction[*],[**]

Amir Pnueli[1,2]

[1] New York University, New York
amir@cs.nyu.edu
[2] Weizmann Institute of Science

Abstract. Predicate abstraction has become one of the most successful methodologies for proving safety properties of programs. Unfortunately, it cannot be used for verifying all liveness properties. In order to handle liveness properties, we introduce the method of *ranking abstraction*. This method augments the analyzed system by a "progress monitor" which observes whether a given ranking function decreases or increases at any step of the program. The fact that the ranking function ranges over a well-founded domain is expressed by a *compassion* (strong fairness) requirement, which states that a function over a well-founded domain cannot decrease infinitely many times without also increasing infinitely many times. In analogy to predicate abstraction which uses a predicate base $\mathcal{P} = \{P_1, \ldots, P_m\}$ consisting of a set of predicates, we augment the program with a *ranking core* $\Delta = \{\delta_1, \ldots, \delta_n\}$ consisting of several ranking components. The augmented system is then abstracted using standard predicate abstraction, but retaining all the compassion requirements. The abstracted augmented system is then model checked for an arbitrary LTL property. The ranking abstraction method is shown to be sound and (relatively) complete for proving all LTL properties, including safety and liveness.

In the presented talk we focus on the strong analogy between predicate abstraction and ranking abstraction. Predicate abstraction can be viewed as a process which determines the best inductive invariant which can be formed as a boolean combination of the predicate base. In a similar way, ranking abstraction can be viewed as a search for the best well-founded global ranking function which can be formed as a lexicographic combination of the ranking components included in the ranking core Δ. In the talk, we present an algorithm for an explicit construction of such a global ranking function. Another important element of the predicate abstraction methodology is that of *abstraction refinement* by which, a coarse abstraction can be refined by analyzing a spurious counterexample. We show that ranking abstraction also possesses an analogous refinement process. We discuss how a spurious counter example can lead to a refinement of either the current predicate base or ranking core.

The talk is based on results obtained through joint research with I. Balaban, Y. Kesten, and L.D. Zuck.

---

[*] The full version of this paper is included in the proceedings of FORTE'05.
[**] This research was supported in part by NSF grant CCR-0205571, ONR grant N00014-99-1-0131, and Israel Science Foundation grant 106/02-1.

Termination and Invariance Analysis of Loops

Aaron Bradley and Zohar Manna

Computer Science Department, Stanford University

Abstract. Deductive verification aims to prove deep properties about programs. The classic Floyd-Hoare-style approach to verifying sequential programs reduces program validity queries to first-order validity queries via verification conditions. Proving that a program is totally correct requires proving the safety aspect with invariants and the progress aspect with invariants and ranking functions. Where do the invariants and ranking functions come from?

A verifying compiler that reads program annotations enables the programmer to write desired properties as assertions. Unfortunately, verifying a safety property requires strengthening it to an inductive assertion, while proving termination requires finding ranking functions. The strengthening process often involves writing many tedious facts, while ranking functions are not always intuitive. In practice, programmers do not want or are unable to invent inductive assertions and ranking functions. Instead, the ideal verifying compiler strengthens the given assertions with facts learned through static analysis. Invariant generators are a class of static analyzers that automatically synthesize inductive invariants. Ranking function generators automatically synthesize ranking functions, sometimes with supporting invariants. Together, they reduce the burden on the programmer by automatically learning facts about programs.

In this talk, we discuss our approach to invariant and ranking function generation. A constraint-based method labels program points with parameterized expressions, which encode the shape of the desired inductive assertions or ranking functions. For example, the shape of an inductive invariant could be an inequality between affine combinations of program variables, while the shape of a ranking function could be an affine combination of program variables. It then generates a set of parameterized verification conditions and solves for the parameter values that make them valid. Instantiating the parameterized expressions with these values results in a set of inductive assertions or ranking functions. We discuss recent work for analyzing termination of programs that manipulate variables via affine expressions. We also discuss a constraint-based analysis for programs with integer division and modulo operators. Finally, we present experimental evidence indicating that invariant and ranking function generation is a powerful technique for scaling deductive verification to large programs.

D.A. Peled and Y.-K. Tsay (Eds.): ATVA 2005, LNCS 3707, p. 2, 2005.
© Springer-Verlag Berlin Heidelberg 2005

Some Perspectives of Infinite-State Verification

Wolfgang Thomas

RWTH Aachen, Lehrstuhl Informatik 7, 52056 Aachen, Germany
thomas@informatik.rwth-aachen.de

Abstract. We report on recent progress in the study of infinite transition systems for which interesting properties (like reachability of designated states) can be checked algorithmically. Two methods for the generation of such models are discussed: the construction from simpler models via operations like unfolding and synchronized product, and the internal representation of state spaces by regular sets of words or trees.

1 Introduction

The method of model-checking has developed largely in the domain of finite system models, and its success in industrial applications is built on highly efficient data structures for system representation. Over infinite models, the situation is different, and for practical applications the field is still in its beginnings. Even simple properties may be undecidable over infinite state spaces, and thus a careful preparatory analysis is necessary in order to determine the possible range of fully automatic verification.

The purpose of the present short survey is to report on some techniques which yield classes of infinite models such that the model-checking problem is decidable for interesting properties. Our presentation is far from complete; it is biased towards results which were obtained in the author's research group and collaborations with other groups (mostly that of D. Caucal, Rennes). We focus on system models in the form of edge-labelled transition graphs; thus a central aspect is the investigation of structural properties of infinite graphs. An alternative and equally fundamental approach for introducing infinite models, which is not discussed in this paper, is to extend finite transition graphs by infinite data structures, for example over the natural or real numbers (as in timed systems).

Transition graphs are considered in the format $G = (V, (E_a)_{a \in \Sigma})$ where V is the set of states (vertices) and where E_a (for a symbol a from a finite alphabet Σ) is the set of a-labelled edges. We write E for the union of the E_a. State-properties may be introduced by subsets V_a of V, where a is from a second label alphabet Γ.

The logics we consider allow to express the reachability relation E^*, the reflexive transitive closure of E, since reachability is the most fundamental property arising in verification. A prominent logic of this kind is monadic second-order logic MSO. It encompasses most standard temporal logics. On the other end,

D.A. Peled and Y.-K. Tsay (Eds.): ATVA 2005, LNCS 3707, pp. 3–10, 2005.

as a kind of minimal logic in this context, we consider FO(R) ("first-order logic with reachability"), the extension of first-order logic by a relation symbol for E^*.

We shall address two methods for constructing infinite transition graphs where model-checking (with respect to MSO or FO(R)) is decidable. First we review the effect of fundamental model constructions – namely, interpretation, unfolding, and synchronized product – on the existence of model-checking procedures. Secondly, we discuss model-checking as based on "regular" internal representations of infinite transition graphs, using finite automata over strings or trees, respectively.

2   Operations on Graphs

2.1   Interpretations

Rabin's Tree Theorem [19] states that the MSO-theory of the infinite binary tree T_2 is decidable (or in other terminology: that model-checking the binary tree with respect to MSO-properties is decidable). We can view T_2 as a graph $(\{1,2\}^*, S_1, S_2)$, where $\{1,2\}^*$ is the set of vertices and S_1, S_2 the successor relations with $S_i = \{(v, vi) \mid v \in \{1,2\}^*\}$. Many other theories were shown decidable (already in [19]) using interpretations in the tree T_2. To show that the model-checking problem for a structure S with respect to formulas of a logic L is decidable one proceeds as follows: One gives an MSO-description of S within the binary tree T_2, and using this one provides a translation of L-formulas φ into MSO-formulas φ' such that $S \models \varphi$ iff $T_2 \models \varphi'$. Taking $L = $ MSO, we see that an MSO-interpretation (i.e., a model description using MSO-formulas) preserves decidability of model-checking with respect to MSO-formulas.

As a simple example of interpretation consider the n-ary branching tree T_n (for $n > 2$), with vertices in the set $\{1, \ldots, n\}^*$ rather than $\{1, 2\}^*$ as for T_2. We may represent the vertex $i_1 \ldots i_r$ of T_n by $1^{i_1}2 \ldots 1^{i_r}2$ in T_2. It is easy to give an MSO-definition of the range of this coding in T_2 and to supply the translation $\varphi \mapsto \varphi'$ as above. As a second example, consider a pushdown automaton A with stack alphabet $\{1, \ldots, k\}$ and states $q_1, \ldots, q_m$. Let $G_A = (V_A, E_A)$ be its configuration graph; here V_A consists of A-configurations $(q_j, i_1 \ldots i_r)$ (with state q_j and stack content $i_1 \ldots i_r$, reading i_1 as top symbol), and we restrict to those configurations which are reachable from the initial one (say $(q_1, 1)$). The edge relation E_A is the one-step transition relation of A between configurations. Choosing $n = \max(k, m)$, we can exhibit an MSO-interpretation of G_A in T_n: Just represent configuration $(q_j, i_1 \ldots i_r)$ by the vertex $i_r \ldots i_1 j$ of T_n. Note that then the A-steps lead to local moves in T_n, from one T_n-vertex to another, e.g. in a push step from vertex $i_r \ldots i_1 j$ to a vertex $i_r \ldots i_1 i_0 j'$. These moves are easily definable in MSO, and reachability (from the initial vertex 11) as well. Due to this interpretation, we obtain the fundamental result of Muller and Schupp ([18]): *For the configuration graph of a pushdown automaton, checking MSO-properties is decidable.*

It is known that the ε-closures of the pushdown transition graphs capture precisely those graphs which are MSO-interpretable in T_2 (or equivalently in T_n);

see Section 3 below. We do not consider here a slightly more general version of MSO-interpretation, the "MSO-definable transduction" in the sense of Courcelle [7]; such a transduction from S to T involves a description of S in a k-fold copy of T rather than T itself.

2.2   Unfoldings

In the previous section we explained how to generate a model "within" a given one, via defining formulas. A more "expansive" way of model construction is the unfolding of a graph $(V, (E_a)_{a \in \Sigma})$ from a given vertex v_0, yielding a tree $T_G(v_0) = (V', (E'_a)_{a \in \Sigma})$: V' consists of the vertices $v_0 a_1 v_1 \ldots a_r v_r$ with $(v_{i-1}, v_i) \in E_{a_i}$, and E'_a contains the pairs $(v_0 a_1 v_1 \ldots a_r v_r, v_0 a_1 v_1 \ldots a_r v_r a v)$ with $(v_r, v) \in E_a$. The unfolding operation has no effect in bisimulation invariant logics, but is highly nontrivial for MSO. Consider, for example, the singleton graph G_0 over $\{v_0\}$ with a 1-labelled and a 2-labelled edge from v_0 to v_0. Its unfolding is the infinite binary tree. While checking MSO-formulas over G_0 is trivial, this is quite difficult over T_2. A powerful result due to Courcelle and Walukiewicz [8] says: *If model-checking MSO-formulas over G is decidable and v_0 is an MSO-definable vertex of G, then model-checking MSO-formulas over $T_G(v_0)$ is decidable.* The result holds also for a slightly more general construction ("tree iteration") which can also be applied to relational structures other than graphs (see [1,24]).

MSO-interpretations and unfoldings are two operations which preserve decidability of MSO model-checking. Caucal [4] studied the structures generated by applying both operations, alternating between unfoldings and interpretations. (In [4] a more special type of interpretation was used; the link to MSO was supplied by Carayol and Wöhrle in [9]; for a detailed treatment see [25].) Starting with the class of finite graphs, one first obtains the regular infinite trees by unfoldings, then a class of graphs containing all pushdown transition graphs by interpretations, then the algebraic trees by unfoldings, and so on. The process yields many more complicated structures, all with a decidable MSO-theory. It is known that this "Caucal hierarchy" of graphs and trees is strict and quite rich, but we do not really have an overview which structures belong to it. An introduction with some examples is given in [23]. We also know of a few infinite graphs outside the Caucal hierarchy which still have a decidable MSO-theory (see [9]).

A related problem is to find more extensive classes of transition graphs for which the unfolding operation also preserves decidability of model-checking, but now for suitably chosen weaker logics than MSO. Note that MSO covers more than reachability properties (for example, one can express the existence of global colorings satisfying local constraints) and thus is more expressive than needed for many practical purposes.

2.3   Products

Products of transition graphs with different synchronization constraints are ubiquitous in system modelling, in particular for representing distributed systems.

While this construction causes fundamental complexity problems when the components are finite-state ("state space explosion"), undecidability may arise over infinite state spaces.

As an example, consider the successor structure $(\mathbb{N}, S)$ over the natural numbers with $S = \{(i, i+1) | i \in \mathbb{N}\}$, whose MSO-theory is known to be decidable (Büchi's Theorem; see [21]). The asynchronous product of $(\mathbb{N}, S)$ with itself is the structure $(\mathbb{N} \times \mathbb{N}, E)$ where $((i, j), (k, l)) \in E$ iff either $i = k$ and $l = j + 1$, or $j = l$ and $k = i + 1$. This is the infinite grid, where the model-checking problem with respect to MSO-properties is undecidable (see e.g. [21]). Thus, if product formation should preserve decidability of model-checking, then MSO is too strong.

If products should preserve decidability of model-checking, the task is to compose model-checking algorithms for the component structures to a corresponding algorithm for the product. Such composition results have a long tradition in logic, starting with the work of Feferman and Vaught [11] in first-order model theory. The situation is more complicated when second-order aspects enter (as involved in reachability properties).

Builing on the approach of [11], a preservation result on decidability of model-checking is shown in [26] for the logic FO(R) (first-order logic with reachability). In each component graph G_i $(1 \leq i \leq n)$, synchronizing and local actions are distinguished by a partition of the label alphabet Σ_i. Transitions may be executed locally via local labels, or else via a "synchronization constraint" $(c_1, \ldots, c_n)$ where each c_i is either a synchronizing label or ε. A corresponding execution leaves the states identical in the components with entry ε and involves a c_i-transition for each of the other components G_i. We speak of a finitely synchronized product if for each constraint $(c_1, \ldots, c_n)$ and each $c_i \neq \varepsilon$, only from finitely many vertices in G_i a c_i-labelled transition exists. This assumption applies to products of infinite systems where synchronization can only be realized within finite parts of the components. In [26], the following is shown: *If the graphs $G_1, \ldots, G_n$ have a decidable model-checking problem with respect to FO(R)-specifications, then this holds also for any finitely synchronized product of the G_i.*

This result is sharp in several ways. First, the assumption on finite synchronization cannot be weakened. If there is just one component which shares infinitely many synchronized transitions, the result fails. Also it is not possible to generalize the logic in any essential way; for example, the result fails if the reachability operator is restricted to regular sets of label sequences or if universal path quantification enters (see [26,20]).

In all the decidability results mentioned above, very high lower bounds for the complexity are known. One of the main tasks in the field is to single out cases which are both practically significant and at the same time allow more efficient procedures than those derived from the first decidability proofs.

3   Regular Presentations

Automata provide a natural framework for finite representations of infinite structures. For graphs (V, E), the idea is to represent the vertex set as a regular language and the edge set by some sort of "regular relation". Since there are many versions of finite-state transducers, there are several options for the latter; for an introduction see e.g. [22]. One choice, leading to the "automatic structures", is based on the "automatic" (or "synchronized rational") relations. Here an edge relation E is defined by an automaton which processes a given word pair (u, v) synchronously in both components letter by letter (and one assumes that, if necessary, a dummy letter is used to extend the shorter word to the same length as the longer word). An automatic structure has a decidable first-order theory (see [2]); however, already the point-to-point-reachability problem ("Given vertices u, v, is there a path from u to v?") may be undecidable for an automatic structure. As an example, one can use the transition graph U of a universal Turing machine: Its configuration space is a regular language, and the one-step relation between configurations is clearly automatic. The halting problem for Turing machines can be reduced to the point-to-point reachability problem over U.

The one-step transition relation over Turing machine configurations is an in-fix rewriting relation. Restricting to prefix rewriting, as it occurs in pushdown transition graphs, the reachability problem becomes decidable. This follows already from classical work of Büchi [3] on his "regular canonical systems". If for the graph $G = (V, (E_a)_{a \in \Sigma})$ the vertex set is presented as a regular language, and the edge relations E_a by finite prefix-rewriting systems, then G has a decidable MSO-theory; this is shown by an interpretation in T_2 as in Section 2.1 above. As observed by Caucal [5], the prefix-rewriting rules can even be generalized to the form $U_1 \to U_2$ for regular sets U_1, U_2, meaning that a prefix $u_1 \in U_1$ can be replaced by any $u_2 \in U_2$. The "prefix-recognizable" graphs arising this way coincide with those which can be obtained from the binary tree T_2 by an MSO-interpretation (see, for example, [15]).

The idea of prefix-rewriting underlies many decidability results in infinite-state model-checking. It can be generalized in several ways while keeping (at least some of) the mentioned decidability properties. We present two such generalizations, the higher-order pushdown systems, and the ground tree rewriting graphs.

3.1 Higher-Order Pushdown Systems

Higher-order pushdown automata are a classical model of computation which arises in the evaluation of higher-order recursion schemes (see [10,14]). The idea is to generalize the stack symbols of a pushdown automaton to be again of stack format, and so on iteratively, which yields stacks of stacks of stacks etc. If k levels of stacks occur, we speak of a level-k pushdown automaton. For example, in a transition of a level-2 pushdown automaton, one can access the topmost symbol of the topmost stack, can modify the topmost stack in the usual way, or can execute global operations on the topmost stack, by deleting it or adding a copy of it as new topmost stack.

The configuration graphs of higher-order pushdown automata, called higher-order pushdown graphs, are of bounded out-degree (since only finitely many successor configurations can be reached directly from a given one). When we consider the ε-closure, i.e. we allow ε-moves and compress sequences of ε-moves into a single transition, then transition graphs of infinite degree are generated. Surprisingly, the hierarchy of these transition graphs (for increasing level k) coincides with the Caucal hierarchy of graphs mentioned in Section 2.2: In [9] (and with full proof in [25]) it is shown that *a graph can be generated from finite graphs by k applications of unfolding and MSO-interpretation iff it is the transition graph of the ε-closure of a level-k pushdown automaton*. Of course, it follows that model-checking a higher-order pushdown graph with respect to MSO-properties is decidable.

3.2   Ground Term Rewriting Graphs

The transition graphs generated by higher-order pushdown automata are still tightly connected with infinite trees – in fact, they can be generated for a given level k from a single tree structure via MSO-interpretations. So these graphs are too restricted for many purposes of verification (excepting applications on the implementation of recursion).

A more flexible kind of model is generated when the idea of prefix-rewriting is generalized in a different direction, proceeding from word rewriting to tree rewriting (which we identify here with term rewriting). Instead of modifying the prefix of a word by applying a prefix-rewriting rule, we may rewrite a subtree of a given tree, precisely as it is done in ground term rewriting. A ground term rewriting graph (GTRG) has a vertex set V which is given by a regular tree language, and each edge relation E_a is defined by a finite ground term rewriting system.

A simple example of a GTRG is the infinite grid: It is generated from the tree $f(c, d)$ by applying the rules $c \to g(c)$ and $d \to g(d)$, which produces the trees $f(g^i(c), g^j(d))$ in one-to-one correspondence with the elements (i, j) of $\mathbb{N} \times \mathbb{N}$. Thus over GTRG's, model-checking MSO-properties is in general undecidable.

In work of C. Löding (see [16,17]), the structural and logical properties of GTRG's are investigated. As it turns out, *the model-checking problem over GTRG's is decidable for a logic which covers reachability and even recurrent reachability.* The atomic formulas of this logic refer to regular state properties (specified by finite tree automata), and the connectives are, besides the boolean ones, EX_a, EF, and EGF (in CTL-like notation). This result is optimal in the sense that adding universal quantification (for example, when adjoining the operator AF) leads to undecidability of the model-checking problem. On the other hand, it is possible – as for pushdown graphs – to generalize the rewriting rules without affecting the decidability results: Instead of allowing replacement of a single subtree by another one, one may use rules of the form $T \to T'$ for regular tree languages T, T', meaning that an occurrence of subterm $t \in T$ can be replaced by any $t' \in T'$. More results, also connecting GTRG's with asynchronous products of pushdown graphs, are shown in [6].

4   Conclusion

The above-mentioned results are as yet mosaic pieces of a picture which hopefully will grow into an esthetically pleasing and practically useful algorithmic theory of infinite models (which the author would call "algorithmic model theory"). It seems that the two approaches mentioned – global model construction and local descriptions based on automata theoretic concepts – can be developed much further and also be combined in new ways.

There is, of course, a different approach for infinite-state model-checking, based on the admission of infinite data structures (like counters over the natural numbers, or addition and inequalities over the real numbers). An interesting direction of current work aims at establishing bridges between that approach and the results treated in the present paper. As an example, we mention the recent paper [13] where transition graphs arising from monotonic counters are discussed.

A dual track of research is to destillate efficient model-checking procedures from the general decidability results mentioned above, by restricting both the models and the logics to simple but relevant cases.

References

1. D. Berwanger, A. Blumensath, The monadic theory of tree-like structures, in: [12], 285-302.
2. A. Blumensath, E. Grädel, Automatic structures, in: *Proc. 15th LICS*, IEEE Comput. Soc. Press 2000, 51-62.
3. J.R. Büchi, Regular canonical systems, *Z. Math. Logik Grundl. Math.* 6 (1964), 91-111.
4. D. Caucal, On infinite terms having a decidable theory, in: *Proc. 27th MFCS*, Springer LNCS 2420 (2002), 265-176.
5. D. Caucal: On infinite transition graphs having a decidable monadic theory., *Theor. Comput. Sci.* 290 (2003), 79-115.
6. Th. Colcombet, On families of graphs having a decidable first order theory with reachability, in: *Proc. 29th ICALP*, Springer LNCS 2380 (2002), 98-109.
7. B. Courcelle, Monadic second-order graph transductions: a survey, *Theor. Comput. Sci.* 126 (1994), 53-75.
8. B. Courcelle, I. Walukiewicz, Monadic second-order logic, graph coverings and unfoldings of transition systems, *Ann. Pure Appl. Logic* 92 (1998), 51-65.
9. A. Carayol, S. Wöhrle, The Caucal hierarchy of infinite graphs in terms of logic and higher-order pushdown automata, in: *Proc. 23rd FSTTCS*, Springer LNCS 2914 (2003), 112-123.
10. W. Damm, A. Goerdt, An automata theoretical characterization of the OI-hierarchy, *Inf. Contr.* 71 (1986), 1-32.
11. S. Feferman, R. Vaught, The first-order properties of products of algebraic systems, *Fund. Math.* 47 (1959), 57-103.
12. E. Grädel, W. Thomas, Th. Wilke (Eds.), *Automata, Logics, and Infinite Games*, Springer LNCS 2500 (2002).
13. W. Karianto, Adding monotonic counters to automata and transition graphs, *Proc. 9th Conf. on Developments in Language Theory*, Springer LNCS 3572 (2005), 308-319.
14. T. Knapik, D. Niwinski, P. Urzyczyn, Higher-order pushdown trees are easy, in: *Proc. 5th FOSSACS*. Springer LNCS 2303 (2002), 205-222.
15. M. Leucker, Prefix recognizable graphs and monadic logic, in: [12], 263-284.

16. C. Löding, *Infinite Graphs Generated by Tree Rewriting*, Dissertation, RWTH Aachen 2002.
17. C. Löding, Reachability problems on regular ground-tree rewriting graphs, *Theory of Computing Systems* (to appear).
18. D. Muller, P. Schupp, The theory of ends, pushdown automata, and second-order logic, *Theor. Comput. Sci.* 37 (1985), 51-75.
19. M.O. Rabin, Decidability of second-order theories and automata on infinite trees, *Trans. Amer. Math. Soc.* 141 (1969), 1-35.
20. A. Rabinovich, On compositionality and its limitations, *ACM Trans. on Computational Logic* (to appear).
21. W. Thomas, Automata on infinite objects, in: *Handbook of Theoretical Computer Science, Vol. B* (J.v. Leeuwen, Ed.), Elsevier, Amsterdam 1990, 133-191.
22. W. Thomas, A short introduction to infinite automata, in: *Proc. 5th Conf. on Developments in Language Theory* Springer LNCS 2295, 130-144
23. W. Thomas, Constructing infinite graphs with a decidable MSO-theory, in: *Proc. 28th MFCS*, Springer LNCS 2747 (2003), 113-124.
24. I. Walukiewicz, Monadic second-order logic on tree-like structures, *Theor. Comput. Sci.* 275 (2002), 311-346.
25. S. Wöhrle, *Decision Problems over Infinite Graphs: Higher-Order Pushdown Systems and Synchronized Products*, Dissertation, RWTH Aachen 2005.
26. S. Wöhrle, W. Thomas, Model checking synchronized products of infinite transition systems, in: *Proc. 19th LICS*, IEEE Comp. Soc. 2004, 2-11.

Verifying Very Large Industrial Circuits Using 100 Processes and Beyond

Limor Fix[2], Orna Grumberg[1], Amnon Heyman[3], Tamir Heyman[2],
and Assaf Schuster[1]

[1] Computer Science Department, Technion, Haifa, Israel
[2] Logic and Validation Technology, Intel Corporation, Haifa, Israel
[3] Phonedo, Herzliya, Israel

Abstract. Recent advances in scheduling and networking have cleared the way for efficient exploitation of large-scale distributed computing platforms, such as computational grids and huge clusters. Such infrastructures hold great promise for the highly resource-demanding task of verifying and checking large models, given that model checkers would be designed with a high degree of scalability and flexibility in mind.

In this paper we focus on the mechanisms required to execute a high-performance, distributed, symbolic model checker on top of a large-scale distributed environment. We develop a hybrid algorithm for slicing the state space and dynamically distribute the work among the worker processes. We show that the new approach is faster, more effective, and thus much more scalable than previous slicing algorithms. We then present a checkpoint-restart module that has very low overhead. This module can be used to combat failures which become probable with the size of the computing platform. However, checkpoint-restart is even more handy for the scheduling system: it can be used to avoid reserving large numbers of workers, thus making the distributed computation work-efficient. Finally, we discuss for the first time the effect of reorder on the distributed model checker and show how the distributed system performs more efficient reordering than the sequential one.

We implemented our contributions on a network of 200 processors, using a distributed scalable scheme that employs a high-performance industrial model checker from Intel. Our results show that the system was able to verify real-life models much larger than was previously possible.

1   Introduction

This paper presents several novel techniques to enhance distributed reachability computation. The techniques enable effective use of a network of 100 computers for the verification of large industrial hardware designs that could not be verified by previously available tools.

For a long time the state explosion problem has been the showstopper of BDD-based (symbolic) model checking [3]: The BDD structures simply cannot squeeze into the RAM available to a single computer. SAT-based model checking [2] can find errors in very large systems, but is limited when used for

D.A. Peled and Y.-K. Tsay (Eds.): ATVA 2005, LNCS 3707, pp. 11–25, 2005.

verification [9]. In fact, BDD-based model checking is usually superior, when verification is required. Larger systems usually have longer diameters and therefore SAT-based bounded model checking can cover smaller parts of their state space.

In recent years, several distributed BDD-based reachability algorithms have been introduced [8,7,6] for networks of communicating computers with distributed memory. Reachability is an important problem because model checking of all temporal safety properties can be reduced to it [1]. Distributed reachability exploits the memory modules and the computation power of a heterogeneous cluster of computers, where more and more machines can be employed on demand. The collective storage offered by the cluster RAM is utilized in a memory- and work-efficient manner, essentially operating as a yet another layer in the memory hierarchy.

However, if these algorithms are to be scaled for very large models that require hundreds of computers, then several enhancements are required. First, fast and effective slicing is needed, in order to accommodate frequent splits in the memory content of overflowed computers. Second, a checkpoint/restart mechanism is needed to recover from a single computer failure and in order to better utilize clusters of computers when memory requirements vary significantly during computation. Finally, dynamic BDD variable reordering should be adapted to work well with the distributed algorithm.

Our work provides solutions for all of these requirements. We developed a *hybrid* algorithm for slicing very large sets quickly and effectively. The user provides the algorithm with measures for an effective slicer, and the algorithm searches for an adequate one. The algorithm is designed to spend as little time as possible in finding an adequate slicer, not necessarily the best one. It starts with a fast estimated computation. If no adequate slicer is found, it gradually applies more precise computations. We compare our hybrid algorithm with the fast estimating algorithm Est [5]. We show that our algorithm produces far fewer duplications. We also compare our algorithm to the exhaustive algorithm Exh [8], which is better than or equal to other exhaustive algorithms [4,11,10]. We show that it is faster than Exh, and, in fact, the difference in run time increases when the size of the BDD or the size of its support increase.

We also propose a non-coordinated checkpoint/restart mechanism as part of the distributed reachability computation. In the distributed reachability analysis [8], each worker *owns* a subset of the state space and iteratively computes the set of reachable states within its ownership. It may also find states owned by others workers, which it sends to them. Likewise, it receives owned states, found by others. The checkpoint mechanism consists of occasionally freezes by each worker. The worker stores its configuration, including the set of states it owns, the set of states computed so far, the iteration number, and the BDD variable ordering. Restart is performed by finding a set of configurations, all taken from the same iteration, whose ownership covers the whole state space. A set of new free workers is then initialized with these configurations and resumes the computation.

The checkpoint/restart mechanism is particularly useful when running on a non-dedicated network. Two tasks running on such a network may reach their memory peak at the same time, thus blocking each other. It then might be necessary to freeze one of them and enable the other to continue. When the memory requirement of the active task decreases, the frozen one can be resumed. In addition, when memory requirements vary significantly during computation, an effective utilization will require clusters of varying sizes. Changing the cluster size is done by freezing the active workers and restarting them on a different cluster with an appropriate size.

In order to maintain effective dynamic reordering, we propose a distributed paradigm to control the points at which dynamic variable reordering is performed. In sequential computation, reorder is invoked after garbage collection, if the BDD size exceeds a certain threshold. The distributed computation applies the same policy. In addition, for each worker, it uses two new controlling operations: enforcing reorder when an overflow occurs; and updating the threshold following an action that reduces the BDD size. Reorder when overflow occurs may save unnecessary splits.

Another improvement to the BDD package enforces timeout on BDD operations that do not terminate within a reasonable time. Usually this is due to the size of their operands. We then split the BDDs and resume the operations on two smaller BDDs.

We demonstrated the utility of our scheme by implementing it as a large-scale distributed engine that consists of more than 100 computers and uses a high-performance model checker. We ran our experiments on clusters composed of ordinary PCs. Our results show that the system can *verify* (apply full reachability to) much larger models than could previously be verified. In addition, our results show that in some cases, when the distributed algorithm needs more processes than available, it still reaches a further step than SAT-base bounded model checking does.

In summary, the contributions of the paper are:

- Fast and effective slicing with small memory overhead.
- A checkpoint/restart mechanism.
- An enhanced BDD package: adaptive dynamic variable reorder and timeout on BDD operations.
- Orthogonality to high-performance model checking: all features of sequential model checking remain effective in the distributed framework.

All of the above allows the *verification* of large industrial components.

The rest of the paper is organized as follows. Section 2 presents a new algorithm for fast and effective slicing of very large sets. Sections 3 describes the checkpoint/restart mechanism. Finally, Section 4 presents our distributed reachability analysis, including a paradigm for dynamic variable reordering, and presents our experimental results on verification of large industrial designs.

2   Hybrid Algorithm for Slicing Very Large Sets

In this section we present a new algorithm for slicing very large sets quickly and effectively. The approach makes use of user-supplied measures of effectiveness: the algorithm simply searches for a slicer that meets the measures. The algorithm attempts to reduce the time spent finding a sufficiently effective slicer; it does not necessarily search for the best one. Rather than checking all variables in the support of the set to be sliced, as was done previously, the proposed algorithm makes use of the abundance of good slicers in the support to pick one from a randomly selected sample.

The algorithm gets as its input a set of states as a characteristic function f and returns a variable v called slicer, which slices f into two subsets: $f \wedge v$ and $f \wedge \overline{v}$. Such slicing is *effective* if two requirements are fulfilled. First, the size of each of the subsets is smaller than the size of f itself: $\frac{\max |f \wedge v|, |f \wedge \overline{v}|}{|f|} < \delta_1$. Second, the amount of *duplication* is not too big: $\frac{|f \wedge v| + |f \wedge \overline{v}|}{|f|} < \delta_2$. The minimum reduction factor and the maximum duplication factor δ_1, δ_2 are provided by the user, or by the higher-level procedure calling the algorithm.

The algorithm proceeds through a sequence of three phases. In each consecutive phase the algorithm spends more time trying to find an effective slicer. Once an effective slicer is found the algorithm declares success and terminates. After three unsuccessful phases the algorithm returns the best slicer it has found so far.

In order to test the effectiveness of a candidate slicer, the BDDs of $f \wedge v$ and $f \wedge \overline{v}$ must be built and their relative sizes measured. This consumes time and memory. In contrast, one can estimate the sizes of the slices in a single scan of the BDD of f without creating a new BDD [12]. Estimation is a lot faster than precise calculation and requires far fewer resources.

In the first phase the algorithm employs the method **Est** [5] to search for an effective slicer. This method initially computes an estimate of the size of $f \wedge v$ and $f \wedge \overline{v}$, for each variable v in the support of f. Then it selects as a slicer, among all other variables, the variable v for which the maximum estimates for $f \wedge v$ and $f \wedge \overline{v}$ is minimal. Next, a precise calculation is used to determine whether v is an effective slicer. If v is found to be effective, the algorithm terminates; otherwise it proceeds to the next phase.

In the second phase, the algorithm randomly selects a subset *varSet* of variables out of the support of f. The *varSet*'s size depends on the required confidence degree in finding at least one effective variable (See Subsection 2.1). *effectiveSet* holds all the variables in *varSet* that were first estimated as effective, and only those that seem to be effective are checked precisely. If *effectiveSet* is empty, the second phase ends unsuccessfully. Otherwise, the best slicer from *effectiveSet* is selected by **Exh**. We remark that the **Exh** procedure itself is no different than the slicing mechanisms described in [8]. Thus, in this paper, we use it as a black box.

The third phase is similar to the second. The difference is that *effectiveSet* now holds all the variables from *varSet* that slice effectively using a precise cal-

```
function Hybrid(f)
 1   v=Est(f)
 2   if effective(v, precise) return v
 3   varSet=randomselect(support(f))
 4   effectiveSet={v | v ∈ varSet ∧ effective(v, fast) ∧ effective(v, precise)}
 5   if effectiveSet ≠ ∅
 6      return Exh(f, efectiveSet)
 7   effectiveSet={v | v ∈ varSet ∧ effective(v, precise)}
 8   if effectiveSet ≠ ∅
 9      return Exh(f, efectiveSet)
10   return MEff(f, efectiveSet)
```

Fig. 1. Pseudo–code for the slicing algorithm Hybrid

culation. Finally, if the third phase fails and none of the variables is effective, the most effective variable, MEff, is selected among the variables that were computed in the third phase and this variable is returned.

Figure 1 describes the algorithm Hybrid for finding a slicer. Lines 1-2 describe the first phase, which uses the Est method to select a slicer v. If v is found to be effective, the algorithm terminates. Lines 3-6 describe the second phase where $varSet$ is randomly selected from the variables in the support of f. Then $effectiveSet$ gets only the variables that are effective slicers. This computation is done by first applying a fast estimated check and only then a precise check. The precise check is applied only on slicers that are estimated to be effective. Finally, the algorithm Exh is used to find the best slicer out of $effectiveSet$. Lines 7-9 describe the third phase where a precise check is applied to all variables in $varSet$. If the third phase fails, the most effective slicer found so far is returned in line 10.

2.1   Size of the Randomly Selected Subset

In this section we discuss the relation between the confidence in finding at least one effective variable and the number of samples. Lemma 1 defines this relation.

Lemma 1. *[Sample size required] Let sup be the size of the support of a set. Let ef be the number of effective slicers in the support (ef ≤ sup). Let s be the number of randomly selected variables(s ≤ sup). Let pr be the confidence in finding at least one effective slicer out of s samples. Then, $pr \geq 1 - \left(1 - \frac{ef}{sup}\right)^s$.*

The proof is straightforward and is omitted for lack of space.

Our experimental results (Figures 5(a), 5(b), explained later) show that the minimum percentage of effective slicers is 4%. Therefore, confidence in finding at least one effective variable converges to 100% exponentially fast in the number of samples. More importantly, it does not depend on the number of variables. If, for example, we want 90% confidence that we will get at least one effective variable and 5% of the variables are effective, we need only 45 samples.

2.2   Experimental Results

We compare three slicing algorithms. The new algorithm Hybrid, presented in Figure 1; the exhaustive algorithm Exh when working on the entire set of support; and the fast estimation Est when working on the entire set of support.

Table 1. Benchmark suite characteristics. For each set of examples we give the BDD size of the sets of states and the support size.

Set	BDD size range	Support size range	Number of sets of states
Small	0.5 - 3 Million	70	25
Large	0.5 - 6 Million	239 - 255	46
Extra large	0.5 - 7 Million	687 - 712	18

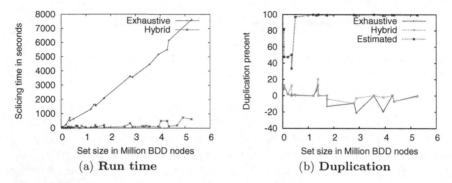

(a) **Run time**   (b) **Duplication**

Fig. 2. Comparing the slicing algorithms for support size 687 - 712

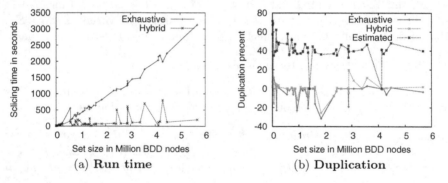

(a) **Run time**   (b) **Duplication**

Fig. 3. Comparing the slicing algorithms for support size 239 - 255

We use three sets of examples, each with different support size. Each set includes varying BDD sizes, from half a million to 7 million nodes. The characteristics of the three sets are presented in Table 1.

Slicing Efficiency and Memory Overhead. We now analyze the run time and the duplication by the different slicing algorithms. Figures 2(a), 3(a) display the run time of the slicing algorithms. In each graph the run times of Hybrid, and Exh algorithms can be seen in relation to the size of the set being sliced.

Figures 2(a), 3(a) show that the run time of the Exh algorithm increases proportionally to the BDD size and increases proportionally to the support size, while the Hybrid algorithm runs in constant time.

Percentage of duplication is the difference between the size of the set being sliced and the sum of the subsets, in proportion to the size of the set being sliced: $\left(\frac{|f \wedge v| + |f \wedge \bar{v}|}{|f|} - 1 \right) * 100$. Figures 2(b), 3(b) compare the percentage of duplication obtained by the Est algorithm to that obtained by the Hybrid algorithm. In each graph, the percentages of duplication in the Est and in the Hybrid algorithms can be seen in relation to the size of the set being sliced. The graphs show that when the support size increases, the slicing by the Est algorithm generates much more duplication than Hybrid. When the size of the support is 239 - 255 variables (Figure 3(b)), the Est algorithm has 50% duplication on average, while, while the Hybrid algorithm creates 7 percentage of duplication on average. When the size of the support is 687 - 712 variables (Figure 2(b)), the average percentage of duplication by the Est algorithm is 89, while the Hybrid algorithm creates 3 percentage of duplication on average.

Figures 2(b), 3(b) compare the percentage of duplication obtained by the Exh algorithm and the Hybrid algorithm. The percentages of duplication of the Exh and the Hybrid algorithms are shown in relation to the size of the set being sliced. We set the maximum duplication factor δ_2 to be 1.2. We set the minimum reduction factor δ_1 to be 0.85. For all set sizes that are not too small (larger than 100K BDD nodes), the resulting slicer creates less duplication than the maximum duplication factor. When the set size is very small, no effective slicer is found by any of the three phases. Thus, the final phase finds a slicer with duplication factor of 1.5. The small memory requirement of such small sets means that slicing them is not effective.

In some cases the percentage of duplication may be negative. This means that the sum of the sizes of the two subsets is less than the original set size. The Exh algorithm finds slicers with a very small percentage of duplication — as low as 30%. In other words, the sum is 30% smaller than the original set size. Because the Hybrid algorithm stops as soon as it finds an effective slicer, it may miss these.

Changing the Measures of Effectiveness. Figures 4(a), 4(b) present the effect of different values for maximum duplication factor, 120% and 105%, on run time and on percentage of duplication. In each graph the duplications are shown in relation to the size of the set being sliced. Figure 4(a) presents the duplications when the maximum duplication factors are 105% and 120%. For all set sizes, the final slicer creates duplication which is smaller than the maximum duplication factors; hence, the duplication with 105% is less than or equal to the duplication with 120%.

Figure 4(b) presents the run time for duplication factors 105% and 120%. In most cases the run time of the algorithm is longer when the maximum duplication factor is 105%. In cases when the algorithm needs to run more phases, the run time with 105% can take up to five times longer than that with 120%. Since the algorithm uses a random selection, different runs may terminate with different results. Sometime the run time takes comparably longer when using larger maximum duplication, but these are rear and caused by the randomization of the algorithm.

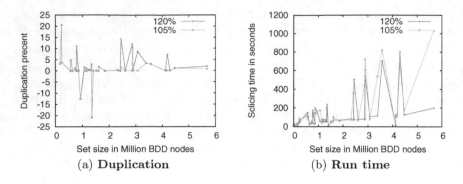

(a) **Duplication**   (b) **Run time**

Fig. 4. Support size 239 - 255. 105 means maximum duplication factor 105%. 120 means maximum duplication factor 120%.

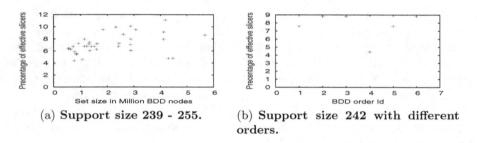

(a) **Support size 239 - 255.**   (b) **Support size 242 with different orders.**

Fig. 5. Percentage of effective slicers

Percentage of Effective Slicers. The experiments presented in this section demonstrate that for different set sizes, regardless of the BDD order, at least 4% of the variables are effective slicers. Figure 5(a) presents the percentage of effective slicers in different sets. The percentage of effective slicers is given in relation to the size of the set being sliced. Figure 5(a) shows, that regardless the set size, a minimum of 4% of the slicers are effective. This means that the confidence in finding at least one effective slicer converge to 100% exponentially fast in the number of samples (see Section 2.1).

Figure 5(b) presents the percentage of effective slicers in a single set with different BDD orders. This example has 242 variables in the support and the set size is 2.4 million BDD nodes with the best order. The percentage of effective slicers is given for each order. Figure 5(b) shows that even when we change the BDD order, as happens in the distributed reachability algorithm, a minimum of 4% of effective slicers is maintained.

3   The Checkpoint Restart Algorithm

In this section we briefly describe the iterative BDD-based distributed algorithm for reachability [7]. We explain how to extend this algorithm with checkpoints and how to exploit these checkpoints in order to restart the reachability algorithm when needed, according to some scheduling policy. Finally we present experimental results which show that the associated overhead is negligible.

The basic paradigm followed by the algorithm is to compute the set of states which are reachable from a given set of initial states. At each iteration, starting from the set of initial states, the set R is computed. R consists of reachable states found so far. In addition, the set N of *undeveloped* states is computed. These are states that do not belong in R and are reachable from R in a single step, whose successors have not yet been found.

The distributed algorithm runs on a network of communicating workers with distributed memory. A set of *window functions* defines for each worker the subset of states it *owns*. This set is *complete*, meaning that it covers the whole state space. Worker id with window function W_{id} computes the sets R_{id} and N_{id}, both subsets of W_{id}.

Three coordinators control the distributed operation: the *pool manager* keeps track of the free processes; the *exchange coordinator* maintains the window functions of the active workers, and the *small coordinator* joins the windows of workers whose memory utilization decreases below a certain threshold.

Figure 6 describes an extension of the distributed algorithm with checkpoint-restart capability, called **reach_checkpt**. The pseudo–code is described for a single worker. For brevity, we omit the worker subscript id from R_{id}, N_{id}, and W_{id}. We remark that the sets R and N, and the window function W, may change during the execution.

The algorithm uses two utility functions to transfer BDDs between a sender and a receiver whose BDD orders may be different: **bdd2msg** translates a BDD into a compact **msg** data and **msg2bdd** translates the **msg** data back to a BDD after it has been transferred. We remark that the functions **bdd2msg** and **msg2bdd** themselves are not different from the functions described in [8]. Thus, in this paper, we use them as a black box.

The algorithm follows the same lines of the distributed reachability algorithm, except at the end of each iteration workers sometimes store checkpoints. The data stored in a checkpoint consists of R, N, W, the iteration number $\#it$, and its current BDD order *bdd_order* (line 9). The checkpoint of a worker may be stored on a persistent storage system, e.g., a distributed file system such as NFS, or simply on the private disk of a peer worker (in which case it is assumed the peer worker does not crash when the worker does).

Recall that the basic reachability paradigm is an iterative, synchronous process. Thus, the collection of all checkpoints from all workers at the end of an iteration forms a consistent view of the global reachability process at that point.

If a restart is needed because of a failure, or due to rescheduling of the reachability process on another distributed system, the collection of checkpoints may set a starting point for pursuing the computation. The restart algorithm searches for a set of checkpoints taken from the same iteration, which forms a complete set of window functions. If an incomplete set is found, indicating that some but not all the workers succeeded in storing checkpoints for the corresponding iter-

```
function reach_checkpt(R, W, N)
 1  Loop until termination()
 2      N = Image(N), split if needed
 3      send non-owned states (N \ W) to their owners
 4      N=N∪ (received states in W from others), split if needed
 5      N=N \ R
 6      R=R ∪ N
 7      Collect_small(R, W, N)
 8      if (W = ∅) return to pool
 9      Check_point(R, W, N, #it, bdd_order)
```

Fig. 6. Pseudo–code for a worker in the distributed reachability computation with checkpoints

ation previous to the abort, then the algorithm searches for a complete set that was stored at the end of a previous iteration. Such a set is guaranteed to exist because the workers follow the same policy, at the end of which iteration checkpoints are stored, and because a previous checkpoint is never removed before the current global checkpoint is known to be complete (e.g., at the end of the next iteration).

Every active worker in the restarted process is restored using its local checkpoint data, and is replaced by a worker from the free pool in the new distributed system. The new worker restores R and N according to the BDD order *bdd_order* and assumes W as its window function.

3.1   Experimental Results

The resources consumed by the distributed algorithm are evaluated by considering the following two figures. The *reserved size* is the number of machines carrying out the computation. These machines are either actively taking part in the computation, or they are part of the free pool. If they are part of the free pool, they might not be carrying out any useful computation because they are being reserved as potential additional resources for the reachability computation. The *utilized size* is the number of active non-free workers that are actually taking part in the reachability computation. Of course, at any point during computation the utilized size is less than the reserved size.

Figure 7(a) presents the utilized size and reserved size during the distributed reachability computation. The graph shows how the checkpointing mechanism is used in order to reduce reserved size to a minimum. Checkpointing is used to vary the number of workers reserved, starting from a small cluster with only 10 machines. When more than 10 machines are required, the run temporarily halts, a cluster with more machine is reserved, the last checkpoint is moved to new cluster, and the computation is resumed on that cluster. With the larger cluster, the run can reach a further step, while it utilizes at least 10 machines. This way the free pool (of idle machines) is kept small compared to the number of reserved workers.

Yet another contribution of the checkpoint restart mechanism is in the case of termination as a result of failure in one of the resources. In case of a fail, the amount of wasted resources is the accumulate of reserved size in each iteration

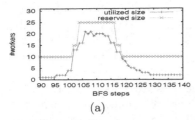
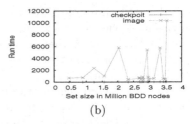

(a)   (b)

Fig. 7. (a) *reserved size* is the number of machines carrying out the computation. *utilized size* is the number of active non-free workers. (b) Run time of image computation and the time to store the checkpoint data.

from the first one till the iteration where the failure appeared. Furthermore, the more machines take part in the computation, and the more iterations involved in the computation, the higher the chance of a failure. Thus, the importance of the checkpoint restart mechanism increases with the number of iterations to fixpoint, and with the scale of the model checked (as indicated by the reserved size).

Figure 7(b) compares the run time of image computation and the time it takes to store the checkpoint data. For each set size, the graph shows the run time required for image computation and the run time required to store the checkpoint data. The graph shows that for all set sizes the checkpoint run time takes less than 20 seconds. Moreover, if there is no job failure, there is almost no overhead for storing checkpoints.

4   Distributed Reachability Analysis for Very Large Circuites Using 100 PCs

In the previous sections two enhancements to distributed reachability analysis were discussed. This section describes the extensions to the algorithm **reach_checkpt**. These extensions enable high performance distributed reachability analysis for very large circuits using 100 PCs. With these extensions, the algorithm verifies circuits that could not be verified by any other tool. Furthermore, although an overflow in the required number of workers occurs in several cases, the distributed scheme still reaches a much further iteration than that reached by the sequential BDD based model checker.

In order to have our distributed scheme scale out, two additional extensions to **reach_checkpt** are needed: *distributed reorder* and *BDD operations timeout*. We discuss the two extensions and then give experimental results.

4.1   Distributed Dynamic Variable Reordering

The dynamic variable reorder suggested by Rudell [13] works well for the sequential algorithm. Here we show how to use it with our distributed approach.

Rudell's algorithm is called by the BDD package according to the growth in the number of BDD nodes. A dynamic reorder threshold dr_th determines where the next threshold should be triggered. The threshold is examined after each garbage collection cycle, and variable reordering is triggered if the number of nodes allocated after the garbage collection is greater than dr_th. After each invocation of reorder, a new value for dr_th is set according to the number of nodes in the new order.

In the distributed scheme the BDD package uses Rudell's algorithm in the same way. However, since there are events such as splits and joins which affect the size of the BDD package, the distributed algorithm also controls the value of dr_th externally. The worker forces the BDD packages to adjust the value of dr_th after splitting a worker, after which the number of nodes decreases dramatically, and after exchanging nonowned states, after which the number of nodes may decrease or increase.

In addition, in case of overflow during image computation, triggering reorder may reduce the size of the BDD and thus avoid the costly splitting. Therefore, when an overflow occurs after many micro-steps but before the image computation is completed, the worker invokes reorder and then tries to complete the image computation. However, if the BDD package triggers reorder just before the micro-step overflowed, the worker avoids the additional reorder since it is unlikely to prevent the splitting.

4.2   Escape from BDD Operation Livelock Using Timeouts

BDD engines use a cache for previously executed BDD operations. When this cache is used, the run time commonly becomes linear in the sizes of the BDD operators, rather than exponential. Since the size of the cache cannot hold all the BDD operations, the engine replaces old results with new ones. If the result of a replaced BDD operation is required, it will be recalculated. Recalculation increases the run time, and in some cases, can cause the execution of a single BDD operation to proceed for hours.

In the distributed scheme a split can help a single worker if it got stuck on a single BDD operation, because the size of the cache is effectively doubled as a result of the split, and because the split reduces the BDD operation operands. A single micro-step is stopped if it turns out to be too long and split is invoked, just as if a memory overflow occurred. Our experiments show that cases in which a large number of recalculations take hours can be efficiently avoided in this way.

4.3   Experimental Results

Our parallel testbed consists of 100 PC machines, each consisting of a two-way 2.4GHz Pentium 4 processors with 1GB memory. For optimal utilization of this configuration we let two workers execute on the same machine. A fast Ethernet connection is used for communication between the nodes. The sequential runs use a PC machine consisting of four way 3.1GHz Pentium 4 processors with 4GB memory.

The distributed algorithm that we tested uses **reach_checkpt** enhanced with the algorithm `Hybrid`, as well as distributed dynamic reordering and the microsteps timeout. The external model checker used by the distributed algorithm is a high-performance industrial tool from Intel.

We conducted our experiments using examples for which the fixpoint had never been reached before, such as the s1423 design from the ISCAS89 benchmarks. We remark that other examples from this benchmark suite, such as s3330, s1269 and s5378, require only a single process when using Intel's high-performance model checker. Thus, they are not suitable as benchmarks for the distributed system. In addition to s1423, we experimented with six large examples which are components in Intel's designs.

The characteristics of the six test cases are given in Table 2.

Table 2. Benchmark suite characteristics. In each example we give the step in which the memory requirements by the sequential model checker overflow and the size of the BDD representing the set of reachable states R at that step.

Circuit	#vars	Overflow step	Overflow $\mid R \mid$
H21	274	55	3,203,064
H20	276	44	3,922,742
I1	147	98	8,006,120
H11	300	44	5,211,955
I3	793	46	5,557,672
I3s	439	54	7,076,762
s1423	88	14	9,705,214

The distributed reachability analysis results are given in Table 3. Four examples reached fixpoint and the verification is completed. Three examples required more workers than were available to us at this point (we did not always have all 100 machines at our disposal), Therefore worker overflow occurred at some step, but always at a much further step than that reached by the sequential model checker.

We next compare the results in Table 3 to the results of the high performance industrial SAT model checker tool of Intel. The SAT model checker could not complete the verification of any of the examples. Computing bounded model checking with timeout of 10,000 seconds, SAT reached the bounds of 85 and 94 on I3s and I3, respectively.

Finally we compare these results to previous distributed symbolic model checking [7] and [8]. In [8] a high performance model checker was used by the distributed algorithm, yet s1423 reached only step 17, while the new distributed algorithm reached step 19. Additional examples from ISCAS89 are so small that they were completed by the sequential model checker. Other examples from [8] were not made available to the public. In [7] a non-sophisticated model checker was used. Therefore a relatively small example such as s3330 required 54 workers to complete. The high performance model checker used in this work can complete this example using a single worker.

It is especially interesting to compare Tables 2 and 3. It turns out that at the point where the sequential algorithm overflows, the aggregate space requirement for the distributed algorithm (given in the tables as the size of R in BDD nodes) is

Table 3. Distributed reachability on the benchmark suite. Four examples reached fixpoint and verification was completed. Three examples required more workers than were available to us and therefore worker overflow occurred. The Max workers column indicates the maximum number of active workers during the computation. The run time when the verification is completed is given in hours. Run time is time elapsed since the first worker starts to run until the last worker finishes the run. Two measures are given for the iteration at which the sequential algorithm overflows: The sum of the sizes of the BDDs representing the subsets of reachable states, and the number of active workers at this iteration.

Circuit	Fixpoint	Max workers	Time	$\max_{ite} \sum_i |R_i|$	at Seq Overflow	
					$\sum_i |R_i|$	#workers
H21	85	3	23h			
H20	85	9	11h			
I1	139	25	70h	15.5M	6.6M	3
H11	98	7	28.5h	4.4M	1.3M	4
I3	WOvf(60)	>50		47.2M	7.1M	5
I3s	WOvf(118)	>150		358.8M	7.1M	4
s1423	WOvf(19)	>200		208.3M	8.8M	8

smaller than the corresponding size in the sequential algorithm! This means that the distributed algorithm is more efficient in maintaining its data structures (the BDD which holds R,N), sometimes to a factor of two or more. This comes as a surprise, since common wisdom tells us to expect some overhead and duplication of work, rather than increased efficiency.

The explanation, however, is straightforward. Recall that with the distributed scheme reorder is optimized individually at every worker, taking into account the worker data only. In this way, BDD reordering by the distributed algorithm is much more efficient than by the sequential algorithm because every worker finds a better order when looking only at its data. The overall effect is an aggregate reduction in the number of BDD nodes, which implies improved overall efficiency.

Acknowledgement. We would like to thank Moshe Vardi for many creative and helpful discussions. We would also like to thank Inessa Chernoguz, Ilan Harari, Alexander Barapp, Eran Galon and Ohad Livnat from Intel, for enabling us to perform our experiments.

References

1. I. Beer, S. Ben-David, C. Eisner, and A. Landver. Rulebase: An Industry-Oriented Formal Verification Tool. In *33rd Design Automation Conference*, pages 655–660, 1996.
2. A. Biere, A. Cimatti, E. M. Clarke, M. Fujita, and Y. Zhu. Symbolic Model Checking using SAT Procedures Instead of BDDs. In *36th Design Automation Conference*, pages 317–320, 1999.

3. J.R. Burch, E.M. Clarke, K.L. McMillan, D.L. Dill, and L.J. Hwang. Symbolic model checking: 10^{20} states and beyond. *Information and Computation*, 98(2):142–171, June 1992. Special Issue: Selections from 1990 IEEE Symposium on Logic in Computer Science.

4. G. Cabodi, P. Camurati, and S. Quer. Improved Reachability Analysis of Large FSM. In *Proceedings of the IEEE International Conference on Computer Aided Design*, pages 354–360. IEEE Computer Society Press, June 1996.

5. R. Fraer, G. Kamhi, B. Ziv, M.Y. Vardi, and L. Fix. Prioritized Traversal: Efficient Reachability Analysis for Verification and Falsification. In *Proc. of the 12th International Conference on Computer Aided Verification, LNCS*, 2000.

6. O. Grumberg, T. Heyman, N. Ifergan, and A. Schuster. Achieving speedups in distributed symbolic reachability analysis through asynchronous computation. In *CHARME (to appear)*, 2005.

7. O. Grumberg, T. Heyman, and A. Schuster. A Work-Efficient Distributed Algorithm for Reachability Analysis. In *Proc. of the 15th International Conference on Computer Aided Verification, LNCS*, 2003.

8. T. Heyman, D. Geist, O. Grumberg, and A. Schuster. Achieving Scalability in Parallel Reachability Analysis of Very Large Circuits. *Formal Methods in System Design*, 21(2):317–338, November 2002.

9. K.L. McMillan. Interpolation and SAT-Based Model Checking. In *Proc. of the 15th International Conference on Computer Aided Verification, LNCS*, 2003.

10. A. Narayan, A. Isles, J. Jain, R. Brayton, and A. L. Sangiovanni-Vincentelli. Reachability Analysis Using Partitioned-ROBDDs. In *Proceedings of the IEEE International Conference on Computer Aided Design*, pages 388–393. IEEE Computer Society Press, June 1997.

11. A. Narayan, J. Jain, M. Fujita, and A. L. Sangiovanni-Vincentelli. Partitioned-ROBDDs. In *Proceedings of the IEEE International Conference on Computer Aided Design*, pages 547–554. IEEE Computer Society Press, June 1996.

12. Kavita Ravi, Kenneth L. McMillan, Thomas R. Shiple, and Fabio Somenzi. Approximation and Decomposition of Binary Decision Diagrams. In *35th Design Automation Conference*, pages 445–450, 1998.

13. R. Rudell. Dynamic Variable Ordering for Ordered Binary Decision Diagrams. In *Intl. Conf. on Computer Aided Design*, Santa Clara, Ca., November 1993.

A New Reachability Algorithm for Symmetric Multi-processor Architecture

Debashis Sahoo[1], Jawahar Jain[3], Subramanian Iyer[2], and David Dill[1]

[1] Stanford University, Stanford CA 94305, USA
[2] University of Texas at Austin, Austin, TX 78712, USA
[3] Fujitsu Labs of America

Abstract. Partitioned BDD-based algorithms have been proposed in
the literature to solve the memory explosion problem in BDD-based verification. A naive parallelization of such algorithms is often ineffective
as they have less parallelism. In this paper we present a novel parallel
reachability approach that lead to a significantly faster verification on
a Symmetric Multi-Processing architecture over the existing one-thread,
one-CPU approaches. We identify the issues and bottlenecks in parallelizing BDD-based reachability algorithm. We show that in most cases
our algorithm achieves good speedup compared to the existing sequential
approaches.

1 Introduction

A common approach to formal verification of hardware is checking invariant
properties of the design. Unbounded model checking [1, 2] of invariants is usually performed by doing a reachability analysis. This approach finds all the states
reachable from the initial states and checks if the invariant is satisfied in these
reachable states. However, exhausting the state space using the reachability approach is an intractable problem. Not surprisingly, such approaches suffer from
the so-called *state explosion problem* for representing large state sets.

In practice, reachability analysis is typically done using *Reduced Ordered
Binary Decision Diagrams* (OBDDs) [3, 4]. A more compact representation of
boolean functions, *Partitioned-OBDDs* (POBDDs) [5] leads to further improvement in reachability analysis [6]. Various improvements to BDD data structures,
variable ordering schemes, as well as the reachability algorithm itself have also
been suggested to improve capturing the total reachable state space using reachability based verification. However, in practice the verification problem typically
consumes far more resources than are typically available for even small sized
problems of 100 state variables, and the gap between requirement and performance is continually growing.

The growing prevalence of, increasingly powerful, clustered high performance
SMP (Symmetric Multi-Processing) machines appears to be an inevitable trend.
However, it is not straightforward to devise a reachability algorithm to mean-
ingfully use a very large number of processors.

D.A. Peled and Y.-K. Tsay (Eds.): ATVA 2005, LNCS 3707, pp. 26–38, 2005.
© Springer-Verlag Berlin Heidelberg 2005

Given the above two trends, it is important to develop efficient parallel verification algorithms that can appropriately exploit the SMP architecture. Though the intractability of the problem will remain, the verification time can get reduced by a significant factor.

In this paper, we show that the naive parallelization of the POBDD-based reachability analysis doesn't have good parallelism. We present a novel parallel reachability approach that improves the parallelism. Our algorithm also improves the performance of sequential POBDD based approaches drastically in some cases. This is because, in sequential POBDD-based algorithms, the relative order in which the partitions are analyzed plays a critical role in the overall performance. Finding an optimal schedule is a very hard problem. Therefore, any heuristic to find a good schedule is likely to not perform well in all cases. In a few cases, the approach can get stuck in some difficult partition and, hence, many remaining states which otherwise could have been easily computed are not reached at all. Our algorithm clearly obviates this *scheduling problem* since it runs all partitions in parallel. Also, in a parallel shared-memory environment, using our techniques of *Early Communication* and *Partial Communication*, state space traversal in some partitions can continue even while remaining partitions are proving to be difficult.

We show that in most cases our algorithm performs much better than the corresponding sequential run using 8 processors. Using our approach, we can locate error states significantly faster than other BDD based methods. We can also show that our results are much better than the standard reachability algorithms in many passing cases as well. Finally, we show that our method is more robust than the standard sequential POBDD-based reachability algorithm as it is able to solve various easy reachability instances which prove to be problematic for current POBDD approaches.

2   Preliminaries

Reachability analysis is usually based on a breadth-first traversal of finite-state machines [4, 2]. The algorithm takes as inputs the set of initial states and a transition relation (TR) that relates the next states a system can reach from each current state. The set of reachable states is obtained by repeatedly performing image computations until a fixed point is reached [4, 2]. This is termed as the *Least Fixed Point* computation. Verification based on reachability can often be improved by the use of POBDDs [7, 6, 8]. Essentially, the POBDD based-reachability algorithm performs as many steps as possible of image computation within each partition i in a step of *least fixed point* within the partition. When no more images can be thus computed, it synchronizes between partitions by considering the transitions that originate in partition i and lead out from there. The term *Communication* refers to these cross-partition image computations that are followed by transferring the computed BDDs to other partitions. Notice that the POBDD-based reachability algorithm performs a BFS which is local to individual partitions, and then synchronizes to add states that result from transitions crossing over from one partition to another. We may characterize this as a region-based BFS, where individual regions of the state space, *i.e,* the partitions, are traversed independently in a breadth first manner. We term the computation within individual partitions as a *local Least Fixed Point* computation or a local LFP computation in short.

Related Work

Several methods have been proposed to do parallel verification. Stern and Dill [9] parallelize an explicit model checker. In [10], parallelized BDDs are used for reachability analysis. Verification using parallel reachability analysis has been studied in [11, 12, 13]. A scalable parallel reachability analysis is presented in [12]. They perform distributed reachability using the classical BFS traversal of the state space in a parallel environment, using distributed memory. A different disjunctive partitioning approach based on iterative squaring is explored in [14]. A thread-based approach has been applied to Constraint-Based Verification in [15].

We implemented our algorithm as a multi-threaded program. We would like to compare our algorithm with other distributed approaches. However, at the time of submission of this paper, we didn't have an implementation of other distributed algorithms to compare with our approach. Therefore, we keep this as a future work.

3   Improving Parallelism in the Reachability Analysis

The reachability analysis involves construction of a TR and the actual reachability steps using the TR. We use the standard sequential approach of building the transition relation. We keep the parallelization of the construction of the transition relation as a future work. In this paper we parallelize the reachability algorithm using various heuristic improvement.

The POBDD-based algorithm given in [6] is naturally parallelizable. The local LFP computation of each partition combined with their *communication* can be processed in parallel. We have to wait for all the partitions to finish their local LFP computation and the *communication* to begin transferring the communicated states to the appropriate partition. However, empirically we find that this simple parallelization of the algorithm in [6] doesn't have much parallelism. This may be due to following reasons

High Variation of BDD Computations
The performance of the image computations inside each partition depend on the BDD variable order. We call a partition an *easy partition* if the BDDs inside the partition are compact and a hard partition otherwise. For a majority of circuits, the complexity of the BDD computations can have significant variations between different partitions. In such cases, all easy partitions wait for the hard partitions to finish their image computation, which reduces the parallelism significantly.

Depth of the local LFP computation
Another reason for the reduced parallelism may be because the depth of the local LFP computation can vary a lot between partitions. In this case the partition

with smaller depth finish faster whereas the partitions with larger depth take longer time. This results in many idle processors which reduces the parallelism.

In practice we find that a large number of partitions wait for a few hard partitions. To address this issue we use following heuristics[16] to improve the parallelism.

Early Communication: Communicate states to other partition after the least fixed point.
Partial Communication: Initiate a partial communication in an idle processor.

3.1   Early Communication

After a partition finishes its local LFP computation, we allow the partition to immediately communicate its states to the other partitions. Each partition accepts this communicated states asynchronously during their local LFP computation. This would enable the easy partitions to make progress with their subsequent local LFP computation without waiting for the hard partitions to finish. Therefore, the early communication from easy partitions to other easy partitions enables all such partitions to reach a fixed point. This is very difficult to achieve in sequential partitioned reachability analysis because such scheduling information is difficult to obtain.

If new states are *communicated* during early communication, then we restart the current image computation after adding these states. Such augmentation can make a harder image computation significantly easier in some cases. This may be because the states that would have been hard to compute in one partition can be more easily computed in another partition and then communicated to the first partition.

3.2   Partial Communication

Even after applying the above technique, we found that some partition that have completed the local LFP on their current states were waiting for other partitions to communicate some states, so that they can continue their local LFP computation. This case arises when all the easy partition finish their local LFP and need communication from a hard partition to make further progress. To improve parallelism, the active partition initiates a *communication* in an idle processor using a small subset of the state space of the hard partition. The *communication* introduces new states in the easy partitions. This enables easy partitions to make progress further with their collective least fixed point from the communicated states. Intuitively this tries to accelerate the activity among easy partitions. We found that communicating the full BDD to a different partition is very hard. Therefore, we find a small subset of state space that can be expressed with a compact BDD (High Density BDD[17]). This heuristic tries to keep all the processors busy there by improving the parallelism. Further, this heuristic can increase the number of early communication instances. Thus, the combined effect of the partial communication and early communication improves the parallelism significantly.

```
Parallel-Reachability(n, TR, InitStates) {
    Create n partitions for InitStates
    Run in parallel for each partition i{
        After every microsteps runs
                ImproveParallelism(i) {
                Get all the communicated states
                Calculate LeastFixedPoint(Rch) in partition i
                Compute cross-over states from i to all parts
            }
        } until (No new state is found in any partition);
}
ImproveParallelism(n: Partition Number) {
    check and add all the communicated states
        if new states are added
                restart current image computation
    request a waiting partition to initiate
        partial communication procedure
}
```

Fig. 1. Parallel Reachability Algorithm

3.3   Parallel Reachability Algorithm

We present our complete parallel POBDD-based reachability algorithm as shown in Figure 1 using the techniques discussed in last section.

We run the local LFP computation combined with the *Communication* in parallel. All computation inside a partition is managed by a dedicated processor. Each processor polls for the communicated states from the other processor. After every micro-step of the image computation, each processor calls a function *ImproveParallelism* that implements two heuristics for improving parallelism. The first heuristic is to do early communication. As a part of the first heuristic, the function checks whether other processors have communicated some states to the current partition. If it finds any processors, then it transfer all the communicated states from their corresponding partitions to the current partition. This simple check and update subroutine performed by each processor implements the early communication heuristic. The second heuristic is to do partial communication. As a part of this heuristic, every active processor checks for an idle thread. If an idle processor is found, then it gives a small subset of the state space from the current partition to the idle processor. The idle processor start a *Communication* from this subset of states to the partition associated with the idle processor.

3.4   Termination Condition

In our approach, each processor manages a partition. The processor goes back to idle state if no new states are communicated to the partition associated with that processor. One of the processor manages the global termination conditions. The processor asserts a global termination flag if all the processors are idle.

4   Engineering Issues

Our implementation of the POBDD-data structure and algorithms uses VIS-2.0 package. The VIS-2.0 package uses CUDD [18] for the BDD operations. We implemented our parallel reachability algorithm as a multi-threaded program in a symmetric multi-processing (SMP) architecture. SMP systems can be programmed using several different methods. In a multi-threaded approach, the program divides the work across the processors by spawning multiple light-weight threads, each executing on a different processor and performing part of the calculation. Since all threads share the same program space, there is no need for any explicit communication calls. However, designing a multi-threaded FV approach using BDDs poses significant challenges.

BDD Issues in Multi-threaded Reachability: The CUDD BDD package is designed for use in a non-thread based environment. Further, there are various optimization features in CUDD, that prevent it to function correctly in a multi-threaded environment. It uses many global variables, which needs to be synchronized in a multi-threaded environment. Nevertheless, fixing this problem enables the program to behave correctly provided each thread work on their respective BDD-managers. However, this leads to a non-deterministic behavior in the BDD-computation.

The CUDD package uses various memory based optimization to boost its performance. However, such optimizations behave non-deterministically in a multi-threaded environment. Therefore, the produced computation trace is often non-reproducible and the program becomes very difficult to debug. It also results in many orders of magnitude difference in run times. Thus, the program behavior is not predictable. However, deterministic behavior of the program is very important for the evaluation of its performance. We re-engineered all the relevant features in the CUDD package that leads to a non-deterministic behavior. This enables the BDD-package to be safe to run in a multi-threaded environment and makes the program more conveniently analyzable. However, this was surprisingly painful to implement.

In addition to the above, each thread needs to synchronize based on a deterministic measure before communicating to another thread. Otherwise, the program would behave non-deterministically because of the non-determinism in the thread scheduling. We synchronize the threads using a fixed count based on the number of BDD conjunction operations and the number of sift operations during variable reordering. Further, we find that the deterministic version of the program performs as good as the non-deterministic program as described in Section 5.2.

Performance Issues on SMP Machine: Further, the scheduling of the threads in an SMP machine, although improved significantly over the years, might not be optimal for our application. Each thread, in our case use separate BDD managers for carrying out various BDD operations. Therefore, if the system thread scheduler assigns the thread to a different processor, then the thread would loose all its cached data and the new processor would re-fetch all the necessary data to carry out the BDD operations. Thus, assigning a thread to a new processor would incur unnecessary large overhead. However, a very simple scheduling strategy of assigning each thread to an exclusive processor would reduce the overhead generated by the heavy cache misses significantly. On the other hand, it is quite difficult to quantify the performance penalty due the non-optimality of scheduling threads.

Performance Issues on Uniprocessor Machine: Furthermore, the simulated parallel execution of the multi-threaded algorithm in a uniprocessor machine may perform better than other sequential algorithm because of the scheduling flexibility. However, the program may have large overhead due to the cache misses because of the frequent switching of threads in one processor. We find that reducing the frequency of switching of threads in a uniprocessor machine significantly improve the results. Moreover, a simulated sequential approach in an 8-CPU machine, where each thread can potentially use different processor cache improves the results further. We use explicit locks to run one thread at a time in the 8-CPU machine. We find that the performance in this simulated case is 2-6 times faster than the corresponding uniprocessor run. Thus, the uniprocessor performance is significantly penalized by the cache overhead. Therefore, we provide results from this simulated sequential approach in the 8-CPU machine in our final table to give a good overview of the parallelism achieved. However, the performance in any uniprocessor machine is much worse than the simulated sequential case in an 8-CPU machine.

5   Experimental Results

We run our experiments using default cluster size of 5000, lazy sift reordering, MLP image method on a 8-way SMP Linux machine based on Intel(R) Xeon(TM) MP CPU 2.20GHz and 8GB RAM. We run all the sequential algorithms on a Linux box with Intel(R) XEON(TM) CPU 2.20GHz and 2GB RAM. We report results only on a few VIS-verilog [19] and industrial circuits because of limited time. In keeping with the typical timeout limits set in our in-house verification tools, we set a timeout of 5000 seconds on all circuits. For sake of brevity, we present our results only on those circuits where VIS requires more than 100 seconds. Results are omitted for the circuits where all the methods timeout. We use 8 different partitions for all POBDD-based approaches. We select the partitioning variable using the method in [6]. We use same partitioning strategy for all partitioned approaches in order to perform a fair comparison.

5.1   Overview of Table

Table 1 shows our invariant check results on various public and industrial circuits. In Table 1, we separate the total reachability time into the transition relation construction time and the actual reachability time. We compare the actual reachability time taken by the following approaches: the standard approach of VIS, the simple partitioning approach and our parallel POBDD-based reachability algorithms. We compare the naive parallel approach with the successive

Table 1. Time (in sec) for Invariant Checking on a few VIS-verilog and Industrial Circuits using 8 CPUs

ckts	TR time	vis	seq pobdd	Parallel 8 CPUs (naive)	Parallel 8 CPUs (early comm)	(early comm + partial comm) Parallel 8 CPUs	Simulated Seq
(a) Industrial Circuits							
c1	36	371	T/O	T/O	T/O	**227**	286
c2	12	3346	1789	1564	93	**917**	917
c3	17	2540	T/O	T/O	T/O	**62**	228
c4	11	2236	2084	1174	161	**161**	509
(b) Few VIS-benchmark Circuits							
spprod	5	891	61	53	93	**440**	510
am2910	9	T/O	281	122	204	**356**	386
palu	3	273	4	9	8	**9**	9
s1269b-1	2	3635	T/O	T/O	59	**60**	72
s1269b-5	2	2287	T/O	T/O	55	**55**	67
blkjack-3	2	T/O	1213	470	340	**70**	98
(c) Simple Industrial Circuits							
d1	11	6	T/O	T/O	13	**13**	13
d2	15	10	11	13	45	**30**	39
d3	12	15	21	23	100	**100**	130
d4	8	11	T/O	T/O	39	**38**	60
d5	7	12	16	15	34	**37**	37

(T/O = Timeout of 5000 sec)

introduction of the two heuristics for communication – early communication and partial communication. The columns in the table are arranged in the same order. The first column is the circuit name, followed by transition relation construction time, *vis*, *se*quential POBDDs, *naive* parallelization, the parallel approach with just early communication and finally with both techniques. The final column has two parts – *8 CPUs* and *Simulated Seq*, which report, respectively, the total reachability time in a parallel environment using 8 CPUs and the time in a simulated sequential approach in an 8-CPU machine. The simulated sequential approach is discussed in section 4. Note that many of the sequential results are better than standard POBDD-based reachability because of the partition and communication scheduling flexibility. The details of the processor utilization are presented in Section 5.3 using Gantt charts.

5.2 Efficiency Issues

Table 1 is composed of three different sections. Section (a) and (c), respectively shows the results on a few hard and easy industrial circuits. Section (b) shows the

Table 2. Time (in sec) for Invariant Checking on the Industrial Circuits using different redundancy value in a parallel and sequential framework

	redundancy [6]					
	0.3		0.5		0.7	
	Parallel	seq	Parallel	seq	Parallel	seq
c1	227	288	226	286	229	292
c2	73	386	917	917	2569	2570
c3	1492	1493	62	228	1407	T/O
c4	2967	2970	161	509	158	520
d1	26	28	13	13	92	138
d2	30	40	30	39	31	39
d3	53	67	100	130	102	133
d4	29	37	38	60	38	59
d5	13	13	37	37	37	38
s1269b-1	61	73	60	72	165	183
sp_prod	446	510	440	510	259	260

(T/O = Timeout of 5000 sec)

results on a few VIS-verilog benchmark circuits. As can be seen from the table, the resulting parallel run times with all the heuristics, *i.e*, the last column of the table have no timeouts. They are also clearly superior to classical partitioned-reachability. The proposed parallel approach will all heuristics, is also usually superior to the less sophisticated parallel techniques. The parallel approach with only early communication, i.e the 6th column in Table 1, often works well and have fewer timeouts compared to the naive parallel approach. Consider the circuit *blkjack-3*, which represents the best scenario, where the results improve with each successive addition of the heuristics. We find that the parallel approach is usually more robust than the sequential approaches. Note that the last column shows the results of simulated sequential approach in an 8-CPU machine to demonstrate the parallelism achieved. The corresponding uniprocessor results are 2-6 times worse than the simulated sequential approach. We find that the parallelism is very small and hope to improve it in a future work.

Scheduling is a Problem Even on Easy Functions: Consider the results of some properties from an industrial design whose OBDDs are fairly small as shown in Table 1 (c). The partitioned reachability for such cases gets harder. Both the standard sequential POBDD-based reachability and naive parallel reachability falls in the trap of an inefficient computation. An early communication often helps in this case, as can be seen from the table. However, both early communication and partial communication are needed to finish all the circuits. The reachability of small circuits using 8 partitions might contribute to some overhead in the partitioned reachability approaches.

Further, we will like to comment on the relative speedup of the multi-threaded 8-CPU approach over the simulated sequential approach. This speedup is not only proportional to the algorithm but also to the choice of partitioning variables.

Table 3. Time (in sec) for Invariant Checking on the Industrial Circuits using the non-deterministic and the deterministic program

	Time in sec	
ckts	non-det	det

(a) Industrial Circuits

c1	T/O	**227**
c2	962	**917**
c3	809	**62**
c4	903	**161**

(b) Simple Industrial Circuits

d1	13	**13**
d2	24	**30**
d3	84	**100**
d4	30	**38**
d5	13	**37**

(T/O = Timeout of 5000 sec)

For the same algorithm, even though the *same* partitioning variables may be provided to both the approaches, depending on the splitting choices, the amount of parallelism that is generated can vary dramatically. For example, in Table 2 it can be seen that for almost half of the entries, by varying redundancy and balancedness, the two parameters that are calculated for evaluating partitioning variables, the amount of parallelism that is generated can vary dramatically. This points to the need for an approach which can dynamically evaluate different choices in deciding the partitioning variables. Such an idea is motivated by the strong results presented in Sahoo et al. [8], where it was shown the successful BDD decisions can be taken if we generate different short traces of reachability computation for each choice and then make the required decision.

Finally, we show that the deterministic version of our program doesn't loose the performance by a great margin to the non-deterministic version. Table 3 shows the results of Invariant checking on the industrial circuits using both the non-deterministic and the deterministic version of our program. As we can see from the table, the performance of non-deterministic program is very similar to the deterministic program in the simple circuits, i.e. Table 3 (b). However, the performance of the deterministic program is better than the non-deterministic version in the hard circuits in Table 3 (a). Therefore, we strongly prefer the deterministic version to the non-deterministic version.

5.3 Improving Parallelism

Consider the reachability analysis of *s1269b-5* from the VIS Verilog benchmark suite. As shown in Table 1 (b), we perform reachability analysis using 8 partitions, each of which runs in a separate thread.

Figure 2 shows the Gantt charts of three parallel reachability analysis on *s1269b-5* circuit. We use the three charts to show the effect of the two heuris-

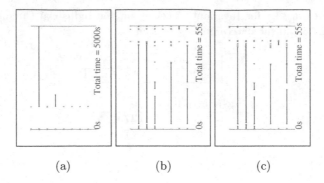

(a)   (b)   (c)

Fig. 2. Parallel Reachability with successive addition of each heuristics

tics added successively to the reachability algorithm. Figure 2(a) shows Gantt chart of the naive parallel reachability. Figure 2(b) shows the Gantt chart of reachability analysis when early communication is allowed. Figure 2(b) shows the Gantt chart of reachability analysis when both early communication and partial communication are allowed. Each partition is represented by a vertical broken line. The filled segment represents the *cpu time* for the partition to perform a computation. At the end of each such stage, a small cross indicates the communication of states to other partitions. A break in the line indicates that the corresponding processor is idle. However, in a multi-threaded uniprocessor environment, the processor can immediately schedule another thread for execution. The total time is the reachability time on a multi-processor machine. As we can see from the figure, more gaps are being filled with the addition of each heuristic. This shows a clear trend of improved parallelism in each case.

6   Conclusion

Partitioning based state space traversal approaches where reachability on each partition is processed independently appear very suited for parallelization. However, we find that a naive parallelization of such algorithms is often ineffective. In this paper we discuss an algorithm suitable for parallel reachability on a symmetric multi-processing architecture. We show that in most cases our algorithm achieves good speedup in a multi-processor shared memory environment, compared to the corresponding sequential run. Further, the parallel algorithm is significantly faster than both the standard sequential reachability algorithm as well as the existing partitioned approaches especially when the property is erroneous. We have made the multi-threaded program behavior deterministic. We found that the performance of both the non-deterministic and the deterministic program is similar.

Our investigation, one of the first in the area of a parallel reachability algorithm exploiting SMP architecture reveals that there are significant areas of performance improvements. These include improving scheduling of threads on various processors, selecting window functions that can potentially enhance parallelism, and communication strategies between threads to decrease number of idle CPUs.

Acknowledgments

The authors thank Fujitsu Laboratories of America, Inc for their gifts to support the research. Prof. Dill thanks the NSF for support via grants CCR-012-1403. Any opinions, findings, and conclusions or recommendations expressed in this publication are those of the author(s) and do not necessarily reflect the views of the National Science Foundation.

References

[1] Clarke, E., Emerson, E.: Design and synthesis of synchronization skeletons using branching time temporal logic. In: Proc. IBM Workshop on Logics of Programs. Volume 131 of Lecture Notes in Computer Science. (1981)

[2] McMillan, K.L.: Symbolic Model Checking. Kluwer Academic Publishers (1993)

[3] Bryant, R.: Graph-based Algorithms for Boolean Function Manipulation. IEEE Transactions on Computers **C-35** (1986) 677–691

[4] Coudert, O., Berthet, C., Madre, J.C.: Verification of sequential machines based on symbolic execution. In: Proc. of the Workshop on Automatic Verification Methods for Finite State Systems. (1989)

[5] Jain, J.: et. al., Functional Partitioning for Verification and Related Problems. Brown/MIT VLSI Conference (1992)

[6] Narayan, A.: et. al., Reachability Analysis Using Partitioned-ROBDDs. In: IC-CAD. (1997) 388–393

[7] Iyer, S., Sahoo, D., Stangier, C., Narayan, A., Jain, J.: Improved symbolic Verification Using Partitioning Techniques. In: Proc. of CHARME 2003. Volume 2860 of Lecture Notes in Computer Science. (2003)

[8] Sahoo, D., Iyer, S.: et. al., A Partitioning Methodology for BDD-based Verification. In: FMCAD. (2004)

[9] Stern, U., Dill, D.L.: Parallelizing the murphy verifier. In: CAV. (1997)

[10] Stornetta, T., Brewer, F.: Implementation of an efficient parallel BDD package. In: DAC. (1996) 641–644

[11] Garavel, H., Mateescu, R., Smarandache, I.: Parallel state space construction for model-checking. In: SPIN workshop on Model checking of software, Springer-Verlag New York, Inc. (2001) 217–234

[12] Heyman, T., Geist, D., Grumberg, O., Schuster, A.: Achieving scalability in parallel reachability analysis of very large circuits. In: CAV. (2000)

[13] Yang, B., O'Hallaron, D.R.: Parallel breadth-first bdd construction. In: symposium on Principles and practice of parallel programming, ACM Press (1997) 145–156

[14] Cabodi, G., Camurati, P., Lavagno, L., Quer, S.: Disjunctive partitioning and partial iterative squaring: An effective approach for symbolic traversal of large circuits. In: DAC. (1997) 728–733

[15] Pixley, C., Havlicek, J.: A verification synergy: Constraint-based verification. In: Electronic Design Processes. (2003)

[16] Sahoo, D., Jain, J., Iyer, S.K., Dill, D.L., Emerson, E.A.: Multi-threaded reachability. In: To appear In DAC. (2005)

[17] Ravi, K., Somenzi, F.: High-density reachability analysis. In: ICCAD. (1995) 154–158

[18] Somenzi, F.: CUDD: CU Decision Diagram Package ftp://vlsi.colorado.edu/pub (2001)

[19] VIS: Verilog Benchmarks http://vlsi.colorado.edu/~ vis/ (2001)

Comprehensive Verification Framework for Dependability of Self-optimizing Systems*

Y. Zhao, M. Kardos, S. Oberthür, and F.J. Rammig

Heinz Nixdorf Institute, University of Paderborn, Paderborn, Germany

Abstract. By integrating formal specification and formal verification into the design phase of a system development process, the correctness of the system can be ensured to a great extent. However, it is not sufficient for a self-optimizing system that needs to exchange its components safely and consistently over time. Therefore, this paper presents a comprehensive verification framework to guarantee the dependability of such a self-optimizing system at the design phase (off-line verification) as well as at the runtime phase (on-line verification). The proposed verification framework adopts AsmL as intermediate representation for the system specification and on-the-fly model checking technique for alleviating the state space explosion problem. The *off* and the *on* -line verifications are performed at (RT-UML) model level. The properties to be checked are expressed by RT-OCL where the underlying temporal logic is restricted to time-annotated ACTL/LTL formulae. In particular, the on-line verification is achieved by running the on-the-fly model checking interleaved with the execution of the checked system in a pipelined manner.

1 Introduction

Mechatronic systems represent a special class of complex cross-domain embedded systems. The design of such systems involves a combination of design techniques and technologies used in mechanical and electrical engineering as well as in computer science. The increasing complexity, even emphasized by the system heterogeneity, is one of the major problems in today's mechatronic industry (e.g., automotive industry). To deal with this complexity, one approach is to build mechatronic systems in a self-reflecting, self-adapting and self-optimizing way. In the Collaborative Research Center 614 of the German National Science Foundation (DFG), entitled "Self-optimizing concepts and structures in mechanical engineering", we are investigating such an approach. The main focus is put on self-optimizing applications with highly dynamic software components which are optimized and even replaced at runtime. Moreover, the considered applications run under real-time constraints. As failures of these technical systems usually

---

* This work is developed in the course of the Collaborative Research Center 614 - Self-Optimizing Concepts and Structures in Mechanical Engineering - Paderborn University, and is published on its behalf and funded by the Deutsche Forschungsgemeinschaft (DFG).

D.A. Peled and Y.-K. Tsay (Eds.): ATVA 2005, LNCS 3707, pp. 39–53, 2005.

have severe consequences, dependability is of paramount importance. This puts new demands on verification of such complex and highly dependable systems.

For real-time systems with a dynamic task set, acceptance tests with respect to schedulability are state of the art in RTOS. In reconfigurable and dependable systems the safety and consistency after component replacement has to be checked as well. This extends the classical area of on-line acceptance testing. Traditionally in real-time systems one tries to execute as many checking activities as possible off-line. In systems of dynamic structure this would mean that all components that may be used in a substitution have to be checked *correct* (e.g., using conventional model checking) in an arbitrary context, i.e., in the most general context. Of course, this very general correctness requirement would result in highly over-dimensioned and thus inefficient components, what would be a contradiction to the overall objective of self-optimization.

It is well known that formal methods for specifying and verifying complex systems can offer a greater assurance of correctness than traditional simulation and testing. In the Collaborative Research Center 614, a design technique [1] has been presented for self-optimizing systems, which integrates formal specification (RT-UML) and formal verification (Model Checking) into the early design phase of a system development. This paper concerns the formal verification methodology applicable to the design technique and consequently presents a comprehensive verification framework to ensure the safety and consistency of the self-optimizing systems not only at the design phase but also at execution phase. The former is named off-line verification and the latter on-line verification. The proposed verification framework adopts AsmL as intermediate representation to bridge the gap between the RT-UML models and the model checking tools on the one hand, and on-the-fly model checking methods to alleviate the state space explosion problem on the other hand. Simply speaking, both off and on -line verification are performed at model level. The properties to be checked are expressed by RT-OCL where the underlying temporal logic is restricted to time-annotated ACTL/LTL formulae. In particular, the on-line verification works as service of a real-time operating system (RTOS) so that the on-the-fly model checking can run interleaved with the execution of the checked system in a pipelined manner.

The remainder of this paper is organized as follows: section 2 outlines the preliminaries; section 3 details the comprehensive verification framework; section 4 addresses the on-line verification mechanism; section 5 discusses the related work; finally, section 6 ends with the conclusion.

2   Preliminaries

2.1   Real-Time UML Statechart

According to the design technique used [1], the self-optimizing systems are designed with the CASE tool Fujaba[1] based on the modeling concepts of UML 2.0. That is, the architecture of a system is specified by a component diagram

---

[1] http://www.fujaba.de/

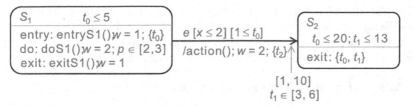

Fig. 1. Part of real-time UML statechart

together with the definitions for ports and connectors; the overall behavior of the system is specified by UML state machines with real-time extension, called RT-UML statecharts, associated to each component, port and connector. In fact, the whole behavior of a component C is the parallel composition of the RT-UML statecharts M_i^r ($1 \leq i \leq m$), which are the refinements of the corresponding protocol state machines associated to the ports P_i ($1 \leq i \leq m$) of C, and the internal synchronization statechart M^s of C, i.e., $M_C = M_1^r \parallel M_2^r \parallel \cdots \parallel M_m^r \parallel M^s$. It is easy to reason that the overall behavior of the system model just is the parallel composition of such a set of RT-UML statecharts.

As far as RT-UML statecharts are concerned, there are many different variants to extend the usual UML statechart with timing constraints in the literature. Here we introduce the RT-UML statechart presented in [2] and realized in the Fujaba tool suite as plug-in. Simply speaking, a RT-UML statechart is obtained by adding real-time annotations to the usual UML statechart. Without loss of generality, Fig. 1 illustrates a typical part of a RT-UML statechart. The state S_1 has the time invariant $t_0 \leq 5$ (time units) and S_2 has the time invariant $t_0 \leq 20$ and $t_1 \leq 13$, where t_0 and t_1 are global clocks. The entry action entryS1() of S_1 has the worst case execution time (wcet) $w = 1$ (time unit) and the clock t_0 is reset while entering S_1, the do activity doS1() of S_1 has $w = 2$ together with period $p \in [2,3]$ and the exit action exitS1() of S_1 has $w = 1$. Similarly, the clocks t_0 and t_1 are reset while exiting S_2. The transition from S_1 to S_2 is triggered whenever the event e is available and the guard $x \leq 2$ and the time guard $1 \leq t_0$ are held. In the mean time, the clock t_2 is reset and the action with $w = 2$ is executed. The firing of the transition has to be finished within the time interval $[1, 10]$ and whenever the clock $t_1 \in [3, 6]$. By default, the transition is urgent and has the priority 1.

2.2   Real-Time OCL

Real-time OCL (RT-OCL) [3] is a state-oriented temporal extension to the usual Object Constraint Language by introducing additional bounded temporal logic operators over the sequence of active state configurations of RT-UML statecharts. E.g., the following invariant requires that for each instance of the class C, at each time point of the next 20 time units, on all possible execution paths, the states S_1 and S_2 must be subsequently entered:

context C
inv:
$self@post[1, 20] \rightarrow forall(p : OclPath \mid p \rightarrow includes(Sequence\{S_1, S_2\}))$

The introduced notations are compliant with the syntax of the OCL 2.0 Proposal and are mapped to real-time CTL (RTCTL) [4], a discrete time variant of the Computation Tree Logic, for further application to model checking. In the future, we'll further extend the RT-OCL [3] to cover timed linear temporal logic.

2.3   Abstract State Machine Language

The Abstract State Machine Language (AsmL) [5] is an executable specification language built upon the theory of Abstract State Machines (ASMs) [6], a formal method for high-level modeling and specification that has proven its strong modeling and specification abilities in various application domains. The main strength of AsmL resides in its rich and expressive syntax, formally underpinned by the ASM theory, which gives user the ability to create precise and comprehensible specifications at any desired level of abstraction. Among other things, AsmL provides a powerful type system that facilitates a wide scale of designs ranging from pure mathematical specifications of algorithms to the complex object-oriented software specifications. Besides the language features, the AsmL comes with a tool support that allows usual validation via specification execution as well as enhanced model-based testing. Moreover, the AsmL tool suite provides a functionality to drive the exploration of the model state space. This feature can be used for constructing a corresponding *Kripke* structure from the given specification so that it can further serve as basis for model checking.

3   Comprehensive Verification Framework

3.1   Overview

The comprehensive verification framework in Fig. 2 illustrates our verification mechanism for the RT-UML models designed with the Fujaba tool suite. First of all, the RT-UML statecharts of the modeled system and the related RT-OCL constraints are exported from the Fujaba Tool Suite in the form of the XML documents and then translated into the corresponding AsmL models and real-time ACTL/LTL formulae respectively at the *Translation* phase. Afterwards, the *Verification Engine* is launched to fulfill the verification task under the assistance of the efficient model checking tools.

To alleviate the state space explosion problem on model checking for complex systems, we adopt on-the-fly model checking for time-annotated ACTL/LTL formulae in our verification framework. For this purpose, the *Kripke* structure of each AsmL model is derived by applying the exploration functionality to the AsmL model and the ACTL/LTL formulae to be verified are transformed into *Büchi* automata. Note that the time-annotated ACTL formulae are just RTCTL (Real-time Computation Tree Logic) [4] formulae with only universal quantifiers allowed and the time-annotated LTL is defined in a similar way. That is, a time interval of the form $[a, b]$, where a and b are *Integers* and $a \leq b$, is attached to the usual temporal operators, named bounded temporal operators. E.g., the formula $AG(p \rightarrow AF_{[0,t]}q)$ specifies that p always leads to q within t time steps.

However, to avoid the fairness conditions caused by the *eventuality* operators, we require that the *eventuality* operators must be bounded ones if any. In this way, the bounds on the *eventuality* operators prevents indefinite postponement. In a word, the verification engine provides the on-the-fly model checker with *Kripke* structures and *Büchi* automata as shown in Fig. 2. Finally, the checking result is reported to the Fujaba tool suite by the verification engine if necessary. As for a negative result, a counterexample is also reported to the Fujaba tool suite and is analyzed there to help figure out the possible problems in the system model. Consequently, the system model is modified and then checked again. This process is repeated until the system model does satisfy the given properties.

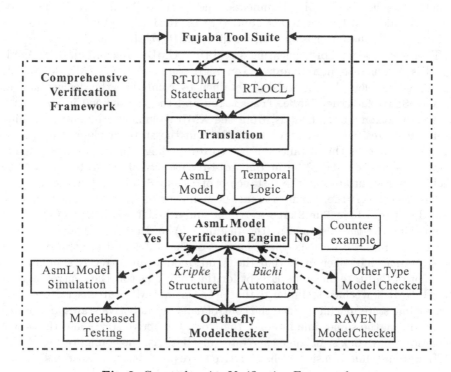

Fig. 2. Comprehensive Verification Framework

In this verification framework, AsmL model plays essentially a role as an intermediate representation from the perspective of model checking. As a result, model checking can be done based on the resulting *Kripke* Structure derived from the AsmL model, which makes it independent of any model checker's input format. Hence, our verification framework can be easily extended by binding other model checking tools. In particular, instead of modifying the internal decision algorithm of a given model checker, many advanced model checking techniques, such as abstraction, compositional and incremental model checking, can be fulfilled at verification engine level. In addition, AsmL model simulation and model-based testing supported by the AsmL tool suite can provide a complement to model checking if needed. Also, using AsmL model as intermediate representation makes the updating of the RT-UML statechart and RT-OCL transparent to model checkers and vice versa.

3.2 Translation Approach

By using the Fujaba tool suite, we can conveniently design individual RT-UML statecharts of a given system and then export them as the corresponding XML documents. Considering that the translation from RT-OCL to Temporal Logic formulae is straightforward, here we mainly focus on the translation approach to convert an RT-UML Statechart into an AsmL model, i.e., to derive AsmL models from the above XML documents. The resulting AsmL model consists of two AsmL files: `declaration.asml` and `instantiation.asml` where the former is common and the latter is special, for different RT-UML statecharts.

Therefore, the goal of translating a real-time UML statechart into an AsmL model is to generate an `instantiation.asml` from the given XML document. Then, the complete AsmL model is obtained by combining the declarations of classes `StateMachine`, `State`, `Transition` and the like defined in the AsmL file `declaration.asml`. That is, from the XML document, the state machine itself, the states, the transitions and others in the state machine are derived and instantiated as the instances of the corresponding classes `StateMachine`, `State`, `Transition` and so on in `instantiation.asml`. E.g., state s in a state machine is instantiated as the instance `s` of class `State` and transition t as the instance `t` of class `Transition`; the behavior of state s (transition t) is defined as procedure `Run_State_s()` (procedure `Run_Transition_t()`), which is associated to the instance `s` (the instance `t`) in `instantiation.asml`. Of course, we also need to make the behaviors of the states and the transitions in the state machine coherent so that the AsmL model can correctly simulate the behavior of the state machine. Except for the timing factor, the control logic of the RT-UML statechart is similar to that of the usual UML statechart. Note that, in real-time state machine, since the control can stay in active states and active transitions in the same time interval, therefore, the active states and the active transitions may coexist in some time intervals. That is, the configuration of RT-UML state machine consists of both active states and active transitions. As for the timing problem, we define procedure `tick()` to increase the values of all the global and local clocks in the state machine one time unit per *tick*. In this way, the complete AsmL model is the combination of the special `instantiation.asml` with the common `declaration.asml`. Due to the limited space, we just outline the basic idea here and refer to [7] for details.

3.3 Verification Engine

The *verification engine* is the pivot of the whole verification framework. The AsmL models obtained at the *translation* phase are explored to acquire the *Kripke* structures by invoking the AsmL exploration functionality. Note that we implicitly assume that each component in the self-optimizing systems owns one finite state machine. Since we adopt the on-the-fly model checking technique, the composition of the resulting *Kripke* structures can be done on-the-fly according to the guidance of the property automaton to be checked. In this way, only a small portion of the state space could be constructed before a counterexample were found (if any). In fact, the *Kripke* structure here is represented as unit delay state transition graph, in which "next state" is identified with "next time". Therefore, the timing constraints in the extended ACTL/LTL formulae can be expressed in the usual ACTL (LTL) using the *next* operator. In this sense, bounded temporal operators are just abbreviations for nested *next* formulae [4]. Consequently, the construction of *Büchi* automata for our real-time temporal formulae can be done in the similar way as for the usual ACTL [8] (LTL [9]). Of course, efficient simplification techniques are suggested to reduce the size of the resulting *Büchi* automata if necessary. The *Büchi* automata here are also represented as unit delay state transition graph. For convenience, let M stand for the system model and B for the property automaton to be checked. In what follows, we discuss the on-the-fly ACTL and LTL model checking methods respectively.

We do on-the-fly ACTL model checking by checking the simulation preorder between M and B incrementally [10]. That is, the decision problem of checking simulation preorder is converted into the satisfiability problem for weakly negative Horn formulae [11], called NHORNSAT problem. The basic idea is to encode the properties of the simulation relation between M and B into a type of CNF (Conjunctive Normal Form) formula Γ, i.e., weakly negative Horn formula, and then prove on-the-fly in polynomial time that the CNF formula Γ is satisfiable.

Let $X_{p,q}$ be a variable in Γ, where p and q are states in M and B respectively. Then, the clauses in the formula Γ are of the following three types:

1) Positive literal $X_{p,q}$, when (p,q) to be in the simulation relation;
2) Negative literal $\overline{X}_{p,q}$, when (p,q) cannot be in any simulation relation;
3) Implication clause of the form $X_{p,q} \rightarrow \bigvee_{p',q'} X_{p',q'}$, when for (p,q) to be in the simulation relation, one of the (p',q')'s must be also in the simulation relation. Here (p',q') belongs to the successors of (p,q).

It is easy to reason that, starting from the initial states of M and B, we can construct the CNF formula Γ by adding to Γ the proper clauses derived from the reachable pairs of states in $M \times B$ layer by layer in BFS (Breadth First Search) order. An efficient on-the-fly algorithm is presented in [12], which receives one Horn clause at a time and allows fast queries about the satisfiability of the whole formula so far received. Let l be the size of the inserted clause and n the size of the whole formula so far received. Then, the algorithm inserts a clause of size l in $O(l)$ amortized time, propagates the effect of this insertion operation on the previous result in $O(n)$ and decides the satisfiability of the formula heretofore constructed in $O(1)$. This algorithm outperforms by an order of magnitude the best known algorithms for the same problem in [13] and [14]. Similarly, a dualization of the algorithm in [12] also gives an efficient linear time on-the-fly solution to the NHORNSAT problem [10].

We follow the emptiness checking method in [15] for the on-the fly LTL model checking. To do this, the property automaton B is derived from the negation of the LTL formula to be verified. Thus, the emptiness of the intersection of

M and B is checked on-the-fly: the states of the intersection of M and B are computed in BFS order from initial states on demand. Let (p, q) be the current state of the search, where p is a state of M and q a state of B. To continue the search, we compute the successors of the state (p, q) one at a time. Because B is already constructed, the successors $q_1, q_2, \cdots, q_k$ of q have already been computed. Let p' be the successor of p that is calculated next. Then, a successor (p', q_i) $(1 \le i \le k)$ of (p, q) exists if the propositions of p is consistent with those of q_i. If the intersection is not empty, a counterexample is reported directly. The time complexity of this method is linear in the size of the product of M and B.

4   On-line Verification Mechanism

Self-optimizing systems need to adjust themselves to dynamic environments over time by means of exchanging components. If such a dynamic adjustment is safety-critical, the dependability problem becomes paramountly significant. Even if we can off-line check at design phase that the current components of a self-optimizing system really hold the required properties, however, it is still possible that the self-optimizing system might not hold the new required properties after some old components were replaced with some new ones at runtime. Hence, in this section we address an on-line verification mechanism based on the on-the-fly model checking technique mentioned in section 3.3, by which the safety and consistency of the dynamic reconfiguration can be checked even at runtime.

4.1   Case Study

Let's take a typical example in Fig. 3 to show how our on-line verification is applied to the self-optimizing systems with safety-critical requirements. Suppose a real-time application contains four components A, B, C and D running in parallel. Now, due to the environment change, a substitution request is passed to a RTOS at time point t_r that the component C would be replaced by the component E at the t_d'th time step after t_r. Before the replacement is really done at time point $t_r + t_d$, the RTOS will trigger the on-line verification mechanism integrated into the RTOS as system service to check if the system still maintains safe and consistent after the replacement. According to the response from the verification service, Yes, No or $Unknown$, the RTOS would decide to accept or reject the requirement for substitution.

Obviously, the substitution of the component E for the component C will cause the environment of each component in the system to be changed at runtime directly (i.e., B, D and E) or indirectly (i.e., A). For component-based systems, each component is verified *correct* under the given assumptions to the environment of the component. As in our case study, the environment of each component in the system might be changed dynamically due to the runtime reconfiguration. Does the changed environment still satisfy the required assumption? To answer this question, traditional model checking unfortunately is not suitable any more: on the one hand, it is difficult to predict how and when the reconfiguration will happen; on the other hand, it is difficult to check the safety and consistency

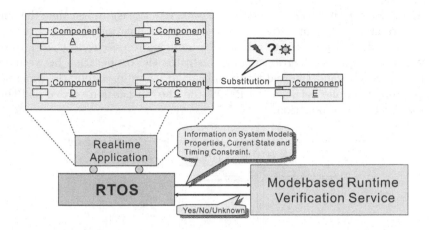

Fig. 3. Case study

of the reconfiguration within the limited time interval. In practice, it is unrealistic to check off-line all the possible cases of the reconfigurations due to the huge time and space complexity. To our knowledge, the state of the art runtime verification [16,17,18,19,20] is also not suitable for our needs. On the one hand, only linear temporal logic formulae as well as trivial assertions and invariants can be checked by tracing the program execution. On the other hand, potential errors can be detected only when they have already happened. In fact, we hope to predict and avoid errors after the reconfiguration. Fortunately, we can resolve this problem by making our on-line verification cooperate in a pipelined working manner with the self-optimizing system via the RTOS as intermediary as shown in Fig. 4.

4.2 Pipelined Working Principle

The self-optimizing operation may cause the system to reconfigure at runtime in many ways. We mainly concern such a case that one component is replaced with another one. Obviously, the replacement may change the environment of every active component in the system directly or indirectly. On the other hand, the only constraint on the components replaceable with each other is that they must follow the compatible protocols, i.e., the protocol of the new one must be the same as or the refinement of the old one. Therefore, it is quite necessary to provide an on-line verification service to make sure that such a reconfiguration does maintain safe and consistent.

Without loss of generality, suppose that a self-optimizing system model M contains n components $C_1, C_2, \cdots, C_n$ ($n \geq 2$) working in parallel and is requested at time point t_r to replace one component C_k ($1 \leq k \leq n$) with another one, say, C'_k at time point t_d relative to t_r, denoted as $M' = M(C'_k/C_k)@(t_r \triangleright t_d)$. Accordingly, let B' be the new property automaton to be satisfied by M'. Consequently, the goal of our on-line verification is to check within the time interval

t_d starting from t_r if $M(C_k'/C_k)@(t_r \triangleright t_d) \models B'$. It is easy to see that the timing constraint is the main barrier for our on-line verification. To leap over this barrier, we adopt a pipelining technique to gain more execution time for verification. The sequence diagram Fig. 4 illustrates the cooperation between the verification service and the real-time application. More precisely, the pipelined working mode is done between the RTOS and the verification service and thus transparent to the application.

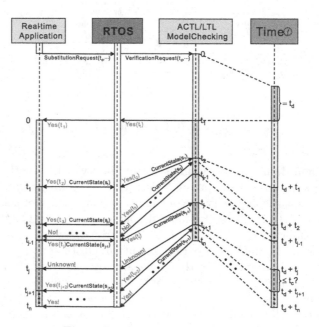

Fig. 4. Pipelined working principle

Whenever the RTOS receives a component substitution request from the application, it will invoke the verification service to check if the substitution is legal or not. The answer must be given within the required timing constraint, say t_d, in our example. If lucky, the verification may finish the checking task before the timing constraint is over. Unfortunately, it might be not the case for more complex systems. Therefore, it is quite possible that, within t_d time units, only the next t_1 time steps starting from the initial states are checked Yes, which means the substitution is safe up to the coming t_1 time steps. In this case, the RTOS does allow the application to make the substitution and execute forward t_1 time steps. During this period, the verification continues to check, say the next $t_2 - t_1$ time steps. Accordingly, the application can then go ahead the next $t_2 - t_1$ time steps. Note that at each time point $t_d + t_i$ ($i \geq 1$) with respect to t_r, the application can report its current state, say s_i, to the verification. Based on this runtime information, the verification can locate in the system model the corresponding state with respect to s_i and thus avoid checking the whole state space of the system model by only checking a sufficient sub-space reachable from this specific state mapped from s_i. In this way, the computation load of the verification can be reduced to a great extent.

The above process is repeated. If at some time point an error is detected, then the verification can be terminated with the answer No to the RTOS. Another situation occurs when at some time point, say $t_d + t_{j+1}$ (relative to t_r), the checking result is still positive, but the time interval $t_{j+1} - t_j$ is less or equal to the pre-defined time constant t_c, which denotes the minimum time steps that the verification must keep ahead of the application. In this case the verification process has to stop and report $Unknown$ to the RTOS. Note that these two cases only mean that the errors might happen in the future, because we check at model level and thus do not know if the errors are spurious or not. To avoid that the errors really happen, we have to conservatively choose to reject the substitution request and inform the application that an error might emerge in the future. That is, an exception will be raised by the RTOS together with a counterexample if necessary. It is possible to let the application to handle the predicted failure in this case, because failure recovery is integrated into the self-optimizing application itself. E.g., for a self-optimizing feedback controller, if the optimization fails, the system would be "near" a critical region (indicated by means of sensor data) and thus could switch into a classical control algorithm in time, which is known to be robust enough (but not optimal or comfortable) to make the system still keep running safely. Finally, if a sufficient sub-space that covers this actual run of the real-time application is successfully checked, then we can report definitely Yes to the RTOS and terminate the verification process. From now on, the application can guarantee to execute safely and consistently after the substitution. In fact, Fig. 4 just illustrates an ideal pipelined cooperation between the application and the verification via the RTOS as intermediary without considering any implementation details.

To make the above on-line verification feasible, the implementation of each component in the system must conform to the corresponding model of the component. In our design environment this is automatically achieved by using Fujaba to generate code directly from the RT-UML model. Therefore, the implementation of a component is the refinement of the model of the component or, put it another way, the model is the abstraction of the corresponding implementation. Thus, an ACTL/LTL formula being $true$ at the model level implies that it is also $true$ at the implementation level, while it being $false$ at the model level does not imply that it is also $false$ at the implementation level. That is, our on-line verification is conservative due to its being applied to model level. However, the benefits of predicting and avoiding errors are gained just due to its being applied to model level. Note that we implicitly assume that the components under consideration own finite state machines and that they have been off-line checked $correct$ under the given assumptions on the environments they depend on at the design phase. In addition, the processing speed for verification is assumed to be faster enough than that for application.

4.3   Improved Model Checking Procedure

It is easy to see that the pipelined working principle between the verification service and the real-time application requires that model checking must be done on-the-fly in a top-down way as mentioned in section 3.3. However, we also need to cooperate the on-the-fly model checking seamlessly with the application via RTOS as intermediary in a pipelined working manner.

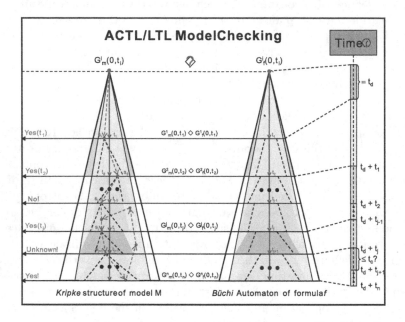

Fig. 5. On-the-fly ACTL/LTL model checking

Due to the limited space, we just use Fig. 5 to intuitively demonstrates how to improve the on-the-fly ACTL/LTL model checking as system service of an RTOS, where "$\diamond$" stands for "$\preceq$" (*simulation relation*) for ACTL model checking and "$\models$" (*satisfaction relation*) for LTL model checking. In order to make the on-line verification efficient, the *Kripke* structures and the *Büchi* automata are stored in a repository in advance. Thus, whenever a verification request from the RTOS is received (Fig. 3), the verification service can fetch the related *Kripke* structures and *Büchi* automata directly from the repository and then immediately start the on-the-fly model checking. As mentioned in Section 4.2, from initial states, only the next t_1 time steps may be checked Yes within the given t_d time units. Similarly, within the next t_1 time units, the next $t_2 - t_1$ time steps may be checked Yes. This procedure is repeated until a definite answer Yes, No, or $Unknown$ is concluded. Note that when the on-the-fly model checking runs to the $(t_d + t_i)$'th ($i \geq 1$) time step, it will know that the current state of the application is s_i. Therefore, model checking can locate the corresponding state mapped from s_i in the system model. For simplicity, we still use s_i to denote its counterpart in the system model. From now on, model checking can continue from this s_i in the system model. In this way, only a part of the state space of the system model needs to be traversed. That is, by introducing the current state s_i from the application, only a subgraph of M' is processed in every checking period. Therefore, in a local view, the time complexity of every checking round is acceptable with respect to the timing constraints. Thus, this runtime ACTL/LTL model checking is feasible in practice. We refer to [21] for details.

5   Related Work

There are two major approaches presented in the literature to translate a (real-time) UML statechart to the input language of a model checker, e.g., SMV, SPIN and UPPAAL. One approach is to flatten the hierarchical UML state machines and then map the flattened statecharts into the input format of a model checker [22,23]. The other approach is to translate each (composite) state into an equivalent ordinary automaton (seen as process) and then use auxiliary signals to synchronize the relevant automata (processes) [24,25]. In addition, there is also the third approach, which translates a UML state machine via an intermediate representation, say ASM, into the input language of a model checker. For instance, [26] adopts XASM [27] to define the formal semantics of the UML statechart diagram and thus model checking can be done based on the semantic model given by XASM.

The related work to traditional (off-line) model checking is well-known and thus omitted here. As for on-line model checking, typically, [16] presents runtime checking for the behavioral equivalence between a component implementation and its interface specification; [17] presents runtime certified computation whereby an algorithm not only produces a result for a given input, but also proves that the result is correct with respect to the given input by deductive reasoning; [18] presents monitoring-oriented programming (MOP) as a lightweight formal method to check conformance of implementation to specification at runtime. Similar to MOP, Temporal Rover [19] is a commercial code generator allowing programmers to insert specifications in programs via comments and then generating executable verification code, which is compiled and linked as part of the application under test, from the specifications. In addition, Java PathExplorer (JPaX) [20] is a runtime verification environment for monitoring the execution traces of a Java program.

6   Conclusion

This paper presents our ongoing work on the comprehensive verification framework for the dependability of the self-optimizing systems with safety-critical requirements. The main characteristics of our verification framework are using AsmL as intermediate representation and using on-the-fly model checking for both ACTL and LTL formulae. For ACTL formulae this means an on-the-fly solution to the NHORNSAT problem, while in the case of LTL formulae, the emptiness checking method is applied. The verification framework provides flexible mechanism to integrate other model checking tools or to extend the current model checking method itself. In particular, the paper extends the verification framework to provide on-line verification service for the self-optimizing systems by introducing the pipelined cooperation between the verification and the application via the RTOS as intermediary. To summarize, our comprehensive verification framework is suitable not only for the off-line model checking at design phase but also for the on-line model checking at runtime phase.

References

1. Giese, H., Tichy, M., Burmester, S., Schäfer, W., Flake, S.: Towards the Compositional Verification of Real-time UML Designs. In: Proceedings of the European Software Engineering Conference (ESEC), Helsinki, Finland (2003)
2. Giese, H., Burmester, S.: Real-time Statechart Semantics. Technical Report tr-ri-03-239, Computer Science Department, Paderborn University (2003)
3. Flake, S., Mueller, W.: An OCL Extension for Real-time Constraints. In Clark, T., Warmer, J., eds.: Object Modeling with the OCL. Number 2263 in LNCS, Heidelberg, Germany, Springer Verlag (2002)
4. Emerson, E.A., Mok, A.K., Sistla, A.P., Srinivasan, J.: Quantitative temporal reasoning. In: Proceedings of the 2nd International Workshop on Computer Aided Verification, London, UK, Springer-Verlag (1991) 136–145
5. Gurevich, Y., Schulte, W., Campbell, C., W.Grieskamp: AsmL: The Abstract State Machine Language Version 2.0. (http://research.microsoft.com/ foundations/AsmL/)
6. Gurevich, Y.: Evolving Algebras 1993: Lipari Guide. In Börger, E., ed.: Specification and Validation Methods. Oxford University Press (1995)
7. Zhao, Y.: Build Asml Model from Real-time UML Statechart. Technical report, Heinz Nixdorf Institute, Paderborn University (2005)
8. Grumberg, O., Long, D.E.: Model Checking and Modular Verification. ACM Transactions on Programming Languages and Systems 16 (1994) 843–872
9. Gerth, R., Peled, D., Vardi, M.Y., Wolper, P.: Simple on-the-fly automatic verification of linear temporal logic. In: Proceedings of the Fifteenth IFIP WG6.1 International Symposium on Protocol Specification, Testing and Verification XV, London, UK, UK, Chapman & Hall, Ltd. (1995) 3–18
10. Shukla, S., Rosenkrantz, D.J., Hunt III, H.B., Stearns, R.E.: A HORNSAT Based Approach to the Polynomial Time Decidability of Simulation Relations for Finite State Processes. DIMACS Series in Discrete Mathematics and Theoretical Computer Science, American Mathematical Society 35 (1997)
11. Schaefer, T.J.: The complexity of satisfiability problems. In: Proceedings of the tenth annual ACM symposium on Theory of computing, New York, NY, USA, ACM Press (1978) 216–226
12. Ausiello, G., Italiano, G.F.: On-line algorithms for polynomially solvable satisfiability problems. J. Log. Program. 10 (1991) 69–90
13. Dowling, W.F., Gallier, J.H.: Linear-time algorithms for testing the satisfiability of propositional horn formulae. J. Log. Program. 1 (1984) 267–284
14. Itai, A., Makowshy, J.A.: Unification as a complexity measure for logic programming. J. Log. Program. 4 (1987) 105–117

15. Courcoubetis, C., Vardi, M., Wolper, P., Yannakakis, M.: Memory-efficient algorithms for the verification of temporal properties. Form. Methods Syst. Des. **1** (1992) 275–288
16. Barnett, M., Schulte, W.: Spying on components: A runtime verification technique. In Leavens, G.T., Sitaraman, M., Giannakopoulou, D., eds.: Workshop on Specification and Verification of Component-Based Systems. (2001)
17. Arkoudas, K., Rinard, M.: Deductive Runtime Certification. In: Proceedings of the 2004 Workshop on Runtime Verification (RV 2004), Barcelona, Spain (2004)
18. Chen, F., Rosu, G.: Towards Monitoring-Oriented Programming: A Paradigm Combining Specification and Implementation. In: Proceedings of the 2003 Workshop on Runtime Verification (RV 2003), Boulder, Colorado, USA (2003)
19. Drusinsky, D.: The Temporal Rover and the ATG Rover. In: SPIN. (2000) 323–330
20. Havelund, K., Rosu, G.: Java PathExplorer — a runtime verification tool. In: Proceedings 6th International Symposium on Artificial Intelligence, Robotics and Automation in Space (ISAIRAS'01), Montreal, Canada (2001)
21. Zhao, Y., Oberthür, S., Kardos, M., Rammig, F.J.: Model-based runtime verification framework for self-optimizing systems. In: Proceedings of the 2005 Workshop on Runtime Verification (RV2005), Edinburgh, Scotland, UK (2005)
22. Diethers, K., Goltz, U., Huhn, M.: Model checking UML statecharts with time. In Jürjens, J., Cengarle, M.V., Fernandez, E.B., Rumpe, B., Sandner, R., eds.: Critical Systems Development with UML – Proceedings of the UML'02 workshop, Technische Universität München, Institut für Informatik (2002) 35–52
23. Knapp, A., Merz, S., Rauh, C.: Model checking - timed uml state machines and collaborations. In: Proceedings of the 7th International Symposium on Formal Techniques in Real-Time and Fault-Tolerant Systems, London, UK, Springer-Verlag (2002) 395–416
24. David, A., Möller, M.O.: From HUPPAAL to UPPAAL: A translation from hierarchical timed automata to flat timed automata. Technical Report RS-01-11, BRICS (2001)
25. Schäfer, T., Knapp, A., Merz, S.: Model checking UML state machines and collaborations. Electronic Notes in Theoretical Computer Science **55** (2001) 13 pages
26. Shen, W., Compton, K.J., Huggins, J.: A toolset for supporting uml static and dynamic model checking. In: COMPSAC. (2002) 147–152
27. Anlauff, M.: Xasm - an extensible, component-based asm language. In: Proceedings of Abstract State Machine Workshop. (2000) 69–90

Exploiting Hub States in Automatic Verification

Giuseppe Della Penna[1,*], Igor Melatti[1], Benedetto Intrigila[2],
and Enrico Tronci[3]

[1] Dip. di Informatica, Università di L'Aquila, Coppito 67100, L'Aquila, Italy
{dellapenna, melatti}@di.univaq.it
[2] Dip. di Matematica, Università di Roma "Tor Vergata",
Via della Ricerca Scientifica, 00133 Roma, Italy
intrigil@mat.uniroma2.it
[3] Dip. di Informatica, Università di Roma "La Sapienza",
Via Salaria 113, 00198 Roma, Italy
tronci@di.uniroma1.it

Abstract. In this paper we present a new algorithm to counteract *state explosion* when using *Explicit State Space Exploration* to verify protocol-like systems.

We sketch the implementation of our algorithm within the Caching Murφ verifier and give experimental results showing its effectiveness.

We show experimentally that, when memory is a scarce resource, our algorithm improves on the time performances of Caching Murφ verification algorithm, saving between 16% and 68% (45% on average) in computation time.

1 Introduction

State Space Exploration (*Reachability Analysis*) is at the very heart of all algorithms for automatic verification of concurrent systems.

As well known, the main obstruction to automatic verification of *Finite State Systems* (FSS) is the huge amount of memory required to complete state space exploration (*state explosion*).

For protocol and hybrid systems verification, *Explicit* State Space Exploration often outperforms *Symbolic* (i.e. OBDD based, [4,5]) State Space Exploration [1,13,8]. Since here we are mainly interested in protocol verification we focus on explicit state space exploration. Tools based on explicit state space exploration are, e.g., SPIN [17,23] and Murφ [11,19].

In our context, roughly speaking, two kinds of approaches have been studied to counteract (i.e. delay) state explosion: *memory saving* and *auxiliary storage*.

In a memory saving approach essentially one tries to reduce the amount of memory needed to represent the set of visited states. Examples of the memory saving approach are, e.g., in [30,7,18,28,26,16,12].

---

* Corresponding Author: Giuseppe Della Penna. Tel: +39 0862 43 3130 Fax: +39 0862 43 3057.

D.A. Peled and Y.-K. Tsay (Eds.): ATVA 2005, LNCS 3707, pp. 54–68, 2005.

In an auxiliary storage approach one tries to exploit disk storage as well as distributed processors (network storage) to enlarge the available memory (and CPU). Examples of this approach are, e.g., in [24,25].

1.1 Background

In [27,10,9] we presented verification algorithms exploiting statistical properties of protocol transition graphs to save on RAM usage as well as to speed up disk based *Breadth First* (BF) state space exploration. Our algorithms have been implemented within the Murφ verifier. We call CMurφ (Caching Murφ [6]) the resulting verifier.

Shortly, CMurφ takes advantage of a statistical property of protocol transition graphs, namely the *transition locality*. That is, w.r.t the levels of a BF state space exploration, state transitions tend to be between states belonging to close levels of the transition graph. Thus, CMurφ replaces the hash table used in a BF state space exploration with a cache memory (i.e. no collision detection is done) and uses auxiliary (disk) storage for the BF queue. The rationale behind this approach is that a cache maintains only *recently visited* states. Thanks to transition locality this is sufficient, in most cases, to complete the verification task. Our experimental results [27,9] show that, with the same amount of RAM, CMurφ can verify systems more than 40% larger than those that can be handled using a hash table based approach. On the other hand, CMurφ verification time can be up to twice that of standard Murφ.

Note that CMurφ caching techniques is not an alternative to state compression techniques (e.g. hash compaction [28,26,16,12]) or to state space reduction techniques (e.g. symmetry and multiset reduction [7,18], partial order reduction [22]). On the contrary, caching is intended to be used together with the available reduction options [27,9]. The only thing that *caching* does is storing data in the cache. Such data can be full states, state signatures, or anything else. This is not relevant to the caching schema. This, of course, may be relevant for the effectiveness of the caching schema. As long as the implemented BF search uses a hash table to store visited states (or their signatures) CMurφ caching scheme can be used. For this reason CMurφ can reuse all state reduction procedures implemented in the standard Murφ verifier [27].

1.2 Goal

CMurφ memory saving stems from the fact the *most* transitions are local. On the other hand, CMurφ time penalty stems from the fact the *not all* transitions are local. A nonlocal transition leading to a rather old state that has been overwritten (and thus *forgotten*) in CMurφ cache may trigger revisit of large portions of the transition graph and may even lead to nontermination because of loops in the transition graph. The higher CMurφ cache *collision rate* (i.e. the ratio between collisions and insertions) the higher the probability of revisiting already visited states because of nonlocal transitions.

When the collision rate is high (i.e. close to 1) it means that we do not have enough RAM to hold all visited states. So our only hope to decrease the time penalty due to revisiting in such a situation is to make a better use of the available RAM.

Quite clearly a (large) fraction of the available RAM must be used to store recently visited states. This is indeed what CMurφ already does. Here we propose to use a (small) fraction of the available RAM to store *hub states*, that is states that have an *in-degree* (i.e. number of incoming transitions) much greater than the average in-degree of the set of reachable states. The rationale behind such proposal is that *many* nonlocal transitions will lead to hub states. Thus avoiding revisiting hub states (and so their successors) may be an effective way to reduce CMurφ time penalty when the collision rate is high.

Note that when the collision rate is low (close to 0) it means that we have (almost) enough RAM to store *all* reachable states. In such a case CMurφ does not incur any time penalty. That is, verification with CMurφ takes the same amount of time as with standard Murφ [19].

Unfortunately our goal of storing hub states faces a substantial obstruction: we do not know *before hand* if a state is a hub or not. Thus, to carry out our goal we need a both time and memory effective way to select hub states among the states visited so far. In other words, the obstruction here is not in storing (the few) hub states, but rather in recognizing that a state seen during the visit is indeed a hub state.

In this paper we show that protocol-like systems do have hub states and present an effective algorithm to select hub states among the states visited so far.

Intuitively, we use a *hard to write* cache L2, that is a cache in which an insertion request is actually carried out with (a small) insertion probability p. This means that states that are frequently *seen* during our visit will have a greater chance than seldom seen states of actually making their way into L2. As a result, statistically speaking, L2 will tend to store the hub states among the states visited so far. Of course not all hub states will be in L2 nor all states in L2 will be hubs. Still, we can show experimentally that L2 is an effective way to catch hub states.

1.3   Main Results

Our main results can be summarized as follows.

In *Section 3* we show experimentally that protocol-like systems do have hub states. We support our claim by measuring the distribution of the in-degree of the reachable states for the set of protocols included in the Murφ verifier distribution [19].

In *Section 4* we present our algorithm to select hub states among the states visited so far.

In *Section 5* we show how an appropriate value for the insertion probability p in L2 can be computed.

We implemented our algorithm within the CMurφ [6] verifier. We call HubCMurφ the resulting verifier. In *Section 6* we give experimental results on HubCMurφ as compared to CMurφ. Our experimental results show that when the collision rate is high typically HubCMurφ allows between 16% and 68% (45% on average) of saving in the verification time. Of course when the collision rate is low HubCMurφ behaves essentially as CMurφ.

1.4   Related Works

A rather systematic study of statistical properties of transition graphs is presented in [21]. The author of [21] concludes that there are no hubs in transition graphs. Note however that the definition of hub state used in [21] is different form ours. For us a reachable state s is a hub state if its in-degree is *much higher* than the average in-degree of the reachable states whereas [21] also requires the s in-degree to be *not too smaller* than the number of (reachable) states.

Of course what is the *right* definition of hub depends on the intended application. Anyway, because of this different definition of hub states there is no contradiction between our results about hub existence and those in [21].

Moreover the focus of our paper is not proving or disproving hub existence but rather finding ways to exploit the fact that there are states whose in-degree is much higher that the average one. Finally, the issue of exploiting statistical properties of transition graphs is not investigated in [21].

A survey on caching schemes is presented in [15]. Note however that [15] studies *Depth First* (DF) search with a linked list based hash table. Caching Murφ [27,9] instead uses a BF search with an open addressing hash table. As remarked in [15] this is a quite different scenario. In fact, CMurφ caching schema works quite well [27,9] with open addressing *and* BF search and does not seem to work with a DF search (SPIN like).

Note that we do not reduce the state space using our hub states. So our approach has nothing to do with *Partial Order* (PO) reduction [22] techniques. On the other hand we can exploit hub states (if any) in a PO reduced state space.

Finally, [3], using static analysis techniques, studies the issue of which states should be stored in order to save RAM. The results in [3] are orthogonal to ours, note however that the two approaches can be usefully combined.

2   Background

In this section we give some basic definitions that will be useful in the following.

For our purposes, a protocol is represented as a *Finite State System*.

Definition 1

1. A *Finite State System* (FSS) $\mathcal{S}$ is a 4-tuple $(S, I, \mathcal{A}, R)$ where: S is a finite set (of states), $I \subseteq S$ is the set of initial states, $\mathcal{A}$ is a finite set (of transition labels) and R is a relation on $S \times A \times S$. R is usually called the *transition relation* of $\mathcal{S}$.
2. Given states $s, s' \in S$ and $a \in A$ we say that *there is a transition from s to s' labeled with a* if and only if $R(s, a, s')$ holds. The set of successors of state s (notation $\texttt{next}(s)$) is the set of states s' such that there exists $a \in A$ such that $R(s, a, s')$ holds.

3. The set of *reachable states* of $\mathcal{S}$ (notation $\mathbf{Reach}(\mathcal{S})$) is the set of states of $\mathcal{S}$ reachable in 0 (zero) or more steps from I. Formally, $\mathbf{Reach}(\mathcal{S})$ is the smallest set such that

   1. $I \subseteq \mathbf{Reach}(\mathcal{S})$,   2. for all $s \in \mathbf{Reach}(\mathcal{S})$, $\text{next}(s) \subseteq \mathbf{Reach}(\mathcal{S})$.

```
FIFOQueue Q; HashTable T;
bfs(FSS S) { let S = (S, I, A, R);
  foreach s in I {Enqueue(Q, s); Insert(T, s);} /*init*/
  while (Q is not empty) { s = Dequeue(Q);
   foreach s' in next(s) { if (s' is not in T) {
    Insert(T, s'); Enqueue(Q, s'); }}}}
```

Fig. 1. Basic Breadth First Search

In the following we will always refer to a given system $\mathcal{S} = (S, I, \mathcal{A}, R)$. Thus, for example, we will write **Reach** for $\mathbf{Reach}(\mathcal{S})$. Also, we may speak about the set of initial states I as well as about the transition relation R without explicitly mentioning $\mathcal{S}$.

The core of all automatic verification tools is the *reachability analysis*, that is the computation of **Reach** given a definition of $\mathcal{S}$ in some language.

Since the transition relation R of a system defines a graph (*transition graph*), computing **Reach** means visiting (exploring) the transition graph starting from the initial states in I. This can be done, e.g., by using a *Depth–First* (DF) search or a *Breadth–First* (BF) search. For example, Murφ [19] and (the latest version of) SPIN [23] may use a DF as well as a BF search.

In the following we will focus on BF search. The Murφ algorithm for the BF visit is shown in Figure 1. Namely, function **bfs** of Figure 1 takes as input a FSS $\mathcal{S}$ and performs a BF visit of $\mathcal{S}$ transition graph. To this end, it uses a FIFO queue **Q** and a hash table **T**. The first maintains the BF front (i.e. the states to be expanded), while the latter stores the visited states, so avoiding to revisit the same states. Thus, state explosion occurs on **T** and **Q**. Finally, note that, if **T** and **Q** fit in the available memory, **bfs** will surely terminate, since the set of reachable states is finite.

3   Hub States

Inspired by [14,2,29] we call *hub* a reachable state which in-degree is much higher than the average in-degree of all reachable states. Note that, as discussed in Section 1.4, our definition of hub state is different from the one used in [21].

In this section we show experimentally that for protocol-like systems hub states do exist. We do this by showing that all our benchmark protocols indeed have hub states. We use as benchmark protocols all those available in the Murφ verifier distribution [19]. The protocols tested cover a wide range of concurrent software typologies such as synchronization, authentication, cache coherence, distributed locks, etc. Thus we have a fairly representative benchmark set.

3.1   Measuring Hub States Presence

In this section we give the basic definitions needed to understand the experimental results in Section 3.2.

Definition 2. *Let $\mathcal{S} = (S, I, A, R)$ be an FSS, and let $s \in S$ be a state. We call* in-degree *of the state s the number* $\mathtt{indeg}(s)$ *of transitions leading to s. That is:* $\mathtt{indeg}(s) = |\{(r, a) \in \mathbf{Reach}(\mathcal{S}) \times A \mid R(r, a, s)\}|$.

Our goal is to study the in-degree distribution in protocol-like systems. As usual when reporting statistical results, to make distributions relative to different systems easily comparable we replace the absolute number of states with the fraction x of reachable states and the actual in-degree value with its fraction of the maximum in-degree. In this way all quantities lie in the interval $[0, 1]$.

To build the in-degree distribution we proceed in the standard way. Namely, we divide the interval $[0, 1]$ in $\lceil \frac{1}{\Delta} \rceil$ subintervals of length Δ and, for each subinterval k, we compute the fraction of the reachable states whose fraction of the maximum in-degree falls in interval k. The following definition gives the formal details.

Definition 3. *Let $\mathcal{S} = (S, I, A, R)$ be an FSS, $M_{\mathtt{indeg}} = \max\{\mathtt{indeg}(t) | t \in \mathbf{Reach}(\mathcal{S})\}$ be the maximum in-degree of $\mathcal{S}$ and $\Delta \in [0, 1]$.*

- *We define function $\theta : (0, 1] \times \mathbb{N} \to [0, 1]$ as follows:*

$$\theta(\Delta, k) = \frac{|\{s \in \mathbf{Reach}(\mathcal{S}) \mid (k - 1)\Delta M_{\mathtt{indeg}} < \mathtt{indeg}(s) \leq k\Delta M_{\mathtt{indeg}}\}|}{|\mathbf{Reach}(\mathcal{S})|}$$

  Function $\theta(\Delta, k)$ returns the fraction of reachable states whose in-degree is a fraction $y \in ((k - 1)\Delta, k\Delta]$ of the maximum in-degree. In other words, $\theta(\Delta, k)$ returns the probability that a reachable state has an in-degree which is a fraction $y \in ((k - 1)\Delta, k\Delta]$ of the maximum in-degree. Thus, technically speaking, $\theta(\Delta, k)$ is a probability density. Of course, for us, function $\theta(\Delta, k)$ is only interesting when $k \leq \frac{1}{\Delta}$.
- *We define function $\tau : (0, 1] \times [0, 1] \to [0, 1]$ as follows:*

$$\tau(\Delta, x) = \theta\left(\Delta, \left\lceil \frac{x}{\Delta} \right\rceil\right)$$

  We also write $\tau_\Delta(x)$ for $\tau(\Delta, x)$ and denote with τ_Δ function $\lambda x. \tau(\Delta, x)$. That is, $\tau_\Delta : (0, 1] \to [0, 1]$ is defined as $\tau_\Delta(x) = \tau(\Delta, x)$. Note that function τ_Δ is completely defined once we know the values $\tau_\Delta(\Delta)$, $\tau_\Delta(2\Delta), \ldots \tau_\Delta(1)$.

3.2   Experimental Results About Hub States

To carry out our plan we modified the Murφ verifier so as to compute function τ in Definition 3. Namely, we compute $\tau_{\frac{1}{n}}(\frac{1}{n}), \ldots, \tau_{\frac{1}{n}}(\frac{n-1}{n}), \tau_{\frac{1}{n}}(1)$ while performing state space exploration. In our experiments, we set $n = 20$.

Our results are shown in Figure 2 where, for each protocol in our benchmark, we plot $\tau(\frac{1}{n}, x)$ (y-axes) versus the fraction x of the maximum in-degree (x-axes).

The graphs in Figure 2 show that most reachable states have an in-degree that is a rather small fraction of the maximum in-degree. However there is a small fraction of states that have an in-degree that is close to the maximum in-degree.

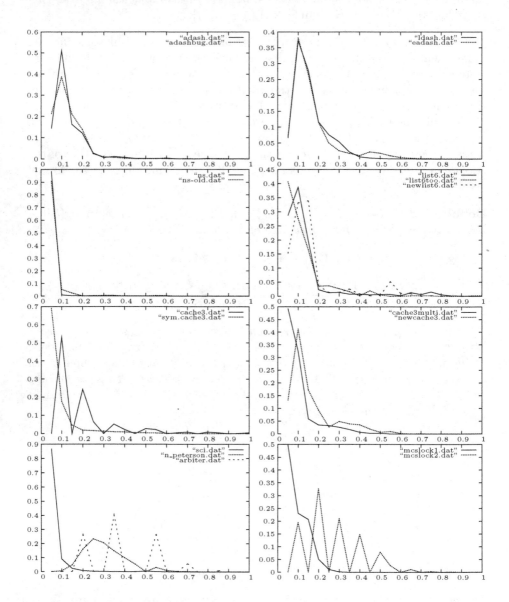

Fig. 2. Density of probability $\tau_{\frac{1}{20}}$ graphs for protocols included in the Murφ distribution. The curves show the fraction of reachable states y which in-degree is a fraction x of the max in-degree. Thus, by definition $y > 0$ when $x = 1$. Note log scale on y axes.

4   Exploiting Hub States in State Space Exploration

In this section we present an algorithm that is able to effectively select hub states among the states visited so far. Note that the correctness of our algorithm does not depend on the results in Section 3. However such results will help us to understand why the proposed algorithm is effective on protocol-like systems.

Before describing our algorithm, in Figure 3 we briefly recall the CMurφ [9] one. With respect to Figure 1, we have that in Figure 3 the queue is now implemented on disk, and the hash table T is replaced by a cache. That is, if the insertion of a state s' causes a collision because of a state t already in cache T, then t is overwritten (and thus *forgotten*). This implies that, if t is reached again, it will be revisited, since it is not in our cache anymore. This means that in general cache T may not be able to prevent nontermination of our visit. As shown in Figure 3, to guarantee termination in CMurφ, the main while cycle is guarded by the *collision rate*, i.e. the ratio between the number of collisions and the number of insertions in cache T. In fact, when the collision rate becomes too high, we are visiting over and over the same set of states. In this case we should give up our verification task because of lack of memory.

In order to improve CMurφ time performances, we present a new two-level caching algorithm. The rationale behind this algorithm is the one discussed in Section 1.2.

To implement the ideas in Section 1.2 we proceed as follows. We modify the cache based BF algorithm in Figure 3 as shown in Figures 4 and 5. Namely, we split cache T in two parts, L1 and L2, with a split ratio $0 < p_h < 1$. Thus, if M was the amount of RAM dedicated to T, then $p_h M$ is now dedicated to L1 and $(1 - p_h)M$ to L2. In our experiments, we set $p_h = 0.7$. This is a reasonable value, since hub states are always a very small subset of the reachable states (see Figure 2).

The idea is to use L1 to store the recently visited states, so inheriting the goal of T (i.e. to exploit transition locality) in CMurφ, and L2 (our *hard to write* cache) to store the hub states. To this end, the algorithm now stores the visited states in L1 (function Insert in Figure 4) and, when the insertion of a state s' causes a collision in L1 on state t, t is passed to L2 *before* being overwritten. If this causes a collision also in L2 on a state r, r will be overwritten by t with a fixed probability p_ovrwrt (functions Insert_L2 and prob_decide in Figure 5). Of course a state is considered visited if it can be found in L1 or L2 (see functions Insert and Lookup_L2 in Figures 4 and 5, respectively).

In this way, if state t is a hub, it will have a high probability of being eventually inserted in L2 and remaining there. In fact, since t will be reached more often than the other states, it will be often present and overwritten in L1 and, as a result, it will attempt insertion in L2 many times. This gives t more chances of entering L2 since it will compete more times for the insertion.

We implemented the algorithm of Figures 4 and 5 within the CMurφ verifier [6], calling HubCMurφ the resulting verifier.

```
FIFOQueue Q;          Cache T;
collision_rate = 0.0;  /* #collisions on T */
                          #insertions in T
cbfs(FSS S) { let S = (S, I, A, R);
 foreach s in I {Enqueue(Q, s); Insert(T, s);}
 while ((Q is not empty) and (collision_rate <= 0.9)) {
 s = Dequeue(Q);
  foreach s' in next(s) if (s' is not in T) {
                      Insert(T, s'); Enqueue(Q, s');}}}
```

Fig. 3. Cache based Breadth First Search

```
Insert(s) {h = hash_key(s);
 if (L1[h] == s) { /*cache hit (state found)*/
  return true; /* report a cache hit */
 } else { /* s not in L1 */
  if (Lookup_L2(s)) { /* but s is in L2 */
   return true; /* report a cache hit */
  } else { /*s is neither in L1 nor in L2, insert it*/
   if (L1[h] is empty) {L1[h] = s;
   } else { /* the slot is full, overwrite it */
    s' = L1[h];
    /* before overwriting s', pass it to L2 */
    Insert_L2(s'); L1[h] = s; }}
  return false; /* report a cache miss */ }}
```

Fig. 4. Function Insert

```
Lookup_L2(s) { h = hash_key2(s);
 if (L2[h] == s) return true; else return false; }

Insert_L2(s) { h = hash_key2(s);
 if (L2[h] == s) return true; /* report a cache hit */
 else if (L2[h] is empty) L2[h] = s;
  else /* slot full, we may choose to overwrite */
  if (prob_decide(p_ovrwrt)) L2[h] = s;
 return false; /* report a cache miss */ }

prob_decide(p) {
  return true with probability p, false otherwise;}
```

Fig. 5. Functions Lookup_L2, Insert_L2 and prob_decide

5 Tuning the Overwrite Probability

As already said in Section 4, a state that causes a collision in the L2 cache is overwritten with a fixed probability p_ovrwrt. To make L2 effective in finding and retaining hub states, it is important to choose a suitable value of p_ovrwrt.

We carried out a set of experiments to determine a reasonable value for p_ovrwrt. In particular, Figure 6 shows the collision rate as a function of the fraction of visited reachable states for values of p_ovrwrt in $\{10^{-4}, 10^{-3}, 10^{-2}, 10^{-1}, 1\}$. When p_ovrwrt $\leq 10^{-5}$ the collision rate becomes soon pretty high and the visits stops. This is because when p_ovrwrt s *too small* it is almost like not having L2 at all. For this reason we only plotted p_ovrwrt in the range $\{10^{-4}, 10^{-3}, 10^{-2}, 10^{-1}, 1\}$. Note that the protocol set used in these experiments is the same one used in Section 6 to assess performances of our algorithm.

Figure 6 shows that when p_ovrwrt is 1 there are cases in which verification does not terminate. For example this happens for protocols mcslock1, mcslock2 and newlists6 in Figure 6.

Note that setting p_ovrwrt to 1 is equivalent two using the standard *victim cache* approach in processor design [20]. However, this does not work in our setting, since in this way the algorithm will overwrite too many states (hubs included) thus leading to nontermination.

On the other hand if p_ovrwrt is *too small* (namely less than 10^{-4}) then L2 will (almost) never be used and, all in all, we have wasted a fraction p_h (see Section 4) of our RAM.

Finally, if p_ovrwrt is *small enough*, only states that are encountered many times during the exploration process will make their way to L2. Summing up, in our experiments we choose to set p_ovrwrt $= 10^{-4}$.

6 Experimental Results

We report the experimental results we obtained using HubCMurφ (Section 4).

We want to measure how much time and (RAM) memory we can save by using our approach. To make the results from different protocols comparable we proceed as follows.

First, for each protocol we determine the minimum amount of memory needed to complete verification using the Murφ verifier (namely Murφ version 3.1 from [19]).

Let M be the amount of memory and g (in $[0, 1]$) be the fraction of M used for the queue (i.e. g is gPercentActive using a Murφ parlance). We say that the pair (M, g) is *suitable* for protocol p iff the verification of p can be completed with memory M and queue gM. For each protocol p we determine the least M s.t. for some g, (M, g) is suitable for p. In the following we denote with $M(p)$ such M.

Of course $M(p)$ depends on the compression options one uses. Murφ offers *bit compression* (-b) and *hash compaction* (-c). However, since in our scenario

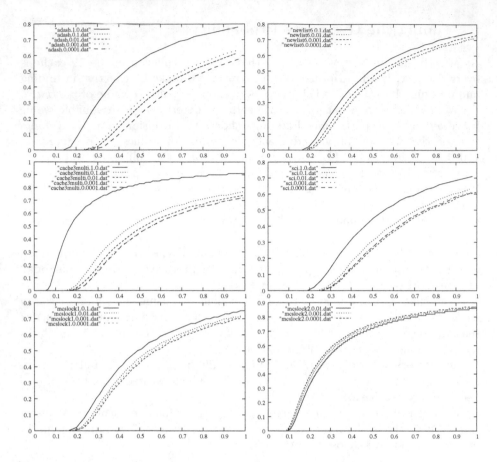

Fig. 6. Collision rate as a function of the fraction of visited protocol states. Each graph shows the collision rate for values of p_ovrwrt in $\{10^{-4}, 10^{-3}, 10^{-2}, 10^{-1}, 1\}$. A missing line indicates that the verifier was unable to complete the verification with the corresponding value of p_ovrwrt.

RAM is a scarce resource, in the following we only consider the case in which both options are enabled on all verifiers (i.e. Murφ, CMurφ, HubCMurφ). Moreover, in order to visit all reachable states, all experiments have been carried out with deadlock detection disabled (-ndl).

Our results are in Figure 7, where we only show protocols requiring at least 10 kilobytes of RAM and a nonnegligible amount of time to complete state space exploration. In Figure 7, column **M** gives the minimum amount of memory (in kilobytes) needed to complete state space exploration and column **T** gives the time (in seconds) to complete state space exploration when using memory M. Finally, column **Reach** gives the number of reachable states.

Our next step is to run each protocol p with less and less memory using both HubCMurφ and CMurφ. That is we run protocol p with memory limits $\alpha M(p)$, $\alpha \in [0, 1]$, with the new (L1+L2) and the old (just CMurφ L1) cache based algorithm. This approach allows us to easily compare the experimental results obtained from different protocols.

The results obtained in such a way are in Fig. 9. Note that in these experiments the value used for g (**gPercentActive**) is not relevant since the queue is implemented on disk. We give the meaning of rows and columns in Fig. 9.

Column α (with $\alpha \in [0,1]$) gives information about the run of protocol p with memory $\alpha M(p)$ (for this reason, the row heading is **Mem**).

Row **States** gives $\frac{N_{hub}}{N_{nohub}}$, where N_{nohub} is the number of visited states using CMurφ and N_{hub} is the number of visited states using HubCMurφ.

Row **Time** gives $\frac{T_{hub}}{T_{nohub}}$, where T_{nohub} is the computation time needed by CMurφ and T_{hub} is the computation time needed by HubCMurφ.

A verifier (CMurφ or HubCMurφ) is stopped when its collision rate becomes greater than 0.99. We mark with a $*$ superscript the data obtained when CMurφ gives up state space exploration because its collision rate exceeds the given threshold (0.99) and, on the contrary, HubCMurφ succeeds in completing the verification. In such cases, instead of giving a ratio, rows **States** and **Time** display, respectively, the absolute values for the visited states and the computation time (in seconds) of HubCMurφ. Note that there was no case in which only CMurφ completed the verification.

We are interested in the case in which the collision rate is high, since this means that we do not have enough RAM to store all visited states. For this reason when comparing CMurφ and HubCMurφ performances we only consider the results obtained from the experiments relative to the least α in which both CMurφ and HubCMurφ terminate. This means that column (α - 0.01) is marked with a $*$ (only HubCMurφ terminates). When the collision rate is low (i.e. we do have enough memory to store *most* of the visited states) CMurφ and HubCMurφ have similar performances. This can be seen from Figure 9 by looking at the column with the largest value of α (namely the leftmost column).

The experimental results in Figure 9 show that, with respect to CMurφ, HubCMurφ typically saves from 16% to 68% (45% on average) in computation time. Note also that for all protocols there are cases in which, with the available memory, only HubCMurφ is able to terminate.

Of course there are protocols (e.g. **n_peterson** in Figure 9) where HubCMurφ is less efficient than CMurφ. We conjecture that this is due to the shape of the in-degree distribution curves in Figure 2. First, we should note that, technically speaking, the curves in Figure 2 are *density* of probabilities. Now, for each protocol p we can compare the curve for p in Figure 2 with HubCMurφ performances for p as from Figure 9. From this we see that if the curve of p is rather *concentrated* (i.e., has a small *variance*) then HubCMurφ performs well on p (e.g., as for protocol **sci**). On the other hand, if p curve has a large variance (e.g. as for **mcslock2** and **n_peterson**) then HubCMurφ does not perform well on p.

We also wanted to test our approach with a large protocol that heavily loads our machine. The results are in Fig. 8. We used protocol **sci** with parameter **MemorySize** set to 5. As shown in [10], this protocol has 75,081,011 reachable

Protocol	Reach	M	T
n_peterson	163298	813	273.32
adash	10466	55	62.98
cache3multi	13738	73	35.11
newlist6	13044	67	18.34
mcslock1	23644	120	16.76
mcslock2	540219	2693	237.48
sci	18193	94	28.17

Fig. 7. Results on a SUN Sparc machine with 512M RAM

Mem	0.41	0.37
States	80430178*	84045856*
Time	47129*	46604*
Mem	**0.33**	**0.29**
States	92322597*	120543398*
Time	51009*	66676*

Fig. 8. HubCMurφ experimental results for protocol `sci-31151` with parameter `MemorySize = 5`

mcslock1

	Mem	0.60	0.59	0.58	0.57	0.56	0.55	0.54	0.53	0.52	0.51	0.50	0.49
	States	0.603	0.352	72358*	104019*	134834*							
	Time	0.69	0.42	3.89*	5.62*	7.36*							

cache3multi

	Mem	0.60	0.59	0.58	0.57	0.56	0.55	0.54	0.53	0.52	0.51	0.50	0.49
	States	0.828	0.89	0.769	0.77	66687*	87096*						
	Time	0.83	0.92	0.78	0.79	19.39*	25.22*						

mcslock2

	Mem	0.60	0.59	0.58	0.57	0.56	0.55	0.54	0.53	0.52	0.51	0.50	0.49
	States	0.99	0.976	0.956	0.93	0.919	0.885	0.805	0.714	1164348*	1397335*	2085105*	
	Time	1.19	1.16	1.14	1.12	1.09	1.05	0.96	0.84	39.67*	47.92*	72.06*	

newlist6

	Mem	0.60	0.59	0.58	0.57	0.56	0.55	0.54	0.53	0.52	0.51	0.50	0.49
	States	0.697	0.296	48882*	63843*								
	Time	0.75	0.32	5.14*	6.69*								

adash

	Mem	0.60	0.59	0.58	0.57	0.56	0.55	0.54	0.53	0.52	0.51	0.50	0.49
	States	0.87	0.873	0.421	0.584	21362*	32166*						
	Time	0.88	0.91	0.44	0.61	11.52*	17.27*						

sci

	Mem	0.49	0.48	0.47	0.46	0.45	0.44	0.43	0.42	0.41	0.40	0.39	0.38
	States	0.914	0.799	0.833	0.797	0.693	0.818	0.626	0.305	34019*	41096*	47845*	91666*
	Time	0.95	0.8	0.84	0.8	0.69	0.86	0.64	0.32	5.28*	6.42*	7.39*	14.17*

n_peterson

	Mem	0.70	0.69	0.68	0.67	0.66	0.65	0.64	0.63	0.62	0.61	0.60	0.59
	States	1.079	1.078	1.028	1.311	1.071	0.663	1.635	1.188	1.032	5588575*		
	Time	1.2	1.2	1.14	1.46	1.18	0.73	1.82	1.32	1.14	368.17*		

Fig. 9. Comparison of CMurφ and HubCMurφ experimental results on an INTEL Pentium 3.2GHz machine with 512M RAM

states and requires 563 Megabytes of memory to be verified with standard Murφ in 35,905 seconds.

CMurφ was not able to complete verification with less than 225 Megabytes, that is 40% of the required (563MB) memory.

On the other hand, as shown in Fig. 8, HubCMurφ completed the verification with about 163 MB, that is 29% of the required memory, and a time penalty (w.r.t. standard Murφ with 563MB of RAM) of 85%.

This suggests that for large protocols HubCMurφ can achieve huge (about 71% in our example above) memory savings, possibly at the expense of time. This is better than being left with an *out of memory* message after hours of computation.

7 Conclusions

We presented a novel explicit verification algorithm that exploits hub states (Section 3) to save on memory usage (Sections 4, 5). We implemented our algorithm within the CMurφ verifier [6] and call HubCMurφ the resulting verifier.

Our experimental results (Section 6) show that, with respect to CMurφ, HubCMurφ typically saves from 16% to 68% (45% on average) in computation time.

Acknowledgments

We gratefully acknowledge discussing with Alan Hu during CHARME 2001 conference the possibility of using a small *victim cache* in order to improve CMurφ performances. Although in its basic form a victim cache does not meet our goals here, it is also quite clear that our *hard to write* second level cache is a sort of (*lucky*) victim cache.

References

1. A.J. Hu, G. York, and D.L. Dill. New Techniques for Efficient Verification with Implicitly Conjoined BDDs. In *31st ACM/IEEE Design Automation Conference (DAC)*, San Diego, CA, USA, 1994.
2. Albert-Laszlo Barabasi. *Linked*. Perseus Publishing, 2002.
3. G. Behrmann, K. G. Larsen, and R. Pelánek. To store or not to store. In *Proc. of 15th Int. Conf. on: Computer Aided Verification (CAV)*, volume 2725 of *Lecture Notes in Computer Science*, Boulder, CO, USA, July 2033. Springer.
4. R. Bryant. Graph-based algorithms for boolean function manipulation. *IEEE Trans. on Computers*, C-35(8):677–691, Aug 1986.
5. J. R. Burch, E. M. Clarke, K. L. McMillan, D. L. Dill, and L. J. Hwang. Symbolic model checking: 10^{20} states and beyond. *Inf. Comput.*, 98(2):142–170, 1992.
6. Caching murphi web page: http://www.dsi.uniroma1.it/~tronci/cached.murphi.html, 2004.
7. C.N. Ip and D.L. Dill. Better verification through symmetry. In *Computer Hardware Description Languages and their Applications*, Ottawa, Canada, 1993. Elsevier Science Publishers B.V., Amsterdam, Netherland.
8. G. Della Penna, B. Intrigila, I. Melatti, M. Minichino, E. Ciancamerla, A. Parisse, E. Tronci, and M. Venturini Zilli. Automatic verification of a turbogas control system with the murφ verifier. In *Hybrid Systems: Computation and Control, HSCC, Proc.*, volume 2623 of *Lecture Notes in Computer Science*. Springer, 2003.
9. G. Della Penna, B. Intrigila, I. Melatti, E. Tronci, and M. Venturini Zilli. Exploiting transition locality in automatic verification of finite state concurrent systems. *STTT*, 6(4), 2004.
10. G. Della Penna, B. Intrigila, E. Tronci, and M. Venturini Zilli. Exploiting transition locality in the disk based murφ verifier. In *Formal Methods in Computer-Aided Design, FMCAD'02, Proc.*, volume 2517 of *Lecture Notes in Computer Science*. Springer, 2002.
11. D. L. Dill, A. J. Drexler, A. J. Hu, and C. Han Yang. Protocol verification as a hardware design aid. In *Proc. of the 1991 IEEE Int. Conf. on Computer Design on VLSI in Computer & Processors*. IEEE Computer Society, 1992.
12. Peter C. Dillinger and Panagiotis Manolios. Bloom filters in probabilistic verification. In *Formal Methods in Computer-Aided Design, FMCAD, Proc.*, volume 3312 of *Lecture Notes in Computer Science*. Springer, Nov 2004.
13. Cindy Eisner and Doron Peled. Comparing symbolic and explicit model checking of a software system. In *SPIN Workshop, Proc.*, Lecture Notes in Computer Science. Springer, 2002.
14. Michalis Faloutsos, Petros Faloutsos, and Christos Faloutsos. On power-law relationships of the internet topology. In *SIGCOMM '99: Proc. of the Conf. on Applications, technologies, architectures, and protocols for computer communication*, New York, NY, USA, 1999. ACM Press.

15. Jaco Geldenhuys. State caching reconsidered. In *SPIN Workshop, Proc.*, volume 2989 of *Lecture Notes in Computer Science*. Springer, 2004.
16. Gerard J. Holzmann. An analysis of bitstate hashing. *Form. Methods Syst. Des.*, 13(3):289–307, 1998.
17. Gerard J. Holzmann. *The SPIN Model Checker: Primer and Reference Manual.* Addison Wesley Professional, 2004.
18. C. N. Ip and D. L. Dill. Efficient verification of symmetric concurrent systems. In *Proc. of the IEEE Int. Conf. on Computer Design: VLSI in Computers and Processors*, Cambridge, MA, October 1993. IEEE Computer Society Press.
19. Murphi web page: http://sprout.stanford.edu/dill/murphi.html, 2004.
20. David A. Patterson and John L. Hennessy. *Computer architecture: a quantitative approach.* Morgan Kaufmann Publishers Inc., 1996.
21. Radek Pelánek. Typical structural properties of state spaces. In *SPIN Workshop, Proc.*, volume 2989 of *Lecture Notes in Computer Science*. Springer, 2004.
22. D. Peled. Ten years of partial order reduction. In *Computer Aided Verification, CAV, Proc.*, volume 1427 of *Lecture Notes in Computer Science*. Springer, 1998.
23. Spin web page: http://spinroot.com, 2004.
24. U. Stern and D. Dill. Parallelizing the murφ verifier. In *Computer Aided Verification (CAV), Proc*, volume 1254 of *Lecture Notes in Computer Science*. Springer, 1997.
25. U. Stern and D. Dill. Using magnetic disk instead of main memory in the murφ verifier. In *Computer Aided Verification (CAV), Proc.*, volume 1427 of *Lecture Notes in Computer Science*. Springer, 1998.
26. U. Stern and D. L. Dill. A new scheme for memory-efficient probabilistic verification. In *IFIP TC6/WG6.1 Joint Int. Conf. on: Formal Description Techniques for Distributed Systems and Communication Protocols, and Protocol Specification, Testing, and Verification*, volume 69 of *IFIP Conference Proceedings*. Kluwer, 1996.
27. E. Tronci, G. Della Penna, B. Intrigila, and M. Venturini Zilli. Exploiting transition locality in automatic verification. In *Correct Hardware Design and Verification Methods, CHARME, Proc.*, volume 2144 of *Lecture Notes in Computer Science*. Springer, 2001.
28. U. Stern and D.L. Dill. Improved Probabilistic Verification by Hash Compaction. In *Correct Hardware Design and Verification Methods*, volume 987, Stanford University, USA, 1995. Springer-Verlag.
29. D. J. Watts. *Small Worlds: The Dynamics of Networks Between Order and Randomness.* Princeton Univ. Press, Princeton, NJ, USA, 1999.
30. Pierre Wolper and Dennis Leroy. Reliable hashing without collision detection. In *Computer Aided Verification (CAV), Proc.*, volume 697 of *Lecture Notes in Computer Science*. Springer, 1993.

An Approach for the Verification of SystemC Designs Using AsmL

Ali Habibi and Sofiène Tahar

Concordia University, Montreal, Quebec, H3G 1M8 Canada
{habibi, tahar}@ece.concordia.ca

Abstract. The spectacular advancement in microelectronics resulted in the creation of new system level design languages, such as SystemC, which put fourth new design and verification challenges. In this paper, we present an approach verifying SystemC designs using model checking and assertion based verification. Such verification is enabled through two transformations from SystemC to AsmL (the Abstract State Machines Language) and vice-versa. The soundness of these transformations, proved using abstract interpretation, guarantees the correctness of the model checking results and the validity of the generated assertion monitors (to be checked by simulation). We illustrate our approach on the SystemC/AsmL modeling and verification of the widely used Accelerated Graphics Port (AGP) standard. The verified AGP model can be either refined to implement an AGP core or used to validate existent compatible device.

1 Introduction

SystemC [18] is an object-oriented system level language for embedded systems design and verification. It is expected to make a stronger effect in the area of architecture, co-design and integration of hardware and software. The SystemC library is composed of a set of classes and a simulation kernel extending C++ to enable the modeling of complex systems at a higher level of abstraction than state-of-the-art HDLs. Nevertheless, except for small models, the verification of SystemC designs is a serious bottleneck in the system design flow. While simulation is the mostly widely used verification technique, it is unable to guarantee the correctness of the design with respect to its specification. On the other hand, model checking is considered as a relevant technique to cover for simulation insufficiencies. Nevertheless, direct model checking of SystemC is not feasible due to the complexity of this library. Besides, the state explosion problem led, for complex systems, to the use of assertion based verification (ABV) where the property under verification is turned into a monitor, checked by simulation and evaluated using coverage metrics. The soundness of ABV relies, in particular, on the correctness of the generation of the SystemC monitor from the property.

In order to enable the model checking of a SystemC design, we translate it to an intermediate representation in AsmL [16]. This latter is an object-oriented abstract state machines (ASM) [2] description language providing features to

D.A. Peled and Y.-K. Tsay (Eds.): ATVA 2005, LNCS 3707, pp. 69–83, 2005.

capture the behavioral semantics of programming and modeling languages where systems are modeled at a high level of abstraction allowing easier validation and verification operations.

The AsmL language is integrated with Microsoft's software development environment and integrated with the Asmlt tool [16] offering a reachability algorithm, able to generate an FSM of the model that can be adapted to perform model checking. When a state explosion happens the design properties are translated to SystemC assertion monitors and verified by simulation. This is made possible through the embedding of the property specification language (PSL [1]) in the same formalism.

The soundness of our approach is established using abstract interpretation by proving the correctness of both transformations: (1) from the original SystemC design to its AsmL representation; and (2) from the PSL property, in AsmL, to the generated monitor, in SystemC.

To illustrate our approach, we considered the AGP bus [14] that was, as far as we know, only verified by simulation due to its complexity and very large state space. We will show that our technique combined with the abstraction features of AsmL allows, using an inductive proof, the model checking of a set of properties on the bus. These properties are also translated to a SystemC monitor that can be used as a separate Intellectual Property (IP) to validate AGP compatible devices.

The rest of this paper is organized as follows: Section 2 discusses related work. Section 3 presents our verification approach. Section 4 contains the proofs of the transformation from SystemC to AsmL. Section 5 describes the application of the proposed methodology for the case of an AGP bus modeled in SystemC. Finally, Section 6 concludes the paper.

2   Related Work

Related work to ours concerns both finite-state verification and assertion based verification. Concerning the first issue, we cite in particular the Bandera [5] project that aims at interfacing Java code to model checking tools like SMV [3] and SPIN [13] by applying program analysis, abstraction, and transformation techniques. In its actual status, Bandera cannot handle SystemC designs because any analysis of a SystemC code must go through the whole simulation environment as well as SystemC defined data-types and classes. Besides, using SMV as an internal model checking tool is a big handicap for Bandera to handle large state space systems. We are not aware of any related work using a sound syntactical transformation from SystemC to AsmL and vice-versa to perform either model checking or ABV.

In [7] an approach is presented to add assertion checkers to SystemC. This previous work is different from our methodology mainly in two aspects: (1) The properties in [7] are restricted to the notation of property checker from Infineon Technologies AG then translated to synthesizable SystemC instructions while we consider any PSL property; and (2) SystemC is considered in [7] as a low level

HDL language while in this paper we do not put any restriction on any subset of SystemC.

In [19], [12] and [10] several approaches were proposed to verify, respectively, a PCI bus monitor in Verilog, a PCI bus model and Look-aside interface [17] (both in SystemC). In [19], the bus was implemented in Verilog with all the properties embedded as part of the code which makes its modification or upgrade a very complex task. Besides, the verified Verilog model includes only two agents (one master and one slave), which does not allow the verification of the properties related to the bus arbitration, for example, and radically reduces the designs state space.

In both [12] and [10] a top-down approach was used where the verification was integrated as part of the design process and AsmL models were first designed and verified then translated to SystemC. In this paper, we consider a bottom-up approach where starting from an existent AGP IP in SystemC we generate internally the AsmL model and verify the system property at the ASM level. Besides, the designs in [19], [10] and [17] were relatively small in comparison to AGP, with a width of 256 for data read, data write and command queues has a minimum of $2^{256 \times 32}$ states. Furthermore, AGP includes a number of additional features making its verification a non-trivial task, such as pipelining. Hence, direct model checking of AGP properties is with no doubt impossible due to the state-explosion problem. The verification technique proposed in this paper takes advantage of the high level of abstraction offered by AsmL which enables both data abstraction and proofs by induction.

3   Verification Methodology

AsmL [9] is one of the very latest languages developed for Abstract State Machines (ASM) [8]. It is supported by a tester (Asmlt) that can be used to generate FSMs and test cases. It supports object-oriented modeling at higher level of abstraction in comparison to C++ and Java. In our verification methodology (Figure 1) we perform the model checking of SystemC by translating the original design to an intermediate representation that omits all the details of the SystemC simulator. The target (or transformed) program is modeled in AsmL to be cross-produced with the system properties that will be verified over the whole system's state space. To model the properties, we used the PSL [1] standard. PSL properties are embedded in the design as external monitors; hence, they can be used as stand-alone IP block(s) to validate other devices, either at the AsmL level by model checking or at the SystemC level by assertion based verification.

3.1   Model Checking

To enable the integration of both the model and the properties at the ASM level, we embedded the PSL semantics in AsmL. At this level, it is possible to verify these properties using model checking. For instance, we encode the properties evaluation in every state, which enables checking its correctness on-the-fly while

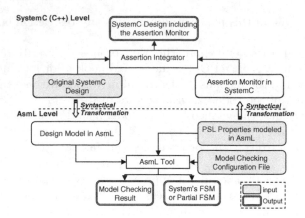

Fig. 1. Verification Methodology

executing the FSM generation algorithm (part of the AsmL tool). An incorrect property detection stops the reachability algorithms and outputs a sub-portion from the complete FSM, which represents a scenario for a counter-example.

PSL properties are defined in a hierarchical way inspired from the hardware design modular concept. For this reason we defined the embedding in a similar structure, where all the components are defined as objects and every PSL layer *extends* its lower layer using the inheritance feature of AsmL. The main layers include the Boolean layer, the temporal layer and the verification layer [1].

We encapsulate sequences in the verification unit as an assertion, which is embedded in the design. Given a set of Boolean items $x_1, x_2, \ldots, x_n$, and $y_1, y_2, \ldots, y_m$ belonging to the Boolean layer, and the sequences, S_1 and S_2 belonging to the temporal layer, we can define: $S_1 = \{x_1, x_2, \ldots, x_n\}$, and $S_2 = \{y_1, y_2, \ldots, y_m\}$ and then use assertions to check any PSL operation between S_1 and S_2 such as $S_1 \; OP \; S_2$, where OP is a PSL operator (e.g., implication (:), or equivalence ($\Leftrightarrow$)). The assertion is built as follows:

1. Add all the Boolean items to the sequences:
   $\forall \; i \; in \; 1 \; to \; n : \; S_1.AddElement(x_i)$
   $\forall \; j \; in \; 1 \; to \; m : \; S_2.AddElement(y_j)$
2. Create the property: $P := S_1 \; OP \; S_2$
3. Define the *verification unit* as an assertion, say A, that includes the above property: $A.Add(P)$

Each property is embedded in every state in the FSM generated by the AsmL tool and is represented by two Boolean state variables P_{eval} and P_{value} (stating, respectively, if the property can be evaluated and the value of the property in the current state). A violated property is detected once $P_{eval} = true$ and $P_{value} = false$. The previous condition is a filter for the FSM generation algorithm stopping the generation when an error is detected. In this case, the generated portion of the state machine can be used to identify the problem through a scenario of a counter-example. For multiple properties, the filter is set as the

conjunction of all the conditions for the separate properties. This technique minimizes radically the number of state variables (the FSM size and its generation
time). A successful verification process results in the generation of the system's
FSM (according to the configuration file constraints). This approach may seem
to be based on an ad-hoc model checking algorithm while more advanced techniques and approaches have been used in tools like SMV and VIS. We believe
there are many reasons that make our approach more efficient, in particular:
(1) It is impossible to use these tools with AsmL considering the OO nature
of the language. Therefore, a translation to the language supported by the tool
(mostly a very low HDL) is mandatory. This operation will prohibit using some
advanced features AsmL offers (e.g., data abstraction, etc.)
(2) Generating the counter-example as an FSM provides a complete path of the
error starting from the entry point to the state where the error took place [6].
(3) The configuration of the FSM generation algorithm can be set by the user
in order to stress the verification only in some particular portions of the state
space (through restricting some variables to have certain range for example) [6].

3.2   Assertion Based Verification

The proposed methodology to integrate and verify PSL assertions for SystemC
designs is given in Figure 2. It consists of the following three main steps:

(1) Updating the SystemC design in order to interface it with the assertion
monitor.
(2) Generating the assertion as a C# code from its ASM description.
(3) Integrating the C# assertion in the SystemC design.

The assertion under verification is a PSL property embedded in AsmL as a
read-only separate module. In order to guarantee that we are verifying the same
property specified in AsmL as the corresponding SystemC model, we need to:
(1) prove the correctness of the transformation from AsmL to SystemC; and
(2) connect the assertion monitor correctly to the original SystemC design. The

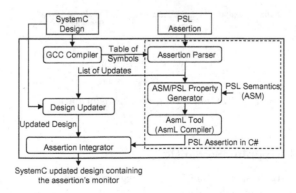

Fig. 2. Assertion Based Verification Approach

second step requires updating the SystemC design to interface to the assertion and integrating the assertion in the design. For instance, we validate the assertion syntactically by generating the list of the variables involved. Then, we perform a type check to make sure the variables are well instantiated in the SystemC design. For instance, the signals (variables) that are used in the assertion must be seen as external signals so that they can be input to the assertion monitor. Hence, we modify the SystemC design to make the required variables visible to the monitor. Once the design is updated, we add the required instantiation of the assertion to bind it to the existing SystemC design modules. The assertion monitor, acting as part of the design, can do the following: (1) stop the simulation when the assertion is fired; (2) write a report about the assertion status and all its variables; and (3) send a warning signal to other modules (if required).

4   Correctness of the SystemC/AsmL and AsmL/SystemC Transformations

The work of Patrick and Radhia Cousot in [4] is the essence for any program transformation using abstract interpretation. The tactical choice of using semantics to link the subject program to the transformed program is very smart in the sense that it enables proving the soundness proof of the transformation, related to an observational semantics. The transformation from SystemC to AsmL, and vice-versa, represents an online program transformation which corresponds to the approach described in Section 3.9 of [4]. Figure 3 displays a projection of that generic methodology on a SystemC subject program and an AsmL transformed program. The same figure can be used to perform the soundness of a transformation and also to construct it. In both cases, we need to define the syntax, semantics and observation functions for both AsmL and SystemC.

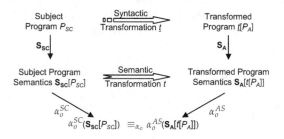

Fig. 3. Online Program Transformation

4.1   SystemC Fixpoint Semantics

Syntactical Domains. SystemC has a large number of syntactical domains. However, they are all based on the single SC_Module domain. Hence, the minimum representation for a general SystemC program is as a set of modules.

Definition 1. *(SystemC Module: SC_Module)*
A SystemC Module is a set ⟨*DMem*, **Ports**, **Chan**, **Mth**, *SC_Ctr*⟩, *where DMem is a set of the module data members,* **Ports** *is a set of ports,* **Chan** *a set of SystemC Chan,* **Mth** *is a set of methods (function) definition and SC_Ctr the module constructor.*

Definition 2. *(SystemC Port: SC_Port)*
A SystemC Port is a set ⟨*IF*, *N*, *SC_In*, *SC_Out*, *SC_InOut*⟩, *where IF is a set of the virtual methods declarations, N is the number of interfaces that may be connected to the port, SC_In is an input port (provides only a* **Read** *method), SC_Out is an output port (provides only a* **Write** *method) and SC_InOut is an input/output port (provides* **Read** *and* **Write** *methods).*

In contrast to default class constructors for OO languages, the SystemC module constructor SC_Ctr contains the information about the processes and threads that will be executed during simulation.

Definition 3. *(SystemC Constructor: SC_Ctr)*
A SystemC Constructor is a set ⟨*Name*, *Init*, *SC_Pr*, *SC_SSt*⟩, *where Name is a string specifying the module name, Init is a default class constructor, SC_Pr a set of processes and SC_SSt is a set of sensitivity statements (to set the process sensitivity list SC_SL).*

Definition 4. *(SystemC Process: SC_Pr)*
A SystemC process is a set ⟨*PMth*, *PTh*, *PCTh*⟩, *where PMth is a method process (defined as a set* ⟨*Mth*, *SC_SL*⟩ *including the method and its sensitivity list), PTh is a thread process (accepts a wait statement in comparison to the method process), PCTh is a clocked thread process (sensitive to the clock event).*

Definition 5. *(SystemC Program: SC_Pg)*
A SystemC program is a set ⟨L_{SC_Mod}, *SC_main*⟩, *where L_{SC_Mod} is a set of SystemC modules and SC_main is the main function in the program that performs the simulator initialization and contains the modules declarations.*

Fixpoint Semantics. In this section, we define the semantics of the whole SystemC program, $\mathbb{W}$ ⟦SC_Pg⟧, and the SystemC module, $\mathbb{M}_{SC}$⟦m_sc⟧. Then, present the proofs (or proof sketches) of the soundness and completeness of $\mathbb{M}_{SC}$⟦m_sc⟧.

Definition 6. *(Delta Delay: δ_d)*
The SystemC simulator considers two phases evaluate *and* update. *The separation between these two phases is called* delta delay.

Definition 7. *(SystemC Environment: SC_Env)*
The SystemC environment is the summation of the default C++ environment (Env) as defined in [15] and the signal environment (Sig_Store) specific to SystemC: SC_Store = Env + Sig_Env = [Var → Addr]+ [SC_Sig → (Addr,Addr)], where Var is a set of variables, SC_Sig is a set of SystemC signals and Addr ⊆ ℕ is a set of addresses.

Definition 8. *(SystemC Store: SC_Store)*
The SystemC store is the summation of the default C++ store (Store) as defined in [15] and the signal store (Sig_Store): SC_Store = Store + Sig_Store = [Addr → Val]+ [(Addr, Addr) → (Val,Val)], where Val is a set of values such that SC_Env ⊆ Val.

Let $R_0 \in \mathcal{P}(\text{SC\_Env} \times \text{SC\_Store})$ be a set of initial states, pc_{in} be the entry point of the main function and $\rightarrow \subseteq$: (SC_Env×SC_Store)×(SC_Env×SC_Store) be a transition relation.

Definition 9. *(Whole SystemC Program Semantics: $\mathbb{W}$ SC_Pg)*
Let SC_Pg = $\langle L_{SC\_Mod}, SC\_main \rangle$ be a SystemC program. Then, the semantics of SC_Pg, $\mathbb{W}$ SC_Pg $\in \mathcal{P}(SC\_Env \times SC\_Store) \rightarrow \mathcal{P}(T(SC\_Env \times SC\_Store))$ is:

$$\mathbb{W}SC\_Pg(R_0) = lfp \,\overset{\subseteq}{_\emptyset} \lambda X. \ (R_0) \cup \{\rho_0 \rightarrow \ \dots \ \rho_n \rightarrow \rho_{n+1}| \ \rho_{n+1} \in$$
$$(SC\_Env \times SC\_Store) \wedge \{\rho_0 \rightarrow \ \dots \ \rho_n\}$$
$$\in X \wedge \rho_n \rightarrow \rho_{n+1}\}$$

Both definitions of the semantics of process declaration ($\mathbb{P}_R$ [[SC_Pr]]) and SystemC module constructor ($\mathbb{P}_{Ctr}$ [[SC_Ctr]]) are given in [11]. In contrast to the semantics definition of an OO object in [15], a SystemC method can be activated either by the default context or by the SystemC simulator through the sensitivity list of the process. A complete definition of the semantics of a SystemC module object ($\mathbb{O}_{SC}$[[o_sc]]) through the definition of a transition function $\text{next}_{sc}(\sigma)=\text{next}(\sigma) \cup \text{next}_{sig}(\sigma)$, including both parts C++ related and SystemC specific functions, can be found in [11].

Definition 10. *(SystemC Module Semantics: $\mathbb{M}_{SC}$ m_sc))*
Let m_sc = $\langle DMem, Ports, Chan, Mth, SC\_Ctr \rangle$ be a SystemC module, then its semantics $\mathbb{M}_{SC}$ m_sc) $\in \mathcal{P}(T(\Sigma))$ is:

$$\mathbb{M}_{SC}\text{m\_sc}= \{\mathbb{O}_{SC}\,o\_sc(v_{sc}, s_{sc}) \mid o\_sc \text{ is an instance of m\_sc, } v\_sc \in D\_in,$$
$$s\_sc \in SC\_Store\}$$

Theorem 1. *(SystemC Module semantics in fixpoint)* [1] *Let*

$$G_{sc}\langle S \rangle = \lambda T. \ \{S_0 \langle v, s \rangle \mid \langle v, s \rangle \in S \ \} \cup \{\sigma_0 \overset{l_0}{\rightarrow} \dots \overset{l_{n-1}}{\rightarrow} \sigma_n \overset{l'}{\rightarrow} \sigma'|$$
$$\sigma_0 \overset{l_0}{\rightarrow} \dots \overset{l_{n-1}}{\rightarrow} \sigma_n \in T, \ \text{next}_{sc}(\sigma_n) \ni \langle \sigma', l' \rangle\}$$

Then $\mathbb{M}_{SC}\text{m\_sc}(v_{sc}, s_{sc}) = lfp \,\overset{\subseteq}{_\emptyset} \ G_{sc} \langle \ D_{in} \times Store \rangle$

The last step in the SystemC fixpoint semantics is to relate the module semantics to the whole SystemC program semantics. Hence, we consider an updated version of the function *abstract* (α°) as defined in [15]. The new function is upgraded to support the SystemC simulation semantics, environment and store. The complete definitions of α_SC° can be found in [11].

Theorem 2. *(Soundness of $\mathbb{M}_{SC}$ m_sc) Let M_{SC} be a whole SystemC program and let $m_{SC} \in M_{SC}$. Then:*
$\forall \ R_0 \in SC\_Env \times SC\_Store. \ \forall \ \tau \in T(SC\_Env \times SC\_Store). \ \tau \in \mathbb{W}SC\_Pg(R_0) : \exists \tau'$
$\in \mathbb{M}_{SC} m_{SC} \ . \ \alpha\_SC^\circ(\{\tau\}) = \{\tau'\}$

---

[1] The proofs of the theorems presented in this paper are available in [11].

Theorem 3. *(Completeness of* $\mathbb{M}_{SC}$*) Let* m_{SC} *be a SystemC module. Then* $\forall \tau \in \mathcal{T}(\Sigma).\tau \in \mathbb{M}_{SC} m_{SC}$:

$\exists\ SC\_P \in \langle L_{SC\_Pg} \rangle.\ \exists \rho_0 \in SC\_Env \times SC\_Store.\ \exists\ o_{SC}$ *instance of* m_{SC}.

$\exists\ \tau' \in \mathcal{T}(SC\_Env \times SC\_Store).\ \tau' \in \mathbb{W}\rho_0 \wedge \alpha\_SC^{\circ}(\{\tau'\}) = \{\tau\}$

4.2 AsmL Fixpoint Semantics

Syntactical Domains.

Definition 11. *(AsmL Class: AS_C)*
An AsmL class is a set $\langle AS\_DMem, AS\_Mth, AS\_Ctr \rangle$*, where AS_DMem is a set of the module data members, AS_Mth a set of methods (functions) definition and AS_Ctr is the module constructor.*

One of the important features that we are going to use in AsmL corresponds to the methods pre-conditions (Boolean proposition verified before the execution of the method).

Definition 12. *(AsmL Method: AS_Mth)*
An AsmL method is a set $\langle AS\_M, AS\_Pre, AS\_Pos, AS\_Cst \rangle$*, where AS_M is the method's core, AS_Pre is a set of pre-conditions, AS_Pos is a set of post-conditions and AS_Cst is a set of constraints.*

Note that AS_Pre, AS_Pos and AS_Cst share the same structure. They are differentiated in the methods by using a specific keyword for each of them (e.g., *require* for pre-conditions).

Definition 13. *(AsmL Program: AS_Pg)*
An AsmL Program is a set $\langle L_{AS\_C}, INIT \rangle$*, where* L_{AS_C} *is a set of AsmL classes and INIT is the main function in the program.*

Fixpoint Semantics. Similar to the notion of delta delay (δ_d) of SystemC, AsmL considers two phases: *evaluate* and *update*. The program will be always running in the *evaluate* mode except if an update is requested. There are two types of updates, total and partial.

Definition 14. *(AsmL Environment: AS_Env)*
The AsmL Environment is a modified OO environment $AS\_Env = [Var \rightarrow Addr, Addr]$*, where Var is a set of variables and* $Addr \subseteq \mathbb{N}$ *is as set of addresses (two addresses store the current and new values of* $v \in Var$*).*

Definition 15. *(AsmL Store: AS_Store)*
The AsmL store is $AS\_Store = [(Addr, Addr) \rightarrow (Val, Val)]$*, where Val is a set of values such that* $AS\_Env \subseteq Val$.

The whole AsmL program semantics ($\mathbb{W}_{AS}$ [[AS_Pg]]), method semantics ($\mathbb{M}_{AS}$ [[.]]) and object semantics ($\mathbb{O}_{AS}$[[o_AS]]) through the definition of a transition function $\text{next}_{\text{as}}(\sigma)$ can be found in [11]. The AsmL class constructor can be defined according to the Definition 3.8 in [15].

Definition 16. *(AsmL Class Semantics: $\mathbb{C}_{AS}\,c\_as$)*
Let $c\_as = \langle as\_dmem,\ as\_mth,\ as\_ctr\rangle$ be an AsmL class, then its semantics
$\mathbb{C}_{AS}\,c\_as) \in \mathcal{P}(\mathcal{T}(\Sigma))$ *is:* $\mathbb{C}_{as}\,c\_as= \{\mathbb{O}_{AS}\,o\_as(v\_as, s\_as) \mid o\_as$ *is an instance*
of c_as, $v\_as \in D\_in$, $s\_as \in SC\_Store\}$

Theorem 4. *(AsmL Class semantics in fixpoint) Let*
$$H_{as}\langle S\rangle = \lambda T.\ \{S_0\langle v, s\rangle \mid \langle v, s\rangle \in S\ \} \cup \{\sigma_0 \xrightarrow{l_0} \ldots \xrightarrow{l_{n-1}} \sigma_n \xrightarrow{l'} \sigma' \mid$$
$$\sigma_0 \xrightarrow{l_0} \ldots \xrightarrow{l_{n-1}} \sigma_n \in T,\ next_{as}(\sigma_n) \ni \langle \sigma', l'\rangle\}$$
Then $\mathbb{C}_{AS}\,c\_as(v_{as}, s_{as}) = lfp \overset{\subseteq}{_\emptyset}\ H_{as}\langle\ D_{in}\times Store\rangle$

The function α_AS° is an updated version of the function *abstract* (α°) defined in [15]. The complete definition of α_AS° is given in [11].

Theorem 5. *(Soundness of $\mathbb{C}_{AS}\,c\_as$) Let P_{AS} be a whole AsmL program and*
let $c_{AS} \in C_{AS}$. Then $\forall\ R_0 \in AS\_Env\times AS\_Store.\ \forall\ \tau \in \mathcal{T}(AS\_Env\times AS\_Store).$
$\tau \in \mathbb{W}AS\_Pg(R_0) : \exists \tau' \in \mathbb{C}_{AS}\,c_{AS}\ .\ \alpha\_AS^\circ(\{\tau\}) = \{\tau'\}$

Theorem 6. *(Completeness of $\mathbb{C}_{AS}$) Let c_{AS} be a AsmL class. Then*
$$\forall \tau \in \mathcal{T}(\Sigma).\ \tau \in \mathbb{C}_{SC}\,c_{SC} : \exists\ AS\_P \in \langle L_{AS\_Pg}\rangle.\ \exists \rho_0 \in AS\_Env\times AS\_Store.\ \exists$$
$$o_{AS}\ instance\ of\ c_{AS}.\ \exists\ \tau' \in \mathcal{T}(AS\_Env\times AS\_Store).\ \tau' \in \mathbb{W}\rho_0$$
$$\wedge\ \alpha\_AS^\circ(\{\tau'\}) = \{\tau\}$$

4.3   Program Transformation

The equivalence in behavior, with respect to an observation α_o, between the source SystemC program and the target AsmL program is required to ensure the soundness of any verification result at the AsmL level. Our objective is to define a relation between the SystemC processes active for certain delta cycle and the set of methods allowed to be executed in the AsmL model. Hence, we will map every thread (method, sensitivity list) in the SystemC design to a method (method core, pre-conditions) in the AsmL model.

The SystemC observation function needs to see all the active processes at the beginning of a delta-cycle by checking for the end of the update phase.

Definition 17. *(SystemC observation function: α_o^{SC})*
Let $SC\_Pg= \langle L_{SC\_Mod},\ SC\_main\rangle$ be a SystemC program, the observation function
$\alpha_o^{SC} \in \mathcal{P}(SC\_Env\times SC\_Store) \to \mathcal{P}(\mathcal{T}(SC\_Env\times SC\_Store))$ *is*
$$\alpha_o^{SC}\,SC\_Pg(R_0) = lfp \overset{\subseteq}{_\emptyset}\lambda X.\ R_0 \cup \{\tilde{\rho}_0 \to \ldots \tilde{\rho}_n \mid \forall \tilde{\rho}_i \in (SC\_Env\times$$
$$SC\_Store) \exists\ \{\rho_0^i \to \ldots \rho_m^i\} \in X\ \wedge$$
$$\rho_m^i \to \tilde{\rho}_i \wedge \{\ m\_sc\ in\ \mathbb{M}_{SC} \mid \exists o\_sc \in$$
$$\mathbb{M}_{SC}.\ o\_sc(\rho_m^i()) \neq \{\epsilon\}\ \} = \emptyset\}$$

In the previous definition, α_o^{SC} is only tracing the initial states of a simulation cycle. For instance, the third condition ensures that the list of process ready to run is empty. Similarly, we define an observation function α_o^{AS} for an AsmL program.

Definition 18. *(AsmL observation function: α_o^{AS})*
Let $AS\_Pg= \langle L_{AS\_C},\ INIT \rangle$ *be an AsmL program, the observation function* α_o^{AS}
$\in \mathcal{P}(AS\_Env \times AS\_Store) \rightarrow \mathcal{P}(\mathcal{T}(AS\_Env \times AS\_Store))$ *is*

$$\alpha_o^{AS} AS\_Pg(R_0) = lfp\ _{\emptyset}^{\subseteq} \lambda X.\ (R_0) \cup \{\tilde{\rho}_0 \rightarrow \dots\ \tilde{\rho}_n|\ \forall \tilde{\rho}_i \in (SC\_Env \times$$
$$AS\_Store)\ \exists\ \{\rho_0^i \rightarrow\ \dots\ \rho_m^i\} \in X\ \wedge$$
$$\rho_m^i \rightarrow \tilde{\rho}_i \wedge \{\ m\_as\ in\ \mathbb{C}_{AS}\ |\ \exists o\_as \in$$
$$\mathbb{C}_{AS}.\ o\_as(\rho_m^i()) \neq \{\epsilon\}\ \} = \emptyset\ \}$$

Next, we define the notion of equivalence between the two observations. Although, SystemC and AsmL have different environment and store structures, it is possible to ensure that they contain the same information.

Definition 19. *(Equivalence w.r.t.* α_o: $\equiv_{\alpha_o}$)
Let SC_Pg *be a SystemC program,* V_sc *a set of its variables,* AS_Pg *be an AsmL program and* $Dout\_as$ *a set of its output variables.*
$prog\_sc \equiv_{\alpha_o} prog\_as$ *if*
$\quad \forall R_0^{SC}$ *set of initial states of* SC_Pg. $\forall R_0^{AS}$ *set of initial states of* AS_Pg.
$\quad \forall \tilde{\rho} \in \{\tilde{\rho}_0 \rightarrow\ \dots\ \rightarrow \tilde{\rho}_n\} \in \alpha_o^{SC} SC\_Pg(R_0^{SC})$.
$\quad \exists \hat{\rho} \in \{\hat{\rho}_0 \rightarrow\ \dots\ \rightarrow \hat{\rho}_n\} \in \alpha_o^{AS} AS\_Pg(R_0^{AS})\ |\ \forall\ vsc \in V\_sc.\ \exists\ vas \in V\_as\ |$
$\quad\quad if\ vsc \in SC\_Sig\ then\ \tilde{\rho}(vsc) = (vl1,vl2) \wedge \hat{\rho}(vas) = (vl1,vl2)$
$\quad\quad if\ vsc \in AS\_DMem\ then\ \tilde{\rho}(vsc) = vl1 \wedge \hat{\rho}(vas) = (vl1,vl1)$

The observation function ensures that the AsmL program is mimicking the *evaluate* and *update* phases (same length n of the ρ sets). The first if condition takes care of the SystemC signals while the second one concerns basic C++ variables.

Theorem 7. *(Existence of transformed AsmL program w.r.t.* α_o^{SC}) *Let* SC_Pg *be a whole SystemC program,* SC_Din *a set of inputs and* SC_Dout *a set of outputs. Then* $\exists$ AS_Pg, *an AsmL program, such that* $SC\_Pg \equiv_{\alpha_o} AS\_Pg$

Theorem 8. *(Existence of transformed SystemC program w.r.t.* α_o^A) *Let* AS_Pg *be a whole AsmL program,* AS_Din *a set of inputs and* AS_Dout *a set of outputs. Then* $\exists$ SC_Pg, *a SystemC program, such that* $AS\_Pg \equiv_{\alpha_o} SC\_Pg$

Theorem 9. *(Soundness of the transformations) Let* SC_Pg *be a whole SystemC program and let* AS_Pg *be a whole AsmL program. Then*
$\quad SC\_Pg \equiv_{\alpha_o} AS\_Pg$:
$\quad \forall\ Prop(V\_sc,\tilde{\rho})\ |\ \tilde{\rho} \in \alpha_o^{SC} SC\_Pg$.
$\quad SC\_Pg \vdash Prop(V\_sc,\tilde{\rho})$
$\quad : AS\_Pg \vdash Prop(V\_as,\hat{\rho})\ |\ \hat{\rho} \in \alpha_o^{AS} AS\_Pg$.
where: $Prop$ *is a program's property,* V_sc *is a set of variables of the SystemC program,* V_as *are their corresponding variables in the AsmL program.*

5 Application: AGP Bus Verification

5.1 Bus Description

AGP (Accelerated Graphics Port) [14] was introduced to meet consumer demand for high-resolution 3D graphics in home computers. New software programs (especially games) require more and more video bandwidth for fancy textures, high frame rate animations, etc. It has the advantage of allowing large amounts of graphics data to be transferred directly between the computer's main memory and the AGP video card. The AGP bus is designed strictly for video processing and does not have to share available bandwidth with other connected devices. Both AGP bus transactions and PCI bus transactions may be run over the AGP interface. An AGP master (graphics) device may transfer data to the system memory using either AGP transactions or PCI transactions. The corelogic can access the AGP master device only with PCI transactions. Traffic on the AGP interface may consist of a mixture of interleaved AGP and PCI transactions. In addition to the PCI features, AGP includes:

(1) Direct Memory Execute (DME) that gives AGP chips the capability to access the main memory directly for complex operations of texture mapping.

(2) Pipelining and sideband addressing of directly accessing texture maps in system memory.

(3) Multiple requests for data during a bus or memory access.

(4) A dedicated non-shared bandwidth with other devices.

5.2   Model Checking

In order to verify the bus properties, we first used a direct model checking approach by considering a set of properties to verify all the possible transactions scenarios. These cover two main classes: (1) PCI transactions and (2) AGP transactions including both modes DMA and execute. We succeeded to prove the first class of properties with a direct approach while we failed to prove the second set due to state explosion. Therefore, we introduce a proof by induction. Performing the verification of the whole model failed to complete due to a state explosion problem. The main reason for that is the huge size of the read, write and commands queues (each of width 256) present in both the AGP device and the corelogic. By reducing the queues width to three, however, we succeeded to verify all the properties. For more general verification, we defined an induction based approach taking advantage from the abstract data types of AsmL.

We define DRQ: Device Read Queue, DWQ: Device Write Queue, $DReQ$: Device Request Queue, CRQ: Controller Read Queue, CWQ: Controller Write Queue and $CReQ$: Controller Request Queue. The maximum width of the queues is $Q.Wd$. The number of packets in each queue is $XXQ.Np$ (where $XX \in \{DR, DW, DReq, CR, CW, CReq\}$). P is the list of properties under verification.

- Step 1: Verify $P = true$, $\forall$ $DRQ.Np$, $DWQ.Np$, $DReQ.Np$, $CRQ.Np$, $CWQ.Np$, $CReQ.Np \in [0, 1]$.
- Step 2:
  - Hypothesis: Consider $N \in \mathbb{N}$ / $0 < N < Q.Wd$
    $\forall x \in \{DRQ.Np, DWQ.Np, DReQ.Np, CRQ.Np, CWQ.Np, CReQ.Np\}$, $x < N : P$ is true.
  - Prove: $\forall x \in \{DRQ.Np, DWQ.Np, DReQ.Np, CRQ.Np, CWQ.Np, CReQ.Np\}$, $x < N + 1 : P$ is true.

5.3   Experimental Results[2]

Model Checking. The CPU time used for the generation of the model checking for queues widths in {1,2,3,6} is given in Table 1. The first three rows are required to ensure the correctness of the initialization conditions. The fourth row, queue width equal to six, is given to illustrate the effect of the numbers of states and transitions increase exponentially as function of the queue size. This clearly illustrates the impossibility of generating the complete FSM for a width of 256. In Table 2.(a) every row corresponds to the proof of a particular queue. Generally, the CPU time, Nodes and number of transitions is close to the case when the queue width is equal to three (see Table 1). Table 2.(b) presents the verification information for the PCI mode which is optional for AGP. A direct proof for this case was possible thanks to the relative simplicity of the PCI, which does not include any queue structure.

Table 1. Validity of Initialization Conditions

Queue width	CPU Time (s)	Number of FSM Nodes	Transitions
1	5.78	34	37
2	30.89	173	193
3	105.20	504	563
6	1758.78	4325	5223

Table 2. Model Checking Results

(a) AGP Mode

Proof for the Queue	CPU Time (s)	Number of FSM Nodes	Trans.
DRQ	341.01	1156	1304
DWQ	345.25	1294	1325
DReQ	347.78	1302	1346
CRQ	457.89	1503	1425
CWQ	462.07	1653	1433
CReQ	487.01	1859	1481

(b) PCI Mode

Masters	Slaves	CPU Time (s)	Nodes	Transitions
1	1	2.31	20	25
1	2	2.94	39	53
3	1	26.01	236	341
2	2	26.84	293	449
2	3	101.38	658	1117
3	2	574.18	1881	3153

Assertion Based Verification. We have been able to verify all the AGP bus structure by model checking. However, when the model checking fails, it is possible to use the properties as assertion monitors that can be checked by simulation on the original SystemC model. Using the syntactical transformation defined in [11], we generate the SystemC modules corresponding to the PSL properties. Then, we update the design and integrate the properties as read-only monitors to the global system. We illustrate in Table 3 the simulation statistics

---

[2] All experiments presented in this section were conducted on a platform consisting of a 2.4 GHz Pentium IV and 512 MB of RAM (PC2700).

Table 3. Simulation Results

Number of		Average Execution
Masters	Slaves	Time per Clock Cycle (10^{-9}s)
1	1	29.321
3	1	32.221
2	2	33.889
2	3	36.568
3	2	38.005
3	3	41.287

of running the new model (combining the original design and the integrated PSL properties) with a random input. The AGP controller can be seen as a slave or a master according to the transaction. The other masters and slaves are just PCI compatible devices. The CPU time confirms the high speed of the SystemC model simulation, which is a direct result from the C++ implementation of the library. Note that the set of assertion monitors including all the properties can be considered as a stand-alone verification IP that can be used to validate other AGP compatible devices either modeled in SystemC or even in Verilog or VHDL.

6   Conclusions

In previous work [10] we introduced a top-down approach similar to the presented in this paper where the verification was integrated as part of the design process and AsmL models were first designed and verified then translated to SystemC. In this paper, we consider a bottom-up approach where starting from an existent SystemC design we generate internally a model in AsmL, an Object-Oriented language used to model systems, and verify the system property at the ASM level. We defined a sound syntactical transformation between SystemC and AsmL to enable model checking at the ASM level. Both the model and its PSL properties were defined in AsmL and checked using a reachability algorithm available in the AsmL tool. We proposed also to translate the same properties used for model checking back to SystemC in order to serve for assertion based verification of the original SystemC design or to serve as a stand-alone verification IP block. We illustrated our approach on the verification of an AGP bus, where we performed a proof by induction to tackle the state explosion problem. Finally, we believe that our approach is an important step towards enabling an efficient formal and semi-formal verification of SystemC. Our future work concerns enhancing the ABV coverage using the FSM generated AsmL models.

References

1. Accellera Organization. Accellera property specification language reference manual, version 1.01. www.accellera.org, 2004.
2. E. Boerger and R. Staerk. *Abstract State Machines: A Method for High-Level System Design and Analysis.* Springer Verlag, 2003.

3. E. Clarke, O. Grumberg, and D. Long. Verification tools for finite-state concurrent systems. In *A Decade of Concurrency - Reflections and Perspectives*, pages 124–175, Berlin, Germany, 1993.
4. P. Cousot and R. Cousot. Systematic design of program transformation frameworks by abstract interpretation. In *Proc. Symposium on Principles of Programming Languages*, pages 178–190, USA, 2002.
5. M. Dwyer, J. Hatcliff, R. Joehanes, S. Laubach, C. Pasareanu, and R. W. Visser amd H. Zheng. Tool-supported program abstraction for finite-state verification. In *Proc. International Conference on Software Engineering*, pages 177–187, Toronto, Canada, 2001.
6. W. Grieskamp, Y. Gurevich, W. Schulte, and M. Veanes. Generating finite state machines from abstract state machines. *Software Engineering Notes*, 27(4):112–122, 2002.
7. D. Große and R. Drechsler. Checkers for systemc designs. In *Proc. Formal Methods and Models for Codesign*, pages 171–178, San Diego, USA, 2004.
8. Y. Gurevich. Evolving Algebras 1993: Lipari Guide. In *Specification and Validation Methods*, pages 9–36. Oxford University Press, 1995.
9. Y. Gurevich, B. Rossman, and W. Schulte. Semantic Essence of AsmL. Technical report, Microsoft Research Tech. Report MSR-TR-2004-27, March 2004.
10. A. Habibi, A.I. Ahmed, O. Ait-Mohamed, and S. Tahar. On the design and verification of the look-aside interface. In *Proc. Design Automation and Test in Europe*, pages 290–295, Germany, 2005.
11. A. Habibi and S. Tahar. On the Transformation of SystemC to AsmL using Abstract Interpretation. Technical report, ECE, Concordia University, December 2004 (www.ece.concordia.ca/~habibi/techrp/TR0404/).
12. A. Habibi and S. Tahar. Design for verification of SystemC transaction level models. In *Proc. Design Automation and Test in Europe*, pages 560–565, Germany, 2005.
13. G. J. Holzmann. *The Spin Model Checker: Primer and Reference Manual*. Addison-Wesley, 2003.
14. Intel Corp. AGP v3.0 interface specification, 2002.
15. F. Logozzo. *Anhalyse Statique Modulaire de Langages a Objets*. PhD thesis, Ecole Polytechnique, Paris, France, June 2004.
16. Microsoft Corp. AsmL for Microsoft .NET Framework. research.microsoft.com, 2004.
17. Network Processing Forum. *Look-Aside (LA-1) Interface, Implementation Agreement, Revision 1.1*. Kluwer Academic Publishers, April 15, 2004.
18. Open SystemC Initiative. www.systemc.org, 2004.
19. K. Shimizu, D. L. Dill, and A. J. Hu. Monitor-based formal specification of PCI. In *Formal Methods in Computer-Aided Design*, pages 335–353. LNCS 1954, Springer-Verlag, 2000.

Decomposition-Based Verification of Cyclic Workflows

Yongsun Choi[*] and J. Leon Zhao

Dept. of Systems Management & Engineering, Inje University, Kimhae, Korea
yschoi@inje.ac.kr
Dept. of MIS, University of Arizona, Tucson AZ 85721, USA
lzhao@eller.arizona.edu

Abstract. A critical challenge in workflow analysis and design is the verification of workflow models, considering commercial workflow systems merely provide a simulation tool for validating workflow models through trial and error. As a result, the current workflow technology does not guarantee that workflow models do not fail or will behave in a manner expected by the modeler. While a couple of verification methods have been reported in the recent literature, how to verify cyclic workflow models remains an open research question. In this paper, we propose a novel integrated approach of hierarchical decomposition and verification of cyclic workflows. This result is significant since it helps close the research gap that other known workflow verification methods fail to deal with cyclic workflow models.

1 Introduction

The recent surge in corporate e-business engineering has resulted in the automation of thousands of business processes by means of workflow management systems (WfMS), both within and across corporate boundaries ([5], [7], [9], [14], [24], [26]). WfMS enable the design, analysis, optimization, and execution of business processes. The basic WfMS functions include the separation between the business process logic and business applications, management of relationships among process participants, integration of internal and external process resources, and monitoring and control of process performances ([19], [28]).

Workflow models must be correctly defined before being deployed in a workflow management system to avoid any costly maintenance delays due to runtime errors in the process model ([18], [23]). Therefore, it is essential to verify the workflow model before its deployment. Despite the importance of workflow verification, few commercial workflow systems provide formal verification tools. This lack of verification support can be attributed to the fact that most of the more than 250 commercially available WfMS use a vendor-specific ad-hoc modeling techniques [5] without a theoretical framework for the representation, analysis, and manipulation of workflow systems [8]. Although some of them allow the simulation of processes under through trial and error, they usually do not support formal workflow analyses. While process simulation can

---

[*] The first author's work was supported in part by the 2004 Inje University research grant.

D.A. Peled and Y.-K. Tsay (Eds.): ATVA 2005, LNCS 3707, pp. 84–98, 2005.

provide useful insight about the process behavior, it does not address questions about the interrelationships among process components [8].

There are two research approaches to ensure control flow correctness in workflow models – *build it correctly*, or *check it completely* [25]. The former ([13], [17]), relying on strict rules in composing the model, may not model certain processes due to syntactical restrictions [17] and may not be very suitable for practical implementation in the industry [25]. The latter, like Petri nets ([1], [4], [6], [21], [27]) or the graph-theoretic techniques ([8], [12], [20], [23]), on the contrary, appeals more by allowing the user tremendous flexibility in expressing process requirements and confronts significant challenges at the same time [25].

The Petri-nets-based workflow verification depends on the formalism of Petri nets, which has yet to be adopted by commercial WfMS. The majority of business processes in previous research have been restricted to acyclic (i.e. loop-free) free-choice nets, a special class of Petri nets that enjoys the added advantage that *soundness* can be verified in polynomial time [1]. Additionally, establishing soundness in a free-choice net implies that the net is free from deadlock, and is also alive, i.e., no dead tasks [2]. However, the modeling of exceptions or precedence partially destroys the free-choiceness of the equivalent Petri net mapping. Moreover, modeling iteration necessitates the presence of loops in the control flow model, a problem that is yet to be satisfactorily addressed [25]. Graph reduction ([20], [23]) or block-wise abstraction [12] has been proposed to identify structural conflicts in workflow graphs, but both approaches are limited to acyclic models [3]. In summary, there is a critical need for workflow verification techniques applicable to generic graph-based workflow models.

In this paper, we propose an integrated and iterative approach of workflow abstraction and verification of control flows represented in directed graphs. By *workflow abstraction*, we refer to the identification of reducible blocks in a given workflow model. A reducible block refers to a subset of nodes and associated links in a workflow model that can potentially be abstracted into a *'block activity'* node. By *workflow verification*, we refer to the detection of potential structural conflicts such as deadlocks and lack of synchronizations. Our approach of integrating workflow abstraction and workflow verification in the same analysis is unique and has a number of important features:

- Our method applies verification to each block structure, which is much easier to comprehend and verify individually than the whole workflow model in general. This decomposition feature has not been seen in any existing workflow verification method. In each iteration, our method identifies a reducible block, verifies any structural conflicts in the block, and abstracts it into a block activity. This simplifies the workflow graph and makes it easier to analyze.
- We also introduce several pattern-based verification rules that can save verification effort if a block or the simplified whole model, after abstractions, matches certain patterns specified by those rules.
- Our method handles cyclic workflow models, even for nested structures, by partitioning the given model into acyclic subgraphs, such enabling our method to handle only acyclic subflows one by one when verifying a workflow block.

The rest of the paper is organized as follows. In Section 2, we present the preliminary concepts such as the directed graph representation and summarizes on the partitioning of a cyclic workflow graph into acyclic subgraphs. In Section 3, we extend the concept of reducible blocks to the analysis of cyclic workflow models and present the associated theorems. Section 4 delineates the unified framework for process abstraction and verification. Section 5 discusses our contributions, related work, and future research.

2   Partitioning a Cyclic Workflow Graph into Acyclic Graphs

2.1   Directed Workflow Graphs

A workflow graph is a directed graph $WG = (N, T)$ with a set of nodes N and a set of edges $(i, j) \in T$, where $i, j \in N$. Each edge, called as a *transition*, links two nodes and represents the execution order of nodes. A *node* is classified into task and coordinator. A *task*, represented by a rectangle, stands for the work to be done. A *coordinator*, represented by a circle, is a point of path choice or merge of paths. Nodes are classified into *sequence*, *AND-split*, *AND-join*, *XOR-split*, and *XOR-join* (Fig. 1). *Start* and *End* nodes indicate the beginning and the end of workflow, respectively ([20], [23]).

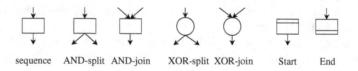

sequence   AND-split   AND-join   XOR-split   XOR-join   Start   End

Fig. 1. Classification of nodes in workflow graphs

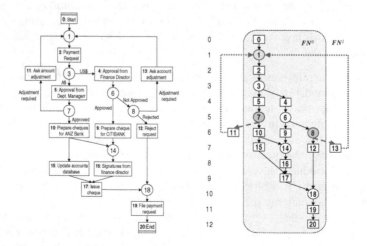

Fig. 2. (a) An example cyclic workflow graph; and (b) the normalized graph

Fig. 2(a) illustrates an example workflow with cycles, with two feedback paths added to an example found in [23]. We make a simplifying assumption on the workflow graph that a node cannot be a join and split at the same time, since such a node can be converted into a join node and a split node with a transition between them.

2.2 Structural Conflicts in Workflow Graphs

In this paper, we focus on the verification of three types of structural conflicts, deadlock, lack of synchronization, and livelock as illustrated in Fig. 3 ([1], [16], [23]). *Deadlock* refers to a situation in which a workflow instance gets into a stalemate such that no further activity can be executed. This happens when only some partial subset of the join paths to an AND-Join is executed, the AND-Join node k will wait forever and block the continuation of the process (Fig. 3a). *Lack of synchronization* refers to a situation in which the concurrent flows are joined by an XOR-Join, resulting in unintentional multiple executions of activities following the node k (Fig. 3b). *Livelock* refers to a situation in which certain loop(s) of tasks are continuously performed, and there is no execution path leading to termination or cannot terminate properly (Fig. 3c). Note that a livelock is associated with cyclic structures. Other types of structural conflicts such as *dangling* nodes are relatively easy to detect by examining the reachability of nodes.

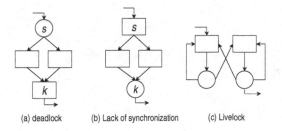

(a) deadlock   (b) Lack of synchronization   (c) Livelock

Fig. 3. Types of structural conflicts

2.3 Partitioning into the Acyclic Subgraphs

Cycles in workflow models are needed for purposes of rework and information feedback, but makes it difficult to analyze. Choi [11] introduced a novel method to partition a cyclic workflow graph into acyclic subgraphs. The proposed algorithm first identifies and temporarily cuts off those transitions, called *feedback join transitions*, which complete each corresponding simple cycle [15] from the given model. The set of nodes that can reach the *End* node in the temporarily resulting acyclic graph is called as *the 0-th order Feedback Nodes*, denoted by FN^0. Note that the subgraph spanned by the nodes in FN^0, called as *the main flow* or *the 0-th order Feedback Flow from Start to End* and denoted by $FF^0(Start, End)$, is acyclic. The algorithm also identifies the set of nodes in FN^0 that have a transition toward or from any node not contained in FN^0, *the 0-th order Feedback Splits*, denoted by FS^0, and *the 0-th order Feedback Joins*, denoted by FJ^0, respectively. The other subgraph spanned by the nodes in FS^0, FJ^0, and those not contained in FN^0 is further partitioned into several smaller subgraphs, each composing a smaller workflow graph starting from $fs \in FS^0$ and ending at $fj \in FJ^0$. If all these derived subgraphs are acyclic, the algorithm stops. Unless, the algorithm proceeds to any cyclic subgraph $FF^{1+}(fs, fj)$[§] in similar way, recursively. By this way, the algorithm classifies all the nodes in the given model into FN^n and derives all acyclic subgraphs of $FF^n(fs, fj)$, where the *feedback order n* is increased by 1 for each recursive call.

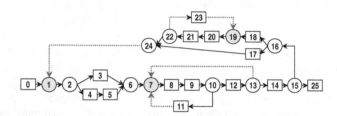

(a) A workflow with nested cycles

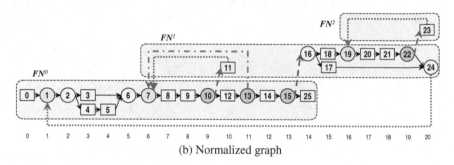

(b) Normalized graph

Fig. 4. Normalization of a workflow graph with nested cycles

Fig. 2(b) shows the normalized graph of Fig. 2(a), with nodes rearranged by its rank shown to the left. The nodes are classified into FN^0 and FN^1, and $FJ^0 = \{ 1 \}$, $FS^0 = \{ 7, 8 \}$. Fig. 4 shows another example with nested cycles. After first iteration, the algorithm derives three acyclic subgraphs and one cyclic subgraph of FF^{1+} (15, 1), which is partitioned into two additional acyclic subgraphs after the first recursive call, resulting total five acyclic subgraphs. Table 1 summarizes the results.

A workflow with an AND- feedback join node *fj* will *deadlock* at *fj*. A workflow with an AND- feedback split node *fs* will potentially result in an *infinite loop* or *multiple instances* [11]. While partitioning a cyclic workflow graph, we can identify those structural anomalies without any additional computation. The verification phase of our integrated method, to be described in Section 4, deals with workflow models that contain only XOR- feedback splits and XOR- feedback joins.

[§] $FF^1(fs, fj)$ represents the main acyclic subgraph partitioned from the cyclic $FF^{1+}(fs, fj)$.

Table 1. Summary of partitioning

Case	Target graph	Classified nodes	Derived subgraphs
Workflow of Fig. 2	$WG(N,T)$	$FJ = \{ 1 \}$; $V - FN^0 = \{ 11, 13 \}$, $FJ^0 = \{ 1 \}$, $FS^0 = \{ 7, 8 \}$.	FF^0 (0, 20) FF^1 (7, 1) FF^1 (8, 1)
Workflow of Fig. 4	$WG(N,T)$	$FJ = \{ 1, 7, 19 \}$; $V - FN^0 = \{ 11, 16, 17, 18, 19, 20, 21, 22, 23, 24 \}$, $FJ^0 = \{ 1, 7 \}$, $FS^0 = \{ 10, 13, 15 \}$.	FF^0 (0, 25) FF^1 (10, 7) FF^1 (13, 7) FF^{1+} (15, 1)
	FF^{1+} (15, 1)	$FN^1 = \{ 11, 16, 17, 18, 19, 20, 21, 22, 24 \}$, $FJ^1 = \{ 19 \}$, $FS^1 = \{ 22 \}$; $FN^1 = \{ 23 \}$.	FF^1 (15, 1) FF^2 (22, 19)

3   Identification and Abstraction of Reducible Block Structures

Our workflow abstraction and verification method utilizes the concept of inline blocks. An *inline block* is a subset of nodes and transitions among those nodes that satisfies the blocked transition property [29]. According to the Workflow Management Coalition, the *blocked transition property* states that any *inward transition* to the inline block can only occur to the start node of the block and that any *outward transition* from the inline block can only occur at the end node of the block. In order to handle cyclic workflows, this property needs to be extended as described later in this section. An inline block is *reducible* to a *block activity* node or may be modeled as a sub-process of the original process definition. This helps in managing a large-scale model, including verification of structural conflicts, being represented as a hierarchy of simple smaller models. Identifying inline blocks manually from a complex workflow [2] is a difficult task even for an experienced process designer. Next, we extend the blocked transition property in the presence of cyclic workflows, leading to extended inline blocks.

3.1   Candidates of Inline Blocks with Cycles

Our method first configures potential inline blocks with one of the *Split nodes* (except Feedback Splits) or *Feedback Joins* as the block start node, called the *source*; and one of the *Join nodes* (except Feedback Joins) or *Feedback Splits* as the block end node, called the *sink*. Those potential inline blocks are referred to as *candidate blocks* because they may or may not satisfy the blocked transition property. Although the source or the sink can be a sequential node, we focus on candidate blocks with split and join nodes as the border nodes that can be easily extended without further verification effort by adding sequential nodes at the borders. This way of composing candidate blocks can reduce computational cost significantly by focusing on the core candidate blocks. Further, deadlock and lack of synchronization problems occur due to the incompatibility of split and join nodes, as described in section 2. This is another reason we focus on candidate blocks with split and join nodes as the border nodes. As candidate block is a fundamental concept of our method, we define it formally.

Definition 1. For any node $i \in FN^n$, let **Fwd** (i) denote the set of nodes in FN^n that can be reached from i by the transitions in T. Let **Bwd** (i) denote the set of nodes in FN^n that can reach to i by the transitions in T.

Definition 2. Let CB_M (σ, κ) denote a subgraph spanned by the set of nodes $\{\sigma, \kappa\} \cup$ ($Fwd(\sigma) \cap Bwd(\kappa)$), where $\sigma \in FN^n$ and $\kappa \in Fwd(\sigma)$. Let CB_F (σ, κ) denote $\cup_{fs, fj}$ $FF^{(n+1)+}(fs, fj)$ where $fs \in FS^n$, $fj \in FJ^n$, and $fs, fj \in CB_M$ (σ, κ). Finally, let *Candidate Block* be CB $(\sigma, \kappa) = CB_M$ $(\sigma, \kappa) \cup CB_F$ (σ, κ).

For convenience, the set of nodes that spans the candidate block CB (σ, κ) will be also denoted as CB (σ, κ), without confusion. For example, CB $(1, 7) = CB_M$ $(1, 7) \cup CB_F$ $(1, 7) = \{1, 2, 3, 5, 7\} \cup \{1, 7, 11\} = \{1, 2, 3, 5, 7, 11\}$ for the workflow of Fig. 2. The number of candidate blocks will grow as the number of split nodes and that of join nodes in the workflow model increase. We will also show that given a candidate block that violates the blocked transition property, we may exclude additional candidate blocks from further analysis to enhance computational efficiency.

3.2 Blocked Transition Property for Cyclic Workflows

The statements on the *blocked transition property* by WfMC [29], i.e., no disallowed inward and outward transitions should exist, assures that a block is an independent unit of tasks that can be separated as a subprocess. To assure this property for cyclic workflow models, all the tasks in a cycle should be kept together in the same block. Therefore, the blocked transition property should be imposed with additional constraints for cyclic workflows. More formally, we have the following four constraints for an inline block. If a candidate block CB (σ, κ), with $\sigma, \kappa \in FN^n$, satisfies these four constraints, we say that CB (σ, κ) is an inline block.

$$pred(i) \subset CB\ (\sigma, \kappa), \forall\ i \in CB\ (\sigma, \kappa) \text{ and } i \neq \sigma, \tag{1}$$
$$succ(i) \subset CB\ (\sigma, \kappa), \forall\ i \in CB\ (\sigma, \kappa) \text{ and } i \neq \kappa, \tag{2}$$
$$i \in CB\ (\sigma, \kappa), \forall\ (i, \sigma) \in FJT, \tag{3}$$
$$i \in CB\ (\sigma, \kappa), \forall\ (\kappa, i) \in FST, \tag{4}$$

where $pred(i) = \{j \mid (j, i) \in T\}$, $succ\ (i) = \{j \mid (i, j) \in T\}$, and FJT (or FST) are the sets of feedback join (or split) transitions, respectively. Note that constraints (3) and (4) are applied to only cyclic workflow process models, as explained above.

3.3 Composing an Inline Block by Node Splitting

In case violations of the above four constrains happen only at the source or the sink, of more than two associated links, we can compose an inline block by splitting the source or the sink. Fig. 5 shows the cases of composing an inline block by splitting the source σ, the sink κ, or both of them of CB (σ, κ). The transition from node A or the transition to node B, where A, B $\notin CB$ (σ, κ), does not violate the blocked transition property for the resulting inline block of CB (σ', κ), CB (σ, κ'), or CB (σ', κ'), respectively. Figures 5(a) and 5(b) are for the cases when conditions (1) or (2) are violated, and Fig. 5(c) is for the cases when conditions (3) or (4) are violated, at the sink or at the source, respectively. The newly added σ' and κ' in Fig. 5(b) are null activities of no tasks to perform. Note that it is not necessary the source σ and sink κ are of same node type and is worth for splitting only at the source or at the sink.

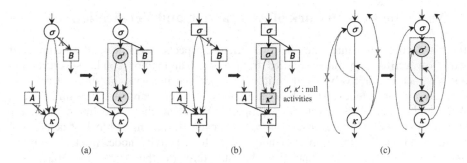

(a)   (b)   (c)

Fig. 5. Composing an inline block by splitting the source or the sink

3.4   Exclusion of Additional Candidate Blocks from Evaluation

When a candidate block **CB** (σ, κ) does not satisfy blocked transition property, additional candidate blocks **CB** (σ, κ') or **CB** (σ', κ) should be excluded from the evaluation. This will reduce the computational efforts significantly, particularly when the number of split and join nodes are large and/or the given workflow model is more unstructured [12]. The following two theorems are given for this purpose.

Theorem 1. If there exists an inward transition toward **CB** (σ, κ), where $\sigma, \kappa \in FN^n$, from an outside node $i \in FN^n$ to an inside node $j \neq \sigma$, this inward transition violation also exists toward **CB** (σ, κ'), for any $\kappa' \in Fwd(\kappa)$. Consequently, candidate block **CB** (σ, κ') is not an inline block.
Proof: The given supposition of $(i, j) \in T$ with $i \notin CB$ (σ, κ) and $i \in FN^n$, $j \in CB$ (σ, κ) and $j \neq \sigma$ implies that $i \notin Fwd(\sigma)$, unless $i \in CB$ (σ, κ), and subsequently $i \notin CB$ (σ, κ'). Further, with $\kappa' \in Fwd(\kappa)$, it is clear that $j \in Bwd(\kappa')$ and subsequently $j \in CB$ (σ, κ'). Therefore, it is certain that transition (i, j) also violates condition (5) for **CB** (σ, κ') and **CB** (σ, κ') could never be an inline block.   //

For **CB** $(6, 14)$ in Fig. 2, as an example, violation of condition (1) by transition $(10, 14)$ results in the exclusion of **CB** $(6, 17)$ and **CB** $(6, 18)$ from further analysis.

Theorem 2. If there exists an outward transition from an inside node $i \neq \kappa$ to an outside node $j \in FN^n$, this outward transition violation also exists for **CB** (σ', κ), for any $\sigma' \in Bwd(i)$. Consequently, candidate block **CB** (σ', κ) is not an inline block.
Proof: The given supposition of $(i, j) \in T$ with $i \in CB$ (σ, κ) and $i \neq \kappa$, $j \notin CB$ (σ, κ) and $j \in FN^n$ implies that $j \notin Bwd(\kappa)$, unless $j \in CB$ (σ, κ), and subsequently $j \notin CB$ (σ', κ). Further, with $\sigma' \in Bwd(i)$, it is clear that $i \in Fwd(\sigma')$, and subsequently $i \in CB$ (σ', κ). Therefore, it is certain that transition (i, j) also violates condition (7) for **CB** (σ', κ) and **CB** (σ', κ) could never be an inline block.   //

For **CB** (6, 14) in Fig. 2, as an example, violation of condition (2) by transition (6, 8) results in the exclusion of **CB** (3, 14) and **CB** (1, 14) from further analysis.

4   An Unified Framework of Abstraction and Verification

In this section, we integrate the two related aspects, workflow abstraction and workflow verification, into a unified framework. Our method conducts verification and abstraction iteratively based on inline blocks, starting with the simplest one and extending to larger ones. At each iteration, the algorithm searches for an inline block that satisfies the blocked transition property. We then check the inline block for structural conflicts. Whatever the verification result is, this inline block structure will be replaced with a single abstract node, i.e., block activity node, marked with the verification result. This simplifies the structure of the workflow graph and subsequently the evaluation of other larger inline blocks containing the already condensed ones. The algorithm then proceeds to abstract further inline blocks and verify all the structural conflicts in the given workflow model.

4.1   Decomposed Verification by Inline Blocks and Acyclic Partitioning

We apply the decomposed approach by verifying each inline block in the workflow model. Further, verification of structural conflicts for any reducible block $CB(\sigma, \kappa)$, with $\sigma, \kappa \in FN^n$, will be handled by verifying $CB_M (\sigma, \kappa)$ and each $FF^{(n+1)+}(fs, fj)$, where $fs \in FS^n$, $fj \in FJ^n$, and $fs, fj \in CB_M (\sigma, \kappa)$, that is each feedback flow originated from and merged into $CB_M (\sigma, \kappa)$. Theorem 3 below argues the correctness of this approach formally.

Theorem 3. If there exist no structural conflicts in both $CB_M (\sigma, \kappa)$ and $CB_F (\sigma, \kappa)$, then there exist no structural conflict in the integrated model $CB (\sigma, \kappa)$.
Proof: It is clear that additional deadlock conflict will not be caused by combining each $FF^{(n+1)+}(fs, fj) \subset CB_F (\sigma, \kappa)$ to $CB_M (\sigma, \kappa)$, through XOR- coordinators. After early stage verification explained at the end of subsection 2.3, each $FF^{(n+1)+}(fs, fj)$ splits from an XOR feedback split fs, merges at an XOR feedback join fj, and does not cross another feedback flow by an AND-split or an AND-join. Therefore, there is no chance that any additional Lack of Synchronization conflict would be caused in $CB (\sigma, \kappa)$ by adding any $FF^{(n+1)+}(fs, fj) \subset CB_F (\sigma, \kappa)$ to $CB_M (\sigma, \kappa)$.   //

To be described in detail next section, our method iteratively composes candidate blocks from the simplest one to more complex ones by utilizing the rank of nodes in selecting the source and the sink. Whatever the verification result, our method abstracts out each reducible block into a new block activity node. In this way with partitioned verification approach, we only need to verify condensed feedback flows, with any previously abstracted block activity nodes, which are all acyclic as well as $CB_M (\sigma, \kappa)$. That is the block-wise decomposition and feedback-partitioning method enables the verification of whole workflow process with the verification of only acyclic structures in each inline block.

4.2 Verification with Block Instance Flows

Each $FF^{n+}(fs, fj)$ or CB_M (σ, κ) composing the CB (σ, κ), after prior abstractions of contained blocks, is a smaller acyclic workflow. To verify any of them, we can adopt any verification method previously proposed, such as the graph reduction techniques by Lin et al. [20] or Petri-net-based approach [1], with some conversion effort if necessary. We introduced an instance-flow-based method that verifies structural conflicts by examining the instance flows of each partitioned acyclic structure of an inline block in [12]. An *instance flow* is the instantiation of certain paths in the workflow model and the resulting graph is called an *instance graph*. Fig. 6 (b), (d) and (e) are three instance flows for the acyclic block CB (1, 11) represented in Fig. 6 (a). Instance flows of Fig. 6 (d) and (e) are derived by instantiating XOR-split node 5 from Fig. 6 (c). Note that *acyclic block instance flows* to be handled in our method are much simpler, in general, than the instance flows of the whole model, which even may not be defined for the cyclic workflow models. .

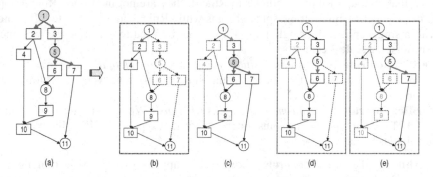

Fig. 6. Derivation of three instance flows (b, d, e) of an acyclic block structure represented in (a)

Two types of structural conflicts, deadlock and lack of synchronization, are identified using the two identification rules below. Note that a livelock occurs due to inadequate connection of feedback flows, which should have been detected and corrected earlier as described at the end of subsection 2.3.

Deadlock identification rule: A *deadlock* can be identified in an instance flow graph when the number of instantiated paths leading to an AND-Join is less than the total number of join paths in the original workflow model.

LOS identification rule: A *lack of synchronization* can be identified in an instance flow graph when the number of instantiated paths leading to an XOR-Join is more than one.

For the instance graph in Fig. 6(d), it can be identified that a 'deadlock' conflict occurs at node 10. Consequently, it is concluded that the inline block CB (1, 11) will incur a deadlock conflict at node 10 for the instance flow of nodes {1, 3, 5, 6, 8, 9, 10, 11}. Note that every structural conflict is detected with the exact location and the instance flow where it happens.

4.3   Verification with Pattern Rules

To further improve verification efficiency, we have created several verification rules. If an inline block (or any acyclic structure of the block) or the whole model after abstractions matches certain patterns specified by these rules, there will be no need of further verification effort..

Verification rule 1: <*Sequential Flow*> If every node is on a sequential path, no structural conflict occurs in this flow.

Verification rule 2: <*Single split and single join*> When the source is the only split and the sink is the only join in the inline block, the given inline block is free from structural conflicts if the split and join are of same control type, i.e. either 'AND' or 'XOR'. Otherwise, a structural conflict occurs at the join node due to incompatibility of the split and the join, as explained in Section 2.

Verification rule 3: <*All splits and joins of the same type*> If all split and join nodes are of the same type in an inline block, there will be no structural conflict in the block. Note that although Rule 3 is similar to Rule 2, they are not the same. Rule 3 applies to inline blocks with multiple splits or joins while Rule 2 applies only to inline blocks with a single split and a single join. Rule 2 can be used to conclude the existence of conflicts, but Rule 3 cannot.

Verification rule 4: <*Direct transition from source to sink of distinct type*> If there is a direct transition from the source to the sink of different type, structural conflict occurs.

Verification rule 5: <*Non-matching splits or joins*> When there are some splits (or joins) of certain type and no joins (or splits) for that type in an inline block, structural conflict also occurs in the block.

Although the verification rules above can be applied to any verification algorithm, these rules become more powerful with our block-based decomposed approach, which handles much simpler structure than the whole workflow model. Consecutive abstractions will further simplify other inline blocks containing those structures, thus increasing the chance of applying the above verification rules.

4.4   Unified Algorithm with an Illustrative Example

A block chart of the unified algorithm of abstraction and verification is given in Fig. 7. The algorithm starts with the simplest CB (σ, κ), with σ as one of the candidate sources of maximum rank and κ as one of the candidate sinks, i.e. $Fwd(\sigma)$, of minimum rank. At the next iteration, new candidate block is selected by fetching new sink κ' of the next higher rank, from $Fwd(\sigma)$, with the same source σ of the current candidate block; when all candidate blocks with σ as source are evaluated or excluded, The algorithm fetches new source σ' of the next lower rank from the stack of candidate sources and proceeds forward.

An inline block that does not contain any other inline block is referred to as a 1st-*order inline block*, and an inline block that contains at least one first-order (and no higher order) inline block is called a 2nd-*order inline block*. Similarly, an nth-*order inline block* is the one that contains at least one $(n-1)^{th}$-order (and no higher order) inline block.

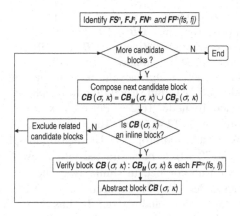

Fig. 7. Illustration of the unified algorithm

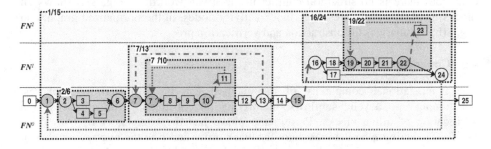

(a) All blocks indicated in the normalized graph

Rank of source	Source	Candidate sinks[1]	Blocks checked	Violation for a block or verification result	Excluded blocks or new block activity node
16	19	22, 24	(19, 22)	No conflict (each by Rule 1)	Abstracted into "19/22"
14	16	_22_, 24	(16, 24)	No conflict (by Rule 2)	Abstracted into "16/24"
6	7	10, 13, 15	(7, 10)	Violates condition (3); No conflict after splitting node 7 (each by Rule 1)	Abstracted into "7'/10"
			(7, 13)	No conflict (each by Rule 1)	Abstracted into "7/13"
2	2	6, _10_, _13_, 15	(2, 6)	No conflict (by Rule 2)	Abstracted into "2/6"
1	1	_6_, _10_, _13_, 15	(1, 15)	No conflict (each by Rule 1)	Abstracted into "1/15"

[1] Underlined numbers represent the candidate sinks ignored by prior abstractions

(b) Summary of abstraction and verification process

Fig. 8. Abstraction and verification for the workflow with nested cycles in Fig. 4

Fig. 8 shows the abstraction and verification process for the workflow graph with nested cycles of Fig. 4 to be partitioned as shown in Table 1.

The algorithm starts with the simplest candidate block CB (19, 22) that satisfies the blocked transition property. Since CB_M (19, 22) and FF^2(22, 19) = CB_F (19, 22) are free from structural conflicts by Rule 1, CB (22, 19) is found to be free from structural conflicts and reduced into a new 1st-order block activity node "19/22". At the next iteration, CB (16, 24), which is acyclic with the just abstracted block activity node "19/22", is found to be free from structural conflicts by Rule 2 and reduced into a new 2nd-order block activity node "16/24". For the next candidate block CB (7, 10), the inward transition from node 13 $\notin CB$ (7, 10) to the source, i.e. node 7, is the only violation for the blocked transition property, The algorithm splits node 7 and builds new candidate block CB (7′, 10), to be abstracted into a new 1st-order block activity node "7′/10" marked with no conflict. In similar way, next candidate block CB (7, 13), containing abstract node "7′/10" is reduced into a new 2nd-order abstract node "7/13" marked with no conflict, and so on. In this way, the unified algorithm identifies and abstracts three 1st-order inline block, two 2nd-order inline block, and one 3rd-order inline block "1/15", verifies all of them by verification rules, and concludes there is no structural conflict in the given workflow. Fig. 8(a) shows all blocks, marked with the resulting block activity nodes, in the normalized graph, and Fig. 8(b) summarizes the abstraction and verification process.

4.5 Comments on Complexity

The computational complexity of our method can be estimated in 3 phases: partitioning into acyclic subflows; identifying and abstracting inline blocks; and verification of inline blocks. Partitioning phase has the complexity of $O(qr|T|) < O(|N| \cdot |T|)$, letting q be the maximum feedback order and r be the average number of subgraphs that need to be further partitioned after identifying FN^n, $n < q$ [11]. Identifying and reducing inline blocks will have the complexity of $O(c \cdot n \cdot t)$, which is less than $O(|N|^2 \cdot |T|)$, letting c be the number of candidate blocks checked, n be the average number of nodes in candidate block, and t be the average number incoming and outgoing transitions of a node in the given workflow. Exclusion of candidate blocks by two Theorems or by prior abstracted blocks will contribute to reduce this complexity. Block decomposition and feedback partitioning reduces the complexity of verification stage as a matter of n, not of $|N|$ found in the other approaches, such as $O((|N|+|T|)^2 \cdot |N|^2)$ even limited to acyclic models ([3], [20]). As noted above, this complexity is related with the control flow structure of the given workflow graph, such as the number of inline blocks. Simplified models with prior abstractions and introduction of simple pattern-based verification rules will further reduce this complexity.

5 Concluding Remarks

Our integrated algorithm of abstraction and verification is decomposition-oriented and can deal with workflows with nested feedback structures. Our verification algorithm can discover potential structural conflicts by analyzing each acyclic structure of blocks further simplified with prior abstractions and do not require prior recognition of complex process patterns whereas the graph reduction technique [23] relies on.

Our work is related to three main studies in workflow verification, namely the graph reduction approach ([20], [23]), the Petri nets approach ([1], [4], [6], [27]), and the logic-based approach ([10], [22]). While the block-based decomposition-oriented approach we proposed in this paper has unique strengths compared with these existing approaches such as the ability to deal with cycles, the use of activity-based models, and the ability to do blockwise decomposition. Furthermore, our work unifies process abstraction and verification while other verification techniques focus mainly on process verification.

We plan to extend our research in two directions. First, we will expand our algorithm to handle OR-nodes, which can be done by extending the lower-level algorithms without changing the overall procedure. Although the Workflow Management Coalition (WfMC) standard does not yet contain OR-nodes, some researchers have proposed the explicit support of OR-nodes in workflow systems [6]. Second, we plan to integrate a prototype system we have developed with a full-fledged workflow system to test its scalability and usability in the presence of complex workflow patterns.

References

[1] Aalst, W. M. P. van der, "The Application of Petri Nets to Workflow Management", *The Journal of Circuits, Systems and Computers*, vol. 8, no. 1, pp. 21-66, 1998.

[2] Aalst, W. M. P. van der, "Workflow Verification: Finding Control-Flow Errors using Petri-net-based Techniques", *Lecture Notes in Computer Science*, vol. 1806, pp. 161-183, 2000.

[3] Aalst, W. M. P. van der, "An alternative way to analyze workflow graphs," *14th Int. Conf. On Adv. Info. Sys. Eng.*, pp. 535-552, 2002.

[4] Aalst, W. M. P. van der and A. H. M. ter Hofstede, "Verification of workflow task structures: A Petri-Net-based Approach," *Information Systems*, vol. 25, no. 1, pp. 43-69, 2000.

[5] Aalst, W.M.P. van der, A.H.M. ter Hofstede, and M. Weske, "Business Process Management: A Survey", *Lecture Notes in Computer Science*, vol. 2678, pp. 1-12, 2003.

[6] Adam, N. R., V. Atluri, and W. Huang. "Modeling and Analysis of Workflows using Petri Nets," *Journal of Intelligent Information Systems*, vol. 10, pp. 131-158, 1998.

[7] Aissi, S., P. Malu, and K. Srinivasan. "E-business process modeling: the next big step," *IEEE Computer*, vol. 35, no. 5, pp. 55-62, 2002.

[8] Basu, A. and R. W. Blanning, "A formal approach to workflow analysis," *Information Systems Research*, vol. 11, no. 1, pp. 17-36, 2000.

[9] Basu, A. and A. Kumar, "Research commentary: Workflow management issues in e-Business," *Information Systems Research*, vol. 13, no. 1, pp. 1-14, 2002.

[10] Bi, H. H. and J. L. Zhao, "Mending the Lag between Commerce and Research: A Logic-based Workflow Verification Approach," *Computational Modeling and Problem Solving in the Networked World*, Kluwer Academic Publishers, pp. 191-212, 2003.

[11] Choi, Y., "A Two Phase Verification Algorithm for Cyclic Workflow Graphs", *Proc. of ICEB 2004*, pp. 137-143.

[12] Choi, Y. and J. L. Zhao, "Matrix-based abstraction and verification of e-business processes," *Proc. the 1st Workshop on e-Business*, pp. 154-165, 2002.

[13] Fan, W. and S. Weinstein, "Specifying and reasoning about workflows with path constraints", *Lecture Notes in Computer Science*, vol. 1749, pp. 13-15, 1999.

[14] Georgakopoulos, D., M. Hornick, and A. Sheth, "An overview of workflow management: from process modeling to workflow automation infrastructure", *Distributed and Parallel Databases,* vol. 3, pp.119-153, 1995.

[15] Gondran, M. and M. Minoux, *Graphs and Algorithms*, John Wiley & Sons Ltd., 1984.

[16] Hofstede, A. H. M. ter, M. E. Orlowska, and J. Rajapakse, "Verification Problems in Conceptual Workflow Specifications," *Data and Knowledge Engineering*, vol. 24, no. 3, pp. 239-256, 1998.

[17] Kiepuszewski, B., *Expressiveness and Suitability of Languages for Control Flow Modelling in Workflows*, PhD thesis, Queensland University of Technology, Brisbane, Australia, 2002.

[18] Kumar, A., and J. L. Zhao, "Dynamic Routing and Operational Controls in Workflow Management Systems," *Management Science*, vol. 45, no. 2, pp. 253-272, 1999.

[19] Leymann, F., D. Roller, and A. Reuter, *Production Workflow: Concepts and Techniques*, Prentice-Hall, Englewood Cliffs, NJ, 2000.

[20] Lin, H., Z. Zhao, H. Li, and Z. Chen, "A novel graph reduction algorithm to identify structural conflicts," *Proc. of the 35th Hawaii Int. Conf. On Sys. Sci.*, pp. 289, 2002.

[21] Murata, T., "Petri nets: Properties, analysis, and applications", *Proceedings of the IEEE*, vol. 77, no. 4, pp. 541-580, 1989.

[22] Mukherjee S., H. Davulcu, M. Kifer, P. Senkul, and G. Yang, "Logic Based Approaches to Workflow Modeling and Verification", In *Logics for emerging applications of databases* (editors, Chomicki et al.), Springer-Verlag, LNCS, 2003.

[23] Sadiq, W. and M. E. Orlowska, "Analyzing process models using graph reduction techniques," *Information Systems,* vol. 25, no. 2, pp.117-134, 2000.

[24] Sheth, A. P., W. M. P. van der Aalst, and I. B. Arpinar, "Processes driving the networked economy," *IEEE Concurrency*, vol. 7, no. 3, pp. 18–31, 1999.

[25] Sivaraman, E. and M. Kamath, " On the use of Petri nets for business process modeling", *11th Annual Industrial Engineering Research Conference*, Orlando, Florida. 2002

[26] Stohr, E. A. and J. L. Zhao, "Workflow automation: Overview and research issues," *Information Systems Frontiers*, vol. 3, no. 3, pp. 281-296, 2001.

[27] Verbeek, H. M. W., T. Basten, and W. M. P. van der Aalst, "Diagnosing workflow processes using Woflan," *Computer Journal*, vol. 44, no. 4, pp. 246-279, 2001.

[28] Workflow Management Coalition, *Glossary. Document Number WfMC-TC-1011*, 1999.

[29] Workflow Management Coalition, *Interface 1: Process Definition Interchange Process Model. Document Number WfMC TC-1016-P,* 1999.

Guaranteed Termination in the Verification of LTL Properties of Non-linear Robust Discrete Time Hybrid Systems*

Werner Damm[1], Guilherme Pinto[1], and Stefan Ratschan[2]

[1] Carl v. Ossietzky Universität, Oldenburg, Germany
[2] Max-Planck-Institut für Informatik, Saarbrücken, Germany

Abstract. We present a novel approach to the automatic verification and falsification of LTL requirements of non-linear discrete-time hybrid systems. The verification tool uses an interval-based constraint solver for non-linear robust constraints to compute incrementally refined abstractions. Although the problem is in general undecidable, we prove termination of abstraction refinement based verification and falsification of such properties for the class of *robust non-linear hybrid systems*, thus significantly extending previous semi-decidability results. We argue, that safety critical control applications *are* robust hybrid systems. We give first results on the application of this approach to a variant of an aircraft collision avoidance protocol.

1 Introduction

This paper significantly extends previous semi-decidability results for LTL verification of non-linear discrete time hybrid systems. Even though this problem is in general undecidable (by reduction from 2 counter machines), we show, that by exploiting the natural property of *robustness* of real-life hybrid systems, an abstraction-refinement based approach—employing both approximations from above and below—is guaranteed to terminate, either establishing the truth of the requirement, or exhibiting a concrete counterexample, even for non-linear hybrid systems. In contrast, results from Fränzle [8, 9]—also based on robustness arguments—only handle polynomial flows (in a dense time setting). It also improves over other approaches to hybrid systems verification [6, 16, 1, 15] in that termination is guaranteed even for a very rich class of models.

The presented approach primarily targets safety critical control applications, such as collision avoidance systems, where designs must guarantee separation of traffic agents by safety margins even in the presence of noise and (bounded) inaccuracies of sensors and actuators. Intuitively, for such applications, small variances in measurements or small deviations of actuator settings may not lead

---

* This work was partly supported by the German Research Council (DFG) as part of the Transregional Collaborative Research Center "Automatic Verification and Analysis of Complex Systems" (SFB/TR 14 AVACS). See www.avacs.org for more information.

D.A. Peled and Y.-K. Tsay (Eds.): ATVA 2005, LNCS 3707, pp. 99–113, 2005.

to a violation of safety margins between traffic agents. We will give a formal definition of this intuitive concept of robustness, which will be instrumental in establishing termination. The approach will be illustrated by an air traffic conflict resolution example [10], where aircraft follow circular trajectories along opposite directions, leading to a non-linear hybrid system.

As mathematical model we use *discrete time hybrid automata*, which in each time step of fixed duration update a set of real-valued variables as determined by assignments occurring as transition labels, allowing possibly non-linear arithmetic expressions. This subsumes the capability to describe the evolvement of plant variables by difference equations. Transition guards can be non-linear arithmetic constraints. Steps of the automata are assumed to take a fixed time-period (also called cycle-time), intuitively corresponding to the sampling period of the control unit, and determine the new mode and new outputs (corresponding to actuators) based on the sampled inputs (sensors). We allow arbitrary first-order LTL formulas as requirements. Atoms are arithmetic constraints over the variables of the hybrid automaton, thus allowing to both express response time requirements (such as "*when crash sensor is activated, the airbag will be ignited within 3 cycles*"), stability properties such as "the aircraft will be maintained at preselected height", as well as safety properties (such as "*the distance between two aircraft will always be greater than 10 km*").

The decision to base our analysis on discrete time models of hybrid systems is motivated from an application perspective. Industrial design flows for embedded control software typically entail a transition from continuous time models in early analysis addressing control law design, to discrete time models in modeling tools such as Scade™, ASCET™, or TargetLink™[1], as a basis for subsequent autocode generation. Current industrial practice relies on informal verification of this design step, typically by simulation. For example, if design engineers have decided to implement a certain control law as a periodic task with periodicity δ, then simulation would be used to "verify" that stability of the controller is maintained in spite of the now limited observability of the plant at the chosen sampling rate δ. The methods of this paper replace this informal validation step. They allow to formally prove that—even under the limited discrete time visibility of the plant—LTL requirements, and thus both stability properties as well as safety requirements, are guaranteed by the controller.

To our knowledge, the previous work on abstraction (and refinement) for hybrid systems consider a *continuous* time model. Because of this, a direct comparison of the employed algorithms is not possible. We can, nevertheless, observe some differences w.r.t. the way they compute the abstraction.

While, for example, also tools such as Hypertech [10] and Checkmate [5] do support analysis of non-linear systems, with Checkmate offering the highly optimized flow-pipe representation technique, none of these can guarantee termination for proving temporal properties of hybrid systems. We also note the potential unsafeness of the Checkmate approach in the construction of the ab-

---

[1] Scade is a trademark of Esterel Technologies, France, ASCET is a trademark of ETAS GmbH, Germany, TargetLink is a trademark of dSpace GmbH, Germany.

stract transition relation due to rounding errors – in contrast, our constraint solver guarantees, that rounding errors are conservatively over-approximated in refinement steps. The high potential of interval-based evaluation methods for hybrid system verification has already been demonstrated for chemical plant applications [16] for a more restricted logic, and without termination guarantees.

There are mechanisms for approximating non-linear continuous-time hybrid systems by rectangular automata arbitrarily closely [11]. However, the approximation has to be done manually, and even verifying only rectangular safety properties on the resulting approximation is still an undecidable problem.

Due to the page limit, we could not include all proofs and formalizations, and had to be selective on the included references.

The paper is organized as follows: Section 2 elaborates the notion of *robust hybrid systems*, leading to a new notion of *robust satisfaction* and *robust falsification* of LTL properties; Section 3 shows how to approximate robust satisfaction from above and robust falsification from below by exact satisfaction/falsification on finite approximations, and proves, that for any property that is robustly satisfied (falsified) by a (non-linear) robust hybrid system, one can find a finite approximation that establishes this fact; Section 4 casts this into a terminating abstraction refinement algorithm and illustrates its power by application to a non-linear collision avoidance example; and Section 5 concludes the paper.

2   Robust Hybrid Systems

The authors have substantial experience in analyzing industrial control unit designs for automotive [2–...] and avionics applications [3–...]. Based on this, we derive the following observations:

- For any sensor inputs, a combination of filtering, plausibility checking and voting will be used to derive what is often called *validated inputs*.
- This preprocessing will in particular guarantee a minimal separation between values assumed by validated inputs, in the following sense: assume, that $v \leq 5$ appears as guard of a transition, then altering the guard to $v \leq 5 \pm \varepsilon$ for some ε smaller than a sensor-dependent constant does not change the mode-switching behavior of the system.
- To take into account noise on actuators and un-modeled disturbances, the controller will enforce a safety margin, separating all legal undisturbed runs from forbidden plant regions by some minimal application dependent constant (catering for noise and disturbances). To this end, deviations induced by disturbances and noise on actuators are detected using closed-loop control, and correcting actions to avoid forbidden states are designed to cater for this difference between ideal and measured trajectories.

Designers hence solve the task to guarantee a safety property φ even in the presence of noise on sensors and actuators and un-modeled disturbances. This entails, that the classical notion of satisfiability is in fact too weak. What is called for, is a notion of *robust satisfiability*, which guarantees φ even in the presence of small bounded uncertainties. In the remainder of this section, we will derive a formal definition of such a notion of robust satisfiability.

For formally modeling discrete time hybrid systems we assume a finite set $\{m_1, \ldots, m_n\}$ of *modes*, and a finite set $X = \{x_1, \ldots, x_k\}$ of *real-valued variables* (in the formal development, we do not further distinguish between sensors, variables, and actuators). We use constraints to specify the transition relation, with primed variables describing the successor mode, respectively constraints on new valuations of variables. We also explicate the predicates observable on the hybrid system, which define the atomic predicates to be used in first-order LTL requirement specifications on our systems.

Definition 1

- *An* arithmetic expression *over a set of variables V is a term (in the predicate-logical sense) over these variables with function symbols in* $\{+, \times, \hat{\ }, \sin, \cos, \exp\}$.
- *An* atomic arithmetic state space constraint *over a set of variables V is of the form $e \; r \; c$, where e is an arithmetic expression over V, $r \in \{\neq, =, <, > , \leq, \geq\}$ is a relational operator, and c is a real-valued constant.*
- *A* mode constraint *over a set of variables $Mode$ is of the form $mode = m_j$, where $mode \in Mode$.*
- *A* state space constraint *over a set of variables V and a set of variables $Mode$ is a Boolean combination of atomic arithmetic state space constraints over V and mode constraints over $Mode$.*
- *A* transition constraint *over V and $Mode$ is a state-space constraint over $V \cup V'$ and $Mode \cup Mode'$, where the primed sets denote the set of primed variables of the corresponding unprimed sets.*

Definition 2 (discrete time hybrid system). *A discrete time hybrid system S is a tuple $S = (\tau, \pi_0, \pi_1, \ldots, \pi_k, \delta)$ where*

- τ *is a disjunction of transition constraints over X and $\{mode\}$ of the form $mode = m \wedge guard \wedge mode' = m' \wedge transitions$ where*
  - *$guard$ is a conjunction of atomic arithmetic state space constraints over X,*
  - *$transitions$ is a conjunction of atomic arithmetic state space constraints over $X \cup X'$.*
- π_0 *is a state space constraint over X and $\{mode\}$, restricting the initial valuation, and*
- $\pi_1, \ldots, \pi_k$ *are additional state space constraints over X and $\{mode\}$, over which we will later form LTL queries (the observed propositions),*
- δ *is the sampling rate in time units, a positive real number.*

Discrete time hybrid systems are sufficiently expressive to express both plant dynamics as well as (possibly hybrid) controllers. Time is modeled implicitly, in that each step corresponds to a fixed unit delay δ, as motivated in the introduction.

Our example is a discretized variant of an aircraft collision avoidance protocol [10] exhibiting non-linear dynamics. Two aircraft, flying in a straight line

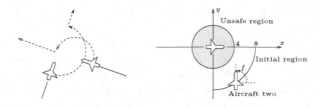

Fig. 1. Air traffic control protocol

and orthogonal trajectories at the same altitude, initiate a collision avoidance maneuver when the distance between them reaches 8 miles. Both aircraft turn 90 degrees to the right and start a semi-circle trajectory to the left, as shown in Fig. 1, with fixed angular velocities. The linear velocity is also fixed and the same for both aircraft. After completing the semi-circle, they resume their original trajectories.

We want to assure that their distance never becomes smaller than 4 miles. Let the angular velocity of aircraft one be 0.95 rad/s and that of aircraft two be 1 rad/s (note that, since they have equal linear velocity, they will follow trajectories with different radius). The relative position of aircraft two (x, y) (i.e., the plant dynamics), illustrated in Fig. 1, is given by the constraint below,

$$f' = f + \delta * (0.05) \ \wedge \ x' = x + \delta * (y - 1 + \cos(f)) \ \wedge \ y' = y + \delta * (\sin(f) - x)$$

where f is the angle between the vector speed of aircraft two relative to the vector speed of aircraft one, δ is the sampling period of the controller in seconds, which determines the three difference equations; and the initial region is $f = 1.57 \ \wedge \ x^2 + y^2 = 64 \ \wedge \ x > 0 \ \wedge \ y < 0$, which models an initial distance of 8 miles, restricted to the cases where the intersection of the trajectories lies ahead of both aircraft.

Definition 3

- A valuation σ is a mapping $X \cup \{mode\} \to \mathbb{R} \cup \{m_1, \ldots, m_n\}$ assigning a real value to each variable in X and a mode to the variable mode. We denote the set of all valuations by Σ.
- We denote by $[\![\pi]\!]$ the set of all valuations satisfying a state space constraint π, and similarly by $[\![\tau]\!]$ the set of pairs of valuations $\langle \sigma, \sigma' \rangle$ satisfying the transition constraint τ, where primed (resp. unprimed) variables are interpreted over σ' (resp. σ).
- Given a set Γ, we call a tuple $(\to, Q_0, Q_1, \ldots, Q_k)$, with $\to \subseteq \Gamma \times \Gamma$, and $Q_0, \ldots, Q_k \subseteq \Gamma$, an (extended) transition system over Γ
- Given a hybrid system $(\tau, \pi_0, \pi_1, \ldots, \pi_k, \delta)$ we denote by $[\![(\tau, \pi_0, \pi_1, \ldots, \pi_k, \delta)]\!]$ the transition system $([\![\tau]\!], [\![\pi_0]\!], \ldots, [\![\pi_k]\!])$ over Σ.
- A run of a system $(\tau, \pi_0, \pi_1, \ldots, \pi_k, \delta)$ is a mapping $\theta : \mathbb{N} \to \Sigma$ such that for all $t \in \mathbb{N}$, $\langle \theta(t), \theta(t+1) \rangle \in [\![\tau]\!]$.

We use first-order LTL formulas such as $G \neg x \geq 10$ to formalize requirements on discrete time hybrid systems. Still, the results of this paper hold for any temporal logic using only universal path quantifiers, such as ACTL*. Since steps have a defined duration, real-time constraints can be expressed using the next-time operator. As atoms we allow the observed propositions $\pi_0, \ldots, \pi_k$. We employ standard syntax and semantics of LTL as can be found in various textbooks [7]—the needed adaption to our definition of extended transition system is a trivial exercise. Especially we write $T \models \varphi$ to signify that the extended transition system T satisfies φ.

Note that we do not treat the state space constraint π_0 that specifies the initial states special in any way (e.g., by allowing only runs that start in an initial state). Instead, we encode initial states into the queries by using LTL formulae of the form $\pi_0 \rightarrow \varphi$ (i.e., $\neg \pi_0 \vee \varphi$).

Robustness of a hybrid system S is defined relative to a temporal specification φ: it requires, that the validity of φ does not depend on small perturbations of S's transition relation. The formal definition is based on a metric between arithmetic constraints [13]. For S to be *robust wrt.* φ requires the existence of a bound ε, such that if φ holds in S, then it must also hold in any S' whose transition predicate has distance at most ε from the transition predicate of S. Intuitively, this entails that avoiding forbidden plant states may not depend on small inaccuracies of sensors or actuators. Indeed, controller designs in which changing a guard of the form $e\ r\ c$ to $e\ r\ (c \pm \varepsilon)$ (mirroring sensor inaccuracy) or changing an actuator setting from $a' = e$ to an assignment $a' = e \pm \varepsilon$ (modeling a small error in actuator settings) causes forbidden states to be reached would not be acceptable (and not "robust", under our formal definition).

We now define these concepts more formally;

Definition 4

- *The distance between two valuations σ_1, σ_2 is defined by $d(\sigma_1, \sigma_2) \doteq$*
  - *∞, if $\sigma_1(mode) \neq \sigma_2(mode)$, and*
  - *$\sup\{d(\sigma_1(x), \sigma_2(x)) \mid x \in X\}$, where $d(a, b) \doteq |a - b|$, otherwise.*
- *The distance between two atomic arithmetic constraints $e\ r\ c$ and $e'\ r'\ c'$ (we assume that all arithmetic constraints have been brought into this form) is defined by $d(e\ r\ c, e'\ r'\ c') \doteq \infty$, if $e \neq e'$ or $r \neq r'$, and $d(c, c')$, otherwise.*
- *The distance between two mode constraints $mode = m_i$ and $mode = m_j$ is ∞ if $m_i \neq m_j$ and 0, otherwise.*
- *The distance between two constraints ϕ, ϕ' is defined by $d(\phi, \phi') \doteq$*
  - *∞, if ϕ and ϕ' have a different Boolean structure or do not have mode constraints at the same places, and*
  - *the maximum of the distance between two corresponding atomic (arithmetic or mode) constraints, otherwise.*

The key definition of this paper, reported below, captures our intuition that safety properties should be guaranteed even under disturbances, as long as these are bounded by some ε. To this end, we define a *non-standard semantics* of discrete time hybrid systems that allows transitions that miss the original transition predicate only by a slight margin below some ε. For a safety property to be robustly satisfied, there must exist a degree of perturbation $\varepsilon > 0$ such that the safety property is true in all ε-perturbed systems.

Definition 5. *A set P is an ε-perturbed solution set of a constraint ϕ iff*

- *for every $x \in P$, there is a constraint ϕ^* with $d(\phi, \phi^*) \leq \varepsilon$ and an x^* with $d(x, x^*) \leq \varepsilon$ such that $x^* \models \phi^*$, and*
- *for every $x \notin P$, there is a constraint ϕ^* with $d(\phi, \phi^*) \leq \varepsilon$ and an x^* with $d(x, x^*) \leq \varepsilon$ such that $x^* \not\models \phi^*$.*

Definition 6. *A transition system $(\rightarrow, Q_0, Q_1, \ldots, Q_k)$ is an ε-perturbed manifestation of a hybrid system $(\tau, \pi_0, \pi_1, \ldots, \pi_k)$ iff $\rightarrow$ is an ε-perturbed solution set of τ, and for each $i \in \{0, \ldots, k\}$, Q_i is an ε-perturbed solution of π_i.*

From now on let S be a hybrid system of the form $(\tau, \pi_0, \pi_1, \ldots, \pi_k, \delta)$.

Definition 7. *An LTL formula φ is satisfied by S with robustness ε ($S \models_\varepsilon \varphi$) iff for all ε-perturbed manifestations T of S, $T \models \varphi$. An LTL formula φ is robustly satisfied by S ($S \models \varphi$) iff there is an $\varepsilon > 0$ such that $S \models_\varepsilon \varphi$.*

For example, a system that starts in state $x = 0$ and evolves according to the transition constraint $x' = x$, satisfies the LTL formula $G\neg x \geq 1$, but does *not* robustly satisfy it, because any transition constraint of the form $x' = x + \varepsilon$, with $\varepsilon > 0$, will eventually violate the constraint $\neg x \geq 1$.

Definition 8. *An LTL formula φ is falsified by S with robustness ε iff for all ε-perturbed manifestations T of S, $T \not\models \varphi$. An LTL formula φ is robustly falsified by S iff there is an $\varepsilon > 0$ such that φ is falsified by S with robustness ε.*

For example, a system that starts in a state fulfilling $0 \leq x \leq 1$, and evolves according to the transition constraint $x \leq x' \wedge x' \leq x + 1/10$ robustly falsifies the LTL formula $G\neg x \geq 10$.

3   Effective Construction of Finite Abstractions with Bounded Imprecision

Our approach follows the abstraction refinement paradigm. In contrast to previous approaches, we are able to prove termination of the refinement loop. In this section we introduce the key instrument—a bound on the degree of imprecision introduced by abstraction. By proving that incremental refinements make the degree of imprecision converge to zero, any desired degree of precision can be reached. We also show in this section, that such abstractions can be efficiently computed even for non-linear hybrid systems, using interval arithmetic. Section 4 puts all pieces together in defining an algorithm for proving robust first-order LTL properties and proving its termination.

From now on, we fix a discrete time hybrid system $S = (\tau, \pi_0, \pi_1, \ldots, \pi_k, \delta)$, and a LTL requirement φ on S over the atoms $\pi_0, \ldots, \pi_k$. For the rest of the development, it will be convenient to assume, that negations occur only in literals, and that all atoms appear under the scope of a negation (this can easily be achieved by adapting the relational operators in arithmetic constraints). This allows us to over-approximate the behavior of a hybrid system by over-approximating the observed propositions $\pi_0, \ldots, \pi_k$ in the same direction as the transition relation τ, allowing more uniformity in the algorithms and proofs. So, by over-approximating the solution set of π_0 and π_1 in a query of the form $G(\neg\pi_0 \vee F\neg\pi_1)$, we under-approximate the literals $\neg\pi_0$ and $\neg\pi_1$.

It is easy to prove that the ε-perturbed solution sets of a constraint have a maximal and a minimal element wrt. the partial order $\subseteq$. This holds for every constraint defining a hybrid system, and so we denote the transition system given by the resulting maximal elements by $\overline{[\![S]\!]}_\varepsilon$, and the transition system give by the resulting minimal elements by $\underline{[\![S]\!]}_\varepsilon$.

For checking satisfiability/falsification with a certain robustness ε it suffices to check it on the maximal perturbed system $\overline{[\![S]\!]}_\varepsilon$/the minimal perturbed system $\underline{[\![S]\!]}_\varepsilon$:

Lemma 1. $S \models_\varepsilon \varphi$ iff $\overline{[\![S]\!]}_\varepsilon \models \varphi$, $S \not\models_\varepsilon \varphi$ iff $\underline{[\![S]\!]}_\varepsilon \not\models \varphi$.

However, it is as hard to check LTL formulae against the maximal/minimal perturbed system as against the original, unperturbed system.

Hence we use abstractions that approximate the behavior of the original system, and then we measure the approximation error introduced by these abstractions. For this we formalize the intuition that one system can show all the behavior of another system. Here we use a notion of simulation that is slightly different from the usual one in the literature which allows a uniform treatment of the initial state predicate and the other (explicitly defined) observables of the system.

Definition 9. *Let T be a transition system over Γ of the form $(\rightarrow, Q_0, \ldots, Q_k)$ and let T' be a transition system of the form $(\rightarrow', Q'_0, \ldots, Q'_k)$ over Γ'. Then a relation $H \subseteq \Gamma \times \Gamma'$ is a (uniform) simulation relation iff*

- *for every $i \in \{0, \ldots, k\}$, for all s, s' such that $H(s, s')$, $s \in Q_i$ implies $s' \in Q'_i$, and*
- *for all s, s_1 with $s \rightarrow s_1$ there are s', s'_1 with $s' \rightarrow s'_1$, $H(s, s')$ and $H(s_1, s'_1)$.*

If there is such a simulation relation then we say that T' simulates T ($T' \succeq T$, $T \preceq T'$).

Analogously to classical simulation (c.f., e.g. Clarke et. al. [7–chapter 11]), we have:

Lemma 2. *For every transition system T and T', for every LTL formula φ, if $T \preceq T'$ then $T' \models \varphi$ implies $T \models \varphi$.*

So, for showing satisfiability we will try to construct transition systems that simulate the original system, and for falsification transition systems that are simulated by the original system.

We start with the problem of showing satisfiability. Here we use predicate abstraction, tuned to our application domain of hybrid systems. In this framework, the abstract state space is given by a finite set of first-order predicates P, which jointly cover the concrete state space, that is for all σ in Σ there is a $p \in P$ such that $\sigma \in [\![p]\!]$. Different approaches for finding P have been discussed in the literature. For example, an initial set of predicates can be derived from transition guards and atomic formulas in the specification logic [4]; or a certain class of predicates, such as convex polyhedra [5], or hyper-rectangles [15] can be used.

For a given set of predicates P, we construct an abstraction $\overline{\alpha}_P(S)$ (*tightest abstraction*) simulating $[\![S]\!]$. It is a transition system whose transition relation is the set of all $\langle p, p' \rangle$ for which there is a pair $\langle \sigma, \sigma' \rangle \in [\![\tau]\!]$ such that $\sigma \models p$ and $\sigma' \models p'$. The set of initial states, and the observed propositions are defined canonically as the set of all p for which there is a $\sigma \in [\![\pi_i]\!]$ such that $\sigma \models p$. It is obvious that the satisfaction relation $\models \subseteq \Sigma \times P$ defines a simulation relation between the concrete infinite state transition system $[\![S]\!]$ and $\overline{\alpha}_P(S)$, hence for all first-order LTL formulas φ, $\overline{\alpha}_P(S) \models \varphi$ implies $S \models \varphi$.

Note that here the abstract transition relation also might contain self-loops, that is transitions from a predicate to itself.

We now introduce the notion of the *diameter* of predicate abstraction to later measure the degree of imprecision introduced by an abstraction.

Definition 10. *The diameter $diam(p)$ of a predicate $p \in P$ is defined as the supremum of $\{d(\sigma, \sigma^*) \mid \sigma \in [\![p]\!], \sigma^* \in [\![p]\!]\}$. The diameter $diam(P)$ of a predicate abstraction over P is defined as the maximal diameter of a predicate in P.*

To bound the degree of imprecision of abstraction we will ensure that for every $\varepsilon > 0$ the abstraction eventually only represents a ε-perturbation of S. Hence, the query will eventually be proven on the abstraction. Here we will measure the perturbations against the original system not from the abstraction directly, but from the following system represented by the abstraction:

Definition 11. *A transition system $(\rightarrow, Q_0, Q_1, \ldots, Q_k)$ over a set of predicates P represents the transition system*

$$\gamma(\rightarrow, Q_0, \ldots, Q_k) \doteq (\gamma(\rightarrow), \gamma(Q_0), \gamma(Q_1), \ldots, \gamma(Q_k)),$$

where $\gamma(R) = \bigcup_{p \in R} [\![p]\!]$.

It is not hard to prove that, using $\models$ (i.e., $\models$ with switched arguments) as a simulation relation, for every transition system T over P, $\gamma(T)$ simulates T. Hence any query φ that is satisfied by $\gamma(T)$ is also satisfied by T, and in particular $\gamma(\overline{\alpha}_P(S)) \models \varphi$ implies that model checking the abstraction will succeed, that is $\overline{\alpha}_P(S) \models \varphi$.

So we are left with the task of showing that $\gamma(\overline{\alpha}_P(S))$ will be sufficiently close to $[\![S]\!]$. Here we use the result that the distance between the tightest abstraction of S over predicates P and S itself is bounded by the diameter of P.

Theorem 1. $\overline{[\![S]\!]}_{diam(P)}$ *simulates* $\gamma(\overline{\alpha}_P(S))$.

We do not include the proof since it can be adapted from the proof of Theorem 2 below. To sum up, an abstraction $\overline{\alpha}_P(S)$ only introduces bounded perturbations since it can be sandwiched between the exact system $[\![S]\!]$ and its perturbed version $\overline{[\![S]\!]}_{diam(P)}$ due to the simulation result $[\![S]\!] \preceq \overline{\alpha}_P(S) \preceq \gamma(\overline{\alpha}_P(S)) \preceq \overline{[\![S]\!]}_{diam(P)}$.

The tightest abstraction can be constructed effectively, if we do not allow the transcendental function symbols $\sin, \cos, \exp$ in our constraints. For this we decide satisfiability of $p(x_1, \ldots, x_k) \wedge \tau(x_1, \ldots, x_k, x_1', \ldots, x_k') \wedge p(x_1', \ldots, x_k')$ for defining the abstract transition relation, respectively $p \wedge \pi_i$ for determining the set of initial states and observed propositions. However, due to the huge complexity of the corresponding decision procedure, this approach is not viable in practice.

Consider thus a predicate abstraction of S, where each predicate p is a hyper-rectangle, or *box*, of the form $\bigwedge_{i \in \{1, \ldots, k\}} c_{i,l} \leq x_i \leq c_{i,u}$. Assume furthermore, that the state space is bounded by a box B_0. In this case the computational effort in constructing the abstract transition relation can be drastically reduced by using interval arithmetic based tests instead of full decision procedures (the cost of a single test reduces from non-elementary in the number of variables to linear in the expression size). Moreover, this does not restrict the allowed function symbols to addition and multiplication. In this approach, transitions from box p to box p' are only added, if they cannot be excluded by interval arithmetic. We thus further abstract from the concrete transition behavior.

More specifically, we evaluate terms over boxes by extending all function symbols f to corresponding functions f^I over intervals. For example, the arithmetic expression $xy + 1$ for a box that restricts x to $[-1, 1]$, and y to $[1, 2]$, evaluates to $[-1, 1][1, 2] +^I [1, 1] = [-2, 2] +^I [1, 1] = [-1, 3]$. Given an arithmetic expression e and a box B we denote by $I(e)(B)$ the interval evaluation of e over B.

The properties of interval evaluation of terms have been widely studied [12]. Here we use a version that is extended to constraints. Using the Booleans $\{\mathbf{F}, \mathbf{T}\}$ with the order $\mathbf{F} < \mathbf{T}$ one can form Boolean intervals, which allows us to extend relations and connectives to intervals in a similar way as above. Hence we can evaluate Boolean combinations of equalities and inequalities over intervals. The formalization of this is a trivial exercise. For example, the evaluation of the constraint $2x \geq 0 \vee x - 2 \geq 0$ over a box restricting x to $[1, 3]$ yields $[2, 2][1, 3] \geq^I [0, 0] \vee^I [1, 3] - [2, 2] \geq^I [0, 0] = [2, 6] \geq^I [0, 0] \vee^I [-1, 1] \geq [0, 0] = [\mathbf{T}, \mathbf{T}] \vee^I [\mathbf{F}, \mathbf{T}] = [\mathbf{T}, \mathbf{T}]$. One can easily incorporate mode constraints by employing mode/box pairs $\langle m, B \rangle$ and evaluating a constraint of the form $mode = m_i$ to $[\mathbf{T}, \mathbf{T}]$ iff $m = m_i$ and to $[\mathbf{F}, \mathbf{F}]$, otherwise.

Whenever such an evaluation yields an interval $[\mathbf{F}, \mathbf{F}]$ we know that the corresponding constraint cannot hold. So we get a conservatively over-approximated satisfaction relation $\models_I$ such that $B \models_I \phi$ iff $\mathbf{T} \in I(\phi)(B)$ (so $B \not\models_I \phi$ tells us that ϕ cannot be satisfied by an element of B, whereas $B \models_I \phi$ does not tell us anything since in the case when $I(\phi)(B) = \{\mathbf{F}, \mathbf{T}\}$, $\mathbf{T}$ might be spurious due to over-approximation).

From Lipschitz continuity of interval evaluation [12–Theorem 2.1.1], it is easy to derive the following convergence result for interval evaluation of terms:

Lemma 3. *For every arithmetic expression e with function symbols in the set $\{+, *, \hat{}, \exp, \sin, \cos\}$, denoting a function $[\![e]\!]$ and box B there is a function $E : \mathbb{R}^+ \to \mathbb{R}^+$ such that $\lim_{x \to 0} E(x) = 0$, and for every box B' with $[\![B']\!] \subseteq [\![B]\!]$, for all $y \in I(e)(B')$, there is an $x \in [\![B']\!]$ such that $d([\![e]\!](x), y) \leq E(diam(B'))$.*

Now we can bound the approximation of interval satisfaction on constraints:

Lemma 4. *For every constraint ϕ, mode m and box B there is a function $E : \mathbb{R}^+ \to \mathbb{R}^+$ with $\lim_{x \to 0} E(x) = 0$, such that for every box B' with $[\![B']\!] \subseteq [\![B]\!]$, $\langle m, B' \rangle \models_I \phi$ implies that there is a ϕ^* with $d(\phi, \phi^*) \leq E(diam(B'))$ and an $x \in [\![B']\!]$ such that $\langle m, x \rangle \models \phi^*$.*

Proof. Let ϕ, m, and B be arbitrary but fixed. Let us first assume that ϕ is an atomic arithmetic constraint of the form $e \geq c$. Choose E as provided by Lemma 3, let B' be arbitrary, but fixed, and assume $B' \models_I e \geq c$. In the case when $I(\phi)(B') = \{\mathbf{T}\}$, the rest is trivial. In the case when $I(\phi)(B') = \{\mathbf{F}, \mathbf{T}\}$, $c \in I(e)(B')$ and we can choose $y = c$ in Lemma 3, which provides a corresponding $x \in [\![B']\!]$ such that $d([\![e]\!](x), c) \leq E(diam(B'))$. This implies $[\![e]\!](x) \geq c - E(diam(B'))$. Choosing ϕ^* as $e \geq c - E(diam(B'))$ clearly $d(\phi, \phi^*) \leq E(diam(B'))$ and $\langle m, x \rangle \models \phi^*$.

The case of other atomic constraints with different relation symbols are similar, and the case of mode constraints is trivial. In the case where ϕ is non-atomic we can choose E as the maximum of the E's of its atomic sub-constraints and choose ϕ^* by taking for each atomic constraint the corresponding constraint constructed above. □

Note that in practice—in order to ensure efficiency—interval arithmetic is usually implemented using floating point arithmetic. In that case, all the necessary operations are rounded outwards. So, differently from other methods, we preserve correctness also under the presence of rounding. Still, it might be necessary to increase the precision during computation in order to ensure convergence. However, experience has shown that this case does not arise in practice except for specifically constructed examples.

Now, by using the over-approximated satisfiability $\models_I$ we get another abstraction $\overline{\alpha}_P^I(S)$ for a given set of boxes P. Since $\models_I$ over-approximates $\models$, also $\overline{\alpha}_P^I(S) \supseteq \overline{\alpha}_P(S)$, and hence $\gamma(\overline{\alpha}_P^I(S)) \supseteq \gamma(\overline{\alpha}_P(S))$. Still, we can bound the over-approximation introduced by interval abstraction:

Theorem 2. *There is a function $E : \mathbb{R}^+ \to \mathbb{R}^+$ with $\lim_{x \to 0} E(x) = 0$, such that given a set of boxes P, $\overline{[\![S]\!]}_{E(diam(P))}$ simulates $\gamma(\overline{\alpha}_P^I(S))$.*

Proof. Let $\overline{\alpha}_P^I(S)$ be of the form $(\to, Q_1, \ldots, Q_k)$. Let E_τ be the function given by Lemma 4 for the transition constraint τ of S and the box B_0 bounding the state space, and $E_{\pi_1}, \ldots, E_{\pi_k}$ be the functions given by Lemma 4 for the state space constraints $\pi_1, \ldots, \pi_k$ of S and the bound of the state space B_0. Let $E(x) \doteq \max\{x, E_\tau(x), E_{\pi_1}(x), \ldots, E_{\pi_k}(x)\}$. We prove that $[\![S]\!]_{E(diam(P))} \supseteq \gamma(\overline{\alpha}_P^I(S))$, with $\supseteq$ interpreted element-wise.

- For an arbitrary, but fixed $i \in \{0, \ldots, k\}$, for proving that every element σ of $\gamma(Q_i)$ is in the corresponding element of $[\![S]\!]_{E(diam(P))}$, we prove that it is an element of an $E(diam(P))$-perturbed solution set of the corresponding state space constraint π_i. Observe that, by Definition 11, there is a corresponding element p of Q_i such that $\sigma \models p$. By definition of interval abstraction, $p \models_I \pi_i$. So, by Lemma 4, there is a π_i^* with $d(\pi_i, \pi_i^*) \leq E_{\pi_i}(diam(P))$, and σ^* with $\sigma^* \models \pi_i^*$. Since $diam(p) \leq diam(P)$, also $d(\sigma, \sigma^*) \leq diam(P)$. So, by Definition 5, every element σ of $\gamma(\pi_i)$ satisfies the transition constraint up to $E(diam(P))$.
- For proving that every element $\langle \sigma, \sigma' \rangle$ of $\gamma(\rightarrow)$ is in the corresponding element of $[\![S]\!]_{E(diam(P))}$, we have to prove that it is an element of an $E(diam(P))$-perturbed solution set of the transition constraint τ. Observe that by Definition 11 there is a corresponding transition $\langle p, p' \rangle$ in $\rightarrow$ such that $\sigma \models p$, and $\sigma' \models p'$. By definition of interval abstraction, $\langle p, p' \rangle \models_I \tau$. So, by Lemma 4, there is a constraint τ^* with $d(\tau, \tau^*) \leq E_\tau(diam(P))$, and $\langle \sigma^*, \sigma'^* \rangle$ with $\langle \sigma^*, \sigma'^* \rangle \models \tau^*$. Since $diam(p) \leq diam(P)$ and $diam(p') \leq diam(P)$, also $d(\sigma, \sigma^*) \leq diam(P)$ and $d(\sigma', \sigma'^*) \leq diam(P)$. So, by Definition 5, every element $\langle \sigma, \sigma' \rangle$ of $\gamma(\rightarrow)$ satisfies the transition constraint up to $E(diam(P))$. $\square$

We have thus shown how to construct a finite abstraction of non-linear discrete time hybrid systems that simulates the original system and whose precision can be arbitrarily increased. In the next section, we will use these results in the development of an algorithm for proving robust satisfaction of LTL formulas of discrete time hybrid systems.

Now we also construct a finite abstraction that under-approximates the original system, that is, that is simulated by it. For this choose a sample point $s(p)$ for every predicate $p \in P$. Then let $\underline{\alpha}_P$ be the transition system whose transition relation is the set of all $\langle s(p), s(p') \rangle$ such that $p, p' \in P$, and $\langle s(p), s(p') \rangle \models \tau$, and for which for every $i \in \{0, \ldots, k\}$, the i-th observed proposition contains the set of all $s(p)$ such that $p \in P$, $s(p) \models \pi_i$. Then we have:

Theorem 3. $[\![S]\!]_{diam(P)} \preceq \underline{\alpha}_P(S) \preceq [\![S]\!]$

Proof. Assume that $[\![S]\!]_{diam(P)}$ has the form $(\rightarrow, Q_0, Q_1, \ldots, Q_k)$, and $\underline{\alpha}_P(S)$ has the form $(\rightarrow', Q_0', Q_1', \ldots, Q_k')$. Proving $\underline{\alpha}_P(S) \preceq [\![S]\!]$ is easy, using the identity simulation relation. For proving $[\![S]\!]_{diam(P)} \preceq \underline{\alpha}_P(S)$ we use the simulation relation $H \doteq \{(x, s(p)) \mid p \in P, x \models p\}$:

- Let $i \in \{0, \ldots, k\}$ be arbitrary, but fixed. Let $x \in Q_i$. Due to the definition of $[\![S]\!]_{diam(P)}$ we know that for all constraints π_i^* with $d(\pi_i, \pi_i^*) \leq diam(P)$ and

x^* with $d(x, x^*) \leq diam(P)$, $x^* \models \pi_i^*$. We have to prove that for all x' with $H(x, x')$, x' is in the corresponding element Q_i' of $\underline{\alpha}_P(S)$. By definition of H this means to prove that for all p with $p \in P$ and $x \models p$, $s(p) \in Q_i'$. Clearly this holds since the distance between x and $s(p)$ is smaller than $diam(P)$, and hence $s(p) \models \pi_i$, that is, $s(p) \in Q_i'$.

- Let x, x_1 be such that $x \rightarrow x_1$. Due to the definition of $[\![S]\!]_{diam(P)}$ we know that for all constraints τ^* with $d(\tau, \tau^*) \leq diam(P)$ and x^*, x_1^* with $d(x, x^*) \leq diam(P)$ and $d(x_1, x_1^*) \leq diam(P)$, $\langle x^*, x_1^* \rangle \models \tau^*$. Let x' be such that $H(x, x')$, and x_1' such that $H(x, x_1')$. We prove that $x' \rightarrow' x_1'$. By definition of H this means to prove that for all p, p_1 with $p, p_1 \in P$, $x \models p$, and $x_1 \models p_1$ we have that $s(p) \rightarrow' s(p_1)$. Clearly this holds since the distance between x and $s(p)$ is smaller than $diam(P)$, and the distance between x_1 and $s(p_1)$ is smaller than $diam(P)$, and hence $\langle s(p), s(p_1) \rangle \models \tau$, that is, $s(p) \rightarrow' s(p_1)$. □

Hence, instead of falsifying an LTL formula against the original system S we can check it against $\underline{\alpha}_P(S)$. Moreover, by letting the diameter of P go to zero, this check will eventually succeed for robust systems.

4   Proving Robust Satisfaction and Falsification

Now assume as given a temporal specification $\varphi \in LTL$, with the arithmetic atoms $\Pi = \{\pi_0, \ldots, \pi_n\}$ occurring negatively. Since the aim of the current paper is to establish the overall approach, we only give a basic algorithm for abstraction refinement, which can be significantly improved according to the directions outlined below. The key result of this section is, that the abstraction refinement algorithm is guaranteed to terminate, if φ is robustly satisfied by S.

The basic algorithm creates a sequence of finer and finer partitions $P_0, P_1, \ldots$. If at a certain iteration m, $\underline{\alpha}_{P_m}(S)$ falsifies φ, we terminate with the result that φ is robustly falsified in S. If $\overline{\alpha}_{P_m}^I$ satisfies φ, we terminate with the result that φ is robustly satisfied by S. Here we start with $P_0 = \{B_0\}$ as the initial partition, and refine a given partition by splitting the largest box in P_m along the biggest side-length to obtain P_{m+1}.

The following main result opens a new line of attack to the verification of non-linear hybrid systems.

Theorem 4. *The basic algorithm is guaranteed to terminate with definite answer if S robustly satisfies φ or φ is robustly falsified by S.*

Proof. The abstraction refinement procedure ensures that the diameter of the abstraction goes to zero. If S robustly satisfies φ, the fact that $\gamma(\overline{\alpha}_{P_m}^I(S))$ simulates $\overline{\alpha}_{P_m}^I(S)$ due to Theorem 2, and transitivity of simulation implies that $\overline{\alpha}_{P_m}^I(S)$ is simulated by $[\![S]\!]_\varepsilon$ with ε going to zero as m goes to infinity. Let $r > 0$ be such that $[\![S]\!]_r \models \varphi$ which is ensured by robustness. Thus, there is an m, from which on ε will be smaller than r. Then $\overline{\alpha}_{P_m}(S) \models \varphi$ and the algorithm succeeds. The case where φ is robustly falsified in S is similar. □

Note that this theorem also includes robust progress properties. In that case, the algorithm will eventually remove all unnecessary transitions in the abstraction that lead from a predicate to itself.

Clearly, further work is needed, to make this algorithm practically efficient. Still—in order to evaluate its efficiency potential—we have implemented it, with small improvements similar to the continuous time case [15], and based on the constraint propagation engine of RSOLVER [14]. Already in this basic form, the algorithm yields promising results for realistic examples.

For our example, for $\delta = 0.6$, our interval arithmetic prototype computes in about 20 seconds an abstraction having only 100 boxes, whose safety can be easily checked with a finite state model checker like NuSMV. This proves the safety of the discretized version of the problem, demonstrating that a safety margin of the planes is maintained.

The base algorithm is compatible with many of the optimization techniques for abstraction refinement. Promising directions for optimization currently under investigation in the large scale collaborative research project AVACS include:

Initial Partitioning: We refine B_0 to approximately discriminate all guards and arithmetic constraints in Π, over-approximating their shapes by boxes. This approach is already realized as part of another research activity for verification of hybrid systems based on predicate abstraction techniques [4].

Counterexample guided abstraction refinement: We incrementally analyze counterexample fragments for concretization [6]. We do so, by applying the constraint propagation based solver for non-linear constraints [14] to the corresponding first-order formula. If the constraint is unsolvable, we dismiss the counterexample fragment as spurious by encoding the corresponding information into an automata representation of the abstraction.

Local search for counter-examples: Instead of just testing samples in the abstract states for counter-examples, we use local search (based on a Newton-like method) to find samples that form counter-examples.

5   Conclusion

This paper opens a novel line of attack to the verification of non-linear hybrid systems. We have argued for the naturalness of the notion of robust satisfaction, and demonstrated how to construct a series of increasingly more accurate abstractions, guaranteed to converge to a sufficiently precise model to prove temporal specifications of hybrid systems in a rich specification logic with first-order arithmetic constraints, able to express real-time requirements. Though we have chosen LTL as the temporal framework in this paper, the development only exploits safeness of the constructed abstractions; it is well known [7], that also ACTL* properties are preserved under the performed abstractions.

We see this paper hence as a promising starting point in exploiting the usage of interval-based constraint solving techniques for the verification of non-linear hybrid systems.

References

1. E. Asarin, T. Dang, and O. Maler. The d/dt tool for verification of hybrid systems. In *CAV'02*, number 2404 in LNCS, pages 365–370. Springer, 2002.
2. T. Bienmüller, J. Bohn, H. Brinkmann, U. Brockmeyer, W. Damm, H. Hungar, and P. Jansen. Verification of automotive control units. In E.-R. Olderog and B. Steffen, editors, *Correct System Design*, volume 1710 of *LNCS*, pages 319–341. Springer, 1999.
3. T. Bienmüller, U. Brockmeyer, W. Damm, et al. Formal verification of an avionics application using abstraction and symbolic model checking. In F. Redmill and T. Anderson, editors, *Towards System Safety—Proc. of the 7th Safety-critical Systems Symp.*, pages 150–173. Springer, 1999.
4. J. Bohn, W. Damm, O. Grumberg, et al. First-order-CTL model checking. In V. Arvind and R. Ramanujam, editors, *Foundations of Software Techn. and Theor. Comp. Sc.*, volume 1530 of *LNCS*, pages 283–294. Springer, 1998.
5. A. Chutinan and B. H. Krogh. Computing polyhedral approximations to flow pipes for dynamic systems. In *The 37th IEEE Conference on Decision and Control: Session on Synthesis and Verification of Hybrid Control Laws (TM-01)*, 1998.
6. E. Clarke, A. Fehnker, Z. Han, B. Krogh, O. Stursberg, and M. Theobald. Verification of hybrid systems based on counterexample-guided abstraction refinement. In H. Garavel and J. Hatcliff, editors, *TACAS 2003*, number 2619 in LNCS, pages 192–207, 2003.
7. E. M. Clarke, O. Grumberg, and D. A. Peled. *Model Checking*. MIT Press, 1999.
8. M. Fränzle. Analysis of hybrid systems: An ounce of realism can save an infinity of states. In J. Flum and M. Rodriguez-Artalejo, editors, *Computer Science Logic (CSL'99)*, number 1683 in LNCS. Springer, 1999.
9. M. Fränzle. What will be eventually true of polynomial hybrid automata. In N. Kobayashi and B. C. Pierce, editors, *Theoretical Aspects of Computer Software (TACS 2001)*, number 2215 in LNCS. Springer-Verlag, 2001.
10. T. A. Henzinger, B. Horowitz, R. Majumdar, and H. Wong-Toi. Beyond HyTech: hybrid systems analysis using interval numerical methods. In N. Lynch and B. Krogh, editors, *Proc. HSCC'00*, volume 1790 of *LNCS*. Springer, 2000.
11. T. A. Henzinger and S. Sastry, editors. *HSCC'98 - Hybrid Systems: Computation and Control*, number 1386 in LNCS. Springer, 1998.
12. A. Neumaier. *Interval Methods for Systems of Equations*. Cambridge Univ. Press, Cambridge, 1990.
13. S. Ratschan. Quantified constraints under perturbations. *Journal of Symbolic Computation*, 33(4):493–505, 2002.
14. S. Ratschan. Rsolver. http://rsolver.sourceforge.net, 2004. Software package.
15. S. Ratschan and Z. She. Safety verification of hybrid systems by constraint propagation based abstraction refinement. In M. Morari and L. Thiele, editors, *Hybrid Systems: Computation and Control*, volume 3414 of *LNCS*. Springer, 2005.
16. O. Stursberg, S. Kowalewski, and S. Engell. On the generation of timed discrete approximations for continuous systems. *Mathematical and Computer Models of Dynamical Systems*, 6:51–70, 2000.

Computation Platform for Automatic Analysis of Embedded Software Systems Using Model Based Approach

A. Dubey, X. Wu, H. Su, and T.J. Koo

Embedded Computing Systems Laboratory,
Institute for Software Integrated Systems,
Department of Electrical Engineering and Computer Science,
Vanderbilt University, Nashville, TN 37212
{abhishek.dubey, xianbin.wu, hang.su, john.koo}@vanderbilt.edu

Abstract. In this paper, we describe a computation platform called ReachLab, which enables automatic analysis of embedded software systems that interact with continuous environment. Algorithms are used to specify how the state space of the system model should be explored in order to perform analysis. In ReachLab, both system models and analysis algorithm models are specified in the same framework using Hybrid System Analysis and Design Language (HADL), which is a meta-model based language. The platform allows the models of algorithms to be constructed hierarchically and promotes their reuse in constructing more complex algorithms. Moreover, the platform is designed in such a way that the concerns of design and implementation of analysis algorithms are separated. On one hand, the models of analysis algorithms are abstract and therefore the design of algorithms can be made independent of implementation details. On the other hand, translators are provided to automatically generate implementations from the models for computing analysis results based on computation kernels. Multiple computation kernels, which are based on specific computation tools such as d/dt and the Level Set toolbox, are supported and can be chosen to enable hybrid state space exploration. An example is provided to illustrate the design and implementation process in ReachLab.

1 Introduction

Embedded software systems are becoming an integral and ubiquitous part of modern society. They are often used in safety critical tasks such as in airplanes and nuclear reactors. Typically, they consist of one or more discrete software components performing computation on a real-time operating system (RTOS) to control the continuous environment. Fig. 1 shows a typical embedded software system, in which the continuous state of plant is controlled by software control tasks. The control task and the plant exchange information of continuous state x and input u via sensors and actuators. In a very simple case, the sensor can be a periodic sampler, while the actuator can be a zero order hold.

D.A. Peled and Y.-K. Tsay (Eds.): ATVA 2005, LNCS 3707, pp. 114–128, 2005.

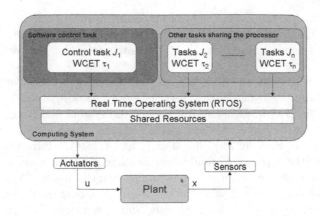

Fig. 1. A typical embedded software system

To ensure high confidence in these systems, rigorous analysis is required before deployment. However, it is often infeasible to perform analysis on the actual system due to its scale and complexity. Model based approach has been advocated for design and analysis of these complex systems in order to produce confidence in the design and reduce development costs. In this approach, representative models of the system are judiciously used to predict its behavior and analyze various properties. Hybrid automaton [1, 2, 13] has been used to model and analyze embedded systems in which discrete and continuous components are tightly coupled.

In order to automate the analysis of hybrid automata, algorithmic approach has been developed. Algorithmic approach can be classified into two categories: reductionist methods and symbolic methods [3]. The former reduces the infinite hybrid (discrete and continuous) state space to an equivalent finite bisimulation and then explores the resulting finite quotient space, while the latter performs direct exploration of this infinite state space. Even though the reductionist method based algorithms are guaranteed to terminate, the classes of systems to which they can be applied are very limited. Therefore, symbolic method based algorithms are generally used. Various computation tools with vastly different implementations have been developed for symbolic method based analysis. For example, d/dt [5] computes reachable sets by approximating reachable states based on numerical integration and polyhedral approximation; whereas the Level Set toolbox [4], which applies the level set methods [14], computes the evolution of a continuous set by solving the associated partial differential equation on grid structure. Due to these implementation differences in computation method, data structure as well as analysis purpose, designing new analysis algorithms by using or modifying existing tools becomes infeasible or inefficient. Furthermore, designing a common interchange format [8] for these tools is difficult.

In order to resolve the analysis problem, the computation platform called ReachLab is designed to enable (i) separating the concern of algorithm design for analysis of hybrid automaton model from any specific computation implementation; (ii) separating the design of algorithm from specific hybrid automaton model so that the same algorithm can be reused for other system models. ReachLab is developed based on the Model Integrated Computing (MIC) [6, 7] approach.

MIC approach is based on models and automatic generation of useful artifacts. In this approach, models are used not only to design and represent the system, but also to synthesize and implement the system using a modeling language tailored to the needs of a particular domain. These modeling languages, termed as Domain Specific Modeling Languages (DSML), have necessary constructs to allow the capture of useful information of a system as model particular to that domain. One can perform *system analysis* on this model. When this modeling capability is augmented with the capability of model transformation, even *automated synthesis of other design models*, and *generation of executable system* can be performed [7].

Based on MIC approach, the domain specific modeling language for analyzing hybrid systems called Hybrid System Analysis and Design Language (HADL) is introduced. Specified by meta-models, it provides a rich library comprising of abstractions of entities and operations commonly found in the symbolic method based computation tools, so that it enables effective design of symbolic method based analysis algorithm for systems modeled as hybrid automata. Then, we will focus more on ReachLab which utilizes this language to design system models and corresponding analysis algorithms, and provides various model translators to implement the models using the facilities provided by Generic Modeling Environment (GME) [9], which provides an end-end solution for building and deploying MIC applications. By keeping the implementation of computation method of computation tools, and enriching them with additional features such as support for comprehensive data structures implemented by existing functions provided in these tools, various computation kernels have been supported by ReachLab, such as d/dt kernel and Level Set kernel. Model translators are used to automatically generate model implementations for these computation kernels. Fig.2 shows

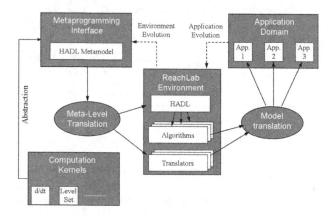

Fig. 2. Design of the ReachLab platform using the MIC multigraph architecture

how MIC approach is applied to encapsulate HADL and automate the design and implementation process based on the MIC multigraph architecture [10].

This architecture has three model development stages, namely meta-model, domain specific models and the executable artifacts. The first level is the meta-programming interface, which is used to define the meta-model of HADL. This meta-model is based on abstract entities found in the symbolic method based computation kernels and is later implemented as the domain specific modeling language, HADL, using the meta-translation facility provided by GME. Model-Integrated Program Synthesis (MIPS) environment [11] is the second level and provides tools to build and modify system models and the analysis algorithms using HADL in a graphical manner. This level also supports construction of model translators. The last level is the different applications (implementations) that can be generated by translators from these models. Environment evolution refers to modification of HADL meta-model to update features. The models of algorithms can also be refined to evolve the analysis application.

The remainder of this paper is organized as follows: Section 2 gives an introduction to HADL. Section 3 presents the architecture of ReachLab and the details about ReachLab construction, including the model translation process. An example is provided to illustrate the design and implementation process in ReachLab in Section 4. Finally, we conclude our work with the future goals for this platform.

2   Introduction to HADL

HADL is a language that enables the design and analysis of hybrid automata. For this design and analysis purpose, HADL is used to specify models of hybrid automata and corresponding analysis algorithm models. In [13], the mathematical definition of a hybrid automaton is given as a collection $H = (Q, \mathbb{X}, f, I, E, G)$ where $Q = \{q_1, \ldots, q_N\}$ is a set of discrete modes; $\mathbb{X} \subseteq \mathbb{R}^n$ is the continuous state space; $f : Q \to (X \to \mathbb{R}^n)$ assigns each discrete mode a Lipschitz continuous vector field on $\mathbb{X}$; $I : Q \to 2^{\mathbb{X}}$ assigns each $q \in Q$ an invariant; $E \subseteq Q \times Q$ is a collection of discrete transitions; $G : E \to 2^{\mathbb{X}}$ assigns each $e = (q, q') \in E$ a guard. The analysis algorithm model specified in HADL is hierarchical in nature, and complex algorithms can be composed from existing algorithms by using them as subroutines. Data variables used in analysis algorithms are strong-typed, and currently, only global scoping is supported. However, in the future, it will allow local scoping as well.

HADL has been formalized as a five tuple of concrete syntax (C), abstract syntax (A), semantic domain (S), semantic mapping (M_S) and syntactic mapping (M_C) [16]:

$$L = < C, A, S, M_S, M_C > .$$

Concrete syntax (C) defines the graphical notation used to specify the models. Abstract syntax (A) specifies all the syntactical elements of the language, as well as the integrity constraints. Semantic domains (S) is defined by formalism which provides meaning to a correct sentence in the language. The mapping $M_S : A \to S$ relates every element of abstract syntax to a specific meaning in the semantic domain. Model translators are used for this semantic mapping. The mapping $M_C : A \to C$ assigns a notational construct to every elements of abstract syntax.

Advocated by the MIC approach, HADL is formalized by meta-models. It is designed to enable the use of multiple aspects [7, 9] to help decompose any analysis application designed in HADL into three separate components – data (data aspect), the system model (system aspect) and algorithm model (programming aspect). Hence, the abstract syntax of HADL can be written as a three tuple

$$A =< L_{data}, L_{system}, L_{program} > .$$

The semantic domain S of HADL is any chosen supported computation kernel. Model translators can be used to provide the semantic mapping $M_s : L_{data} \times L_{system} \times L_{program} \to S$. Hence, a translator is required for each semantic domain.

As part of the HADL's abstract syntax, integrity constraints can be checked by using Object Constraint Language (OCL) [18], which guarantees the correctness of designed models. The other part of the abstract syntax, the syntactical elements in these three aspects, provide basic notions and constructs to specify hybrid automaton models, analysis algorithms as well as the data variables used in these algorithms. To be specific, these elements are comprehensively listed in Table 1.

HADL has been provided with precise mathematical semantics, which are generic and not dependent on implementation details. For example, the discrete

Table 1. HADL Language Syntactical Elements

Aspect	Model of	Syntactical Elements
Data	Data	Primitive data types: integer, float, Boolean; Data structure: multi-dimensional list.
System	Hybrid automaton	Discrete mode, associated with invariant; Discrete transition, associated with guard and reset; Continuous set and initial continuous set; Analysis set, as a specialization of continuous set; Computation parameters.
Programming	Control flow	Routine, hierarchical in nature; Looping: "*while*" loop; Branching: "*if-then-else*";
	Operators	Primitive data operations: $+, -, *$; Logical operations: equal, less than, and, or, not; Multi-dimensional list operations: new, delete, append, element; Reachable set operations: discrete successor and predecessor, (constraint) continuous successor and predecessor in a single step (in bounded time), reset, projection, visualization; Boolean set operations: intersection, union, complement.

successor operation in HADL, denoted as $Post_d$, is defined as $Post_d(q_i) = \{q \in Q \mid \exists e \in E \ s.t. \ e = (q_i, q)\}$. This operation specifies the collection of reachable discrete states of the hybrid automaton in a single discrete transition. Similarly, the constraint continuous successor operation in a single step Δt, notated as $cPostc_{\Delta t}$, is defined as $cPostc_{\Delta t}(q_i, P, X_\psi) = \{x \in \mathbb{X} \mid \exists t \in [0, \Delta t], \exists y \in P \ s.t. \ x = \phi(t, y) \land \forall z \in [0, t], \phi(z, y) \in I(q) \cap X_\psi\}$ where P is the initial continuous set, $\frac{d}{dt}\phi(t, y) = f(q_i, \phi(t, y))$, and $X_\psi = \{x \in \mathbb{X} \mid \psi(x) \leq 0\}$ defines the constraint continuous set. This operation specifies the collection of reachable continuous state set of the hybrid automaton in a single time step Δt. By using such reachability operations and algorithmic approach, many properties of a hybrid automaton can be revealed, such as safety or liveness. However, it is known that computation of exact or even approximate continuous successor sets is a difficult problem due to representing continuous sets and computing the evolution of the sets. Existing computation kernels adopt different methods to approximate it. For example, kernels like Level Set kernel and d/dt kernel are tailored to their own analysis needs and computation capacities so that the implementations of these reachable set operations as well as Boolean set operations (such as union and intersection) are quite different. HADL is defined based on the mathematical definitions of these operations and HADL is designed to ensure there exists a correspondence between the semantics of these kernels and the semantics of HADL. Therefore, one can use the semantics of HADL to anchor the semantics of these kernels, which is referred to as *semantic anchoring* in [17]. Because of this feature, we can design analysis algorithms by using the mathematical semantics of these operations instead of considering the detailed implementation. Furthermore, HADL enriches the functions of its computation kernels by providing constructs and operations more than these computation kernels, such as multi-dimensional list and its corresponding operations. These constructs and operations will be mapped to a collection of entities in the computation kernel rather than a direct mapping.

The advantage of using this language is that (i) algorithms are designed independently from implementation and hence can be used with any supported computation kernel; (ii) analysis algorithms can be reused for different systems; (iii) more complex algorithms can be constructed by using other existing algorithms.

3   Construction of ReachLab

In this section, the architecture of ReachLab is introduced and the construction issues related to model traversal and semantic mapping are presented.

3.1   ReachLab Architecture

By utilizing the language defined by HADL, a computation platform called ReachLab has been developed, and its architecture, as shown in Fig.3, is designed to separate the concerns of algorithm design from implementation details. The

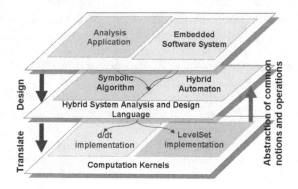

Fig. 3. The three-layer ReachLab architecture

MIPS environment of ReachLab, facilitated by GME, provides support to build graphical algorithm and system models. Different graphical model entities and components are connected according to the rules specified by HADL meta-model. Therefore, models can be designed in ReachLab graphically according to HADL specification. Besides model design, the other key process is the use of translators to automatically translate the models into executable artifacts. This translation process requires mapping of the abstract entities into concrete implementations for the target domain of a computation kernel. In [7], the translation process has been summarized as a graph transformation: (i) *Creation of "input graph"* : The models with different interconnected components are implicitly represented by a graph structure. (ii) *Model traversal and Semantic mapping* : The translation process requires creation of a "target graph" (data structure for the executable artifact) from an "input graph". This requires the translator to traverse various objects in the "input graph", recognize their patterns and calculate attributes of output objects in the "target graph" using semantic mapping. The "target graph" corresponds to the data structure required to represent the output form of the executable artifacts.(iii) *Printing the product* : In this step, the translator serializes the "target graph" to generate executable artifacts pertaining to the related domain.

In ReachLab, the traversal process uses the data structures provided by GME to store the "input graph" along with necessary information. These data structures are very generic and remain the same for different translators. However, the data structures used to store the "target graph" vary due to implementation differences among different computation kernels.

In the next subsection, we will explain in detail how model traversal is done to fulfill model translation process.

3.2 Model Traversal

Translators need to perform the traversal of all three aspects in order to understand the patterns and collect all useful information. This traversal process is

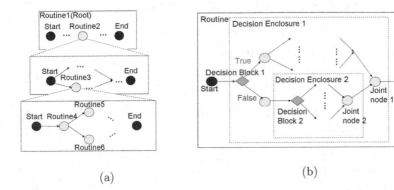

Fig. 4. (a) The components of a routine are interconnected as a DAG. Routines may be hierarchical leading to a hierarchical graph; (b) The decision enclosure is sub-graph starting from a decision block and ending at its corresponding joint-node.

based on graph search techniques such as depth first search [12]. The complete process can be broken down into four sub-tasks reviewed below.

Traversal of Data Aspect: All the data are defined in one single data folder as a list. Translator traverses this list in a linear fashion to collect all useful information about the data elements.

Traversal of System Aspect: The hybrid automaton model specified in the system aspect can be understood as a graph, in which the discrete modes are vertices and the discrete transitions of hybrid automaton are the edges. The translators traverse this graph by using depth first search starting from the initial discrete state to collect all useful information.

Traversal of Control Flow of Algorithms: The traversal of programming aspect is more complex. Every algorithm has a root *routine* which is the entry point to the algorithm. *Routines* can be hierarchical and may contain other sub-routines as shown in Fig.4(a). The control flow inside each *routine* routes from a *"start"* to an *"end"*. However, there might be other exit routes from a *routine* through *"break-exit"*, which is used in the same way as the break in many programming languages. For example, the constraint continuous successor set operation in bounded time T, denoted as $cPostc_T$, can be implemented by iterating $T/\Delta t$ times by calling $cPostc_{\Delta t}$, which is previously defined. Therefore, the routine to implement $cPostc_T$ can use the routine of $cPostc_{\Delta t}$ as its sub-routine. The language also provides a specialization of *routine* called *while routine* for implementation of looping constructs such as *do-while* which is traversed in the same manner as a *routine*. The control flow inside a routine is sequential, however it can have multiple branches due to *decision blocks*. Cycles in the control flow are disallowed to demote the use of sudden jumps such as "goto". Therefore, the control flow inside each routine is a directed acyclic graph (DAG) [12] with its directed edges depicting the route of control flow and each node depict-

Table 2. Decision-Enclosure Algorithm

Input:
$DecisionBlock$ = the starting node of the enclosure
Initialization:
$InitPath := DecisionBlock$
$Paths := \{InitPath\}$
Start:
While $true$ do
For each $path$ in $Paths$ do
$Fringe :=$ the tail of $path$
$Succ :=$ successor nodes of $Fringe$
If $Succ \neq \phi$ then
Add $Succ[0]$ to the fringe of $path$
$Succ := Succ - Succ[0]$
For each s in $Succ$ do
$path' := path$
Add s to the fringe of $path'$
Add $path'$ to $Paths$
End For
If $\exists s \in Succ$ s.t. $\forall p \in Paths, s \in p$ then
Return s as the joint-node
End If
End If
End For
End While

ing a block of algorithm. Since routines can contain other routines, the overall control flow of the complete algorithm is a hierarchical DAG. The translators traverse the graph structure of algorithms in a depth-first search manner to extract information. In each routine, the traversal starts from *"start"* block and follows the directed edges. If any of the traversed entity is hierarchical, translators will traverse its subcomponents in a depth-first manner. *Decision blocks* are used inside routines to design a logical branching in the control flow sequence. For each of these blocks, the branching starts from itself, and finally merges at a *joint-node*. The sub-graph enclosed by the *decision block* and the joint-node in the DAG is called a *decision-enclosure*. This is illustrated by Fig. 4(b). The traversal algorithm has to recognize the *"if true"* and *"if false"* part of each *decision block* so that they can be mapped to the corresponding decision logic in the implementation. This requires knowledge of its *decision-enclosure*. Table 2 gives an algorithm based on breadth first search technique for determining *decision-enclosure* of each *decision block*. This algorithm has a complexity of $O(n^2)$, where n is the number of blocks in the DAG.

The key of this algorithm is to find the joint-node, and since a joint-node is where all branches from the *decision block* merge, by using breath-first search and keeping all branching paths from the *decision block*, the first block that belongs to every recorded branching paths is the joint-node.

Traversal of Operators: Operators are used for data manipulation. Every assignment expression forms a tree structure, with the left-hand-side data variable as the root of the tree. All data variables on the right-hand-size of the expression correspond to the leaves of this tree, and operators on the right-hand-side correspond to the internal nodes of the tree. The expression itself can be restored to reverse-polish notation by post-order traverse.

The operators have different semantic meanings depending on the input data types. And since HADL is "strong-typed", the data types of the tree leaves, which are predefined, will finally determine the input data type of the operator connected to the root data. Therefore, it is important to propagate the data type information from leaves to the root in a post-order manner [12].

3.3   Semantic Mapping

Since the semantics of a computation kernel are anchored to the semantics of HADL, we can find a corresponding implementation for HADL constructs in the computation kernel. These constructs include sequential programming features, boolean operations on state sets, as well as the reachable set operations. However, in some cases, the operations, such as data structure manipulation operations, are not directly supported by the computation kernel and have to be specifically added to the computation kernel as new functions. The process of associating the HADL constructs to its implementation in computation kernel is akin to providing a meaning to them and is therefore referred to as semantic mapping.

We will illustrate some of the aspects of the semantic mapping process by using the example of Level Set kernel. Level Set kernel has been implemented as Matlab functions. It supports all the basic data types in HADL except the multi-dimensional list structure, which we have to specifically implement along with the relevant operations in Matlab. The hybrid system specific data types such as *discrete mode* and *continuous set* are mapped to Matlab *struct* and *mesh* on analysis space, respectively. This *mesh* is an internal structure used by Level Set kernel. The control flow inside a routine is mapped to the sequential flow of logical commands inside a function. We use *"if-else-end"* statement in Matlab to implement branching and *"while-end"* statement in Matlab to implement looping. Boolean operations on state sets and reachable set operations are mapped to their corresponding implementation in Level Set kernel. However, for some of the operations defined in HADL, there are no straight-forward mappings, therefore we have to write specialized functions for them by using operations provided by the kernel.

4   Design and Implementation Process in ReachLab

In this section, we will illustrate the design and implementation process for analysis algorithms in ReachLab by designing a forward reachability analysis algorithm for the embedded software system shown in Fig.5(a).

Depending on the current state of the plant, it determines input $u \in \{\sigma_1, \sigma_2\}$. By considering the direct interaction between the control task and the plant, we

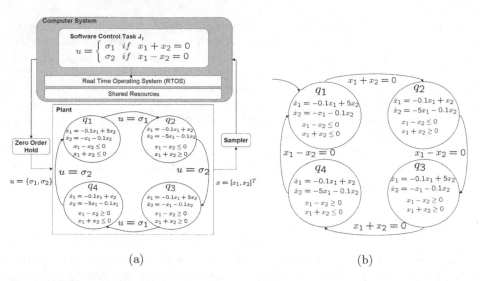

(a)   (b)

Fig. 5. (a) An embedded software system. The plant on the bottom has four running modes with different continuous dynamics, controlled by the software control task J_1; (b) Hybrid automaton model for the control task and plant. It has four discrete modes corresponding to the four running modes of the plant, and one continuous state $x = [x_1, x_2]^T \in \mathbb{R}^2$.

can model the system as a hybrid automaton as shown in Fig.5(b). Multiple tasks which share common resource with the control task, the scheduler and the interface elements such as sampler and the zero order hold can be modeled by a more complex hybrid automaton.

It has been shown in [15] that this system is stable in the sense of Lyapunov. Starting from anywhere in the continuous state space, the continuous state of the automaton moves toward the origin in a flower-like trajectory. For this system, we are interested in computing forward reachable set using symbolic methods based algorithms, in order to verify that starting from certain initial state, whether or not the system can eventually enter some desired set.

Table 3 gives the specification of a generic forward reachability algorithm for hybrid automaton. It uses the concepts of both discrete and continuous successor set and finds the reachable set starting from a given initial set. This algorithm unfolds the hybrid automaton into a tree like structure and explores it by using breadth first search. Termination of this algorithm is guaranteed because of the limit M on the depth of this tree. The data structure *Reach* is used to store the reachable set. It can be noted that this specification does not delve into the actual implementation method of reachable set operations. However, the process of semantic mapping will relate those operations to a specific implementation method based on the concerned computation kernel. This algorithm can be used to verify if the system would ever execute into some desired state. In order to perform verification, the algorithm systematically explore the hybrid state space and check if the forward reachable set overlaps with the desired set. The

Table 3. Algorithm for computing forward reachable set

Input:
$\quad$ $H_A, Q_S, X_S, Q_F, X_F, X_B$, where
$\quad$ Q_S is list of initial discrete modes, X_S is list of initial continuous sets, Q_F is
$\quad$ list of final discrete modes, X_F is list of final continuous sets, and X_B is bad set.
Constant:
$\quad$ T as time limit for $cPost_T c$, M as search depth limit
Initialization:
$\quad$ $Reach = X_S, List = \{\}, Successors = \{\}, R = \phi, Queue = Q_S$
$\quad$ $Depth = 1, i = 0, j = 0$
Start:
$\quad$ While $\neg Empty(Queue)$ do
$\quad\quad$ $List = \text{PopAll } Queue$
$\quad\quad$ For $i = 1 : \text{Size}(List)$ do
$\quad\quad\quad$ $R = cPostc_T(List(i), Reach(i))$
$\quad\quad\quad$ $Successors = Postd(List(i))$
$\quad\quad\quad$ For $j = 1 : (\text{Size}(Successors)$ do
$\quad\quad\quad\quad$ If $R \cap Guard_{List(i), Successors(j)} \neq \phi$ Then
$\quad\quad\quad\quad\quad$ Push $Successors(j) \to Queue$
$\quad\quad\quad\quad\quad$ Append $R \cap Guard_{List(i), Successors(j)} \to Reach$
$\quad\quad\quad\quad$ End If
$\quad\quad\quad$ End For
$\quad\quad$ End For
$\quad\quad$ $Depth = Depth + 1$
$\quad\quad$ If $Depth > M$ Then
$\quad\quad\quad$ Stop
$\quad\quad$ End If
$\quad\quad$ Pop first $\text{Size}(List)$ elements of $Reach$
$\quad$ End While

main concern with this type of algorithms is termination. But if we perform the computation in an *Eulerian* framework (one in which the underlying coordinate system is fixed) within a bounded continuous state space, the algorithms will terminate due to the fact that the partition of state space has finite number of representative elements.

4.1   Design Steps

To analyze the safety property of the hybrid automaton model in Fig.5(b) by using the forward reachability algorithm, we need to design its hybrid automata model in the system aspect and design the algorithm in the programming aspect. The data used in both of the system model and the algorithm are defined in the data aspect. The entire process can be summarized into three steps:

1. **Obtaining system model and algorithm specification**:
   Fig.5(b) and Table 3 provide the hybrid automaton and analysis algorithm specifications for this example.

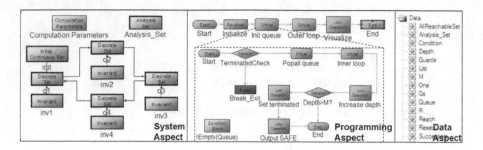

Fig. 6. Hybrid automaton model for the corresponding plant in the system aspect, forward reachability analysis algorithm model in the programming aspect, and data used in the data aspect of ReachLab

2. **Design phase**:
   – Design of the system model: A hybrid automaton is drawn in the system aspect with discrete transitions connecting discrete modes, as in Fig.6.
   – Design of the analysis algorithm: The analysis algorithm, which is hierarchical in nature, is modeled in the programming aspect by using ReachLab library elements. Fig.6 also gives part of the algorithm model for the algorithm given in Table 3, and the data required by both the hybrid automaton and the algorithm model.
   – Specification of computation parameters: Input parameters to the algorithm and the computation kernels have to be specified before translation, such as the bounded time (T) for $cPost_{cT}$ operator, the analysis region, and how the analysis region is partitioned into finite number of representative elements.

3. **Implementation phase**:
   Translators are used to convert the designed models into implementation for a certain computation kernel. For this example, we translate the system and algorithm model into the d/dt implementation. Fig.7 shows the computa-

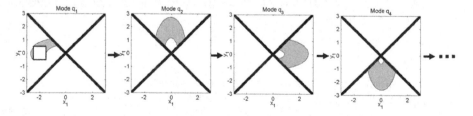

Fig. 7. The reachable set computed by using d/dt kernel. The white box is the initial set, [-2.5,-1.5]x[-0.5, 0.5]. Each sub-figure denotes the reachable set in the corresponding discrete mode. Eventually, the reachable set will reach the origin. The analysis region is $[-3,3] \times [-3,3]$, the size of a representative elements in each dimension is 0.001, and the bounded time T is 5 seconds. Time taken for execution: 180 minutes on Pentium IV 2.59 GHz machine with 2 GB RAM.

tion result. This result can be used to examine system behaviors, such as approaching the origin while evolving. It can also be used to verify system stability properties by testing intersection between the reachable set and the desired set.

5 Conclusion

In this paper, we presented the computation platform called ReachLab for enabling automatic analysis of embedded software systems modeled as hybrid automata. It implements the meta-model based language HADL whose abstract entities allow users to model their algorithms and the system in an implementation independent manner. These models are then translated to implementations for different computation kernels. Translation is performed by using model traversal and sematic mapping. Currently, d/dt kernel and Level Set kernel are supported by ReachLab. In the future, we will expand this platform to other computation kernels for more effective and efficient computation. In order to model networked hybrid automata, shared variable could be introduced to ReachLab for specifying communication protocols between hybrid automata. We are also interested in expanding the capabilities of HADL to capture a larger class of embedded software systems so that more sophisticated system features can be described.

Acknowledgments

This work is supported by NSF's Faculty Early Career Development (CAREER) Program, Award No. 0448234, and Department of EECS, Vanderbilt University.

References

1. T. HENZINGER. The theory of hybrid automata. In *Proceedings of the 11th Annual IEEE Symposium on Logic in Computer Science*, (1996), pp. 278–292.
2. R. ALUR, D. L. DILL. A theory of timed automata. *Theoretical Computer Science 126*, (1994), pp. 183–235.
3. T.A. HENZINGER, R. MAJUMDAR. A classification of symbolic transition systems. In *Proceedings of the 17th International Conference on Theoretical Aspects of Computer Science* (2000), pp. 13–34.
4. I. MITCHELL, J. A. TEMPLETON. A toolbox of Hamilton-Jacobi solvers for analysis of nondeterministic continuous and hybrid systems. In *Hybrid Systems: Computation and Control*, (2005), pp. 480–494.
5. E. ASARIN, T. DANG, O. MALER. The d/dt tool for verification of hybrid systems. In *Computer Aided Verification*, (2002), vol. 2404 of *LNCS*, Springer-Verlag, pp. 365–370.
6. G. KARSAI, A. AGRAWAL, A. LEDECZI. A metamodel-driven MDA process and its tools. Workshop in Software Model Engineering, (2003).
7. G. KARSAI, J. SZTIPANOVITS, A. LEDECZI, T. BAPTY. Model-integrated development of embedded software. In *Proceedings of the IEEE*, (2003), pp. 145–164.

8. A. PINTO, A. L. SANGIOVANNI-VINCENTELLI, L. P. CARLONI, R. PASSERONE. Interchange formats for hybrid systems: Review and proposal. In *Hybrid Systems: Computation and Control*, (2005), pp. 526–541.

9. A. LEDECZI, M. MAROTI, A. BAKAY, ET AL. Generic modeling environment. In *International Workshop on Intelligent Signal Processing*, (2001).

10. J. SZTIPANOVITS, G KARSAI, C. BIEGL, T. BAPTY, A. LEDECZI, D. MALLOY. Multigraph: an architecture for model-integrated computing. In *Proceedings of the 1st International Conference on Engineering of Complex Computer Systems*, (1995), pp. 361–368.

11. J. SZTIPANOVITS, G. KARSAI, H. FRANKE. Model-integrated program synthesis environment. In *Proceedings of the IEEE Symposium and Workshop on Engineering of Computer Based Systems*, (1996), pp. 348–355.

12. T. H. CORMEN, C. E. LEISERSON, R. L. RIVEST, C. STEIN . Introduction to Algorithms, Second Edition, (2001), The MIT PRESS.

13. J. LYGEROS. Lecture Notes on Hybrid Systems. Cambridge, 2003.

14. S. OSHER, R. FEDKIW. Level Set Methods and Dynamic Implicit Surfaces. Springer, 2003.

15. A.RANTZER, M. JOHANSSON. Piecewise linear quadratic optimal control. In *IEEE Transactions on Automatic Control*, (2000), pp. 629–637.

16. T Clark, A Evans, S Kent, and P Sammut. The mmf approach to engineering object-oriented design languages. In *Workshop on Language Descriptions, Tools and Applications.LDTA*, Genova, Italy, 2001. Available via http://www.puml.org.

17. Kai Chen, Janos Sztipanovits, and Sandeep Neema. Toward a semantic anchoring infrastructure for domain-specific modeling languages. Fifth International Conference on Embedded Software (EMSOFT05), Jersey City, New Jersey, September 2005. (Accepted for publication).

18. ET A.L, R. S. C. *Object Constraint Language Specification ver 1.1*, Sept 1997.

Quantitative and Qualitative Analysis of Temporal Aspects of Complex Activities

Andrei Voinikonis

University of Leipzig, Department of Computer Science
Augustusplatz 10-11, D-04109 Leipzig, Germany
voinikon@informatik.uni-leipzig.de

Abstract. A preparation of the consistent task schedule is significant for the proper functioning of reminder systems. Two problems have to be solved thereby: avoiding temporal task overlapping; preventing task generation with an unlimited task execution time. Each task consists of complex activities combining temporally linked actions. The article introduces a method for formal description of such activities. To limit the execution time of the activities, definitions of timer transitions were included in the action specification. The expiration of the timer causes a transition to a specified action. The fact that the actual timer depends on the actions performed before complicates the analysis. A timed automaton can be built for each complex activity based on the introduced description. This automaton is applied to quantitative and qualitative analysis of temporal aspects of the activities. The article presents an algorithm for calculating the duration limits of the activities and for detecting the unlimited activities.

1 Introduction

Automated distributed reminder systems with mobile components are growing in importance in the modern world of aging population [1]. Such systems can be applied for care for patients with memory deficits and for support of treatment of the chronic patients [2]. The systems can find a possible application in the corporate work.

A reminder system is intended to prompt a person to perform the scheduled tasks at the appointed time. Thereby, the significant aspect is the task scheduling [1] because the majority of people cannot perform several tasks simultaneously and the tasks can hinder each other. Thus, the temporal overlapping of the tasks has to be avoided, if it is possible [3].

The Mobile Memory Aid System MEMOS[1] [4] is specially developed to assist patients with memory deficits by task execution. It is also intended to support caregivers by task generation and execution control. The idea is to furnish each patient with a mobile device (PDA with GPRS [5] modem) connected to the central server via Internet. This allows to remotely set the tasks. The mobile device downloads the tasks

---

[1] MEMOS is supported by the German Ministry of Education and Research (BMB+F). The author takes the responsibility for the content of this publication.

D.A. Peled and Y.-K. Tsay (Eds.): ATVA 2005, LNCS 3707, pp. 129–143, 2005.

from the server, requests the patient to perform a task and retrieves the result of its execution, providing feedback to the caregivers.

The complex tasks are split into some autonomous uninterruptible parts - subtasks - called *decks* defining an organized structure of temporal linked actions to achieve sub-goals of a task. Each deck describes a "complex activity". It consists of *cards*: each card represents a single interaction with the patient. The card describes a single step/action within the task execution and offers the patient the possibility to react, e.g. to confirm or reject the step. Each offered reaction specifies a reference to another card that can belong to another deck of the task. Fig.1. shows an example of a task for medicine taking.

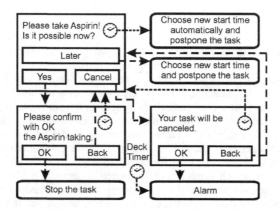

Fig. 1. Simplified description of task for medicine taking

The mobile component handles decks as independent jobs: each reference to another deck terminates presentation of current deck and returns the control to the main program with request to start presentation of the referred deck.

The server of the system stores the tasks and manages the task schedule. To avoid temporal conflicts, the overlapping of the tasks (between decks, further the term "task" is applied to refer decks because they are handled as the independent tasks) has to be detected and reported to the caregivers in order to solve them. To detect task overlapping, the duration of the tasks has to be calculated. Another problem to solve is generation of correct task descriptions because mistakes in the task can confuse the patients: e.g. they can lead to infinite repetition of some steps.

This article proposes the method for formal description of such tasks and introduces an algorithm for the qualitative and quantitative analysis of the task description. The algorithm is based on the application of timed automata [6] to the task analysis. The proposed formal description is applied as the basis for construction of the necessary timed automata.

First, the special features of the introduced task model required by the specific of system application and task design issues will be discussed. Further, the method for formal description is introduced. After that, the method for construction of the 2-level timed automaton is proposed. The original algorithm for determination of clock constraints for transitions is introduced for the automaton. The qualitative characteristics of these constrains allow to draw conclusions about the maximal and minimal task duration, task termination in finite time and reachability of particular actions.

2 Task Model

Each task describes a complex human activity. Description of the complex activity consists of descriptions of particular actions. The description of an action consists of an instruction to perform the action and a list of possible reactions such as confirmation, rejection or transitions to alternative actions: they are presented to a user as control elements, e.g. as buttons. The actions are connected together according the specified reactions: the choice of a particular reaction causes the transition to the corresponding action description. The user can cause only the events that are specified by the action description (*DI1*).

The actions may form cycles to provide ability of return to a description of a previous action if an alternative action is not suitable. Duration of the activities has to be limited in order to handle user inactivity and to make possible execution of other scheduled tasks.

To limit duration of the actions, a local timer is assigned to each action. An additional task range timer (further the global timer) is introduced to limit duration of the action cycles. Specification of the action descriptions contains the specification of routines for handling of timer events. These routines (further the global or local timer handler) specify transition targets: task stop or the action descriptions that are shown after timer event. The start of presentation of each action description causes reset of the local timer and can cause reset of the global timer with simultaneous updating of the transition targets for the timer events. Expiration of the timers causes the transition to the action pointed to by the corresponding event handler. After expiration of a timer, no events are to be expected until the timer will be reset. In order to simplify design of the task description and the task generation at the runtime, each value for the global timer in its definitions is counted from the moment of the task start (*DI2*), not from the moment of the timer setting. It allows controlling task duration by the repeated visiting of the action description with a definition of the global timer better.

As mentioned above, the objects of the analysis of such complex activities are:

- **Quantitative aspect:** The task overlapping has to be avoided in order to produce the consistent task schedule. For it, durations for the scheduled tasks have to be calculated. Based on the calculated durations and specified start times, the task overlapping can be detected and the detected conflicts can be solved, if possible.
- **Qualitative aspect:** Each task has to be executed in the finite time. The loops without temporal limitation in a task description can lead to infinite repetition of actions. Thereby, the object of qualitative analysis is to detect the tasks, whose execution time can be infinite.

To start the analysis, the task description should be formalised. The complex activity without time aspects can be described as an automaton, where the states present the actions and the transitions present the handlers of the events caused by user reactions.

The automaton for complex activity is a tuple:

$$A^c = (\Sigma, S, S^0, F, E)$$

where

Σ - an alphabet of the events caused by user input,

S - a set of the states, each of them corresponds to the single action,

S^0 - a set of start states, $S^0 \subset S$,[2]

F - a set of end states, $F \subset S$, $F = \{ s^e \}$ consists of single state, that corresponds to the stop of the task. The state s^e has not any exit transitions,

E - a set of the transitions $E \subseteq \Sigma \times S\backslash F \times S$. Each transition $e_{ij} = (\sigma, s_i, s_j)$ consists of a source state s_i, a target state s_j and corresponds to an event $\sigma \in \Sigma$. The transition e_{ij} is entry transition for state s_j and is exit transition for state s_i.

To handle the temporal aspects, the system of temporal transitions T^c is defined over the automaton A^c. A problem arises by definition of the global timer handlers: the timer initiated at the start of a particular action remains valid for all following actions until it will be reset or expires.

Furthermore, the current global timer handler for some states that can be reached by several different paths depends on the path to these states because these paths can contain the different specifications of global timer handlers.

System with temporal transitions is a tuple:

$$T^c = (A^c, C, M, \varepsilon, T)$$

where

C - a set of decreasing timers, e.g. as in [7], which run monotonically down to 0 and stop at 0, $C = \{ x^L, x^G \}$, where
$C^L = \{ x^L \}$ corresponds to the local timer and
$C^G = \{ x^G \}$ corresponds to the global timer,

M - a set of cells, $M = \{ m^L, m^G \}$, where
$M^L = \{ m^L \}$ contains the transition target for the local timer and
$M^G = \{ m^G \}$ contains the transition target for the global timer,

ε - an entry guard function for setting of the temporal transitions,
$\varepsilon \subset S\backslash F \times C \times R \times M \times S$, $\varepsilon = \varepsilon^L \cup \varepsilon^G$, where:
R – the set of real numbers;
$\varepsilon^L \subset S\backslash F \times C^L \times R \times M^L \times S$ - an entry guard function for setting of the local temporal transition, so that:

1. $\forall s_i \in S\backslash F \rightarrow \exists z_i \in \varepsilon^L$;

2. If exists a value $z_i = (s_i, x^L, t_{ij}, m^L, s_j) \in \varepsilon^L$, the transition in the state s_i causes:

   • setting of a transition pointer corresponding to expiration of the local timer $m^L := s_j$

   • reset of the local timer $x^L := t_{ij}$

---

[2] Transfer of the control to the task can be considered as transitions from a single start state, but they are irrelevant for the analysis. However, the analysis can be performed successively for each $s \in S^0$ due to this condition.

$\varepsilon^G \subset S\backslash F \times C^G \times R \times M^G \times S$ - an entry guard function for setting of the global temporal transition, so that:

1. ε^G can contain some elements;
2. If exists a value $z_i = (s_i, x^G, t_{ij}, m^G, s_j) \in \varepsilon^G$ the transition in the state s_i causes:
   - setting of a transition pointer corresponding to expiration of the global timer $m^G := s_j$
   - reset of the global timer according formula:

$$x^G := \begin{cases} 0, & \text{if } t_{ij} - t_{current} \leq 0, \\ \\ t_{ij} - t_{current}, & \text{if } t_{ij} - t_{current} > 0, \end{cases}$$

according design issue *DI2* all values for the global timer are defined from the moment of the task start, where $t_{current}$ is the time elapsed from the task start,

T - a set of temporal transitions, $T \subset C \times M$, $T = \{(x^G, m^G), (x^L, m^L)\}$ specifies that the transition to the state pointed to by content of a cell m takes place at expiration of a timer x.

The definition of T^c can be hardly applied for analysis directly, but is very useful as the base for further construction of the required timed automaton.

3   Construction of the Timed Automaton

A timed automaton is built on the base of T^c for further analysis that is carried out for each start state $s_{cur} \in S^0$ repeatedly. The *idea* is to build for each start state $s_{cur} \in S^0$ a 2-level timed automaton (further the second level timed automaton or CTA^S) on the base of the defined system of temporal transitions T^c, whose locations are timed automata too (further the first level timed automata or TA^F).

First, the clocks of the timed automata can take each value from $R^\circledast = R \cup \{ \otimes \}$, where value $\otimes$ shows that the clock is stopped and R is the set of real numbers.

The CTA^S is defined as a tuple:

$$CTA^S = (\Sigma'', L'', L^{0''}, F'', E'', C'')$$

where

Σ'' is an alphabet of events, $\Sigma'' = \Sigma' \cup \{ \textbf{\textit{gt}} \}$, $\Sigma' = \Sigma \cup \{ \textbf{\textit{lt}} \}$,
    lt is event corresponding expiration of the local timer,
    gt is event corresponding expiration of the global timer,
L'' is a set of locations, each of them is TA^F,
$L^{0''}$ is a set of start locations,
F'' is a set of end locations,
C'' is a set of clocks that increase strictly monotonically e.g. as in [6, 8], $C'' = \{ x^{S''}, x^{L''}, x^{G''} \}$, $x^{L''}, x^{G''}$ correspond to the timers $x^L, x^G \in C$ of T^c respectively, $x^{S''}$ is a system clock that is set to 0 at the start of CTA^S,

E"   is a set of transitions $E" \subset L"\times L" \times S \times \Sigma" \times \Omega" \times \Phi(C")$, element from S of A^c applied to mark the source state of a transition, $\Omega" \subset Pow(C"\times R)$, $\Omega" = \{\{(x", r) \mid x \in \{ x^{L"}, x^{G"} \}, r \in R\}\}$ is entry guard function that sets the clock $x" \in C"$ on value $r \in R^{\circledast}$, $\Phi(C")$ is a set of clock constrains $\delta"$ defined inductively by

$$\delta" ::= \boldsymbol{true} \mid \boldsymbol{false} \mid x \geq c \mid c \geq x \mid x = c \mid \delta"_1 \wedge \delta"_2 \mid \delta"_1 \vee \delta"_2,$$

where x is a clock in C" and c is a parameterised constant in R.

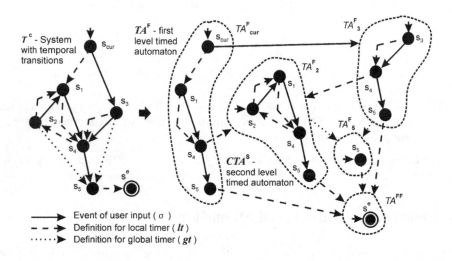

Fig. 2. Construction of the required timed automaton on the base of the defined system with the temporal transitions. The system with the temporal transitions is shown left; the built 2-level timed automaton is shown right. The TA^F_2 and TA^F_3 present the scopes of the global timers; TA^F_{cur} corresponds to the start state; TA^F_5 corresponds to the target state for the transitions of the global timers; TA^{FF} presents the end state.

Each state of CTA^S is a timed automaton TA^F that is defined as a tuple:

$$TA^F = (\Sigma', L', L^{0'}, F', E', C')$$

where

Σ' is an alphabet of events, $\Sigma' = \Sigma \cup \{ \boldsymbol{lt} \}$,
    $\boldsymbol{lt}$ is event corresponding expiration of the local timer,
L' is a set of locations $L' \subset S$ defined below,
$L^{0'}$ is a set of start locations,
F' is a set of end locations,
C' is a set of clocks that increases strictly monotonically, $C' = \{ x^{L"}\}$, $x^{L"}$ corresponds to the timer $x^L \in C$ of T^c,
E' is a set of transitions $E' \subset L' \times L' \times \Sigma' \times \Omega(C') \times \Phi(C')$,
    $\Omega(C') = \{(x^{L"}, 0), (x^{L"}, \otimes)\}$ is entry guard function that stops the clock $x^{L"}$ if $s_i = s^e$ or sets the clock $x^{L"}$ on 0 otherwise,
    $\Phi(C')$ is a set of clock constrains δ' defined by

$$\delta' ::= c \geq x^{L''} \mid x^{L''} = c$$

where c is a constant in R.

Further, the set of locations for the first level automata is refined. First, the set of successors for a state $s_i \in S$ is defined as follows:

$$succ(s_i) = \{ s_j \mid \exists (\sigma, s_i, s_j) \in E \vee \exists (s_i, x^L, t_{ij}, m^L, s_j) \in \varepsilon^L \}.$$

The set contains also the elements referred by the entry guard function for setting of local temporal transitions in T^c. Because this clock is reset by entry of *each* state $s_i \in S\backslash F$, the transition corresponding to the local timer may be handled just as the transitions corresponding to the events of user input.

The elements of the timed automata are built on the base of T^c as in example shown on the Fig. 2. The second level timed automaton obtains the locations:

- for the current start state,
- for the end state,
- for each state where is defined the entry guard function for setting of a global temporal transition,
- for each state that is used as the transition target by definition of the entry guard functions for setting of a global temporal transition.

These states are the start states for the corresponding first level timed automata. Thus, one TA^F is built as a location for CTA^S for each element from the set $S'' \subset S$:

$$S'' = \{s_{cur}\} \cup \{s^e\} \cup \{s_i \mid \exists(s_i, x^G, t_{ij}, m^G, s_j) \in \varepsilon^G\} \cup \{s_j \mid \exists(s_i, x^G, t_{ij}, m^G, s_j) \in \varepsilon^G\},$$

$$L'' = \{ TA^F_i \mid L^{0i}_i = \{s_i\} \wedge s_i \in S'' \}.$$

The set of the start locations $L^{0''}$ of CTA^S consists of the TA^F built on the base of the current start state s_{cur}, the set of end locations F'' of CTA^S consists of the TA^F built on the base of s^e:

$$L^{0''} = \{ TA^F_i \mid L^{0i}_i = \{ s_{cur} \}\},$$

$$F'' = \{ TA^{FF} \mid L^{0i} \text{ is a set of start locations of } TA^{FF}, L^{0i} = \{ s^e \}, TA^{FF} \in L''\},$$

$$TA^{FF} = (\Sigma', \{ s^e \}, \{ s^e \}, \{ s^e \}, \varnothing, C').$$

The location set of each first level timed automaton TA^F_i are the set $L'_i = Succ^*(s_i)$ consisting of the states that are reachable from the start state $s_i \in S''\backslash F$ of this automaton and another entry guard functions for setting of global temporal transitions are not defined for these states. The end state s^e does not belong to any TA^F_i except TA^{FF}. Thus, such a set presents the reachable region where the global timer will be not reset. It is defined recursively by:

$$Succ^*(s_i) = \{s_i\} \cup \{s_j \mid s_j \in succ(s_k) \wedge s_k \in Succ^*(s_i) \wedge \neg\exists(s_j, x^G, t_{jm}, m^G, s_m) \in \varepsilon^G \wedge s_j \neq s^e\}.$$

Thereby, the set of start location for TA^F_i is the set $L^{0i}_i = \{ s_i \}$. Further, s_i is applied to designate the start location of for TA^F_i. The set of end locations F'_i for TA^F_i is the subset of states L'_i that have a transition to the state s^e or to some state for that the entry guard function for setting of the global temporal transition is defined:

$F'_i = \{s_k \mid s_k \in L'_i \wedge \exists\, s_j \in \text{succ}(s_k) \wedge ((\exists(s_j, x^G, t_{jm}, m^G, s_m) \in \varepsilon^G \wedge s_j \neq s_i) \vee s_j = s^e)\}$.

The set of transitions E' for TA^F_i are defined as follows:

- The TA^F_i obtains a transition for each corresponding transition from A^c, if source and target states of this transition belong to L'_i. The clock constraint for such transitions is $x^{L''} < t_{kj}$ - the edge may be passed until the local timer expires.
- The TA^F_i obtains also a transition, if entry guard function for setting of the local timer defines the temporal transition and its source and target states belong to L'_i. The clock constraint for such transitions is $x^{L''} = t_{kj}$ - the transition may be passed at expiration of the local timer.

$E' = \{(s_k, s_j, \textbf{\textit{lt}}, (x^{L''}, g(s_j)), x^{L''} = t_{kj}) \mid s_k \in L'_i \wedge\ s_j \in L'_i \wedge\ \exists(s_k, x^L, t_{kj}, m^L, s_j) \in \varepsilon^L,$
$\textbf{\textit{lt}} \in \Sigma'\} \cup \{(s_k, s_m, \sigma, (x^{L''}, g(s_j)), x^{L''} < t_{kj}) \mid s_k \in L'_i \wedge\ s_j \in L'_i \wedge\ \exists(\sigma, s_k, s_m) \in E,$
$\qquad\qquad (s_k, x^L, t_{kj}, m^L, s_j) \in \varepsilon^L, \sigma \in\ \Sigma\},$

where

$$g(s_j) = \begin{cases} \otimes, \text{ if } s_j = s^e, \\ \\ 0, \text{ otherwise.} \end{cases}$$

The set of transitions E" for CTA^S is defined as follows (the clock constraints will be defined later):

- The CTA^S obtains a transition for each corresponding edge from A^c, if source and target states of this edge belong to different TA^F and entry guard function for setting of the global timer is defined for the target state or target state is s^e (ψ_1).
- The CTA^S obtains also a transition:
  - if entry guard function for setting of the local timer defines the temporal transition, and the target state of this transition has a definition of entry guard function for setting of the global timer or target state is s^e (ψ_2) and
  - if source and target states of this transition belong to different TA^F.
- The CTA^S obtains transitions for each definition of a temporal transition for the global timer (ψ_3).

$E" = (\, TA^F_i, TA^F_j,\ s_k, \sigma, \{(\, x^{L''}, g(TA^F_j)),(\, x^{G''}, f(TA^F_j, t_{jn}, x^{S''}))\}, \delta"_1)\mid \psi_1\,\} \cup$
$\{(\, TA^F_i, TA^F_j,\ s_k, \textbf{\textit{lt}}, \{(\, x^{L''}, g(TA^F_j)),(\, x^{G''}, f(TA^F_j, t_{jn}, x^{S''}))\}, \delta"_1)\mid \psi_2\,\} \cup$
$\{(\, TA^F_i, TA^F_j,\ s_i, \textbf{\textit{gt}}, \{(\, x^{L''}, g(TA^F_j)),(\, x^{G''}, f(TA^F_j, t_{jn}, x^{S''}))\}, \delta"_2)\mid \psi_3\,\}$

where

$$g(TA^F_j) = \begin{cases} \otimes, \text{ if } TA^F_j = TA^{FF}, \\ \\ 0, \text{ otherwise;} \end{cases}$$

$$f(TA^F_j, t_{jn}, x^{S''}) = \begin{cases} x^{S''}, \text{ if } t_{jn} > x^{S''} \wedge\ \exists(s_j, x^G, t_{jn}, m^G, s_n) \in \varepsilon^G,\ L^{0'}_j = \{s_j\}, \\ t_{jn}, \ \text{ if } t_{jn} \leq x^{S''} \wedge\ \exists(s_j, x^G, t_{jn}, m^G, s_n) \in \varepsilon^G,\ L^{0'}_j = \{s_j\}, \\ \otimes, \ \ \text{ if } \neg\exists\, (s_j, x^G, t_{jn}, m^G, s_n) \in \varepsilon^G,\ L^{0'}_j = \{s_j\}; \end{cases}$$

note that no transitions with $\sigma \in \Sigma'$ exist to the locations of CTA^S without the global timer excepts TA^{FF} according the construction method of CTA^S,

$\psi_1 = \exists(\sigma, s_k, s_j) \in E \wedge s_k \in L'_i \wedge s_j \in L^{0_r}_j \wedge s_i \neq s_j \wedge \exists(s_j, x^G, t_{jn}, m^G, s_n) \in \varepsilon^G, \sigma \in \Sigma;$

$\psi_2 = \exists(s_k, x^L, t_{kj}, m^L, s_j) \in \varepsilon^L \wedge s_k \in L'_i \wedge s_j \in L^{0_r}_j \wedge s_i \neq s_j \wedge$
$\qquad \wedge \exists(s_j, x^G, t_{jn}, m^G, s_n) \in \varepsilon^G, lt \in \Sigma';$

$\psi_3 = \exists (s_i, x^G, t_{ij}, m^G, s_j) \in \varepsilon^G \wedge s_i \in L^{0_r}_i \wedge s_j \in L^{0_r}_j, gt \in \Sigma'';$

$\delta''_2 := x^{G''} = t_{ij}, (s_i, x^G, t_{ij}, m^G, s_j) \in \varepsilon^G.$

Explanation for the term $s_i \neq s_j$ is that no transitions for CTA^S has to be added if a start location is referred by transitions with $\sigma \in \Sigma'$ from its corresponding TA^F. However, if a transition for global timer points to its definition state, the corresponding transition should be added to CTA^S.

It remains to calculate the clock constraints for the transitions of the first level timed automata and for the transitions of the second level automaton.

4 Determination of the Clock Constraints

To determine the clock constraints for CTA^S with respect to $x^{S''}$, the minimal and maximal passing times of each exit transition of TA^F_i have to be calculated first for each TA^F_i. The minimal and maximal passing times are defined recursively as follows:

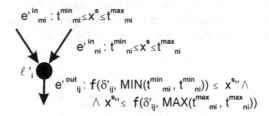

Fig. 3. Calculation of the maximal and minimal exit times for exit transition e'^{out}_{ij} of the location l'_i based on the maximal and minimal entry times and maximal stay time for this location. The stay time limited by the expiration of the local timer is taken into account by the clock constraint δ'_{ij}

The *idea* is to define a passing time (minimal or maximal) for each exit transition based on corresponding reachability times of its source location defined to each entry transition of this location (Fig. 3.). If some reachability times are not defined, they have to be defined first and stored for further use. The operation has to be applied recursively until the start location of this automaton is reached. If some *passed* locations are reached again during execution - the automaton contains a cycle. Maximal passing time for this transition is not limited. That is applied for the qualitative analysis: CTA^S for the complex activities has not to contain such automata with the undefined transition for the global timer that has to limit the cycle passing. The algorithm can be written in general as follows:

function Calculate
    if *start location of the automaton is reached*
        calculate *maximal and minimal exit times for the current exit transition*
        based on maximal and minimal parameterised entry times.
        return *defined values.*
    for the current exit transition
    calculate *the possible maximal and minimal passing times*
    counted from task start
    based on maximal and minimal entry times of its source location and
    on maximal stay time for this location (ref. Fig. 3)
    with respect to a possible limitation
    if *the passing times is undefined for some entry transitions of this location*
        for each *of these transitions*
            apply *function* Calculate *recursively,*
                /* the entry transition will be handled as the exit transition
                by the next call of the function Calculate thereby. */
    termination: *after termination the parameterised maximal and minimal passing*
    times of exit transitions of a first level automaton are defined

The algorithm for definition of the clock constraints by calculation of the passing times for the exit transitions of the first level automata with $\sigma \in \Sigma'$ in CTA^S with respect to the system clock $x^{S"}$ and parameterised minimal and maximal entry times (T^{min}_i parameter for minimal entry time for TA^F_i; T^{max}_i parameter for maximal entry time for TA^F_i) is shown on the listing 1. The clock constraints for these transitions depend on the internal structure of the first level automata in contrast to the transitions with $\sigma = gt$. Fig. 4. illustrates the program run for TA^F_3 built in example of Fig.2.

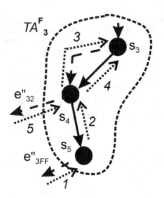

Fig. 4. Recursive calculation of entry times for the first level timed automaton TA^F_3. Calculation for the transition $e"_{32}$ will be stopped at the location s_4 because the times for entry transitions of this location are already calculated.

```
for each TA^F_i ∈ L"\ F"
    T^min_i parameter for minimal entry time for TA^F_i
    T^max_i parameter for maximal entry time for TA^F_i
```

for each e'': $(TA^F_i, TA^F_j, s_k, \sigma, \ldots, \delta''_1)$, $e'' \in E''$, $\sigma \in \Sigma'$

  t^{min}_{ik} minimal stay time for TA^F_i for s_k

  t^{max}_{ik} maximal stay time for TA^F_i for s_k

  create *Results*

  create *Passed_Locations*

  define *pseudo-transition* e' *corresponding to* e''-

$$e'_{kj}: (s_k, s_j, \sigma, \ldots, \delta'_k), \sigma \in \Sigma',$$

  Min_Max_Time mmt :=

      calc_Min_Max_Time($Results$, $Passed\_Locations$, e')

  t^{min}_{ik} := $mmt.min$, t^{max}_{ik} := $mmt.max$

  if $\exists\, (s_i, x^G, t_{ij}, m^G, s_j) \in \varepsilon^G$, $s_i \in L^{0'}_i$

      $\delta''_1 := T^{min}_i + t^{min}_{ik} \leq x^{S''} \wedge x^{S''} \leq T^{max}_i + t^{max}_{ik} \wedge t_i > T^{min}_i + t^{min}_{ik} \wedge x^{S''} < t_{ij}$

  else

        if $mmt.max = \infty$

            error *"Infinite unlimited path."*

        else

            $\delta''_1 := T^{min}_i + t^{min}_{ik} \leq x^{S''} \wedge x^{S''} \leq T^{max}_i + t^{max}_{ik}$.

function calc_Min_Max_Time($Results$, $Passed\_Locations$, e')

/* e' *has form* $(s_k, s_j, \sigma_{kj}, \ldots, \delta'_{kj})$ */

if result for e' **in** *Results*

/* *no repeated calculation* */

    return *Min_Max_Time* **for** e'

Min_Max_Time mmt:

    $mmt.min = \infty$,

    $mmt.max = 0$

if start state s_i of TA^F_i is reached: $s_i = s_k$

    if exists a cycle: $\exists\, (s_j, s_i, \sigma_{ji}, \ldots) \in E'_i$, $\sigma_{ji} \in \Sigma'$

          $mmt.max := \infty$

          /* *it can be walked infinitely* */

    else

          $mmt.max := t_{kj}$,

          /* δ'_{kj} *for* e' *has form* $x^{L''} = t_{kj}$ *or* $x^{L''} < t_{kj}$ */

    $mmt.min := 0$

    store mmt **in** *Results*

    return mmt.

  for each $e'_{lk} = (s_l, s_k, \sigma_{lk}, \ldots, \delta'_{lk})$, $e'_{lk} \in E'_i$ of TA^F_i

    if exists a cycle: s_l **in** *Passed_Locations* **or** $s_l = s_k$

          $mmt.max := \infty$ /* *it can be walked infinitely* */

    else

          add s_k **to** *Passed_Locations*

          Min_Max_Time ret := calc_Min_Max_Time(

              $Results$, $Passed\_Locations$, e'_{lk})

          remove s_k **from** *Passed_Locations*

          $ret.max := ret.max + t_{kj}$,

          /* δ'_{kj} *has form* $x^{L''} = t_{kj}$ *or* $x^{L''} < t_{kj}$ */

          if $\sigma_{kj} = lt$

                $ret.min := ret.min + t_{kj}$,

```
                    /* δ'kj has form xL" = tkj */
              if mmt.min > ret.min
                    mmt.min := ret.min
              if mmt.max < ret.max
                    mmt.max := ret.max
    store mmt in Results
    return mmt.
```

Listing. 1. Algorithm for definition of clock constraints for exit transitions with $\sigma \in \Sigma'$ for the first level timed automata

It remains to define the values of parameters T^{min}_i, T^{max}_i for δ''_1 and the clock constraints δ''_2 for the transitions with $\sigma = \boldsymbol{gt}$ with respect to $x^{S''}$. The algorithm is built on the similar strategy as before; it is shown on the listing 2. If some transitions cannot be passed, the minimal and maximal passing times for such transitions are set to -1. It can occur if e.g. a minimal passing time for a transition with $\sigma \in \Sigma'$ exceeds the value of the global timers for a corresponding $\boldsymbol{TA^F}$ (a transition with $\sigma \in \Sigma'$ is impassable) or if a maximal passing time for the transition with $\sigma \in \Sigma'$ is less than the value of the global timers for a corresponding $\boldsymbol{TA^F}$ (a transition with $\sigma = \boldsymbol{gt}$ is impassable).

```
for each s ∈ S⁰
  build CTAˢ
  create Results
  create Passed_Locations
  calculate clock constraints /* according Listing 1 */
  for each transition with target location
            TAᶠᶠ: e":= (TAᶠ_i, TAᶠᶠ, σ, ... , δ"_i), σ ∈ Σ", e" ∈ E"
  Min_Max_Time mmt :=
        calc_Global_Times (Results, Passed_Locations, e")
    store returned Min_Max pair
  if all entry transitions unreachable
    error "Task can not terminate.".
  find least minimum and greatest maximum
  among stored pairs with exception of
  unreachable transitions and store in mmt
  mmt contains now the maximal and minimal duration of
  current CTAˢ
find least minimum and greatest maximum among CTAˢ
that defines the maximal and minimal duration of Tᶜ.


function calc_Global_Times (Results, Passed_Locations, e")
  /* e" has form (TAᶠ_i, TAᶠ_j, σ_ij, ... , δ"_ij), σ_ij ∈ Σ" */
  if Results contains result for e"
  /* no repeated calculation */
      return Min_Max_Time for e"
  Min_Max_Time mmt, ret
  if start state of CTAˢ_i is reached: TAᶠ_i ∈ Lᴼ"
      if exists a cycle: ∃ (TAᶠ_i, TAᶠ_i, gt,...) ∈ E" V
                V (∃ (TAᶠ_l, TAᶠ_i, σ_li,...) ∈ E" ∧
                ∧ TAᶠ_l in Passed_Locations, σ_li ∈ Σ")
```

```
                error "Cycle found."
    mmt := define_Constraints(0,0, e")
    store mmt in Results
    return mmt.
if state without entry transitions is reached
    transition unreachable: mmt.min:= -1, mmt.max:= -1
    store mmt in Results
    return mmt.
```

for each $e''_{mi} : (TA^F_m, TA^F_i, \sigma_{mi}, \ldots, \delta''_{mi})$, $e''_{mi} \in E''$

```
    if exists a cycle:
```
$$TA^F_m \textbf{ in } Passed\_Locations \textbf{ or } TA^F_m = TA^F_i$$
```
            error "Cycle found."
```
add TA^F_i **to** Passed_Locations

Min_Max_Time ret := calc_Global_Times(
                    Results, Passed_Locations, e''_{mi})

remove TA^F_i **from** Passed_Locations

```
    store returned Min_Max pair
if all entry transitions unreachable
    all exit  transitions unreachable too:
    mmt.min = -1, mmt.max = -1
    store mmt in Results
    return mmt.
find least minimum and greatest maximum
    among returned pairs with exception of
    unreachable transitions and store in ret
mmt := define_Constraints( ret.min, ret.max, e")
store mmt in Results
return mmt.
```

function define_Constraints(min, max, e")

/* e" has form $(TA^F_i, TA^F_j, \sigma_{ij}, \ldots, \delta''_{ij})$, $\sigma_{ij} \in \Sigma''$ */

Min_Max_Time mmt

if $\exists\, (TA^F_i, TA^F_l, gt, \ldots, \delta''_{il}) \in E''$ **and** $(s_i, x^G, t_{il}, m^G, s_l) \in \varepsilon^G$

   if $\sigma_{ij} = gt$

```
            if max + MAXk (F'i, t maxik )3 < til
                transition unreachable:
                mmt.min := -1, mmt.max := -1
            else
                mmt.min := til, mmt.max := MAX (til, max)
```
     /* $\delta''_2 := t_{il} \leq x^{S''} \wedge x^{S''} \leq$ MAX (t_{il}, max) */

   else

     /* $\delta''_1 := min + t^{min}_{ij} \leq x^{S''} \wedge x^{S''} \leq t^{max}_{ij} + max \wedge t_{il} > min + t^{min}_{ij} \wedge x^{S''} < t_{il}$ */

       if $t_{il} \leq min + t^{min}_{ij}$

```
                transition unreachable:
                mmt.min := -1, mmt.max := -1
            else
```
         mmt.min := $min + t^{min}_{ij}$,

         mmt.max := MIN$(t_{il}, max + t^{max}_{ij})$

---

[3] The function chooses the maximal passing time through the corresponding first level automaton calculated earlier.

```
/* δ"₁:= min + t min ij ≤x S" ∧ x S" ≤ MIN(t il, max + t max ij)   */
else
    mmt.min := min + t min ij, mmt.max := max + t max ij
/* δ"₁:= min + t min ij ≤ x S" ∧ x S" ≤ max + t max ij */
return mmt.
```

Listing. 2. Algorithm for definition of the clock constraints for the transitions of the second level timed automaton

Thus, the least minimal and greatest maximal passing times of the transitions, whose target is the TA^{FF}, calculated for all start states in S^0 characterises the maximal and minimal duration of the complex activity T^c. The objects of the qualitative analysis are also reached by application of the described algorithm: if the TA^{FF} cannot be reached or reachability time is infinitely or an error is reported, the corresponding task must not be accepted by system.

Finally, complexity of the algorithm should be estimated. Each transition will be passed only once because the calculation results are stored for each passed transition and will be reused if they are required; complexity of the result search is $O(1)$. The upper limit for the number of TA^F is $2 \times |\varepsilon^G| + 2$ according the method of construction of TA^F. The number of transitions in each TA^F does not exceed $|E| + |\varepsilon^L|$; the number of transitions in CTA^S does not exceed $|E| + |\varepsilon^L| + |\varepsilon^G|$ (propagation of the transitions to TA^{FF} can be neglected). Therefore, the number of the passed transitions during calculation can be estimated as $|S^0| \times ((2 \times |\varepsilon^G| + 2) \times (|E| + |\varepsilon^L|) + (|E| + |\varepsilon^L| + |\varepsilon^G|))$. Thus, the complexity of the algorithm can be estimated as $O(|S^0| \times |\varepsilon^G| \times (|E| + |\varepsilon^L|))$ because $|S^0| \ll |E| + |\varepsilon^L|$ and $|\varepsilon^G| \ll |E| + |\varepsilon^L|$.

The algorithm was implemented in Java. The test runs have demonstrated a good agreement between manually and automatically calculated values for the applied tasks.

5 Summary

The proposed method for the analysis of the reminder tasks allows to define the duration limits of the task execution. Thereby, the tasks with an unlimited execution time can be detected. The pursuance of analysis allows preparing the consistent task schedule: temporal task overlapping can be avoided; generation of the tasks with the unlimited execution time can be prevented. The approach to construction of the 2-level timed automata allows handling dependency of the actual timer definition on the actions performed before. The article introduces also the efficient algorithm for the analysis.

References

1. J. Pineau,, M. Montemerlo, M. Pollack,N. Roy, S. Thrun, Towards robotic assistants in nursing homes: Challenges and results, Proc. of Robotics and Autonomous Systems 42, 2003, p. 271–281.
2. A. Voinikonis, A Generic Approach to a Mobile Monitoring System, Proc. of 2nd IASTED International Conference on Biomedical Engineering BioMED 2004, Acta-Press, Innsbruck, Austria, February, 2004

3. A.Voinikonis, A Generic Data Model and a Supporting Server Architecture for the Mobile Memory Aid System, Proc. of 9th IASTED International Conference on Internet and Multimedia Systems and Applications EuroIMSA 2005, Acta-Press, Grindelwald, Switzerland, February, 2005
4. H. Schulze, A. Voinikonis, T. Hoffmann, K. Irmscher, Modeling a Mobile Memory Aid System, Proceedings zur 13. ITG/GI-Fachtagung "Kommunikation in Verteilten Systemen" (KiVS2003). 25.-28.02.2003, Universität Leipzig. Springer-Verlag, Reihe Informatik aktuell. Berlin, Heidelberg, New York, 2003. p. 143-153.
5. 3GPP, GPRS Service Description, 3G TS 22.060 v. 3.3.0, Mar. 2000.
6. R. Alur and D.L. Dill, A theory of timed automata, Theoretical Computer Science, 1994, 126, p. 183-235.
7. A.Th. Henzinger, It's About Time: Real-time Logics Reviewed, Proc. of the 10th International Conference on Concurrency Theory, LNCS 1466, Springer, 1998, pp. 439-454
8. E. Asarin, O. Maler, A. Pnueli. Symbolic controller synthesis for discrete and timed systems. In Hybrid Systems II, LNCS 999, Springer 1995, pp. 1-20.

Automatic Test Case Generation with Region-Related Coverage Annotations for Real-Time Systems

Geng-Dian Huang[1,2] and Farn Wang[1]

[1] Dept. of Electrical Engineering, National Taiwan University, Taiwan, ROC
[2] Inst. of Information Science, Academia Sinica, Taiwan, ROC
Ph: +886-2-27883799 ext. 2105
gdhuang@ntu.edu.tw

Abstract. Testing is the mainstream of verification techniques used for real-time systems in the industry because it allows the engineers to directly observe how their system implementations react to various test cases. In this paper, we investigate how to use symbolic techniques to automatically generate test cases for real-time systems. Especially, our test cases have two annotations that can be useful in the construction of powerful test cases. First, events in our test cases are labeled with symbolic timing constraints which can either be conveniently used in picking event occurrence times or be used for choosing boundary timing values in domain analysis. Second, our test cases are annotated with region-related coverage estimations which support high precision in detecting some timing bugs. Finally, we have implemented our ideas with BDD-like data-structures which could lead to performance advantage for testing complex embedded systems.

1 Introduction

Nowadays, as the verification cost has grown to over 50 percent of the total development budget in most industrial projects for complex embedded systems, the ability to control the verification process has become the major factor in the competitiveness of most high-tech companies. Of the many verification techniques, *testing* [14, 3] has been the mainstream in the software industry over the last few decades. The major reason is that testing is directly applied to the software engineers' major product, i.e., programs, which the software engineers feel most comfortable with. In contrast, other verification techniques, like simulation [5] and formal verifications [2, 6], usually work on artefacts, like virtual models and mathematical logics, which do not fuse easily with the existing development cycles in many companies. However, the complexity of new-generation embedded systems has driven the cost of testing to bigger and bigger proportions in their development budgets. But even having spent huge money on testing, people still found that they usually did not have time and resources to run enough test cases for the confidence in their products. One way to overcome the challenges of verification in the industry without disrupting the existing development cycles is

D.A. Peled and Y.-K. Tsay (Eds.): ATVA 2005, LNCS 3707, pp. 144–158, 2005.

to use formal verification techniques to enhance the quality of test case generation. In this work, we investigate how to use symbolic techniques for flexible automatic test cases generation for real-time systems.

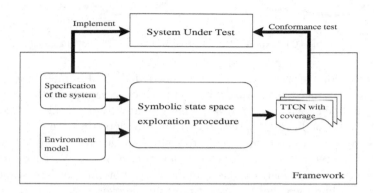

Fig. 1. Framework of conformance testing

In fig 1, we show our framework of *conformance testing* [17] for embedded systems. Both the *SUT (System under test)* and the environment are specified as *communicating timed automata (CTA)* [23,24]. We apply a symbolic state space exploration procedure to generate symbolic trace-trees annotated with coverage estimations. Every symbolic trace from the root to a leaf in the symbolic trace-tree is mapped to a test case. The test cases are then fed to the SUT to check whether the SUT's behavior conforms with the specification. The generated test cases are sequences of input events and expected output events. Specifically, our test cases have the following two annotations.

- *Flexible timing-constraints of all the events.* The constraints annotated with the input/output events are specified as Boolean combinations of event occurrence time differences. The constraints can be conveniently used in both picking the input event occurrence times and checking the correctness of the output event occurrence times of the SUT. Test cases with specific input event occurrence times may hardly give development teams strong confidence in the correctness of the timing behaviors of their SUT. Usually, engineers would like to efficiently check how their SUT behaves with respect to the extreme cases of data-values. Thus our annotations of flexible constraints of input events can thus be used as a basis for domain and boundary analysis of input/output event occurrence times.
- *Region-related coverage estimations.* In the before, people suggested to use coverage metrics for untimed systems, like transition coverage, to measure the progress of testing real-time systems [4,20]. However, there can be special timing bugs that could escape testing with such metrics. A general characteristic of such timing bugs can be illustrated with the simple CTA in figure 2. The periods of the first and the second processes are 3 and 5 respectively. Thus the global period of the whole system is 15. At the 5'th time unit,

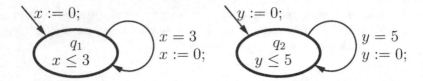

Fig. 2. An example that exposes the imprecision of the transition coverage metric

the transition coverage has already reached 100% and implies that no more test cases are needed. However, if a bug can only happen in the 14'th time unit, specified with $x = 2 \wedge y = 4$, then apparently the transition coverage metric will not have the precision to help us detecting the bug. Our test cases are all annotated with region-related coverage estimations [23] and can be shown precise enough to detect such timing bugs. We have employed two such coverage metrics, one roughly corresponding to dense-time state coverage while the other to dense-time branch coverage.

We have implemented the ideas in this article with symbolic techniques and BDD-like data-structures, which have been proven more efficient than DBM [8] against several benchmarks [25]. We have developed a technique to combine an iteration of abstract forward analysis with an iteration of backward analysis. This technique helps us focusing on the test cases related to the reachability of risk conditions. Our experiment data corroborates this claim since the technique leads to smaller test plans[1] in the experiment. We have also experimented to use abstraction techniques to control the sizes of the test plans. Abstraction techniques may remove some state information, make the state-equivalence relation coarser, and in turn generate fewer test cases to guarantee coverage.

The rest of this paper is structured as follows. We review related work in section 2. We review the basic building blocks of this work, including the formal specification language CTA, the symbolic state space exploration procedure, and the symbolic state coverage estimation techniques in section 3. Then, we present techniques to extract test cases from symbolic traces in section 4. We report our implementation and experiment in section 5. Finally, we present the conclusion and discuss the future work in section 6.

2   Related Work

To automatically generate test cases, we need a formal specification of the SUT and then a mechanical procedure to read in the formal specification and generate the test cases. For testing real-time systems, people have used the popular *timed automata (TA)* [1] and its variations as the formal specification languages. People have also adapted the existing test-case generation algorithms for untimed algorithms. The idea is to discretize the state space before applying the untimed test case generation algorithms. In [15], the discretization is achieved through

---

[1] A test plan can be viewed as a sequence of the test cases.

digital clock automata. In [21], Springintveld et al. discretized timed automata into finite grid automata and then applied untimed test case generation algorithm. Both of these methods encounter the state explosion problem even with small systems since they partition the state space with fine granularity.

Hessel et al. [10] used the fastest diagnostic trace facility of the UPPAAL [19], a model checker for real-time systems with DBM-technology [8], to generate time optimal test cases. Test cases can be selected through manually formulated test purposes or automatically from three coverage metrics: edge coverage, location coverage, definition-use pair coverage. The test cases are annotated specific time-delay values between events. The timing constraints are preserved from symbolic traces to test cases through summations of specific time-delay values between events. In this work, we deduce flexible timing constraints on event occurrence times instead of specific time-delay values. Such flexibility could support domain and boundary analysis in the latter stage of test case generation.

Nielsen et al. [18] proposed a method to generate test cases for real-time systems, specified as event-recording automata, in which every event has a corresponding clock to record the elapsed time since its last occurrence. No internal events are permitted. The state space is partitioned, according to the triggering conditions on the transitions, for constructing an equivalence-class graph. Then symbolic techniques are used to construct the reachability graph out of the equivalence-class graph. Finally, test cases are generated to cover all equivalence classes.

3   Review of the Basic Technology

In this section, we review some of the basic technology, on which we build this work. In section 3.1, we give the definition of our specification language, CTA. In section 3.2, we review the basic symbolic techniques to explore the dense state space. In section 3.3, we then review the three coverage metrics implemented in our test case generation algorithm. Finally, in section 3.4, we review the symbolic state space exploration procedure.

3.1   CTA as a Specification Language

A *communicating timed automaton (CTA)* is a set of *process timed automata (PTA)*, equipped with a finite set of clocks (with nonnegative real-values) and synchronization channels. A PTA is structured as a directed graph whose nodes are *modes (control locations)* and whose arcs are *transitions*. The modes are labeled with *invariance conditions* while the transitions are labeled with *triggering conditions* and a set of clocks to be reset during the transitions. The invariance conditions and triggering conditions are Boolean combinations of inequalities comparing clocks with integers. At any moment, each PTA can stay in only one *mode* (or *control location*). In its operation, one of the transitions can be triggered when the corresponding triggering condition is satisfied and its input/output events are synchronized. Upon being triggered, the PTA instantaneously transits from one mode to another and resets some clocks to zero. In between transitions, all clocks increase their readings at a uniform rate.

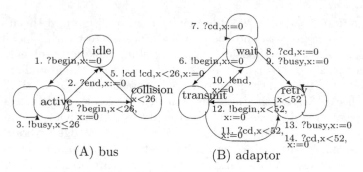

Fig. 3. Specification of a bus-contending protocol

In figure 3, we draw two PTAs for specifying a bus-contending protocol. One is for the bus and the other one is for the adaptor. The circles represent modes while the arcs represent transitions, which may be labeled with synchronization symbols (e.g., !begin, ?end, ...), triggering conditions (e.g., $x < 52$), and assignments (e.g., $x := 0$;). For convenience, we have labeled the transitions with numbers. In the system, an adaptor process may synchronize through channel begin with the bus to start sending signal on the bus. While one adaptor is using the bus, the second one may also synchronize through channel begin to start placing message on the bus and corrupting the bus contents. When this happens, the bus then signals bus collision (cd) to all the adaptors.

In the following, we give a brief definition of CTA. For detailed definition, please refer to [23, 24]. For convenience, given a set Q of modes and a set X of clocks, we use $B(Q, X)$ as the set of all Boolean conjunctions of inequalities of the forms $\mathtt{mode}_p = q$ and $x - x' \sim c$, where $\mathtt{mode}_p$ is a special auxiliary variable to record the current mode of process p, $q \in Q$, $x, x' \in X \cup \{0\}$, '$\sim$' is one of $\leq, <$, and c is an integer constant. $\mathcal{R}^+$ is the set of nonnegative real numbers.

Definition 1. process timed automata (PTA) A PTA A is given as a tuple $\langle X, E, Q, I, \mu, T, \lambda, \tau, \pi \rangle$. X is the set of clocks. E is the set of synchronization channels. Q is the set of modes. $I \in B(Q, X)$ is the initial condition. $\mu : Q \mapsto B(\emptyset, X)$ defines the invariance condition of each mode. $T \subseteq Q \times Q$ is the set of transitions. $\lambda : (E \times T) \mapsto \mathcal{Z}$ defines the message sent and received at each process transition. When $\lambda(e, t) \leq 0$, it means that process transition t receives $|\lambda(e, t)|$ events through channel e. When $\lambda(e, t) > 0$, it means that process transition t sends $\lambda(e, t)$ events through channel e. $\tau : T \mapsto B(\emptyset, X)$ and $\pi : T \mapsto 2^X$ respectively define the triggering condition and the clock set to reset of each transition. ∎

Definition 2. communicating timed automata (CTA) A CTA of m processes is a tuple $\langle E, A_1, A_2, \ldots, A_m \rangle$, where E is the set of synchronization channels and for each $1 \leq p \leq m$, $A_p = \langle X_p, E, Q_p, I_p, \mu_p, T_p, \lambda_p, \tau_p, \pi_p \rangle$ is the PTA for process p. ∎

A *valuation* of a set is a mapping from the set to another set. Given an $\eta \in B(Q, X)$ and a valuation ν of X, we say ν *satisfies* η, in symbols $\nu \models \eta$, iff η is evaluated *true* when the variables in η are interpreted according to ν.

Definition 3. states Suppose we are given a CTA $C = \langle E, A_1, A_2, \ldots, A_m \rangle$ such that for each $1 \leq p \leq m$, $A_p = \langle X_p, E, Q_p, I_p, \mu_p, T_p, \lambda_p, \tau_p, \pi_p \rangle$. A state ν of C is a valuation of $\bigcup_{1 \leq p \leq m} (X_p \cup \{\text{mode}_p\})$ such that

- $\nu(\text{mode}_p) \in Q_p$ is the mode of process p in ν; and
- for each $x \in \bigcup_{1 \leq 1p \leq m} X_p$, $\nu(x) \in \mathcal{R}^+$ such that $\nu \models \bigwedge_{1 \leq p \leq m} \mu_p(\nu(\text{mode}_p))$.

For any $t \in \mathcal{R}^+$, $\nu + t$ is a state identical to ν except that for every clock $x \in X$, $(\nu + t)(x) = \nu(x) + t$. ∎

A *global transitions* Φ of a CTA is a mapping from process indices p, $1 \leq p \leq m$, to $T_p \cup \{\bot\}$, where $\bot$ means no transition (i.e., a process does not participate in a global transition). A legitimate global transition has to be *synchronized*, that is, each output event from a process is received by exactly one unique corresponding process with a matching input event. Formally speaking, in a global transition Φ, for each channel e, the number of output events must match that of input events. Or in arithmetic, $\forall e \in E, \sum_{1 \leq p \leq m; \Phi(p) \neq \bot} \lambda(e, \Phi(p)) = 0$. Moreover, to be compatible with the popular interleaving semantics, we require that two synchronized global transitions are not allowed to occur at the same time. In the following, whenever we say "global transition", we actually mean "legitimate global transition" for briefness.

We define the transition relation $\overset{\delta}{\hookrightarrow}$ of a CTA as follows. δ is either a time-delay t or a global transition Φ. Given two states ν and ν', we say that $\nu \overset{t}{\hookrightarrow} \nu'$ iff $\nu' = \nu + t$ for $t \in \mathcal{R}^+$. We say that $\nu \overset{\Phi}{\hookrightarrow} \nu'$ iff

- $\nu \models \bigwedge_{1 \leq p \leq m; \Phi(p) \neq \bot} \tau_p(\Phi(p))$, and
- ν is identical to ν' except that for all $1 \leq p \leq m$ and $\Phi(p) \neq \bot$, $(\nu(\text{mode}_p), \nu'(\text{mode}_p)) = \Phi(p)$ and $\nu'(x) = 0$ if $x \in \pi_p(\Phi(p))$.

3.2 Symbolic Trace Computation

Since we assume that time is continuous in a CTA (i.e., the domain of the clocks is positive real numbers), there are infinitely many states. In order to analyze a CTA, we use *zones* to represent state-space. A zone z is a state-space described by a set of constraints in either of the following two forms.

- $\text{mode}_p = q_p$, for some $1 \leq p \leq m$ and $q_p \in Q_p$.
- $x - x' \sim c$ for clock differences, where x and x' are clocks or 0, '$\sim$'$\in \{\leq, <, =, >, \geq\}$, and c is an integer.

Many model-checkers for CTAs have been built on the symbolic manipulation procedures of zones [19, 22, 26]. Our symbolic trace computation is also based on a well-discussed symbolic procedure, called `post()`, to compute a symbolic post-condition of a zone after a global transition and time-progress [12]. Given a zone z and a global transition Φ,

$$\text{post}(z, \Phi) = \{\nu'' | \nu \overset{\Phi}{\hookrightarrow} \nu' \overset{t}{\hookrightarrow} \nu'', \nu \in z, \text{ and } t \in \mathcal{R}^+\}.$$

Note that the result of the post-condition procedure can also be represented as a zone. For briefness, we use $z \xrightarrow{\Phi} z'$ to denote $z' = \mathrm{post}(z, \Phi)$ and a symbolic trace can be described as $z_0 \xrightarrow{\Phi_1} z_1 \xrightarrow{\Phi_2} \ldots \xrightarrow{\Phi_n} z_n$.

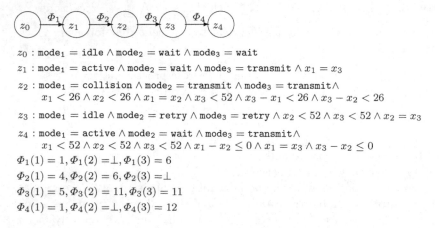

$z_0 : \mathrm{mode}_1 = \texttt{idle} \land \mathrm{mode}_2 = \texttt{wait} \land \mathrm{mode}_3 = \texttt{wait}$

$z_1 : \mathrm{mode}_1 = \texttt{active} \land \mathrm{mode}_2 = \texttt{wait} \land \mathrm{mode}_3 = \texttt{transmit} \land x_1 = x_3$

$z_2 : \mathrm{mode}_1 = \texttt{collision} \land \mathrm{mode}_2 = \texttt{transmit} \land \mathrm{mode}_3 = \texttt{transmit} \land$
$\qquad x_1 < 26 \land x_2 < 26 \land x_1 = x_2 \land x_3 < 52 \land x_3 - x_1 < 26 \land x_3 - x_2 < 26$

$z_3 : \mathrm{mode}_1 = \texttt{idle} \land \mathrm{mode}_2 = \texttt{retry} \land \mathrm{mode}_3 = \texttt{retry} \land x_2 < 52 \land x_3 < 52 \land x_2 = x_3$

$z_4 : \mathrm{mode}_1 = \texttt{active} \land \mathrm{mode}_2 = \texttt{wait} \land \mathrm{mode}_3 = \texttt{transmit} \land$
$\qquad x_1 < 52 \land x_2 < 52 \land x_3 < 52 \land x_1 - x_2 \leq 0 \land x_1 = x_3 \land x_3 - x_2 \leq 0$

$\Phi_1(1) = 1, \Phi_1(2) = \bot, \Phi_1(3) = 6$

$\Phi_2(1) = 4, \Phi_2(2) = 6, \Phi_2(3) = \bot$

$\Phi_3(1) = 5, \Phi_3(2) = 11, \Phi_3(3) = 11$

$\Phi_4(1) = 1, \Phi_4(2) = \bot, \Phi_4(3) = 12$

Fig. 4. A symbolic trace of the bus-contending protocol

In figure 4, we show a symbolic trace of the bus-contending protocol (in figure 3) and the related derivation. There are three PTAs, A_1 for the bus while A_2, A_3 for the adaptors. For briefness, $x = x'$ is a shorthand for $x - x' \leq 0 \land x' - x \leq 0$ and $x \sim c$ is a shorthand for $x - 0 \sim c$, where x and x' are clocks or 0. The initial zone z_0 describes that the bus process is in the $\texttt{idle}$ mode and the two adaptor processes are in the $\texttt{wait}$ mode. With global transition Φ_1, A_3 synchronizes through channel $\texttt{begin}$ with A_1 to start sending signal on the bus. At zone z_1, $x_1 = x_3$ since both x_1 and x_3 are reset at Φ_1. If A_2 also starts sending signal with Φ_2 before A_3 can be sure of the total access to the bus in 52 time units, a collision happens at global transition Φ_3 and bumps all transmitting adaptors to the $\texttt{retry}$ mode. In the $\texttt{retry}$ mode, A_3 tries to retransmit signals with global transition Φ_4 in 52 time units. Similarly, $x_1 = x_2$, $x_2 = x_3$, and $x_1 = x_3$ are true respectively at zones z_2, z_3, and z_4. At z_2, $x_1 < 26$ since $\mathrm{mode}_1 = \texttt{collision}$ and $\mu_1(\texttt{collision})$ is $x_1 < 26$. For the same reason, $x_2 < 52$ and $x_3 < 52$ are true at z_3.

3.3   Coverage Estimation

In the following, we briefly discuss three coverage metrics, ACM, RCM, and TCM. For more details, readers can refer to [24].

Arc coverage metric (ACM). This is a straightforward adaptation from the *FSM (finite-state machine) arc coverage* [4, 20] of VLSI simulation and testing. Conceptually, we transform a circuit to an FSM and measure the set of executed transitions. The same definition of FSM arc coverage can be readily copied for the test case analysis of CTAs. That is, we can also use the global transitions of CTAs to estimate coverage in ACM.

Region coverage metric (RCM). Another extreme that can also be adapted from VLSI verification technology is the *visited-state coverage* metric, which measures the reachable states in FSM. The states are discrete and countable in VLSI's models while they are dense and uncountable in CTAs. Instead of measuring the reachable states directly, region-equivalence relation [1] can be used to partition the dense-time state-space into finite set of equivalent states, and we measure the reachable regions in RCM. We use the symbolic procedure in [24] to estimate the number of regions in a zone.

Triggering-condition coverage metric (TCM). The third coverage metric is called *triggering-condition coverage metric (TCM)*, which is a hybrid measure composed of ACM and RCM. Unlike ACM, in which a global transition is covered once it is executed, we take the triggering conditions into account. When a global transition is executed, we use TCM to estimate the regions that have been covered in the triggering condition of the corresponding global transitions.

3.4 Symbolic State Space Exploration Procedure

From each zone, there could be many successor zones. Thus the symbolic traces constructed in section 3.2 constitute a directed graph of zones. The following symbolic procedure returns a traversing tree of the directed graph for a given CTA and risk condition.

Symbolic_trace_tree(C, η) /* C is a CTA with $I = z_1 \vee \ldots \vee z_n$; η is the risk condition. */ {
    let $V := \{z_1, \ldots, z_n\}$; $F := \emptyset$;
    while (true) {
        select a zone $z \subseteq V \wedge \text{abstract}(\neg \eta)$ and a global transition Φ
            such that $\text{post}(z, \Phi) \neq \textit{false}$ and $\text{post}(z, \Phi) \not\subseteq V$;   (a)
        if there is no such a z, return $\langle V, F \rangle$;
        $z' := \text{abstract}(\text{post}(z, \Phi))$; $V := V \cup \{z'\}$; $F := F \cup \{(z, z')\}$;   (b)
    }
}

The zone z and the global transition Φ are fed to $\text{post}()$ to compute the next-step state space after transition and time-progress in statement (b). The while loop continues until the generated symbolic traces have covered all reachable state space up to the risk condition. There are two features of this procedure.

- In statement (a), we allow for the flexibility of various traversing strategies in choosing z and Φ. With different strategies, the procedure generates different trace-trees. The leaves of a traversing tree generated from this procedure represent those zones which either have already been traversed (and recorded in V) or are contained in the risk conditions. Typical traversing orders are depth-first traversing, breadth-first traversing, etc.

- In statement (b), we may use abstraction techniques through procedure abstract() to simplify the representation of V. This abstraction option certainly may over-approximate the state-space representations. Abstraction techniques have been used widely to make state-space analysis and test-case generation feasible with practical resource assumptions. Typical abstraction techniques include convex-hull approximation [13] and discretization [7].

4   Test Case Generation

We now use the building blocks in subsections 3.2, 3.3, and 3.4 to design our test case generation procedure. In the framework of conformance testing, we inject the inputs to an SUT and observe if the outputs of the SUT conform with our expectation. Given a CTA that specifies a system and its environment and a risk condition, we can use procedure Symbolic_trace_tree() in subsection 3.4 to construct a trace-tree of the CTA. In this section, we show how to step by step extract a test case from a symbolic trace of a CTA with coverage information. Each test case consists of (1) the input events and the expected output events, and (2) the timing constraints between events. This is done in three steps.

1. The symbolic trace should be strengthened by stronger constraints such that the symbolic trace corresponds to true computations of the CTA.
2. The events of the trace and their timing constraints are extracted. Since our CTAs allow for internal events, we need a projection procedure to eliminate the internal events while preserving the interval timing information.
3. Finally, assuming a certain order of the test cases generated in the 2nd step, we calculate the (region-related) coverage estimation of each steps in each test case.

We present the three steps in subsections 4.1, 4.2, and 4.3 respectively.

4.1   Backward Analysis

Now, we present the first step. A symbolic trace $z_0 \xrightarrow{\Phi_1} z_1 \xrightarrow{\Phi_2} \ldots \xrightarrow{\Phi_n} z_n$ is computed forwardly with procedure post() so that every state $\nu' \in z_i$ has a preceding state $\nu \in z_{i-1}$. If we want to map each symbolic trace to a test case, we want to make sure that the reverse is also true. However, the reverse is not true. For example, a state ν satisfying $\nu(\mathtt{mode_1}) = \mathtt{active} \wedge \nu(\mathtt{mode_2}) = \mathtt{wait} \wedge \nu(\mathtt{mode_2}) = \mathtt{transmit} \wedge \nu(x_1) = 26 \wedge \nu(x_2) = 26 \wedge \nu(x_2) = 26$ is in z_1. But it can not reach z_2 through Φ_2 since the triggering condition of $\Phi_2(1)$ is not satisfied at ν. If we extract a test case from the symbolic trace with states that breaks the execution of the symbolic trace, we may generate an invalid test case that the implementations are not supposed to pass.

In order to exclude the states that can not reach z_n, we need a procedure $\mathtt{pre}(z, \Phi) = \{\nu | \nu \xrightarrow{t} \nu' \xrightarrow{\Phi} \nu'', \nu'' \in z, \text{ and } t \in \mathcal{R}^+\}$ to compute the pre-condition so that every state $\nu \in \mathtt{pre}(z, \Phi)$ has a succeeding state $\nu'' \in z$. Like $\mathtt{post}()$, the result of $\mathtt{pre}()$ can be represented as a zone. In the following, based on $\mathtt{pre}()$, we present procedure $\mathtt{Backward\_Prune}$ that prunes redundant states that break the execution of a symbolic trace.

$\mathtt{Backward\_Prune}(z_0 \xrightarrow{\Phi_1} z_1 \xrightarrow{\Phi_2} \ldots \xrightarrow{\Phi_n} z_n)$ {

   for $(z'_n := z_n, i := n; i > 0; i := i - 1)$ $z'_{i-1} := z_{i-1} \wedge \mathtt{pre}(z'_i, \Phi_i)$;

   return $z'_0 \xrightarrow{\Phi_1} z'_1 \xrightarrow{\Phi_2} \ldots \xrightarrow{\Phi_n} z'_n$;

}

Intuitively, the procedure computes the pre-conditions iteratively and backwardly from z_n through $\Phi_n, \Phi_{n-1}, \ldots, \Phi_1$. In short, we backwardly propagate the pre-conditions from z_n to z_0. As a result, all states in the restricted symbolic trace $z'_0 \xrightarrow{\Phi_1} z'_1 \xrightarrow{\Phi_2} \ldots \xrightarrow{\Phi_n} z'_n$ can reach z'_n (i.e., z_n) in this symbolic trace. When we apply $\mathtt{Backward\_Prune}()$ to the trace in figure 4, we get a restricted symbolic trace $z'_0 \xrightarrow{\Phi_1} z'_1 \xrightarrow{\Phi_2} \ldots \xrightarrow{\Phi_n} z'_4$. This restricted symbolic trace differs from the original symbolic trace in z'_1 and z_1. z'_1 have extra constraints, $x_1 < 26$ and $x_3 < 26$, that is the pre-conditions of z_2.

4.2   Projection from Traces to Test Cases

From each symbolic trace, we can construct the following *trace constraint*, which is a pair (K, Θ) and contains enough information to generate a test case. Given a symbolic trace $z_0 \xrightarrow{\Phi_1} z_1 \xrightarrow{\Phi_2} \ldots \xrightarrow{\Phi_n} z_n$, (K, Θ) is defined as follows.

- K is a sequence $\Phi_0 \Phi_1 \ldots \Phi_n$ of global transitions, where Φ_0 is an initial global transition that resets all clocks to zero.
- Θ is a set of inequalities, which specify the timing constraints between global transitions in K. Let t_i denote the variable that records the time when Φ_i is executed. Then $t_i - t_j$ is the time duration between Φ and Φ'. Given an index i and a clock x, $K[i, x] = j$ such that $j \le i$ and x is reset in Φ_j but not in $\Phi_{j+1}, \ldots, \Phi_i$. Θ consists of the following inequalities.
  - $t_{K[i,x]} - t_{K[i,x']} \sim c$, if $x' - x \sim c$ is a constraint in z_i;
  - $t_{i'} - t_{K[i'-1,x]} \sim c$, if $x - 0 \sim c$ is a constraint in $z_{i'-1}$;
  - $t_{K[i'-1,x]} - t_{i'} \sim c$, if $0 - x \sim c$ is a constraint in $z_{i'-1}$,
  where $0 \le i \le n$ and $0 \le i' < n$.

We now want to extract the test-case-related information from trace constraints like (K, Θ). This can be done by removing all global transitions which are not related to the interactions among processes. In K, a global transition is caused by either an internal action or an interaction between the environment processes and the system processes. Here the environment processes refer the PTAs that model the environment, while the system processes refer to the PTAs that specify the behavior of the system. A global transition is *internal* if it does not involve both environment processes and system processes. For blackbox testing (and hence conformance testing), test cases only check the interaction between the SUT and the environment. So our projection step eliminates those global transitions that represent only internal actions from K. Since some global transitions are to be eliminated, all the timing constraints with reference to the eliminated global transitions also have to be eliminated from Θ. Suppose the global transitions in K that are not internal are $\Phi_{i_1}, \Phi_{i_2}, \ldots, \Phi_{i_k}$. Conceptually, the elimination can be carried out with Fourier-Motzkin elimination [12] that projects Θ to the space of dimensions $t_{\Phi_{i_1}}, \ldots, t_{\Phi_{i_k}}$. The following procedure Project() realizes this elimination process.

```
Project(Φ₀Φ₁...Φₙ,Θ) {
    Φ'₀ := Φ₀; Θ' := Θ; j := 1;
    for (i := 1; i ≤ n; i := i + 1)
        if Φᵢ is internal, Θ' := Fourier-Motzkin-elimination(Θ', t_Φᵢ);
        else { Φ'ⱼ := Φᵢ; j := j + 1; }
    return (Φ'₀Φ'₁...Φ'ⱼ,Θ');
}
```

Take the restricted symbolic trace in section 4.1 as an example, its trace constraint is $(\Phi_0\Phi_1\Phi_2\Phi_3\Phi_4, \{t_2 - t_1 < 26, t_3 - t_2 < 26, t_3 - t_1 < 52, t_4 - t_3 < 52\})$. Assume that we want to generate test cases for a network adaptor. We use A_1 and A_2 as environment processes while A_3 as the system process. Project() eliminates Φ_2 and its time variable t_2 from the trace constraint since they are internal to the environment processes.

After we have generated a trace constraint (K, Θ) from Project(), we can further map all global transitions in K to test statements in sequence. Here we use the TTCN [14] test language to explain the mapping. Assume there is a system clock called Time. There are two TTCN commands, START (to start the ticking of a clock from zero) and READTIMER() (to read the current reading of a clock). Given a trace constraint $(\Phi_0\Phi_1 \ldots \Phi_n, \Theta)$, first we start clock Time with statement "START Time" at time t_0. Then iteratively for each $1 \leq i \leq n$,

1. print out the input and output events of Φ_i;
2. print out "READTIMER Time(t_i)" to record the occurrence time of Φ_i; and
3. print out all timing constraints in Θ of the form $x_i - x_j \sim c$ and $x_j - x_i \sim c$, with $j < i$, to check if any timing constraints are violated.

For example, to continue with the restricted symbolic trace in section 4.1, we get the following test case in TTCN format.

```
START Time
?begin
READTIMER Time(t₁)
!collision
READTIMER Time(t₃)
[t₃ - t₁ < 52]
```

?begin
READTIMER Time(t_4)
$[t_4 - t_3 < 52]$

The test case checks if an adaptor retries the transmission within 52 time unit after a bus collision is detected.

4.3   Coverage Annotations of Test Cases

We have presented how to extract a test case from a symbolic trace. Now, we combine all the components to present our algorithm to generate test cases with coverage annotations. The algorithm is as follows.

```
Test_case_generation(C, η) /* C is a CTA; η is the risk condition. */ {
    Let ⟨V, F⟩ := Symbolic_trace_tree(C, η); Coverage := 0;
    While there is still an unchosen trace in ⟨V, F⟩ {
```
Choose a trace $z_0 \overset{\Phi_1}{\rightarrow} z_1 \overset{\Phi_2}{\rightarrow} \ldots \overset{\Phi_m}{\rightarrow} z_m$
```
        from ⟨V, F⟩ that has not been chosen before;
        Let Coverage := the new coverage estimation considering z₀;
        For (i := 0; i ≤ m; i := i + 1) {
            Coverage := the new coverage estimation considering zᵢ and Φᵢ;
            Annotate both zᵢ and Φᵢ in the trace with Coverage;
        }
        Eliminate the internal global transitions form the trace
            to generate a test case with the coverage annotations;
    }
}
```

First, we construct trace-tree with procedure `Symbolic_trace_tree()` in subsection 3.4. Then, we enumerate symbolic traces in the symbolic trace-tree to generate test cases. Here, we specifically leave the flexibility to allow for various policies in generating the test plans in using the test cases in particular orders. The coverage estimation annotated on the test cases are computed according to a chosen test plan.

In our implementation, we adopt the test plan that orders the test cases according to the depth-first ordering of the leaves of their corresponding symbolic traces. This approach has the following advantage in black-box testing. It tends to generate long test cases which could save us time in restarting the SUT. In contrast, if we use several short test cases to reach the same coverage as a long one, then we need to restart the SUT for each of the short ones.

5   Experiment

We have implemented our ideas in **RED** [22, 23, 25], a model-checker/simulator for CTAs and linear hybrid systems. **RED** adopts BDD-like data-structures,

Table 1. Experiment result of the generated test cases

Specification	Trace-tree strategies	Exploration time(s)	Generation time(s)	Steps	# test cases
Audio	*All*	2.21	6.73	131	40
	Risk	1.2	0.99	89	37
	Abstraction	1.94	6.62	122	37
L2CAP	*All*	>3hr	Not available		
	Risk	>3hr			
	Abstraction	13.56	229.07	169	127

CRD (Clock-Restriction Diagrams) for CTAs and HRD (Hybrid-Restriction Diagrams) for linear hybrid systems. We have experimented with two benchmarks, the Philips audio protocol [11, 16] and the Bluetooth L2CAP [9, 24].

In table 1, we show the performance data, which was collected on a Pentium 4 3.2G machine running Mandrake 10. We have implemented the following three strategies to generate the trace-trees.

- *All*: With this strategy, we generate traces to cover the whole reachable state-space.
- *Risk*: We only generate traces that are related to the reachability of a risk test property. Specifically, we use an abstract backward reachability procedure from the risk conditions to compute an approximation of the state space which are backward reachable from a risk state. Then when we do the trace-tree construction, we refine our exploration in this approximation. This makes sure that our test cases, generated from the trace-tree, are highly related to the reachability of the risk condition [24]. The test property used for the Philips audio protocol is that the receiver enters the "ERROR" state. The one for the L2CAP is that the master stays in the "OPEN" state, but the slave enters the "W4_L2CA_DISCONNECT_RSP" state.
- *Abstraction*: We adopt the `Game-Abstraction` technique [23] to simplify the zone representations in the trace exploration. This strategy may sometimes reduce the time for a symbolic trace exploration.

"Exploration time" and "Steps" are the time spent in symbolic trace exploration and the number of calls to `post()` in symbolic trace exploration. "Generation time" is the time spent in test case generation and "# test cases" is the number of generated test cases. For the audio specification, we have explored less symbolic states and generated less test cases when strategies *Risk* and *Abstraction* are adopted. For L2CAP specification, it takes more than three hours in symbolic trace exploration when strategies *All* and *Risk* are adopted. This is due to the sheer size of the CTA for the L2CAP specification. But with strategy *Abstraction*, we have effectively generated test cases for the L2CAP.

We have also collected coverage data in running our test cases. Due to page-limit, we only show two of the charts. Figure 5 shows the cumulative coverage estimations for the Philips audio protocol SUT with strategy *All*. After we have executed the first 4 test cases, we get about 60% coverage in TCM. The ACM

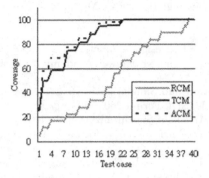
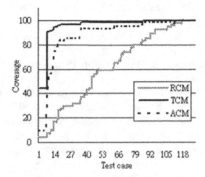

Fig. 5. Accumulative coverage values of the test cases for the Philips audio protocol, strategies is "All"

Fig. 6. Accumulative coverage values of the test cases for the L2CAP protocol, strategies is "Abstraction"

and TCM coverage estimations reach 100% before all test cases are applied to the Philips audio SUT. This is because ACM and TCM are both based on covered transitions and could be less precise in discerning bugs related to dense-time behaviors. Figure 6 shows the estimations for the L2CAP SUT with strategy *Abstract*. The same pattern as in figure 5 is observed. That is, after the first few test cases, we already have a quite high coverage in both TCM and ACM.

On the other hand, the RCM estimations grow much slower than TCM and ACM estimations. This implies that RCM usually have better precision in discerning bugs related to dense-time behaviors. However, for large-scale systems, when the number of global transitions is already pushing the limit of state of the art, ACM and TCM may still offer basic confidence check of the SUT.

6   Conclusion

In this paper, we investigate how to use symbolic techniques to automatically generate test cases for real-time systems. The test cases are annotated with symbolic timing constraints and coverage estimations. Our framework does leave the pace for future work. Especially, the design of various test plans, abstraction techniques, and traversing orders to construct the trace-trees. It will be very interesting to see how the flexibility left in the framework can accommodate various techniques for the test case generation in real-world projects.

References

1. R. Alur, C. Courcoubetis, D.L. Dill. Model Checking for Real-Time Systems. IEEE LICS, 1990.
2. J.R. Burch, E.M. Clarke, K.L. McMillan, D.L.Dill, L.J. Hwang. Symbolic Model Checking: 10^{20} States and Beyond. IEEE LICS, 1990.

3. G.V. Bochmann, A. Petrenko. Protocol Testing: Review of Methods and Relevance for Software Testing. Proceedings of the 1994 ACM SIGSOFT international symposium on Software testing and analysis.
4. L. Bening, H. Foster. Principles of Verifiable RTL Design: a Functional Coding Style Supporting Verification Processes in Verilog,li 2nd ed. Kluwer Academic Publishers, 2001.
5. G. Bucci, A. Fedeli, E. Vicario. Specification and Simulation of Real Time Concurrent Systems Using Standard SDL Tools. SDL Forum 2003: 203-217.
6. E. Clarke, E.A. Emerson, Design and Synthesis of Synchronization Skeletons using Branching-Time Temporal Logic. Proceedings of the Workshop on Logic of Programs, LNCS 131, Springer-Verlag.
7. E. M. Clarke, O. Grumberg, S. Jha, Y. Lu, H. Veith. Counterexample-Guided Abstraction Refinement for Symbolic Model-Checking. J. Assoc. Comput. Mach., vol. 50, no. 5, pp. 752V794, Sept. 2003.
8. D.L. Dill. Timing Assumptions and Verification of Finite-state Concurrent Systems. CAV'89, LNCS 407, Springer-Verlag.
9. J. Haartsen. Bluetooth Specification, version 1.0. http://www.bluetooth.com/.
10. A. Hessel, K.G. Larsen, B. Nielsen, P. Pettersson, A. Skou. Time-Optimal Real-Time Test Case Generation Using Uppaal. FATES 2003.
11. P.-H. Ho, H. Wong-Toi. Automated Analysis of an Audio Control Protocol. CAV 1995, LNCS 939, Springer Verlag, 1995.
12. T.A. Henzinger, X. Nicollin, J. Sifakis, S. Yovine. Symbolic Model Checking for Real-Time Systems. IEEE LICS 1992.
13. H. Wong-Toi. Symbolic Approximations for Verifying Real-Time Systems. Ph.D. dissertation, Stanford Univ., Stanford, CA, 1995.
14. ISO/IEC 9646:IT-OSI-Conformance testing methodology and framework,1996.
15. M. Krichen, S. Tripakis. Black-box Conformance Testing for Real-Time Systems. In SPIN'04 Workshop on Model Checking Software.
16. K.G. Larsen, P. Pettersson, W. Yi. Diagnostic Model-Checking for Real-Time Systems. In Proceedings of the 4th DIMACS Workshop on Verification and Control of Hybrid Systems, New Brunswick, New Jersey, 22-24 October, 1995.
17. D. Lee, M. Yannakakis. Principles and Methods of Testing Finite State Machines - A Survey. Proceedings of The IEEE, Vol. 84, No. 8, August 1996, pp. 1090-1123.
18. B. Nielsen, A. Skou. Automated Test Generation from Timed Automata. International Journal on Software Tools for Technology Transfer (STTT), 4, 2002.
19. P. Pettersson, K.G. Larsen, UPPAAL2k. in Bulletin of the European Association for Theoretical Computer Science, volume 70, pages 40-44, 2000.
20. P. Rashinkar, P. Paterson, L. Singh. System-on-a-chip Verificatoin, Methodology and Techniques. Kluwer Academic Publishers, 2001.
21. J. Springintveld, F. Vaandrager, P.R. D'Argenio Testing Timed Automata. Theoretical Computer Science, Vol. 254, Issue 1-2, 2001.
22. F. Wang. Symbolic Verification of Complex Real-Time Systems with Clock-Restriction Diagram, in Proceedings of FORTE, August 2001, Cheju Island, Korea.
23. F. Wang, G.-D. Huang, F. Yu. Symbolic Simulation of Real-Time Concurrent Systems. RTCSA2003, LNCS 2968, Springer-Verlag.
24. F. Wang, G.-D. Huang, Fang Yu. Numerical Coverage Estimation for Dense-Time Systems. in proceedings of FORTE'2003, LNCS 2767, Springer-Verlag.
25. F. Wang. Symbolic Parametric Safety Analysis of Linear Hybrid Systems with BDD-like Data-Structures. CAV 2004, LNCS 3114, Springer-Verlag.
26. S. Yovine. Kronos: A Verification Tool for Real-Time Systems. International Journal of Software Tools for Technology Transfer, Vol. 1, Nr. 1/2, October 1997.

Selective Search in Bounded Model Checking
of Reachability Properties*

Maciej Szreter

Institute of Computer Science, PAS
Warsaw, Poland

Abstract. Bounded Model Checking (BMC) encodes a model checking
problem in the propositional logic. Diagnosing the resulting formula to
be satisfiable provides a counterexample. While surprisingly efficient for
many complex systems, in general BMC still fails to be complete and is
a method of falsification rather then validation. The major obstacle is
satisfiability testing (SAT). The paper introduces a selective search to
the standard DLL SAT algorithm, allowing to profit from several optimization techniques proposed for non-symbolic methods. Partial-order
reductions are shown as an example of selective search. Preliminary experimental results confirm that the selective search can significantly improve the effectiveness of BMC.

1 Introduction

The general idea of BMC is to encode in the propositional logic a model checking
problem. Because models can be huge, usually the search takes into account only
a part of the whole state space, increasing the range of search if the evaluated
fragment was proved not to contain any counterexample or returning the found
one. The practical realization of the method is possible thanks to developing
efficient SAT-testing algorithms (solvers).

Many algorithms reducing the state space searched were invented for explicit-
state model checking. One of the most successful optimization approaches is a
selective search – constructing a reduced model preserving the properties of the
full one. The reduction consists in restricting the transition relation, exploring
only a subset of system transitions enabled in a state. A natural question is
whether this techniques could be applied to logic-based symbolic verification.
The formulation of the optimization problem is different in this case. Symbolic
representation and relevant operations deal with sets of states, so it must be
guaranteed that the reduction is correct with respect to all the system states.
There is no direct access to processed states (no notion of a searched state nor
a search stack) and determining states described by symbolic formulas may be
costly.

---

* Partly supported by the Ministry of Science and the Information Society Technologies under the grant No. 3T11C01128.

D.A. Peled and Y.-K. Tsay (Eds.): ATVA 2005, LNCS 3707, pp. 159–173, 2005.

In this paper the problem of efficient SAT testing in BMC reachability checking is examined. The general idea consists in supplying the solver with additional
information characterizing the structure of a tested formula. When a general approach sees a solver as a "black box", we loose generality with hope of improving
the efficiency. [Str00] introduces a simple strategy of free variable decision – a
step towards DFS symbolic search. Our original contribution extends it to the
full DFS search (Alg. SAT-DFS-2), and finally parametrizes it with a selective
search method (Alg. SAT-POR). The reduction is obtained by assigning subformulas of a formula encoding an instance of BMC with information about depth
on the symbolic path and actions they encode, and using this information by the
modified solver. Partial order reductions are chosen as a selective search realization, which is possible thanks to enforcing the DFS search order. Preliminary
results show that the selective search can significantly improve the efficiency
particularly in the case of unsatisfiable formulas, and justify the future research
on efficient implementing the presented ideas.

Related Work. BMC was introduced in [BCCZ99] and is a subject of intensive
research. [BCC+03] offers good introduction and discussion of related research.
Despite many optimizations, in most cases BMC remains incomplete.

Partial order reductions constitute a group of optimization methods reducing
the size of the state space to be searched by model checking algorithms. The
most important groups of methods are the *stubborn set*, the *ample set* and the
persistent set approaches [CGMP99]. All the above-mentioned methods were
proposed in the context of DFS exploration. There were however attempts to
change the search algorithm to BFS, which allows for applying symbolic model
checking methods [ABH+97].

2   Preliminaries

2.1   Propositional Logic

Let $\mathcal{PV}$ be a set of propositional *variables*. $\mathcal{F}$ is a set of *propositional formulas*,
and for $\alpha \in \mathcal{F}$, we denote by $\mathcal{PV}(\alpha)$ the set of propositional variables in α. An
assignment A is a function assigning to every variable a logical value of 1 or
0. This function is extended to formulas. A formula is *satisfiable* iff there is an
assignment for which it is assigned with 1. For a variable v, v and $\neg v$ are *literals*.
A *clause* is a disjunction of literals, and a formula in *Conjunctive Normal Form*
(CNF) is a conjunction of clauses.

Satisfiability-preserving conversion to CNF. The majority of SAT algorithms work with CNF formulas. The efficient transformation [PG86] is usually
used to test satisfiability: given a formula $\gamma \in \mathcal{F}$, it produces a satisfiability-
preserving CNF formula $toCNF(\gamma)$ of polynomial length, over the set of propositional variables extending the propositional variables $\mathcal{PV}(\gamma)$ with fresh vari-
ables from the set $\mathcal{PV}^C \subseteq \mathcal{PV}$ ($l_\alpha \in \mathcal{PV}^C$ represents a subformula α of γ,
$p \in \mathcal{PV}$ is denoted by l_p for simplicity of notation, but we do not introduce a

new literal). Let us define a function $properClauses : \mathcal{F} \to 2^C$ assigning to every non-propositional subformula of γ a set of clauses (we show the case of propositional variables and conjunction, the remaining ones can be found in [PG86]):

$$properClauses(\gamma) = \begin{cases} true & \text{for } \gamma \in \mathcal{PV}, \\ (l_\alpha \vee \neg l_\gamma) \wedge (l_\beta \vee \neg l_\gamma) \wedge (l_\gamma \vee \neg l_\alpha \vee \neg l_\beta) & \text{for } \gamma = \alpha \wedge \beta, \end{cases} \tag{1}$$

Let $\mathcal{PV}^C(\alpha)$ denote the literals introduced by the translation of α. The function $toCNF : \mathcal{F} \to 2^C$ is defined as follows:

$$toCNF(\gamma) = \begin{cases} true & \text{for } \gamma \in \mathcal{PV}, \\ toCNF(\alpha) \wedge properClauses(\gamma) & \text{for } \gamma = \neg\alpha, \\ toCNF(\alpha) \wedge toCNF(\beta) \wedge properClauses(\gamma) \\ \quad \text{for } \gamma = \alpha \sim \beta, \text{ and } \sim \in \{\vee, \wedge, \implies, \Leftrightarrow\} \end{cases} \tag{2}$$

For any assignment A of $toCNF(\alpha)$, for every subformula α of φ, if $A(toCNF(\alpha)) = 1$, then we have $A(\beta) = A(l_\beta)$ for every subformula β of α (in particular, $A(\alpha) = A(l_\alpha)$). $\alpha \in \mathcal{F}$ is satisfiable iff the formula $toCNF(\alpha) \wedge l_\alpha$ is satisfiable.

Davis-Loveland-Logemann (DLL) SAT algorithm

The DLL algorithm forms the basis for most modern SAT solvers. Practically efficient implementations appeared about three decades after inventing the theoretical framework, providing clever solutions of key operations: **variable decision (VD)**, **Boolean constraint propagation (BCP)** and **conflict-based learning (CBL)**. It is based on a DFS search through the space of assignments, taking advantage of advanced optimization and implementation techniques. Alg. 1 presents the generic $SAT()$. The formula φ to be checked is given in the CNF form. Below the main parts of the algorithm are briefly explained:

```
input: χ =
          toCNF(φ) ∧ l_φ
deduce();
while true do
    d = d + 1;
    if decide() =
    ALL-ASSIGNED
    then
        ⌊ return A;
    if deduce() =
    CONFLICT then
        (d, c_l) =
        diagnose();
        if d = 0 then
            ⌊ return ∅;
        erase(d);
        ⌊ χ = χ ∧ c_l;
```

Algorithm 1. $SAT(\varphi)$

(VD) The search is driven by assigning a logical value to a free variable chosen by $decide()$ (when no free variables, ALL-ASSIGNED is returned). Many heuristics were proposed to this aim. The *decision level* is the number of decided variables in the current assignment.

(BCP) BCP efficiently propagates every assigned variable, in order to identify *unit clauses*, i.e., the clauses of one unassigned literal only and the other literals evaluating to 0. Obviously, a clause composed of one unassigned literal is unit. An unassigned literal in a unit clause must be assigned 1 in order for the formula to be satisfied. If for some variable, BCP implies both logical values of 0 and 1, a *conflict* is detected.

(CBL) CBL on the basis of a conflict assignment produces a *learned clause* (added to the working set of clauses), which excludes partial assignments which imply the current conflict. *diagnose*() identifies a partial assignment responsible for the conflict, returns a learned clause and computes the decision level to which the search backtracks. *erase*(d) unassigns the variables assigned at the levels greater than d.

The above procedures are repeated until either a satisfying assignment is found or a conflict occurs at the level 0 (not dependent on any decision). Implementation details can be found in [MMZ$^+$01].

2.2 Models of Systems

A *Kripke structure* is a triple $\mathcal{K} = (S, s^0, \longrightarrow)$, where S is a set of *states*, $s^0 \in S$ - an *initial state* , and $\longrightarrow \subseteq S \times \Sigma \times S$ is a labeled transition relation for same fixed set Σ of *actions*. Elements of $\longrightarrow$ are called *transitions*. Given a set of propositional variables $\mathcal{PV}$, a *model* for a Kripke structure $\mathcal{K}$ is a pair $\mathcal{M} = (\mathcal{K}, V)$, where $V : S \longrightarrow 2^{\mathcal{PV}}$ is *a labeling function*. We call $V(s)$ the *valuation* of the state $s \in S$.

Some actions of the modeled system can be not relevant from the point of view of tested properties. $a \in \Sigma$ is a *label of invisible transition*, if for each pair of states s, s' such that $s \xrightarrow{a} s'$, we have $V(s) = V(s')$. We say that $e \in \longrightarrow$ is *enabled* in $s \in S$ if $\exists s' \in S$ s.t. $e = s \longrightarrow s'$, and by *enabled*(s) $\subseteq \Sigma$ we denote the set of actions labeling transitions enabled in s. A *path* in $\mathcal{K}$ is a (finite or infinite) sequence $\pi = s_0 \longrightarrow s_1 \longrightarrow \ldots$, where $s_0, s_1, \ldots \in S$. We use the standard notions related to paths. A state $s \in S$ is *reachable*, if there is a path in the model from s^0 to s. The set of all reachable states of $\mathcal{K}$ is denoted by $Reach_\mathcal{K}$.

A set of structures can be used to model a concurrent system, with every structure modeling a process. These structures can be composed into a global (*product*) structure by a standard multi-synchronization approach: the transitions that do not correspond to a shared action are interleaved, whereas the transitions labeled with a shared action are synchronized. Also the valuation function is extended, with disjoint sets of labels in components. The detailed definition is given in [PWZ02] (for more general case of timed automata).

2.3 Bounded Model Checking of Reachability Properties

Let $\mathcal{M} = (\mathcal{K}, V)$ be a (possibly product) model of a system, and let $\varphi \in \mathcal{F}$ over the set of propositions labeling states of $\mathcal{K}$ be a *reachability property*. For $v \in \mathcal{PV}(\varphi)$ and a state s, we say that v is satisfied in s iff $v \in V(s)$. This notion naturally extends to Boolean connectives. A reachability property φ is true in $\mathcal{M}$ iff $\exists s \in Reach_\mathcal{K}$ such that φ holds in s.

Let denote by $d(\mathcal{M})$ the length of the longest loop-free path in $\mathcal{M}$ starting from the initial state. Formally, let π' be a maximal path $\pi = s_0, \ldots, s_m$ with $s_0 = s^0$ and $s_i \neq s_j$ for $i \neq j$. Then $d(\mathcal{M}) = m$. It is obvious that a state s is reachable in $\mathcal{M}$ iff it is reachable on a k-path for $k \leq d(\mathcal{M})$. BMC reachability testing is based on this fact. A sequence $\mathbf{w}[1], \ldots, \mathbf{w}[n]$ of $\mathcal{PV}$ variables is a *state vector*, and a function $\theta : S \to \{1, 0\}^g$ uniquely assigns a Boolean encoding over $g = \lceil log_2(|S|) \rceil$ bits to every state. Let $\mathbf{w}_0, \ldots, \mathbf{w}_k$ be a *symbolic k-path* of state vectors representing all the k-paths in $\mathcal{M}$.

The formula $I_s(\mathbf{w})$ encodes a state s over $\mathbf{w}$, that is is satisfied in an assignment A iff $A(\mathbf{w}) = \theta(s)$. The formula $T(\mathbf{w}, a, \mathbf{w}')$ encodes the transition $a \in \Sigma$: it is satisfied in an assignment A iff $A(\mathbf{w}) = \theta(s)$, $A(\mathbf{w}') = \theta(s')$ and $s \xrightarrow{a} s'$. $\longrightarrow$ is encoded by a disjunction of encoded actions over Σ: $T(\mathbf{w}, \mathbf{w}') = \bigvee_{a \in \Sigma} T(\mathbf{w}, a, \mathbf{w}')$. The symbolic path representing all the k-paths in $\mathcal{M}$ beginning in s^0 is encoded by $path_k = I_{s_0}(\mathbf{w}_0) \wedge \bigwedge_{i=0}^{k-1} T(\mathbf{w}_i, \mathbf{w}_{i+1})$. Concerning the property to be verified, expressed by a formula $\varphi \in \mathcal{F}$, the propositional formula $[\varphi](\mathbf{w}_k)$ encodes over the vector $\mathbf{w}_k$ the set of states of $\mathcal{M}$ in which φ is true. For the implementations of $I_s(\mathbf{w})$, $T(\mathbf{w}, \mathbf{w}')$ and $[\varphi](\mathbf{w})$, see [PWZ02].

The formula φ_k represents a symbolic k-path, with the property φ satisfied in the final state: $\varphi_k = path_k \wedge [\varphi](\mathbf{w}_k)$.

Lemma 1. *The formula φ_k is satisfiable iff there is a k-path $\pi = s_0, \ldots, s_k$ in $\mathcal{M}$, with $s_0 = s^0$ and φ is satisfied in s_k.*

BMC encodes φ_k for k iteratively increased from 1 to $d(\mathcal{M})$ and tests for satisfiability. If this formula is satisfied, the property φ holds in the system, and the algorithm stops, otherwise the property is diagnosed to not hold in the system if the diameter is reached. The important problem of detecting the latter fact is not discussed in this paper.

3 Selective Search in BMC

In this section the main ideas of the paper are presented. First, we introduce functions describing the structure of the formula φ_k. Secondly, $SAT()$ (Alg. 1) is extended to SAT-DFS-1 (partial DFS, [Str00]), SAT-DFS-2 (full DFS) and finally to SAT-POR using a selective search. The idea of selective search is that when checking the property in the state s of a model $\mathcal{M} = ((S, s^0, \to), V)$ of a concurrent system, instead of exploring all the transitions corresponding to $enabled(s)$, a subset $ample(s) \subseteq enabled(s)$ suffices to determine whether the property holds.

3.1 Assigning the Structure Information to φ_k

Depth on search path. We assign a depth on the symbolic k-path to the subformulas of φ_k, as well as to the clauses and variables of $toCNF(\varphi_k)$:

⋄ **subformulas of** φ_k The partial function $depth : \mathcal{F} \to 2^{\mathbb{N}}$ assigns to every subformula α of φ_k depths[1] on the symbolic path encoded by α:

$$depth(\alpha) = \{k \mid \alpha \text{ is a subformula of } [\varphi](\mathbf{w}_k)\} \cup$$
$$\{i \mid \alpha \text{ is a subformula of } T(\mathbf{w}_{i-1}, \mathbf{w}_i), \text{ for } \alpha \notin \mathbf{w}_{i-1}\} \cup$$
$$\{0 \mid \text{ for the remaining subformulas of } \varphi_k\}.$$

The last case includes the formulas $I_{s^0}(\mathbf{w}_0)$, $\bigwedge_{i=0}^{k-1} T(\mathbf{w}_i, \mathbf{w}_{i+1})$[2], $path_k$ and $path_k \wedge [\varphi](\mathbf{w}_k)$ Notice that each subformula of φ_k may have at most two depths assigned (because φ_k is defined over vectors $\mathbf{w}_i$ as propositional variables, a subformula can encode at most both postcondition of some action and precondition of another action at some depth); moreover, $depth(v) = \{i\}$ for each $v \in \mathbf{w}_i$.

⋄ **clauses of** $toCNF(\varphi_k)$ In $toCNF(\alpha)$ (p. 161) we applied the function $properClauses$ assigning to every subformula of α a set of clauses. Because every clause of $toCNF(\alpha)$ is generated by exactly one formula, we can also define the function $properClauses^{-1} : C \to \mathcal{F}$.

We define the partial function $depth^C : C \to 2^{\mathbb{N}}$ assigning to a clause of $toCNF(\varphi_k)$ depths of the formula which generated this clause:

$$depth^C(c) = depth(properClauses^{-1}(c))$$

A partial function $depth\_clauses : \mathbb{N} \to 2^C$ returns the clauses associated with a depth: $depth\_clauses(i) = \{c \in toCNF(\varphi_k) \mid i \in depth^C(c)\}$.

⋄ **variables of** $toCNF(\varphi_k)$ The function $depth$ assigns depth on the symbolic path to the variables of $\mathcal{PV}(\varphi_k) = \bigcup_{0 \le i \le k} \mathbf{w}_i$ (these variables are subformulas of φ_k). Now we extend $depth()$ to the literals of $\mathcal{PV}^C(\varphi_k)$:

$$depth(l) = \{d \mid (\exists c \in toCNF(\varphi_k)) \ l \in c \text{ and } d \in depth^C(c)\}$$

A function $CNF\_vars : \mathbb{N} \to 2^{\mathcal{PV}^C}$ associates with each depth the clause variables occurring in the clauses of this depth. Formally $CNF\_vars(i) = \{v \in \mathcal{PV}^C \mid (\exists c \in C) \ c \in depth\_clauses(i) \text{ and } v \in c\}$. A function $depth\_vars : \mathbb{N} \to 2^{\mathcal{PV}^C(\varphi_k)}$ gives the variables associated with a depth: $depth\_vars(i) = \mathbf{w}_i \cup CNF\_vars(i)$.

Encoded actions of a depth in the path. Given a depth on the search path, we define functions assigning to subformulas, clauses and variables actions encoded by these, in way analogous as we did for depths:

⋄ **subformulas of** φ_k The partial function $action : \mathcal{F} \times \mathbb{N} \to 2^{\Sigma}$ assigns the encoded actions to the subformulas of φ_k:

$$action(\beta, i) = \{a \mid \beta \text{ is a subformula of } T(\mathbf{w}_{i-1}, a, \mathbf{w}_i)\} \text{ for } 1 \le i \le k \quad (3)$$

---

[1] The notion of *depth* should not be confused with the decision *level* (Alg. $SAT()$) representing the number of decision variables in the current assignment (see p. 161).

[2] But not the formulas $T(\mathbf{w}_i, \mathbf{w}_{i+1})$.

Notice that for variables $v \in \mathbf{w}_i$, $action(v,i) = \Sigma$, because for every $a \in Act$, the formula $T(\mathbf{w}_i, a, \mathbf{w}_{i+1})$ is defined over both $\mathbf{w}_i$ and $\mathbf{w}_{i+1}$.

$\diamond$ **clauses of** $toCNF(\varphi_k)$ We define a function $action^C : C \times \mathbb{N} \to 2^\Sigma$ as follows:

$$action^C(c,i) = action(properClauses^{-1}(c),i)$$

A partial function $action\_clauses : \Sigma \times \mathbb{N} \to 2^C$ returns the clauses encoding an action a at the depth i: $action\_clauses(a,i) = \{c \in C \mid a \in action^C(c,i)\}$.

$\diamond$ **variables of** $toCNF(\varphi_k)$ State variables of φ_k have actions already assigned, because are subformulas of φ_k. We extend the function $action$ to the literals of $\mathcal{PV}^C(\varphi_k)$:

$$action(l,i) = \{a \mid (\exists c \in toCNF(\varphi_k))\ l \in c \text{ and } a \in action^C(c,i)\}$$

A function $action\_vars : \mathcal{PV}^C \times \mathbb{N} \to 2^\Sigma$ assigns actions to variables. Formally for $v \in \mathcal{PV}^C$, $action\_vars(v,i) = \{a \in \Sigma \mid (\exists c \in C)\ action^C(c,i) = a \text{ and } v \in c\}$.

3.2   SAT Algorithms Using Formula Structure Information

Now we present algorithms extending $SAT()$ (Alg. 1) by making use of the structure information concerning φ_k. We give general ideas with only preliminary implementation techniques, so there is much space for improvements.

SAT-DFS-1: variable decision. [Str00] discusses many changes to the general SAT algorithm. A step towards DFS by changing the order of free variable selection proved to be successful. The standard procedure $decide()$ can result in stepwise construction of the fragments of the path, which may lead to a conflict because these parts do not respect the transition relation. So $decide()$ is changed: a variable $currD \in [0,k]$ represents the smallest depth on the symbolic path such that for $0 \le i < currD$, every variable from the set $depth\_var(i)$ is assigned. The correct value of $currD$ is maintained: increased after assigning the last variable of the current depth and decreased after backtracking, if necessary. The modified procedure $decide\_dfs()$ chooses an unassigned variable from the set $depth\_vars(currD)$. It suffices to decide only state variables of $\mathbf{w}_{currD+1}$, the remaining ones are implied.[3] The experimental results given in Sect. 5 confirm the claim of [Str00] that SAT-DFS-1 alone improves the overall performance. For us, however, it is a prerequisite for application of a selective search.

SAT-DFS-2: postponing deduction. SAT-DFS-1 implements a partial DFS, because is restricted to VS. In Fig. 1 it is depicted a fragment of a symbolic path $..., \mathbf{w}_1, \mathbf{w}_2, \mathbf{w}_3, ...$ Braces at the left side represent the depths assigned to subformulas. Gray fragments depict subformulas already assigned. Fig. **a)** shows

---

[3] Notice that the depth assignments of the variables of $depth\_vars(0)$ are determined by the encoding of the initial state, so there is no variable decision on this depth. When there is no free variable of $\mathbf{w}_{currD+1}$, $currD$ is incremented.

that (assuming $currD = 1$) deducing clauses of $currD > 1$ may lead to assignments which must be withdrawn when there will be no assignment of $\mathbf{w}_2$ consistent with the transition relation. SAT-DFS-2 (Alg. 2) extends SAT-DFS-1 by restricting deduction to clauses of $depth^C(currD)$ and performing *postponed deductions* after increasing $currD$. Our solution is to stepwise extend the search to clauses and variables encoding consecutive depths. In Fig. **b)**, having assigned the depth 1, the search proceeds at the depth 2. After completing it (Fig. **c)**), the postponed deduction is performed in order to assign the variables and clauses of the depth 3 induced by assigned variables of lower depths (notice that some variables may already be assigned, namely those encoding two depths).

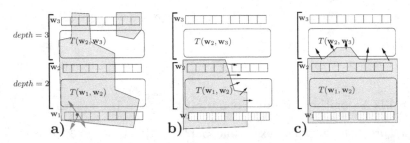

Fig. 1. a) *deduce*() not restricted to $currD$, **b)** *deduce*() restricted to $currD = 2$, **c)** postponed deduction after increasing $currD$ to 3

⋄ **deduction restricted to the current depth** − *deduce_dfs*(). A clause $c \in toCNF(\varphi_k)$ is taken into account by BCP iff $currD \in depth^C(c)$. Learned clauses are never ignored. Notice that no depths are assigned to learned clauses and to literals on the basis of learned clauses.

An *assignment stack* is a data structure used by the solver: it contains vectors of variables assigned at all the levels; first element is a decision variable for every level with the exception of level 0 where all variables are implied by unit clauses. In $SAT()$, the stack grows only at the current level. The consequence of the above deduction scheme is that it can grow at all decision levels when performing postponed deductions. This is shown in Fig. 2 for an example system[4]. The path depth 1 is completed after deciding the variables v_1, v_2 and v_3 (these decision variables imply further assignments, possibly conflicts happen and are resolved). The subformulas of depths 2 and 3 are uniquely determined by decision variables of the depths 0 and 1, possibly because some learned clauses were added earlier.

For the use in backtracking, we maintain the information how are depths and levels related in the current assignment: first, a function $initDepth : \mathbb{N} \rightarrow \mathbb{N}$ assigns to each level the value of $currD$ when the level was initiated. Secondly, for every initiated depth we maintain the size of the search stack at all levels: the function n_j^i gives the number of assigned variables for the level i when the depth j was initiated.

---

[4] Notice that all the variables of the depth 0 are implied without a decision, because the initial state s^0, uniquely determines assignments of $\mathbf{w}_0$ variables.

◇ **postponed deduction** – *PostponedDeduction*(). As soon as $currD$ is incremented, it is checked whether some clauses of the new depth are unit or conflicting. This is done by re-assigning already assigned variables beginning from the decision level 0, so that each implied variable is assigned at the depth of this implication. If a clause is found to be unit, the implied variable is assigned at the maximal search level of literals in the clause. For example, if the clause $(v_1 \lor v_2 \lor v_3)$ is unit because v_1 is assigned at the level 1 and v_2 is assigned at the level 2, v_3 is implied at the level 2 – when re-assigning v_1, the unit implication waits for v_2 to be re-assigned.

◇ **conflict analysis** – *diagnose_dfs*(). If during the postponed deduction a conflict occurs when re-assigning a variable assigned at the decision level n smaller than the current decision level, we set the decision level to n (erasing variables assigned at depths bigger than n, that is executing $erase\_dfs(n + 1)$). Moreover it can happen that conflicting implied literals (v and $\neg v$ for some variable v) are assigned at different decision levels. In such a case, we perform the conflict analysis on the higher level.

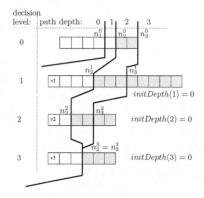

Fig. 2. Assignment stack with path depths. Variables assigned at $currD \in \{2, 3\}$ are shown in gray.

◇ **backtracking** – *erase_dfs*(). When returning to the level i, we reduce the path depth to $c = initDepth(i)$, unassigning all the variables assigned at levels greater than i, and for every level $j < i$, variables assigned after n_c^j. We reduce the number of conflicts in this way, because variables corresponding to depths greater than c are removed from the assignment stack.

For example in Fig. 2, assume that a conflict occurs at the level 3 for $currD = 3$, and the search returns to the level 2. The path depth is reduced to $initDepth(2) = 0$ and the variables assigned at levels 0, 1 and 2 corresponding to depths 2 and 3 can be withdrawn (in gray in the figure), resulting in smaller numbers of conflicts.

SAT-POR: selective search. SAT-POR (Alg. 3) extends SAT-DFS-2 by processing only variables and clauses of φ_k relevant not because of the basis of depth, but also the encoded actions, with subset of relevant actions chosen by the selective search.

◇ **selective search** – *CalculateSelected*(). The selective search is introduced: after incrementing $currD$, the assignments current assignment A of $\mathbf{w}_{currD-1}$ determines the global system state $s_{currD-1}$ (i.e. $s_{currD-1} = \theta^{-1}(A(\mathbf{w}_{currD-1}))$). Below we describe how the search is reduced to formulas encoding the actions from the reduced set $selected(currD) \subseteq \Sigma$, choosen by the selective search $selected(currD) = ample(s_{currD-1})$. [5]

$\diamond$ **deduction restricted to selected actions of the current depth** – $deduce\_por()$. The aim is not to consider clauses and variables encoding only ignored actions. Thus BCP considers a clause cl iff either

- $action(cl, currD) \cap selected(currD) \neq \emptyset$ (clause encodes some selected actions), or
- $action(cl, currD) = \emptyset$ (clause does not encode actions at all - it may encode the reachability property φ or disjunction of formulas encoding actions).

Learned clauses are treated in the same way as in $deduce\_dfs()$.

input: $\chi = toCNF(\varphi_k) \wedge l_{\varphi_k}$
$deduce\_dfs()$;
while *true* **do**
    $d = d + 1$;
    if $decide\_dfs() =$
    $ALL\text{-}ASSIGNED$ **then**
       if $currD = k$ **then**
       return A;
       $currD = currD + 1$;
       $PostponedDeduction()$;
    if $deduce\_dfs() =$
    $CONFLICT$ **then**
       $(d, c_l) =$
       $diagnose\_dfs()$;
       if $d = 0$ **then** return $\emptyset$;
       $currD = erase\_dfs(d)$;
       $\chi = \chi \wedge c_l$;

Algorithm 2. Alg. $SAT(\varphi_k)$ implementing BMC-DFS-2

input: $\chi = toCNF(\varphi_k) \wedge l_{\varphi_k}$
$deduce\_por()$;
while *true* **do**
    $d = d + 1$;
    if $decide\_dfs() =$
    $ALL\text{-}ASSIGNED$ **then**
       if $currD = k$ **then**
       return A;
       $currD = currD + 1$;
       $CalculateSelected()$;
       $RestrictT()$;
       $PostponedDeduction()$;
    if $deduce\_por() =$
    $CONFLICT$ **then**
       $(d, c_l) =$
       $diagnose\_por()$;
       if $d = 0$ **then** return $\emptyset$;
       $currD = erase\_dfs(d)$;
       $\chi = \chi \wedge c_l$;

Algorithm 3. Alg. $SAT(\varphi_k)$ implementing DFS-POR

$\diamond$ **variable decision** – $decide\_dfs()$. In order to comply with the general reduction rule no variables encoding only ignored actions should be decided. The simplest solution is to choose only variables of $\mathbf{w}_{currD}$ (the same as in SAT-DFS-2).

$\diamond$ **restricting transition relation** – $RestrictT()$. Assume that the depth $currD = i$ is completed and $currD = i + 1$ is to be explored. In order to restrict the search to selected actions the formula $T(\mathbf{w}_i, \mathbf{w}_{i+1})$ is substituted with

---

[5] Notice that a reduction is obtained even without applying the selective search, namely disabled actions are ignored: $selected(currD) = enabled(s_{currD-1})$.

$T_{red}(\mathbf{w}_i, \mathbf{w}_{i+1}) = \bigvee_{a \in selected(i)} T(\mathbf{w}_i, a, \mathbf{w}_{i+1})$. We remove from the working set χ the clauses of $toCNF(T(\mathbf{w}_i, \mathbf{w}_{i+1}))$ and add ones of $toCNF(T_{red}(\mathbf{w}_i, \mathbf{w}_{i+1}))$, we also add the clause $(l_{T_{red}(\mathbf{w}_i, \mathbf{w}_{i+1})})$. The above clauses are removed when backtracking to the depth i. Removing and adding clauses is a costly operation and a more advanced solution should be applied.

◇ **conflict analysis** − $diagnose\_por()$. SAT-DFS-2 worked with all the variables and clauses, changing the order of exploration. SAT-POR chooses relevant variables and clauses depending on the current assignment. The consequence is that the conflict analysis must be extended, because some decision variables although not present in a learned clause, may implicate the resolved conflict (states on the path and ample set selection depend on them). We applied the very simple solution: substituted a search-based learned clause generation algorithm with returning disjunction of all the decision variables negated with respect to their assignment. In this way the learned clause is always associated with sets of actions selected when the conflict occurred.

4 Partial Order Reductions

So far we used an abstract notion of a selective search. Now we apply the well known approach of partial order reductions.

In the interleaving semantics the executed actions are interleaved in all possible ways. The method consists in constructing a reduced state graph, potentially smaller than the full state graph. Usually algorithms choosing ample sets are characterized *conditions* which must be fulfilled in order to preserve the required class of properties. For preserving reachability, the following conditions suffice: [CGMP99]

- **C0 (Emptiness)**: $ample(s) = \emptyset$ iff $enabled(s) = \emptyset$.
- **C1 (Faithful decomposition)**: for every path starting from the state s, a transition that is dependent on some transition in $ample(s)$ cannot be executed before a transition from $ample(s)$.
- **C2 (Cycle closing)**: for every cycle in the reduced state space there is at least one fully expanded node.
- **C3 (Visibility)**: if $ample(s)$ contains a visible transition, then the state s is fully expanded, that is $ample(s) = enabled(s)$.

Combining BMC and POR. Let φ_k encode the BMC problem introduced above and be tested by SAT-POR. Because the search for a satisfying assignment is performed in DFS mode, the current assignment of vectors $\mathbf{w}_0, \ldots, \mathbf{w}_{currD}$ always determines a path $s_0, \ldots, s_{currD}$ of the model. In $CalculateSelected()$, **C2** is checked on the path $s_0, \ldots, s_{currD}$ while the remaining conditions are calculated with respect to s_{currD}.

Concerning invisible actions, we restrict the notion of invisibility only to propositions occurring in the reachability property.

5   Experimental Results

The DLL algorithm outlined in Alg. 1 has been implemented in many solvers. We implemented the described algorithms into ZChaff. Verics [NNP+04] BMC module was extended in order to provide necessary information. Our experiments were performed on a Linux machine with 600 MHz clock and 256 MB memory. The following parameters are given: n is the number of processes, k - path length, and L_1, L_2 denote the number of local transitions added to the model sequentially to the local transitions, in order to show how increasing the effectiveness of the selective search influences the effectiveness of the BMC algorithm. ML is maximal search level, and ND, NI, NC and NL are numbers of variable decisions, implications, learned clauses added and literals in learned clauses, respectively.

5.1   Mutual Exclusion Benchmark (Table 1)

The system consists of $n + 1$ automata modeling n processes P_i and a shared variable X coordinating exclusive access to the critical resource (Fig. 3).

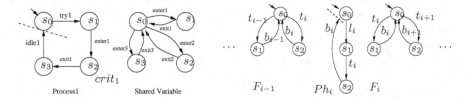

Fig. 3. Simplified Fischer's mutual exclusion (left), Dining Philosophers (right)

The following reduction is applied: if a local transition is enabled, it is choosen as a singleton ample set. **C0** is trivially satisfied. **C1** holds, because every local action is the only one locally enabled in a component state, and it cannot prevent from executing any other action. **C2** holds because every cycle in the reduced space involves a state where for all processes no local action is enabled, thus all actions *enter* are in the ample set. **C3** holds because processes enter end exit their critical sections by synchronous transitions.

Property describing unreachable states. Our simple mutex system is correct, as it guarantees that no pair of processes is in their critical sections. In states violating this property the following formula is satisfied: $\varphi^1 = \bigvee_{1 \le i, j \le n, i \ne j} crit_i \wedge crit_j$.

Property describing reachable states. The formula $\varphi^2 = crit_1$ represents global states in which P_1 is in its critical section. In the full model, the state in which φ^2 holds, is reachable with two transitions, namely P_{i_1} performs *try* and *enter*. In the reduced model, the state is reachable by $n + 1$ transitions, because the reduction first chooses the *try* in all the processes and only then *enter* becomes selected. DFS-POR is slower than the other algorithms, but for the same instances of φ_k less operations are executed. In the satisfying assignment found by DFS-POR, 467 of 1282 variables remain free.

Exploring the model's diameter. In order to consider a reachability property true only in the last state of every path of model depth we have modified the system by cutting cycles (dashed line) and adding an additional state s_4 so that the action *idle* leads from the state s_3 to s_4. The proposition *final* is true in s_4 and the property $\varphi^3 = \bigwedge_{i=1}^{n} final_i$ expresses that all the processes reach their final states. This state is reachable by a path of the length equal to the diameter and is on top of all the "diamonds" formed by independent actions - so we can relax **C3** and choose a visible transition *leave* to ample sets.

Table 1. Time bold–formula SAT, numbers in exp notation rounded

	SAT				DFS-SAT-1				DFS-POR			
k	ML/ND	NI	NC/NL	time	ML/ND	NI	NC/NL	time	ML/ND	NI	NC/NL	time
φ^1, $n = 4$, $L_1/L_2 = 0/0$, $d(\mathcal{M}) = 16$												
2	8/50	3068	33/367	0.004	9/15	1632	15/166	0.002	0/0	135	0/0	0.006
4	15/541	63059	356/5618	0.065	19/101	14573	102/1671	0.012	0/0	213	0/0	0.013
8	28/7730	1.8e6	6697/3.3e6	5.07	39/558	1.4e5	545/1e4	0.13	3/8	1791	5/9	0.12
12	32/5.5e4	1.7e7	4.9e5/4.6e6	129	59/1106	5e5	1084/2.2e4	0.57	6/37	7088	25/85	0.83
16	39/3.6e5	1.3e8	3.4e5/4.8e7	1987	79/1644	1.1e6	1604/3.5e4	1.58	9/153	28548	105/549	5.171
φ^1, $n = 3$, $L_1/L_2 = 2/0$, $d(\mathcal{M}) = 18$												
17	46/1.6e4	5.4e6	12499/7.6e5	16.62	67/955	6.7e5	922/2.1e4	0.85	4/25	8105	16/36	1.3
18	52/3.5e4	1.3e7	2.9e4/2.5e6	63	71/1027	7.7e5	990/2.3e4	1	4/25	8422	16/36	1.49
φ^1, $n = 3$, $L_1/L_2 = 2/2$, $d(\mathcal{M}) = 24$												
22				> 300	87/2095	2.3e6	2025/6.0e4	4.06	4/25	11022	16/36	2.5
24				> 300	95/2316	2.9e6	2257/6.9e4	5.24	4/25	1.5e4	16/286	4.77
φ^2, $n = 3$, $L_1/L_2 = 0/0$												
2	5/9	311	1/5	0.001	2/3	315	2/16	0.001	0/1	72	0/0	0.02
3									0/2	100	0/0	0.06
4									0/4	164	0/0	0.13
φ^3, $n = 4$, $L_1/L_2 = 0/0$, $d(\mathcal{M}) = 16$												
15	38/8.1e4	3.0e7	7.3e4/9.2e6	255	54/1325	9.2e5	1160/3.6e4	1.15	9/231	27201	65/414	3.83
16	38/468	48029	164/2096	0.05	48/49	3071	0/0	0.01	9/12	1125	3/20	0.11

5.2 Dining Philosophers Benchmark (Table 2)

The benchmark models n ($n \geq 2$) philosophers Ph_i sitting around a table (Fig. 3), with n forks F_i lying between them. The actions t_i and b_i model taking and laying back the i-th fork, respectively. The reduction consists in choosing a single enabled local action to an ample set or taking all enabled actions. The reduction conditions hold with the same explanation as in the previous example, because the structures of systems are similar (processes with local actions form cycles).

Property describing unreachable states. The unreachable property $\varphi^4 = \bigvee_{i=1}^{n} eats_i \wedge eats_{(i+1) \bmod n}$ is satisfied in states where a pair of neighbour philosophers eats simultaneously.

An interesting phenomenon can be seen for $n = 4, L_1/L_2 = 2/0$. For $k \leq 12$, only local transitions of philosophers are selected to singleton ample sets. DFS-POR profits on it, as no variable decision occurs and the unsatisfiability is diagnosed without adding learned clauses.

Property describing reachable states. $\varphi^5 = \bigvee_{1 \leq i,j \leq n, i \neq j} eats_i \wedge eats_j$ is satisfied when a pair of philosophers eats simultaneously. Provided that they are not neighbours, this does not violate the mutual exclusion.

Exploring the model's diameter. Similar to the case of mutual exclusion, we examine a reachability property satisfied only by path of the full model depth. The system is modified by cutting the cycle in P_i (dashed line) and adding s_3 so that the action b_i leads from s_2 to s_3. The proposition $final$ is true in s_3 and the property $\varphi^6 = \bigwedge_{i=1}^{n} final_i$ expresses that all the philosophers reach their final states.

Table 2. Time in **bold**-formula SAT, numbers in exp notation rounded

	SAT				DFS-SAT-1				DFS-POR			
k	ML/ND	NI	NC/NL	time	ML/ND	NI	NC/NL	time	ML/ND	NI	NC/NL	time
$\varphi^4, n = 4, L_1/L_2 = 0/0, d(\mathcal{M}) = 12$												
11	43/1.2e4	4.6e6	6.5e4/6.1e5	13.175	96/731	2.7e5	565/1.0e4	0.27	22/231	3.4e4	321/3384	4.68
12	51/1.6e4	6.8e6	1.4e4/9.5e5	21.8	105/811	3.1e5	634/1.2e4	0.345	27/789	7.6e4	789/9931	10.9
$\varphi^4, n = 4, L_1/L_2 = 2/0, d(\mathcal{M}) = 20$												
4	15/276	2.3e4	112/993	0.02	41/160	2.1e4	110/1883	0.02	0/0	344	0/0	0.02
12	52/9354	3.4e6	6919/3.8e5	8.2	129/2524	1.5e6	2116/6.1e4	2.43	0/0	883	0/0	0.11
13	57/1.0e4	4.3e6	7870/4.6e5	10.6	140/2886	2.0e6	2454/7.3e4	3.4	4/6	3779	6/12	0.51
20	97/6.3e4	3.4e7	5.2e4/6.0e6	165	217/5423	7.6e6	4771/1.6e5	17	20/260	3.2e4	260/2647	8.2
$\varphi^4, n = 4, L_1/L_2 = 2/2, d(\mathcal{M}) = 28$												
26				>2000	283/1.8e4	3.5e7	1.6e4/7.3e5	109.5	20/218	5.9e4	218/2077	18.8
27				>2000	294/1.9e4	4.0e7	1.7e4/7.8e5	124.8	22/362	1.0e5	362/3734	35.11
28				>2000	305/2.1e4	4.4e7	1.8e4/8.3e5	139.1	24/890	2.7e5	890/9338	98.8
$\varphi^5, n = 4, L_1/L_2 = 0/0$												
2	6/36	2991	25/145	0.005	15/25	2471	18/168	0.002	0/0	171	0/0	0.01
4	15/80	6040	31/216	**0.007**	33/43	2130	13/100	**0.003**	0/0	276	0/0	0.01
6									3/3	607	1/3	**0.03**
$\varphi^6, n = 4, L_1/L_2 = 0/0, d(\mathcal{M}) = 12$												
11	42/8695	3.3e6	7318/4.0e5	7.74	45/637	2.8e5	483/11696	0.28	14/533	6.3e4	210/1136	9.35
12	46/727	3.4e4	104/986	**0.04**	45/46	2543	0/0	**0.009**	7/11	1211	4/20	**0.16**
$\varphi^6, n = 4, L_1/L_2 = 2/0, d(\mathcal{M}) = 20$												
15	58/4.1e4	2.5e7	3.7e4/4.3e6	120	96/3263	2.7e6	2788/1.1e5	4.74	9/42	8506	22/95	1.3
19				>500	98/3629	5.4e7	3208/1.2e5	9.42	13/611	1.1e5	254/1523	23.4
20	78/2106	2.4e5	563/7479	**0.33**	90/91	5503	0/0	**0.025**	9/13	1957	4/24	**0.38**

6 Conclusions and Future Work

For almost all examined unsatisfiable formulas DFS-POR reduces the number of implications, decided variables and conflicts in the case of unsatisfiable formulas comparing to SAT and SAT-DFS-1. The differences are often significant. The running time is better comparing to SAT and in some cases better comparing to SAT-DFS-1. It can be observed that the effectiveness of SAT-POR depends on the scale of reduction provided by the selective search. Moreover, the solver implementation is highly optimized and the presented ideas also require advanced optimizations – mainly restricting the transition relation and performing postponed implications. The preliminary results justify further work. Not only can the time usage be significantly reduced, but also the algorithm efficiency parameters (e.g. number of blocking clauses) can be improved.

For satisfiable formulas SAT and SAT-DFS-1 perform better - in particular, find counterexamples on shorter paths. Our approach is aimed at improving the overall effectiveness of BMC, where testing unsatisfiable formulas is the major bottleneck.

Future Work. A natural question is whether can the presented approach be used for richer specification languages. While extending it to LTL seems to be possible (only one symbolic path is encoded), it is doubtful in the case of ACTL – more than one symbolic paths are encoded and partial order reductions are less effective.

A couple of possible research directions can be proposed based on the connection we made between the problem and its propositional formula encoding. It is worth considering other selective search algorithms (sleep sets, stubborn sets, symmetry reductions).

References

[ABH+97] R. Alur, R. Brayton, T. A. Henzinger, S. Qadeer, and S. Ramajani, *Partial order reduction in symbolic state-space exploration*, Proc. of the 9th Int. Conf. on Computer Aided Verification (CAV'97), LNCS, vol. 1254, Springer-Verlag, 1997.

[BCC+03] A. Biere, A. Cimatti, E. Clarke, O. Strichman, and Y. Zhu, *Bounded model checking*, Highly Dependable Software, Advances in Computers, vol. 58, Academic Press, 2003.

[BCCZ99] A. Biere, A. Cimatti, E. Clarke, and Y. Zhu, *Symbolic model checking without BDDs*, Proc. of the 5th Int. Conf. on Tools and Algorithms for the Construction and Analysis of Systems (TACAS'99), LNCS, vol. 1579, Springer-Verlag, 1999.

[CGMP99] E. Clarke, O. Grumberg, M. Minea, and D. Peled, *State space reduction using partial order techniques*, Software Tools for Technology Transfer **2(3)** (1999), 279–287.

[MMZ+01] M. Moskewicz, C. Madigan, Y. Zhao, L. Zhang, and S. Malik, *Chaff: Engineering an efficient SAT solver*, Proc. of the 38th Design Automation Conference (DAC'01), June 2001.

[NNP+04] W. Nabiałek, A. Niewiadomski, W. Penczek, A. Półrola, and M. Szreter, *VerICS 2004: A model checker for real time and multi-agent systems*, Proc. of the Int. Workshop on Concurrency, Specification and Programming (CS&P'04), Informatik-Berichte, vol. 170(1), Humboldt University, 2004.

[PG86] D. Plaisted and S. Greenbaum, *A structure-preserving clause form translation*, Journal of Symbolic Computation **2(3)** (1986), 293–304.

[PWZ02] W. Penczek, B. Woźna, and A. Zbrzezny, *Towards bounded model checking for the universal fragment of TCTL*, Proc. of the 7th Int. Symp. on Formal Techniques in Real-Time and Fault Tolerant Systems (FTRTFT'02), LNCS, vol. 2469, Springer-Verlag, 2002.

[Str00] O. Strichman, *Tuning SAT checkers for bounded model checking*, Proc. of the 12th Int. Conf. on Computer Aided Verification (CAV'00), LNCS, vol. 1855, Springer-Verlag, 2000.

Predicate Abstraction of RTL Verilog Descriptions Using Constraint Logic Programming*

Tun Li, Yang Guo, SiKun Li, and GongJie Liu

National University of Defense Technology, 410073 ChangSha, HuNan, China
tunli@nudt.edu.cn

Abstract. A major technique to address state explosion problem in model checking is abstraction. Predicate abstraction has been applied successfully to large software and now to hardware descriptions, such as Verilog. This paper evaluates the state-of-the-art constraint logic programming (CLP) techniques to improve the performance of predication abstraction of hardware designs, and compared it with the SAT-based predicate abstraction techniques. With CLP based techniques, we can model various constraints, such as bit, bit-vector and integer, in a uniform framework; we can also model the word-level constraints without flatting them into bit-level constraints as SAT-based method does. With these advantages, the computation of abstraction system can be more efficient than SAT-based techniques. We have implemented this method, and the experimental results have shown the promising improvements on the performance of predicate abstraction of hardware designs.

1   Introduction

Formal verification techniques are widely applied in the hardware design industry. Among the techniques, model checking [1], is the widely used one. However, model checking suffers from state explosion problem. Therefore, abstraction techniques, which can reduce the state space, have become one of the most important techniques for successfully applying formal methods in software and hardware verification. Abstraction techniques reduce the state space by mapping the set of states of the actual, concrete system to an abstract, and smaller, set of states in a way that preserves the relevant behaviors of the system. In the software domain, the most successful abstraction technique for large systems is predicate abstraction [2]. In the hardware domain, the mostly used localization reduction is a special case of predicate abstraction.

Traditionally, predicate abstraction is computed using a theorem prover such as Simplify [3] or Zapato [4]. The typical techniques and applications can be found in [2], [5], [6], [7], and there are some typical tools such as SLAM [8], BLAST [9] and Magic [10].

---

* This work is supported by the National Science Foundation of China (NSFC) under grant No. 60403048 and 60303013.

D.A. Peled and Y.-K. Tsay (Eds.): ATVA 2005, LNCS 3707, pp. 174–186, 2005.

In hardware domain, the SAT based abstraction method is first proposed in [11]. Then, [12] proposed SAT-based predicate abstraction techniques, and applied it to the verification of ANSI-C programs. The main idea is to form a SAT equation containing all the predicates, a basic block, and two symbolic variables for each predicate, one variable for the state before the execution of the basic block, and one variable for the state after its execution. The SAT solver is then used to obtain all satisfying assignments in terms of the symbolic variables. In [13], the method has been applied for word-level predicate abstraction and verifying RTL Verilog.The technique has also been applied to SpecC [14], which is a concurrent version of ANSI-C used for hardware design.

However, there are some limitations when using theorem prover and SAT for predicate abstraction. Firstly, theorem prover based method has to call the theorem prover many times during abstraction, which will make the abstraction process inefficient. Secondly, theorem provers model the variables using unbounded integer numbers. Overflow or bit-wise operators are not modeled. However, hardware description languages like Verilog provide an extensive set of bit-wise operators. Thirdly, although SAT based method can only call the SAT solver one time during abstraction, it has to flatten the word-level constraints into bit-level constraints to model word-level variables and operations, which will lose most word-level information and the runtime of this process typically grows exponentially in the number of predicates.

In this paper, following the work of [13], we focus on applying constraint logic programming (CLP) [15] to predication abstraction of RTL Verilog descriptions, especially using CLP to solving the abstraction computation constraints obtained from circuit model and predicates. First, we build the formal model of the circuit using decision diagrams (DD) models [16] extracted from Verilog descriptions. Then following the method proposed in [13], we convert the abstraction computation formula into CLP constrains and apply CLP solver to solve them.

The advantage of CLP-based method is: Firstly, it can model bit, bit-vector and bounded integer in a uniform framework, and can support various arithmetic and logic operations. Secondly, the word-level constraints are solved with word-level information and without flattening them into bit-level constraints. With these advantages, we can compute the abstraction model of concrete RTL Verilog designs very quickly. Experimental results have shown that the runtime of abstraction process grows linearly in the number of predicates. Finally, CLP combines the expressiveness of logic programming and the constraints solving techniques, our method bridges the gap between EDA research and the research progress in constraint satisfaction problem and artificial intelligence area.

The rest of the paper is organized as follows. In section 2, we formalize the semantics of the subset of Verilog that we handle and introduce how to model Verilog descriptions using DD models. Techniques for building formal models from DD model for Verilog descriptions are described in Section 3. In Section 4, we briefly introduce the SAT-based predicate abstraction with the help of an example. Techniques for translating word-level abstraction constraints into CLP constraints are given in Section 5. We report experimental results in section 6. Finally, we conclude the paper in section 7.

2 Verilog Modeling

The Verilog subset supported in this paper is the same as that used in [13]: synthesizable Verilog with one single clock clk. We assume the clock is only used within either *posedge* or *negedge* event guards, but not both. We also assume that every variable is assigned values only at one place in the description.

Here, we first give the definition of DD model according to [16] with minor modification.

Definition 1. In the general case, a DD that represents function $y=F(X)$ is a directed, non-cyclic graph $G_y=(M, \Gamma, X)$ with set of nodes M, single root node $m_0 \in M$, and relation Γ in M, where $\Gamma(m) \subset M$ denotes the set of successor nodes of m. Non-terminal nodes m for $\Gamma(m) \neq \emptyset$ have variables $x_i \in X$ as labels. Terminal nodes m for $\Gamma(m)=\emptyset$ have variables x_i, functional sub-expressions of $F(X)$, or constants as labels. Let $x(m)$ be the label of node m. In graph G_y, for all non-terminal nodes m for which $\Gamma(m) \neq \emptyset$, a one-to-one correspondence exists between the values of label variable $x(m)$ and the successors, $m_k \in \Gamma(m)$ of m.

Definition 2. Let $m^0 \in \Gamma(m)$ denote the successor of m that corresponds to value $x(m)=0$ and $m^1 \in \Gamma(m)$ denote the successor that corresponds to value $x(m)=1$. We call an output edge from m to m^e, $e \in 0, 1$, activated when label variable $x(m)$ has value e. A path in DD model is activated if all the edges forming this path are activated. A DD model is activated to the value 0 (or 1) if there exists an activated path that includes both the root node and the terminal node labeled by the constant 0 (or 1).

Definition 3. A DD model G_y with nodes labeled by variables $x_1, x_2, , x_n$ represents function $y=f(x)=f(x_1, x_2, , x_n)$, if for each pattern X, the DD model will be activated to the value m^t that equals y.

Definition 4. A collection of DD models $G(S)=G_y$ represents a digital system $S=(F, N)$, if for each function $y=f(x)$ included in F, there exists a DD model G_y. $G(S)=G_y$ is called the DD model of digital system S.

According to the above definitions, we can build DD model for each variable or signal in the designs. The root node of the DD model is the variable or signal it is built for, while the terminal nodes are the expressions assigned to the variable or signal. The non-terminal nodes are the control conditions and statements that guard these assignments, which include *if*, *case* and *loop* statements, *etc.* For our convenience, we do some preprocessing before building DD model, such as translating *case* statement into a series of *ifelse* statements.

Figure 1 gives a Verilog design example which was cited from [13], and the corresponding DD models for the variables used in it. The example and the DD models will be used in the follows descriptions. In the DD models showed in Figure 1, the ellipse nodes correspond to the assignment statements in the Verilog description, the rectangle nodes correspond to the condition statements, and the most-left circle node is the root of the DD model. Readers can refer to [17] for the detailed algorithm for extraction of DD model from Verilog description.

```
module main(clk);
input clk;
reg [7:0] x, y;

initial x = 1;
initial y = 0;

always @ (posedge clk) begin
   y <= x;
   if (x < 100) x <= y + x;
end

endmodule
```

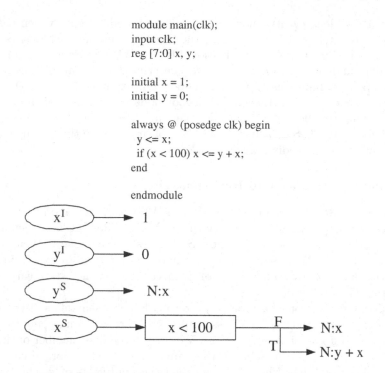

Fig. 1. Verilog example and the corresponding DD models

3 Formal Semantics of Verilog

We use the following formalism to model the concrete circuit: A transition system $T=(S, I, R)$ consists of a set of states S, a set of initial states $I \subseteq S$, and a transition relation R, which relates a current state $s \in S$ to a next-state $s' \in S$.

For different Verilog language constructions, we can build the formal model using different methods based on the corresponding DD models.

3.1 Continuous Assignment

The variable of *wire* type in Verilog can only be assigned by only one continuous assignment. Let w_i be the wire that is assigned by the i-th continuous assignment, and e_i the value that is assigned. If A denotes the semantics of continuous assignment, we have $A := \bigwedge_i (w_i = e_i)$. The formula can be obtained by traversal the DD model for w_i.

3.2 Initial and Always Statements

The statements in the *initial* blocks define the initial values of states, while the statements in the clock events guarded *always* blocks define the transition function (next state function) of the states. For the *always* blocks that do not be guarded by clock events, they define combinational circuits, which will not generate state latches. We can examine the trigger events for each always block to distinguish sequential and combinational logics. When extracting DD models for variables and signals from RTL Verilog descriptions, we can distinguish the two cases by attaching tags on the root nodes. For example, for the DD models in Figure 1, the tag "I" attached to the root node means that this assignment is initial values, while tag "S" means that this assignment is in clock event guarded always block. Similarly, the tag "C" not appeared in the example means assignment in combinational *always* block.

3.3   Finite State Machines Representation

The notion we used here is mainly cited from [13] with minor modification. Let V denote the set of variables, as given in the Verilog file. Let $L \subseteq R$ denote the set of state variables. The set of states S of the state machine is then defined to be: $S := \{0, 1\}^{|L|}$. For a state $s \in S$, we denote the value of an expression e in that particular state by $s(e)$. The set of variables that are not state variables is denoted by C: $C := V - L$.

We define the notion of a process state to define the semantics of the statements in the *initial* and *always* blocks. A process state ϕ is a mapping from the variables $r \in V$ into a pair of expressions. We denote the first member of the pair by $\phi_c(r)$ and the second member of the pair by $\phi_f(r)$. The expression $\phi_c(r)$ is called the current value, while $\phi_f(r)$ is called the final value of r. The two differ in order to distinguish non-blocking assignments from blocking assignments. Non-blocking assignments only update the final value, but not the current value, while blocking assignments update both. For an expression e, $\phi_c(r)$ denotes the evaluation of e in the current state ϕ_c, i.e., all variables v that are found in e are replaced by $\phi_c(v)$.

We can also distinguish non-blocking and blocking assignments by attaching tags on the terminal nodes. For example, the tag "N:" denotes non-blocking assignments, while tag "B:" denotes blocking assignments. With these tags, we can generate FSM models by traversal DD models.

Initial States: The assignments in *initial* blocks are used to assign initial values before execution. For these initial values, we can build formal models as $I := \{s \in S | \bigwedge_{r \in L} s(r) = \phi_f^I(r)\}$. For the example showed in Figure 1, the model for the initial values is $x=1 \wedge y=0$.

Variable Assignments: From the root node of the DD model to the terminal nodes, when a condition node is encountered, an expression of the form "$c?t{:}f$", where c is the condition expression, t and f denote the expression to be assigned when the condition is evaluated to be true or false, respectively. When a terminal node is encountered, the assignment expression is used directly. The detailed DD model traversal algorithm can be found in [17]. The special case to be considered is to distinguish non-blocking and blocking assignment. For the example showed in Figure 1, the expression generated for the x' and y' (we will explain in "Next States Relations") is shown as follows:

$$y' = x \tag{1}$$

$$x' = ((x < 100)?(x + y) : x) \tag{2}$$

Next States Relations: First we can examine the tag of root node of each DD model to distinguish variables and signals belong to set L to form the states space from those used in combinational circuits. For the variables and signals used in combinational circuits, we need the new value of each one to equal to the value after assignments. Then the formal model for the combinational circuits is defined as $C := \bigwedge_{v \in C} s(v) = s(\phi_f^C(v))$.

For the variables and signals in set L, besides generating assignments formula as discussed above, we also need the assignment formula to build the model of transition relations.

The transition relation $R(s, s')$ is defined under the constraints that for each variable $v \in L$, we require that the next state value of v—denoted v'—is the final value of v after the execution of assignments. By adding constraints for combinational circuits and continuous assignments, we can get the transition function as follows:

$$R(s, s') := \bigwedge_{v \in L} s'(v) = s(\phi_v^S(v)) \wedge \bigwedge_{v \in C} s'(v) = s(\phi_v^C(v)) \wedge s(A) \tag{3}$$

For example, for the design showed in Figure 1, the transition relation is defined as follows:

$$R(x, y, x', y') := (x' = ((x < 100)?(x + y) : x)) \wedge (y' = x). \tag{4}$$

4 Predicate Abstraction

The predicate abstraction method is the same as the method proposed in [13]. We briefly introduce the method with some modification.

In predicate abstraction [2], the variables of the concrete program are replaced by Boolean variables that correspond to a predicate on the- + variables in the concrete program. These predicates are functions that map a concrete state $\bar{r} \in S$ into a Boolean value. Let $B = \{\pi_1, \pi_2, ..., \pi_n\}$ be the set of predicates over the given program. When applying all predicates to a specific concrete state, one obtains a vector of Boolean values, which represents an abstract state $\bar{b}$. The abstract model can make a transition from an abstract state $\bar{b}$ to $\bar{b}'$ iff there is a transition from $\bar{r}$ to $\bar{r}'$ in the concrete model and $\bar{r}$ is abstracted to $\bar{b}$ and $\bar{r}'$ is abstracted to $\bar{b}'$. A symbolic variable b_i is associated with each predicate π_i. If the concrete machine makes a transition from state $\bar{r}$ to state $\bar{r}'$, then the abstract machine makes a transition from state $\bar{b}$ to $\bar{b}'$, where $\bar{b}' = pi_i(\bar{r}')$. Finally, let $\hat{T}$ denote the abstract machine, and $\hat{R}$ denote the abstract transition relation of $\hat{T}$, then $\hat{R}$ is defined as follows:

$$\hat{R} = \{(\overline{b}, \overline{b'}) | \exists \overline{r}, \overline{r'} : \bigwedge_{i=1}^{k} b_i = \pi_i(\overline{r}) \wedge R(\overline{r}, \overline{r'}) \wedge \bigwedge_{i=1}^{k} b'_i = \pi_i(\overline{r'}) \} \tag{5}$$

For the example showed in Figure 1, the transition relation is

$$R(x, y, x', y') := (x' = ((x < 100)?(x + y) : x)) \wedge (y' = x) \tag{6}$$

Suppose we want to prove that the concrete system (Verilog program) showed in Figure 1 satisfies **AG(x<100)**. In order to perform predicate abstraction we need a set of predicates. For our example, we take $\{x{<}200, x{<}100, x{+}y{<}200\}$ as the set of predicates. We associate symbolic variables b_1, b_2, b_3 with each predicate, respectively. Then the following equation will be generated:

$$(b_1 \Leftrightarrow (x < 200)) \wedge (b_2 \Leftrightarrow (x < 100)) \wedge (b_3 \Leftrightarrow (x + y < 200))$$
$$\wedge R(x, y, x', y')$$
$$\wedge (b'_1 \Leftrightarrow (x' < 200)) \wedge (b'_2 \Leftrightarrow (x' < 100)) \wedge (b'_3 \Leftrightarrow (x' + y' < 200)) \tag{7}$$

The equation for the initial state is:

$$(b_1 \Leftrightarrow (x < 200)) \wedge (b_2 \Leftrightarrow (x < 100))$$
$$\wedge (b_3 \Leftrightarrow (x + y < 200)) \wedge (x = 1) \wedge (y = 0) \tag{8}$$

Most tools using predicate abstraction for verification use general-purpose theorem provers such as Simplify [4] to compute the abstraction. This approach suffers from the fact that errors caused by bit-vector overflow may remain undetected. Furthermore, bit-vector operators are usually treated by means of uninterpreted functions. Thus, properties that rely on these bit-vector operators cannot be verified. However, we expect that Verilog designs typically use an abundance of bit-vector operators, and that the property of interest will depend on these operations. [13] proposed to use SAT solver to compute abstraction. However, in this method, the word-level abstraction computation formula needs to be flattened into bit-level one, which will generate large bulk of constraints. Especially when the division and multiplication are used in the formula, a division or multiplication circuits will be generated to model these operations. Also, flatten the word-level formula into bit-level will lose most functional information related to word-level structure. Here, we propose to use CLP to compute the abstraction system of RTL Verilog descriptions. This method can support all Verilog bounded integer and bit-vector operators. The CLP constraints generated can be very small. Finally, the bit, bit-vector and various arithmetic and logic operations can be solved under a uniform framework.

5   CLP Constraints Generation

We use GNU Prolog [18] as the constraints solver. For the abstraction formula generated in last section, we first translate them into CLP constraints, and then solve them.

To translate the Verilog expressions into constraint equations according to GNU Prolog format, it is necessary to consider separately the case of bits, bit vectors and integers, because these three types belong to different domains, and are solved in different ways.

Arithmetic operators: The arithmetic operators include addition, subtraction, (scalar) multiplication, division, shift left (right), extraction and concatenation, etc. The translation method must take the **modulo** semantics of Verilog operators into consideration during operation.

Logic operator: For bit operators and logic compare operators, the translation is straightforward, which only substitutes the bit-vector operators with the corresponding CLP predicates. However, for some bit-vector bit-wise operators, we must model them with **modulo** semantics in CLP constrains without violating their original semantics.

Bit: GNU Prolog provides various operations for bit. In this case, for each expression involves bit type, a single GNU Prolog equation is produced. The domain of all constraint variables used in the equations is defined as the Boolean domain $\{0, 1\}$.

Bit-vector: If at least one variable involved in a constraint equation is a bit vector, the situation is more complex. There are two ways that the bit vectors involved in expression:

- *Entire:* The bit vector involves in computation as an entire variables. In this case, if there are integer variables in equation, then the bit-vector will be considered as an integer variable too. Otherwise, if there are other bit-vectors in equation, then the bit-vector will be decomposed into bits and generate constraints for the decomposed bits. For example, if two 4-bit bit-vectors are involved in expression "V1==V2", then the constraint equations generated for this express is shown as following. Vi_j represents each bit in bit-vector, where $i \in \{1, 2\}$ indicating the bit-vector variable, and $j \in \{1, 2, 3\}$ indicating the bit location in each bit-vector.

$$V1\_0 = V2\_0$$
$$V1\_1 = V2\_1$$
$$V1\_2 = V2\_2$$
$$V1\_3 = V2\_3$$
$$2^3 * V1\_3 + 2^2 * V1\_2 + 2^1 * V1\_1 + V1\_0 = V1$$
$$2^3 * V2\_3 + 2^2 * V2\_2 + 2^1 * V2\_1 + V2\_0 = V2 \quad (9)$$

- *Bit Selection:* Bit selection means a portion of a bit-vector is involved in expression. In this case, besides generating constraints for the expression, we will also generate constraints for the selected bits. For example, the constraint equations generated for expression "V[1:0]=2'b00" are as following, where V is a 4-bit bit vector variable.

$$V\_1 = 0$$
$$V\_0 = 0$$
$$2^3 * V\_3 + 2^2 * V\_2 + 2^1 * V\_1 + V\_0 = V \tag{10}$$

Integer: GNU Prolog provides various operations for integer variables. The domain of each integer is also required to be defined.

GNU Prolog provides supports for most of the arithmetic and logical operations used in Verilog. The only thing need to be considered is the operations taken on bit-vector and bounded integer. When concern expressions with these variables or signals, we need to take care of the overflow problem. In GNU Prolog, we can solve this problem by using the *rem* operation built in GNU Prolog. Let the expression we try to translate is of the form "*a op b*", where *a* and *b* are variables of bit-vector or bounded integer type, assume the width of *a* and *b* is *n*, *op* is arithmetic operations such as addition *etc*. Then the translated results is of the form "(*a op b*) *rem* 2^n".

Although the CLP constraints generation method introduced above may also flatten the word-level constraints to bit-level when involving bit-vector signals, we need not flat them into bit ones in most situations.

In general, the abstraction computation formula is a conjunction of a set of equivalent formula. For each equivalent formula in the conjunction formula, we generate a temporal variable for it and then conjunct all the generated temporal variables. Finally, we set the value of the conjunction of the temporal variables to constant 1. By solving the generated CLP constraints with the *findall* predicate of GNU Prolog, we can get all the state transitions for the abstraction system.

```
Z #= (X + Y) rem 256,
Temp1 #<=> ((#\B1) #\/ (X #< 200)) #/\ (B1 #\/ (X #>= 200)),
Temp2 #<=> ((#\B2) #\/ (X #< 100)) #/\ (B2 #\/ (X #>= 100)),
Temp3 #<=> ((#\B3) #\/ (Z #< 200)) #/\ (B3 #\/ (Z #>= 200)),
Y_Bar #= X,
(X #< 100) #==> (X_Bar #= Z), (X #>= 100) #==> (X_Bar #= X),
Z_Bar #= (X_Bar + Y_Bar) rem 256,
Temp4 #<=> ((#\B1_Bar) #\/ (X_Bar #< 200)) #/\ (B1_Bar #\/ (X_Bar #>= 200)),
Temp5 #<=> ((#\B2_Bar) #\/ (X_Bar #< 100)) #/\ (B2_Bar #\/ (X_Bar #>= 100)),
Temp6 #<=> ((#\B3_Bar) #\/ (Z_Bar #< 200)) #/\ (B3_Bar #\/ (Z_Bar #>= 200)),

Out #<=> Temp1 #/\ Temp2 #/\ Temp3 #/\ Temp4 #/\ Temp5 #/\ Temp6,
```

For the example formula generated in last section, the generated CLP constraints according to formula (7) are shown as below. The semantics of the CLP symbols can be known from their syntax. The second line, third line and forth line is the constraint generated for the first, second and third equivalence formula of formula (7), respectively. The first line shows the usage of the *rem* GNU Prolog operation to implement the **modulo** semantics of $x+y$ and a new variable Z is generated to be used in following constraints. The X_Bar and Y_Bar is used to represent the variable x' and y' of formula (7) respectively, Z_Bar is used to represent the value of Z in next state. By defining these new variables, lines 5-7 are constraints for the transition relation. The following 4 lines are constraints for the last three equivalence formulas of the formula (7). In above code segment, the last line is the constraint for the entire formula (7) in conjunction form. By forcing the *Out* to be **1** and solving the generated constraints, we can get the abstraction state transitions.

For the example showed in Figure 1, we can get transition diagrams just the same as in [13], which is shown in Figure 2. We can also get the initial state by solving the initial state computation constraints generated similar to the above process. For the example in Figure 1, we can compute the initial state—"111".

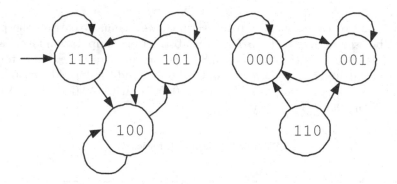

Fig. 2. State transition diagrams for the example

The abstract transition relations and initial states are converted to SMV program, and the property is verified on the abstraction system. For the above example, the property to be verified is $\mathbf{AG}(b_2)$.

6   Implementation and Experimental Results

Based on the system implemented in [18], we have implemented the RTL Verilog CLP-based predicate abstraction prototype system. In order to compare our method with SAT-based method, we follow the method proposed in [12] to translate abstraction computation formula into SAT instance. First we build the circuit model for the abstraction formula, and then synthesis the circuit into BLIF format using VIS [19] system. Finally, we use the modified BLIF2CNF [20] program to convert BLIF into CNF format, which is the acceptable input format for most SAT solver. To use the SAT solver to compute all the satisfiable assignments for the generated CNF, we use zChaff [21] as the SAT solver, and modified it according to the algorithm proposed in [22].

Table 1 shows the characteristics of benchmarks used in our experiment. The 8051 Controller and Viper are publicly available designs. The Decoder is the instruction decoder unit of a 32-bit microprocessor implemented by ourselves. SMU and DCU is the data cache unit and stack manage unit of PicoJava microprocessor [23], respectively.

Table 1. Benchmark Characteristics

Benchmark	Lines of Code	Inputs	Signals
8051 Controller (8051)	350	18	59
Viper Microprocessor(Viper)	400	24	57
Decoder	2092	14	94
SMU	1467	30	217
DCU	3979	43	385

According to the properties to be verified, we manually extract the predicates to be used for abstraction. Then the abstraction computation formula and its corresponding CLP constraints and SAT constraints are generated automatically. We compared the performance of CLP based and SAT based method. The experimental configuration is a Windows 2000 PC with AMD Athlon XP 1.8 GHz CPU and 256MB memory.

Table 2. Circuit statistics

Benchmark	Predicates	CLP Based Method		SAT Based Method	
		Line of Constraints	Time (Sec.)	Literals	Time (Sec.)
8051 Controller (8051)	23	239	10.10	13972	58
Viper Microprocessor (Viper)	25	247	12.34	24719	204
Decoder	25	253	15.47	17527	177
SMU	39	372	23.73	35836	361
DCU	24	255	17.49	21075	236

The experimental results are shown in Table 1. In Table 1, the "Predicates" column shows the predicates used to compute the abstraction system, the "Line of Constraints" column shows the lines of generated CLP constraints, while "Literals" shows the generated SAT literals for the abstraction computation formula. The two "Time" columns under "CLP based method" and "SAT based method" shows the time used to solving the converted constraints, respectively. All times are reported in second.

We can conclude from Table 1 that CLP based abstraction computation can gain promising performance improvements than SAT based method. Although the inefficient implementation of the algorithm proposed in [22] may influence the performance of SAT based method, we believe that the distinct characteristic such as word level modeling and constraints solving capability of CLP based method make it more efficient than SAT based method.

7   Conclusion

In this paper, we proposed to use CLP as the abstraction computation engine for predicate abstraction of RTL Verilog, and the experimental results showed the promising improvements of abstraction computation by our proposed method. In the future, we will intensively research on CLP based predicate abstraction method, such as CLP based abstraction and refinement techniques, unsat core extraction for CLP based method. We will also make our CLP based abstraction system to be more practical.

References

1. E. Clarke, O. Grumberg, and D. Peled. Model Checking. MIT Press, 1999.
2. S. Graf and H. Saidi. Construction of abstract state graphs with PVS. In O. Grumberg, editor, Proc. 9th INternational Conference on Computer Aided Verification (CAV'97), volume 1254, pages 72-83. Springer Verlag, 1997.
3. David Detlefs, Greg Nelson, and James B. Saxe. Simplify: A theorem prover for program checking. Technical Report HPL-2003-148, HP Labs, 2003.
4. Thomas Ball, Byron Cook, Shuvendu K. Lahiri, and Lintao Zhang. Zapato: Automatic theorem proving for predicate abstraction refinement. In Computer Aided Verification. Springer-Verlag, 2004.
5. T. Ball and S.K. Rajamani. Boolean programs: A model and process for software analysis. Technical Report 2000-14, Microsoft Research, February 2000.
6. Cormac Flanagan and Shaz Qadeer. Predicate abstraction for software verification. POPL '02: Proceedings of the 29th ACM SIGPLAN-SIGACT symposium on Principles of programming languages. p 191-202, ACM Press, 2002.
7. Thomas Ball, Rupak Majumdar, Todd D. Millstein and Sriram K. Rajamani. Automatic Predicate Abstraction of C Programs. ACM Conference on Programming Language Design and Implementation, p 203-213, ACM Press, 2001.
8. T. Ball and S. K. Rajamani. Automatically validating temporal safety properties of interfaces. In The 8th International SPIN Workshop on Model Checking of Software, volume 2057 of LNCS, pages 103-122. Springer, 2001.
9. Thomas A. Henzinger, Ranjit Jhala, Rupak Majumdar, and Gregoire Sutre. Software verification with Blast. Proceedings of the Tenth International Workshop on Model Checking of Software (SPIN), Lecture Notes in Computer Science 2648, Springer-Verlag, 235-239, 2003.
10. Sagar Chaki, Edmund Clarke, Alex Groce, Somesh Jha, Helmut Veith. Modular Verification of Software Components in C. IEEE Transactions on Software Engineering, Volume 30, Number 6, p 388-402, June 2004.
11. Edmund Clarke, Muralidhar Talupur, and Dong Wang. SAT based predicate abstraction for hardware verification. In Proceedings of SAT'03, 2003.

12. Edmund Clarke, Daniel Kroening, Natalia Sharygina, and Karen Yorav. Predicate abstraction of ANSI-C programs using SAT. Formal Methods in System Design (FMSD), vol. 25, no. 2-3, p 105-127, Kluwer Academic Publishers, 2004.
13. Edmund Clarke, Himanshu Jain, Daniel Kroening. Predicate Abstraction and Refinement Techniques for Verifying Verilog. Technical report, Carnegie Mellon University, CMU-CS-04-139, June, 2004.
14. Edmund Clarke, Himanshu Jain, Daniel Kroening. Verification of SpecC using Predicate Abstraction. MEMOCODE, June, 2004.
15. J. Jaffar, M. J. Maher. Constraint logic programming: A Survey. The Journal of Logic Programming, 1994, Vol. 19 & 20: 503 582.
16. R. Ubar. Test synthesis with alternative graphs. IEEE Design & Test of Computers, 1996.13(1): 48 57.
17. Li Tun. Research on techniques of VLSI RT-Level automatic functional vectors generation [Ph.D. Thesis]. ChangSha: National University of Defense Technology, 2003.
18. Tun Li, Yang Guo, SiKun Li. Functional Vectors Generation for RT-Level Verilog Descriptions Based on Path Enumeration and Constraint Logic Programming. to appear in Proceedings of 8th EUROMICRO CONFERENCE ON DIGITAL SYSTEM DESIGN, August, 2005, Porto, Portugal.
19. http://vlsi.colorado.edu/ vis.
20. Joao Marques Silva. BLIF2CNF. sat.inesc-id.pt/ jpms/scripts/bin/blif2cnf.
21. M. Moskewicz, C. Madigan, Y. Zhao, L. Zhang, S. Malik. Chaff: Engineering an Efficient SAT Solver. In Proceedings of 39th Design Automation Conference (DAC 2001), Las Vegas, June 2001.
22. McMillan, K. Applying SAT Methods in Unbounded Symbolic Model Checking. In 14th Conference on Computer Aided Verification, Springer-Verlag, p 250-264, 2002.
23. Sun Microsystems. PicoJava technology.
    http://www.sun.com/microelectronics/communitysource/picojava/, 1999.

State Space Exploration of Object-Based Systems Using Equivalence Reduction and the Sweepline Method

Charles A. Lakos[1,*] and Lars M. Kristensen[2,**]

[1] School of Computer Science, University of Adelaide,
Adelaide, SA 5005, Australia
Charles.Lakos@adelaide.edu.au

[2] Department of Computer Science, University of Aarhus,
DK-8200, Aarhus N, Denmark
kris@daimi.au.dk

Abstract. Object-based systems present particular challenges for state space exploration. Objects can be dynamically created and discarded, and can be referenced via object identifiers. Consistent relabelling of object identifiers in a state leads to a state that is superficially different but behaviourally equivalent to the original. Similarly, object-based systems can include garbage which has no effect on subsequent behaviour but which results in unnecessary differentiation of states. Both of these factors can lead to state space explosion.

This paper considers state space exploration for object-based systems based on the Petri Net formalism. It addresses the above issues by using both equivalence reduction and the sweep-line technique. Experimental results are presented for a simple case study of a communication protocol.

1   Introduction

Object-oriented technology has been widely adopted for the modelling and development of software systems, thus motivating the development of formal analysis techniques suitable for verifying such systems. The object-oriented paradigm views a system as composed of autonomous entities which cooperate by exchanging messages, i.e. a concurrent system. In this paper, we focus on object-based rather than object-oriented systems. According to the classification in [26], this means that we do not consider inheritance and dynamic binding, but we do support the notion of autonomous objects whose state and behaviour are defined by classes, which can be dynamically created and destroyed, and which are referenced by *object identifiers* (or *oids*).

A common form of analysis applied to concurrent systems is that of state space exploration [25]. Thus, model checking generates the reachable states (or at least representatives of those states) and then evaluates the desired properties over those states. This approach has a number of advantages (as detailed in [25]), including simplicity, no requirement for specialised domain knowledge, and a high degree of automation. The main disadvantage is the ever-present threat of state space explosion — where the number of states is simply too large to be explored with the available computer memory.

* Supported by an Australian Research Council (ARC) Discovery Grant DP0210524.
** Supported by the Danish Natural Science Research Council.

D.A. Peled and Y.-K. Tsay (Eds.): ATVA 2005, LNCS 3707, pp. 187–201, 2005.
© Springer-Verlag Berlin Heidelberg 2005

In an object-based system, the use of oids leads to state space explosion. The state of a system consists of a set of objects, each with a unique oid. Objects refer to each other via these oids. The oids can be memory addresses, or integers, or some other form of reference. The particular oid value associated with each object is immaterial — any consistent relabelling of the oids leads to an equivalent state. Essentially, the two states are representations of the same *object graph*, where the nodes are the objects and the arcs are the references between objects. Isomorphic graphs should be treated as equivalent. In order to perform state space exploration for such object-based systems, it will be necessary to store only one representative from each set of such equivalent states. This requires some form of equivalence reduction [20,13] or the use of a graph isomorphism algorithm.

An added complication for object-based systems is the approach adopted to destroying or discarding objects. One approach (as in C and C++ [24]) is to require explicit destruction, thus assuming that the designer knows when an object is no longer required. This approach can lead to dangling references or memory leaks, which are difficult to identify and remedy. Another approach (as in Java [8]) is to use garbage collection to remove objects which are no longer reachable from a root object. This approach eliminates the possibility of dangling references and memory leaks but at the cost of run-time overheads. Any retention of non-accessible objects in the state will lead to distinctions between states which are otherwise equivalent (modulo garbage collection).

In this paper, we examine the state space exploration of object-based systems with garbage collection. We capture object behaviour within the Petri Net formalism [22] which has a well-defined semantics, and has been widely used in the modelling and analysis of concurrent systems [23]. While it is not common for Petri Nets to support the dynamic creation and destruction of subnet instances, we adopt a formalism suitable for modelling both mobile and object-oriented systems [19]. The main contributions of the paper consist of the algorithms and experimental results for the state space exploration of such systems. We extend an existing canonicalisation algorithm [9] to cater for Petri Nets and combine it with the sweep-line technique [6,15] with mutual benefits to both.

The paper is organised as follows: Section 2 considers the background and related work. Section 3 presents a case study of a confirmed protocol for establishing connections over a faulty link. Section 4 considers the algorithms for state space exploration while Section 5 presents the experimental results for the analysis of the case study. Section 6 contains the conclusions.

2   Background

There have been a number of proposals for extending Petri Net formalisms to incorporate object-oriented capabilities [1], but very few support any form of automated analysis and, to the best of our knowledge, only one [5] supports state space exploration. The work on *CO-OPN* [3] incorporates algebraic specification of data types and supports verification via theorem proving. The work on *Co-Operative Objects* [2] concentrates on modelling and prototyping, and does not support analysis. The formalism of *Object-Based Petri Nets* [18] restricts the use of references so that garbage collection is not required. Two approaches are built on object-oriented programming languages which means that they have difficulties in providing a complete formal semantics. The tool *Renew* [16] is built on the *Java* language and provides open access to its facilities, but does not support state space exploration. Of particular interest is *PNtalk* [5] which is built on the language *SmallTalk* and *does* consider equivalence-reduced state spaces. However, the published papers do not include the specific algorithms and provide only sparse experimental results (from a prototype implementation).

In this paper, we adopt the formalism of [19], which was designed to model mobile and object-based systems. It has a clearly defined notion of garbage, based on causal dependence. It captures a folded version of Object-Based Petri Nets [17] where each token and each transition firing mode includes the oid of the associated object. This representation is particularly convenient for mapping OBPNs into Hierarchical Coloured Petri Nets (HCPNs) [11], which can then be analysed in the tool Design/CPN [12].

The approach we adopt for the canonicalisation of each state is similar to that employed in the context of *dSPIN* (a Dynamic Extension of SPIN) [10,9]. As [9] observes, earlier approaches to symmetry reduction considered systems composed of a fixed number of active components (processors), variables of a special symmetry-preserving data type, and specification symmetries. More sophisticated techniques along these lines continue to emerge [14]. However, these approaches to symmetry reduction do not consider garbage collection and it is attractive to adopt an algorithm which combines both canonicalisation and garbage collection.

The Iosif approach [9] essentially implements a mark-and-sweep algorithm for garbage collection. The first phase starts from the root object and follows references to all reachable objects, marking them on the way. A subsequent sweep phase examines all objects and discards as garbage those which were not marked. At the same time as marking the reachable objects, Iosif collects a relabelling map, i.e. a mapping from existing object identifiers to new ones. During the sweep phase, the relabelling map is applied to the retained objects. The Iosif approach is not adequate for Petri Nets where places hold an unordered collection of objects. The order of processing affects the so-called relabelling map which in turn affects canonicalisation. We address this issue by extending equivalence reduction and combining it with the sweepline method.

3   Case Study

We illustrate our approach with a simple case study of a typical protocol for the confirmed establishment and discarding of connections. As noted above, the case study is presented as a folded version of an object system [17], which can be represented as a *Hierarchical Coloured Petri Net* (HCPN) [11] and which is then amenable to analysis by the Design/CPN tool [12].

For those unfamiliar with the HCPN formalism, we start by considering the components of the system. In this protocol, the lifecycle of a sender is given by the page (or subnet) shown in Fig. 1. A net consists of places, transitions and arcs, together with annotations of these. The *places* are depicted as ovals and can hold a multiset of tokens of some type, which can consist of arbitrarily complex data values. This marking determines the state of the system. In Fig. 1, the italic annotation adjacent to each place indicates the type of resident tokens, and the non-italic annotation indicates the initial marking (or state). Thus, the place *SenderIdle* holds tokens of type *SenderFree*, and is initialised to hold the two tokens *(2,e)* and *(3,e)*.

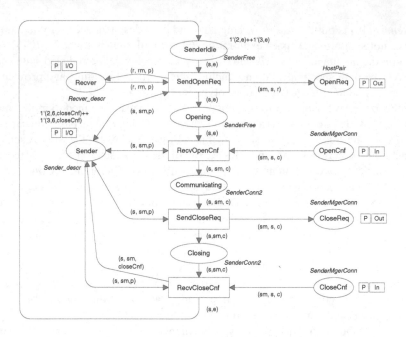

Fig. 1. Subnet for the Sender processes

The *transitions* are depicted as rectangles, and determine the possible changes of state. The incident arcs indicate how the transitions affect the places and are annotated with the multisets of tokens which are added to or removed from the adjacent places. The precise effect of a transition is determined by a firing mode (or binding), which determines the values of variables in the arc annotations. A transition paired with a binding is called a *binding element*. A transition can also be annotated with a guard (in brackets) which constrains the possible firing modes or bindings. In Fig. 1 a binding for transition *SendOpenReq* will specify values for the variables *s*, *r*, *sm*, *rm*, *p*.

In Design/CPN, data types are declared in a variant of Standard ML [12]. For the sender processes, an excerpt of the relevant data type declarations is given in Fig. 2. Object identifiers (the type *OID*) are defined to be a subrange of the integers. Aliases are defined to indicate the usage of oids — *Sender_oid* is used in a sender descriptor to specify the oid for the associated instance, while *Sender_ref* is used as a reference to a sender instance. The type *SenderConn2* is a product involving references to a sender, a sender connection manager and a connection. Variables are also declared for binding to values of particular type, e.g. the variable *s* will be used to refer to a sender.

The state of each sender is indicated by having a token in one of the places *SenderIdle*, *Opening*, *Communicating*, *Closing* (see Fig. 1), which reflects the stage reached in the lifecycle. Initially, sender processes have a token in place *SenderIdle* — the token *(2,e)* for the sender process with oid 2 and *(3,e)* for the process with oid *3*. A sender progresses round its lifecycle by firing the transitions *SendOpenReq*, *RecvOpenCnf*, *SendCloseReq*, *RecvCloseCnf*, each of which uses the variable *s* to ensure that matching tokens for a given sender are consumed and generated.

```
color NoColor = with e declare ms;

(* Basic object identifier types *)
val minOID = 10;                   (* Min unused OID *)
val maxOID = 12;                   (* Max unused OID *)
color OID = int with 0..maxOID;    (* Use zero for no value *)
color FreeOID = int with minOID..maxOID declare ms;

(* Aliases for object identifiers - name determines role *)
color Sender_oid = OID declare same;
color Sender_ref = OID declare same;
color SenderConnMger_oid = OID declare same;
color SenderConnMger_ref = OID declare same;
color ConnPhase = with openReq | openCnf | closeReq | closeCnf;

(* Descriptors + tokens for different classes of objects *)
color Sender_descr = product Sender_oid * SenderConnMger_ref * ConnPhase;
color SenderFree = product Sender_ref * NoColor;
color SenderConn2 = product Sender_ref * SenderConnMger_ref * Conn_ref;
color HostPair = product SenderConnMger_ref * Sender_ref * Recver_ref;
color SenderMgerConn = product SenderConnMger_ref * Sender_ref * Conn_ref;

(* Variable declarations *)
var s : Sender_ref;
var r : Recver_ref;
var sm : SenderConnMger_ref;
var p : ConnPhase;
```

Fig. 2. Excerpt of type definitions relevant to sender processes

In addition to the basic lifecycle described above, the transitions access a place *Sender* which holds tokens which are descriptors for each of the senders. Also they access places *OpenReq, OpenCnf, CloseReq, CloseCnf* which are annotated by the symbol *P* to indicate that they are *port* places and consequently provide an interface to external components. Thus a sender can move from *idle* to *opening* by sending a request via port place *OpenReq*. The sender can progress from *opening* to *communicating* on receipt of a matching confirmation (via port place *OpenCnf*). The steps in closing the connection are analogous. Finally, we note that transition *SendOpenReq* also accesses a place *Recver* which holds the descriptors for the receivers. The sole purpose of this is so that the sender can choose a communication partner for the protocol. The lifecycle of a receiver process is largely the dual of that of the sender — it responds to requests for connection establishment and release rather than initiating them.

A *Hierarchical Coloured Petri Net* (HCPN) allows a system to be modelled as a number of communicating subnets. For the protocol we are studying, the top-level net is shown in Fig. 3. Here, the large rectangles are annotated with a tag *HS* to indicate that they are hierarchical constructs, and specifically *substitution transitions*. Such a transition is substituted by a subnet and the detailed annotation (not shown in the figure) indicates which subnet is being instantiated and how the neighbouring *socket places* of the substitution transitions are fused with the port places of the subnet. In our example, these port assignments can be deduced by the naming. Thus, port node *OpenReq* of Fig. 1 is fused with socket node *OpenReq* of Fig. 3.

On the left of the Fig. 3 is a substitution transition which instantiates the *SenderEntity* subnet for the sender processes from Fig. 1. The senders make requests to the sender

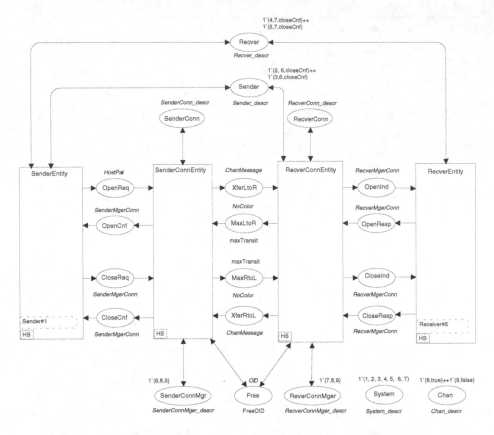

Fig. 3. Top-level net for the object-based protocol model

connection manager and the receivers respond to requests from the receiver connection manager (given by the substitution transitions titled *SenderConnEntity*, *RecverEntity* and *RecverConnEntity* respectively). In our model, we have two sender processes which share the one sender connection manager, and two receiver processes that share the one receiver connection manager. It would be simple to increase the number of each.

Connection establishment and release is confirmed — it is a four stage process involving request, indication, response and confirm primitives. For connection establishment, these primitives are captured by places *OpenReq*, *OpenInd*, *OpenResp*, *OpenCnf*, and similarly places *CloseReq*, *CloseInd*, *CloseResp*, *CloseCnf* are used for releasing connections. The passing of primitives from sender to connection manager and vice versa is error free, while message loss is possible between the connection managers.

The sender connection manager is modeled by the page titled *SenderConnEntity* shown in Fig. 4. On the left are the port places for interacting with the senders, while on the right are port places for interacting with the network channels. Most transitions access the descriptor for the sender connection manager with a side condition to the place *SenderConnMger*. (Exceptions are the transitions *HandleOpenReq* and *Handle-CloseReq* since the sender connection manager is already indicated in the request.)

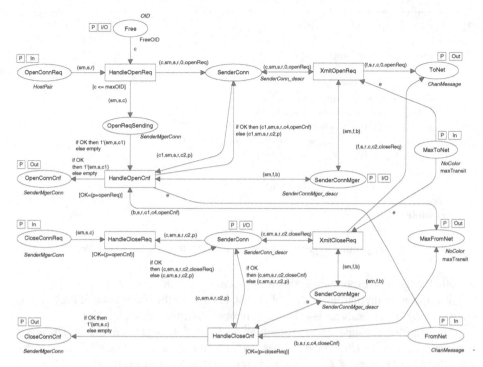

Fig. 4. Subnet for the Sender Connection Manager

An open request (arriving in place *OpenConnReq*) can be accepted (by firing the transition *HandleOpenReq*) if there is an available oid for the connection (in the place *Free*). Connections have local significance — they have identifiers for the local connection, the sender manager, the sender and receiver, the receiver-side connection (when known). They also record the phase reached (i.e. requested or confirmed). Once a sender-side connection indicates that a request has been made, the transition *XmitOpenReq* is enabled to send a message requesting the connection. It can fire repeatedly as long as the sender connection manager is in this state, thus providing a mechanism to overcome potential message loss (by the faulty network channel). In order to avoid an unbounded number of messages in the channel and hence an infinite state space, the place *MaxToNet* has a number of tokens indicating the maximum number of messages that can be in transit (in this case one).

Once an open confirmation has been processed (by firing transition *HandleOpenCnf*), the state of the sender-side connection is modified to *OpenCnf* and thus the transmission of open request messages will be disabled. A similar process handles close requests.

4   State Space Exploration Algorithms

In the context of HCPNs, a state space can be defined as a graph (V, E) where V is a set of vertices corresponding to states and including the initial state M_0. E is a set of

---

```
 1: Nodes = {canon(M₀)}
 2: Arcs = ∅
 3: Unprocessed = {canon(M₀)}
 4: while Unprocessed ≠ ∅ do
 5:    select M ∈ Unprocessed
 6:    Unprocessed ← Unprocessed \ {M}
 7:    for all (t,b) ∈ BE s.t. M[(t,b)⟩M′ do
 8:       if canon(M′) ∉ Nodes then
 9:          Unprocessed = Unprocessed ∪ {canon(M′)}
10:          Nodes = Nodes ∪ {canon(M′)}
11:       end if
12:       Arcs = Arcs ∪ {(M,(t,b),canon(M′))}
13:    end for
14: end while
```

Fig. 5. Algorithm to generate a canonicalised state space for a Petri Net

(labelled) edges corresponding to the occurrence of transitions — $(M_1,(t,b),M_2)$ is in E if transition t with binding b is enabled in state M_1 and the occurrence of the binding element *(t,b)* in M_1 leads to M_2. This is commonly written $M_1[(t,b)⟩M_2$.

An algorithm for state space exploration for Petri Nets is given in Fig. 5. The algorithm maintains a set *Unprocessed* of as-yet unexplored states. At each iteration of the *while* loop, an element of *Unprocessed* is removed and examined for enabled binding elements. If any are found, the relevant arcs are added to the graph and newly reached markings are added both to the graph and set *Unprocessed*, provided they are not already present. The above algorithms stores canonicalised versions of the markings in the state space — if the function *canon* is the identity function, then the algorithm reduces to the basic algorithm for state space exploration for Petri Nets.

The need for canonicalisation can be demonstrated with the stylised excerpt from the state space of our protocol case study as in Fig. 6. The states are (partially) labelled with the state of the two sender processes (s_1 and s_2) and the state of the sender connection manager (sm). The arcs are labelled with the relevant transition together with an indication of the binding of the transition. Thus, the arc between states 1 and 2 indicates that transition *SendOpenReq* occurs with a binding to indicate (among other things) that this is for sender process s_1. On the left is a sequence of states where sender s_1 requests an open connection first and is allocated c_1, followed by sender s_2 which is allocated c_2. On the right is a sequence of states where the senders request the connections in a different order, and are consequently allocated different connections. States 8 and 9 are equivalent since they can be obtained from each other by a consistent relabelling of the object identifiers and the behaviour observable from each will be equivalent.

The number of states can increase significantly depending on the regime adopted for allocating identifiers. In the state space of Fig. 6, the occurrence of transition *HandleOpenReq* in state 2 allocates an identifier for the new connection. This object identifier comes from place *Free* in Figs. 3 and 4. Place *Free* could hold one token for each available oid. With *100* available oids, there would be *100* arcs from state 2, each one ending in a state with a different connection identifier. Alternatively, the oids could be

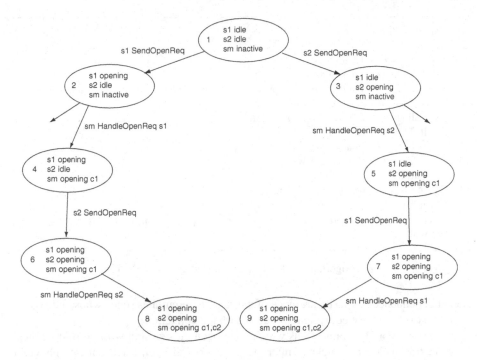

Fig. 6. Excerpt from the state space

allocated in sequence. Then the place *Free* would hold only the next available identifier, and access to this identifier would result in the subsequent identifier being added to the place. This approach significantly reduces the number of states but also limits the concurrent allocation of identifiers.

Thus, in the state space exploration of object-based systems, the choice of object identifiers (oids) is a significant contributor to state space explosion. The consistent relabelling of oids in one system state leads to a (superficially) different derived state which is equivalent to the original. The choice of object identifiers can be affected by many things, including non-determinism in the allocation of oids (here the regime for allocating oids from the place *Free*), and non-determinism in the sequencing of independent activity resulting in different sequences of allocation of objects (here the decision of which sender requests a connection first).

In order to minimise these contributors to state space explosion, it is necessary to generate a condensed state space. One approach is to check each newly generated state for equivalence with an existing state. If so, we do not store this as a separate state. Another approach is to store a canonical representative for each state, as in Fig.5.

A second significant contributor to state space explosion in the analysis of object-based systems is the presence of garbage. We normally consider the root object to be primarily of interest. Anything that cannot affect this object (either directly or indirectly) is considered to be garbage. This can be defined more precisely in terms of

1: $Nodes = \{M_0\}$
2: $Arcs = \emptyset$
3: $Unprocessed = \{M_0\}$
4: **while** $Unprocessed \neq \emptyset$ **do**
5:     select $M \in Unprocessed$ $s.t.$ $\psi(M) = min\{\psi(M') \mid M' \in Unprocessed\}$
6:     $Unprocessed = Unprocessed \setminus \{M\}$
7:     **for all** $(t,b) \in BE$ $s.t.$ $M[(t,b)\rangle M'$ **do**
8:         **if** $M' \notin Nodes$ **then**
9:             $Unprocessed = Unprocessed \cup \{M'\}$
10:            $Nodes = Nodes \cup \{M'\}$
11:        **end if**
12:        $Arcs = Arcs \cup \{(M,(t,b),M')\}$
13:    **end for**
14:    $Nodes = \{M \in Nodes \mid \psi(M) \geq min\{\psi(M') \mid M' \in Unprocessed\}\}$
15: **end while**

Fig. 7. Algorithm for basic sweep-line analysis of a Petri Net

causal dependence [19]. The presence of garbage differentiates states whose behaviour of interest is otherwise equivalent (modulo garbage collection).

In our case study, connections which have been closed (and with no related messages in transit) are no longer of interest, and do not affect the subsequent behaviour of the protocol. Removing these connections will help to reduce the state space. It is worth noting that the sender connection manager of Fig. 4 cannot explicitly discard a closed connection, since there may be messages in transit which refer to it. Note that the *TCP protocol* uses a three-way handshake to establish and release connections so as to minimise this problem of having a closed connection with messages in transit [7].

The approach we have adopted for the canonicalisation of each state is similar to that employed by Iosif in the context of *dSPIN* (a Dynamic Extension of SPIN) [10,9]. This is essentially a mark-and-sweep algorithm for garbage collection. The first phase starts from the root object and follows references to all reachable objects, marking them on the way. A subsequent sweep phase examines all objects and discards as garbage those which were not marked. At the same time as marking the reachable objects, Iosif collects a relabelling map, i.e. a mapping from existing object identifiers to new ones. During the sweep phase, the relabelling map is applied to the retained objects.

This algorithm requires two passes over the state, where each pass has a linear time complexity depending on the size of the state. In the case of dSPIN, this algorithm is sufficient and optimal because the components of each object are fixed and hence can be traversed in a fixed order, thus guaranteeing a unique canonical relabelling.   For Petri Nets, places can hold an unordered multiset of tokens, each of which can hold references to other objects. The order of traversing the tokens will not affect the determination of garbage, but will affect the relabelling of the state. Thus, the algorithm will no longer be linear or will not guarantee to produce a unique canonical representative. The use of non-optimal equivalence algorithms may be appropriate in avoiding the possible exponential costs of an optimal algorithm on pathological scenarios [14].

We seek to ameliorate the inefficiencies of a non-optimal equivalence algorithm, by combining it with the sweep-line method [6], which reduces the memory demands for state space exploration.[1] This approach is predicated on the observation that systems often exhibit the notion of progress. A progress measure can be defined on states such that, as the state space exploration proceeds, the progress value for states increases. Formally, a *progress measure* is a tuple $\mathcal{P} = (\psi, O, \sqsubseteq)$ where $(O, \sqsubseteq)$ is a total order, and $\psi : V \to O$ is a mapping assigning a *progress value* to each state in V. The total order is *monotonic* if $(M_1, (t, b), M_2) \in E$ implies $\psi(M_2) \geq \psi(M_1)$. In other words, a progress measure is monotonic if it is always the case that the successor of a state has a greater or equal progress measure. In this case, states which have a lesser progress measure than the minimum of the unexplored states can never be revisited. The states that can never be revisited can be deleted from memory, thus reducing the storage and time demands of state space exploration. The basic sweep-line algorithm is shown in Fig. 7 [21,4]. Note that the markings in set *Unprocessed* are now examined in the order of increasing progress, and that just prior to the end of the *while* loop, the nodes which cannot be revisited because of their progress value are removed.

The above algorithm has been generalised to cater for so-called *regress* edges in the state space, where one state has a greater progress measure than its successor [15]. In this case, the target states of the regress edges are stored persistently and some parts of the state space may be traversed more than once. Even with regress edges, the sweep-line method can provide substantial efficiency gains for state space exploration.

There are benefits in combining the sweep-line method with equivalence reduction [21,4]. A progress measure is *compatible* with an equivalence relation if equivalent states have the same progress measure. Whether compatible or not, the two techniques can be used in combination, with beneficial results. We show that if the progress measure is *not* compatible with the equivalence relation, it can be used to choose the canonical representative (see Section 5).

5 Experimental Results

This section presents experimental results for the communication protocol example of Section 3. The experimental result have been obtained using the Design/CPN [12] computer tool which supports full state space construction, equivalence class reduction, and the sweep-line method for CPN models. The results presented in this section were obtained on an Intel Xeon 3Ghz Linux PC with 2 Gb of memory.

As discussed in Section 4, the regime adopted for allocating oids can have a significant impact on the size of the state space. We have experimented with both the regimes discussed in Section 4. The first variant allocates oids in any order — here, the place *Free* in Fig. 3 holds one token for each available oid, and a transition may access any of these for assigning to a newly-generated object. The second variant allocates oids in sequence — the place *Free* holds one token which indicates the next available oid, and any transition that accesses this token will need to replace it with the subsequent oid.

---

[1] The reader should not confuse the terms *mark-and-sweep*, which refers to an algorithm for garbage collection in a state of an object-based system, and the *sweep-line* method, which is an algorithm for reducing storage requirements during state space exploration.

Table 1. Sweep-line results — oids allocated in arbitrary order, and in sequence

Free	Full			Sweep-Line ψ_1		Sweep-Line ψ_2		Sweep-Line ψ_3	
	Nodes	Arcs	Sec	Peak	Sec	Peak	Sec	Peak	Sec
3	9,897	28,716	9	8,088	12	2,976	11	2,304	13
4	256,617	826,540	1,794	226,320	1,925	54,528	1,767	61,152	3,145
3	3,153	8,064	2	2,352	2	720	2	768	2
4	48,725	155,680	89	45,572	100	10,752	112	12,112	123
5	87,029	284,272	403	60,788	543	16,576	557	15,840	459
6	>251,500		>1 hr						

We have also experimented with three progress measures. The function ψ_1 defines a generic measure for object-based systems — the number of oids in use. Progress is made as new objects are generated. The function ψ_2 defines a simple application-specific measure for the protocol case study. Each connection (held in places *Sender-Conn* and *RecverConn* in Fig. 3) is in one of four states — *OpenReq*, *OpenCnf*, *CloseReq* or *CloseCnf*. These states are assigned the numbers 1 through 4, and then ψ_2 is the weighted sum of all the connections. Finally, the function ψ_3 is a refined, application-specific measure. It identifies 16 stages that a sender goes through in the process of establishing and releasing a connection. ψ_3 is the weighted sum for the two senders.

Finally, we have experimented with two canonicalisation functions. $Canon_1$ performs a straightforward depth-first scan of each state in collecting a relabelling map (as in [10,9]). It does not use heuristics to choose the order for scanning the tokens in a place. The function $Canon_2$ determines the progress of the two senders (as in function ψ_3), and then scans the senders in the order of decreasing progress. Thus, the most advanced sender (in terms of the connection stages) ends up with the lowest oid.

Table 1 gives the results for the three sweep-line measures — the top half is for oids allocated in arbitrary order, while the bottom half is for oids allocated in sequence. The table consists of four parts. The *Free* column specifies the system parameter which is the number of available oids (i.e. $maxOID - minOID + 1$ from Fig. 2). The *Full* part lists the number of nodes and arcs in the state space, and the CPU time in seconds it took to generate the state space. The *Sweep-Line ψ_1*, *Sweep-Line ψ_2*, *Sweep-Line ψ_3* parts list the peak number of states stored with the sweep-line method and the CPU time it took to explore the state space in each case. The function ψ_1 is clearly too coarse to reduce the memory requirements by much, while functions ψ_2 and ψ_3 perform much better. However, on their own, they are not enough because the number of nodes and arcs explored with the sweep-line method is the same as for the full state space.

Table 2 gives the results for the canonicalisation functions $Canon_1$ and $Canon_2$ — again, the top half is for oids allocated in an arbitrary order, while the bottom half is for oids allocated in sequence. These tables consists of four parts. The *Free* column and the *Full* part are as before. The $Canon_1$, $Canon_2$ parts list the number of nodes and arcs in the state space together with the CPU time. The *Combined $Canon_1$, ψ_2* part lists the results for combining canonicalisation function $Canon_1$ with progress measure given by ψ_2. Table 3 provides other combinations. Canonicalisation clearly has a significant

Table 2. Canonicalisation results — oids allocated in arbitrary order, and in sequence

Free	Full			Canon₁			Canon₂			Combined Canon₁, ψ₂			
	Nodes	Arcs	Sec	Nodes	Arcs	Sec	Nodes	Arcs	Sec	Nodes	Arcs	Peak	Sec
3	9,897	28,716	9	1,538	4,532	1	421	1,230	1	3,074	9,056	445	3
4	256,617	826,540	1,794	7,524	24,896	7	2,053	6,755	1	15,046	49,784	2,223	17
5				8,982	32,806	10	2,467	8,953	2	17,962	65,604	2,999	23
6				10,712	42,820	13	2,981	11,803	3	21,420	85,624	4,171	30
7				10,720	48,268	14	2,989	13,368	3	21,436	96,518	4,179	31
16				10,720	96,940	24	2,989	27,093	6	21,436	193,844	4,179	55
3	3,153	8,064	2	1,538	4,480	1	421	1,213	1	3,074	8,952	445	3
4	48,725	155,680	89	7,524	24,096	7	2,053	6,523	1	15,046	48,184	2,223	16
5	87,029	284,272	403	8,982	30,786	9	2,469	8,378	2	17,962	61,564	2,999	21
6	>251,500		>1 hr	10,712	36,736	12	2,981	10,116	3	21,420	73,458	4,171	25
7				10,720	37,592	12	2,989	10,408	3	21,436	75,170	4,179	27
16				10,720	37,592	12	2,989	10,408	3	21,436	75,170	4,169	27

Table 3. Combined results — oids allocated in arbitrary order, and in sequence

Free	Combined Canon₁, ψ₃				Combined Canon₂, ψ₂				Combined Canon₂, ψ₃			
	Nodes	Arcs	Peak	Sec	Nodes	Arcs	Peak	Sec	Nodes	Arcs	Peak	Sec
3	2,774	8,124	301	1	840	2,452	125	1	753	2,175	89	1
4	18,613	61,304	1,957	23	4,101	13,485	598	4	5,092	16,660	493	5
5	20,515	75,474	2,189	28	4,934	17,887	808	5	5,673	20,683	551	7
6	24,107	97,320	2,603	35	5,955	23,560	1,199	7	6,741	26,898	735	9
7	24,139	108,966	2,611	38	5,972	26,692	1,207	8	6,759	30,234	739	10
16	24,283	213,060	2,611	66	5,972	54,124	1,207	14	6,798	59,621	738	17
3	2,774	8,020	301	2	840	2,418	125	1	753	2,141	89	1
4	18,613	59,048	1,957	21	4,102	13,025	598	4	5,092	16,024	493	5
5	20,507	69,850	2,189	25	4,933	16,733	808	5	5,674	19,125	551	6
6	24,091	82,222	2,603	30	5,956	20,198	1,199	6	6,741	22,763	735	8
7	24,107	83,562	2,611	31	5,971	20,778	1,207	7	6,756	23,250	739	8
16	24,107	83,562	2,611	31	5,971	20,778	1,207	7	6,756	23,250	739	8

impact on the size of the state space, with a fixed point being reached in the number of nodes once $Free \geq 7$. It is also notable that with the more refined progress measure ψ_3, some states are revisited multiple times (see the discussion in [15]). Here, it leads to time penalties, but on more memory-constrained machines, we have observed a five-fold improvement in performance. In other words, even though function $Canon_2$ is based on the refined progress measure ψ_3, the combined use of the sweep-line method with the same ψ_3 can produce significant time improvements because of the decreased memory requirements.

6 Conclusion

This paper has examined the state space exploration of object-based systems with garbage collection. We have used a folded representation of such systems in a Petri

Net formalism which makes it possible to build on their extensive use in the modelling and analysis of concurrent systems. Specifically, our representation of such systems has made it possible to perform state space exploration with existing tools.

We have demonstrated that the combination of equivalence reduction and the sweepline method can ameliorate the state explosion problem for object-based systems. A simple progress measure based on the number of used oids was too coarse, at least for our case study. Application-dependent progress measures were more effective in reducing the peak number of nodes that needed to be stored. A significant benefit of this combination is that the effort expended in the determination of a discriminating progress measure can help to achieve a much better canonicalisation function. This is important given that optimal canonicalisation functions may require exponential time.

Future work will apply these algorithms to more realistic case studies incorporating more dynamic components. We also intend to explore other heuristics and equivalence reduction algorithms for producing more optimal canonicalisation functions.

Acknowledgements

The authors are pleased to acknowledge early discussions with Thomas Mailund about state space exploration of Object-Based systems, and early efforts by Garen Derharoutian and Joern Freiheit in implementing a combination of equivalence reduction and the sweep-line method in the Design/CPN tool.

References

1. G. Agha, F. De Cindio, and G. Rozenberg, editors. *Concurrent Object-Oriented Programming and Petri Nets*, volume 2001 of *Lecture Notes in Computer Science*. Springer-Verlag, Berlin, 2001.
2. R. Bastide, O. Sy, and P. Palanque. A Formal Notation and Tool for the Engineering of CORBA Systems. *Concurrency: Practice and Experience*, 12:1379–1403, 2000.
3. O. Biberstein, D. Buchs, and N. Guelfi. Object-Oriented Nets with Algebraic Specifications: The CO-OPN/2 Formalism. In G. Agha, F. De Cindio, and G. Rozenberg, editors, *Concurrent Object-Oriented Programming and Petri Nets*, volume 2001 of *Lecture Notes in Computer Science*, pages 70–127. Springer-Verlag, 2001.
4. J. Billington, G.E. Gallasch, L.M. Kristensen, and T. Mailund. Exploiting Equivalence Redution and the Sweep-Line Method for Detecting Terminal States. *IEEE Transactions on System, Man and Cybernetics*, 34(1):23–37, 2004.
5. M. Ceska, V. Janousek, and T. Vojnar. Generating and Using State Spaces of Object-Oriented Petri Nets. *International Journal of Computer Systems Science and Engineering*, 16(3):183–193, 2001.
6. S. Christensen, L. M. Kristensen, and T. Mailund. A Sweep-Line Method for State Space Exploration. In *7th International Conference on Tools and Algorithms for the Construction and Analysis of Systems (TACAS'2001)*, volume 2031 of *Lecture Notes in Computer Science*, pages 450–464. Springer-Verlag, 2001.
7. D. Comer. *Internetworking with TCP/IP: Principles, Protocols and Architectures*, volume 1. Prentice-Hall, Englewood Cliffs, second edition, 1991.
8. J. Gosling, B. Joy, and G. Steele. *The Java^{TM} Language Specification*. Addison-Wesley, Reading Massachussets, 1996.

9. R. Iosif. Exploiting Heap Symmetries in Explicit-State Model Checking of Software. In *16th IEEE Conference on Automated Software Engineeering*, pages 254–261. IEEE, 2001.

10. R. Iosif and R. Sisto. dSPIN: A Dynamic Extension of SPIN. In *6th SPIN Workshop*, volume 1680 of *Lecture Notes in Computer Science*, pages 261–276. Springer, 1999.

11. K. Jensen. *Coloured Petri Nets: Basic Concepts, Analysis Methods and Practical Use — Volume 1: Basic Concepts*, volume 26 of *EATCS Monographs in Computer Science*. Springer-Verlag, Berlin, 1992.

12. K. Jensen, S. Christensen, P. Huber, and M. Holla. *Design/CPN^{TM}: A Reference Manual*. MetaSoftware Corporation, 1992.

13. T.A. Junttila. Finding Symmetries of Algebraic System Nets. *Fundamenta Informatica*, 37:269–289, 1999.

14. T.A. Junttila. New Canonical Representative Marking Algorithms for Place/Transition Nets. In J. Cortadella and W. Reisig, editors, *25th International Conference on the Application and Theory of Petri Nets*, volume 3099, pages 258–277, Bologna, Italy, 2004. Springer.

15. L.M. Kristensen and T. Mailund. A Generalised Sweep-Line Method for Safety Properties. In *11th International Symposium of Formal Methods Europe (FME'2002)*, volume 2391 of *Lecture Notes in Computer Science*, pages 549–567, Copenhagen, 2002. Springer.

16. O. Kummer, F. Wienberg, M. Duvigneau, J. Schumacher, M. Köhler, D. Moldt, H. Rölke, and R. Valk. An extensible editor and simulation engine for Petri nets: Renew. In J. Cortadella and W. Reisig, editors, *25th International Conference on Application and Theory of Petri Nets (ICATPN 2004)*, volume 3099 of *Lecture Notes in Computer Science*, pages 484–493, Bologna, Italy, 2004. Springer.

17. C.A. Lakos. Object Petri Nets Definition and Relationship to Coloured Nets. Technical Report TR94-3, Computer Science Department, University of Tasmania, April 1994 1994.

18. C.A. Lakos. From Coloured Petri Nets to Object Petri Nets. In G. De Michelis and M. Diaz, editors, *16th International Conference on the Application and Theory of Petri Nets*, volume 935 of *Lecture Notes in Computer Science*, pages 278–297, Torino, Italy, 1995. Springer-Verlag.

19. C.A. Lakos. A Petri Net View of Mobility. In *25th IFIP WG 6.1 International Conference on Formal Techniques for Networked and Distributed Systems*, Lecture Notes in Computer Science, Taipei, Taiwan, 2005. Springer (to appear).

20. L. Lorentsen and L. Kristensen. Exploiting Stabilizers and Parallelism in State Space Generation with the Symmetry Method. In *2nd International Conference on Application of Concurrency to System Design*, pages 211–220, Newcastle, U.K., 2001. IEEE Computer Society.

21. T. Mailund. Analysing Infinite-State Systems by Combining Equivalence Reduction and the Sweep-Line Method. In J. Esparza and C. Lakos, editors, *23rd International Conference on the Application and Theory of Petri Nets*, volume 2360 of *Lecture Notes in Computer Science*, pages 314–334, Adelaide, Australia, 2002. Springer.

22. W. Reisig and G. Rozenberg, editors. *Lectures on Petri Nets I: Basic Models*, volume 1491 of *Lecture Notes in Computer Science*. Springer, Berlin, 1998.

23. W. Reisig and G. Rozenberg, editors. *Lectures on Petri Nets II: Applications*, volume 1492 of *Lecture Notes in Computer Science*. Springer, Berlin, 1998.

24. B. Stroustrup. *The C++ Programming Language (Second Edition)*. Addison-Wesley, New York, 1991.

25. A. Valmari. The State Explosion Problem. In W. Reisig and G. Rozenberg, editors, *Lectures on Petri Nets I: Basic Models*, volume 1491 of *Lecture Notes in Computer Science*, pages 429–528. Springer, Dagstuhl, 1998.

26. P. Wegner. Dimensions of Object-Based Language Design. In N. Meyrowitz, editor, *OOPSLA 87*, pages 168–182, Orlando, Florida, 1987. ACM.

Syntactical Colored Petri Nets Reductions

S. Evangelista[1], S. Haddad[2], and J.-F. Pradat-Peyre[1]

[1] CEDRIC - CNAM Paris, 292, rue St Martin, 75003 Paris
[2] LAMSADE-CNRS UMR 7024 Université Paris-Dauphine,
Place du Maréchal de Lattre de Tassigny, 75775, Paris Cedex 16

Abstract. In this paper, we develop a syntactical version of elaborated reductions for high-level Petri nets. These reductions simplify the model by merging some sequential transitions into an atomic one. Their conditions combine local structural ones (e.g. related to the actions of a thread) and global algebraic ones (e.g. related to the threads synchronization). We show that these conditions are performed in a syntactical way, when a syntax of the color mappings is given. We show also how our method outperforms previous ones on a recent case study with regard both to the reduction ratio and the automatization of their application.

1 Introduction

The concurrent programming paradigm is a powerful tool for the implementation of complex software. However it may lead to applications where the interaction between threads or processes produces subtle behaviours that are difficult to predict. In this context, it is necessary to include in the application development life cycle a complete and systematic verification step.

Two kinds of verification techniques are usually performed: state enumeration based methods and structural methods. The state enumeration based methods lead to a complete verification of the modeled system but the analysis is restricted by the combinatory explosion factor (i.e. the number of control states may grow exponentially w.r.t. the number of threads and the size of the application). The structural methods are generally efficient but they do not ensure the complete correctness of the system. Thus an attractive trade-off is to combine both methods.

In this context, an efficient strategy is to examine the structure of the model for reducing the number of execution traces that are to be analyzed. The obtained reduction ratio depends on the kind of considered properties. The more specific are the properties, the greater is the reduction.

Again, two distinct approaches can be followed to obtain such a reduction. On the one hand, it's possible to apply on-the-fly techniques when building the state graph. These techniques are based on the detection that in a given state,

- some enabled actions may be forgotten since they lead to an already visited state [GW93],
- some enabled actions may be safely delayed [Val93],
- some enabled actions may be executed simultaneously [VM97].

D.A. Peled and Y.-K. Tsay (Eds.): ATVA 2005, LNCS 3707, pp. 202–216, 2005.

On the other hand, one can work at the model level in order to simplify it before building a reduced state graph. In this framework, a frequent approach is the merging of consecutive statements into a virtual atomic one whose effect is the composition of the effects of these statements. Such a transformation presents the following advantages:

- the combinatory explosion is drastically reduced by the elimination of the intermediate states,
- the induced overhead computation is negligible w.r.t. the cost of the state graph building,
- this abstraction is potentially applicable to "parameterized" programs (e.g. independent of the number of instances of a process class) and **this feature is not covered by the on-the-fly techniques**.

We have chosen to explore this approach by proposing new colored Petri nets reductions that simplify the model by merging some sequential transitions [EHPP04]. These reductions enlarge earlier ones by weakening application conditions but also by defining precisely which conditions are sufficient to preserve some specific properties (i.e. liveness and linear temporal formulae defined on maximal or infinite sequences) We show here, that given a syntax for colored net, application conditions and transformation rules of these reductions can performed with only fully automatic syntactical operations.

The paper is organized as follows. In Section 2 we recall the definition of colored nets and the definition of the colored post-agglomeration. Section 3 shows how to define syntactical conditions enabling the manipulation of colored mapping with a well chosen syntax for colored Petri nets. Section 4 highlights the interest of our reductions by applying them on a recently published case study. Before concluding, we present in Section 5 related works.

2 Colored Petri Nets and Agglomerations

We assume that the reader is familiar with Petri nets and usual mathematics notions such as multisets or powersets. We denote by $Bag(S) = \mathbb{N}^S$ the set of multisets over the finite set S, and by $\mathcal{P}(S) = \{true, false\}^S$ the set of powersets over S.

We first give in this Section some definitions related to colored Petri nets. Then, we recall some definitions concerning color mappings properties and handling. At last, we detail the application conditions of the post-agglomeration. For space constraint, the pre-agglomeration will not be mentioned in this paper. The pre-agglomeration is treated in [EHPP04].

2.1 Colored Petri Nets

Definition 1. *A colored Petri net (CPN for short) is a tuple* $N = \langle P, T, \Sigma, C, W^-, W^+ \rangle$ *where P is a finite set of* **places***; T is a finite set of* **transitions***, with* $P \cap T = \emptyset$*; Σ, the* **colors set***, is a finite set of finite and non empty sets; C, the* **color domain** *application, is a mapping from* $P \cup T$ *to* Σ*; W^- and W^+, the* **backward and forward incidence matrixes** *associate to each* $(p,t) \in P \times T$ *a color mapping from* $C(t)$ *to* $Bag(C(p))$*.*

A couple (e,c) with $e \in P \cup T$ and $c \in C(e)$ is called an instance of e. In the remainder of the paper mappings from C to $Bag(C')$ will be extended to mappings from $Bag(C)$ to $Bag(C')$ by the two following rules : $f(\lambda.c) = \lambda.f(c)$ and $f(c_1 + c_2) = f(c_1) + f(c_2)$. Given a place p, the sets $^\bullet p$ and $p^\bullet$ are defined as usual as $\{t \in T | W^+(p,t) \neq 0\}$ and $\{t \in T | W^-(p,t) \neq 0\}$. The same notations for a transition can be given in a straightforward way. A marking of a CPN associates to each of its places a multi-set over its color domain. The firing rule defines the dynamic of the net.

Definition 2. *Let $N = \langle P,T,\Sigma,C,W^-,W^+,m_0 \rangle$ be a CPN. A **marking** of N is a mapping which associates each $p \in P$ to an element of $Bag(C(p))$. The set of markings of a net N is denoted by $\mathbb{M}_N$. A **colored marked net** is a couple $\langle N, m_0 \rangle$ with N a CPN and $m_0 \in \mathbb{M}_N$ the initial marking of the net.*

Definition 3. *Let $N = \langle P,T,\Sigma,C,W^-,W^+ \rangle$ be a CPN, $t \in T$, $c_t \in C(t)$, and $m \in \mathbb{M}_N$. The instance (t,c_t) is **firable** at m, denoted by $m[(t,c_t)\rangle$, if and only if $\forall p \in P, m(p) \geq W^-(p,t)(c_t)$. The **firing** of (t,c_t) at m leads to the marking m', denoted by $m[(t,c_t)\rangle m'$, defined by: $\forall p \in P, m'(p) = m(p) + W(p,t)(c_t)$. The **reachability set** of $\langle N, m_0 \rangle$, denoted by $Reach(N,m_0)$, is the set $\{m_0\} \cup \{m \in \mathbb{M}_N | \exists m' \in Reach(N,m_0), t \in T, c_t \in C(t) | m'[(t,c_t)\rangle m\}$.*

Application conditions of agglomerations rely on the existence on some flows that induce invariants.

Definition 4. *A **colored flow** $\mathcal{F}$, on the color domain $C_{\mathcal{F}}$, is a vector over P, denoted by the formal sum $\mathcal{F} = \sum_{p \in P} \lambda_p.\mathcal{F}_p.p$, where $\forall p \in P, \lambda_p \in \mathbb{Z}$ and $\mathcal{F}_p$ is a mapping from $Bag(C(p))$ to $Bag(C_{\mathcal{F}})$ such that: $\forall t \in T, \sum_{p \in P} \lambda_p.\mathcal{F}_p \circ W(p,t) = 0$ [1]. The colored flow $\mathcal{F}$ is **positive** if $\forall p \in P, \lambda_p \geq 0$.*

Definition 5. *A colored flow $\mathcal{F}$, on the domain $C_{\mathcal{F}}$, induces the invariant:*
*$\forall m \in Reach(N,m_0), \sum_{p \in P} \lambda_p.\mathcal{F}_p(m(p)) = \sum_{p \in P} \lambda_p.\mathcal{F}_p(m_0(p))$. This invariant is a **binary** invariant if $\forall c \in C_{\mathcal{F}}, \sum_{p \in P} \lambda_p.\mathcal{F}_p(m_0(p))(c) = 1$; a **synchronization** invariant if $\forall c \in C_{\mathcal{F}}, \sum_{p \in P} \lambda_p.\mathcal{F}_p(m_0(p))(c) = 0$. When no confusion is possible (i.e. the initial marking is given), we will not distinguish a colored flow and its induced invariant.*

For instance, given the right model of figure 1(b) we can automatically compute the positive flow (on the domain ε) $\mathcal{F} = mb + \langle All_C \rangle.q2$ which induces the binary invariant $\forall m \in Acc(N,m_0), m(mb) + \sum_{c \in C} m(q2(c)) = 1$. This invariant ensures that when place mb is marked then place $q2$ is not, and then, that transition $d1d2$ is not fireable when $q2$ is marked.

2.2   Color Mappings Properties and Handling

Reductions techniques for Petri nets are characterized by : (1) some application conditions, (2) the characterization of the reduced net, (3) the properties preserved. For ordinary Petri nets, the application conditions rely on the structure of the net, i.e., the physical links between the places and transitions of the net, and on algebraic conditions

---

[1] 0 denotes here the null mapping from $C(t)$ to $Bag(C_{\mathcal{F}})$.

given by the invariants of the net. When reasoning with colored nets, the color mappings also have to be considered since the structure of the colored net does not necessarily reflect the structure of the underlying ordinary Petri net. There is then two possibilities : unfold the net, apply reductions on the unfolded net and fold it back; or define conditions on the colored net that ensure correct ordinary agglomerations in the underlying net. Thus operations on natural numbers, e.g., $W^-(p,t).W^+(q,t) > 0$ becomes operations on color mappings, e.g., $W^-(p,t) \circ {}^t(W^+(q,t)) \neq 0_{Bag(C(q)) \to Bag(C(p))}$.

Firstly, we define a set of properties that are used in agglomerations definition. These properties can give some precious hints on the structure on the underlying net. For instance, a quasi-one-to-one mapping that labels an arc between a place p and a transition t, implies that two different instances of t cannot be linked to the same instance of p.

Definition 6. *Let f be a mapping from C to $Bag(C')$. f is*

- **unitary** *when $\forall c \in C, f(c)(c') \leq 1$*
- **orthonormal** *when $\forall c \in C \exists c' \in C'$ such that $f(c)(c') = 1$ and $\forall c' \in C' \exists c \in C$ such that $f(c)(c') = 1$*
- **ortho-projection** *when $f = g \circ h$ with h an orthonormal mapping from C to $Bag(C)$ and g an orthonormal mapping from C to $Bag(C')$*
- **quasi-one-to-one** *when $\forall c_1, c_2 \in C, c' \in C', f(c_1)(c') = 0 \vee f(c_2)(c') = 0$*
- **quasi-onto** *when $\forall c' \in C', \exists c \in C$ such that $f(c)(c') > 0$*

Secondly, a frequent need is to symbolically follow a path in the underlying net. That can be achieved by using the transposition and composition operators. The transposition is used to find the instances of a place linked to a transition instance, e.g., ${}^t W^+(p,h)$. The composition enables to find, for example, the instances of a transition linked to another one by an intermediary place instance, e.g., ${}^t W^+(p,h) \circ W^-(p,f)$.

Definition 7 (Transposition and composition). *If f is a mapping from $Bag(C'')$ to $Bag(C')$, and g is a mapping from $Bag(C)$ to $Bag(C'')$ then $f \circ g$ is a mapping from $Bag(C)$ to $Bag(C')$ defined by $\forall c \in C, c' \in C', (f \circ g)(c)(c') = \sum_{c'' \in C''} f(c'')(c') \cdot g(c)(c'')$. If h is a mapping from $Bag(C)$ to $Bag(C')$, then ${}^t h$ is a mapping from $Bag(C')$ to $Bag(C)$ defined by $\forall c \in C, c' \in C', {}^t h(c')(c) = h(c)(c')$.*

At last, we are usually not interested in the exact numbers of tokens produced in a place, but rather in the fact that tokens are actually produced. The $\bar{f}$ operation can be used for this purpose.

Definition 8. *Let $f \in S \to Bag(S')$. $\bar{f} \in S \to \mathcal{P}(S')$ is defined by: $\forall s \in S, \bar{f}(s) = \{s' \in S' \mid f(s)(s') > 0\}$.*

It is also useful to check if the image of a mapping f from $\mathcal{P}(C)$ to $\mathcal{P}(C')$ is included in the image of a mapping g from $\mathcal{P}(C)$ to $\mathcal{P}(C')$; we denote this by $f \sqsubseteq g$ and it is defined by $f \sqsubseteq g$ iff $\forall c \in C, \bar{f}(c) \subseteq \bar{g}(c)$.

2.3   The Post-Agglomeration Reduction

We recall now application conditions of the post-agglomeration. The transformation rule and the definition of the other transitions agglomeration (the pre-agglomeration) are presented in [EHPP04].

The basic hypothesis of the post-agglomeration is that the set of transitions of the net is partitioned as: $T = T_0 \uplus H \uplus F$. The underlying idea of this decomposition is that transitions of H and transitions of F are causally dependent: an occurrence of $f \in F$ in a sequence of firings may always be related to a previous occurrence of some $h \in H$ in this sequence. Thus, in the reduced net, one fires f immediately after the firing of some $h \in H$.

The definition of the net obtained by the agglomeration of H with F is straightforward. Thus for space constraint we will not give it in this paper. For the same reasons, we will not detail the properties preserved by the post-agglomeration. We simply recall that if all the mentioned conditions are verified by the net, both the reduced and the original net will be equivalent in terms of Petri net liveness and languages of maximal and infinite sequences which do not observe transitions of F. Indeed, since the idea of the post-agglomeration is to advance the firing of any transition $f \in F$, the sequence remains equivalent with respect to transitions which are not in F. The curious readers may find these additional informations in [EHPP04].

The post-agglomeration is based on four hypotheses: the **potential agglomerability**, the F-**independence**, the F-**continuation** and the HF-**interchangeability**.

Firstly we impose that the net is **potentially agglomerable**. This hypothesis ensures that a transition $f \in F$ in a sequence of firings is related to a previous occurrence of some $h \in H$ in this sequence. The first point ensures that the place p models an intermediate state between the firing of a transition in H and the firing of a transition in F. The second one ensures that the firing of a transition h produces only one token in place p (conditions on H) and that two different tokens in place p cannot be consumed by a same firing of f (conditions on F).

Definition 9. *A colored net is **potentially agglomerable** (p-agglomerable) if $\exists p \in P$ such that*

1. $\bullet p = H$, $p^\bullet = F$ *and* $m_0(p) = 0$;
2. $\forall f \in F$, $C(f) = C(p) \times C_f$, $W^-(p,f)$ *is an ortho-projection from* $C(f)$ *to* $C(p)$ *and* $\forall h \in H$, $C(h) = C(p)$, $W^+(p,h)$ *is orthonormal*

The F-**independence** hypothesis ensures that when the place p is marked, no transition that can produce tokens useful for the firing of a transition in F can be fired. Given $c \in C(p)$, $\phi(c)$ is exactly the set of firing instances of t producing tokens useful for the firing of (f,c). Similarly, given $c \in C(p)$, $\psi(c)$ is exactly the set of firing instances of t which can not be fired when a token colored by c is present in p. Additionally, the strong independence ensures that the place p is safe, i.e. there is at most one token per color present in p.

Definition 10. *A p-agglomerable colored net is F-**independent** if $\forall f \in F$, $\forall q \in (\bullet f \setminus \{p\})$, $\forall t \in \bullet q \setminus F$, $\exists p_t \in \bullet t$, $\exists \mathcal{F} = \sum_{r \in P} \mathcal{F}_r.r$ a binary positive flow on a domain D such that if $\phi = {}^t W^+(q,t) \circ W^-(q,f) \circ {}^t W^-(p,f)$ and $\psi = {}^t W^-(p_t,t) \circ {}^t \mathcal{F}_{p_t} \circ \mathcal{F}_p$ then $\phi \sqsubseteq \psi$. Furthermore, if there exists a binary positive invariant $\mathcal{F}'$ on the domain $C(p)$ such that ${}^t \mathcal{F}'_p$ is a quasi-onto mapping then the net is **strongly** F-independent.*

The F-**continuation** hypothesis means that an excess of occurrences of $h \in H$ can always be reduced by subsequent firings of transitions of F, i.e. when the place p is marked, a transition of F is necessarily fireable.

Definition 11. *A p-agglomerable colored net is F-**continuable** if $\exists f \in F$ such that $\,^\bullet f = \{p\}$ or $\exists\, F_s \subset F$ such that:*

1. $\forall f \in F_s, \exists p_f \neq p \in P,\; ^\bullet f = \{p, p_f\}$,
2. $\forall f \in F_s, {}^t W^-(p_f, f)$ is an unitary quasi-one-to-one mapping;
3. there exists a flow on $C(p)$, $\mathcal{F} = \sum_{f \in F_s} \mathcal{F}_{p_f} \cdot p_f - \lambda \cdot X_{C(p)} \cdot p$ with
   $\forall f \in F_s, {}^t\overline{\mathcal{F}_{p_f}} \sqsubseteq \overline{W^-(p_f, f)} \circ {}^t W^-(p, f)$ and such that
   (a) either $\lambda = 0$ and $\mathcal{F}$ induces a binary positive invariant
   (b) or $\lambda = 1$ and $\mathcal{F}$ induces a synchronization invariant

At last, the HF-**interchangeability** hypothesis mainly restricts either the set H or F to be a singleton in order to avoid the case where $h \in H$ and $f \in F$ are live in the original net whereas the transition hf is not live in the reduced net.

Definition 12. *A p-agglomerable colored net is HF-**interchangeable** if either $H = \{h\}$ or $F = \{f\}$, $C(f) = C(p)$ (thus $W^-(p, f)$ is orthonormal since it is p-agglomerable)*

3 Syntactical Rules for Agglomerations Implementation

Computing the transposition of a color mapping, or the composition of two color mappings is impossible for general colored Petri nets, i.e., with unstructured color domains or color mappings. In order to enable to perform such computations in a symbolic way without unfolding the net, we first define in this section a restricted class of colored Petri nets with well defined color domains and mappings. In the second and third part of the section, we will see that this class allows us to check basic mapping properties such as orthonormality in a straightforward way, and to perform operations on color mappings in a syntactic manner.

3.1 Quasi Well Formed Colored Nets (QWNs)

Quasi well formed nets are a restriction of the well-known well formed nets class. QWNs are characterized by a good structuring of color domains and mappings.

At first, to such a net is associated a set of finite color classes (e.g. a set of processes) that will be denoted $Cl = \{C_1, \dots, C_N\}$. The sizes of these classes are the parameters of the net (denoted n_i for C_i). Each class can be enumerated starting from any color with the help of a successor mapping $succ$, i.e. $\forall c \in C_i$, $C_i = \{c, succ(c), \dots, succ^{n_i-1}(c)\}$.

A color domain C is a cartesian product of color classes. For the sake of simplicity, we assume that these domains are built upon the order of Cl, i.e., each color domain C can be written as $C = C_1 \times \cdots \times C_1 \times \cdots \times C_N \times \cdots \times C_N$. Since we allow repeated occurrences of a class, e_i denotes the number of occurrences of C_i in C.

Color mappings are built using simpler mappings called elementary mappings. Four kinds of elementary mappings are allowed: the projection, the successor (or predecessor), the constant mapping, and the broadcast mapping.

Definition 13. *Let C be a color domain, and C_i be a color class. The set of **elementary color mappings** from C to $Bag(C_i)$ is the set*
$$\{X_i^j\}_{j \in [1..e_i]} \cup \{X_i^j \oplus n\}_{j \in [1..e_i], n \in \mathbb{N}} \cup \{All_i\} \cup \{\mathbb{1}_{c_i}\}_{c_i \in C_i}$$

It is defined by $\forall c = \langle c_1^1, \ldots, c_N^{e_N} \rangle \in C$:

- $X_i^j(c) = \{c_i^j\}$ *(a **projection** mapping)*
- $X_i^j \oplus n(c) = X_i^j \ominus -n(c) = \{succ^n(c_i^j)\}$ *(a **successor** mapping)*
- $All_i(c) = \sum_{c_i \in C_i} c_i$ *(the **broadcast** mapping)*
- $\mathbb{1}_{c_i}(c) = \{c_i\}$ *(a **constant** mapping)*

Definition 14. *Let C be a color domain and $c = \langle c_1^1, \ldots, c_N^{e_N} \rangle \in C$ then an **elementary guard** G on C, a mapping from C to $\mathbb{B} = \{true, false\}$, is:*

- *either $(X_i^j = X_i^{j'} \oplus n)$ defined by $(X_i^j = X_i^{j'} \oplus n)(c) = (c_i^j = succ^n(c_i^{j'}))$,*
- *or $(X_i^j = \mathbb{1}_{c_i})$ with $c_i \in C_i$ defined by $(X_i^j = \mathbb{1}_{c_i})(c) = (c_i^j = c_i)$*

A general guard is a boolean combination of elementary guards.

The general syntax of color mappings is based on elementary mappings and guards with the help of three constructors: the tuple constructor, the product of a tuple by a scalar and the sum of tuples.

Definition 15. *Let C and C' be two color domains. The syntax of a **QWN color mapping** f from C to $Bag(C')$ is:*

$f = \sum_{k=1}^{K} \alpha_k . [G_k] \langle f_{1,k}^1, \ldots, f_{N,k}^{e_N'} \rangle$ *with $\forall k \in [1..K], i \in [1..N], j \in [1..e_i'], \alpha_k > 0, G_k$ a guard on C and $f_{i,k}^j$ is an elementary color mapping from C to $Bag(C_i)$. It is defined by:*

$$f(c) = \sum_{k=1}^{K} \alpha_k \sum_{\{c \in C | G_k(c)\}} \langle f_{1,k}^1, \ldots, f_{N,k}^{e_N'} \rangle(c)$$

3.2 Checking Color Mappings Properties

The good structuring of quasi well formed nets allows us to easily check color mapping properties. The straightforward proof of these propositions can be found in [Eva04]. In all the propositions, we consider a quasi well formed color mapping f from $Bag(C)$ to $Bag(C')$.

A simple condition to ensure that f is unitary is to impose that it is composed of a single tuple of which valuation is 1.

Proposition 1. *If $f = [G]\langle f_1^1, \ldots, f_N^{e_N'} \rangle$ then f is **unitary**.*

To ensure orthonormality, we must have $C = C'$, f composed of a single non guarded tuple and each variable of the transition must appear in this tuple.

Proposition 2. *If $C = C'$, $f = \langle f_1^1, \ldots, f_N^{e_N'} \rangle$ and $\forall i \in [1..N], j \in [1..e_i], \exists j' \in [1..e_i], n \in \mathbb{N}$ such that $f_i^j = X_i^{j'} \oplus n$ then f is **orthonormal**.*

If f is a single non guarded tuple in which only variables appear and such that the same variable can not appear at two different positions in the tuple then it is an ortho-projection.

Proposition 3. *If $f = \langle f_1^1, \ldots, f_N^{e_N'} \rangle$ and $\forall i \in [1..N], j \in [1..e_i'], f_i^j = X_i^{j'} \oplus n$ and $\nexists j'' \in [1..e_i']$ such that $f_i^{j''} = X_i^{j'} \oplus m$ then f is an **ortho-projection**.*

A single tuple in which all the variables of the transition appear is quasi-one-to-one.

Proposition 4. *If* $f = \alpha.[G]\langle f_1^1, \ldots, f_N^{e'_N}\rangle$ *and* $\forall i \in [1..N], j \in [1..e_i], \exists j' \in [1..e'_i], n \in \mathbb{N}$ *such that* $f_i^{j'} = X_i^j \oplus n$ *then* f *is* **quasi-one-to-one**.

At last, f is quasi-onto if there is a non guarded tuple in it which is such that no constant appear in it and no variable can appear at two different positions in it.

Proposition 5. *If* $f = \alpha.\langle f_1^1, \ldots, f_N^{e'_N}\rangle + g$ *such that these two conditions are fulfilled*

1. $\forall i \in [1..N], j \in [1..e'_i], f_i^j = All_i$ or $f_i^j = X_i^{j'} \oplus n$
2. $\nexists i \in [1..N], j \in [1..e'_i], j' \in [1..e'_i]$ *such that* $f_i^j = X_i^{j''} \oplus n$ *and* $f_i^{j'} = X_i^{j''} \oplus m$

then f *is* **quasi-onto**.

3.3   Computing Structural Relations

Syntactic Transposition. We now focus on the specification of a symbolic transposition. At first, we notice that the transpose of a linear combination of mappings is the linear combination of the transposes. Thus we restrict ourselves to a guarded tuple. We now focus on the guard. We remark that if $f = [G]\langle f_1^1, \ldots, f_N^{e'_N}\rangle$ then f can be viewed as the following composition: $f = \langle f_1^1, \ldots, f_N^{e'_N}\rangle \circ [G]\langle X_1^1, \ldots, X_1^{e_1}, \ldots, X_N^1, \ldots, X_N^{e_N}\rangle$. Thus $^t f = {}^t[G]\langle X_1^1, \ldots, X_1^{e_1}, \ldots, X_N^1, \ldots, X_N^{e_N}\rangle \circ {}^t\langle f_1^1, \ldots, f_N^{e'_N}\rangle$. By a straightforward evaluation, one remarks that:

$$^t[G]\langle X_1^1, \ldots, X_1^{e_1}, \ldots, X_N^1, \ldots, X_N^{e_N}\rangle = [G]\langle X_1^1, \ldots, X_1^{e_1}, \ldots, X_N^1, \ldots, X_N^{e_N}\rangle$$

Hence supposing that the composition can be handled, we restrict the symbolic transposition to non guarded tuples.

We make a new observation. Let g be a mapping from C to C' and h be a mapping from D to D'. Suppose that f is a mapping from $C \times D$ to $C' \times D'$ defined by $f(c,d) = \langle g(c), h(d)\rangle$. Then $^t f(c', d') = \langle {}^t g(c'), {}^t h(d')\rangle$. As it is the case for QWN mappings (that can be viewed as tuple of mappings from C^{e_i} to $C^{e'_i}$), we can restrict ourselves to mappings where a single class occurs (with possible repetitions) in its domain and its codomain.

Proposition 6 (Symbolic transposition). *Let* $C = C_i^e$ *and* $C' = C_i^{e'}$ *be two color domains. Since we deal with a single class C_i, we omit in the sequel the subscript i.*

Let $f = \langle f^1, \ldots, f^{e'}\rangle$ *be a mapping from* $Bag(C)$ *to* $Bag(C')$ *with* f^k *being either* $All, X^{\mu(k)} \oplus m_{k'}$ *or* $\mathbb{1}_n$. *The transposition of* f *is defined by:*

$$^t f = [\bigwedge_{k=1}^{e} G_k \bigwedge_{k'=1}^{e'} H_{k'}]\langle g^1, \ldots, g^e\rangle]$$

where:

- **if** $\mu^{-1}(k) = \emptyset$ **then** $g^k = All$ and $G_k = true$
- **else** $(\mu^{-1}(k) = \{j_1, \ldots, j_q\})$ $g^k = X^{j_1} \ominus m_{j_1}$ and $G_k = \bigwedge_{k'=2}^{q}(X^{j_{k'}} \ominus n_{j_{k'}} = X^{j_1} \ominus m_{j_1})$

and

- **if** $f^{k'} = \mathbb{1}_n$ **then** $H_{k'} = (X^{k'} = \mathbb{1}_n)$
- **else** $H_{k'} = true$

Example 1. Let us compute the transpose of the mapping f from
$Bag(C_1 \times C_1 \times C_2 \times C_3 \times C_3)$ to $Bag(C_1 \times C_1 \times C_2 \times C_2 \times C_3)$ defined by

$$f = \langle X_1^1 \ominus 3, X_1^1 \oplus 1, X_2^1, All_2, \mathbb{1}_{3,1} \rangle$$

- We first consider the mapping f_1 from $Bag(C_1 \times C_1)$ to $Bag(C_1 \times C_1)$ defined by
  $f_1 = \langle X_1^1 \ominus 1, X_1^1 \oplus 1 \rangle$.
  Using previous notations, $\mu_1(1) = 1$ and $\mu_1(2) = 2$. So,
  - $\mu_1^{-1}(1) = \{1,2\}$ and then $g_1^1 = X_1^1 \oplus 3$ and $G_1 = (X_1^2 \ominus 1 = X_1^1 \oplus 3)$
  - $\mu_1^{-1}(2) = \emptyset$ and then $g_1^2 = All_1$
  - No constant appears in f_1 so $H_1 = true$.
- We consider then the mapping from $Bag(C_2)$ to $Bag(C_2 \times C_2)$ $f_2 = \langle X_2^1, All_2 \rangle$.
  - $\mu_2^{-1}(1) = \{1\}$ and then $g_2^1 = X_2^1$ and $G_2 = true$
  - No constant appears in f_2 so $H_2 = true$.
- At last consider the mapping from $Bag(C_3 \times C_3)$ to $Bag(C_3)$ $f_3 = \langle \mathbb{1}_{3,1} \rangle$. We obtain
  - $\mu_3^{-1}(1) = \mu^{-1}(2) = \emptyset$ so $g_3^1 = g_3^2 = All_3$.
  - As $f_3^1 = \mathbb{1}_{3,1}$ then $H_3 = (X_3^1 = \mathbb{1}_{3,1})$.

So we obtain as result to our calculus:

$$^t f = [(X_1^2 \ominus 1 = X_1^1 \oplus 3) \wedge (X_3^1 = \mathbb{1}_{3,1})] \langle X_1^1 \oplus 3, All_1, X_2^1, All_3, All_3 \rangle$$

Syntactic Composition. Computing the composition $f \circ g$ of two mappings can raise syntactical problems. For instance, if g is a mapping from $Bag(\varepsilon)$ to $Bag(C_1)$ and f a mapping from $Bag(C_1)$ to $Bag(C_1 \times C_1)$ defined by $f = \langle X_1^1, X_1^1 \rangle$ and $g = \langle All_1 \rangle$, we clearly have $f \circ g = \sum_{c \in C_1} \langle c, c \rangle$ which cannot be expressed in our syntax. In the same way, $\langle All_i \rangle \circ \langle All_i \rangle = n_i . \langle All_i \rangle$ which is also not allowed in our syntax. So we impose for the computation of $f \circ g$ that

$$\forall i, k, g_i^k = All_i \Rightarrow (\exists ! j, n \text{ such that } f_i^j = X_i^j \oplus n) \text{ and} (\forall j, f_i^j \neq All_i)$$

With this additional constraint, we can compute the transposition of any two tuples as follows (the proof can again be found in [EHPP04]): Using linearity of QWN mappings we restrict our self to the composition of tuples of elementary mappings.

Proposition 7 (Symbolic tuples composition). *Let* $g = \langle g_1^1, \ldots, g_N^{e_N''} \rangle$ *from* $Bag(C)$ *to* $Bag(C'')$ *and* $f = \langle f_1^1, \ldots, f_N^{e_N'} \rangle$ *from* $Bag(C'')$ *to* $Bag(C')$ *be two QWN mappings. Then* $h = f \circ g = \langle h_1^1, \ldots, h_N^{e_N'} \rangle$ *is defined by :*

$$\forall i,j \in [1..e_i'], h_i^j = \begin{cases} \text{if } f_i^j = X_i^{j'} \oplus n \text{ then } \begin{cases} \text{if } g_i^{j'} = X_i^{j''} \oplus m \text{ then } X_i^{j''} \oplus (n+m) \\ \text{if } g_i^{j'} = All_i \quad\quad \text{then } All_i \\ \text{if } g_i^{j'} = \mathbb{1}_m \quad\quad \text{then } \mathbb{1}_{n+m} \end{cases} \\ \text{if } f_i^j = All_i \quad\quad \text{then } All_i \\ \text{if } f_i^j = \mathbb{1}_n \quad\quad \text{then } \mathbb{1}_n \end{cases}$$

Example 2. Let $f = \langle X_1^1, X_1^1 \oplus 1, X_2^1 \rangle$ from $Bag(C_1 \times C_2)$ to $Bag(C_1 \times C_1 \times C_2)$ and $g = \langle X_1^3, All_2 \rangle$ from $Bag(C_1 \times C_1 \times C_1 \times C_2)$ to $Bag(C_1 \times C_2)$. The mapping $h = f \circ g$ from $Bag(C_1 \times C_1 \times C_1 \times C_2)$ to $Bag(C_1 \times C_1 \times C_2)$ is $h = \langle X_1^3, X_1^3 \oplus 1, All_2 \rangle$.

Others complications appear when computing the composition of two guarded tuples $[G_f]f \circ [G_g]g$ when there is a predicate $[X_i^j \oplus n = X_i^{j'} \oplus n']$ in G_f and when $g_i^j = g_i^{j'} = All_i$. For instance, if $f = [X_1^1 = X_1^2]\langle X_1^1, All_1 \rangle$ and $g = \langle All_1, All_1 \rangle$ (from $Bag(C_1)$ to $Bag(C1 \times C_1)$) then $(f \circ g) = \sum_{c \in C_1} \langle c, c \rangle$ which is not a quasi well formed mapping. Thus we have to introduce a second constraint for the computation:

$$G_f = [(X_i^j = X_i^{j'} \oplus n)] \Rightarrow (g_i^j \neq All_i \text{ or } g_i^{j'} \neq All_i)$$

Proposition 8 (Symbolic guarded tuples composition). *Let* $g = \langle g_1^1, \ldots, g_N^{e_N''} \rangle$ *from* $Bag(C)$ *to* $Bag(C'')$ *and* f *from* $Bag(C'')$ *to* $Bag(C')$ *be two QWN mappings. Then* $h = [G_f]f \circ [G_g]g = [G \wedge G_g]f \circ g'$ *where* g' *is defined by* $g'^j_i = g_i^j$ *except for some indices where a substitution occurs and where G is defined as follows (note that due to symmetry of guards we just consider non symmetrical cases for g_i^j and $g_i^{j'}$, and that the negation of a guard is easily defined from these constructions):*

– G_f is $(X_i^j = X_i^{j'} \oplus n)$:

if $g_i^j = X_i^k \oplus m$ then
$\begin{cases} \text{if } g_i^{j'} = X_i^{k'} \oplus m' & \text{then} \quad G = (X_i^k \oplus m = X_i^{k'} \oplus (n+m')) \\ \text{if } g_i^{j'} = All_i & \text{then} \quad G = G_f \\ \text{if } g_i^{j'} = \mathbb{1}_m & \text{then} \quad G = (X_i^k = \mathbb{1}_{n+m}) \end{cases}$

if $g_i^j = \mathbb{1}_n$ then
$\begin{cases} \text{if } g_i^{j'} = All_i & \text{then} \quad G = true \text{ and } g'^{j'}_i = \mathbb{1}_n \\ \text{if } g_i^{j'} = \mathbb{1}_{n'} & \text{then} \quad G = (n = n') \end{cases}$

– G_f is $(X_i^j = \mathbb{1}_n)$:

if $g_i^j = X_i^k \oplus m$ then $G = (X_i^k \oplus m = \mathbb{1}_n)$

if $g_i^j = All_i$ then $G = true$ and $g'^{j'}_i = \mathbb{1}_n$

if $g_i^j = \mathbb{1}_{n'}$ then $G = (n = n')$

Mapping Inclusion. Our last need is to be able to check that two QWN color mappings f and g are such that $\overline{f} \sqsubseteq \overline{g}$. This is the case if for every tuple tup_f of f there is a tuple tup_g of g which is such that the guard of tup_g is true and at each position in the co-domain of f and g, the elementary mapping in tup_g is either the broadcast mapping either the same mapping as in tup_f.

Proposition 9. *Let f and g be two QWN color mappings from C to C' such that*

– $f = \sum_{k=1}^{K_f} \alpha_{k,f}.[G_{k,f}]\langle f_{1,k}^1, \ldots, f_{N,k}^{e_N'} \rangle$

– $g = \sum_{k=1}^{K_g} \alpha_{k,g}.[G_{k,g}]\langle g_{1,k}^1, \ldots, g_{N,k}^{e_N'} \rangle$

If $\forall k \in [1..K_f], \exists k' \in [1..K_g]$ such that $G_{k',g} = true$, and $\forall i \in [1..|Cl|], j \in [1..e_N']$, either $g_{i,k'}^j = All_i$, either $g_{i,k'}^j = f_{i,k}^j$ then $f \sqsubseteq g$.

4   Cases Studies

Flanagan and Qadeer proposed in [FQ03a] the following example where a counter *count* can be either read, incremented or decremented. Two shared variables, *a* and *b*, keep track of the number of increments or decrements performed on the counter.

```
int a, b, ma, mb, count = 0;
```

```
void incr(){            void decr(){            void read(){
  acquire (ma);           acquire (mb);           acquire (ma); int x = a;
  int x = a ;             int y = b;              acquire (mb); int y = b;
  count++;                count--;                release (mb);
  a = x+1;                b = y+1;                release (ma);
  release (ma); }         release (mb); }         return (tx-ty); }
```

The corresponding colored Petri net is depicted Fig. 1(a) and, for simplicity, we have duplicated some places on the figure (ma, mb, a, b and count). Note that the value of the local variables (x and y) is modeled by the coloration of the token contained in the places p2,...,p4, q2,...,q4 and u3,...,u5. One aims to reduce this net, to check that a property that does not observe the five variables declared holds.

We first perform four post-agglomerations (i4 with i5, d4 with d5, r5 with r6 and r4 with r5r6 (the result of the agglomeration of r5 with r6). These agglomerations are possible mainly because the transitions corresponding to f in these reductions have a single input: the place corresponding to p in the agglomeration scheme.

Then we perform three post-agglomerations (i1 with i2, d1 with d2, r1 with r2 and r3 with r4r5r6). Let us detail the post-agglomeration of $i1$ with $i2$:

1. the p-agglomerability is obviously fulfilled;
2. concerning the F-independence, we use the following positive flow (on the domain ε) $\mathcal{F} = ma + p2 + \langle All_C \rangle.p3 + \langle All_C \rangle.p4 + u2 + \langle All_C \rangle.u3 + \langle All_C \rangle.u4$ which induces the binary positive invariant $\forall m \in Acc(N,m_0), m(ma) + \sum_{x \in C}(m(p2)(x) + m(p3)(x) + m(p4)(x)) + \sum_{x \in C}(m(u3)(x) + m(u4)(x)) = 1$. With the help of this invariant, we check for instance that (using notations of definition 10) for $q = a$, $t = i4$, $p_t = p4$ then $\Phi = {}^t(\langle X+1 \rangle) \circ (\langle X \rangle) \circ {}^t(\langle \Pi_\varepsilon \rangle) = All_C$ and $\Psi = {}^t(\langle X \rangle) \circ {}^t(\langle All_C \rangle) \circ \langle X_\varepsilon \rangle = All_C$ and then $\phi \sqsubseteq \psi$ (note again that these computations are performed using only the syntax of the mappings).
3. the F-continuation is verified with the help of the flow $\langle All_C \rangle.a$ which induces the binary invariant $\forall m \in Acc(N,m_0), \sum_{x \in C} m(a)(x) = 1$.
4. the HF-interchangeability is ensured since $|H| = \{i1\}$

The reduced net is depicted Fig. 1(b).

In this last model, we perform a pre-agglomeration of d1d2 with d4d5. This reduction is possible since r3r4r5r6 is a neutral transition and since mb induces a binary invariant ensuring that d4d5 is not fireable when d1d2 is fireable. Then we suppress the place mb (now an implicit place see [Had90]) and we apply a parallel pre-agglomeration of r1r2 with r3r4r5r6, and i1i2 with i4i5. So we suppress *ma* (now an implicit place) and we obtain a net reduced to three transitions (Fig.1(c)). Note that contrary to the results proposed in [FQ03a], our reduction process is fully automatic and, in addition to serializability, it preserves Petri nets liveness, deadlocks, as well as other properties expressed with the help of maximal or infinite sequences.

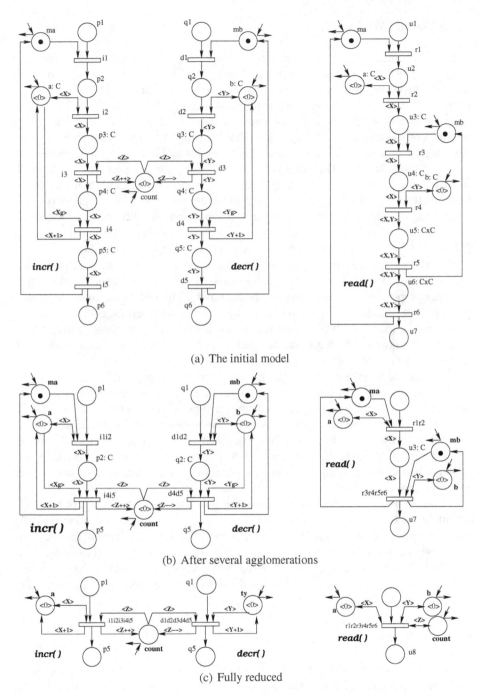

(a) The initial model

(b) After several agglomerations

(c) Fully reduced

Fig. 1. The Flanagan and Qadeer's example

5   Related Works

The first theoretical work concerning reduction of sequences into atomic actions for simplification purpose was performed by Lipton in [Lip75]. Lipton focused only on deadlock property preservation. Using parallel program notations of Dijkstra he defined "left" and "right" movers. Roughly speaking, a "left" (resp. "right") mover is a local process statement that can be moved forward (resp. delayed) w.r.t. statements of others processes without modifying the halting property. Lipton then demonstrated that, in principle, the statement P(S), where S is a semaphore, is a "left" mover and V(s) is a "right" mover. Then Lipton proved that some parallel program are deadlock free by moving P(S) and V(S) statements and by suppressing atomic statements that have no effect on variables. However, two difficulties arise: the reduction preserves only the existence of deadlocks and the application conditions are difficult to be automatically checked. Thus, this work has been extended and adapted to different formalisms [CL98], [SC03], or to programming languages [SC03], [FQ03b], [FQ03a].

In Petri nets formalism, the first works concerning reductions have been performed by Berthelot [BRV80, Ber85]. The author focused only the preservation of specific Petri net properties such as liveness or boundedness. The link between transition agglomerations (the most effective reductions) and general properties, expressed in LTL formalism, is done in [PPP00]. However, these reductions rely on "pure" structural application conditions, which are, on the one hand, very efficient, but in the other hand, lead to a quite narrow application area.

Esparza and Schröter [ES01], simplify one point in the original pre-agglomeration conditions. However, they consider only 1-safe Petri nets (each place is bounded by 1), the application conditions remain purely structural, and as the authors focus only on infinite sequences preservation, their reductions do not even preserve the existence deadlock[2].

Orthogonally, Schnoebelen and Sidorova [SS00] characterize reductions by means of bisimulation. The interest in this approach is that one only needs to consider a particular subset of the markings and thus, can obtain a very abstract model. On the other hand, the applicability of these reductions is quite limited.

Recently we proposed in [HPP04] new Petri nets reductions that cover a large range of patterns by introducing algebraic conditions whereas the previously defined ones rely solely on structural conditions. We adapt them to colored nets in [EHPP04] and we show here how to automatize their applications with a well chosen syntax for colored Petri nets. Note that the expressiveness of colored Petri nets is sufficient to model concurrent software. Thus, these colored Petri nets reductions are a very efficient supplementary material for simplifying software model checking.

6   Conclusion

We have presented in this paper how new colored Petri nets reductions can be automatically performed using a precise syntax of colored net. In particular, we showed that a precise syntax of colored nets allows us to transform functional calculus into syntactical operations.

---

[2] Note moreover that being 1-safe is not a stable characteristic w.r.t. reductions.

We have illustrate on a recent and significant example that the use of these reductions leads to a very effective way to simplify model (and thus concurrent programs) while preserving general properties of the model (expressed for instance with an action-based linear time temporal logic).

The next step in our researches in this area will be to define directly in high-level languages (such as Ada or Java) equivalent conditions allowing to automatically infer transactions for simplifying software model checking.

References

[Ber85]   G. Berthelot. Checking properties of nets using transformations. In G. Rozenberg, editor, *Advances in Petri nets*, volume No. 222 of *LNCS*. Springer-Verlag, 1985.

[BRV80]   G. Berthelot, G. Roucairol, and R. Valk. Reduction of nets and parallel programs. In Brauer, W., editor, *LNCS: Net Theory and Applications*, volume 84, pages 277–290, Berlin, Heidelberg, New York, 1980. Springer-Verlag.

[CL98]   Ernie Cohen and Leslie Lamport. Reduction in TLA. In *International Conference on Concurrency Theory*, pages 317–331, 1998.

[EHPP04]   S. Evangelista, S. Haddad, and J.F. Pradat-Peyre. Colored Petri nets reductions for concurrent software validation. Technical report, CEDRIC, CNAM, Paris, 2004.

[EKPPR03]   S. Evangelista, C. Kaiser, J. F. Pradat-Peyre, and P. Rousseau. Quasar: a new tool for analysing concurrent programs. In *Reliable Software Technologies - Ada-Europe 2003*, volume 2655 of *LNCS*. Springer-Verlag, 2003.

[ES01]   J. Esparza and C. Schröter. Net Reductions for LTL Model-Checking. In T. Margaria and T. Melham, editors, *Correct Hardware Design and Verification Methods (CHARME'01)*, volume 2144 of *Lecture Notes in Computer Science*, pages 310–324. Springer-Verlag, 2001.

[Eva04]   S. Evangelista. Syntactical rules for colored Petri nets manipulation. Technical Report 641, CEDRIC, CNAM, Paris, 2004.

[FQ03a]   Cormac Flanagan and Shaz Qadeer. Transactions for software model checking. In Byron Cook, Scott Stoller, and Willem Visser, editors, *Electronic Notes in Theoretical Computer Science*, volume 89. Elsevier, 2003.

[FQ03b]   Cormac Flanagan and Shaz Qadeer. A type and effect system for atomicity. In *Proceedings of the ACM SIGPLAN 2003 conference on Programming language design and implementation*, pages 338–349. ACM Press, 2003.

[GW93]   Patrice Godefroid and Pierre Wolper. Using partial orders for the efficient verification of deadlock freedom and safety properties. *Form. Methods Syst.*, 2(2):149–164, 1993.

[Had90]   S. Haddad. A reduction theory for colored nets. In Jensen and Rozenberg, editors, *High-level Petri Nets, Theory and Application*, volume 424 of *LNCS*, pages 399–425. Springer-Verlag, 1990.

[HPP04]   S. Haddad and J.F. Pradat-Peyre. Efficient reductions for LTL formulae verification. Technical report, CEDRIC, CNAM, Paris, 2004.

[Lip75]   Richard J. Lipton. Reduction: a method of proving properties of parallel programs. *Commun. ACM*, 18(12):717–721, 1975.

[PPP00]   D. Poitrenaud and J.F. Pradat-Peyre. Pre and post-agglomerations for *LTL* model checking. In M. Nielsen and D Simpson, editors, *High-level Petri Nets, Theory and Application*, number 1825 in LNCS, pages 387–408. Springer-Verlag, 2000.

[SC03]   Scott D. Stoller and Ernie Cohen. Optimistic synchronization-based state-space reduction. In H. Garavel and J. Hatcliff, editors, *TACAS'03*, volume 2619 of *Lecture Notes in Computer Science*, pages 489–504. Springer-Verlag, April 2003.

[SS00]   P. Schnoebelen and N. Sidorova. Bisimulation and the reduction of petri nets. In M. Nielsen and D Simpson, editors, *High-level Petri Nets, Theory and Application*, number 1825 in LNCS, pages 409–423. Springer-Verlag, 2000.

[Val93]   Antti Valmari. On-the-fly verification with stubborn sets. In *Proceedings of the 5th International Conference on Computer Aided Verification*, pages 397–408. Springer-Verlag, 1993.

[VM97]   François Vernadat and François Michel. Covering step graph preserving failure semantics. In *Proceedings of the 18th International Conference on Application and Theory of Petri Nets*, pages 253–270. Springer-Verlag, 1997.

Algorithmic Algebraic Model Checking II: Decidability of Semi-algebraic Model Checking and Its Applications to Systems Biology[*]

V. Mysore[1], C. Piazza[2], and B. Mishra[1,3]

[1] Courant Institute, New York University, New York, NY, U.S.A
[2] Dept. of Mathematics and Computer Science, University of Udiné, Udine, Italy
[3] NYU School of Medicine, New York University, New York, NY, U.S.A
vm40@nyu.edu, piazza@dimi.uniud.it, mishra@nyu.edu

Abstract. Motivated by applications to systems biology, and the emergence of *semi-algebraic hybrid systems* as a natural framework for modeling biochemical networks, we continue exploring the decidability problem for model-checking with TCTL (Timed Computation Tree Logic) over this broad class of *semi-algebraic hybrid systems*. Previously, we had introduced these models, demonstrated the close connection to the goals of systems biology. However, we had only developed the techniques for bounded reachability, arguing for the adequacy of such an approach in a majority of the biological applications. Here, we present a semi-decidable symbolic algebraic dense-time TCTL model checking algorithm, which satisfies two desirable properties: it can be derived automatically from the symbolic description, and it extends to and generalizes other versions of temporal logics. The main mathematical device at the core of this approach is Tarski-Collins' real quantifier elimination employed at each fixpoint iteration, whose high complexity is the crux of its unfortunate limitation. Along with these results, we prove the undecidability of this problem in the more powerful "real" Turing machine formalism of Blum, Shub and Smale. We then demonstrate a preliminary version of our model-checker Tolque on the Delta-Notch example.

1 Prologue

It has been said[1], "Biologists have generally eschewed the possibility, or even the value, of an overarching theory of life." Biology is considered complex and not amenable to systematic dissection to reveal a unifying principle. However, as complex interconnected interactions among various biological entities begin to be cataloged from a diverse set of experiments, patterns emerge: sequences are

---

[*] The work reported in this paper was supported by grants from NSF's ITR program, Defense Advanced Research Projects Agency (DARPA), the US Air Force (AFRL), National Institutes of Health (NIH) and New York State Office of Science, Technology & Academic Research (NYSTAR). C.P. was partially supported by the MIUR FIRB grant RBAU018RCZ and the MIUR PRIN'04 grant 2004013015.
[1] *Making Sense of Life*, E.F. Keller, Harvard Press, MA, 2002.

D.A. Peled and Y.-K. Tsay (Eds.): ATVA 2005, LNCS 3707, pp. 217–233, 2005.

aligned; genes are clustered; genes are grouped in modules; proteins are placed in families; motifs of interaction are listed; polymorphisms are partitioned into blocks; chromosomal aberrations and methylation patterns are segmented. The picture, however, remains frozen in time.

On the other hand, much less has been inferred about the temporal interactions of these entities. There are two problems: a mathematically precise, but somewhat idealized description of these interactions is often presented in a form, that is neither succinct nor easy to analyze. We lack both theoretical frameworks and efficient implementations for developing automatic computational tools that will allow a scientist to explore important phenomenological properties of these models.

The subject *Algorithmic Algebraic Model Checking* focuses on these issues as it examines connections between systems biology, dynamical systems, modal logic and computability, and how they can be useful in the biological context. Towards this aim, we began by addressing the symbolic bounded reachability problem for a new class of hybrid models arising in systems biology – *semi-algebraic hybrid systems*, introduced in the first paper of this "AAMC" (Algorithmic Algebraic Model Checking) series [28]. There, we aimed to characterize the widest range of automata that admit sound albeit expensive mathematical techniques, as opposed to focusing on a very narrow class of systems that often prematurely sacrifice generalizability for the sake of efficiency. It was shown that the bounded reachability problem can be solved using real algebraic techniques like Taylor series approximation and quantifier elimination. It was found sufficiently powerful in analyzing such systems as the Delta-Notch protein interaction example [10,14,19]. It was expected that, building upon this algebraic bounded reachability algorithm [28] and other recent techniques (e.g. some of Fränzle's ideas [13]), we can address the algebraic model-checking problem over the dense time logic *TCTL* [1]. The current paper deals with this subject.

We build upon and integrate many existing ideas: we use Henzinger et al.'s characterization of the *Until* operator as a fixpoint expression involving the *one-step until* operator [17]. Exploiting the power of a symbolic[2] approach, we retain all parameters as variables thus obtaining an algebraic expression representing the possible solutions. The ability to perform an entirely symbolic analysis of arbitrary polynomial hybrid systems over a full temporal logic, limited only by computational power, distinguishes our approach from the other methods in literature. Furthermore, to study decidability, we use Blum et al.'s "real" Turing machine (or equivalently, finite-dimensional machine over a field) formalism [7] – a more apt approach to analyzing problems involving real computations. We find that reachability is undecidable even in this more powerful computational model. The rest of the paper is organized as follows: the main ingredients of the paper – semi-algebraic hybrid automata, the Blum-Shub-Smale model of "real" computation and TCTL – are reviewed in *Section 2*; the technical proofs of our main results along with a literature survey are provided in *Section 3*; we

---

[2] This is in contrast to traditional *symbolic* model-checking where we refer to the use of BDDs as opposed to explicit enumeration of states as being *symbolic*.

demonstrate our software system Tolque over the same Delta-Notch example in *Section 4* (additional results are recorded in the *Appendix*) and conclude with a discussion in *Section 5*.

2   Technical Preliminaries

The temporal properties of a network of interacting biochemicals are typically captured by relating two neighboring system-states at time instants t and $t + \delta$, and the biochemical interactions (synthesis, degradation, multimerization, etc.) which occur in that short time interval δ. The dynamics resulting from these interactions can be described as a set of differential equations and discrete states [25]. Nonetheless, a direct model of transitions and flows, given through their symbolic description, can be computationally manipulated (either numerically or symbolically) to derive logical conclusions about global temporal properties, that may not have been obvious in the instantaneous description. The exact structure of this approach depends on the complexity of the three underlying frameworks: description of the dynamical system, the expressivity of the temporal logic and the basic operations of the models of computation. In a conventional "numerical" approach, starting with an initial system-state, successive states are chased by an integration scheme (eg. Runge-Kutta). Conclusions about the behavior of the network are then made by tracing the trajectories over a suitable time-frame and verifying temporal properties (eg. the Simpathica tool [5]). The "symbolic" alternative to the numerical procedure instead uses algebraic methods to characterize the transition of the system with time. The appropriate frameworks for this setting consist of the following: semi-algebraic hybrid automata which allow polynomial expressions, TCTL logic to capture the continuous changes, and the "real" Turing machine model that computes a semi-algebraic operation in one unit step. Their formal definitions follow.

Definition 1. Semi-algebraic Set.[26] *Every quantifier-free boolean formula composed of polynomial equations and inequalities defines a semialgebraic set (i.e., unquantified first-order formulæ over the reals - $(\mathbb{R}, +, \times, =, <)$).* $\square$

Definition 2. Semi-algebraic Hybrid Automata. [28] *A k-dimensional hybrid automaton is a 7-tuple, $H = (Z, V, E, Init, Inv, Flow, Jump)$, consisting of the following components:*

- $Z = \{Z_1, \ldots, Z_k\}$ *and* $Z' = \{Z'_1, \ldots, Z'_k\}$ *are two finite sets of variables ranging over the reals* $\mathbb{R}$
- (V, E) *is a directed graph of discrete states and transitions*
- *Each discrete state* $v \in V$ *is labeled by "Init"(initial), "Inv"(invariant) and "Flow" labels of the form* $Init_v[Z]$, $Inv_v[Z]$, *and* $Flow_v[Z, Z', t, h]$
- *Each edge* $e \in E$ *is labeled by a "Jump" condition of the form* $Jump_e[Z, Z'] \equiv Guard_e(Z) \wedge Reset_e(Z, Z')$
- *Init, Inv, Flow, and Jump are semi-algebraic.* $\square$

For ease of expression and clarity, we have enhanced the semantics presented in [28].

Definition 3. Semantics of Hybrid Automata. *Let $H = (Z, V, E, \text{Init}, \text{Inv}, \text{Flow}, \text{Jump})$ be a hybrid automaton of dimension k.*

- *A location ℓ of H is a pair $\langle v, R \rangle$, where $v \in V$ is a discrete state and $R \in \mathbb{R}^k$ is an assignment of values to the variables of Z. A location $\langle v, R \rangle$ is said to be* admissible, *if $\text{Inv}_v(R)$ is satisfied.*
- *The* continuous reachability transition relation $\xrightarrow[C]{h}$ *forces the discrete state invariant to hold at every location except the end-location, along the evolution curve determined by the flow equations during the $h(> 0)$ time units from the current time t_0:*

$$\langle v, R \rangle \xrightarrow[C]{h} \langle v, S \rangle \quad \text{iff}$$

$$\left(\text{Flow}_v(R, S, t_0, h) \land \forall Z', h' \in [0, h) \ \text{Flow}_v(R, Z', t_0, h') \Rightarrow \text{Inv}_v(Z') \right),$$

where $\text{Flow}_v(Z, Z', T, h)$ is the flow label of v.
- *The* discrete reachability transition relation $\xrightarrow[D]{0}$ *ensures that both parts of the zero-time* jump – *the guard condition which needs to be satisfied just before the transition is taken, and the reset condition which determines the values after the transition, are satisfied.*

$$\langle v, R \rangle \xrightarrow[D]{0} \langle u, S \rangle \quad \text{iff} \quad \langle v, u \rangle \in E \land \text{Jump}_{v,u}(R, S).$$

- *The* transition relation T *of H connects the possible values of the system variables before and after one step - a discrete step for a time $h = 0$ or a continuous evolution for any time period $h > 0$:*

$$T(\ell \xrightarrow{h} \ell') = \{ h = 0 \land \ell \xrightarrow[D]{0} \ell' \} \lor \{ h > 0 \land \ell \xrightarrow[C]{h} \ell' \}.$$

- *A* trace *of H is a sequence $\ell_0, \ell_1, \ldots, \ell_n, \ldots$ of admissible locations such that*

$$\forall i \geq 0, \ \exists h_i \geq 0, \ T(\ell_i \xrightarrow{h_i} \ell_{i+1}). \qquad \square$$

Remark 1. Few remarks about this definition of *trace* are in order: It admits two continuous transitions to occur consecutively, which is necessary for compositionality of traces. Further, two consecutive continuous transitions of time-steps h_1 and h_2 are *not* necessarily equivalent to one continuous transition of time-step $h_1 + h_2$ in the case of non-linear approximation errors in $\xrightarrow[C]{h}$.

When a *semi-algebraic* relation $\text{Flow}_v(R, S, t, h)$ is used between the continuous states R at time t and S at time $t + h$ in a discrete state v, it may have been "derived" in two ways: (1) *Solution Is A Polynomial*: The equation describing the continuous evolution of the variables in a discrete state is a polynomial, say

$Y(t)$, and $Flow_v(Z, Z', t, h) \equiv \{ Z = Y(t) \wedge Z' = Y(t+h) \}$. Or, (2) *Differential Equation Is A Polynomial*: Differential equations describing the continuous evolution are *approximated* in $Flow_v$ using one of the symbolic integration schemes (e.g., the *Taylor* series in [28] or based on a direct integration scheme such as the linear *Euler* or the higher degree *Runge-Kutta*). The error is controlled by an upper bound (say Δ) on the time spent in one continuous step, as we aim for over- or under-approximating the flow equations. The Lagrange Remainder Theorem can be used to estimate errors [23].

We now report the basic definitions of the temporal logics TCTL and $T\mu$-Calculus which we use to study properties of our semi-algebraic hybrid automata.

Definition 4. TCTL[1]. *It has the following syntactic structure:*

$$\phi ::= p \mid \neg\phi \mid \phi_1 \vee \phi_2 \mid \phi_1 \exists \mathcal{U} \phi_2 \mid \phi_1 \forall \mathcal{U} \phi_2 \mid z.\phi.$$

Its associated semantics are described below:

- **z.**: *The freeze quantification "z." binds the associated variable z to the current time. Thus the formula $z.\phi(z)$ holds at time t iff $\phi(t)$ does.*
- $\phi_1 \forall \mathcal{U} \phi_2$ *and* $\phi_1 \exists \mathcal{U} \phi_2$: *universal (on all paths) and existential (on at least one path) "until" operators. For $\phi_1 \mathcal{U} \phi_2$ to be true on a path, ϕ_2 is required to be true somewhere along the path, and ϕ_1 is required to be true all along the path up to (but not necessarily at) that location.* □

Remark 2. The basic notations are often extended by the following syntactic abbreviations [1].

1. $p \exists \mathcal{U}_{\leq max} q \equiv p \exists \mathcal{U} (q \wedge z.(z \leq max))$ and $p \forall \mathcal{U}_{\leq max} q \equiv p \forall \mathcal{U} (q \wedge z.(z \leq max))$: "subscripted" *Until* operators (max is the time-bound).
2. $\forall \mathcal{F} \equiv true \forall \mathcal{U} p$ and $\exists \mathcal{F} \equiv true \exists \mathcal{U} p$: "eventuality" operators.
3. $\forall \mathcal{G} \equiv \neg \exists \mathcal{F} \neg p$ and $\exists \mathcal{G} \equiv \neg \forall \mathcal{F} \neg p$: "invariance" operators.

Definition 5. Single-Step Until Operator, ▷, [17]. *The formula $p \triangleright q$ holds if $p \vee q$ is true all along "one step" of the hybrid system and q is true at the end of the transition.* □

Definition 6. $T\mu$-Calculus Syntax: [17]. $\phi ::= X \mid p \mid \neg\phi \mid \phi_1 \vee \phi_2 \mid \phi_1 \triangleright \phi_2 \mid z.\phi \mid \mu X.\phi$, *where μ is the* least-fixpoint *operator. Thus,*

- *The* greatest-fixpoint ν *can be expressed as* $\neg\mu X.(\neg\phi[X := \neg X])$.
- Existential Until: $p \exists \mathcal{U} q = \mu X.(q \vee (p \triangleright X))$
- Universal Until: $p \forall \mathcal{U} q = \neg(\neg q \exists \mathcal{U} (\neg p \wedge \neg q))$ □

Notice that the translation of the universal until is valid only when q is "finitely variable" over all premodels [17].

The undecidability result we will prove is based on the model of finite-dimensional machines over a field $\mathcal{R}$, which in our case will be $\mathbb{R}$, and on the undecidability of the Mandelbrot set over these machines. (We only introduce these "real" Turing Machines here, and refer the interested reader to [7].)

Definition 7. Finite-Dimensional Machine Over $\mathcal{R}$: [7]. *A finite dimensional machine M over $\mathcal{R}$ consists of a finite directed connected graph with four types of nodes:* input, computation, branch *and* output. *The unique input node has no incoming edges and only one outgoing edge. All other nodes have possibly several incoming edges. Computation nodes have only one outgoing edge, branch nodes exactly two, Yes and No, and output nodes none. In addition the machine has three spaces:* input space $\mathcal{I}_M$, state space $\mathcal{S}_M$ *and* output space $\mathcal{O}_M$ *of the form $\mathcal{R}^n, \mathcal{R}^m, \mathcal{R}^l$, respectively, where n, m and l are positive integers. Associated with each node of the graph are maps of these spaces and* next node *assignments.*

1. *Associated with the* input node *is a linear map $I : \mathcal{I}_M \rightarrow \mathcal{S}_M$ and a unique next node β_1.*
2. *Each* computation node η *has an associated* computation map, *a polynomial (or rational) map $g_\eta : \mathcal{S}_M \rightarrow \mathcal{S}_M$ given by m polynomials (or rational functions) $g_j : \mathcal{R}^m \rightarrow \mathcal{R}, j = 1, \cdots, m$, and a unique next node β_η. If g is a rational map associated with a computation node (in the case $\mathcal{R}$ is a field), we assume each g_j is given by a fixed pair of polynomials (p_j, q_j), where $g_j(x) = (p_j(x))/(q_j(x))$.*
3. *Each* branch node η *has an associated* branching function, *a nonzero polynomial function $h_\eta : \mathcal{S}_M \rightarrow \mathcal{R}$. The next node along the Yes outgoing edge, β_η^+, is associated with the condition $h_\eta \geq 0$ and the next node along the No outgoing edge, β_η^-, with $h_\eta(z) < 0$.*
4. *Each* output node η *has an associated linear map $\mathcal{O}_\eta : \mathcal{S}_M \rightarrow \mathcal{O}_M$ and no next node.* □

Definition 8. The Mandelbrot Set [24], $\mathcal{M}$ *is the subset of the set of complex numbers $\mathcal{C}$ that remains bounded when subject to the following iterative procedure: $f_0(C) = C$, $f_{n+1}(C) = f_n(C)^2 + C$. Formally, the complement $\mathcal{M}'$ of the Mandelbrot set is defined as*

$$\mathcal{M}' = \{C \in \mathcal{C} | f_n(C) \rightarrow \infty \text{ as } n \rightarrow \infty\}.$$ □

It is to be noted that $f_i(C) \geq 2$ implies that eventually $f_n(C) \rightarrow \infty$.

In what follows, when we refer to the Mandelbrot set we mean the 2-dimensional set of real numbers corresponding to the Mandelbrot set, i.e., the set of pairs of the form $\langle C_r, C_i \rangle$ such that $C = C_r + iC_i$ is in the Mandelbrot set.

Theorem 1. Undecidability Of The Mandelbrot Set: [7]. *The Mandelbrot set cannot be expressed as the countable union of semi-algebraic sets over $\mathbb{R}$, and hence not decidable over $\mathbb{R}$.* □

3 Symbolic Algebraic Model Checking

Our main results for semi-algebraic hybrid systems may be summarized thus: (1) Reachability is *undecidable* even in Blum et al.'s "real" Turing machine formalism. (2) The "existential" segment of TCTL (including reachability) and the negation of the "universal" segment are *semi-decidable*. Further, all subscripted operators become *decidable* in the absence of zeno-paths. (3) Finally, a *quantifier elimination* tool (e.g. Qepcad [18],Redlog [12]) may be used to perform the fixpoint iterations of a TCTL query. The technical details are presented below.

The symbolic route to model-checking TCTL-specifications of hybrid systems is via the fixpoint expression for the *until* operator, which uses the standard *single-step until* operator ▷ [17] (also, see [28,13]). The exact expression for the ▷ operator for semi-algebraic hybrid systems proves the basis of our approach: ▷ *corresponds to a semi-algebraic expression and is hence decidable.*

Definition 9. ▷ for Semi-algebraic Hybrid Systems. *The expression $p \triangleright q$ is* True *at the current continuous state R if q is true now, or*

- *For one of the possible current discrete states v, there exists at least one discrete state u to which a transition can be taken such that q holds at the end, or*
- *For one of the possible current discrete states v, there exists a continuous transition (of at most Δ time units when we need to upper-bound the flow-approximation error) all along which $p \vee q$ holds, with q being true at the end[3].*

$$p \triangleright q = q(R) \bigvee_{\forall v}$$
$$\left(\{\exists S \bigvee_{\forall u} \langle v, R \rangle \xrightarrow[D]{0} \langle u, S \rangle \wedge q(S)\} \bigvee \right.$$
$$\{\exists S, h \ (0 < h \leq \Delta) \wedge \langle v, R \rangle \xrightarrow[C]{h} \langle v, S \rangle \wedge q(S) \wedge$$
$$\left. \forall S', h' \ ((0 \leq h' < h) \wedge \langle v, R \rangle \xrightarrow[C]{h'} \langle u, S' \rangle) \Rightarrow (p(S') \vee q(S'))\} \right) \square$$

Remark 3. The upperbound Δ on h should be *omitted* if there is no error in the $Flow_v$ expression. Also, since the discrete jump is instantaneous, $p(R)$ does not appear in the discrete-jump expression (second line).

Theorem 2. *The* one-step-until *operator ▷ is decidable for semi-algebraic hybrid systems if p and q are also semi-algebraic.*

Proof. Semi-algebraic sets are closed under boolean operations and quantifier elimination. Since *Jump, Inv* and *Flow* are semi-algebraic, so are the expressions $\xrightarrow[C]{t}$ and $\xrightarrow[D]{0}$. Thus $p \triangleright q$ is semi-algebraic since p and q are also semi-algebraic. Since quantifier elimination over semi-algebraic sets is decidable [32], $p \triangleright q$ is decidable.   □

Corollary 1. *For semi-algebraic hybrid systems:*

1. *$\exists \mathcal{U}$, $\exists \mathcal{F}$, $\exists \mathcal{G}$ and their subscripted versions $\exists \mathcal{U}_{\leq z}$, $\exists \mathcal{F}_{\leq z}$ and $\exists \mathcal{G}_{\leq z}$ are semi-decidable.*

---

[3] The last term in the formula, $p(S') \vee q(S')$, can be replaced with just $p(S')$ for evaluating $\exists \mathcal{U}$ over semi-algebraic hybrid systems.

2. *The* negations *of* $\forall \mathcal{U}$, $\forall \mathcal{F}$, $\forall \mathcal{G}$ *and their subscripted versions* $\forall \mathcal{U}_{\leq z}$, $\forall \mathcal{F}_{\leq z}$ *and* $\forall \mathcal{G}_{\leq z}$ *are semi-decidable.*
3. *All subscripted operators become* decidable *in the absence of* zeno *paths.*

Proof. The conclusions can be drawn as follows:

- The $\exists \mathcal{U}$ operator can be evaluated by iterating (indefinitely) over the decidable "one-step-until" operator $\triangleright$ as per the fixpoint characterization $p \exists \mathcal{U} q \equiv \mu X.(q \vee (p \triangleright X))$. Hence it is semi-decidable i.e. the computation procedure is guaranteed to converge if the query is *True*.
- Since $p \forall \mathcal{U} q \equiv \neg(\neg q \exists \mathcal{U} (\neg p \wedge \neg q))$, it can be guaranteed to converge only when it is *False*. Thus the negation of $\forall \mathcal{U}$ is semi-decidable by our procedure.
- Since $\exists \mathcal{F} p \equiv true \exists \mathcal{U} p$, reachability is semi-decidable.
- $\forall \mathcal{F} p \equiv true \forall \mathcal{U} p$ and is not semi-decidable since $\forall \mathcal{U}$ is not.
- Since $\exists \mathcal{G} p \equiv \neg \forall \mathcal{F} \neg p$, we can guarantee that it will converge if it is *True* since $\forall \mathcal{F}$ is guaranteed to converge if it is *False*. Thus it is semi-decidable.
- Since $\forall \mathcal{G} p \equiv \neg \exists \mathcal{F} \neg p$, it is guaranteed to converge only when it is *False*.
- A new variable *time* is introduced, with *initial* value 0, *flow* 1 in all discrete states and identity resets. This allows the interpretation of *freeze* ($z.X$) and *subscripted until* ($U_{\leq a}$) operators.
- In non-zeno systems, every path of a specified time-length can be explored fully. Hence all subscripted operators are decidable.   □

Remark 4. Purely symbolic reachability cannot be convergent as many sets (including the Mandelbrot set) cannot be expressed as the finite union of semi-algebraic sets [7]. Similarly, the solution of many coupled, non-linear differential equations and simple discrete difference equations are inexpressible even using exponential and trigonometric terms [30], let alone as a finite union of polynomial inequalities. However, the conventional semi-decidability notion only applies to cases where the query can be answered as *True* or *False*. It was under this default assumption (also used by Fränzle while discussing "polynomial" hybrid systems [13]) that the above results were derived.

3.1   General Undecidability of Reachability

System-state (or equivalently, "location") reachability is undecidable for hybrid automata with just two clocks [16], as the Turing machine halting-problem can be encoded as a reachability query. It becomes pertinent to ask if this undecidability result holds for the more powerful "real" computing machines of Blum et al.[7], where semi-algebraic sets appear naturally in the computability definition (see *Path Decomposition Theorem* [7]). In the following construction, we present a semi-algebraic hybrid system and encode the Mandelbrot set as a reachability query. Since Blum and Smale have proved that the *Mandelbrot set is undecidable* [7], this proves that reachability over semi-algebraic hybrid systems is also undecidable, *even* under the "real" Turing Machine model.

Definition 10. The Mandelbrot Hybrid Automaton. *Let* $C = \langle C_r, C_i \rangle$ *be a pair of real numbers. The* Mandelbrot Hybrid Automaton M_C *consists of*

- *One discrete state s_0 with invariant* False *and two continuous variables Z_1 and Z_2.*
- *$Flow_1$: { $Z'_1 = Z_1$ ∧ $Z'_2 = Z_2$ } (no continuous evolution).*
- *One Discrete State Transition: $1 \rightarrow 1$ with $Jump_1$: $(Z'_1 = Z_1^2 - Z_2^2 + C_r)$ ∧ $(Z'_2 = 2Z_1 Z_2 + C_i)$.*   □

Notice that in M_C the only possible trace is the infinite zeno path of self-loops.

Theorem 3. General Undecidability Of Reachability. *For semi-algebraic hybrid systems, reachability is undecidable even in Blum et al.'s "real" Turing machine formalism.*

Proof. Consider the Mandelbrot hybrid automaton M_C defined above. Let $S(t) = (Z_1(t), Z_2(t))$ be the point reached after t discrete transitions from the initial location $\langle s_0, (0,0) \rangle$. After one more discrete transition (self-loop), we get

$$S(t+1) = S'(t) = \{Z_1(t)^2 - Z_2(t)^2 + C_r\} + \imath.\{2Z_1(t)Z_2(t) + C_i\}$$
$$= \{Z_1(t) + \imath.Z_2(t)\}^2 + \{C_r + \imath.C_i\}$$

In other words, if we consider the pairs of real numbers as complex numbers, we have $S'(t) = S^2(t) + C$ which is the defining equation of the *Mandelbrot Set*. Clearly, there exists an evolution where $|S(t)| \geq 2$ if and only if $C = C_r + iC_i$ does not belong to the Mandelbrot set, i.e., the decidability of the reachability query[4] $(Z_1^2 + Z_2^2 \geq 4)$ would imply the decidability of the Mandelbrot set, thus resulting in a contradiction.   □

3.2   Literature Review

While semi-algebraic hybrid systems have been suggested in one form on another before [20,4,13,22], the full potential of this formalization is only beginning to be appreciated [28]. Beyond timed, multirate and initialized rectangular automata [2,29], the linearity of the continuous dynamics is another extensively studied restriction [3,6]. Controllable linear systems [31], some families of linear vector fields [22] and o-minimal hybrid automata [21] have also been shown to be decidable for the reachability query. In the case of o-minimal hybrid automata, the decidability is guaranteed by the decidability of the underlying theory and by the fact that the resets are constant. In semi-algebraic hybrid automata, we do not have any restriction on the resets. However, o-minimal systems admit more complex functions (beyond polynomials) in the flows, invariants and guards.

While the above methods find efficient solutions by restricting the dynamics, over- or under-approximating methods assume that the reachable region has a (mathematically) convenient geometric shape such as a polyhedron, a level set or an ellipsoid [6,8,9]. Bisimulation on the other hand is an intelligent partitioning of the concrete system-state space of the hybrid system into fewer abstract discrete-states such that the properties of interest continue to hold in the simpler smaller

---

[4] $Reachable(p) \equiv \exists \mathcal{F}(p)$.

model [15]. Predicate abstraction has also been frequently used to map a hybrid automaton into a discrete one [33,3].

On the algebraic side, Jirstrand [20] demonstrated the use of Qepcad for problems in control system design. Anai [4] and Fränzle [13] independently suggested the use of quantifier elimination for the verification of polynomial (semi-algebraic) hybrid systems, while Lafferiere et al. [22] have described a quantifier-elimination-centric method for symbolic reachability computation of linear vector fields.

4   Tolque: A Symbolic Algebraic TCTL Model Checker

A preliminary version of a symbolic algebraic model checker that uses the TCTL model-checking approach outlined in the previous section has been implemented. This quantifier-elimination-centric model checker, christened Tolque, takes as input a semi-algebraic hybrid automaton specification (with the flow equations already approximated if necessary) and an *Existential Until* ($p \; \exists \mathcal{U} \; q$) query. It then computes the fixpoint $p \; \exists \mathcal{U} \; q \; = \; \mu X.(q \vee (p \triangleright X))$ [17] by using Qepcad [18] to perform the quantifier elimination in $p \triangleright X$. The entire process is automated in this $C/C++$ implementation that runs in *Linux*.

A Case Study: The Delta-Notch Protein Signaling

Here we examine the Delta-Notch protein interaction system, the primary basis of biological pattern formation. Ghosh et al. [14,19] analyzed a simplified piece-wise linear hybrid automaton model (derived from Collier et al.'s work [10]) with the following properties: (1) The Delta (concentration v_D) production is turned on by low Notch concentration (v_N) in the same cell i.e. when $-v_N > h_D$; (2) The Notch production is turned on by high Delta concentration in the cell environment (neighbors) i.e. when $\Sigma_i u_D^i > h_N$. Here, h_D and h_N are the thresholds, and u_D^i denotes the Delta concentration in each (i-th) neighbor.

In this section, we show how some interesting properties of the one-cell and two-cell Delta-Notch model of Ghosh et al. [14,19] can be formulated as temporal logic queries, that Tolque can answer. Unfortunately, Qepcad cannot support the queries necessary to analyze system properties more complex than those documented here. Approximate methods (such as those discussed in AAMC-III [27]), reduction in the computational complexity of quantifier elimination, and greater computing power will help overcome this computational bottleneck. Rather than providing new insight about the model, at this point, Tolque is only seen to support a more elegant and general way of thinking about system properties. (Please see the appendix for a complete list of results.)

One-Cell System. In the hybrid automaton modeling the one-cell system [14], there are 2 dynamic variables v_D and v_N corresponding to the Delta and Notch concentration in the cell, 4 discrete states corresponding to the 2×2 possibilities resulting from Delta and Notch production being switched "on" or "off". The external variable u_N is assumed to be static. We will denote the upper bound on the continuous time-step by Δ.

1. **Pruned Transition Map.** When the state invariants are non-overlapping, an evolution path from discrete state i to j is possible iff $Inv_i \wedge \{Inv_i \,\exists\mathcal{U}\, Inv_j\}$. Notice that invariants can be made non-overlapping by introducing a new environmental variable "discrete-state" that is reset to the destination discrete state number during discrete state transitions, with flow always 0.

   - **Discrete Transition** $1 \xrightarrow[\mathcal{D}]{0} 2$
     $[-v_N \leq h_D \wedge u_N \leq h_N] \,\exists\mathcal{U}\, [-v_N \geq h_D \wedge u_N \leq h_N]$
     After k iterations, we get the requirement $v_N \leq -h_D/(1 - \Delta l_N)^k$ which is *True* when $k \, (\geq -\log(h_D/v_N)/\log(1 - \Delta l_N))$. Thus the transition from 1 to 2 is possible.
   - **Discrete Transition** $2 \xrightarrow[\mathcal{D}]{0} 1$
     $[-v_N \geq h_D \wedge u_N \leq h_N] \,\exists\mathcal{U}\, [-v_N < h_D \wedge u_N < h_N]$ converges after two iterations to *False*. Thus, it is not possible to jump to state 1 from state 2.

2. **Estimating Continuous-State Equilibrium Concentrations.** When the state invariants are non-overlapping, an equilibrium of the continuous state exists in state i iff $Inv_i \wedge \neg\{Inv_i \,\exists\mathcal{U}\, (v'_D \neq v_D \vee v'_N \neq v_N)\}$, where v'_D and v'_N are the values after one step of the hybrid automaton.

   Remark 5. We have extended the TCTL notation to allow more complex temporal queries that can describe the values of the variables before and after one step of evolution. The semi-algebraic quantifier elimination based model-checking supports this without *any* additional work.

   State 1: $\neg\{[-v_N \leq h_D \wedge u_N \leq h_N] \,\exists\mathcal{U}\, [v'_D \neq v_D \vee v'_N \neq v_N]\}$ converges to *False* – implying the non-existence of an equilibrium in this state.

   State 2: $\neg\{[-v_N \geq h_D \wedge u_N \leq h_N] \,\exists\mathcal{U}\, [v'_D \neq v_D \vee v'_N \neq v_N]\}$ converges to $v_D l_D - r_D = 0 \wedge v_N \leq 0$. Thus we get the equilibrium concentrations as $v_D^* = r_D/l_D, v_N^* = 0$.

3. **Discrete State Equilibria.** When the invariants are non-overlapping, a system can stay forever in the discrete state i iff $Inv_i \wedge \neg\{Inv_i \,\exists\mathcal{U}\, \neg Inv_i\}$.

   State 1: $[-v_N \leq h_D \wedge u_N \leq h_N] \,\exists\mathcal{U}\, [-v_N > h_D \vee u_N > h_N]$ returns $v_N \leq -h_D/(1 - \Delta l_N)^k$ after k iterations, effectively evaluating to *True*. Thus the system always evolves out of state 1 and hence it does not correspond to any equilibrium.

   State 3: $[-v_N \leq h_D \wedge u_N \geq h_N] \,\exists\mathcal{U}\, [-v_N < h_D \vee u_N > h_N]$ is non-convergent and returns $v_N \leq (-h_D - \Delta r_N)/(1 - \Delta l_N)$ after one iteration. So, for such a path out of state 3 to not exist, there should be no way of satisfying the above inequality when $-v_N < h_D$. So we get $(-h_D - \Delta r_N)/(1 - \Delta l_N) < -h_D$ which simplifies to $h_D > -r_N/l_N$.

Two-Cell System. The above exercise can be repeated for a two cell model, where there are 4 dynamic variables n_1, d_1, n_2 and d_2, which stand for the Notch and Delta concentrations in cell 1 and 2 respectively. Due to the limitations of Qepcad, we use the numerical parameter values courtesy Hwang et al. [19] to demonstrate our approach. In particular, we set $\lambda_N = \lambda_D = r_N = r_D = 1, h_D = -\frac{1}{2}, h_N = \frac{1}{5}, \Delta = \frac{1}{2}$.

1. **Equilibrium Concentration Estimation**
   State q_{10} (3,2): $\neg\{[-2n_1 > -1 \wedge 5d_1 < 1 \wedge -2n_2 < -1 \wedge 5d_1 > 1]\exists\mathcal{U}[d_1' \neq d_1 \vee n_1' \neq n_1 \vee d_2' \neq d_2 \vee n_2' \neq n_2]\}$ converges to $[n_1 \leq 0 \wedge d_2 \leq 0 \wedge d_1 - 1 = 0 \wedge n_2 - 1 = 0]$. Thus $n_1^* = d_2^* = 0$ and $d_1^* = n_2^* = 1$.
   State q_{15} (4,3): $\neg\{[-2n_1 > -1 \wedge 5d_2 > 1 \wedge -2n_2 < -1 \wedge 5d_1 > 1]\exists\mathcal{U}[d_1' \neq d_1 \vee n_1' \neq n_1 \vee d_2' \neq d_2 \vee n_2' \neq n_2]\}$ converges to *False*, implying that in this discrete state the variables can never be in equilibrium.

2. **Are Equilibria Reversible?**
   State q_7 (2,3): $[-2n_1 > -1 \wedge 5d_2 < 1 \wedge -2n_2 < -1 \wedge 5d_1 > 1]$ $\exists\mathcal{U}$ $[-2n_1 = -1 \vee 5d_2 = 1 \vee -2n_2 = -1 \vee 5d_1 = 1]$ converges to *False* after 2 iterations implying that this is an irreversible discrete state equilibrium.
   State q_{16} (4,4): $[-2n_1 > -1 \wedge 5d_2 > 1 \wedge -2n_2 > -1 \wedge 5d_1 > 1]$ $\exists\mathcal{U}$ $[-2n_1 = -1 \vee 5d_2 = 1 \vee -2n_2 = -1 \vee 5d_1 = 1]$ converges to *True* implying that the two-cell Delta-Notch system will always leave this discrete state.

3. **Choice Of Equilibrium.** We can "verify" that the wrong equilibrium cannot be reached from a given initial relation between n_1 and n_2, and d_1 and d_2. When the invariants are non-overlapping, the initial conditions that allow a path to discrete state i but not to discrete state j are given by $\{\text{True} \exists\mathcal{U} \, Inv_i\} \wedge \neg\{\text{True} \exists\mathcal{U} \, Inv_j\}$.
   State q_7 (2,3): At iteration 2 of $\text{True} \exists\mathcal{U} [-2n_1 > -1 \wedge 5d_2 < 1 \wedge -2n_2 < -1 \wedge 5d_1 > 1]$, we get: $n_1 - 1 \leq 0 \wedge [[2n_1 - 5d_1 \leq 0 \wedge 5d_2 - 1 \leq 0 \wedge 8n_2 - 5d_2 - 3 \geq 0 \wedge n_2 + n_1 - 1 = 0] \vee [8n_1 - 5d_1 - 3 \leq 0 \wedge 4d_2 + d_1 - 1 = 0 \wedge 2n_2 - 1 \geq 0 \wedge 8n_2 + 5d_1 - 5 \geq 0] \vee [5d_1 - 1 \geq 0 \wedge 2n_1 - 5d_1 \leq 0 \wedge 5d_2 + 2n_1 - 2 \leq 0 \wedge 2n_2 - 1 \geq 0] \vee [5d_1 - 1 \geq 0 \wedge 2n_1 - 1 \leq 0 \wedge 5d_2 - 1 \leq 0 \wedge 8n_2 - 5d_2 - 3 \geq 0] \vee [2n_1 - 1 \leq 0 \wedge 5d_2 - 1 \leq 0 \wedge 8n_2 - 5d_2 - 3 \geq 0 \wedge 8n_2 + 5d_1 - 5 \geq 0] \vee [2n_1 - 5d_1 \leq 0 \wedge 5d_2 - 1 \leq 0 \wedge 2n_2 - 1 \geq 0 \wedge 8n_2 + 5d_1 - 5 \geq 0]] \equiv f_7$.
   State q_{10} (3,2): At iteration 2 of $\text{True} \exists\mathcal{U} [-2n_1 < -1 \wedge 5d_2 > 1 \wedge -2n_2 > -1 \wedge 5d_1 < 1]$, we get: $n_2 - 1 \leq 0 \wedge [[2n_1 - 1 \geq 0 \wedge 5d_2 + 8n_1 - 5 \geq 0 \wedge d_2 + 4d_1 - 1 = 0 \wedge 2n_2 + 5d_1 - 2 \leq 0] \vee [2n_1 - 1 < 0 \wedge 8n_1 - 5d_1 - 3 \geq 0 \wedge 5d_2 + 8n_1 - 5 \geq 0 \wedge n_2 + n_1 - 1 = 0] \vee [8n_1 - 5d_1 - 3 \geq 0 \wedge 5d_2 + 8n_1 - 5 < 0 \wedge 5d_2 + 2n_1 - 2 \geq 0 \wedge n_2 + n_1 - 1 = 0] \vee [2n_1 - 1 \geq 0 \wedge 5d_2 - 1 \geq 0 \wedge 2n_2 + 5d_1 - 2 \leq 0 \wedge n_2 + n_1 - 1 < 0] \vee [5d_1 - 1 \leq 0 \wedge 2n_1 - 1 \geq 0 \wedge 5d_2 + 8n_1 - 5 \geq 0 \wedge 2n_2 - 5d_2 \leq 0] \vee [5d_1 - 1 \leq 0 \wedge 2n_1 - 1 \geq 0 \wedge 5d_2 + 8n_1 - 5 \geq 0 \wedge 2n_2 - 1 \leq 0] \vee [8n_1 - 5d_1 - 3 \geq 0 \wedge 5d_2 - 1 \geq 0 \wedge 2n_2 + 5d_1 - 2 \leq 0 \wedge 2n_2 - 1 \leq 0]] \equiv f_{10}$.
   State q_7 and not State q_{10}: The initial conditions that lead only to q_7 and not q_{10} are thus given by $f_7 \wedge \neg f_{10}$. Since we have assumed no upper bound on the initial values and since we have been able to compute only two iterations, this formula does *not* evaluate to *True* given the correct initial partition $n_1 < n_2 \wedge d_1 > d_2$. However, when Qepcad simplifies the above formula assuming that $n_1 > n_2 \wedge d_1 < d_2$, it evaluates to *False*.

5   Conclusion

The real limitation of this quantifier-elimination-based model-checking comes from the computational complexity of Collins' cylindrical algebraic decomposition (CAD) algorithm, with its double-exponential dependence on the number of variables [11]. In our experience, Qepcad failed to support fully symbolic analysis of the two-cell Delta-Notch system. However, it is to be noted that even this preliminary version of Tolque was able to support a very uniform way of asking about a good spectrum of interesting temporal properties of a biologically significant hybrid system. We are in the process of rewriting Tolque in *Lisp* and integrating it with Simpathica[5]. These modifications will allow biochemical networks to be easily represented, stored and analyzed in keeping with our initial "Systems Biology" motivation. Based on the results of this paper, we can focus on complexity improvement through other meaningful approximations. The next paper in the AAMC series focuses on approximate methods like bisimulation-partitioning, space discretization (using grids and polyhedra) and time discretization [27]. Eventually, we plan to implement our own symbolic algebra system to work hand in hand with the different *quantifier elimination, Gröbner basis* and *characteristic set* tools that can systematically simplify the formulæ at each fixpoint iteration.

To summarize, the "semi-algebraic" method, outlined here, enables sophisticated symbolic algebraic model checking of a large class of hybrid automata, well beyond the capabilities of current applications of symbolic methods in this area. The semi-decidability results for the TCTL operators and the introduction of the Blum-Shub-Smale model are expected to spark further investigations of the relations between dynamical systems, topology and complexity. Our approach is general: it can be extended beyond TCTL model-checking to dense-time LTL; and it can be further enhanced by allowing non-linear (but polynomial) expressions in the temporal queries that can involve the values before and after one step of the hybrid system.

Finally, although the state of the art of algebraic hybrid systems model-checking can only be compared to that of *boolean finite-state model-checking* in the early 80s, we believe that the approach will make quick and important strides, and yield deep insights in biological areas before the end of this decade.

References

1. R. Alur, C. Courcoubetis, and D. Dill. Model-Checking for Real-Time Systems. In *International Symposium on Logic in Computer Science*, 5, pages 414–425. IEEE Computer Press, 1990.
2. R. Alur, C. Courcoubetis, N. Halbwachs, T. A. Henzinger, P.-H. Ho, X. Nicollin, A. Olivero, J. Sifakis, and S. Yovine. The Algorithmic Analysis of Hybrid Systems. *Theoretical Computer Science*, 138:3–34, 1995.
3. R. Alur, T. Dang, and F. Ivancic. Progress on Reachability Analysis of Hybrid Systems Using Predicate Abstraction. In O. Maler and A. Pnueli, editors, *Hybrid Systems: Computation and Control (HSCC'03)*, volume 2623 of *LNCS*, pages 4–19. Springer-Verlag, 2003.

4. Hirokazu Anai. Algebraic approach to analysis of discrete-time polynomial systems. In *ECC Karlsure (Germany)*, 1999.

5. M. Antoniotti, A. Policriti, N. Ugel, and B. Mishra. Reasoning about Biochemical Processes. *Cell Biochemistry and Biophysics*, 38:271–286, 2003.

6. E. Asarin, T. Dang, O. Maler, and O. Bournez. Approximate Reachability Analysis of Piecewise-Linear Dynamical Systems. In B. Krogh and N. Lynch, editors, *Hybrid Systems: Computation and Control (HSCC'00)*, volume 1790 of *LNCS*, pages 20–31. Springer-Verlag, 2000.

7. L. Blum, F. Cucker, M. Shub, and S. Smale. *Complexity and Real Computation*. Springer-Verlag, 1997.

8. O. Bournez, O. Maler, and A. Pnueli. Orthogonal Polyhedra: Representation and Computation. In F. Vaadrager and J. van Schuppen, editors, *Hybrid Systems: Computation and Control (HSCC 1999)*, volume 1596 of *LNCS*, pages 19–30. Springer-Verlag, 1999.

9. A. Chutinan and B. Krogh. Verification of Polyhedral-Invariant Hybrid Automata Using Polygonal Flow Pipe Approximations. In F. W. Vaandrager and J. H. van Schuppen, editors, *Hybrid Systems: Computation and Control (HSCC'99)*, volume 1569 of *LNCS*, pages 76–90. Springer-Verlag, 1999.

10. J. R. Collier, N. A. M. Monk, P. K. Maini, and J. H. Lewis. Pattern Formation by Lateral Inhibition with Feedback: a Mathematical Model of Delta-Notch Intercellular Signalling. *Journal of Theor. Biology*, 183:429–446, 1996.

11. G. E. Collins. Quantifier Elimination for the Elementary Theory of Real Closed Fields by Cylindrical Algebraic Decomposition. In *Proceedings of the Second GI Conference on Automata Theory and Formal Languages*, volume 33 of *LNCS*, pages 134–183. Springer-Verlag, 1975.

12. Andreas Dolzmann and Thomas Sturm. REDLOG: Computer algebra meets computer logic. *SIGSAM Bulletin (ACM Special Interest Group on Symbolic and Algebraic Manipulation)*, 31(2):2–9, 1997.

13. Martin Fränzle. What will be eventually true of polynomial hybrid automata? In Naoki Kobayashi and Benjamin C. Pierce, editors, *Theoretical Aspects of Computer Software, 4th International Symposium, TACS 2001, Sendai, Japan, October 29-31, 2001, Proceedings*, volume 2215 of *Lecture Notes in Computer Science*, pages 340–359. Springer, 2001.

14. R. Ghosh and C. Tomlin. Lateral Inhibition through Delta-Notch signaling: A Piecewise Affine Hybrid Model. In M. D. D. Benedetto and A. Sangiovanni-Vincentelli, editors, *Int.l Workshop on Hybrid Systems: Computation and Control (HSCC'01)*, volume 2034 of *LNCS*, pages 232–246. Springer-Verlag, 2001.

15. Esfandiar Haghverdi, Paulo Tabuada, and George J. Pappas. Bisimulation relations for dynamical, control, and hybrid systems. *Theoretical Computer Science*, November 2003.

16. T. Henzinger, P. W. Kopke, A. Puri, and P. Varaiya. What's Decidable about Hybrid Automata. In *Symposium on the Theory of Computing (STOC)*, pages 373–382, 1995.

17. T. A. Henzinger, X. Nicollin, J. Sifakis, and S. Yovine. Symbolic Model Checking for Real-time Systems. In *7th Annual IEEE Symposium on Logic in Computer Science*, pages 394–406. IEEE, IEEE Computer Society Press, June 1992.

18. H. Hong. Quantifier elimination in elementary algebra and geometry by partial cylindrical algebraic decomposition, version 13. *WWW site* www.eecis.udel.edu/~saclib, 1995.

19. Inseok Hwang, Hamsa Balakrishnan, Ronojoy Ghosh, and Claire Tomlin. Reachability analysis of delta-notch lateral inhibition using predicate abstraction. *Lecture Notes in Computer Science*, 2552:715–724, Jan 2002.

20. Mats Jirstrand. Nonlinear control system design by quantifier elimination. *J. Symb. Comput.*, 24(2):137–152, 1997.

21. G. Lafferiere, G. J. Pappas, and S. Sastry. O-minimal Hybrid Systems. *Mathematics of Control, Signals, and Systems*, 13(1):1–21, March 2000.

22. Gerardo Lafferriere, George J. Pappas, and Sergio Yovine. Symbolic reachability computation for families of linear vector fields. *J. Symb. Comput.*, 32(3):231–253, 2001.

23. R. Lanotte and S.Tini. Taylor approximation for hybrid systems. In *HSCC*. LNCS, 2005.

24. B. Mandelbrot. *The Fractal Geometry of Nature*. Freeman Co., San Francisco, 1982.

25. B. Mishra. A Symbolic Approach to Modeling Cellular Behavior. In S. Sahni, V. K. Prasanna, and U. Shukla, editors, *High Performance Computing (HiPC'02)*, volume 2552 of *LNCS*, pages 725–732. Springer-Verlag, 2002.

26. B. Mishra. *Computational Real Algebraic Geometry*. CRC Press, Boca Raton, FL, 2004.

27. V. Mysore and B. Mishra. Algorithmic Algebraic Model Checking III: Approximate Methods. In *Third International Symposium on Automated Technology for Verification and Analysis (ATVA)*, 2005.

28. C. Piazza, M. Antoniotti, V. Mysore, A. Policriti, F. Winkler, and B. Mishra. Algorithmic Algebraic Model Checking I: The Case of Biochemical Systems and their Reachability Analysis. In *17th International Conference on Computer Aided Verification (CAV)*, 2005.

29. A. Puri and P. Varaiya. Decidebility of hybrid systems with rectangular differential inclusions. *Computer Aided Verification*, pages 95–104, 1994.

30. C. Robinson. *Dynamical Systems: Stability, Symbolic Dynamics, and Chaos*. CRC Press, Boca Raton, 1995.

31. Paulo Tabuada and George J. Pappas. Model checking ltl over controllable linear systems is decidable. *Hybrid Systems : Computation and Control, Lecture Notes in Computer Science*, 2623, April 2003.

32. A. Tarski. *A Decision Method for Elementary Algebra and Geometry*. University of California Press, second edition, 1948.

33. A. Tiwari and G. Khanna. Series of Abstraction for Hybrid Automata. In C. J. Tomlin and M. Greenstreet, editors, *Hybrid Systems: Computation and Control (HSCC'02)*, volume 2289 of *LNCS*, pages 465–478. Springer-Verlag, 2002.

Appendix

One-Cell Delta-Notch Analysis in Tolque

1. **Pruned Transition Map**
   - **Discrete Transition** $1 \xrightarrow[\mathcal{D}]{0} 2$

     $[-v_N \leq h_D \wedge u_N \leq h_N] \; \exists \mathcal{U} \; [-v_N \geq h_D \wedge u_N \leq h_N]$

     After k iterations, we get the requirement $v_N \leq -h_D/(1 - \Delta l_N)^k$ which is *True* when $k \; (\geq -\log(h_D/v_N)/\log(1 - \Delta l_N))$. Thus the transition from 1 to 2 is possible.

– **Discrete Transition** $2 \xrightarrow[D]{0} 1$

$[-v_N \geq h_D \wedge u_N \leq h_N]$ $\exists \mathcal{U}$ $[-v_N < h_D \wedge u_N < h_N]$ converges after two iterations to *False*. Thus, it is not possible to jump to state 1 from state 2.

2. **Estimating Continuous-State Equilibrium Concentrations**

   State 1: $\neg\{[-v_N \leq h_D \wedge u_N \leq h_N]$ $\exists \mathcal{U}$ $[v_D' \neq v_D \vee v_N' \neq v_N]\}$ converges to *False* – implying the non-existence of an equilibrium in this state.

   State 2: $\neg\{[-v_N \geq h_D \wedge u_N \leq h_N]$ $\exists \mathcal{U}$ $[v_D' \neq v_D \vee v_N' \neq v_N]\}$ converges to $v_D l_D - r_D = 0 \wedge v_N \leq 0$. Thus we get the equilibrium concentrations as $v_D^* = r_D/l_D, v_N^* = 0$.

   State 3: $\neg\{[-v_N \leq h_D \wedge u_N \geq h_N]$ $\exists \mathcal{U}$ $[v_D' \neq v_D \vee v_N' \neq v_N]\}$ converges to $v_D \leq 0 \wedge v_N l_N - r_N = 0$. Thus $v_D^* = 0, v_N^* = r_N/l_N$ are the equilibrium values.

   State 4: $\neg\{[-v_N \geq h_D \wedge u_N \geq h_N]$ $\exists \mathcal{U}$ $[v_D' \neq v_D \vee v_N' \neq v_N]\}$ converges to the equilibrium condition $v_N^* l_N - r_N = 0 \wedge h_D + v_N^* \neq 0 \wedge v_D^* l_D - r_D = 0 \wedge h_N - u_N \neq 0$.

3. **Discrete State Equilibria**

   State 1: $[-v_N \leq h_D \wedge u_N \leq h_N]$ $\exists \mathcal{U}$ $[-v_N > h_D \vee u_N > h_N]$ returns $v_N \leq -h_D/(1 - \Delta l_N)^k$ after k iterations, effectively evaluating to *True*. Thus the system always evolves out of state 1 and hence it does not correspond to any equilibrium.

   State 2: $[-v_N \geq h_D \wedge u_N \leq h_N]$ $\exists \mathcal{U}$ $[-v_N < h_D \vee u_N > h_N]$ converges to *False*. Thus there is no path out of state 2 and hence it corresponds to an equilibrium. Note that the transition from 2 to 4 recorded in [14] is not possible in a one-cell model where u_N is not modeled as a dynamic variable.

   State 3: $[-v_N \leq h_D \wedge u_N \geq h_N]$ $\exists \mathcal{U}$ $[-v_N < h_D \vee u_N > h_N]$ is non-convergent and returns $v_N \leq (-h_D - \Delta r_N)/(1 - \Delta l_N)$ after one iteration. So, for such a path out of state 3 to not exist, there should be no way of satisfying the above inequality when $-v_N < h_D$. So we get $(-h_D - \Delta r_N)/(1 - \Delta l_N) < -h_D$ which simplifies to $h_D > -r_N/l_N$.

   State 4: $[-v_N \geq h_D \wedge u_N \geq h_N]$ $\exists \mathcal{U}$ $[-v_N < h_D \vee u_N < h_N]$ is non-convergent and returns $l_N h_D + r_N > 0 \wedge h_D - \Delta v_N l_N + \Delta r_N + v_N \geq 0$ after the second iteration. The second term is just a lower bound on the starting value of v_N which continues to drop with each iteration - effectively being *True*. Hence, for an equilibrium to exist in State 4, the first term must not be satisfiable i.e. $l_N h_D + r_N \leq 0$ which is equivalent to $h_D \leq -r_N/l_N$.

Two-Cell Delta-Notch Analysis in Tolque

1. **Equilibrium Concentration Estimation**

   State q_{10} (3,2): $\neg\{[-2n_1 > -1 \wedge 5d_2 < 1 \wedge -2n_2 < -1 \wedge 5d_1 > 1]\exists \mathcal{U}[d_1' \neq d_1 \vee n_1' \neq n_1 \vee d_2' \neq d_2 \vee n_2' \neq n_2]\}$ converges to $[n_1 \leq 0 \wedge d_2 \leq 0 \wedge d_1 - 1 = 0 \wedge n_2 - 1 = 0]$. Thus $n_1^* = d_2^* = 0$ and $d_1^* = n_2^* = 1$.

State q_7 (2,3): $\neg\{[-2n_1 < -1 \wedge 5d_2 > 1 \wedge -2n_2 > -1 \wedge 5d_1 < 1]\exists \mathcal{U}[d_1' \neq$ $d_1 \vee n_1' \neq n_1 \vee d_2' \neq d_2 \vee n_2' \neq n_2]\}$ converges to $[n_2 \leq 0 \wedge d_1 \leq 0 \wedge d_2 - 1 =$ $0 \wedge n_1 - 1 = 0]$. Thus $n_2^* = d_1^* = 0$ and $d_2^* = n_1^* = 1$.

State q_{15} (4,3): $\neg\{[-2n_1 > -1 \wedge 5d_2 > 1 \wedge -2n_2 < -1 \wedge 5d_1 > 1]\exists \mathcal{U}[d_1' \neq$ $d_1 \vee n_1' \neq n_1 \vee d_2' \neq d_2 \vee n_2' \neq n_2]\}$ converges to *False*, implying that in this discrete state the variables can never be in equilibrium.

2. **Are Equilibria Reversible?**

   State q_7 (2,3): $[-2n_1 > -1 \wedge 5d_2 < 1 \wedge -2n_2 < -1 \wedge 5d_1 > 1]\ \exists \mathcal{U}\ [-2n_1 =$ $-1 \vee 5d_2 = 1 \vee -2n_2 = -1 \vee 5d_1 = 1]$ converges to *False* after 2 iterations implying that this is an irreversible discrete state equilibrium.

   State q_{10} (3,2): $[-2n_1 < -1 \wedge 5d_2 > 1 \wedge -2n_2 > -1 \wedge 5d_1 < 1]\ \exists \mathcal{U}\ [-2n_1 =$ $-1 \vee 5d_2 = 1 \vee -2n_2 = -1 \vee 5d_1 = 1]$ also converges to *False* after 2 iterations implying that the equilibrium is irreversible.

   State q_{16} (4,4): $[-2n_1 > -1 \wedge 5d_2 > 1 \wedge -2n_2 > -1 \wedge 5d_1 > 1]\ \exists \mathcal{U}\ [-2n_1 =$ $-1 \vee 5d_2 = 1 \vee -2n_2 = -1 \vee 5d_1 = 1]$ converges to *True* implying that the two-cell Delta-Notch system will always leave this discrete state.

3. **Choice Of Equilibrium**

   State q_7 (2,3): At iteration 2 of *True* $\exists \mathcal{U}\ [-2n_1 > -1 \wedge 5d_2 < 1 \wedge -2n_2 <$ $-1 \wedge 5d_1 > 1]$, we get: $n_1 - 1 \leq 0 \wedge [[2n_1 - 5d_1 \leq 0 \wedge 5d_2 - 1 \leq 0 \wedge 8n_2 - 5d_2 -$ $3 \geq 0 \wedge n_2 + n_1 - 1 = 0] \vee [8n_1 - 5d_1 - 3 \leq 0 \wedge 4d_2 + d_1 - 1 = 0 \wedge 2n_2 - 1 \geq$ $0 \wedge 8n_2 + 5d_1 - 5 \geq 0] \vee [5d_1 - 1 \geq 0 \wedge 2n_1 - 5d_1 \leq 0 \wedge 5d_2 + 2n_1 - 2 \leq$ $0 \wedge 2n_2 - 1 \geq 0] \vee [5d_1 - 1 \geq 0 \wedge 2n_1 - 1 \leq 0 \wedge 5d_2 - 1 \leq 0 \wedge 8n_2 - 5d_2 - 3 \geq$ $0] \vee [2n_1 - 1 \leq 0 \wedge 5d_2 - 1 \leq 0 \wedge 8n_2 - 5d_2 - 3 \geq 0 \wedge 8n_2 + 5d_1 - 5 \geq$ $0] \vee [2n_1 - 5d_1 \leq 0 \wedge 5d_2 - 1 \leq 0 \wedge 2n_2 - 1 \geq 0 \wedge 8n_2 + 5d_1 - 5 \geq 0]] \equiv f_7$.

   State q_{10} (3,2): At iteration 2 of *True* $\exists \mathcal{U}\ [-2n_1 < -1 \wedge 5d_2 > 1 \wedge -2n_2 >$ $-1 \wedge 5d_1 < 1]$, we get: $n_2 - 1 \leq 0 \wedge [[2n_1 - 1 \geq 0 \wedge 5d_2 + 8n_1 - 5 \geq$ $0 \wedge d_2 + 4d_1 - 1 = 0 \wedge 2n_2 + 5d_1 - 2 \leq 0] \vee [2n_1 - 1 < 0 \wedge 8n_1 - 5d_1 - 3 \geq$ $0 \wedge 5d_2 + 8n_1 - 5 \geq 0 \wedge n_2 + n_1 - 1 = 0] \vee [8n_1 - 5d_1 - 3 \geq 0 \wedge 5d_2 + 8n_1 - 5 <$ $0 \wedge 5d_2 + 2n_1 - 2 \geq 0 \wedge n_2 + n_1 - 1 = 0] \vee [2n_1 - 1 \geq 0 \wedge 5d_2 - 1 \geq 0 \wedge 2n_2 +$ $5d_1 - 2 \leq 0 \wedge n_2 + n_1 - 1 < 0] \vee [5d_1 - 1 \leq 0 \wedge 2n_1 - 1 \geq 0 \wedge 5d_2 + 8n_1 - 5 \geq$ $0 \wedge 2n_2 - 5d_2 \leq 0] \vee [5d_1 - 1 \leq 0 \wedge 2n_1 - 1 \geq 0 \wedge 5d_2 + 8n_1 - 5 \geq 0 \wedge 2n_2 - 1 \leq$ $0] \vee [8n_1 - 5d_1 - 3 \geq 0 \wedge 5d_2 - 1 \geq 0 \wedge 2n_2 + 5d_1 - 2 \leq 0 \wedge 2n_2 - 1 \leq 0]] \equiv f_{10}$.

   State q_7 and not State q_{10}: The initial conditions that lead only to q_7 and not q_{10} are thus given by $f_7 \wedge \neg f_{10}$. Since we have assumed no upper bound on the initial values and since we have been able to compute only two iterations, this formula does *not* evaluate to *True* given the correct initial partition $n_1 < n_2 \wedge d_1 > d_2$. However, when Qepcad simplifies the above formula assuming that $n_1 > n_2 \wedge d_1 < d_2$, it evaluates to *False*.

   State q_{10} and not State q_7   Similarly, $\neg f_7 \wedge f_{10}$ evaluates to *False* assuming $n_1 < n_2 \wedge d_1 > d_2$.

A Static Analysis Using Tree Automata
for XML Access Control

Isao Yagi, Yoshiaki Takata, and Hiroyuki Seki

Graduate School of Information Science,
Nara Institute of Science and technology
{isao-y, y-takata, seki}@is.naist.jp

Abstract. Recently, an access control for XML database is one of the key issues in database security. Given an access control policy and a query expression,
static analysis determines whether the query does not access any elements nor
attributes that are prohibited by the access control policies. In a related work,
policies and queries were modeled as regular sets of paths in trees. However, this
model loses information on the structure of the trees, and some policies cannot
be represented by the model accurately. In this paper, we propose a formal model
for access control of XML databases and provide a static analysis method based
on tree automata theory. Both an access control policy and a query are modeled
as tree automata, and a policy is provided with two alternative semantics; AND-
semantics and OR-semantics. We investigate the computational complexity of the
static analysis problem, and show that the problem in AND-semantics is solvable
in square time while the problem in OR-semantics is EXPTIME-complete.

1 Introduction

Automatic verification has been recognized as an effective and efficient approach to
improving reliability and dependability in system design, and applied to not only hard-
ware/software correctness verification but also areas such as compile time optimization
and security assurance. This paper focuses on static analysis of XML database access
control as a successful application of automatic verification based on tree automata theory to security assurance.

XML is now becoming the *de facto* standard for data exchange format and is also
widely used as a schema language for database of structured documents (XML
database). Since a schema defined by XML is more complex than traditional database
schema such as relational database schema, a few query languages specialized to XML
database are being developed such as XPath[3] and XQuery[2]. Access control is one
of the most important technologies for database security and several models for XML
database access control have been proposed [1,6,10,14]. Usually, an access control policy (e.g., 'a professor can read every record of student files,' and 'a student can read
the record of her/himself only.') is provided to database management system (DBMS)
in advance. When a query is issued, DBMS checks whether the query is valid for the
access control policy. That is, DBMS determines whether the query is accessing only
the portion that the policy permits to access. If the query is valid, then DBMS permits

D.A. Peled and Y.-K. Tsay (Eds.): ATVA 2005, LNCS 3707, pp. 234–247, 2005.

the access, and the query is aborted otherwise. This kind of runtime access control process sometimes brings non-negligible overhead to DBMS. Static analysis is effective in overcoming this problem.

Especially for XML databases, Murata et al. [14] discuss the static analysis problem that, given an access control policy AP, an XML schema S and a query R, decides whether the query R is always valid for (or always against) the policy AP in any XML databases conforming the schema S. In their setting, both a policy and a query are given as XPath expressions and a schema is given as a regular tree grammar (or equivalently, a tree automaton). Then, three finite automata on strings are constructed by extracting regular expressions from these XPath expressions and the tree automaton, and the static analysis problem is reduced to the set-inclusion problem for regular string languages. They also present experimental results on static analysis of XMark queries and show their method is efficient and has enough scalability. It is mentioned in [14] that they did not use tree automata because decision procedures for tree automata need more time and space complexity than string automata. However, using regular expression as approximation of XPath expression and tree automaton loses information on the structure of the original tree. For example, we cannot distinguish the first son labeled with tag 'a' and the second son labeled with the same tag 'a' in the regular expression approximation. More concrete discussion is provided in the following sections.

In this paper, we propose a formal model for access control of XML databases and provide a static analysis method for XML access control based on tree automata theory. As in [14], we consider the node level (or element level) fine-grained access control.

We first model both an access control policy and a query by tree automata (TA), called a *policy TA* and a *query TA*, respectively. For this purpose, we introduce a charged alphabet to distinguish permission/denial in a policy and access/non-access in a query in a simple and uniform way. For simplicity, database schema is not considered in this paper: A schema defined by DTD or XML schema can be represented by a tree automaton, and it is easy to incorporate a schema as a part of a problem instance in our setting. Next, a static analysis problem is defined based on the tree languages accepted by a policy TA and a query TA. We introduce two alternative semantics, AND-semantics and OR-semantics. Generally, an access control policy may contain conflicts, e.g., one rule says that a student file is allowed to read while another rule says no [11,9]. These two semantics provide alternative conflict resolution strategies (if any conflict occurs in a policy). Intuitively, a query is valid for a policy in AND-semantics if for every tree t, every possible run of the query on t meets *all* the individual policies for t. A query is valid for a policy in OR-semantics if for every tree t, every possible run of the query on t meets *one of* the individual policies for t. Finally, we investigate the computational complexity of the static analysis problem and show that the problem in AND-semantics is solvable in square time while the problem in OR-semantics is EXPTIME-complete.

Related Work. Several access control models for XML databases have been proposed [1,6,10,14] but static analysis has not been discussed except [14]. Our model has two alternative semantics (AND-semantics and OR-semantics) for a database administrator to choose an appropriate conflict resolution strategy according to the database under consideration. For a traditional database, more sophisticated conflict resolution methods are proposed [11,9].

The static analysis problem discussed in this paper can also be considered as a model checking problem for infinite state systems. Model checking methods have been proposed for infinite state systems such as pushdown system (PDS), Petri Net and Process Rewrite Systems [12,7,16]. Most of these works are based on automata theory over strings. For example, LTL model checking for PDS can be solved by reducing it to the decision problem on the reachability set of the given PDS, which is known to be a regular string language. The analysis method proposed in this paper uses tree automata instead of automata on strings so that more accurate analysis can be performed by taking tree structure information into consideration.

2   Preliminaries

2.1   Trees

Each XML document can be represented by a tree, whose internal nodes correspond to the elements and the attributes in the XML document and the leaf nodes correspond to the contents of the elements. Such a tree is an *unranked tree*, which is a tree in which the number of children of a node is not bound. In this paper, we consider only the structure of documents and ignore the nodes corresponding to the actual values contained within the elements and the attributes; that is, we only consider trees in which every node is labeled the name of an element or an attribute.

We assume that we are given a finite alphabet Σ and each node label is chosen from Σ. A tree in which each node is labeled a symbol in Σ is called a Σ-*tree*. The set of unranked Σ-trees is denoted by T_Σ. Formally, the unranked Σ-trees are defined as strings which represent the tree structure. T_Σ is the smallest set of strings over Σ and the parenthesis symbols '(' and ')' such that for every $\sigma \in \Sigma$ and $w \in T_\Sigma^*$, $\sigma(w)$ is in T_Σ (T_Σ^* is the Kleenean closure of T_Σ). We abbreviate $\sigma()$ to σ. The set of nodes or positions of a tree t is denoted by $\mathrm{Dom}(t)$. The root node of t is denoted by $root(t)$. For every tree t and every $u \in \mathrm{Dom}(t)$, the label of u in t is denoted by $lab^t(u)$.

2.2   Tree Automata

A nondeterministic tree automaton (NTA) [5,13,15] $M = (Q, \Sigma, \delta, F)$ is a 4-tuple where

- Q is the finite set of states,
- Σ is the alphabet,
- $\delta : Q \times \Sigma \to 2^{Q^*}$ is the transition function such that $\delta(q, a)$ is a regular language over Q, and
- $F \subseteq Q$ is the set of accepting states.

A *run* of M on a Σ-tree t is a labeling $\lambda : \mathrm{Dom}(t) \to Q$ such that for every $v \in \mathrm{Dom}(t)$ and its children $v_1, \ldots, v_n$, $\lambda(v_1) \ldots \lambda(v_n) \in \delta(\lambda(v), lab^t(v))$. A run is accepting if and only if the root is labeled with an accepting state. The set of Σ-trees accepted by M is denoted by $L(M)$ and we say that M recognizes the tree language $L(M)$. A tree language is regular if it is recognized by some NTA. Let $\|M\|$ be the description length of M.

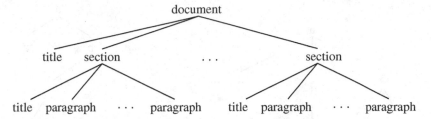

Fig. 1. A schema of tree-structured documents

For example, consider a schema of tree-structured documents illustrated in Fig.1. The set of trees conforming the schema is recognized by an NTA M_t defined as follows. Note that the value of $\delta(q, a)$ for each $q \in Q_t$ and $a \in \Sigma_t$ is denoted by a regular expression (which allows the operator '+' that means one or more repetition). The empty string is denoted by ϵ.

$M_t = (Q_t, \Sigma_t, \delta_t, F_t)$ where

- $Q_t = \{q_t, q_p, q_s, q_d\}$,
- $\Sigma_t = \{document, title, section, paragraph\}$,
- $\delta_t(q_p, paragraph) = \epsilon$,
  $\delta_t(q_t, title) = \epsilon$,
  $\delta_t(q_s, section) = q_t q_p{}^+$,
  $\delta_t(q_d, document) = q_t q_s{}^+$,
  $\delta_t(q, a) = \emptyset$ for any other pair of $q \in Q_t$ and $a \in \Sigma_t$, and
- $F_t = \{q_d\}$.

By this definition, $L(M_t)$ is the set of trees in which the root is labeled *document* and has a leaf child labeled *title* as well as one or more children labeled *section*, and each child of the root labeled *section* has a leaf child labeled *title* as well as one or more leaf children labeled *paragraph*. Fig.2 shows a sample tree t and a run of M_t on t.

It is known that every unranked tree can be converted into a binary tree[15]. Let t^{bin} be the binary tree obtained by this conversion from an unranked tree t. Each node v of an unranked tree t has exactly one corresponding node v_b of t^{bin}. The left child and the right child of v_b represent the eldest child of v and the immediately following sibling of v, respectively. If v has no child but has a younger sibling, then the left child

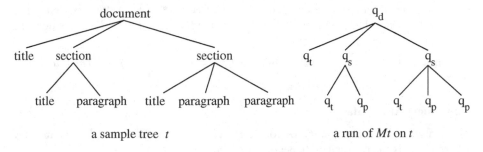

a sample tree t a run of M_t on t

Fig. 2. A run of M_t

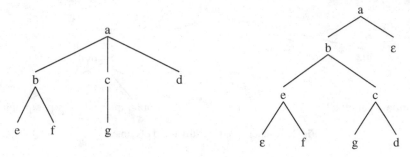

Fig. 3. An unranked tree and its corresponding binary tree

of v_b is labeled ϵ. If v has a child but has no younger sibling, then the right child of v_b is labeled ϵ (Fig.3).

We can convert an NTA $M = (Q, \Sigma, \delta, F)$ for unranked trees into an NTA M_b for binary trees such that $L(M_b) = \{t^{bin} \mid t \in L(M)\}$ and $\|M_b\|$ is at most $O(\|M\|^2)$, if $\delta(q, a)$ is given as a finite automaton over Q for any $q \in Q$ and $a \in \Sigma$. Hence, for simplicity, we consider only tree automata for binary trees. The transition function of a tree automaton for binary trees is restricted to $\delta : Q \times \Sigma \to 2^{\{\epsilon\} \cup (Q \times Q)}$. Note that we use unranked trees in examples for readability.

Similar to regular string languages, regular tree languages have the following good properties[5].

Lemma 1. *For a tree t and a regular tree language L, membership ($t \in L$?) and emptiness ($L = \emptyset$?) are decidable. The class of regular tree languages is closed under boolean operations. Thus, for regular tree languages L_1 and L_2, inclusion ($L_1 \subseteq L_2$?) is also decidable.*

3   Access Control Model Based on Tree Automata

3.1   Charged Alphabet

For a given alphabet Σ, let $\Sigma^{+,-}$ be the alphabet whose elements are the symbols in Σ augmented with the positive and the negative signs ('+' and '−'); that is, $\Sigma^{+,-} = \Sigma \times \{+, -\}$. $\Sigma^{+,-}$ is called the *charged alphabet* of Σ. For readability, we write the augmented symbol $(a, +)$ as a^+ and $(a, -)$ as a^-. Let $\Sigma^+ = \{a^+ \mid a \in \Sigma\}$ and $\Sigma^- = \{a^- \mid a \in \Sigma\}$ (i.e., $\Sigma^{+,-} = \Sigma^+ \cup \Sigma^-$). Each $\Sigma^{+,-}$-tree is called a *charged tree*. The *uncharged tree* of a charged tree τ is the tree obtained from τ by removing all $+$ and $-$ from the node labels of τ. The uncharged tree of $\tau \in T_{\Sigma^{+,-}}$ is denoted by $uc(\tau)$.

Example 1. *Let $\tau_1 = a^+(b^-(c^+d^-)e^+)$ and $\tau_2 = a^+(b^+(c^-d^-)e^-)$. Then $uc(\tau_1) = uc(\tau_2) = a(b(c\,d)e)$.*

3.2   Query Automata

A *query tree automaton (query TA* for short) $M_R = (Q_R, \Sigma^{+,-}, \delta_R, F_R)$ is an NTA where $\Sigma^{+,-}$ is the charged alphabet of a given alphabet Σ.

Intuitively, a query TA M_R specifies the set of nodes accessed by the query for each XML document. For instance, assume that $\tau \in L(M_R)$ and $t = uc(\tau)$. This means that when we apply the query to the XML document represented by t, the query accesses every node u of t such that $lab^\tau(u) \in \Sigma^+$ and does not access any node v such that $lab^\tau(v) \in \Sigma^-$. For example, $a^+(b^-(c^+d^-)e^+) \in L(M_R)$ means that the query accesses exactly the nodes labeled by a, c, and e when it is applied to the tree $a(b(c\,d)e)$. If there exist τ_1 and τ_2 in $L(M_R)$ such that $uc(\tau_1) = uc(\tau_2) = t$, then one of the accesses represented by τ_1 and τ_2 is nondeterministically chosen.

```
<TreatmentAnalysis>
{
    for $r in document("medical_record")/record
    where $r/diagnosis/pathology/@type = "Gastric Cancer"
    return
        $r/diagnosis/pathology, $r//comment
}
</TreatmentAnalysis>
```

Fig. 4. A sample query in [14]

Fig.4 is a sample query taken from [14], which is written in XQuery. We model this query by a query TA described below. As the same as in [14], we consider only XPath location expressions occurring in the FLWR expression (which consists of a FOR, LET, WHERE, and RETURN clause) of the query. This query contains the following XPath location expressions. (Note that /record is substituted for variable $r.) We consider that the query accesses the nodes pointed by these location expressions and does not access any other nodes.

- /record
- /record/diagnosis/pathology/@type
- /record/diagnosis/pathology
- /record//comment

Let Σ be the alphabet of the XML database that is the target of the query, i.e., $\{record,$ $diagnosis, pathology, comment, @type\} \subseteq \Sigma$. A query TA which models the query should accept any $\tau \in T_{\Sigma^{+,-}}$ such that for each node u of $uc(\tau)$, $lab^\tau(u) \in \Sigma^+$ if and only if u is pointed by one of the above location expressions. We can define such a query TA M_q as follows. Note that for any $\tau \in T_{\Sigma^-}$, there exists a run λ of M_q such that $\lambda(root(\tau)) = q_F$, by the third line of the definition of δ_q. Thus M_q accepts any $\tau \in T_{\Sigma^-}$ such that $lab^{uc(\tau)}(root(uc(\tau))) \neq record$.

$M_q = (Q_q, \Sigma^{+,-}, \delta_q, F_q)$ where

- $Q_q = \{q_A, q_R, q_F, q_D, q_{R1}, q_P\}$,
- $\delta_q(q_A, record^+) = q_R{}^*$,
  $\delta_q(q_A, x^-) = q_F{}^*$ for $\forall x \in \Sigma - \{record\}$,
  $\delta_q(q_F, y^-) = q_F{}^*$ for $\forall y \in \Sigma$,
  $\delta_q(q_R, diagnosis^-) = q_D{}^*$,

$\delta_q(q_R, comment^+) = q_{R1}{}^*,$
$\delta_q(q_R, z^-) = q_{R1}{}^*$ for $\forall z \in \Sigma - \{diagnosis, comment\},$
$\delta_q(q_{R1}, comment^+) = q_{R1}{}^*,$
$\delta_q(q_{R1}, u^-) = q_{R1}{}^*$ for $\forall u \in \Sigma - \{comment\},$
$\delta_q(q_D, pathology^+) = q_P{}^*,$
$\delta_q(q_D, comment^+) = q_{R1}{}^*,$
$\delta_q(q_D, v^-) = q_{R1}{}^*$ for $\forall v \in \Sigma - \{pathology, comment\},$
$\delta_q(q_P, @type^+) = q_{R1}{}^*,$
$\delta_q(q_P, comment^+) = q_{R1}{}^*,$
$\delta_q(q_P, w^-) = q_{R1}{}^*$ for $\forall w \in \Sigma - \{@type, comment\},$
$\delta_q(q, a) = \emptyset$ for any other pair of $q \in Q_q$ and $a \in \Sigma^{+,-}$, and
- $F_q = \{q_A\}.$

3.3 Policy Automata

An access control policy determines the set of nodes that a user is allowed to access for a given tree. Murata et al. modeled a policy as a regular set of paths in a tree[14]. However, some policies cannot be represented by their model. For example, it cannot represent a policy such that access permission for a node depends on the states of its sibling nodes, e.g., a user is allowed to access a node labeled d if it has no siblings labeled b. To solve this problem, we model a policy as a tree automaton. An *access control policy tree automaton (policy TA* for short) $M_{AP} = (Q_A, \Sigma^{+,-}, \delta_A, F_A)$ is an NTA where $\Sigma^{+,-}$ is the charged alphabet of a given alphabet Σ. A policy TA M_{AP} specifies the set of nodes which a user is permitted to access for each XML document. When we apply the policy to a tree t and if there is a charged tree $\tau \in L(M_{AP})$ such that $uc(\tau) = t$, then the policy permits a user to access every node u of t such that $lab^\tau(u) \in \Sigma^+$ and prohibits him or her from accessing any node v of t such that $lab^\tau(v) \in \Sigma^-$.

For example, consider a policy which prohibits a user from accessing any subtree rooted by a node labeled d if there exists its sibling labeled b. This policy should include the charged trees in Fig.5. In the policy specification language introduced in [14], this policy can be specified by the following three rules.

- $(s, +r, //*)$
- $(s, -r, //*[b]/d)$
- $(s, -r, //*[b]/d//*)$

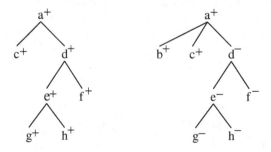

Fig. 5. A sample policy

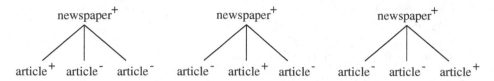

newspaper$^+$

article$^+$ article$^-$ article$^-$

newspaper$^+$

article$^-$ article$^+$ article$^-$

newspaper$^+$

article$^-$ article$^-$ article$^+$

Fig. 6. A part of the policy of a newspaper browsing system

The first rule means that subject s is allowed to access the nodes pointed by the XPath location expression (which points every node in a tree)[1]. The second and third rules denote prohibition. A rule for prohibition for a node overrules any rules for permission for the same node. We show that this policy cannot be represented accurately by the model in [14]. In the model, each location expression in such rules is modeled as a regular expression. For example, the location expressions in the above rules are modeled as $\Sigma^*\Sigma$, $\Sigma^*\Sigma d$, and $\Sigma^*\Sigma d\Sigma^*\Sigma$, respectively (i.e., the predicate [b] is conservatively approximated by 'true'). It means that a user is prohibited from accessing any node pointed by a path denoted by $\Sigma^*\Sigma d\Sigma^*$ in the approximated policy. Thus any node in the subtree rooted by a node labeled d cannot be accessed, even if the node does not have a sibling labeled b. On the other hand, we can define a policy TA that exactly represents this policy.

We provide a policy TA with two alternative semantics: AND-semantics and OR-semantics. In AND-semantics, every charged tree τ_1 in a query (i.e., $L(M_R)$) has to be valid for all charged trees τ_2 such that $uc(\tau_1) = uc(\tau_2)$ in the policy (i.e., $L(M_{AP})$). In OR-semantics, every charged tree τ_1 in a query has to be valid for at least one charged tree τ_2 such that $uc(\tau_1) = uc(\tau_2)$ in the policy. Formal definitions of AND-semantics and OR-semantics are provided in section 3.5.

3.4 Example

A policy of a newspaper browsing system is given by a policy TA as an example. For readability, we use unranked (not binary) trees and tree automata in this section. A newspaper browsing system which distributes electronic newspapers on the Web may have the following policy.

> The system permits users to read exactly one article which they would like to read among all articles, and prohibits them from reading the other articles at the same time.

The policy can be represented by an (infinite) set of charged trees. Fig.6 is a part of the policy that consists of charged trees for a newspaper with three articles. We use OR-semantics in this example, i.e., each query should be valid for at least one of these charged trees. Thus, the user is permitted to access exactly one article among all the three articles. The policy TA of this system is as follows.

$M_n = (Q_n, \Sigma_n^{+,-}, \delta_n, F_n)$ where

- $Q_n = \{q_0, q_1, q_2\}$,
- $\Sigma_n = \{newspaper, article\}$,

---

[1] The letter 'r' in the second component means 'read'.

$$- \delta(q_1, article^+) = \epsilon,$$
$$\delta(q_2, article^-) = \epsilon,$$
$$\delta(q_0, newspaper^+) = q_2^* q_1 q_2^*,$$
$$\delta(q, a) = \emptyset \text{ for any other pair of } q \in Q_n \text{ and } a \in \Sigma_n^{+,-}, \text{ and}$$
$$- F_n = \{q_0\}.$$

3.5 Validity of Query to Access Control Policy

In section 3.2, we stated the two alternative intuitive semantics of a policy TA. In this section, we define them formally. For the rest of this paper, we fix an alphabet Σ.

Definition 1. *For charged trees τ_1 and τ_2 in $T_{\Sigma^{+,-}}$, $\tau_1 \succeq \tau_2$ if and only if the following two properties hold.*

- $uc(\tau_1) = uc(\tau_2)$.
- *For every node u of τ_1, if $lab^{\tau_1}(u) \in \Sigma^+$, then $lab^{\tau_2}(u) \in \Sigma^+$.*

Proposition 1. *The relation $\succeq$ is a partial order over $T_{\Sigma^{+,-}}$.*

Definition 2. *An equivalence relation $\approx_{uc}$ over $T_{\Sigma^{+,-}}$ is defined as $\tau_1 \approx_{uc} \tau_2$ if and only if $uc(\tau_1) = uc(\tau_2)$. A partial order $\succeq$ over $\{+, -\}$ is defined as $- \succeq +$ and $+ \not\succeq -$.*

Example 2. *If $\tau_1 = a^+(b^+c^+)$ and $\tau_2 = a^+(b^-c^+)$, then $\tau_2 \succeq \tau_1$. However, if $\tau_1 = a^+(b^-c^+)$ and $\tau_2 = a^+(b^+c^-)$, then $\tau_1 \not\succeq \tau_2$, because the sign of the node labeled by c in τ_2 is $-$ while the sign of the corresponding node in τ_1 is $+$. Similarly, $\tau_2 \not\succeq \tau_1$ for the latter example.*

Definition 3.   *1. M_R is valid for M_{AP} in AND-semantics if and only if*
$$\forall \tau_1 \in L(M_R), \forall \tau_2 \in L(M_{AP}), \tau_1 \approx_{uc} \tau_2 \Rightarrow \tau_1 \succeq \tau_2.$$
 2. M_R is valid for M_{AP} in OR-semantics if and only if
$$\forall \tau_1 \in L(M_R), \exists \tau_2 \in L(M_{AP}), \tau_1 \succeq \tau_2.$$

Example 3. *Let $\tau_1 = a^+(b^-c^+)$ and $\tau_2 = a^+(b^+c^-)$ as in the latter case of example 2. We consider each combination of three policies $(\emptyset, \{\tau_1\}, \{\tau_1, \tau_2\})$ and two queries $(\{\tau_1\}, \{\tau_1, \tau_2\})$. The validity of M_R to M_{AP} in AND-semantics is summarized in the following table.*

		$L(M_{AP})$		
		$\emptyset$	$\{\tau_1\}$	$\{\tau_1, \tau_2\}$
$L(M_R)$	$\{\tau_1\}$	valid	valid	not valid
	$\{\tau_1, \tau_2\}$	valid	not valid	not valid

In a similar way, the validity of M_R to M_{AP} in OR-semantics is summarized in the following table.

		$L(M_{AP})$		
		$\emptyset$	$\{\tau_1\}$	$\{\tau_1, \tau_2\}$
$L(M_R)$	$\{\tau_1\}$	not valid	valid	valid
	$\{\tau_1, \tau_2\}$	not valid	not valid	valid

For convenience, we define the following relations and operations over the subsets of $T_{\Sigma+,-}$. As stated in lemma 2, $\sqsubseteq$ and $\sqsubseteq_A$ characterize OR-semantics and AND-semantics, respectively. $L\uparrow$ is intuitively the set which contains all upper-bounds (with respect to $\succeq$) of each $\tau' \in L$, while $L\uparrow^A$ is the set which contains all upper-bounds of each equivalent class defined by $\approx_{uc}$ in L.

Definition 4. *Let L, L_1, and L_2 be subsets of $T_{\Sigma+,-}$. We define the following relations and operations.*

- $L_1 \sqsubseteq L_2 \Leftrightarrow \forall \tau_2 \in L_2, \exists \tau_1 \in L_1, \tau_1 \preceq \tau_2$.
- $L_1 \sqsubseteq_A L_2 \Leftrightarrow \forall \tau_2 \in L_2, \forall \tau_1 \in L_1, \tau_1 \approx_{uc} \tau_2 \Rightarrow \tau_1 \preceq \tau_2$.
- $L\uparrow \; = \{\tau \mid \tau' \preceq \tau \; for \; \exists \tau' \in L\}$.
- $L\uparrow^A = \{\tau \mid \tau' \preceq \tau \; for \; \forall \tau' \in L \; such \; that \; \tau \approx_{uc} \tau'\}$.

By the definition, the following lemma holds obviously.

Lemma 2. *M_R is valid for M_{AP} in OR-semantics if and only if $L(M_{AP}) \sqsubseteq L(M_R)$. M_R is valid for M_{AP} in AND-semantics if and only if $L(M_{AP}) \sqsubseteq_A L(M_R)$.*

In the following, we discuss the relationship between the two semantics.

Lemma 3. *$L\uparrow^A \sqsubseteq L'$ if and only if $L \sqsubseteq_A L'$.*

Proof. It is sufficient to show that the following two statements are equivalent.

1. $\forall \tau_2 \in L', \exists \tau_1 \in L\uparrow^A, \tau_1 \preceq \tau_2$.
2. $\forall \tau_2 \in L', \forall \tau_3 \in L, \tau_3 \approx_{uc} \tau_2 \Rightarrow \tau_3 \preceq \tau_2$.

$(1 \Rightarrow 2)$ Assume that statement 1 holds and let $\tau_2 \in L'$. By statement 1, $\exists \tau_1 \in L\uparrow^A$, $\tau_1 \preceq \tau_2$ (and thus $\tau_1 \approx_{uc} \tau_2$). By the definition of $L\uparrow^A$, $\tau_3 \approx_{uc} \tau_1 \Rightarrow \tau_3 \preceq \tau_1$ for $\forall \tau_3 \in L$. Assume that $\tau_3 \in L$ and $\tau_3 \approx_{uc} \tau_2$. Then, $\tau_3 \approx_{uc} \tau_1$ and $\tau_3 \preceq \tau_1 \preceq \tau_2$.

$(2 \Rightarrow 1)$ Assume that statement 2 holds. By the definition of $L\uparrow^A$, $L' \subseteq L\uparrow^A$. Thus, statement 1 holds by letting $\tau_1 = \tau_2$.

Lemma 4. *If L is regular, then $L\uparrow^A$ is also regular.*

Proof. Let $M = (Q, \Sigma^{+,-}, \delta, F)$ be an NTA such that $\underline{L = L(M)}$. We construct an NTA $M_A = (Q_A, \Sigma^{+,-}, \delta_A, F_A)$ such that $L(M_A) = \overline{L\uparrow^A}$ as follows.

- $Q_A = Q \times \{0, 1\}$,
- $F_A = F \times \{1\}$,
- δ_A is the function such that for each $q_A \in Q_A$ and $a_A \in \Sigma^{+,-}$, $\delta_A(q_A, a_A)$ is the smallest set satisfying the followings for any $q, q_1, q_2 \in Q, a \in \Sigma, s_1, s_2 \in \{+, -\}$, and $d_1, d_2 \in \{0, 1\}$.
  - $\delta_A((q, 0), a^{s_1}) \ni \epsilon$ if $\delta(q, a^{s_2}) \ni \epsilon$ and $s_1 \succeq s_2$.
  - $\delta_A((q, 1), a^+) \ni \epsilon$ if $\delta(q, a^-) \ni \epsilon$.
  - $\delta_A((q, max(d_1, d_2)), a^{s_1}) \ni (q_1, d_1)(q_2, d_2)$ if $\delta(q, a^{s_2}) \ni q_1 q_2$ and $s_1 \succeq s_2$.
  - $\delta_A((q, 1), a^+) \ni (q_1, d_1)(q_2, d_2)$ if $\delta(q, a^-) \ni q_1 q_2$.

Note that $max(d_1, d_2)$ denotes the larger value of $d_1, d_2 \in \{0, 1\}$.

Intuitively, M_A behaves as follows. For any $\tau_1 \in T_{\Sigma^{+,-}}$, $\tau_1 \in \overline{L\uparrow^A}$ if and only if there exists a tree $\tau_2 \in L$ such that $\tau_1 \approx_{uc} \tau_2$ and $\tau_1 \not\succeq \tau_2$; that is, there exists a node v of τ_1 such that $lab^{\tau_1}(v) \in \Sigma^+$ and $lab^{\tau_2}(v) \in \Sigma^-$. To accept such τ_1, M_A simulates a run of M on a tree τ_2, by ignoring the positive and negative signs of the node labels, and by the second component of each state, M_A indicates for each node v of τ_2 that $lab^{\tau_1}(v) \in \Sigma^+$ and $lab^{\tau_2}(v) \in \Sigma^-$ or a descendant of v fulfills this property. When this property holds on v, there exists a run λ of M_A such that the second component of $\lambda(v)$ is 1. Thus, M_A exactly accepts $\tau_2 \in \overline{L\uparrow^A}$. By lemma 1, $L\uparrow^A$ is regular, since $\overline{L\uparrow^A}$ is regular.

Theorem 1. *For any policy TA M_{AP} in AND-semantics, we can convert it into an equivalent policy TA M'_{AP} in OR-semantics. On the other hand, there is a policy TA in OR-semantics such that there is no equivalent policy TA in AND-semantics.*

Proof. By lemma 3, $L(M_{AP}) \sqsubseteq_A L(M_R)$ if and only if $L(M_{AP})\uparrow^A \sqsubseteq L(M_R)$ for any query TA M_R. By lemma 4, we can obtain a policy TA M'_{AP} such that $L(M'_{AP}) = L(M_{AP})\uparrow^A$. On the other hand, the policy TA in section 3.4 is an instance such that there is no equivalent policy TA in AND-semantics.

4   Static Analysis

4.1   Problem Statement

The static analysis problem in AND-semantics (resp. OR-semantics) for M_R and M_{AP} is defined as follows.

Input: A query TA M_R and a policy TA M_{AP} over the same charged alphabet $\Sigma^{+,-}$.
Output: "YES" if M_R is valid for M_{AP} in AND-semantics (resp. OR-semantics) and
    "NO" otherwise.

By theorem 1, it is sufficient to give an algorithm for the problem in OR-semantics. We propose such an algorithm and discuss the time complexity of it.

4.2   Decision Algorithm

By the following lemma, we can reduce the static analysis problem in OR-semantics to the set-inclusion problem of regular tree languages.

Lemma 5. $L_1 \sqsubseteq L_2 \Leftrightarrow L_2 \subseteq L_1\uparrow$.

Proof. $L_2 \subseteq L_1\uparrow$ implies $\tau_2 \in L_1\uparrow$ for $\forall \tau_2 \in L_2$. By the definition of $L_1\uparrow$, $\tau_2 \succeq \tau_1$ for some $\tau_1 \in L$, and thus $L_1 \sqsubseteq L_2$. The converse can be shown by the reverse way.

Lemma 6. *If L is regular, then $L\uparrow$ is also regular.*

Proof. Let $M = (Q, \Sigma^{+,-}, \delta, F)$ be an NTA such that $L = L(M)$. We define $M^\uparrow = (Q, \Sigma^{+,-}, \delta^\uparrow, F)$ as follows. For each $q \in Q$ and $a \in \Sigma$,

- $\delta^\uparrow(q, a^-) = \delta(q, a^+) \cup \delta(q, a^-)$, and
- $\delta^\uparrow(q, a^+) = \delta(q, a^+)$.

We can easily show that $L(M^\uparrow) = L\uparrow$.

Theorem 2. *The static analysis problem for M_R and M_{AP} in OR-semantics is decidable.*

Proof. $L(M_{AP})\uparrow$ is regular by lemma 6 and thus $L(M_R) \subseteq L(M_{AP})\uparrow$ is decidable by lemma 1. Therefore, this theorem holds by lemma 2 and lemma 5.

From the proof of theorem 2, we obtain the following algorithm for the static analysis problem in OR-semantics.

Algorithm 1. Perform the following two steps in this order.
  1. Construct an NTA M_b such that $L(M_b) = L(M_R) \cap \overline{L(M_{AP})\uparrow}$.
  2. Decide whether $L(M_b) = \emptyset$ or not.

In the following, we consider the time complexity of the problem.

Lemma 7. [5] *For NTAs M_1 and M_2, we can construct an NTA M such that $L(M) = L(M_1) \cap L(M_2)$ and $\|M\| = O(\|M_1\| \cdot \|M_2\|)$.*

Lemma 8. *For an NTA M, emptiness of $L(M)$ is decidable in $O(\|M\|)$ time.*

The emptiness can be decided by the following algorithm.

1. Mark all the reachable states. A state q is reachable if it satisfies one of the following properties.
    – $\epsilon \in \delta(q, a)$ for some a.
    – $q_1 q_2 \in \delta(q, a)$ for some a and both q_1 and q_2 are reachable.
2. Return "YES" if all accepting states are not marked. Otherwise return "NO".

We can use an efficient method similar to an algorithm for the emptiness check of a context-free language (CFL)[8]. By this method, emptiness of $L(M)$ is decidable in $O(\|M\|)$ time.

On the other hand, step 1 of algorithm 1 would require the construction of an NTA N such that $L(N) = \overline{L(M_{AP})\uparrow}$; however, its size would be exponential to $\|M_{AP}\|$ in general[2]. In fact, the problem is EXPTIME-complete in general as shown below.

Theorem 3. *The static analysis problem in OR-semantics is EXPTIME-complete.*

Proof. We can construct an NTA N such that $L(N) = \overline{L(M_{AP})\uparrow}$ and $\|N\| = O(c^{\|M_{AP}\|})$ for some constant $c > 1$. Thus the problem is in EXPTIME by lemma 7 and lemma 8. EXPTIME-hardness can be shown by transforming the following problem known as EXPTIME-complete[5] to the static analysis problem.

    Regular Tree Language Non-Universality
    Input: An NTA M over a finite alphabet Σ.
    Output: $L(M) \neq T_\Sigma$?

---

[2] If $M_{AP}^\uparrow$ constructed from M_{AP} in the proof of lemma 6 is bottom-up deterministic [5], then the size of N is the same order of $\|M_{AP}\|$. However, $M_{AP}^\uparrow$ is not bottom-up deterministic in general even if M_{AP} is so.

From a given instance M of Regular Tree Language Non-Universality, we construct M_{AP} as the same as M except that its alphabet is Σ^+ and it uses $a^+ \in \Sigma^+$ instead of each $a \in \Sigma$. We let M_R be an NTA such that $L(M_R) = T_{\Sigma^+}$. Obviously, M_R is valid for M_{AP} in OR-semantics if and only if $L(M_{AP}) = T_{\Sigma^+}$, i.e., $L(M) = T_\Sigma$.

In contrast to OR-semantics, the static analysis problem in AND-semantics can be solved in polynomial time.

Lemma 9. $(L\uparrow^A)\uparrow = L\uparrow^A$.

Proof. It is obvious by the definition of $L\uparrow^A$.

Theorem 4. *The time complexity of the static analysis problem for M_R and M_{AP} in AND-semantics is $O(\|M_R\| \cdot \|M_{AP}\|)$.*

Proof. By theorem 1, this problem is equivalent to deciding whether $L(M_{AP})\uparrow^A \sqsubseteq L(M_R)$, which is equivalent to $L(M_R) \subseteq (L(M_{AP})\uparrow^A)\uparrow = L(M_{AP})\uparrow^A$ by lemma 5 and lemma 9. Thus, in step 1 of algorithm 1, it is sufficient to construct an NTA M_b such that $L(M_b) = L(M_R) \cap \overline{L(M_{AP})\uparrow^A}$. As is the way of constructing $L\uparrow^A$ in lemma 4, we can directly construct an NTA M_A from M_{AP} (without determinization and explicit complementation) such that $L(M_A) = \overline{L(M_{AP})\uparrow^A}$ and $\|M_A\| = O(\|M_{AP}\|)$. Therefore, this theorem holds by lemma 7 and lemma 8.

5   Conclusion

In this paper, we defined a formal model for XML database access control by tree automata and defined a static analysis problem for access control. By introducing the notion of charged alphabet, we can concisely and uniformly formalize the distinction of permission/denial in a policy and access/non-access in a query. Also, we provided two alternative semantics, AND-semantics and OR-semantics, and showed that the static analysis problems in AND-semantics and OR-semantics are solvable in square time and EXPTIME-complete, respectively.

Implementation of an analysis tool and empirical evaluation of the proposed method are left as a future study.

References

1. E. Bertino, S. Castano, E. Ferrari and M. Mesiti: Author-X: A Java-based system for XML data protection, IFIP WG 11.3 Working Conf on Database Security, 2000.
2. S. Boag, D. Chamberlin, M. F. Fernandez, D. Florescu, J. Robie, and J. Simeon: XQuery 1.0: An XML query language. W3C working draft 16 august 2002, http://www.w3.org/TR/xquery/, 2002.
3. J. Clark and S. DeRose: XML Path Language (XPath) version 1.0. W3C Recommendation, http://www.w3.org/TR/xpath, 1999.
4. E. M. Clarke, O. Grumberg and D. Peled: *Model Checking,* MIT Press, 2000.
5. H. Comon, M. Dauchet, R. Gilleron, F. Jacquemard, D. Lugiez, S. Tison, and M. Tommasi: Tree Automata Techniques and Applications, http://www.grappa.univ-lille3.fr/tata, 1997.

6. E. Damiani, S. D. C. di Vimercati, S. Paraboschi and P. Samarati: Securing XML documents, EDBT 2000, LNCS 1777, 121–135, 2000.
7. J. Esparza, D. Hansel, P. Rossmanith and S. Schwoon: Efficient algorithms for model-checking pushdown systems, CAV2000, LNCS 1855, 232–247, 2000.
8. J. Hopcroft, R. Motwani, and J. Ullman: Introduction to Automata Theory, Languages, and Computation, Addison-Wesley, 2000.
9. M. Koch, L. Mancini and F. Parisi-Presicce: Conflict detection and resolution in access control policy specifications, FOSSACS2002, LNCS 2303, 223–237, 2002.
10. M. Kudo and S. Harada: XML document security based on provisional authorization, 7th ACM CCS, 87–96, 2001.
11. E. C. Lupu and M. Sloman: Conflicts in policy-based distributed systems management, IEEE Trans. on Software Eng., 25(6), 852–869, 1999.
12. R. Mayr: Process Rewrite System, Inform. & Comput., 156, 264–286, 1999.
13. M. Murata, D. Lee, and M. Mani: Taxonomy of XML schema languages using formal language theory, ACM Trans. on Internet Technology, 5(4), 2005, http://www.cs.wpi.edu/~mmani/publications.html.
14. M. Murata, A. Tozawa, and M. Kudo: XML access control using static analysis, ACM CCS 2003, 73–84, 2003.
15. F. Neven: Automata theory for XML researchers, SIGMOD Record, Vol. 31, No.3, 39–46, 2002.
16. N. Nitta, Y. Takata and H. Seki: An efficient security verification method for programs with stack inspection, 8th ACM CCS, 68–77, 2001.

Reasoning About Transfinite Sequences[*]

(Extended Abstract)

Stéphane Demri[1] and David Nowak[2]

[1] LSV/CNRS UMR 8643 & INRIA Futurs projet SECSI & ENS Cachan, France
[2] Department of Information Science, The University of Tokyo, Japan

Abstract. We introduce a family of temporal logics to specify the behavior of systems with Zeno behaviors. We extend linear-time temporal
logic LTL to authorize models admitting Zeno sequences of actions and
quantitative temporal operators indexed by ordinals replace the standard next-time and until future-time operators. Our aim is to control
such systems by designing controllers that safely work on ω-sequences
but interact synchronously with the system in order to restrict their behaviors. We show that the satisfiability problem for the logics working
on ω^k-sequences is EXPSPACE-complete when the integers are represented
in binary, and PSPACE-complete with a unary representation. To do so,
we substantially extend standard results about LTL by introducing a
new class of succinct ordinal automata that can encode the interaction
between the different quantitative temporal operators.

1 Introduction

Control of physical systems. Modelling interaction between a computer system
and a physical system has to overcome the difficulty of the different time scales.
For example, reasoning about the connection between the physical description
of an electric circuit and its logical description in VHDL (standard language
designed and optimized for describing the behavior of digital systems) needs to
take into account that the two descriptions are dealing with objects running at
distinct speeds. The speeds can be so different that some abstraction consists in
assuming one system evolves infinitely quicker than the other one. Another kind
of interaction consists of controlling a physical system by a computer system.
Usually, a physical system is modelled by differential equations. Solving those
equations can then involve computations of limits. For instance, in the bouncing
ball example [14], in a finite amount of time an infinite number of actions can be
performed. It is a Zeno sequence of actions. However, Zeno behaviors are usually
excluded from the modelling of real-time controllers, which is a quite reasonable
requirement (see e.g. [7]), but also from the modelling of the physical systems,
see some exception in [5]. This is a quite drastic limitation, since Zeno sequences
are often acceptable behaviors for physical systems.

[*] The first author acknowledges partial support by the ACI "Sécurité et Informatique"
CORTOS. The second author acknowledges partial support by the e-Society project
of MEXT. Part of this work was done while the second author was affiliated to LSV,
CNRS & ENS de Cachan.

D.A. Peled and Y.-K. Tsay (Eds.): ATVA 2005, LNCS 3707, pp. 248–262, 2005.
© Springer-Verlag Berlin Heidelberg 2005

Beyond ω-sequences. Our main motivation in this paper is to model Zeno behaviors and ultimately to control physical systems admitting such behaviors. To do so, we introduce a specification logical language that is interpreted on well-ordered linear orderings. Reasoning problems based on this logical language should admit efficient algorithms, as good as those for standard specification languages as linear-time temporal logic LTL. The ω-sequences are already familiar objects in model-checking, see e.g. [28], even though such infinite objects are never manipulated when model-checking finite-state programs. Indeed, most problems on Büchi automata reduce to standard reachability questions on finite graphs. In a similar fashion, the behaviors of physical system are modeled in the paper by sequences indexed by countable ordinals, i.e. equivalence classes of well-ordered linear orderings, even though as we will show most problems will also reduce to questions on finite graphs. For instance, the law of movement of the bouncing ball is modelled by a set of sequences of length ω^2. The specification of the ball, i.e. the set of acceptable behaviors, is also characterized as a set of sequences of the same length ω^2. On the other hand, the controller is a computer system whose complete executions are ω-sequences. In this paper, we allow Zeno behaviors of physical systems and we will present a specification language working on sequences indexed by ordinals greater than the usual first infinite ordinal ω.

Our contribution. We introduce a class of logics $\text{LTL}(\alpha)$ indexed by a countable ordinal α closed under addition whose models are sequences of length α. Quantitative extensions of the standard next-time X and until U operators are considered by allowing operators of the form X^β and U^β with β smaller than α. As shown in the paper, for every $\alpha \leq \omega^\omega$, $\text{LTL}(\alpha)$ can be viewed as a fragment of the monadic second-order theory $\langle \omega^\omega, < \rangle$ known to be decidable, see e.g. [10]. For every $k \geq 1$, we show that $\text{LTL}(\omega^k)$ satisfiability is PSPACE-complete with an unary encoding of integers and EXPSPACE-complete with a binary encoding. This generalizes non-trivially what is known about LTL. We reduce the satisfiability problem to the emptiness problem of ordinal automata recognizing transfinite words [9,13,29,19,8]. The reduction entails that the satisfiability problem has an elementary complexity (by using [11]) but does not guarantee the optimal upper bound. To do so, we introduce a class of succinct ordinal automata of level k, $k \geq 1$ in which the $\text{LTL}(\omega^k)$ formulae can be translated into and we prove that the emptiness problem is in NLOGSPACE. Succinctness allows us to reduce by one exponential the size of the automata obtained by translation which provides us the optimal upper bound. Finally, we introduce and motivate a control problem with inputs a physical system $\mathcal{S}$ modelled by an ordinal automaton working on ω^k-sequences, and an $\text{LTL}(\omega^k)$ formula ϕ describing the desirable behaviors of the system. The problem we introduce is the existence of a controller $\mathcal{C}$ working on ω-sequences such that the system $\mathcal{S} \times_k \mathcal{C}$ satisfies ϕ. The synchronization operation $\times_k$ takes into account the different time scales between $\mathcal{S}$ and $\mathcal{C}$. As a by-product of our results, checking whether a controller satisfies the above conditions can be done effectively but we leave the question of the synthesis of such controllers for future work.

Related work. Our original motivation in this work is the control of systems with legal Zeno behaviors by systems whose complete executions are ω-sequences. The theory of control of discrete event systems was introduced in [25]. In this theory, a process is a deterministic non-complete finite automaton over an alphabet of events. The control problem consists in, given a process P and a set S of admissible behaviors, finding a process Q such that the behaviors of $P \times Q$ are in S and such that Q reacts to all uncontrollable events and cannot detect unobservable events. Extension to specifications from the modal μ-calculus can be found in [2] whereas the control of timed systems (without Zeno behaviors) is for instance studied in [3,7]. It is plausible that the techniques from the above-mentioned works (see also [24]) can be adapted to the control problem we have introduced but the technical contribution of this paper is mainly oriented towards satisfiability and model-checking issues.

The logics we have introduced belong to the long tradition of quantitative versions of LTL. LTL-like logics having models non isomorphic to ω can be found in [1,27,26,20,22]. Temporal operators in the real-time logics from [1,20,22] are indexed by intervals as our logics LTL(α). However, among the above-mentioned works, only Rohde's thesis [27] contains a LTL-like logic interpreted over α-sequences with ordinal α but the temporal operators are simply the standard next-time and until operators without any decoration. It is shown in [27] that the satisfiability problem for such a logic can be decided in exponential-time when the inputs are the formula to be tested and the countable ordinal from which the model is built.

In the paper, we follow the automata-based approach for temporal logics from [28] but we are dealing with ordinal automata recognizing words of length α for some countable ordinal α. So, we extend the reduction from LTL into generalized Büchi automata to the reduction from LTL(ω^k) into ordinal automata recognizing words of length ω^k. Many classes of ordinal automata have been introduced in the literature. We recall below some of them. In [9,13] automata recognizing ω^k-sequences for some $k \geq 1$ are introduced making essential the concept of layer. In [10,29,19], such automata are generalized to recognize α-sequences for α countable. Correspondences between these different classes can be found in [4]. In the paper, we mainly adopt the definitions from [19]. An elegant and powerful extension to automata recognizing words indexed elements from a linear ordering can be found in [8]. As far as we know, automata recognizing sequences of length greater than ω designed to solve verification problems have been first used in [18] to model concurrency by limiting the state explosion problem. Similarly, timed automata accepting Zeno words are introduced in [5] in order to model physical phenomena with convergent execution. The emptiness problem for such automata is shown to be decidable [5].

As LTL can be viewed as the first-order fragment of monadic second order theory over $\langle \mathbb{N}, < \rangle$, theories over $\langle \alpha, < \rangle$ for some countable ordinal α have been also studied by Büchi [9], see also [10,4]. For instance, decidability of monadic second order theories over $\langle \alpha, < \rangle$ for some countable ordinal α is shown in [10].

Decidability status of elementary theories over countable ordinals have been established in [6,12] whereas relationships with other theories are shown in [23]. Because of lack of space, the proofs can be found in [15].

2   Temporal Logics on Transfinite Sequences

2.1   Ordinals

We recall basic definitions and properties about ordinals. An *ordinal* is a totally ordered set which is *well ordered*, i.e. all its non-empty subset have a least element. Order-isomorphic ordinals are considered equals. An ordinal α is a *successor* ordinal iff there exists an ordinal β such that $\alpha = \beta + 1$. An ordinal which is not 0 or a successor ordinal, is a *limit* ordinal. The first limit ordinal is written ω. Addition, multiplication and exponentiation can be defined on ordinals inductively: $\alpha + 0 = \alpha$, $\alpha + (\beta + 1) = (\alpha + \beta) + 1$ and $\alpha + \beta = sup\{\alpha + \gamma : \gamma < \beta\}$ where β is a limit ordinal. Multiplication and exponentiation are defined similarly. ϵ_0 is the closure of $\omega \cup \{\omega\}$ under ordinal addition, multiplication and exponentiation. By the Cantor Normal Form theorem, for any ordinal $\alpha < \epsilon_0$, there are unique ordinals $\beta_1, \ldots, \beta_p$, and unique integers $n_1, \ldots, n_p$ such that $\alpha > \beta_1 > \cdots > \beta_p$ and $\alpha = \omega^{\beta_1}.n_1 + \cdots + \omega^{\beta_p}.n_p$. If $\beta < \omega^\omega$, then the β_i's are integers. Whenever $\alpha \leq \beta$, there is a unique ordinal γ such that $\alpha + \gamma = \beta$. We write $\beta - \alpha$ to denote γ. For instance, $\omega^2 - \omega = \omega^2$, $\omega \times 3 - \omega = \omega \times 2$ and $\omega^2 - \omega^3$ is not defined since $\omega^3 > \omega^2$.

An ordinal α is said to be closed under addition whenever $\beta, \beta' < \alpha$ implies $\beta + \beta' < \alpha$. For instance, 0, 1, ω, ω^2, ω^3, and ω^ω are closed under addition. In the sequel, we shall consider logics whose models are α-sequences, i.e. mappings of the form $\alpha \rightarrow \Sigma$ for some finite alphabet Σ and ordinal α closed under addition.

2.2   Quantitative Extensions of LTL

For every ordinal α closed under addition, we introduce the logic $LTL(\alpha)$ whose models are precisely sequences of the form $\sigma : \alpha \rightarrow 2^{AP}$ for some countably infinite set AP of atomic propositions. The formulae of $LTL(\alpha)$ are defined as follows: $\phi ::= p \mid \neg\phi \mid \phi_1 \wedge \phi_2 \mid X^\beta \phi \mid \phi_1 U^{\beta'} \phi_2$, where $p \in AP$, $\beta < \alpha$ and $\beta' \leq \alpha$. The satisfaction relation is inductively defined below where σ is a model for $LTL(\alpha)$ and $\beta < \alpha$:

- $\sigma, \beta \models p$ iff $p \in \sigma(\beta)$,
- $\sigma, \beta \models \phi_1 \wedge \phi_2$ iff $\sigma, \beta \models \phi_1$ and $\sigma, \beta \models \phi_2$, $\sigma, \beta \models \neg\phi$ iff not $\sigma, \beta \models \phi$,
- $\sigma, \beta \models X^{\beta'} \phi$ iff $\sigma, \beta + \beta' \models \phi$,
- $\sigma, \beta \models \phi_1 U^{\beta'} \phi_2$ iff there is $\gamma < \beta'$ such that $\sigma, \beta + \gamma \models \phi_2$ and for every $\gamma' < \gamma$, $\sigma, \beta + \gamma' \models \phi_1$.

Actually in order to study the decidability/complexity of $LTL(\alpha)$, we restrict ourselves to countable limit ordinals α so that the set of formulae is itself countable. Furthermore, for studying complexity issues, it is necessary to specify the encoding of the ordinals $\beta \leq \alpha$ occurring in $\text{LTL}(\alpha)$ formulae. In the sequel, we use Cantor normal form to encode ordinals $1 \leq \beta \leq \omega^\omega$, and the natural numbers occurring in such normal forms are represented in binary.

Proposition 1. *Satisfiability for* $\text{LTL}(\omega^\alpha)$, $0 \leq \alpha \leq \omega$, *is decidable.*

The model-checking for $\text{LTL}(\alpha)$ takes as inputs an ordinal automaton $\mathcal{A}$ with alphabet AP (see Def. 1) and an $\text{LTL}(\alpha)$ formula ϕ and checks whether there is an α-sequence σ accepted by $\mathcal{A}$ such that $\sigma, 0 \models \phi$.

3   Automata-Based Approach

In this section, we show how to construct an ordinal automaton $\mathcal{A}_\phi$ such that its set of accepted words is precisely the models of ϕ, extending the approach for LTL from [28]. In the rest of this section, $\phi \in \text{LTL}(\omega^k)$ for some $k \geq 1$.

3.1   Ordinal Automata

We define ordinal automata as a generalization of Muller automata.

Definition 1 (Ordinal Automaton). *An ordinal automaton is a tuple* $(Q, \Sigma, \delta, E, I, F)$ *where:*

- *Q is a finite set of states, Σ is a finite alphabet,*
- *$\delta \subseteq Q \times \Sigma \times Q$ is a one-step transition relation,*
- *$E \subseteq 2^Q \times Q$ is a limit transition relation,*
- *$I \subseteq Q$ [resp. $F \subseteq Q$] is a finite set of initial [resp. final] states.*

We write $q \xrightarrow{a} q'$ whenever $\langle q, a, q' \rangle \in \delta$ and $q \rightarrow q'$ iff $q \xrightarrow{a} q'$ for some $a \in \Sigma$. A path of length $\alpha + 1$ is a map $r : \alpha + 1 \rightarrow Q$ such that for every $\beta \in \alpha$, $r(\beta) \rightarrow r(\beta+1)$ and for every limit ordinal $\beta \in \alpha$, there is $P \rightarrow r(\beta) \in E$ s.t. $P = inf(\beta, r)$ with $inf(\beta, r) \stackrel{\text{def}}{=} \{q \in Q : \text{for every } \gamma \in \beta, \text{ there is } \gamma' \text{ such that } \gamma < \gamma' < \beta \text{ and } r(\gamma') = q\}$.

A run of length $\alpha + 1$ is a path of length $\alpha + 1$ such that $r(0) \in I$. If $r(\alpha) \in F$ then r is said to be accepting. The set of sequences recognized by the automaton $\mathcal{A}$, denoted by $L(\mathcal{A})$, is the set of α-sequences $\sigma : \alpha \rightarrow \Sigma$ for which there is an accepting run r of length $\alpha + 1$ verifying for every $\beta \in \alpha$, $r(\beta) \xrightarrow{\sigma(\beta)} r(\beta + 1)$.

Ordinal automata from Definition 1 are those defined in [19].

3.2   Hintikka Sequences

We define below a notion of closure which generalizes the Fisher-Ladner closure [16].

Definition 2 (Closure). *The closure of ϕ, denoted by $cl(\phi)$, is the smallest set of $\text{LTL}(\omega^k)$ formulae such that*

- $\perp, \phi \in cl(\phi)$, and $\neg\psi \in cl(\phi)$ implies $\psi \in cl(\phi)$,
- $\psi \in cl(\phi)$ implies $\neg\psi \in cl(\phi)$ (we identify $\neg\neg\psi$ with ψ),
- $\psi_1 \wedge \psi_2 \in cl(\phi)$ implies $\psi_1, \psi_2 \in cl(\phi)$,
- $\mathsf{X}^\beta \psi \in cl(\phi)$ and $\beta \geq \omega^n$ $(0 \leq n < k)$ imply $\mathsf{X}^{\beta - \omega^n} \psi \in cl(\phi)$,
- $\psi_1 \mathsf{U}^\beta \psi_2 \in cl(\phi)$ and $\beta \geq \omega^n$ $(0 \leq n \leq k)$ imply the formulae below belong to $cl(\phi)$: ψ_1, ψ_2, $\mathsf{X}^{\omega^n}(\psi_1 \mathsf{U}^{\beta - \omega^n} \psi_2)$, $\mathsf{T}\mathsf{U}^{\omega^n} \neg\psi_1$, $\psi_1 \mathsf{U}^{\omega^n} \psi_2$.

It is not difficult to show that the notion of closure introduced above generalizes what is done for LTL. From a formula ϕ, we build an ordinal automata $\mathcal{A}_\phi$ such that $L(\mathcal{A}_\phi)$ is precisely the set of $LTL(\omega^k)$ models satisfying ϕ. Following [28], the states of $\mathcal{A}_\phi$ are subsets of $cl(\phi)$ containing formulae to be satisfied in the future, including the current position. Hence, $cl(\phi)$ is built in such a way that if either $q' \to q$ or $P \to q$ are transitions in $\mathcal{A}_\phi$, then all the formulae to be satisfied in q depending on q' and P are part of $cl(\phi)$.

Definition 3. A set $X \subseteq cl(\phi)$ is said to be locally maximally consistent with respect to ϕ iff it satisfies the conditions below:

(mc1) $\perp \notin X$,
(mc2) for every $\psi \in cl(\phi)$, $\psi \in X$ iff $\neg\psi \notin X$,
(mc3) for every $\psi_1 \wedge \psi_2 \in cl(\phi)$, $\psi_1 \wedge \psi_2 \in X$ iff $\psi_1, \psi_2 \in X$,
(mc4) for every $\mathsf{X}^0 \psi \in cl(\phi)$, $\mathsf{X}^0 \psi \in X$ iff $\psi \in X$,
(mc5) for every $\psi_1 \mathsf{U}^0 \psi_2 \in cl(\phi)$, $\psi_1 \mathsf{U}^0 \psi_2 \notin X$,
(mc6) for all $\psi_1 \mathsf{U}^\beta \psi_2 \in cl(\phi)$ and $\beta \geq \omega^n \geq 1$, $\psi_1 \mathsf{U}^\beta \psi_2 \in X$ iff either $\psi_1 \mathsf{U}^{\omega^n} \psi_2 \in X$ or $\neg(\mathsf{T}\mathsf{U}^{\omega^n} \neg\psi_1), \mathsf{X}^{\omega^n}(\psi_1 \mathsf{U}^{\beta - \omega^n} \psi_2) \in X$,
(mc7) for all $\psi_1 \mathsf{U}^\beta \psi_2, \psi_1 \mathsf{U}^{\beta'} \psi_2 \in cl(\phi)$ with $\beta \leq \beta'$, $\psi_1 \mathsf{U}^\beta \psi_2 \in X$ implies $\psi_1 \mathsf{U}^{\beta'} \psi_2 \in X$,
(mc8) for every $\psi_1 \mathsf{U}^1 \psi_2 \in cl(\phi)$, $\psi_1 \mathsf{U}^1 \psi_2 \in X$ iff $\psi_2 \in X$.

We denote by $maxcons(\phi)$ the set of locally maximally consistent subsets of $cl(\phi)$.

For standard LTL, an Hintikka sequence ρ for a formula ϕ is an ω-sequence of sets of subformulae of ϕ such that ϕ is satisfiable iff ϕ has an Hintikka sequence. Local conditions in ρ between two successive elements of the sequence are easy to handle in Büchi automata with the transition relation. The only global condition, stating that if $\psi_1 \mathsf{U} \psi_2$ occurs in the sequence, then some future element in the sequence contains ψ_2, is handled by the Büchi acceptance condition. Sometimes the non-uniform treatment between local conditions and the global condition is the source of confusion. The Hintikka sequences defined below are based on a similar principle except that we can extend advantageously the notion of locality. The Hintikka sequences ρ are of the form $\rho : \omega^k \to 2^{cl(\phi)}$. Encoding conditions between $\rho(\beta)$ and $\rho(\beta + 1)$ can be performed by one-step transitions in ordinal automata. However, the presence of limit transitions allows us also to admit conditions between $\rho(\beta)$ and $\rho(\beta + \omega^{n'})$ with $0 \leq n' < k$. Hence, the global condition in Hintikka sequences of LTL formulae is replaced by a condition between $\rho(\beta)$ and $\rho(\beta + \omega)$. For transfinite sequences, the local and global conditions can be treated uniformly.

Definition 4 (Hintikka Sequence). *An Hintikka sequence for ϕ is a sequence $\rho : \omega^k \to 2^{cl(\phi)}$ such that*

(hin1) $\phi \in \rho(0)$,
(hin2) *for every $\beta < \omega^k$, $\rho(\beta) \in maxcons(\phi)$,*
(hin3) *for all $\beta < \omega^k$, $\mathrm{X}^{\beta'}\psi \in cl(\phi)$ and $0 \le n' < k$ such that $\beta' \ge \omega^{n'}$,*
$\mathrm{X}^{\beta'}\psi \in \rho(\beta)$ *iff* $\mathrm{X}^{\beta'-\omega^{n'}}\psi \in \rho(\beta + \omega^{n'})$*,*
(hin4) *for all $\beta < \omega^k$ and $\psi_1\mathrm{U}^{\beta'}\psi_2 \in cl(\phi)$, (A) $\psi_1\mathrm{U}^{\beta'}\psi_2 \in \rho(\beta)$ iff (B) there is $\beta \le \beta'' < \beta + \beta'$ such that $\psi_2 \in \rho(\beta'')$ and for every $\beta \le \gamma < \beta''$, $\psi_1 \in \rho(\gamma)$.*

Proposition 2. ϕ *is* $\mathrm{LTL}(\omega^k)$ *satisfiable iff ϕ has an Hintikka sequence.*

3.3 Automaton Construction

We build an ordinal automaton $\mathcal{A}_\phi$ that recognizes only words of length ω^k over the alphabet 2^{AP} (assuming that AP is the finite set of atomic propositions occurring in ϕ). The automaton $\mathcal{A}_\phi = \langle Q, \Sigma, \delta, E, I, F \rangle$ is defined as follows:

- $\Sigma = 2^{\mathrm{AP}}$, $Q = maxcons(\phi) \times \{0, \dots, k\}$,
- $I = \{\langle X, 0 \rangle \in Q : \phi \in X\}$, $F = \{\langle X, n \rangle \in Q : n = k\}$,
- $\langle X, n \rangle \xrightarrow{a} \langle X', n' \rangle \in \delta$ iff (one-step transition)
  (A1) $n < k$ and $n' = 0$,
  (A2) $X \cap \mathrm{AP} = a$,
  (A3) for every $\mathrm{X}^\beta\psi \in cl(\phi)$ such that $\beta \ge 1$, $\mathrm{X}^\beta\psi \in X$ iff $\mathrm{X}^{\beta-1}\psi \in X'$.
- In order to define E, we introduce preliminary definitions. For every $\psi_1\mathrm{U}^\alpha\psi_2 \in cl(\phi)$, we write $P_{\psi_1\mathrm{U}^\alpha\psi_2}$ to denote the set $\{\langle X, n \rangle : \text{either } \psi_2 \in X \text{ or } \neg(\psi_1\mathrm{U}^\alpha \psi_2) \in X\}$. For every $\langle X, n \rangle \in Q$ we write $Q_{\langle X,n \rangle}$ to denote the subset of Q such that for every $\langle X', n' \rangle \in Q$, $\langle X', n' \rangle \in Q_{\langle X,n \rangle} \overset{\mathrm{def}}{\Leftrightarrow}$
  (A4) $n' < n$,
  (A5) for every $\mathrm{X}^\alpha\psi \in cl(\phi)$ with $\alpha \ge \omega^n$, $\mathrm{X}^\alpha\psi \in X'$ iff $\mathrm{X}^{\alpha-\omega^n}\psi \in X$.
  For every $\langle X, n \rangle \in Q$, $Z \to \langle X, n \rangle \in E$ iff
  (A6) $n \ge 1$,
  (A7) $Z \subseteq Q_{\langle X,n \rangle}$,
  (A8) Z contains a state of the form $\langle Y, n - 1 \rangle$,
  (A9) for all $\psi_1\mathrm{U}^\beta\psi_2 \in cl(\phi)$ and $\beta \ge \omega^n$ such that $\neg(\psi_1\mathrm{U}^{\beta-\omega^n}\psi_2) \in X$, $P_{\psi_1\mathrm{U}^\beta\psi_2} \cap Z \ne \emptyset$.

Observe the similarities between (A3) and (A5) and between (A9) and (mc6). For $\mathrm{LTL}(\omega)$, the above construction roughly corresponds to the Muller automaton obtained from the generalized Büchi automaton for the LTL formula ϕ.

The automaton $\mathcal{A}_\phi$ has $2^{2^{O(|\phi|)}}$ states and $2^{2^{2^{O(|\phi|)}}}$ transitions. By [11, Proposition 6], the emptiness problem for ordinal automata is in P. So checking whether $\mathcal{A}_\phi$ accepts at least one word can be done in triple exponential time, which provides an elementary bound but not optimal as shown in the sequel.

Proposition 3. $\mathrm{L}(\mathcal{A}_\phi) = \mathrm{Mod}(\phi)$.

We invite the reader to consult the tedious proof of Proposition 3 in [15] to understand the relationships between the conditions (mc$\star$), (hin$\star$) and (A$\star$).

4   Computational Complexity

In this section, we show complexity results about satisfiability of LTL(ω^k) with $1 \leq k < \omega$.

Theorem 1. *For every ordinal $\alpha \geq 1$, satisfiability for LTL(ω^α) is* EXPSPACE-*hard.*

4.1   Succinct Ordinal Automata of Level k

In order to refine the complexity result from Sect. 3, we define below specialized ordinal automata that recognize ω^k-sequences. Similar automata can be found in the literature, see e.g. [13,19,4].

Definition 5 (Ordinal Automaton of Level k). *An ordinal automaton $\mathcal{A} = \langle Q, \Sigma, \delta, E, I, F \rangle$ is said to be of level $k \geq 1$ iff there is a map $l : Q \to \{0, \ldots, k\}$ such that*

- *for every $q \in F$, $l(q) = k$;*
- *$q \xrightarrow{a} q' \in \delta$ implies $l(q') = 0$ and $l(q) < k$;*
- *$P \to q \in E$ implies*
  1. *$l(q) \geq 1$,*
  2. *for every $q' \in P$, $l(q') < l(q)$,*
  3. *there is $q' \in P$ such that $l(q') = l(q) - 1$.*

The automaton built in Section 3 is of level k when the input formula is in LTL(ω^k). However, $\mathcal{A}_\phi$ is of triple [resp. double] exponential size in $|\phi|$ when integer are encoded in binary [resp. unary] which is still too much to characterize accurately the complexity of LTL(ω^k) satisfiability. That is why we introduce below a special class of ordinal automata which can represent succinctly an exponential amount of limit transitions as the generalized Büchi automata can be viewed as a succinct representation of Muller automata. Hence, we shall construct $\mathcal{A}'_\phi$ such that $L(\mathcal{A}'_\phi) = L(\mathcal{A}_\phi)$, and $\mathcal{A}'_\phi$ is "only" of double [resp. simple] exponential size in $|\phi|$ when integers are encoded in binary [resp. unary].

Definition 6 ($p(\cdot)$-Succinct Ordinal Automaton of Level k). *Given a polynom $p(\cdot)$, a $p(\cdot)$-succinct ordinal automaton of level k is a structure $\mathcal{A} = \langle Q, \Sigma, \delta, E, I, F, l \rangle$ defined as an ordinal automata of level k except that E is a set of tuples of the form $\langle P_0, P_1, \ldots, P_n, q \rangle$ with $n \geq 0$, $q \in Q$ and $P_0, \ldots, P_n \subseteq Q$ such that*

- *$\langle P_0, P_1, \ldots, P_n, q \rangle \in E$ implies*
  1. *$1 \leq l(q) \leq k$,*
  2. *each state in P_0 is of level $l(q) - 1$,*
  3. *each state in $P_1 \cup \cdots \cup P_n$ is of level less than $l(q) - 1$,*
  4. *$n \leq p(|Q|)$,*
- *for every state q of level strictly more than 0, there is at most one tuple in E of the form $\langle P_0, P_1, \ldots, P_n, q \rangle$.*

Each tuple $\langle P_0, P_1, \ldots, P_n, q \rangle$ encodes succinctly the set of limit transitions

$$trans(\langle P_0, P_1, \ldots, P_n, q \rangle) \stackrel{\text{def}}{=}$$

$$\{P \to q : \ P \subseteq Q, \ \forall \, i \ P_i \cap P \neq \emptyset \text{ and } \forall q' \in P, \ l(q') < l(q)\}.$$

In the sequel, given a $p(\cdot)$-succinct ordinal automaton $\mathcal{A}$ of level k, we write $\mathcal{A}^o = \langle Q, \Sigma, \delta, E', I, F, l \rangle$ to denote the ordinal automaton of level k with $E' = \bigcup_{t \in E} trans(t)$. The language recognized by $\mathcal{A}$ is defined as the language recognized by $\mathcal{A}^o$. In that way, a $p(\cdot)$-succinct ordinal automaton of level k is simply a succinct encoding of some ordinal automaton of level k. An important property of such automata rests on the fact that the size of E is in $\mathcal{O}(|Q|^2 \times p(|Q|))$. By contrast, in an ordinary ordinal automaton of level k, the cardinality of the set of limit transitions can be in the worst case exponential in $|Q|$.

The automaton $\mathcal{A}_\phi$ from Sect. 3.3 can be viewed as a $p_0(\cdot)$-succinct ordinal automaton of level k with $p_0(x) = x$.

Lemma 1 below is the key property to obtain the NLOGSPACE upper bound for the emptiness problem of ordinal automata of level k, even in the succinct version. It generalizes substantially the property that entails that the graph accessibility problem and the emptiness problem for generalized Büchi automata can be solved in non-deterministic logarithmic space.

Lemma 1. *Let $\mathcal{A}$ be an automaton of level k and r be a run of length $\omega^{k'} + 1$ for some $1 \leq k' \leq k$. Then, there is a path r' of length $\omega^{k'} + 1$ such that*

- *$r'(0) = r(0)$ and $r'(\omega^{k'}) = r(\omega^{k'})$,*
- *there are $K \leq |Q|$ and $K' \leq |Q|^2$ such that for every $\alpha \geq \omega^{k'-1} \times K$ such that the normal form of α is $\omega^{k'-1} \times n + \beta$, $r'(\alpha) = r'(\omega^{k'-1} \times (n + K') + \beta)$.*

4.2   An Optimal Algorithm to Test Emptiness

In order to test emptiness of the language recognized by an automaton of level k, we introduce a function $acc(q, q')$ (see Fig. 1) that returns $\top$ iff there is a path r of length $\omega^{l(q')}$ such that $r(0) = q$ and $r(\omega^{l(q')}) = q'$. We design the following non-deterministic algorithm:

```
Empty?(A)
Guess q0 ∈ I and qf ∈ F;
InLoop := false;
acc(q0, qf).
```

Nondeterminism is also highly present in the definition of $acc(q_0, q_f)$. A few global variables are used. The variable InLoop is a Boolean equals to true iff q' in a call $acc(q, q')$ belongs in the periodic part of the run. Moreover, for every $i \in \{1, \ldots, k\}$, the variable $\uparrow_i$ contains the address of the occurrence of a state in the leftmost part of a rule $P \to q''$ with $l(q'') = i$: $\mathcal{O}(k \times log|\mathcal{A}|)$ bits are needed in total. Remember that $\mathcal{A}$ is encoded as a string and the address of the occurrence of a state is simply a position in that string, which requires only

$acc(q, q')$ $(l(q') \leq k, l(q) = 0)$

> $k' := l(q') - 1$;
> If $k' \geq 0$ then
>> Guess a rule $P \to q'$;
>> $\uparrow_{k'+1}$ takes the value of the address of the first state in P;
>> Guess $K \leq |Q|$ and $K' \leq |Q|^2$;
>> Guess $q_{k'}^{\text{repeat}} \in P$ such that $l(q_{k'}^{\text{repeat}}) = k'$ (repeating state);
>> $q_0 := q$;
>> For $i = 1$ to K do
>>> Guess $q_{k'} \in P$ of level k';
>>> If $acc(q_0, q_{k'})$ then guess q_0 such that $l(q_0) = 0$ and $q_{k'} \to q_0$;
>> If $q_{k'} \neq q_{k'}^{\text{repeat}}$ then **abort**;
>> If $k' + 1 = k$ then InLoop $=$ **true**;
>> Guess $q_{k'} \in P$ of level k';
>> If InLoop $=$ **true** then (Check&Update(q_0);Check&Update($q_{k'}$));
>> For $i = 1$ to K' do
>>> If $acc(q_0, q_{k'})$ then
>>>> Guess q_0 such that $l(q_0) = 0$ and $q_{k'} \to q_0$;
>>>> $q_{k'}^{\text{aux}} := q_{k'}$;
>>>> Guess $q_{k'} \in P$ of level k';
>>>> If $i \neq K'$ then (Check&Update(q_0);Check&Update($q_{k'}$));
>>> otherwise **abort**;
>> If one of the conditions below fails then **abort** otherwise **accept**
>>> 1. $\uparrow_{k'+1} \neq nil$ (some state in P has not been visited infinitely often),
>>> 2. $q_{k'}^{\text{aux}} \neq q_{k'}^{\text{repeat}}$ (wrong choice of the repeating state of level k')
>> otherwise if $q \to q'$ then **accept** otherwise **abort**.

Fig. 1. Accessibility function

$\mathcal{O}(log|\mathcal{A}|)$ bits. The variable $\uparrow_i$ is updated when the state whose address is $\uparrow_i$ is detected in the periodic part of the run.

In the definition of $acc(q, q')$, in order to test whether there is a path r of length $\omega^{l(q')}$ such that $l(q') \geq 1$, $r(0) = q$ and $r(\omega^{l(q')}) = q'$, Lemma 1 guarantees that the periodic part of r is of length at most $\omega^{l(q')-1} \times |Q|^2$ and the prefix is of length at most $\omega^{l(q')-1} \times |Q|$. This explains the two main loops of $acc(q, q')$. When a state t is guessed in the periodic part of the run, one has to check that t indeed belongs to rules of the form $P \to q''$ with $l(q'') > l(q_t)$ and one updates the variables $\uparrow_i$ since t has been detected (see Fig. 2).

Theorem 2. *For every $k \geq 0$, the emptiness problem for ordinal automata of level k is* NLOGSPACE-*complete.*

Corollary 1. *The emptiness problem for Muller automata is* NLOGSPACE-*complete.*

The discipline on memory space done in the algorithm in Fig. 1 can be adapted to succinct ordinal automata.

Check&Update(q)
For $1 \leq i \leq k$ do
    If $\uparrow_i$ contains the address of an occurrence of q in the leftmost part of a rule
    then $\uparrow_i$ takes the value of the next state in the rule (possibly the rightmost
    state in the rule);
    If $l(q) \leq i - 1$ and q does not occur in the leftmost part of the rule that is
    currently pointed by $\uparrow_i$ then **abort**. (one needs another variable to visit the
    states in the leftmost part of that rule)
accept.

Fig. 2. Update of the variables $\uparrow_i$s

Corollary 2. *For all $k \geq 0$ and polynom $p(\cdot)$, the emptiness problem for $p(\cdot)$-succinct ordinal automata of level k is* NLOGSPACE*-complete.*

4.3 Optimal Complexity Upper Bounds

Theorem 3. *For every $k \geq 1$, the satisfiability problem for* LTL(ω^k) *is* PSPACE-*complete when the integers are encoded in unary and the problem is in* EXPSPACE-*complete when the integers are encoded in binary.*

Corollary 3. *For every $k \geq 1$, the model-checking problem for* LTL(ω^k) *is decidable.*

Since the complexity of the emptiness problem for ordinal automata is not completely characterized (we know it is in P by [11] but P-hardness is open), our decidability proof does not provide a full characterization of the complexity of the model-checking problem for LTL(ω^k). However, with space ressources, it is at most two exponential higher than the satisfiability problem.

Since the languages recognized by x-succinct ordinal automata of level k can be shown to be closed under intersection, we have the following result.

Theorem 4. *For every $k \geq 1$, the model-checking problem for* LTL(ω^k) *restricted to x-succinct ordinal automata of level k is* PSPACE-*complete when the integers are encoded in unary and the problem is* EXPSPACE-*complete when the integers are encoded in binary.*

5   Application: Control of Physical Systems

In this section, we formalize the control problem of a physical system by a computer system by using ordinal automata and the logics LTL(ω^k). Even though it is the original motivation of our investigations on the logics LTL(α), at this point of the paper we have all the necessary definitions and results to state concisely the problem. We model a system by an ordinal automaton recognizing ω^k-sequences. For instance, the law of movement of the bouncing ball corresponds to ω^2-sequences and the set of acceptable behaviors of the ball is modelled by a set of sequences of the same length ω^2. On the other hand, the controller is an operational model working on ω-sequences.

Before stating the control problem, we need to give definitions about the synchronous product between ordinal automata and about the way to transform an ordinal automaton of level 1 into an ordinal automaton of level $k \geq 2$ that has relevant actions only on states in positions of the form $\omega^{k-1} \times n$ (*lifting*). As usual, LTL(ω^k) formulae can be viewed equivalently as ordinal automata of level k and we shall use these different representations depending on the context (see [2] for a similar standard treatment between formulae and automata).

Synchronous product. We define below the synchronous product of two ordinal automata such that if they have the same alphabet then the language recognized by the product is the intersection language. Otherwise, a letter that is present in a single automaton can only affect the state component in the product related to this automaton. This is useful to deal with unobservable actions (see below). Given two ordinal automata $\mathcal{A}_i = \langle Q_i, \Sigma_i, \delta_i, E_i, I_i, F_i \rangle$, for $i = 1, 2$, their synchronous product is defined as $\mathcal{A}_1 \times \mathcal{A}_2 = \langle Q, \Sigma, \delta, E, I, F \rangle$ where:

- $Q = Q_1 \times Q_2$, $\Sigma = \Sigma_1 \cup \Sigma_2$.
- $\langle q_1, q_2 \rangle \xrightarrow{a} \langle q_1', q_2' \rangle \in \delta$ iff either:
  - $a \in \Sigma_1 \cap \Sigma_2$, $q_1 \xrightarrow{a} q_1' \in \delta_1$, and $q_2 \xrightarrow{a} q_2' \in \delta_2$; or
  - $a \in \Sigma_1 \setminus \Sigma_2$, $q_1 \xrightarrow{a} q_1' \in \delta_1$, and $q_2 = q_2'$; or
  - $a \in \Sigma_2 \setminus \Sigma_1$, $q_2 \xrightarrow{a} q_2' \in \delta_2$, and $q_1 = q_1'$.
- $P \rightarrow \langle q_1, q_2 \rangle \in E$ iff there exist $P_1 \rightarrow q_1 \in E_1$ and $P_2 \rightarrow q_2 \in E_2$ such that $\{q : \langle q, q' \rangle \in P\} = P_1$ and $\{q' : \langle q, q' \rangle \in P\} = P_2$.
- $I = I_1 \times I_2$, $F = F_1 \times F_2$.

We write w/Σ for the subword of w consisting only of the letters from Σ.

Proposition 4. $w \in \mathrm{L}(\mathcal{A}_1 \times \mathcal{A}_2) \iff w/\Sigma_1 \in \mathrm{L}(\mathcal{A}_1)$ *and* $w/\Sigma_2 \in \mathrm{L}(\mathcal{A}_2)$.

Lifting. In order to synchronize the system with a controller working on ω-sequences, we need to transform the controller so that its product with $\mathcal{S}$ only constraints states on positions $\omega^{k-1} \times n$, $n \in \mathbb{N}$. The other positions are not constrained.

Let $\mathcal{A} = \langle Q, \Sigma, \delta, E, I, F, l \rangle$ be an automaton of level 1. We define its lifting $lift_k(\mathcal{A})$ at level $k \geq 2$ to be the automaton $\langle Q', \Sigma, \delta', E', I', F, l' \rangle$ by:

- $Q' = (\{0, \ldots, k-1\} \times (Q \setminus F)) \cup F$, $I' = \{k-1\} \times I$,
- $l'(q) = k$ for $q \in F$ and $l'(\langle i, q' \rangle) = i$,
- $\delta' = \{\langle k-1, q \rangle \xrightarrow{a} \langle 0, q' \rangle : q \xrightarrow{a} q' \in \delta\} \cup$,
  $\qquad \{\langle i, q \rangle \xrightarrow{a} \langle 0, q \rangle : 0 \leq i < k, a \in \Sigma, q \notin F\}$
- $E' = \{\{\langle 0, q \rangle, \ldots, \langle i-1, q \rangle\} \rightarrow \langle i, q \rangle : 1 \leq i < k, q \in Q\} \cup \{\{\langle 0, q_1 \rangle, \ldots, \langle k-1, q_1 \rangle, \ldots, \langle 0, q_n \rangle, \ldots, \langle k-1, q_n \rangle\} \rightarrow q \mid \{q_1, \ldots q_n\} \rightarrow q \in E\}$.

Proposition 5. *For all* $w \in \Sigma^{\omega^k}$, $w \in \mathrm{L}(lift_k(\mathcal{A}))$ *iff the word* $w' \in \Sigma^{\omega}$, *defined by* $w'(i) = w(\omega^{k-1} \times i)$, *is in* $\mathrm{L}(\mathcal{A})$.

The control problem. A physical system S is modelled as a structure

$$\langle \mathcal{A}, Act_C, Act_O, Act \rangle$$

where $\mathcal{A}$ is an ordinal automaton of level k with alphabet 2^{Act} where Act is a finite set of actions, $Act_O \subseteq Act$ is the set of observable actions and $Act_C \subseteq Act_O$ is the set of controllable actions. The set of uncontrollable actions is denoted by Act_{nc}. A specification of the system S is naturally an LTL(ω^k) formula ψ. A controller $\mathcal{C}$ for the pair $\langle S, \psi \rangle$ is a system whose complete executions are ω-sequences (typically ordinal automata of level 1) verifying the properties below.

- Only observable actions are present in the controller. Hence, thanks to the synchronization mode, in the product system between S and $\mathcal{C}$, unobservable actions do not change the $\mathcal{C}$-component of the current state. So the alphabet of $\mathcal{C}$ is 2^{Act_O}.
- From any state of $\mathcal{C}$, uncontrollable actions can always be executed: $\forall q \cdot \forall a \subseteq Act_O \setminus Act_C$, there is a transition $q \xrightarrow{b} q'$ in $\mathcal{C}$ such that $b \cap Act_{nc} = a$.
- Finally, the system S controlled by $\mathcal{C}$ satisfies ψ. Because S and $\mathcal{C}$ work on sequences of different length, the controlled system is in fact equal to $lift_k(\mathcal{C}) \times S$. So $lift_k(\mathcal{C}) \times S \models \psi$ should hold. This is equivalent to the emptiness of the language of the product automaton $lift_k(\mathcal{C}) \times S \times \mathcal{A}_{\neg \psi}$.

As a consequence of Corollary 3 we obtain the following result.

Proposition 6. *The problem of checking whether $lift_k(\mathcal{C}) \times S \times \mathcal{A}_{\neg \psi}$ given a physical system S, a controller $\mathcal{C}$ and a specification ψ is decidable.*

We explained how to check that a controller is correct with respect to a specification, but we do not address here the controller synthesis issue. Moreover, by assuming that S and $\mathcal{C}$ are succinct ordinal automata, we can improve considerably the complexity of the above problem (see e.g., Theorem 4).

Example. Consider the system is a bouncing ball [14] with three actions *lift-up*, *bounce* and *stop*, where only *lift-up* is controllable, and only *stop* and *lift-up* are observable. The law of the ball is described by the following LTL(ω^2) formula:

$$\phi = G^{\omega^2}(lift\text{-}up \Rightarrow X^1(G^\omega bounce \wedge X^\omega stop))$$

$G^\alpha \varphi$ is an abbreviation for $\neg(\top U^\alpha \neg \varphi)$. Informally, ϕ states that when the ball is lifted-up, then it bounces an infinite number of times in a finite time and then stops. An equivalent ordinal automaton $\mathcal{A}_\phi$ working on ω^2-sequences can be easily defined. The specification is given by the LTL(ω^2) formula: $\psi = G^{\omega^2} X^1 bounce$. Informally, ψ states that the ball should almost always be bouncing. A possible controller for this system is described by the following LTL formula:

$$\varphi = lift\text{-}up \wedge G^\omega(stop \Rightarrow lift\text{-}up)$$

Informally, φ states that the controller should lift-up the ball at the beginning and then lift-up it again each time it stops. Similarly, an equivalent ordinal automaton $\mathcal{A}_\varphi$ working on ω-sequences can be easily defined.

6   Concluding Remarks

We have introduced a family of temporal logics to specify the behavior of systems by assuming that the sequence of actions is isomorphic to some well-ordered linear ordering (see the bouncing ball example in Sect. 5). Our aim is to control such physical systems by designing controllers that safely work on ω-sequences but interact synchronously with the physical system in order to restrict their behaviors. We have extended linear-time temporal logic LTL to α-sequences for any countable ordinal α closed under addition, by considering quantitative operators indexed by ordinals smaller than α. This is a new class of linear-time temporal logics for which we have shown that LTL(ω^ω) is decidable by reduction to the monadic second-order theory $\langle \omega^\omega, < \rangle$ and for every $k \geq 1$, LTL(ω^k) satisfiability problem is PSPACE-complete [resp. EXPSPACE-complete] when the integers are encoded in unary [resp. in binary] generalizing what is known about LTL. Our proof technique is inspired from [28] with significant extensions in order to deal with the interaction between arithmetics on ordinals and temporal operators. Moreover, we have introduced a new class of succinct ordinal automata in order to fully characterize the complexity of the logics. The treatment of these aspects leads to the most difficult technical parts of the paper.

A lot of work remains to be done even though our logics have been shown to admit reasoning tasks of complexity similar to that of LTL. Synthesis of controllers working on ω-sequences on the line of Sect. 5 is on the top of our priority list. Moreover, LTL is known to be initially equivalent to the first-order theory of $\langle \omega, < \rangle$ by Kamp's theorem [21] and by the separation theorem [17]. Is LTL(ω^k) also initially equivalent to the first-order theory of $\langle \omega^k, < \rangle$?

References

1. R. Alur, T. Feder, and T. Henzinger. The benefits of relaxing punctuality. *Journal of the ACM*, 43:116–146, 1996.
2. A. Arnold, A. Vincent, and I. Walukiewicz. Games for synthesis of controllers with partial observation. *TCS*, 303(1):7–34, 2003.
3. E. Asarin, O. Maler, and A. Pnueli. Symbolic controller synthesis for discrete and timed systems. In *Hybrid systems II*, volume 999 of *LNCS*, pages 1–20. Springer, 1995.
4. N. Bedon. *Langages reconnaissables de mots indexés par des ordinaux*. PhD thesis, Université Marne-la-Vallée, 1998.
5. B. Bérard and C. Picaronny. Accepting Zeno words: a way toward timed refinements. In *MFCS'97*, volume 1295 of *LNCS*, pages 149–158. Springer, 1997.
6. A. Bès. Decidability and definability results related to the elementary theory of ordinal multiplication. *Fundamenta Mathematicae*, 171:197–211, 2002.
7. P. Bouyer, D. D'Souza, P. Madhusudan, and A. Petit. Timed control with partial observability. In *CAV'03*, volume 2725 of *LNCS*, pages 180–192. Springer, 2003.
8. V. Bruyère and O. Carton. Automata on linear orderings. In *MFCS 2001*, volume 2136 of *LNCS*, pages 236–247. Springer-Verlag, 2001.
9. J. Büchi. Transfinite automata recursions and weak second order theory of ordinals. In *Int. Cong. Logic, Methodology and Philosophy of Science, Jerusalem*, pages 3–23, 1964.

10. J. Büchi and D. Siefkes. *The monadic second order theory of all countable ordinals*, volume 328 of *Lecture Notes in Mathematics*. Springer, 1973.

11. O. Carton. Accessibility in automata on scattered linear orderings. In *MFCS 2002*, volume 2420 of *LNCS*, pages 155–164. Springer, 2002.

12. C. Choffrut. Elementary theory of ordinals with addition and left translation by ω. In *DLT'01*, volume 2295 of *LNCS*, pages 15–20. Springer, 2002.

13. Y. Choueka. Finite automata, definable sets, and regular expressions over ω^n-tapes. *JCSS*, 17:81–97, 1978.

14. P. Cuijpers, M. Reniers, and A. Engels. Beyond Zeno-behaviour. Technical report, TU of Eindhoven, 2001.

15. S. Demri and D. Nowak. Reasoning about transfinite sequences. arXiv:cs.LO/0505073, May 2005.

16. M. Fischer and R. Ladner. Propositional dynamic logic of regular programs. *JCSS*, 18:194–211, 1979.

17. D. Gabbay, A. Pnueli, S. Shelah, and J. Stavi. On the temporal analysis of fairness. In *POPL'80*. ACM Press, 1980.

18. P. Godefroid and P. Wolper. A partial approach to model checking. *I&C*, 110(2):305–326, 1994.

19. J. Hemmer and P. Wolper. Ordinal finite automata and languages (extended abstract). Technical report, Université of Liège, 1991.

20. Y. Hirshfeld and A. Rabinovich. Logics for real time: decidability and complexity. *Fundamenta Informaticae*, 62:1–28, 2004.

21. J. Kamp. *Tense Logic and the theory of linear order*. PhD thesis, UCLA, USA, 1968.

22. C. Lutz, D. Walther, and F. Wolter. Quantitative temporal logics: PSPACE and below. In *TIME'05*, 2005. To appear.

23. F. Maurin. The theory of integer multiplication with order restricted to primes is decidable. *The Journal of Symbolic Logic*, 62(1):123–130, 1997.

24. A. Pnueli and R. Rosner. On the synthesis of a reactive module. In *16th ACM POPL, Austin, Texas*, pages 179–190, 1989.

25. P. J. G. Ramadge and W. M. Wonham. The control of discrete event systems. *Proceedings of the IEEE*, 77:81–98, 1989.

26. M. Reynolds. The complexity of the temporal logic with until over general linear time. *JCSS*, 66(2):393–426, 2003.

27. S. Rohde. *Alternating Automata and The Temporal Logic of Ordinals*. PhD thesis, University of Illinois, 1997.

28. M. Vardi and P. Wolper. Reasoning about infinite computations. *I&C*, 115:1–37, 1994.

29. J. Wojciechowski. Classes of transfinite sequences accepted by nondeterministic finite automata. *Annales Societatid Mathematicae Polonae*, pages 191–223, 1984.

Semi-automatic Distributed Synthesis

Bernd Finkbeiner and Sven Schewe

Universität des Saarlandes, 66123 Saarbrücken, Germany
{finkbeiner, schewe}@cs.uni-sb.de

Abstract. We propose a sound and complete compositional proof rule
for distributed synthesis. Applying our proof rule only requires the manual strengthening of the specification into a conjunction of formulas that
can be guaranteed by individual black-box processes. All premises of the
proof rule can be checked automatically.

For this purpose, we give an automata-theoretic synthesis algorithm
for single processes in distributed architectures. The behavior of the
local environment of a process is unknown in the process of synthesis and cannot be assumed to be maximal. We therefore consider reactive environments that have the power to disable some of their own
actions, and provide methods for synthesis (and realizability checking)
in this setting. We establish upper bounds for CTL (2EXPTIME) and
CTL* (3EXPTIME) synthesis with incomplete information, matching
the known lower bounds for these problems, and provide matching upper and lower bounds for μ-calculus synthesis (2EXPTIME) with complete or incomplete information. Synthesis in reactive environments is
harder than synthesis in maximal environments, where CTL, CTL* and
μ-calculus synthesis are EXPTIME, 2EXPTIME and EXPTIME complete, respectively.

1 Introduction

In the synthesis of distributed systems, we transform a given specification into a
collection of finite-state programs that satisfy the specification when composed
according to a given architecture. For some restricted architectures, such as
pipelines and rings in which only one designated process communicates with the
environment [1], synthesis can be done automatically. However, as soon as the
architecture contains an *information fork*, i.e., a pair of processes that have an
incomparable degree of information about the system state, the problem becomes
undecidable [2].

In this paper, we investigate a *semi-automatic* approach where we synthesize
one process at a time. It turns out that the synthesis of a single process can be
done automatically and it is always possible to decompose a realizable specification into a conjunction of properties that can be guaranteed by single processes.
This approach therefore works for all distributed architectures, including those
with information forks.

The problem of synthesizing a single process has been studied in a number
of variations. *Closed synthesis* excludes any interaction with the environment

D.A. Peled and Y.-K. Tsay (Eds.): ATVA 2005, LNCS 3707, pp. 263–277, 2005.

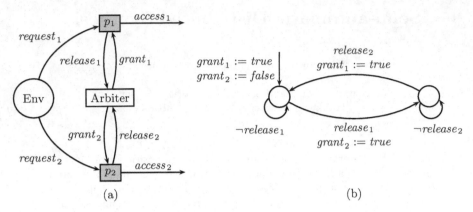

Fig. 1. A simple distributed shared-resource application. (a) The system architecture. An edge between two process nodes p and q labeled with variable v indicates that v is an output variable of process p and an input variable of process q. (b) The implementation of the white-box process Arbiter, represented as a finite-state automaton.

[3,4]. *Open synthesis* finds implementations that satisfy a specification in any environment. For universal specifications (e.g., ACTL*), it suffices to consider the *maximal* environment, which shows all possible behaviors [5,6]. In general, it is necessary to account for *reactive environments*, which may disable some of their responses [7].

We consider the problem of synthesizing a single black-box process in a given distributed *architecture*. An architecture consists of an external environment and a set of system processes, which we partition into subsets of *white-box* and *black-box* processes: each white-box process comes with a known and fixed implementation, while the implementation of the black-box processes is yet to be found.

A single black-box process may interact with the external environment, the white-box processes, and with other black-box processes. Like in open synthesis, we assume that the behavior of the external environment is maximal. The behavior of white-box processes is known beforehand, but may be nondeterministic. The other black-box processes show reactive [7] behavior: in each state, they may disable some (but not all) of their responses. An important difference between synthesizing systems that consist of a single process, and synthesizing a single process within a general architecture is that, while the process has *complete information* about the system state in the former case, it only sees a part of the state as defined by the architecture in the latter case.

Figure 1a shows the architecture of a simple distributed *shared-resource* application. The external environment Env can request *access* to the resource by setting the *request* variable of one of the two black-box processes p_1 and p_2. Mutual exclusion is accomplished using a white-box Arbiter process that alternates a *grant* between p_1 and p_2, such that each process retains the grant until the respective *release* variable is set, as shown in Figure 1b.

We can specify the expected behavior of the shared-resource system as a conjunction $\psi = \psi_1 \wedge \psi_2 \wedge \psi_3$ of three CTL* formulas, where the first two formulas specify that there is a way for both processes to use the resource infinitely often ($\psi_i = \mathrm{EGF}\ access_i$ for $i \in \{0,1\}$) and the third formula specifies mutual exclusion ($\psi_3 = \mathrm{AG}\ \neg(access_1 \wedge access_2)$).

Obviously, neither p_1 nor p_2 can guarantee ψ for *all* possible implementations of the other process (for example, if the other process constantly sets its *access* variable to *true*, mutual exclusion must be violated in some branch). We therefore strengthen ψ into two separate properties φ_{p_1} and φ_{p_2} that can be guaranteed by p_1 and p_2, respectively. A natural assumption to be made by process p_{3-i} about process p_i is that there is path, such that process p_i infinitely often releases the grant ($\alpha_1^{p_i} = \mathrm{EGF}\ release_i$) and that, on every path, p_i only accesses the resource when permitted by Arbiter ($\alpha_2^{p_i} = \mathrm{AG}\ access_i \rightarrow grant_i$). By adding these assumptions, we obtain a strengthened specification $\varphi = \varphi_{p_1} \wedge \varphi_{p_2}$ where

$$\varphi_{p_i} = \quad \alpha_1^{p_i} \wedge \alpha_2^{p_i} \quad \wedge \quad (\alpha_1^{p_{3-i}} \wedge \alpha_2^{p_{3-i}} \;\rightarrow\; \psi).$$

Once the auxiliary formulas φ_{p_1} and φ_{p_2} have been defined, an implementation can be found automatically. For example, process p_i can guarantee φ_{p_i} against any implementation of process p_{3-i}, by setting $access_i$ after each $request_i$ as soon as $grant_i$ becomes *true* and by setting $release_i$ in the immediately following state.

Contribution. We propose a sound and complete compositional proof rule for distributed synthesis. Applying our proof rule only requires the manual strengthening of the specification into a conjunction of formulas that can be guaranteed by individual black-box processes against the other black-box processes. All premises of the proof rule can be checked automatically.

For this purpose, we give an automata-theoretic synthesis algorithm for single processes in distributed architectures. Our environment model builds on open synthesis [5], but combines the maximal external environment with reactive black-box processes. Synthesis in reactive environments was studied before, but only under the assumption of complete information [7].

Our construction turns a specification into an alternating parity automaton accepting exactly the reactive models of a specification. For a specification φ with length $n = |\varphi|$ in CTL, CTL* and μ-calculus this automaton has $n^{O(n)}$, $2^{2^{O(n)}}$ and $n^{O(n^3)}$ states, respectively. We establish 2EXPTIME and 3EXPTIME upper bounds for synthesis with incomplete information in case of CTL and CTL* specifications, respectively. We defer a doubly exponential lower bound for μ-calculus specifications from the doubly exponential lower bound for CTL and establish a matching upper bound.

Overview. In the following section, we formally introduce the synthesis problem studied in this paper. We explain the compositional synthesis rule in Section 3. The synthesis algorithm is presented in Section 4.

2 Setting

In the *distributed synthesis* problem, we decide for a pair (A, φ), consisting of an architecture A and a specification φ, whether there exists a finite-state program (or *strategy*) for each black-box process in A, such that the joint behavior satisfies φ.

Architectures. An architecture

$$A = (B, W, \{I_p\}_{p \in B \uplus W \uplus \{env\}}, \{O_p\}_{p \in B \uplus W \uplus \{env\}}, \{s_w\}_{w \in W})$$

is given as a set of processes $P = B \uplus W \uplus \{env\}$ that is decomposed into a set B of black-box processes that have to be developed, a set W of white-box processes that already have an implementation $\{s_w\}_{w \in W}$, and the external environment *env*. The processes communicate through a set V of shared variables, which also serve as atomic propositions in the specification. Each process $p \in P$ has a fixed set of input and output variables $I_p, O_p \subseteq V$, such that the family of output variables $\{O_p\}_{p \in P}$ decomposes V. The environment is always omniscient $(I_{env} = V)$.

Implementations. A process p is implemented by a (nondeterministic) *strategy*, i.e., a function $s_p : (2^{I_p})^* \rightarrow 2^{2^{O_p}_\emptyset}$ (where $2^X_\emptyset = 2^X \smallsetminus \{\emptyset\}$ denotes the nonempty subsets of a set X). A strategy is *finite-state* if it can be represented by a finite-state automaton. The implementations $\{s_w\}_{w \in W}$ of the white-box processes W are fixed for the architecture. An *implementation* of an architecture is a set of strategies $S = \{s_b\}_{b \in B}$ for the black-box processes.

We use trees as a representation for strategies and computations. As usual, an Υ-*tree* is given as a prefix-closed subset $Y \subseteq \Upsilon^*$ of all finite words over a given set of directions Υ. If the set of directions is not important or clear from the context, we call Y a tree. We define that every non-empty node $x \cdot v$, $x \in \Upsilon^*, v \in \Upsilon$, has the direction $dir(x \cdot v) = v$ and the empty word ε has some designated *root-direction* $dir(\varepsilon) = v_0 \in \Upsilon$. An Υ-tree Y is called *total*, if it contains the empty word $\varepsilon \in Y$ and every element $y \in Y$ of the tree has at least one successor $y \cdot v \in Y, v \in \Upsilon$. If $Y = \Upsilon^*$, the tree is called *full*.

For given finite sets Σ and Υ, a Σ-*labeled* Υ-*tree* is a pair $\langle Y, l \rangle$, consisting of a tree $Y \subseteq \Upsilon^*$ and a labeling function $l : Y \rightarrow \Sigma$ that maps every node of Y to a letter of Σ. The *successor-tree* $\langle Y, sucset \rangle$ of a tree Y is the 2^Υ-labeled Υ-tree, where every node is labeled with the set of its successors $sucset : Y \rightarrow 2^\Upsilon$, $sucset : y \mapsto \{v \in \Upsilon | y \cdot v \in Y\}$.

For a set $\Xi \times \Upsilon$ of directions and a node $x \in (\Xi \times \Upsilon)^*$, $hide_\Upsilon(x)$ denotes the node in Ξ^* obtained from x by replacing (ξ, v) by ξ in each letter of x. For a Σ-labeled Ξ-tree $\langle \Xi^*, l \rangle$ we define the Υ-widening of $\langle \Xi^*, l \rangle$, denoted by $wide_\Upsilon(\langle \Xi^*, l \rangle)$, as the Σ-labeled $\Xi \times \Upsilon$-tree $\langle (\Xi \times \Upsilon)^*, l' \rangle$ with $l'(x) = l(hide_\Upsilon(x))$.

We consider specifications φ that are given as CTL, CTL*, or μ-calculus formulas. Such specifications define a set $\mathcal{M}_\varphi$ of total 2^{AP}-labeled Υ-trees, where $AP = V$ denotes the set of atomic propositions in φ.

Let $S_Q = \bigotimes_{p \in Q} 2_{\emptyset}^{2^{O_p}}$ denote the set of possible common outputs of a set of strategies for the processes in $Q \subseteq B \cup W$. The *composition* $\bigoplus_{p \in Q} s_p = s_Q :$ $(2^V)^* \to S_Q$ of a set of strategies $\{s_p\}_{p \in Q}$ maps the global input history to the common output of the processes in Q: For $\langle (2^V)^*, s'_p \rangle = wide_{2^{V \smallsetminus I_p}}(\langle (2^V)^*, s'_p \rangle)$, $s_Q : y \mapsto \biguplus_{p \in Q} s'_p(y)$ naturally defines a S_Q-labeled 2^V-tree.

A *non-distributed implementation* of the processes B' is a function

$$s_{B'} : (2^{I_{B'}})^* \to S_{B'}, \text{ for } I_{B'} = \bigcup_{b \in B'} I_b.$$

A *(distributed) implementation* is a set of strategies $\{s_b\}_{b \in B'}$ whose composition is the widening of a non-distributed implementation: $\langle (2^V)^*, \bigoplus_{b \in B'} s_b \rangle = wide_{2^{V \smallsetminus I_{B'}}}(\langle (2^{I_{B'}})^*, s_{B'} \rangle)$ for some non-distributed implementation $s_{B'}$.

Realizability. An implementation $s_{B'}$ of a set $B' \subseteq B$ of black-box processes *guarantees φ against the remaining black-box processes*, if for all $S_{B \smallsetminus B'}$-labeled 2^V-trees $\langle (2^V)^*, s_{B \smallsetminus B'} \rangle$, the total 2^V-labeled 2^V-tree $\langle Y, dir \rangle$, whose branching restriction $sucset(y) = (s_{B'} \oplus \bigoplus_{w \in W} s_w \oplus s_{B \smallsetminus B'})(y) \times 2^{O_{env}}$ is defined by the strategies, is a model of φ.

We say that a specification is *realizable by the processes $B' \subseteq B$* for a given architecture $(B, W, \{I_p\}_{p \in B \uplus W}, \{O_p\}_{p \in B \uplus W}, O_{env}, \{s_w\}_{w \in W})$, $(A, B') \vDash \varphi$, if there is a distributed implementation of the processes B' that guarantees φ against $B \smallsetminus B'$. A specification is *realizable* if it is realizable by the entire set of black-box processes B.

3   A Compositional Synthesis Rule

The compositional synthesis rule reduces the realizability of a distributed system, $(A, B) \vDash \psi$, to the realizability of single processes, $(A, \{b\}) \vDash \varphi_b$, for each black-box process $b \in B$. The proof rule requires an auxiliary specification φ_b for each process $b \in B$. If each process b guarantees φ_b against the remaining black-box processes, the distributed system can be implemented to satisfy ψ.

For a distributed architecture A with a set of black-box processes $B = \{b_1, \cdots, b_n\}$, and CTL* or μ-calculus formulas $\psi, \varphi_{b_1}, \ldots \varphi_{b_n}$,

$$
\begin{array}{lll}
\text{(R0)} & (A, \emptyset) & \vDash \bigwedge_{b \in B} \varphi_b \to \psi \\[2mm]
\text{(R1)} & (A, \{b_1\}) & \vDash \varphi_{b_1} \\
\vdots & \vdots & \\
\text{(R}n\text{)} & (A, \{b_n\}) & \vDash \varphi_{b_n} \\
\hline
& (A, B) & \vDash \psi
\end{array}
$$

Premise (R0) shows that the auxiliary formulas $\varphi_{b_1}, \ldots, \varphi_{b_n}$ strengthen the original formula φ and hence any implementation that satisfies $\varphi_{b_1}, \ldots, \varphi_{b_n}$ must also satisfy φ. Premises (R1) through (Rn) prove that there are, for all b_i in B, strategies s_{b_i} that guarantee φ_{b_i} against the remaining black-box processes.

Theorem 1. *The proof rule is sound.*

Proof. Premises (R1) through (Rn) guarantee that, for each $b \in B$, there is an implementation s_b that guarantees φ_b against the remaining black-box processes $B \smallsetminus \{b\}$. Consequently, the strategies can be fixed independently; the distributed implementation thus obtained satisfies φ_b for all $b \in B$ and hence $\bigwedge_{b \in B} \varphi_b$. Premise (R0) guarantees that every non-distributed implementation of $\bigwedge_{b \in B} \varphi_b$ is also an implementation of ψ. As the distributed implementations form a subset of the non-distributed implementations, the claim holds true. □

To show the completeness of the distribution rule, we derive the auxiliary formulas from a given implementation that realizes the specification: for a given architecture, we call a specification *strict*, if it completely determines its implementation. An implementation can be described by a strict LTL specification φ. A distributed implementation can be described by a strict specification φ_b for every black-box component $b \in B$, such that $\varphi = \bigwedge_{b \in B} \varphi_b$ is a strict specification for the implementation.

Theorem 2. *The proof rule is complete.*

Proof. Assume there is a distributed implementation for a specification ψ and $\varphi = \bigwedge_{b \in B} \varphi_b$ is a strict specification for this implementation. Then $(A, \{b\}) \vDash \varphi_b$ holds true for each $b \in B$. The implementation of φ is completely determined and $(A, \emptyset) \vDash \varphi \to \psi$ requires that every specification of φ is an implementation of ψ. As the unique implementation is by definition an implementation of ψ, $(A, \emptyset) \vDash \varphi \to \psi$ also holds true. □

4   Single-Process Synthesis

We now develop a procedure that checks if a specification can be guaranteed by a single black-process b against the remaining black-box processes, $(A, \{b\}) \vDash \varphi$, as required for premises (R1) through (Rn), and a procedure that checks if a specification can be guaranteed by the empty set of black-processes against all black-box processes, $(A, \emptyset) \vDash \varphi$, as required for premise (R0).

Every formula of a temporal logic can be translated into an alternating tree automaton that accepts exactly its set of models. This automaton is the starting point for our construction, which consists of a series of tree automata transformations.

4.1   Tree Automata

An *alternating parity tree automaton* is a tuple $\mathcal{A} = (\Sigma, Q, q_0, \delta, \alpha)$, where Q denotes a finite set of states, $q_0 \in Q$ denotes a designated initial state, δ denotes a transition function, and $\alpha : Q \to C \subset \mathbb{N}$ is a coloring function. The transition function $\delta : Q \times \Sigma \to \mathbb{B}^+(Q \times \Upsilon)$ maps a state and an input letter to a positive boolean combination of states and directions (for a predefined finite set Υ of directions).

An alternating automaton runs on full Σ-labeled Υ-trees. A *run tree* $\langle R, r \rangle$ on a given full Σ-labeled Υ-tree $\langle \Upsilon^*, l \rangle$ is a $Q \times \Upsilon^*$-labeled tree where the root is labeled with (q_0, ε) and where, for each node n with a label (q, y) with the set of labels of its successors $L = \{r(n \cdot \rho) | \rho \in \text{sucset}(n)\}$, there is a set $A \subseteq 2^{Q \times \Upsilon}$ which satisfies $\delta(q, l(y))$ such that $(q', v) \in A \Leftrightarrow (q', y \cdot v) \in L$.

An infinite path fulfills the *parity condition*, if the highest color of the states appearing infinitely often on the path is even. A run tree is *accepting* if all infinite paths fulfill the parity condition. A total Σ-labeled Υ-tree is accepted if it has an accepting run tree.

The set of trees accepted by an alternating automaton $\mathcal{A}$ is called its *language* $\mathcal{L}(\mathcal{A})$. $\overline{\mathcal{L}(\mathcal{A})}$ denotes the set of full Σ-labeled Υ-trees not accepted by $\mathcal{A}$. An automaton is empty, if its language is empty.

The acceptance of a tree can also be viewed as the outcome of a game, where player *accept* chooses, for a pair $(q, \sigma) \in Q \times \Sigma$, a set of atoms of $\delta(q, \sigma)$, satisfying $\delta(q, \sigma)$, and player *reject* chooses one of these atoms, which is executed. The input tree is accepted iff player *accept* has a strategy enforcing a path that fulfills the parity condition. One of the player has a memoryless winning strategy, i.e., a strategy where the moves only depend on the state of the automaton, the position in the tree and, for player *react*, on the choice of player *accept* in the same move.

A *nondeterministic* automaton is a special alternating automaton, where the image of δ consists only of such formulae that, when rewritten in disjunctive normal form, contain exactly one element of $Q \times \{v\}$ for all $v \in \Upsilon$ in every disjunct.

For nondeterministic automata, every node of a run tree corresponds to a node in the input tree. Emptiness can therefore be checked with an *emptiness game*, where player *accept* also chooses the letter of the input alphabet. A nondeterministic automaton is empty iff the emptiness game is won by *reject*.

Symmetric alternating automata are a variant of alternating automata that run on total Σ-labeled Υ-trees. For a symmetric alternating automaton $\mathcal{S} = (\Sigma, Q, q_0, \delta, \alpha)$, Q, q_0, and α are defined as before. The transition function $\delta : Q \times \Sigma \to \mathbb{B}^+(Q \times \{\Box, \Diamond\})$ now maps a state and an input letter to a positive boolean combination over atoms that refer to *some* ($\Diamond$) or *all* ($\Box$) successor states.

A *run tree* on a given Σ-labeled Υ-tree $\langle R, r \rangle$ is a $Q \times \Upsilon^*$-labeled tree where the root is labeled with (q_0, ε) and where, for a node n with a label (q, y) and a set of labels of its successors $L = \{r(n \cdot \rho) | \rho \in \text{sucset}(n)\}$, the following property holds: there is a set of atoms $A \subseteq 2^{Q \times \{\Box, \Diamond\}}$ satisfying $\delta(q, l(y))$ such that $\forall q' \in Q.((q', \square) \in A \Rightarrow \forall v \in sucset(x).(q', y \cdot v) \in L) \wedge ((q', \Diamond) \in A \Rightarrow \exists v \in sucset(x).(q', y \cdot v) \in L)$.

We introduce a function $suc : (Q \times \Sigma \to \mathbb{B}^+(Q \times \{\square, \Diamond\})) \to (Q \times \Sigma \times 2_{\emptyset}^{\Upsilon} \to \mathbb{B}^+(Q \times \Upsilon))$ that translates the transition function of a symmetric alternating automaton running on total Σ-labeled Υ-trees into the corresponding transition function of an alternating automaton running on full $\Sigma \times 2_{\emptyset}^{\Upsilon}$-labeled Υ-trees. For the set $2_{\emptyset}^{\Upsilon} = 2^{\Upsilon} \setminus \{\emptyset\}$ of possible sets of successors, $suc(\delta) : Q \times \Sigma \times 2_{\emptyset}^{\Upsilon} \to \mathbb{B}^+(Q \times \Upsilon)$ maps a state, an input letter and a set of successors to a positive boolean combination of states and directions.

4.2   Overview

We represent the joint behavior of a system as a total 2^V-labeled 2^V-tree $\langle Y, dir \rangle$, where the label is completely determined by the direction. The process strategies determine the tree: By the proper widening of a strategy $s'_p : (2^V)^* \to 2_{\emptyset}^{2^{O_p}}$, each input history (or initial sequence of a path) is mapped to a nonempty subset of 2^{O_p}, restricting the set of successors. The nodes of Y consist of the root and all nodes $y \cdot v$ whose predecessor y is in Y, and whose direction agrees with the decisions of the processes: $y \cdot v \in Y \Leftrightarrow y \in Y \wedge \forall p \in B \uplus W.v \cap O_p \in s'_p(y)$.

We start our construction with a symmetric automaton $\mathcal{S}_{\varphi}$ that accepts the models of the specification φ. Automata transformations are simpler for automata running on full trees; we therefore represent total trees as full trees by decorating each node with its own set of successors. Considering a full $2^V \times 2_{\emptyset}^{2^V}$-labeled 2^V-tree $\langle (2^V)^*, l' \rangle$, where the nodes are additionally decorated with the sets of relevant successors, one can easily determine the original total 2^V-labeled 2^V-tree $\langle Y, l \rangle$, which we call its *characteristic tree*.

We continue with an automaton that accepts those full $2^V \times 2_{\emptyset}^{2^V}$-labeled 2^V-trees whose characteristic tree is a model of φ. The labeling of the nodes $(2^V)^* \setminus Y$ of $\langle (2^V)^*, l' \rangle$ that are not on the characteristic tree has no influence on the acceptance of the tree. We restrict the language under consideration to $2^V \times S_b \times S_W \times S_{B'} \times S$-labeled 2^V-trees, where $S_b, S_W, S_{B'}$ and S describe the possible restrictions on the successor sets induced by the black-box process b, the set of white-box processes W, the remaining black-box processes $B' = B \setminus \{b\}$, and the environment, respectively. By that, we obtain an automaton $\mathcal{A}_{\varphi}$ that accepts $2^V \times S_b \times S_W \times S_{B'} \times S$-labeled 2^V-trees. Since $S_p = 2_{\emptyset}^{2^{O_p}}$ for all processes[1] $p \in B \uplus W$, the sets of possible restrictions can be identified with $S_W = \bigotimes_{w \in W} S_w$, $S_{B'} = \bigotimes_{b \neq b' \in B} S_{b'}$ and $S = \{2^{O_{env}}\}$ (as we assume the environment to be maximal).

It remains to find a strategy s_b such that for its proper widening s'_b, $\langle (2^V)^*, dir \times s'_b \times (\bigoplus_{w \in W} s_w) \times s_{B'} \times \{O_{env}\} \rangle$ is accepted for all strategies $s_{B'} : (2^V)^* \to \bigotimes_{b \neq b' \in B} 2_{\emptyset}^{2^{O_{b'}}}$.

---

[1] For generality, we allow all processes to be nondeterministic. If a subset $D \subseteq B \uplus W$ of the processes is to be deterministic, one can simply choose, for all $p \in D$, the set of singleton subsets of 2^{O_p} instead of the set of non-empty subsets.

We first build an automaton $\mathcal{R}_\varphi$ that accepts a $2^V \times S_b \times S_W$-labeled 2^V-tree, if its complete cylinder is accepted by $\mathcal{A}_\varphi$, establishing independence from the decision of the black-box processes. Sbsequently, we use the determination of the 2^V and S_W fraction of the label to defer an automaton $\mathcal{D}_\varphi$ that accepts all strategy trees $\langle (2^V)^*, s_b \rangle$ that would guarantee φ against the remaining black-box processes if process b were omniscient. This automaton is then transformed into an automaton $\mathcal{B}_\varphi$ accepting the strategies of b ($2^{2^{O_b}}_\emptyset$-labeled 2^{I_b}-trees).

Checking this automaton for emptiness answers the question of realizability. In case of realizability, the emptiness test can be extended to synthesize a finite-state strategy for b.

In summary, our construction consists of seven steps:

1. **From formulas to automata:** We construct a symmetric alternating automaton $\mathcal{S}_\varphi$ that accepts the models of φ.
2. **Characteristic trees:** The alternating automaton $\mathcal{A}_\varphi$ accepts a $2^V \times S_b \times S_W \times S_{B'} \times S$-labeled 2^V-tree if its characteristic tree is accepted by $\mathcal{S}_\varphi$.
3. **Quantification:** The alternating automaton $\mathcal{R}_\varphi$ accepts a $2^V \times S_b \times S_W$-labeled 2^V-tree if all $S_{B'} \times S$ extensions are accepted by $\mathcal{A}_\varphi$.
4. **Adjusting for white-box processes:** The alternating automaton $\mathcal{W}_\varphi$ accepts a $2^V \times S_b$-labeled 2^V-tree if the $2^V \times S_b \times S_W$-labeled 2^V-tree obtained by adding the decisions of the white-box processes is accepted by $\mathcal{R}_\varphi$.
5. **Pruning directions from the labeling:** The alternating automaton $\mathcal{D}_\varphi$ accepts a S_b-labeled 2^V-tree if the $2^V \times S_b$-labeled 2^V-tree obtained by adding the direction of a node to the label is accepted by $\mathcal{W}_\varphi$.
6. **Narrowing:** The alternating automaton $\mathcal{B}_\varphi$ accepts a S_b-labeled 2^{I_b}-tree if its proper widening is accepted by $\mathcal{D}_\varphi$.
7. **Emptiness check:** The realizability claim $(A, \{b\}) \vDash \varphi$ holds true iff $\mathcal{B}_\varphi$ is not empty. To perform an emptiness test, $\mathcal{B}_\varphi$ can be transformed into an equivalent nondeterministic automaton $\mathcal{C}_\varphi$, which can be checked for emptiness by solving the emptiness game. A winning strategy in the emptiness game implies an implementation for the process b.

In the following, we discuss the automata transformations in detail.

4.3   Automata Transformations

From formulas to automata. We use standard constructions to translate a temporal specification φ into a symmetric alternating automaton $\mathcal{S}_\varphi$ that accepts the models of the formula: $\mathcal{L}(\mathcal{S}_\varphi) = \mathcal{M}_\varphi$.

Theorem 3. *Given a CTL specification φ, we can construct a symmetric alternating automaton $\mathcal{S}_\varphi$ with $O(|\varphi|)$ states and two colors such that $\mathcal{L}(\mathcal{S}_\varphi) = \mathcal{M}_\varphi$ [8]. Given a CTL* specification φ, we can construct a symmetric alternating automaton $\mathcal{S}_\varphi$ with $2^{O(|\varphi|)}$ states and five colors such that $\mathcal{L}(\mathcal{S}_\varphi) = \mathcal{M}_\varphi$ [8]. Given a μ-calculus specification φ, we can construct a symmetric alternating automaton $\mathcal{S}_\varphi$ with $O(|\varphi|^2)$ states and $O(|\varphi|)$ colors such that $\mathcal{L}(\mathcal{S}_\varphi) = \mathcal{M}_\varphi$ [6].*   □

Characteristic trees. For a $\Sigma \times \Xi$-labeled Υ-tree $\langle Y, l \rangle$, we denote the Σ-projection $proj_\Sigma : \langle Y, l \rangle \mapsto \langle (Y, l_\Sigma) \rangle$ with $l(y) = (\sigma, \xi) \Rightarrow l_\Sigma : y \mapsto \sigma$ that maps $\Sigma \times \Xi$-labeled Υ-trees to Σ-labeled Υ-trees.

For a full $\Sigma \times 2_\emptyset^\Upsilon$-labeled Υ-tree $\langle \Upsilon^*, l \rangle$, we define the *characteristic tree* as the total Σ-labeled Υ-tree $\langle Y, l_c \rangle = char(\langle \Upsilon^*, l \rangle)$ to be the sub-tree of $proj_\Sigma(\langle \Upsilon^*, l \rangle)$ with $y \in Y \Rightarrow \forall v \in \Upsilon.y \cdot v \in \Upsilon \Leftrightarrow v \in proj_{2_\emptyset^\Upsilon}(\langle \Upsilon^*, l \rangle)$. Intuitively, the second argument in the label defines the set of successors of a node.

Lemma 1. *Given a symmetric alternating automaton $\mathcal{S} = (\Sigma, Q, q_0, \delta, \alpha)$, running on total Σ-labeled Υ-trees, we can construct an alternating automaton $\mathcal{A} = (\Sigma \times 2_\emptyset^\Upsilon, Q, q_0, suc(\delta), \alpha)$ that accepts a full $\Sigma \times 2_\emptyset^\Upsilon$ labeled Υ-tree $\langle \Upsilon^*, l \rangle$, iff $proj_\Sigma(char(\langle \Upsilon^*, l \rangle))$ is accepted by $\mathcal{S}$.*

Proof. Let $\langle T, l_T \rangle = char(\langle \Upsilon^*, l \rangle)$. Then the successor set of a node $x \in T$ is defined by the label: $sucset(x) = proj_{2_\emptyset^\Upsilon}(l_{T(x)}) = proj_{2_\emptyset^\Upsilon}(l(x))$. $\square$

Quantification. To construct an alternating automaton $\mathcal{R}_\varphi$ that accepts a $2^V \times S_b \times S_W$-labeled 2^V-tree if all $S_{B'} \times S$ extensions are accepted by $\mathcal{A}_\varphi$, we

1. complement $\mathcal{A}_\varphi$, i.e., we compute an alternating automaton $\mathcal{I}_\varphi$ with $\mathcal{L}(\mathcal{I}_\varphi) = \overline{\mathcal{L}(\mathcal{A}_\varphi)}$,
2. build a nondeterministic automaton $\mathcal{N}_\varphi$ with the same language $\mathcal{L}(\mathcal{N}_\varphi) = \mathcal{L}(\mathcal{A}_\varphi)$,
3. compute a nondeterministic automaton $\mathcal{P}_\varphi$ that accepts a $2^V \times S_b \times S_W$-labeled 2^V-tree if it is the the $S_{B'} \times S$-projection of a tree accepted by $\mathcal{N}_\varphi$,
4. complement $\mathcal{P}_\varphi$, i.e., we compute an alternating automaton $\mathcal{R}_\varphi$ with $\mathcal{L}(\mathcal{R}_\varphi) = \overline{\mathcal{L}(\mathcal{P}_\varphi)}$.

Lemma 2. *[9] Given an alternating automaton $\mathcal{A} = (\Sigma, Q, q_0, \delta, \alpha)$ that runs on Σ-labeled Υ-trees, the dual automaton $\mathcal{I} = (\Sigma, Q, q_0, \overline{\delta}, \alpha + 1)$, where $\overline{\delta}$ is the function dual to δ, accepts a tree $\langle \Upsilon^*, l \rangle$ iff $\langle \Upsilon^*, l \rangle$ is not accepted by $\mathcal{S}$.* $\square$

Lemma 3. *[2,10] Given an alternating automaton $\mathcal{A}$ with n states and c colors, we can construct an equivalent nondeterministic automaton $\mathcal{N}$ with $n^{O(c \cdot n)}$ states and $O(c \cdot n)$ colors.* $\square$

Lemma 4. *Given a nondeterministic automaton $\mathcal{N} = (\Sigma \times \Xi, Q, q_0, \delta, \alpha)$ that runs on $\Sigma \times \Xi$-labeled Υ-trees, we can construct a nondeterministic automaton $\mathcal{P} = (\Sigma, Q, q_0, \delta', \alpha)$ that accepts a Σ-labeled Υ-tree $\langle \Upsilon^*, l \rangle$ iff there is a $\Sigma \times \Xi$-labeled Υ-tree $\langle \Upsilon^*, l_\Xi \rangle$ accepted by $\mathcal{N}$ with $\langle \Upsilon^*, l \rangle = proj_\Sigma(\langle \Upsilon^*, l_\Xi \rangle)$.*

Proof. $\mathcal{P}$ can be constructed by using δ' to guess the correct tree: we set $\delta' : (q, \sigma) \mapsto \bigvee_{\xi \in \Xi} \delta(q, (\sigma, \xi))$. $\square$

In the following two transformations, the decisions of the white-box processes and the labeling imposed by the directions are deleted from the label.

Adjusting for white-box processes. The S_W fraction of the label represents the decisions made by the white box processes. Consequently, we are only interested in those trees, where the label of every node is in accordance with these decisions. This information is then redundant and can be pruned. We assume that the composed strategy $\bigoplus_{w \in W} s_w$ of the white-box processes is represented as a finite-state automaton $\mathcal{O} = (2^V, O, o_0, d_W, o_W)$, where O is a set of states, o_0 the initial state, the transition function $d_W : 2^V \times O \to O$ is a mapping from the input alphabet and the set of states to the set of states, and the output function $o_W : O \to 2^{2^{O_W}}_{\emptyset}$ maps each state to a nonempty set of output letters. The following operation performs the pruning; the state-space of the resulting automaton is linear in the state-space of the original automaton and the number of states of $\mathcal{O}$, while the set of colors remains unchanged.

Lemma 5. *Given an alternating automaton* $\mathcal{R} = (\Sigma \times \Xi, Q, q_0, \delta, \alpha)$ *over* $\Sigma \times \Xi$*-labeled* Υ*-trees and a finite automaton* $\mathcal{O} = (\Sigma, O, o_0, d_W, o_W)$ *that produces a* Ξ*-labeled* Υ*-tree* $\langle \Upsilon^*, l \rangle$*, we can construct an alternating automaton* $\mathcal{W} = (\Sigma, Q \times O, (q_0, o_0), \delta', \alpha')$ *over* Σ*-labeled* Υ*-trees, such that* $\mathcal{W}$ *accepts* $\langle \Upsilon^*, l' \rangle$ *iff* $\mathcal{R}$ *accepts* $\langle \Upsilon^*, l'' \rangle$ *with* $l'' : y \mapsto (l'(y), l(y))$*.*

Proof. If $\delta : (q, \sigma, \xi) \mapsto b_{(q,\sigma,\xi)}(\{q_i, v_i\}_{i \in I})$, we can set $\delta' : (q, o, \sigma) \mapsto b_{(q,\sigma,o_W(o))}(\{q_i, d_W(\sigma, o), v_i\}_{i \in I})$. The coloring function can simply be set to $\alpha' : (q, o) \mapsto \alpha(q)$. $\qquad\qquad \square$

Pruning directions from the labeling. We are only interested in those trees where the label of every node is in accordance with its direction. This information then becomes redundant and can be pruned. The following operation performs this pruning; the state-space of the resulting automaton is linear in the state-space of the original automaton, while the set of colors remains unchanged.

For a Σ-labeled Υ-tree $\langle \Upsilon^*, l \rangle$, we define the function $xray : \langle \Upsilon^*, l \rangle \mapsto \langle \Upsilon^*, l' \rangle$ with $l'(x) = (dir(x), l(x))$ that maps Σ-labeled Υ-trees to $\Upsilon \times \Sigma$-labeled Υ-trees.

Lemma 6. *[8] Given an alternating automaton* $\mathcal{W} = (\Upsilon \times \Sigma, Q, q_0, \delta, \alpha)$ *over* $\Upsilon \times \Sigma$*-labeled* Υ*-trees, we can construct an alternating automaton* $\mathcal{D} = (\Sigma, Q \times \Upsilon, (q_0, v_0), \delta', \alpha')$ *over* Σ*-labeled* Υ*-trees, such that* $\mathcal{D}$ *accepts* $\langle \Upsilon^*, l \rangle$ *iff* $\mathcal{R}$ *accepts* $xray(\langle \Upsilon^*, l \rangle)$*.* $\qquad\qquad \square$

The transition function $\delta' : Q \times \Upsilon \times \Sigma \to \mathcal{B}^+(Q \times \Upsilon \times \Upsilon)$ can be constructed from $\delta : Q \times \Upsilon \times \Sigma \to \mathcal{B}^+(Q \times \Upsilon)$ by replacing all occurrences of (q, v) in each $\delta(q', v', \sigma')$ by (q, v, v), storing the direction as quasi-input. $\alpha' : (q, c) \mapsto \alpha(q)$ simply evaluates the first component of the new state-space.

Narrowing. The process b is in general not omniscient, and its output may only depend on the history of the input visible to b. The following transformation therefore accepts a 2^{O_p}-labeled 2^{I_p}-tree if its proper widening is accepted by $\mathcal{D}_\varphi$. The state-space and the set of colors remain unchanged.

Lemma 7. *[8] Given an alternating automaton* $\mathcal{D} = (\Sigma, Q, q_0, \delta, \alpha)$ *over* Σ*-labeled* $\Xi \times \Upsilon$*-trees, we can construct an alternating automaton* $\mathcal{B} =$

$(\Sigma, Q, q_0, \delta', \alpha)$ over Σ-labeled Ξ-trees, such that $\mathcal{B}$ accepts $\langle \Xi^*, l \rangle$ iff $\mathcal{W}$ accepts $wide_{\Upsilon}(\langle \Xi^*, l \rangle)$. □

δ' can be constructed from δ by replacing all occurrences of $(q, (\xi, \upsilon))$ by (q, ξ) in $\delta(q', \sigma)$ for all $q, q' \in Q, \sigma \in \Sigma, \xi \in \Xi$ and $\upsilon \in \Upsilon$.

Emptiness check. To perform an emptiness test, $\mathcal{B}_\varphi$ can be transformed into an equivalent nondeterministic automaton $\mathcal{C}_\varphi$.

Theorem 4. *Given a symmetric alternating automaton $\mathcal{S}_\varphi$ that accepts the models of φ, an architecture $(B, W, \{I_p\}_{p \in B \uplus W \uplus \{env\}}, \{O_p\}_{p \in B \uplus W \uplus \{env\}}, \{s_w\}_{w \in W})$ and a designated black-box process $b \in B$, we can construct a nondeterministic automaton $\mathcal{C}_\varphi$ that accepts a full 2^{O_p}-labeled 2^{I_p}-tree $\langle (2^{I_p})^*, s_b \rangle$ iff s_b guarantees φ against $B \setminus \{b\}$. If $\mathcal{S}$ has n states and c colors, $\mathcal{C}$ has $2^{n^{O(n \cdot c)}}$ states and $n^{O(n \cdot c)}$ colors.*

Proof. By applying the transformation steps in the order described in the overview of the algorithm, we obtain an alternating automaton $\mathcal{B}_\varphi$ with $n^{O(n \cdot c)}$ states and $O(n \cdot c)$ colors that accepts an implementation $\langle (2^{I_b})^*, s_b \rangle$ of a process b if it guarantees φ against $B \setminus \{b\}$. A nondeterminisation of $\mathcal{B}_\varphi$ by the construction of Lemma 3 provides the required automaton. □

Theorem 5. *For a given architecture A and a black-box process b, we can check $(A, \{b\}) \models \varphi$ and, if the claim is true, provide an implementation for b guaranteeing φ, in 2EXPTIME in the length $|\varphi|$ if φ is a CTL or μ-calculus specification, and in 3EXPTIME in $|\varphi|$ if φ is a CTL* specification, respectively.*

Proof. By Theorem 3, we can turn a specifications φ in CTL, μ-calculus or CTL* with length $n = |\varphi|$ into a symmetric alternating automaton $\mathcal{S}$ with $O(n)$ states and two colors, $O(n^2)$ states and $O(n)$ colors or $2^{O(n)}$ states and five colors, respectively.

By Theorem 4, we can transform the symmetrical alternating automaton $\mathcal{S}$ into a nondeterministic automaton $\mathcal{C}$, accepting the strategies of b that guarantee φ against the remaining black-box processes. $\mathcal{C}$ has $2^{n^{O(n)}}$ states and $n^{O(n)}$ colors, $2^{n^{O(n^3)}}$ states and $n^{O(n^3)}$ colors or $2^{2^{2^{O(n)}}}$ states and $2^{2^{O(n)}}$ colors, respectively.

The actual emptiness test or the synthesis of a strategy for process n can be done in time polynomial in the state-space and exponential in the number of colors. More precisely, if $\mathcal{C}$ has m states and c colors, a strategy (or the proof of emptiness) can be found in $m^{O(c)}$ time [11]. The overall time complexity is hence $2^{n^{O(n)}}$, $2^{n^{O(n^3)}}$ and $2^{2^{2^{O(n)}}}$, respectively. □

Lower Bounds. To demonstrate that the upper bounds are sharp, we give a reduction from the synthesis problem in reactive environments with complete information, which is known to be 2EXPTIME and 3EXPTIME hard for CTL and CTL*, respectively [7]. In synthesis with reactive environments and complete information, we have only one process b, for which a (deterministic) strategy

$s_b : (2^{O_{env}})^* \rightarrow S_b$ is sought (where S_b is the set of singleton subsets of $2^{O_{env}}$. The environment can react on the input by restricting its actions to a non-empty subset of its output variables O_e, which can be viewed as a non-deterministic strategy $s_e : (2^{O_{env} \cup O_b})^* \rightarrow 2^{2^{O_e}}_\emptyset$). In our terms, a strategy $s_b : (2^{O_{env}})^* \rightarrow S_b$ implements a specification φ if, for all strategies $s_e : (2^{O_{env} \cup O_b})^* \rightarrow 2^{2^{O_{env}}}_\emptyset$ of the environment, $s_b \times s_e$ is a model of φ.

We encode this synthesis problem as the realizability of φ by b against a black-box process e with output O_e and an environment without output. The second black-box process e plays the rôle of the reactive environment. Formally, we define the architecture $A = (\{b, e\}, \emptyset, \{I_b = O_e, I_e = I_{env} = V\}, \{O_b, O_e, O_{env} = \emptyset\}, \emptyset)$. The determinacy of s_b can be guaranteed by the construction (by setting S_b to the set of singleton subsets of 2^{O_b}). Alternatively, we can ensure the determinacy of s_b by strengthening the specification φ such that only deterministic strategies are allowed: For $\psi = \bigwedge_{o \in O_b} AG\,(EXo \rightarrow AXo)$, we can solve the realizability problem for $\varphi' = \varphi \wedge \psi$ (which is linear in φ).

Theorem 6. *The realizability problem* $(A, \{b\}) \models \varphi$ *is 3EXPTIME complete for CTL* and 2EXPTIME complete for CTL and μ-calculus specifications in the size $|\varphi|$ of the specification.*

Proof. The lower bounds for CTL and CTL* follow from the equal lower bounds for the synthesis problem with reactive environments. The lower bound for the μ-calculus is established by the lower bound for CTL. The upper bound is demonstrated by Theorem 5. □

Premise R0. The correctness of premise R0 can be checked along the same lines: we check whether the empty strategy guarantees $\bigwedge_{b \in B} \varphi_b \rightarrow \psi$ against all black-box processes. Since $S_b = \{\emptyset\}$ and $I_b = \emptyset$, the automaton $\mathcal{B}_\varphi$ (with n states and c colors) is an alternating word automaton over the single-letter alphabet, whose emptiness can be checked in $n^{O(c)}$ time. Checking (R0) is therefore in EXPTIME for CTL and μ-calculus specifications and in 2EXPTIME for CTL* specifications, respectively, in $|\bigwedge_{b \in B} \varphi_b \rightarrow \psi|$.

5   Conclusions

In open synthesis, where we synthesize a system that consists of a single process, it is safe to assume that the environment behavior is *maximal*. For the synthesis of a black-box process in the architecture of a general distributed system, the environment model needs two extensions: (1) The other black-box processes add a *reactive* component to the environment and (2) the process only has *incomplete information* about the environment behavior.

Extension (1) turns out to be expensive. Adding the reactive component increases the complexity for CTL specifications from EXPTIME [8] to

2EXPTIME [7], and for CTL* specifications from 2EXPTIME [8] to 3EXPTIME [7]. As shown in Section 4, extension (2) has no extra cost. This settles an open question of [7]: The complexity of synthesizing a single process in a distributed architecture is still 2EXPTIME and 3EXPTIME, respectively.

The complexity of single-process synthesis is especially convincing in comparison to the cost of distributed synthesis: in the rare cases where distributed synthesis is decidable, the cost of synthesizing a distributed system with n processes (with distinguishable degree of information about the system state) is n-exponential in the size of the specification [1,2].

Dividing the synthesis problem into several synthesis problems for single processes therefore appears as a promising approach to cope with the complexity and general undecidability of distributed synthesis. The situation is similar to the *verification* of distributed systems, where the compositional approach is well-established [12]. Our proof rule in Section 3 is a first example of a compositional synthesis technique. The rule is complete and therefore sufficient to decompose any realizable specification. The rule may, however, be less convenient to use than some compositional verification rules that, for example, apply circular assume-guarantee reasoning [13]. Defining such rules for the synthesis problem is an interesting topic of future research.

References

1. Kupferman, O., Vardi, M.Y.: Synthesizing distributed systems. In: IEEE Symposium on Logic in Computer Science. (2001)
2. Finkbeiner, B., Schewe, S.: Uniform distributed synthesis. In: IEEE Symposium on Logic in Computer Science. (2005)
3. Clarke, E.M., Emerson, E.A.: Design and synthesis of synchronization skeletons using branching time temporal logic. In: Proc. IBM Workshop on Logics of Programs. Volume 131 of LNCS., Springer-Verlag (1981) 52–71
4. Wolper, P.: Synthesis of Communicating Processes from Temporal-Logic Specifications. PhD thesis, Stanford University (1982)
5. Kupferman, O., Vardi, M.Y.: Synthesis with incomplete informatio. In: Proc. 2nd International Conference on Temporal Logic (ICTL'97). (1997)
6. Kupferman, O., Vardi, M.Y.: μ-calculus synthesis. In: Proc. 25th International Symposium on Mathematical Foundations of Computer Science. Volume 1893 of LNCS., Springer-Verlag (2000) 497–507
7. Kupferman, O., Madhusudan, P., Thiagarajan, P., Vardi, M.Y.: Open systems in reactive environments: Control and synthesis. In: Proc. 11th Int. Conf. on Concurrency Theory. Volume 1877 of LNCS., Springer-Verlag (2000) 92–107
8. Kupferman, O., Vardi, M.Y.: Church's problem revisited. The bulletin of Symbolic Logic **5** (1999) 245–263
9. Muller, D.E., Schupp, P.E.: Alternating automata on infinite trees. Theor. Comput. Sci. **54** (1987) 267–276
10. Muller, D.E., Schupp, P.E.: Simulating alternating tree automata by nondeterministic automata: new results and new proofs of the theorems of rabin, mcnaughton and safra. Theor. Comput. Sci. **141** (1995) 69–107

11. Jurdziński, M.: Small progress measures for solving parity games. In: 17th Annual Symposium on Theoretical Aspects of Computer Science. Volume 1770 of LNCS., Springer-Verlag (2000) 290–301
12. de Roever, W.P., Langmaack, H., Pnueli, A., eds.: Compositionality: The Significant Difference. COMPOS'97. Volume 1536 of LNCS. (1998)
13. Maier, P.: A Lattice-Theoretic Framework For Circular Assume-Guarantee Reasoning. PhD thesis, Universität des Saarlandes, Saarbrücken (2003)

A New Graph of Classes for the Preservation of Quantitative Temporal Constraints

Xiaoyu Mao[1], Janette Cardoso[2], and Robert Valette[3]

[1] IRIT-UT1/LAAS, Toulouse, France,
[2] IRIT-UT1, 21, allées de Brienne, 31042 Toulouse, France
[3] LAAS-CNRS, 31077 Toulouse, France
xmao@etud.insa-toulouse.fr, jcardoso@univ-tlse1.fr, robert@laas.fr

Abstract. The objective of this paper is to present a new abstract state space for t-time Petri nets which associates with each path in this space a sequence effectively firable in the net. This means that this state space has to exactly (in a quantitative way) define the set of constraints which have to be verified by the firings. After some definitions about the Simple Temporal Networks, the abstract states are defined as well the generation of the abstract space. It is shown that this space does not coincide with the two previously defined spaces (W and A) in TINA.

1 Introduction

For checking some properties of critical embedded systems such as the timeliness property for correct environment interaction, it is frequently necessary to consider specific scenarios of operations and to analyze the temporal constraints which have to be verified by the events composing them [Ri 05].

Other properties (related for example to the fact that a state is not reachable) imply the exhaustive search for all the states of a system. When temporal constraints exist, the states, in an infinite number, can be covered by a finite set of state classes for bounded Petri nets. In this case, a graph of state classes can be built in order to study the system, where nodes are state classes and the arc from a class C to a class C' is labeled by the transition t (leading from C to C'). Several kinds of classes have been proposed according to the kind of properties to be proven (properties expressed in LTL or in CTL for instance) [Me 85, Yo 98, Be 04, Ca 05]. Some approaches allow deriving the temporal constraints associated with a given scenario, directly from the Petri net [PR 99, Ri 01, Ri 05]. However, they cannot be used efficiently for t-time Petri nets with strong semantics and interleaving. In order to correctly delimit the domains of the variables attached to the firing dates in a transition firing sequence, it is necessary, in the case of a t-time Petri net with strong semantics, to know the transition enabling dates. This implies that, for each transition, the date of the firing which has produced the last token is known. In consequence, it is necessary to proceed in the context of interleaving semantics and therefore to explicitly consider states and firing sequences (in contrast with [PR 99, Ri 01] where the approach is based on scenarios i.e. partial orders).

D.A. Peled and Y.-K. Tsay (Eds.): ATVA 2005, LNCS 3707, pp. 278–292, 2005.

It is clear that it is always possible, given a firing sequence possibly derived from a graph of classes, to obtain a set of constraints delimiting the firing dates by considering both the Petri net and the graph of classes [Sc 04]. In this paper, the proposed approach is to construct a graph of classes with sets of constraints attached to its arcs, such that the constraints which have to be verified by the firing dates for any sequence in the net, are directly derived by concatenating the constraints attached to the arcs covered by the corresponding sequence in the graph of classes.

2   Basic Notions

2.1   Simple Temporal Network

Definition 1 (Simple temporal network). *A simple temporal network N is composed of a finite set V of variables v_i and a finite set C of* **binary** *constraints $C_{ij}(v_i, v_j)$ defined as convex intervals $[c_{mij}, c_{Mij}]$ delimiting the possible distance between two variables v_i and v_j of V. Each C_{ij} is therefore equivalent to: $c_{mij} \leq v_j - v_i \leq c_{Mij}$ $v_i, v_j \in V$.*

Definition 2 (Complete network). *A simple temporal network N is complete iff a constraint C_{ij} is associated with each pair of variables.*

Definition 3 (Minimal network). *A complete simple temporal network $N = (V, C)$ is minimal iff $\forall v_i, v_j \in V$ and $\forall c \in C_{ij}$ ($c_{mij} \leq c \leq c_{Mij}$), there is an assignment of values to all the variables of V which verifies all the constraints and such that $v_j - v_i = c$.*

The Floyd-Warshall algorithm, derives a complete and minimal simple temporal network from any consistent (having at least one solution) simple temporal network [De 91, Gh 04]. After applying this algorithm, the new resulting constraint $C_{ij} = [d_{mij}, d_{Mij}]$ is such that d_{mij} is the best possible lower bound, d_{Mij} is the best possible upper bound and these bounds are actually reached for at least one set of assignments of all the variables of V verifying all the constraints of C.

Definition 4 (Intersection). *The intersection of two simple temporal networks $N = (V, C)$ and $N' = (V', C')$ is the simple temporal network $N'' = N \cap N' = (V'', C'')$ such that: i) $V'' = V \cap V'$, ii) $\forall v_i, v_j \in V''$, $C''_{ij} = C_{ij} \cap C'_{ij}$.*

The constraints are given by the intersection of the intervals. If one of these intersections is empty, the simple temporal network N'' is inconsistent in an obvious way.

Definition 5 (Union). *Let us consider two temporal networks $N = (V, C)$ and $N' = (V', C')$ such that: $\forall v_i, v_j \in V \cap V'$, $C_{ij} = C'_{ij}$. The union $N'' = N \cup N'$ is a simple temporal network (V'', C'') such that: i) $V'' = V \cup V'$, ii) $C'' = C \cup C'$.*

It has to be pointed out that as for any pair of variables v_i and v_j belonging both to N and N', the constraints C_{ij} and C'_{ij} are the same in N and N', and the union of the sets of constraints C and C' is always consistent.

2.2   t-Time Petri Nets

Definition 6. *A t-time Petri Net [Be 91, Be 04] is a 3-tuple* $< \mathcal{N}, M_0, I >$ *where:*

- $\mathcal{N} =< P, T, Pre, Post >$ *is a Petri net,*
- M_0 *: is the initial marking,*
- $I : T \rightarrow (Q^+ \cup 0) * (Q^+ \cup \infty)$ *is the static interval function.*

The static interval function I associates with each transition t_i a temporal interval $[a_i, b_i]$ (see figure 1) that represents the set of its possible firing dates counting from its enabling date.

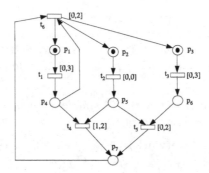

Fig. 1. Example of a t-time Petri net

Typically, for t-time Petri nets, the operational semantics includes the so-called *strong semantics* which enforces the firing of one of the enabled transitions before the earliest of all the latest firing dates for the enabled transitions. This means that a transition cannot remain enabled without being fired after the end of its firing interval. In this paper, it is assumed that there is no memory of the enabling time of a transition in the past and transitions may be enabled concurrently.

In a t-time Petri Net, the following events associated with a transition (and the corresponding temporal variables) must be taken into account: the *enabling date, begin/end of the firing interval* and *firing date*. The following constraints must be verified between the variables corresponding to these events:

- the enabling date of a transition is equal (not greater) to the firing date of the last transition which has contributed to its enabling,
- the transition firing date should be included in its firing interval I.

These relations can be expressed by simple binary constraints when the operational semantics is such that only firing sequences (totally ordered) are considered (interleaving semantics). In consequence, simple temporal networks are an adequate framework to analyze the temporal constraints generated by t-time

Petri nets. In the following, only two types of variables are considered: x_i^k which is the variable denoting the date of the k^{ith} firing of transition t_i and y_i which denotes the upper bound of the firing interval of enabled transition t_i.

3   Definition of States and State Classes

3.1   State of a t-Time Petri Net

Let us consider the execution of a firing sequence $\sigma = t_1 ; \cdots ; t_i ; t_j ; \cdots ; t_n$ in a t-time Petri net. A transition can be fired several times in a sequence. We consider a firing of transition t_i which is the oi^{th} firing of this transition and the next firing in σ is the oj^{th} firing of t_j. The corresponding variables are x_i^{oi} for t_i and x_j^{oj} for t_j.

Given a specific execution of σ, the state after the firing of t_i is the obtained marking associated with the current clock value and the firing dates of all the transitions preceding t_i in σ in order to compute the remaining firing intervals for each enabled transition.

3.2   State Classes

A class is composed of all the states which are reachable by an execution of σ after the firing of t_i and before that of t_j. The class has to allow the accurate definition of all the constraints which have to be verified by the firing date of transitions t_j and by the following ones in σ. This means that it is necessary to be able to derive not only the distance of x_j^{oj} and x_i^{oi}, but also the distance of x_j^{oj} with all the preceding firing dates in σ.

In order to have a finite number of classes, it is necessary to *forget* a part of the past. Instead of keeping all the variables corresponding to the past transition firings and the corresponding simple temporal network, it is possible to only keep a fragment of it.

After having defined this fragment, the paper gives the procedure of construction of the temporal constraints which variable x_j^{oj} must verify. These constraints are attached to the arcs of the graph of classes under the form of a simple temporal network. Then it is proven that the fragment is sufficient, *i.e.* that considering more variables and more constraints about the past events would not modify the simple temporal networks attached to the arcs.

Definition 7. *The initial state class C_0 is defined by the tuple (M_0, Nc_0) where:*

- *M_0 is the initial marking of the net; it is assumed that n_0 transitions are enabled by M_0,*
- *Nc_0 is the temporal network composed only of the variable x_0 representing the time origin.*

The time origin is the event that has enabled all n_0 enabled transition at class C_0 and in a certain way, it is the *beginning of the world*.

Let σ be a firing sequence $t_1 ; \cdots ; t_i$ of a t-time Petri net, t_i the last fired transition in σ and $t_{s(k)}$ the transition that has enabled a transition t_k.

Definition 8. *The* **state class** $\mathcal{C}$, *obtained after the firing of transition* t_i, *is defined by the pair* $\{M, Nc\}$ *where:*

- M *is the current marking of the net; it is assumed that* n *transitions are enabled by* M,
- Nc *is the minimal and complete simple temporal network composed of the following variables and constraints :*
    1. *the variable* x_i^{oi} *associated with the last transition firing* (t_i *firing*),
    2. *for each enabled transition* t_k *from* M, *the variable associated with the firing of transition* $t_{s(k)}$ *which has enabled* t_k, $x_{s(k)}^{osk}$ ($k = 1, \ldots, n$),
    3. *the temporal constraints between these variables (minimal and complete network).*

If $\mathcal{C}_p$ is the class from which transition t_i has been fired, $\mathcal{C}$ is the class obtained by the firing of t_i at date x_i^{oi} and Nt_{i,c_p} the simple temporal network delimiting t_i firing, figure 2 describes the relationships between classes and simple temporal networks.

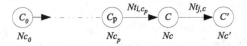

Fig. 2. A piece of a graph of classes

For all classes $\mathcal{C} \neq \mathcal{C}_0$, the representation of the past includes the last transition firing and the firing which has enabled each one of the n enabled transitions at $\mathcal{C}$. There are two cases:

- two transitions t_1 and t_2 have been enabled by the same transition t_a, the corresponding variables $x_{s(1)}^{os1}$ and $x_{s(2)}^{os2}$ are the same, $x_{s(1)}^{os1} = x_{s(2)}^{os2} = x_a^{oa}$;
- the last transition firing (represented by variable x_i^{oi}) is also the event that enables a transition t_j in this class (represented by variable $x_{s(k)}^{osk}$), these variables are the same, $x_i^{oi} = x_{s(k)}^{osk}$.

In the sequel if a transition t_i appears only once in a sequence σ ($o_i = 1$), the corresponding variable is noted x_i instead of x_i^1.

For example, let us consider the t-time Petri net in figure 1, with the firing of sequence $t_2 ; t_3 ; t_1$ from initial class $\mathcal{C}_0$ with initial marking $p_1 p_2 p_3$ and the temporal network Nc_0 given by x_0. The class $\mathcal{C}$ reached by the firing of this sequence has the marking $p_4 p_5 p_6$. The transitions enabled by this marking are t_4 and t_5. The following events must be considered in order to construct Nc:

- the last transition fired in the sequence is $t_i = t_1$, and the corresponding variable is x_1;
- t_4 has been enabled by t_1 firing, so s(4)=1, and $x^{os4}_{s(4)} = x_1$;
- t_5 has been enabled by t_3 firing, so s(5)=3, and $x^{os5}_{s(5)} = x_3$.

The complete definition of the temporal network Nc requires the constraint values associated with variables x_1 and x_3. Nc is a fragment of the temporal network delimiting the last transition firing (t_1 in this example). The definition of the temporal network Nt delimiting the firing of a transition t is defined in the sequel.

3.3   The Temporal Network Delimiting the Firing of t_j

In a reachable marking graph obtained from a classical Petri net (without temporal information), a node corresponds to a marking and an arc between two nodes (n_1, n_2) is labeled by the transition whose firing leads from n_1 to n_2. In the graph of classes obtained from a t-time Petri net, an arc between two classes must be labeled, besides the transition, by temporal information delimiting the firing date of this transition. According to the definition of class and the corresponding definition of temporal information attached to the arc, several graphs of classes have been proposed allowing to prove different properties of a t-time Petri net ([Be 91, Yo 98], etc). In our approach, an arc, labeled by a transition t_j, is also associated with a temporal network $Nt_{j,i}$ delimiting the firing date of t_j from C_i. These constraints reflect the memory of the past necessary to characterize the future events.

Let t_j be a transition among the n enabled transitions at class $\mathcal{C} = (M, Nc)$ (def. 8), with $Nc = (Vc, Cc)$, and let t_l, $l \neq j$ be the other $n - 1$ enabled transitions at $\mathcal{C}$.

Definition 9. *The **simple temporal network** $Nt_{j,c} = (Vt, Ct)$ delimiting the firing of t_j from class $\mathcal{C}$ is composed of the following variables and constraints:*

1. *all variables and constraints from Nc, $Vt = Vc$, $Ct = Cc$,*
2. *the variable x^{oj}_j (firing date of t_j) and the static interval $I(t_j)$ as a constraint between x^{oj}_j and $x^{osj}_{s(j)}$,*
3. *the variable y^{ol}_l corresponding to each enabled transition t_l and the singleton $[d_{Ml}, d_{Ml}]$ (the upper bound of static interval $I(t_l)$) as a constraint between $(x^{osl}_{s(l)}, y^{ol}_l)$,*
4. *the constraint $[0, \infty[$ between x^{oi}_i and x^{oj}_j to express the fact that t_j must be fired after t_i,*
5. *the constraint $[0, \infty[$ between the pairs (x^{oj}_j, y^{ol}_l), $l \neq j$, to express the fact that t_j must be fired before the upper bound of the firing interval of transitions t_l.*

The minimal and complete $Nt_{j,c}$ is obtained after applying Floyd-Warshall algorithm. All variables y_l^{ol} and the constraints to which they are directly connected can be deleted (proved in section 3.4).

Step 1 indicates that Nc is a fragment of $Nt_{j,c}$, $Nc \subseteq Nt_{j,c}$. By the way, variables $x_{s(j)}^{osj}$ and $x_{s(l)}^{osl}$ in Steps 2 and 3 respectively belong to Nc (def. 8), since they correspond to transitions which have enabled one of n enabled transitions in C. Step 4 is imposed by the interleaving semantics and step 5 is imposed by the strong semantics. If the network is not consistent, it means that t_j cannot be fired before the other $n - 1$ transitions t_l.

Let us consider the initial class C_0 of the net in fig. 1, with $M_0 = p_1 p_2 p_3$ and $Nc_0 : x_0$. Let us consider the firing of t_2 (at date x_2), delimited by $Nt_{2,0}$. At the beginning, $Nt_{2,0} = Nc_0 : x_0$ (step 1); node x_2 and arc $(x_0, x_2)=[0\ 0]$ are added ($s(2) = 0$, step 2). As t_1 and t_3 are also enabled at C_0, nodes y_1 and y_3 as well arcs $(x_0, y_1)=(x_0, y_3)=[3\ 3]$ are added ($s(1) = s(3) = 0$, step 3). Arc $(x_0, x_2)=[0\ \infty[$ ($i = 0$, step 4) is also added, as well $(x_2, y_1)=(x_2, y_3)=[0\ \infty[$ (step 5), leading to $Nt_{2,0}$ of fig. 3.a. After Floyd-Warshall algorithm, the obtained $Nt_{2,0}$ is the one of fig. 3.b. The final $Nt_{2,0}$ is represented by the dotted arc of this figure.

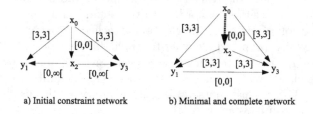

a) Initial constraint network   b) Minimal and complete network

Fig. 3. Temporal network $Nt_{2,0}$ delimiting t_2 firing from C_0

It is important to remark that the simple temporal network Nc' of the class C' reached after the firing of t_j is also included in $Nt_{j,c}$. In fact, all n' enabled transitions at C' have been enabled by the firing of t_j ($x_j \in Nt_{j,c}$) or the firing of a previous transition t in the sequence leading to C ($x \in Nc \subseteq Nt_{j,c}$).

3.4 Proofs

Proving that y_l^{ol} can be Deleted. After Floyd-Warshall execution, variables $x_{s(l)}^{osl}$ and y_l^{ol} are redundant because the constraints connecting them are singletons. Indeed knowing the constraint connecting $x_{s(l)}$ (event that has enabled transition t_l) to x_k is sufficient to derive the triangle in figure 4.a, because:

$$d_{mkl} = d_M - d_{msk} \quad \text{and} \quad d_{Mkl} = d_M - d_{Msk} \tag{1}$$

Proving that the Past can be Forgotten. Let us consider the class C' obtained from the firing of t_j, characterized by the temporal network Nc' in fig. 4.b, with a variable x_k belonging to the forgotten past. The proof that a

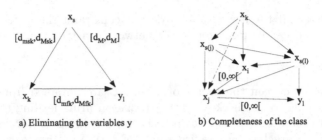

Fig. 4. Temporal network Nt illustrating the proof

part of the past can be forgotten, upon which the definition of class is based, relies on the assumption that x_k cannot restrict the constraints between x_j and the other nodes.

As underlined in section 3.3, the temporal network $Nt_{j,c}$ (delimiting the firing of a transition t_j from a class $\mathcal{C}$) is constructed from the temporal network Nc of the class $\mathcal{C}$ (obtained from the firing of a precedent transition t_i in the sequence).

So, if the variables y_l are not deleted in step 7 of the procedure given in section 3.3, the obtained class $\mathcal{C}'$ is composed by 3 kind of constraints: 1) between x_j and $x_{s(j)}$ (event that has enabled transition t_j), 2) between x_j and x_i (the last transition fired before t_j, interleaving semantics) and 3) between x_j and y_l, $l \neq j$ (strong semantics). Only y_1 is represented in the figure, the other nodes y_l are identical. The constraints C_{kj} is initially equal to $[0, \infty[$.

The longest path of x_k towards x_j thus passes necessarily by $x_{s(j)}$, x_i or one of nodes $x_{s(l)}$. Let us suppose that it is going through $x_{s(j)}$, so $d_{mkj} = d_{mks(j)} + d_{ms(j)j}$ and $d_{Mkj} = d_{Mks(j)} + d_{Ms(j)j}$. Can this constraint restricts $[d_{mij}, d_{Mij}]$, for example? (An arc $(x_i, x_j) = [d_{mij}, d_{Mij}]$ corresponds to two arcs $(x_i, x_j) = d_{Mij}$ and $(x_j, x_i) = -d_{mij} = d_{mji}$.) In this case:

$$d_{mij} = d_{mik} + d_{mkj} = d_{mik} + d_{mks(j)} + d_{ms(j)j} \qquad (2)$$

$$d_{Mij} = d_{Mik} + d_{Mkj} = d_{Mik} + d_{Mks(j)} + d_{Ms(j)j} \qquad (3)$$

As the temporal network Nc characterizing the class $\mathcal{C}$ is complete and minimal, $d_{mis(j)} \geq d_{mik} + d_{mks(j)}$ and $d_{Mis(j)} \leq d_{Mik} + d_{Mks(j)}$, so the lower bound of the path going directly through $x_{s(j)}$ is equal or *bigger* than the one going through x_k (eq. 2), and the upper bound is equal or *smaller* than it (eq. 3).

The other cases are analogous. Let us take into account the case where the longest path between x_j and x_k goes through $x_{s(j)}$ and the one between x_k and y_l goes through $x_{s(l)}$. If x_k can reinforce the constraint between x_j and y_l:

$$d_{mjl} = d_{mjk} + d_{mkl} = d_{mjs(j)} + d_{ms(j)k} + d_{mks(l)} + d_{ms(l)l} \qquad (4)$$

$$d_{Mjl} = d_{Mjk} + d_{Mkl} = d_{Mjs(j)} + d_{Ms(j)k} + d_{Mks(l)} + d_{Ms(l)l} \qquad (5)$$

But $d_{ms(j)s(l)} \geq d_{ms(j)k} + d_{mks(l)}$ and $d_{Ms(j)s(l)} \leq d_{Ms(j)k} + d_{Mks(l)}$, so the lower bound of the path $(x_j, x_{s(j)}, x_{s(l)}, y_l)$ is equal or *bigger* than the one going through x_k, and the upper bound is equal or *smaller* than it.

It is proved that the firing date x_k do not constraint the distance between other nodes, so it can be forgotten in the network construction.

3.5   Restricted Class

The constraints between the events of a class C are obtained from the set of constraints having to be checked by the transition firing leading to C. Indeed, the temporal network Nc of class C, reached from t_i firing, is a fragment of the network Nt_{i,c_p} characterizing the firing date of t_i (from a previous class C_p).

During the construction of a temporal network $Nt_{j,c}$ from the class C, some constraint $C_{k,l}$ between two nodes x_k and x_l can become more restricted than its initial value in the network Nc of C. This means that transition t_j can only be fired from the states of C for which variables x_k and x_l verify this new, more restricted constraint $C_{k,l}$. This defines a sub-class Cr^j restricted in order to permit the firing of t_j.

Let $C = (M, Nc)$ be a class, let t_j be a transition which can be fired from C and whose firing date is delimited by the $Nt_{j,c}$. If $Nt_{j,c} \cap Nc \neq Nc$ (see definition 4) then it is necessary to define a restricted class.

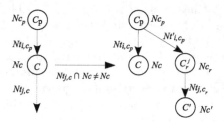

Fig. 5. Restricted class Cr of class C

Definition 10. *The restricted class $Cr^j = (M_r, Nc_r)$ of class C is defined by*

- $M_r = M$,
- Nc_r *is the network $Nt_{j,c} \cap Nc$ after application of Floyd-Warshall*

The class Cr^j characterizes the states from where the transition t_j is firable; these states have been reached by the firing of t_i (preceding t_j in the sequence $\tau = t_1; ...; t_i; t_j$) whose firing date has to be consistent with Cr^j (fig. 5). This means that this date is delimited by the network $Nt'_{i,c_p} = Nt_{i,c_p} \cap Nc_r$, which, after a new application of Floyd-Warshall may be such that $Nt'_{i,c_p} \cap Nc_p \neq Nc_p$ and require so a restricted class C^i_{pr} for C_p and so on.

3.6   Equivalent Classes

Definition 11. *Two classes $C = (M, Nc)$ and $C' = (M', Nc')$, differing from the initial class C_0, with $Nc = (X, C)$ and $Nc' = (X', C')$ are equivalent if:*

1. *they have the same marking,* $M = M'$,
2. *there exists a bijection* τ *between the elements of* X *and* X' *such that*
   - $x_k^{'ok} = \tau(x_i^{oi})$ *implies* $k = i$ *(the variables are firing dates of the same transition)*
   - *if* $x_i' = \tau(x_i)$ *and* $x_j' = \tau(x_j)$ *then* C_{ij}' *(constraint between* x_i' *and* x_j'*) is equal to* C_{ij} *(constraint between* x_i *and* x_j*)*

Definition 12. *A class* $C = (M, Nc)$ *is equivalent to the initial class* $C_0 = (M_0, x_0)$ *if:*

1. *they have the same marking,* $M = M_0$,
2. *the set of variables* X *of* Nc *is a singleton,* $X = \{x_k\}$ *(no past memory).*

In the above definition, the firing of transition t_k leads the system back to the initial marking M_0 and enables all transitions at this marking. That is why it is equivalent to the *beginning of the world*.

3.7   Graph of Classes

The graph of classes is composed by classes $C = (M, \ Nc)$ (def. 7 and 8) and the arcs connecting them. An arc (C, C') is labeled by the transition t (leading from C to C') and $Nt_{i,c}$ delimiting this firing (section 3.3). The graph generator (in Java) can be downloaded at `http://www.irit.fr/~Janette.Cardoso/feria` as well the algorithm description (`AlgoGraphC.pdf`) and the manual (`readme`).

3.8   Sequence Characterization

The temporal network of a sequence $\sigma = t_1; ...; t_i; t_j; ...; t_n$ from a class C is given by the union (see definition 5) of the temporal networks delimiting each transition firing in σ: $Nt_\sigma = Nt_{1,c} \cup ... Nt_{i,ci} \cup Nt_{j,cj} \cup ... \cup Nt_{n,cn}$.

It must be pointed out that this expression is consistent with the union of simple temporal networks because by construction $Nt_{i,ci} \cap C_j = C_j$, $Nt_{j,cj} \cap C_j = C_j$ and $Nt_{i,ci} \cap Nt_{j,cj} = C_j$. This means that the constraints between variables belonging both to $Nt_{i,ci}$ and $Nt_{j,cj}$ are equal, they are those of C_j.

A same sequence σ can be associated with more than one path in the graph of classes. A particular case appear when $\sigma = t_1; ...; t_i$ and the firing of last transition t_i leads to a class C and also to its restricted class Cr. It means that Cr was created in such a way that another transition t_j can be fired after t_i. Two network are obtained, N_σ^1 leading to C and N_σ^2 leading to Cr, but $N_\sigma^1 \supseteq N_\sigma^2$ and so the network characterizing σ is N_σ^1 (see the example in section 4.2).

4   Example

4.1   Construction of the Graph of Classes

Let us consider the example of figure 1, presenting a deadlock and also infinite sequences. Table 1 shows the classes (marking and temporal network Nc) obtained with the proposed approach and figure 6 represents the graph of classes.

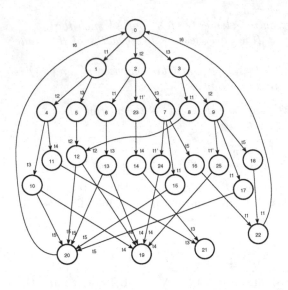

Temporal networks $Nt_{i,k}$ of t_i from C_k

$Nt_{1,0}.(x_0, x_1)=[0\ 0], \qquad Nt_{2,0}.(x_0, x_2)=[0\ 0]$
$Nt_{3,0}.(x_0, x_3)=[0\ 0]$
$Nt_{2,1}.(x_0, x_1)=(x_0, x_2)=(x_1, x_2)=[0\ 0]$
$Nt_{3,1}.(x_0, x_1)=(x_0, x_3)=(x_1, x_3)=[0\ 0]$
$Nt_{1,2}.(x_0, x_2)=[0\ 0],(x_0, x_1)=(x_2, x_1)=[0\ 3]$
$Nt_{3,2}.(x_0, x_2)=[0\ 0],(x_0, x_3)=(x_2, x_3)=[0\ 3]$
$Nt_{1,3}.(x_0, x_3)=(x_0, x_1)=(x_3, x_1)=[0\ 0]$
$Nt_{2,3}.(x_0, x_3)=(x_0, x_2)=(x_3, x_2)=[0\ 0]$
$Nt_{3,4}.(x_0, x_2)=[0\ 0],(x_0, x_3)=(x_2, x_3)=[0\ 2]$
$Nt_{4,4}.(x_0, x_2)=[0\ 0],(x_0, x_4)=(x_2, x_4)=[1\ 2]$
$Nt_{2,5}.(x_0, x_3)=(x_0, x_2)=(x_3, x_2)=[0\ 0]$
$Nt_{3,6}.(x_0, x_1)=(x_0, x_3)=[0\ 3],(x_1, x_3)=[0\ 2]$
$Nt_{1,7}.(x_0, x_3)=(x_0, x_1)=[0\ 3],(x_3, x_1)=[0\ 2]$
$Nt_{5,7}.(x_0, x_3)=(x_0, x_5)=[0\ 3],(x_3, x_5)=[0\ 2]$
$Nt_{2,8}.(x_0, x_1)=(x_0, x_2)=(x_1, x_2)=[0\ 0]$
$Nt_{1,9}.(x_0, x_2)=[0\ 0],(x_0, x_1)=(x_2, x_1)=[0\ 2]$
$Nt_{5,9}.(x_0, x_2)=[0\ 0],(x_0, x_5)=(x_2, x_5)=[0\ 2]$
$Nt_{4,10}.(x_2, x_3)=(x_3, x_4)=[0\ 2],(x_2, x_4)=[1\ 2]$
$Nt_{5,10}.(x_2, x_3)=(x_0, x_1)=(x_2, x_1)=[0\ 2]$
$Nt_{4,12}.(x_2, x_4)=[1\ 2], \qquad Nt_{5,12}.(x_2, x_5)=[0\ 2]$
$Nt_{4,13}.(x_1, x_3)=(x_3, x_4)=[0\ 2],(x_1, x_4)=[1\ 2]$
$Nt_{5,13}.(x_1, x_3)=(x_1, x_5)=(x_3, x_5)=[0\ 2]$
$Nt_{3,14}.(x_0, x_4)=(x_0, x_3)=[1\ 3],(x_4, x_3)=[0\ 2]$
$Nt_{5,15}.(x_3, x_1)=(x_3, x_5)=(x_1, x_5)=[0\ 2]$
$Nt_{1,16}.(x_0, x_5)=(x_0, x_1)=(x_5, x_1)=[0\ 3]$
$Nt_{5,17}.(x_2, x_1)=(x_2, x_5)=(x_1, x_5)=[0\ 2]$
$Nt_{1,18}.(x_0, x_5)=[0\ 2],(x_0, x_1)=(x_5, x_1)=[0\ 3]$
$Nt_{6,20}.(x_5, x_6)=[0\ 2]\ Nt_{6,22}.(x_1, x_6)=[0\ 2]$
$Nt'_{1,2}.(x_0, x_2)=[0\ 0],(x_0, x_1)=(x_2, x_1)=[0\ 2]$
$Nt_{4,24}.(x_3, x_1)=[0\ 1],(x_3, x_4)=(x_1, x_4)=[1\ 2]$
$Nt'_{1,7}.(x_0, x_3)=(x_0, x_1)=[0\ 3],(x_3, x_1)=[0\ 1]$
$Nt_{4,25}.(x_2, x_1)=[0\ 1],(x_2, x_4)=(x_1, x_4)=[1\ 2]$
$Nt'_{1,9}.(x_0, x_2)=[0\ 0],(x_0, x_1)=(x_2, x_1)=[0\ 1]$

Fig. 6. a)Graph of classes preserving firing constraints, b) Temporal networks on arcs

Let us consider the sequence $\sigma_1 = t_2; t_3; t_1; t_4$ in the graph of figure 6, leading to a deadlock $M_{19} = p_6 p_7$. The initial class C_0 (see table 1) is defined by the initial marking $M_0 = p_1 p_2 p_3$ and the network Nc_0 composed by a unique node x_0 corresponding to an initial event creating the tokens of the initial marking. It represents the time origin.

Considering the firing of t_2 (at the date x_2) from C_0, the final temporal network $Nt_{2,0}$ delimiting this firing is represented by the dotted arc in fig. 3.b (as explained in section 3.3. The network Nc_2 of the new class C_2, reached with t_2 firing (obtained from $Nt_{2,0}$) is also represented by the dotted arc in fig. 3.b.

Transitions t_1 and t_3 are enabled at C_2. Let us consider the firing of t_3. The network $Nt_{3,2}$ delimiting t_3 firing (fig. 7.a) brings the system from the class C_2 to class C_7. The networks Nc_2 and Nc_7 are represented in figure 7.a respectively by C_{02} (the bold arc) and C_{03} (the dotted arc).

Let us consider now the firing of t_1 from C_7. The minimal and complete network $Nt_{1,7}$ delimiting the firing date x_1 is given by fig. 7.b. The reached class is C_{15} (bold dotted arc in fig. 7.b).

The firing of t_4 from C_{15} is defined by $Nt_{4,15}$ delimiting the firing date x_4(fig. 7.c). The minimal network $Nt_{4,15}$ has the constraint $C'_{31} = [0\ 1]$ (on arc (x_3, x_1)), that is a reduced value in relation to that defined by Nc_{15} ($C_{31} = [0\ 2]$ or $0 \le x_1 - x_3 \le 2$) of class C_{15}. So, t_4 can be fired after t_1 only if t_1 is fired no more than $[0\ 1]$ unities of time after t_3. The arc (x_3, x_1) defines a *restricted class* C_{24}, with $M_{24} = M_{15}$, and Nc_{24} given by $C'_{31} = [0\ 1]$. This class gathers all the states reached from the initial state by the firing of the sequence t_2 ; t_3 ; t_1 *knowing that transition t_4 can be fired.*

Table 1. Classes preserving the constraints

Class	Marking	Constraints Nc	Class	Marking	Constraints Nc
C_0	$p_1p_2p_3$	x_0	C_{13}	$p_4p_5p_6$	$0 \leq x_3 - x_1 \leq 2$
C_1	$p_2p_3p_4$	$0 \leq x_1 - x_0 \leq 0$	C_{14}	p_3p_7	$1 \leq x_4 - x_0 \leq 3$
C_2	$p_1p_3p_5$	$0 \leq x_2 - x_0 \leq 0$	C_{15}	$p_4p_5p_6$	$0 \leq x_1 - x_3 \leq 2$
C_3	$p_1p_2p_6$	$0 \leq x_3 - x_0 \leq 0$	C_{16}	p_1p_7	$0 \leq x_5 - x_0 \leq 3$
C_4	$p_3p_4p_5$	$0 \leq x_2 - x_0 \leq 0$	C_{17}	$p_4p_5p_6$	$0 \leq x_1 - x_2 \leq 2$
C_5	$p_2p_4p_6$	$0 \leq x_3 - x_0 \leq 0$	C_{18}	p_1p_7	$0 \leq x_5 - x_0 \leq 2$
C_6	$p_3p_4p_5$	$0 \leq x_1 - x_0 \leq 3$	C_{19}	p_6p_7	x_4
C_7	$p_1p_5p_6$	$0 \leq x_3 - x_0 \leq 3$	C_{20}	p_4p_7	x_5
C_8	$p_2p_4p_6$	$0 \leq x_1 - x_0 \leq 0$	C_{21}	p_6p_7	x_3
C_9	$p_1p_5p_6$	$0 \leq x_2 - x_0 \leq 0$	C_{22}	p_4p_7	x_1
C_{10}	$p_4p_5p_6$	$0 \leq x_3 - x_2 \leq 2$	C_{23}	$p_3p_4p_5$	$0 \leq x_1 - x_0 \leq 2$
C_{11}	p_3p_7	$1 \leq x_4 - x_0 \leq 2$	C_{24}	$p_4p_5p_6$	$0 \leq x_1 - x_3 \leq 1$
C_{12}	$p_4p_5p_6$	x_2	C_{25}	$p_4p_5p_6$	$0 \leq x_1 - x_2 \leq 1$

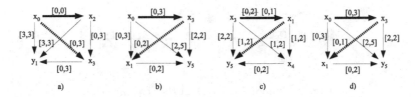

Fig. 7. Temporal networks $a)Nt_{3,2}$, $b)Nt_{1,7}$, $c)Nt_{4,15}$ and $d)Nt'_{1,7}$

Once the restricted class C_{24} was created, a new arc coming from the previous class C_7 to C_{24} must also be created, labeled by the temporal network delimiting the firing of t_1 (considering that transition t_4 can be effectively fired). This network is given by $Nt'_{1,7} = Nt_{1,7} \cap Nc_{24}$ (fig. 7.d). As $Nt_{3,2} \cap Nc_7 = Nc_{24}$, the backward propagation stops.

The class C_{15} is kept in the graph as well as the network $Nt_{1,7}$ labeling the arc (C_7, C_{15}), but there is no output arc from C_{15} labeled by t_4. Instead only the pair (C_{24}, t_4) is appended to the list of hanging nodes.

The firing of t_6 from classes C_{20} and C_{22} leads the system to a class C with $M = M_0$ and Nc given by x_6 (no past memory). Using definition 12, this class is equivalent to the initial class C_0.

4.2   Temporal Network of a Sequence

Let us consider the sequence $\sigma_1 = t_2; t_3; t_1; t_4$ whose temporal network (fig. 8) is obtained by the union of $Nt_{2,0}$, $Nt_{3,2}$, $Nt'_{1,7}$ et $Nt_{4,24}$. Some arcs are represented twice in order to point out that they belong to two networks delimiting firing dates. There is indeed only one value and one constraint. For example, as $Nt'_{1,7} \cap Nt_{4,24} = Nc_{24}$, the arc (x_3, x_1) belongs to two networks and is represented by two doted lines.

Let us now consider the sequence $\sigma_2 = t_2; t_3; t_1$. Two paths in the class graph and in consequence two networks are obtained: $N^1_{\sigma_2} = Nt_{2,0} \cup Nt_{3,2} \cup Nt_{1,7}$

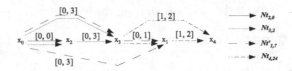

Fig. 8. Temporal network of the sequence σ_1

(leading to C_{15}) and $N^2_{\sigma_2} = Nt_{2,0} \cup Nt_{3,2} \cup Nt'_{1,7}$ (leading to C_{24}). But $N^1_{\sigma_2} \supseteq N^2_{\sigma_2}$, so the network characterizing σ_2 is given by $N^1_{\sigma_2}$.

The figure 9 shows the temporal network N_{σ_3} for the sequence $\sigma_3 = t_2; t_3; t_5; t_1; t_6; t_2; t_3$ where t_2 and t_3 fire twice in the sequence, and the second firings of t_2 and t_3 are represented by x_2^2 and x_3^2 respectively in the temporal network.

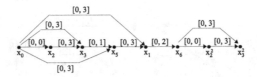

Fig. 9. Temporal network of the sequence σ_3

5   Related Work

Several approaches have been proposed to reduce the potentially infinite state spaces of real time systems to finite states spaces in order to analyze such systems [Me 85], [Be 91], [Yo 98], [Be 04]. All approaches are based on the equivalence of state classes. A first difference with these approaches is that, in the approach presented here, simple temporal network are used instead of geometrical region to deal with temporal information.

[Be 91] and [Be 04] have proposed the tool Tina, with two types of graph of classes, one is called Linear mode (W) and the other Atomic mode (A). They allow LTL and CTL property model checking, respectively. In the W mode, a class is given by its marking, the temporal domain of enabled transitions and the (non redundant) constraints existing between these transitions in the past. In the A mode, a class is given by its marking and a clock for each enabled transition (clock(t)=0 if t is newly enabled, otherwise it takes the previous value). Some classes in this mode correspond to a partition of the ones in W mode. Figure 10 represents both modes for the t-time Petri net of figure 1.

The objective of the A mode is different from the one presented here. In consequence, it differentiates the states for which there is a conflict between two transitions from the states where only one of both are firable. Let us consider classes C_{15} et C_{24} (fig. 6 and table 1). Transition t_5 can be fired from the states of C_{15} (whatever t_4 can or cannot be fired). But C_{24} (the restricted class of C_{15}) has been defined in order to characterize the temporal constraint that must be verified to fire t_4 and so t_5 does not appear as an output of this node. Using

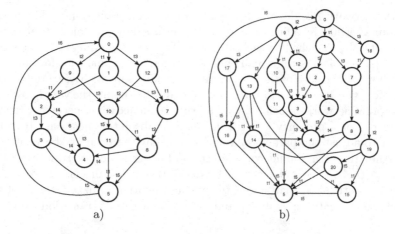

Fig. 10. Graph of classes in Tina : a) linear (W), b) atomic (A)

A mode[1], Class A14 in fig. 10.b gathers up the states where there is a conflict between t_4 et t_5, and A15 the ones where only t_5 can be fired.

Another difference appears in the way the past is memorized. For example, C_{20} and C_{22} correspond[2] to a same class W5 in fig. 10.a. The corresponding temporal constraint networks $Nc_{20} = x_5$ and $Nc_{22} = x_1$ allow to preserve the name of the transition which has enabled t_6. The memory of the past can goes back beyond the last event. For example C_{13} and C_{10} are different even if the last transition fired is t_3. Besides x_3, Nc_{13} has variable x_1 (t_1 has enabled t_4) and Nc_{10} has variable x_2 (t_2 has enabled t_4). But in mode W and also A, there is only one class (W3 and A3 respectively).

[Yo 98] is closer to our approach. There are two differences. In our approach, when a restricted class C_r is created, the initial class C is conserved instead of replacing it for a class that is complementary to C_r. Another difference is that in our approach a class does not keep all the constraints in the past, but only the ones that are necessary to characterize it, as proved in section 3.4.

6   Conclusion

The presented approach presents a graph of classes that allows obtaining the exact temporal constraints that have to be verified by each transition firing with respect to a given firing sequence. A state class in the graph is defined by a marking and a temporal network; an arc between two classes is labeled by a

---

[1] Correspondence between A and C: $W_2 = (A_2, A_{10}, A_{12})$, $W_6 = (A_6, A_{11})$, $W_8 = (A_8, A_{14}, A_{15})$, $W_{10} = (A_{13}, A_{17}, A_{19})$, $W_{11} = (A_{16}, A_{20})$, $W_{12} = A_{18}$. For $i = 0, 1, 3, 4, 5, 7, 9$, Wi=Ai.

[2] Correspondence between W and C mode: W2=(C_6, C_{23}, C_4); W3=(C_{13}, C_{10}); W4=(C_{19}, C_{21}); W5=(C_{20}, C_{22}); W6=(C_{14}, C_{11}); W7=(C_5, C_3); W8=(C_{15}, C_{24}, C_{12}, C_{17}, C_{25}); W10=(C_7, C_9); W11=(C_{16}, C_{18}); W0=C_0; W1=C_1; W9=C_2; W12=C_3.

temporal network Nt_i delimiting the firing date of a transition t_i. The temporal constraints verified by a firing sequence are obtained by the union of the temporal constraints Nt_i attached to each arc along the corresponding path on the class graph. This set of constraints can only be derived after some transformations and calculations in the case of the other graphs of classes in the literature (it was not their objective). It is important to underline another point: the very knowledge of the temporal network associated with a firing sequence is not necessary to answer whether or not a property is verified, but it is absolutely necessary to help the designer to adjust the parameter values such that the property be verified.

Further research should consider the following issues: i) translate this approach to the p-time Petri nets, ii) extend the graph of classes to deal with fuzzy time Petri nets, that associate with a transition a fuzzy interval of firing, allowing to evaluate a possibility and necessity degree of transition firing.

References

[Be 91]   B. Berthomieu, M. Diaz : Modeling and verification of time dependent systems using Time Petri nets *IEEE Trans. on Software Engineering*, Vol 17, No 3 p.259-273 1991.

[Be 04]   B. Berthomieu, P.O. Ribet, F. Vernadat : The tool TINA: construction of abstract state spaces for Petri nets and time Petri nets, IJPR, Vol.42, N°14, pp.2741-2756, 15 Juillet 2004.

[Ca 05]   J. Cardoso, S. Cousy, G.Juanole : Extending time Petri nets to fuzzy time Petri nets: definition of the graph of fuzzy state class, 16th IFAC World Congress, Juillet 2005, Prague.

[De 91]   R. Dechter, I.Meiri, J. Pearl : Temporal constraint networks, Artificial Intelligence, vol 49, p.61-91, 1991.

[Gh 04]   M. Ghallab, D. Nau, P. Traverso : Automated Planning Theory and practice, Morgan Kaufman, 2004 ISBN 1-55860-856-7.

[Me 85]   M. Menasche : PAREDE: an automated tool for the analysis of time Petri nets, International workshop on timed Petri nets Torino July 1985, p. 162-169

[PR 99]   B. Pradin-Chézalviel, R. Valette, L.A. Künzle, Scenario duration characterization of t-timed Petri nets using linear logic, PNPM'99, 8th Int. Workshop on Petri Nets and Performance Models, Zaragoza, Spain, pp.208-217, Sep. 6-10, 1999.

[Ri 01]   N. Rivière, B. Pradin-Chézalviel, R. Valette : Reachability and temporal conflicts in t-time Petri nets, 9th Int. Workshop on Petri Nets and Performance Models, IEEE PNPM'01, Aachen, Allemagne, pp.229-238, 11-14 Sep 2001.

[Ri 05]   N. Rivière, H. Demmou, R. Valette, M. Medjoudj, Symbolic temporal constraint analysis, an approach for verifying hybrid systems, 16th IFAC, Prague, July 2005.

[Sc 04]   V. Schastai, E.A. Lima, L.A. Knzle : Sequence analysis for time Petri nets, IFAC 7th Int. Workshop on Discrete Event Systems WODES'04, France.

[Yo 98]   T. Yoneda, H. Ryuba, CTL Model checking of time Petri nets using geometric regions, *IEICE Trans. inf. & Syst.*, Vol E81-D, No. 3, pp.297-396, 1998.

Comparison of Different Semantics for Time Petri Nets

B. Bérard[1], F. Cassez[2], S. Haddad[1], Didier Lime[3], and O.H. Roux[2]

[1] LAMSADE, Paris, France
{beatrice.berard, serge.haddad}@lamsade.dauphine.fr
[2] IRCCyN, Nantes, France
{Franck.Cassez, Olivier-h.Roux}@irccyn.ec-nantes.fr
[3] CISS, Aalbork, Denmark
Didier@cs.aau.dk

Abstract. In this paper we study the model of Time Petri Nets (TPNs) where a time interval is associated with the firing of a transition, but we extend it by considering general intervals rather than closed ones. A key feature of timed models is the memory policy, i.e. which timing informations are kept when a transition is fired. The original model selects an *intermediate* semantics where the transitions disabled after consuming the tokens, as well as the firing transition, are reinitialised. However this semantics is not appropriate for some applications. So we consider here two alternative semantics: the *atomic* and the *persistent atomic* ones. First we present relevant patterns of discrete event systems which show the interest of these semantics. Then we compare the expressiveness of the three semantics w.r.t. weak timed bisimilarity, establishing inclusion results in the general case. Furthermore we show that some inclusions are strict with unrestricted intervals even when nets are bounded. Then we focus on bounded TPNs with upper-closed intervals and we prove that the semantics are equivalent. Finally taking into account both the practical and the theoretical issues, we conclude that persistent atomic semantics should be preferred.

Keywords: Time Petri Nets, Timed Bisimilarity, Expressiveness.

1 Introduction

Since their introduction, Petri nets have been successfully applied for the design and analysis of discrete event systems. However with the development of critical systems, time has become a significant issue for their correctness. So numerous timed extensions have been proposed for Petri nets. These extensions can be roughly divided into three categories w.r.t. their application field:

- *Timed Petri nets* [17] include a duration associated with each transition in order to model for instance scheduling policies in production management;
- *Stochastic Petri nets* [2] include a probability distribution associated with each transition in order to evaluate the transient or steady-state behaviour of a system where duration of actions are obtained by statistical observations;

D.A. Peled and Y.-K. Tsay (Eds.): ATVA 2005, LNCS 3707, pp. 293–307, 2005.

– *Time Petri nets* [15] include a time interval associated with each transition (specifying the possible time elapsing before firing) in order to model systems which may evolve in a non deterministic way.

The latter model has a lot of alternatives: for instance time constraints may be associated to places [12] or to arcs [1,9], timed synchronisations may be added [10], etc. Here we stick to the original model for which significant theoretical developments [5,16,13,7] have been obtained leading to efficient verification tools on models of large systems [6,11]. Moreover when bounded this model can be translated into timed automata [8] which are also extensively studied with successful applications [3].

More precisely we consider a slight extension of TPNs where any kind of time interval can be associated with the firing of a transition instead of the closed ones in the original definition. Our work focuses on the impact of the memory policy on the expressiveness of the model. The memory policy specifies which timing informations are kept when a transition is fired. The original model selects an intermediate semantics meaning that the transitions disabled after consuming the tokens, and the firing transition, are reinitialised. Here we propose two alternative semantics: the atomic and the persistent atomic ones. We first present significant examples where these semantics are more appropriate than the original one. Then we compare the expressiveness of the three semantics w.r.t. weak timed bisimilarity which is the standard equivalence relation used for such comparisons. First we establish inclusion results in the general case. Furthermore we show that some inclusions are strict with unrestricted intervals even when nets are bounded. The key point of the previous result is the presence of non *upper-closed* intervals. Then we focus on bounded TPNs with upper-closed intervals and we establish that the semantics are equivalent. All our translations are optimal since the size of the produced net is linear w.r.t. the size of the emulated net.

The paper is organised as follows. Section 2 introduces the syntax and semantics of TPNs, timed transition systems and timed bisimilarity. Section 3 is devoted to the comparison between the different semantics for TPNs with general intervals both in the bounded and the unbounded case. In section 4, we prove that the three semantics are equivalent for bounded TPNs with upper-closed intervals. Finally we conclude in section 5.

2   Time Petri Nets

Notations. Let Σ be a finite set (or alphabet). Σ^* denotes the set of finite words on Σ. If $w = a_1 \cdots a_n$, the *length* of w denoted $|w|$, is n. We also use $\Sigma_\varepsilon = \Sigma \cup \{\varepsilon\}$ with $\varepsilon \notin \Sigma$, where ε is the empty word. B^A stands for the set of mappings from A to B. If A is finite and $|A| = n$, an element of B^A is also a vector in B^n. The usual operators $+, -, <$ and $=$ are used on vectors of A^n with $A = \mathbb{N}, \mathbb{Q}, \mathbb{R}$ and are the point-wise extensions of their counterparts in A. The set $\mathbb{B}$ denotes the boolean values $\{\mathsf{tt}, \mathsf{ff}\}$ and $\mathbb{R}_{\geq 0}$ denotes the set of non negative reals. A *valuation* ν over a set of variables X is an element of $\mathbb{R}_{\geq 0}^X$. For $\nu \in \mathbb{R}_{\geq 0}^X$

and $d \in \mathbb{R}_{\geq 0}$, $\nu + d$ denotes the valuation defined by $(\nu + d)(x) = \nu(x) + d$. $\mathbf{0}$ denotes the valuation s.t. $\forall x \in X, \nu(x) = 0$.

An interval I is a $\mathbb{Q}_{\geq 0}$-*interval* of $\mathbb{R}_{\geq 0}$ iff its left endpoint belongs to $\mathbb{Q}_{\geq 0}$ and its right endpoint belongs to $\mathbb{Q}_{\geq 0} \cup \{\infty\}$. We let $I^{\downarrow} = \{x \mid \exists y \in I \wedge y \geq x\}$ be the *downward closure* of I. We denote by $\mathcal{I}(\mathbb{Q}_{\geq 0})$ the set of $\mathbb{Q}_{\geq 0}$-intervals of $\mathbb{R}_{\geq 0}$.

2.1 Timed Transition Systems (TTS) and Weak Timed Bisimulation

Timed transition systems describe systems which combine discrete and continuous evolutions. We present here a standard version.

Definition 1 (Timed Transition Systems). *A* timed transition system *(TTS) over the set of actions Σ_ε is a tuple $S = (Q, q_0, \Sigma_\varepsilon, \longrightarrow)$ where:*

- *Q is a set of states,*
- *$q_0 \in Q$ is the initial state,*
- *Σ_ε is a finite set of actions disjoint from $\mathbb{R}_{\geq 0}$,*
- *$\longrightarrow \subseteq Q \times (\Sigma_\varepsilon \cup \mathbb{R}_{\geq 0}) \times Q$ is a set of edges. If $(q, e, q') \in \longrightarrow$, we also write $q \xrightarrow{e} q'$. For a transition $q \xrightarrow{d} q'$ with $d \in \mathbb{R}_{\geq 0}$, the value d represents a duration.*

We make the following common assumptions about TTS:

- TIME-DETERMINISM: if $q \xrightarrow{d} q'$ and $q \xrightarrow{d} q''$ with $d \in \mathbb{R}_{\geq 0}$, then $q' = q''$,
- 0-DELAY: $q \xrightarrow{0} q$,
- ADDITIVITY: if $q \xrightarrow{d} q'$ and $q' \xrightarrow{d'} q''$ with d, $d' \in \mathbb{R}_{\geq 0}$, then $q \xrightarrow{d+d'} q''$,
- CONTINUITY: if $q \xrightarrow{d} q'$, then for every d' and d'' in $\mathbb{R}_{\geq 0}$ such that $d = d' + d''$, there exists q'' such that $q \xrightarrow{d'} q'' \xrightarrow{d''} q'$.

Due to these properties, a *run* ρ of length $n \geq 0$ can be written as a finite sequence of transitions of the form

$$\rho = q_0 \xrightarrow{d_0} q_0' \xrightarrow{a_0} q_1 \xrightarrow{d_1} q_1' \xrightarrow{a_1} \cdots q_n \xrightarrow{d_n} q_n'$$

where discrete actions alternate with (possibly null) durations. We also write this run as $q \xrightarrow{d_0 a_0 \dots d_n} q'$. *Untimed*$(\rho)$ is the word of Σ^* obtained by concatenation of labels $a_0, \dots, a_{n-1}$ (remember that ε is the empty word). *Duration*$(\rho) = \sum_{i=0}^{n} d_i$.

It is well-known that the concept of weak timed bisimilarity is central among equivalence relations between systems since, for instance, two equivalent TTS are not distinguishable by formulas of most common timed arborescent temporal logics.

Let $S = (Q, q_0, \Sigma_\varepsilon, \longrightarrow)$ be a TTS. We define the relation $\longrightarrow\!\!\!\!\!\!\gg \, \subseteq Q \times (\Sigma \cup \mathbb{R}_{\geq 0}) \times Q$ by:

- $q \xrightarrow{d} q'$ iff there is a run $\rho = q \xrightarrow{\sigma} q'$ with $Untimed(\rho) = \varepsilon$ and $Duration(\rho) = d$,
- $q \xrightarrow{a} q'$ with $a \in \Sigma$ iff there is a run $\rho = q \xrightarrow{\sigma} q'$ with $Untimed(\rho) = a$ and $Duration(\rho) = 0$,

Definition 2 (Weak Timed Bisimilarity). *Let* $S_1 = (Q_1, q_0^1, \Sigma_\varepsilon, \longrightarrow_1)$ *and* $S_2 = (Q_2, q_0^2, \Sigma_\varepsilon, \longrightarrow_2)$ *be two TTS and* $\approx$ *be a binary relation over* $Q_1 \times Q_2$. *We write* $q \approx q'$ *for* $(q, q') \in \approx$. $\approx$ *is a* weak timed bisimulation relation *between* S_1 *and* S_2 *if:*

- $q_0^1 \approx q_0^2$;
- *if* $q_1 \xrightarrow{a}_1 q_1'$ *with* $a \in \Sigma \cup \mathbb{R}_{\geq 0}$ *and* $q_1 \approx q_2$ *then* $\exists q_2 \xrightarrow{a}_2 q_2'$ *such that* $q_1' \approx q_2'$; *conversely if* $q_2 \xrightarrow{a}_2 q_2'$ *with* $a \in \Sigma \cup \mathbb{R}_{\geq 0}$ *and* $q_1 \approx q_2$ *then* $\exists q_1 \xrightarrow{a}_1 q_1'$ *such that* $q_1' \approx q_2'$.

Two TTS S_1 *and* S_2 *are* weakly timed bisimilar *if there exists a weak timed bisimulation relation between* S_1 *and* S_2. *We write* $S_1 \approx_W S_2$ *in this case.*

Let $\mathcal{C}$ and $\mathcal{C}'$ be two classes of TTS. The next definition formalises the relative expressiveness of $\mathcal{C}$ and $\mathcal{C}'$.

Definition 3 (Expressiveness w.r.t. Weak Timed Bisimilarity). *The class* $\mathcal{C}$ *is* more expressive *than* $\mathcal{C}'$ *w.r.t. weak timed bisimilarity if for all* $B' \in \mathcal{C}'$ *there is a* $B \in \mathcal{C}$ *s.t.* $B \approx_W B'$. *We write* $\mathcal{C}' \leq_W \mathcal{C}$ *in this case. If moreover there is a* $B \in \mathcal{C}$ *s.t. there is no* $B' \in \mathcal{C}'$ *with* $B \approx_W B'$, *then* $\mathcal{C}' <_W \mathcal{C}$. *If both* $\mathcal{C}' \leq_W \mathcal{C}$ *and* $\mathcal{C} \leq_W \mathcal{C}'$ *then* $\mathcal{C}$ *and* $\mathcal{C}'$ *are equally expressive w.r.t. weak timed bisimilarity, and we write* $\mathcal{C} \approx_W \mathcal{C}'$.

2.2   Time Petri Nets

Time Petri Nets (TPN) were introduced in [15] and extend Petri Nets with timing constraints on the firings of transitions. In a TPN, a time interval is associated with each transition. An implicit clock can then be associated with each enabled transition, and gives the elapsed time since it was last enabled. An enabled transition can be fired if its clock value belongs to the interval of the transition. Furthermore, time cannot progress if time elapsing would result in leaving the interval of a transition. The following definitions formalise these principles.

Definition 4 (Labeled Time Petri Net). *A Labeled Time Petri Net* $\mathcal{N}$ *is a tuple* $(P, T, \Sigma_\varepsilon, {}^\bullet(.), (.)^\bullet, M_0, \Lambda, I)$ *where:*

- P *is a finite set of* places;
- T *is a finite set of* transitions *with* $P \cap T = \emptyset$;
- ${}^\bullet(.) \in (\mathbb{N}^P)^T$ *is the* backward *incidence mapping;* $(.)^\bullet \in (\mathbb{N}^P)^T$ *is the* forward *incidence mapping;*
- $M_0 \in \mathbb{N}^P$ *is the* initial *marking;*
- $\Lambda : T \to \Sigma_\varepsilon$ *is the* labeling function;
- $I : T \to \mathcal{I}(\mathbb{Q}_{\geq 0})$ *associates with each transition a* firing interval;

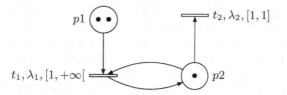

Fig. 1. An example of TPN

We also use $^\bullet t$ (resp. $t^\bullet$) to denote the set of places $^\bullet t = \{p \in P \mid {}^\bullet t(p) > 0\}$ (resp. $t^\bullet = \{p \in P \mid t^\bullet(p) > 0\}$) as it is common in the literature[1].

The net of figure 1 illustrates the graphical representation of a TPN. Each transition is represented with its label and its interval. For instance transition t_1 has label λ_1 and interval $[1, \infty[$.

Semantics of Time Petri Nets. The semantics of TPNs is given in terms of TTS. A *marking* M of a TPN is a mapping in $\mathbb{N}^P$ and $M(p)$ is the number of tokens in place p. A transition t is *enabled* in a marking M iff $M \geq {}^\bullet t$. We denote by $En(M)$ the set of enabled transitions in M. To decide whether a transition t can be fired, we need to know for how long it has been enabled: if this amount of time lies within the interval $I(t)$, t can actually be fired, otherwise it cannot. On the other hand time can progress only if the enabling duration still belongs to the downward closure of the interval associated with an enabled transition. Let $\nu \in (\mathbb{R}_{\geq 0})^{En(M)}$ be a *valuation* such that each value $\nu(t)$ is the time elapsed since transition t was last enabled. A *configuration* of the TPN $\mathcal{N}$ is a pair (M, ν). An *admissible configuration* of a TPN is a configuration (M, ν) s.t. $\forall t \in En(M), \nu(t) \in I(t)^{\downarrow}$. We let $ADM(\mathcal{N})$ be the set of admissible markings. When defining the semantics of a TPN, three kinds of policies must be fixed.

The choice policy concerns the choice of the next event to be fired (scheduled). For TPNs (and also timed automata), this choice is non deterministic (possible alternatives use priorities, probabilities, etc.).

The service policy concerns the possibility of simultaneous instances of a same event to occur. In the context of Petri nets, this is formalised by the enabling *degree* of a transition. Here we adopt the *single-server policy* (at most one instance of a firing per transition in every state). Our results could be extended to the multiple server at the price of intricate notations.

The memory policy concerns the updating of timing informations when a discrete step occurs. The key issue in the semantics is to define when to reset the clock measuring the time since a transition was last enabled. This can only happen when a transition is fired. We let $\uparrow enabled(t', M, t) \in \mathbb{B}$ be true if t' is *newly enabled* by the firing of transition t from marking M, and false otherwise.

---

[1] Whether $^\bullet t$ (resp. $t^\bullet$) stands for a vector of $(\mathbb{N}^P)^T$ or a subset of P will be unambiguously defined by the context.

Let M be a marking and $t \in En(M)$. The firing of t leads to a new marking $M' = M - {}^\bullet t + t^\bullet$. Three semantics are possible:

I: The *intermediate* semantics (I) considers that the firing of a transition is performed in two steps: consuming the input tokens in ${}^\bullet t$, and then producing output tokens in $t^\bullet$. The fact that a transition t' is newly enabled on the firing of a transition $t \neq t'$ is determined w.r.t. the intermediate marking $M - {}^\bullet t$. When a transition t is fired it is newly enabled whatever the intermediate marking. We denote by $\uparrow enabled_I(t', M, t)$ the newly enabled predicate in this case. This mapping is defined by:

$$\uparrow enabled_I(t', M, t) = (t' \in En(M - {}^\bullet t + t^\bullet) \\ \wedge \left(t' \notin En(M - {}^\bullet t) \vee (t = t') \right) \tag{1}$$

A: The *atomic semantics* considers that the firing of a transition is obtained by an atomic step. The corresponding mapping $\uparrow enabled_A(t', M, t)$ is defined by:

$$\uparrow enabled_A(t', M, t) = (t' \in En(M - {}^\bullet t + t^\bullet)) \wedge \left(t' \notin En(M) \vee (t = t') \right) \tag{2}$$

PA: The *persistent atomic semantics* considers that the firing of a transition is also obtained by an atomic step. The difference with the A semantics in only on the value of $\uparrow enabled_A(t', M, t)$ when $t = t'$. The fired transition here is handled as any other one:

$$\uparrow enabled_{PA}(t', M, t) = t' \in En(M - {}^\bullet t + t^\bullet) \wedge (t' \notin En(M)) \tag{3}$$

Note that we have the relation: $(3) \Rightarrow (2) \Rightarrow (1)$ but as we shall see on the example this does not imply any inclusion relation between the different behaviours. We now define the semantics of a TPN, which is parameterised by the choice of the $\uparrow enabled$ predicate.

Definition 5 (Semantics of TPN). *Let $s \in \{I, A, PA\}$. The s-semantics of a TPN $\mathcal{N} = (P, T, \Sigma_\varepsilon, {}^\bullet(.), (.)^\bullet, M_0, \Lambda, I)$ is a timed transition system $S_\mathcal{N} = (Q, q_0, T, \rightarrow)$ where: $Q = ADM(\mathcal{N})$, $q_0 = (M_0, \mathbf{0})$, and $\longrightarrow \in Q \times (\Sigma_\varepsilon \cup \mathbb{R}_{\geq 0}) \times Q$ consists of the discrete and continuous transition relations:*

- $\forall (M, \nu) \in ADM(\mathcal{N}), \forall t \in En(M)$ *s.t.* $\nu(t) \in I(t)$
  the discrete transition relation is defined by:
  $(M, \nu) \xrightarrow{\Lambda(t)} (M - {}^\bullet t + t^\bullet, \nu')$ *where* $\forall t \in En(M - {}^\bullet t + t^\bullet)$,
  $$\nu'(t) = \begin{cases} 0 & \text{if } \uparrow enabled_s(t', M, t), \\ \nu(t) & \text{otherwise.} \end{cases}$$
- $\forall (M, \nu) \in ADM(\mathcal{N}), \forall d \in \mathbb{R}_{\geq 0}$, *s.t.* $\forall t \in En(M), \nu(t) + d \in I(t)^\downarrow$, *the continuous transition relation is defined by:* $(M, \nu) \xrightarrow{d} (M, \nu + d)$

We simply write $(M, \nu) \xrightarrow{w}$ to emphasise that a sequence of transitions w can be fired in $S_\mathcal{N}$ from (M, ν). If $Duration(w) = 0$ we say that w is an *instantaneous firing sequence*. The set of *reachable markings* of $\mathcal{N}$ is $\mathsf{Reach}(\mathcal{N}) = \{M \in$

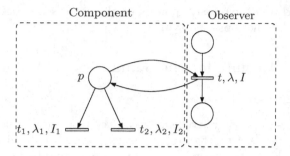

Fig. 2. A case where PA or A are more convenient than I: observation of a component

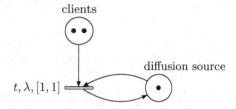

Fig. 3. A case where PA is more convenient than A and I: instantaneous multicast

$\mathbb{N}^P \mid \exists (M, \nu) \mid (M_0, \mathbf{0}) \xrightarrow{w} (M, \nu)\}$. A net is bounded iff there exists an integer B such that $\forall M \in \mathsf{Reach}(\mathcal{N}), \forall p \in P, M(p) \leq B$.

We illustrate the different semantics on the example of fig. 1. $(M_0, \mathbf{0}) \xrightarrow{1t_1 t_1}$ is a run for the PA semantics but not for the other ones since the second firing of t_1 should imply a delay of at least 1 time unit. $(M_0, \mathbf{0}) \xrightarrow{1t_1 t_2}$ is a run for the PA and A semantics but not for the I semantics since as t_1 consumes (and produces again) the token in place p_2 this should imply a delay of at least 1 time unit before the firing of t_2. $(M_0, \mathbf{0}) \xrightarrow{1t_1 1t_2}$ is a run for for the I semantics but not for the other ones since after t_1 fires, t_2 is not newly enabled and time cannot elapse before it is either fired or disabled.

The intermediate semantics I, based on [4,5] is the most common one. However, we provide two significant patterns (among other ones) of discrete event systems where the other semantics are more appropriate. Consider the net of figure 2 which models a component whose state is checked by an observer in order to react (by firing transition t). Let us emphasise that this modeling by a loop is standard in the untimed context. This observation does not interfere with the behaviour of the component using A and PA semantics while the I semantics renitialises the delay of transitions t_1 and t_2.

The subnet of fig. 3 models clients waiting for some information to be produced by a source (in 1 time unit) and then sent to every client (in a negligible time). The two firings of t are performed at the same time only with the PA semantics.

The comparison of expressive powers of the three semantics has not been investigated and is the topic of our work.

3 Inclusion Results for the Semantics *I*, *A* and *PA*

3.1 Large Inclusion Results

We now establish inclusion relations between the three semantics for TPNs.

In order to alleviate the figures, transitions are filled in black when their firing interval is $[0, 0]$ and we omit their label when equal to ε.

Proposition 1. *Let $\mathcal{N}$ be a time Petri net with intermediate semantics. There exists a TPN $\overline{\mathcal{N}}$ with atomic semantics which is weakly timed bisimilar to $\mathcal{N}$. The size of $\overline{\mathcal{N}}$ is linear w.r.t. the size of $\mathcal{N}$. Furthermore if $\mathcal{N}$ is bounded then $\overline{\mathcal{N}}$ is bounded.*

Proof. The construction is quite easy. Let $T' \subseteq T$ be the subset of transitions which have at least one input place. The set of places of $\overline{\mathcal{N}}$ is obtained by adding to the set of places of $\mathcal{N}$ a new place for each transition t from $\mathcal{N}$: $\overline{P} = P \cup \{p_t \mid t \in T'\}$. The transitions of $T \setminus T'$ are unchanged. The transitions T' of $\mathcal{N}$ are duplicated in $\overline{\mathcal{N}}$: $\overline{T} = T'^+ \cup T'^- \cup (T \setminus T')$ and the construction follows Figure 4, from left to right.

We consider the equivalence relation $\mathcal{R}$ which contains all pairs $((M, \nu), (\overline{M}, \overline{\nu}))$ such that:

- for all $p \in P$, $M(p) = \overline{M}(p) + \Sigma_{t \in T'} t^\bullet(p).\overline{M}(p_t)$
- for all $t \in T \setminus T'$, $\nu(t) = \overline{\nu}(t)$ and for all $t \in T' \cap En(M)$, $\nu(t) = \overline{\nu}(t^-)$ if t^- is enabled in $\overline{M}$ and 0 otherwise. The latter case corresponds in $\mathcal{N}$ to a newly enabled transition.

To prove that $\mathcal{R}$ is a bisimulation, we first note that, with the definition above for markings, from any configuration $(\overline{M}, \overline{\nu})$, we can reach instantaneously a configuration $(\overline{M}_1, \overline{\nu}_1)$ such that $\overline{M}_1(p_t) = 0$ for all $t \in T'$, with the firing of a (possibly empty) sequence of transitions in T^+. Moreover, the relation between valuations implies that $(\overline{M}_1, \overline{\nu}_1)$ is still equivalent to (M, ν).

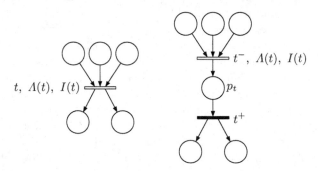

Fig. 4. From *I* to *A*

Consider now a pair $((M,\nu),(\overline{M},\overline{\nu})) \in \mathcal{R}$.

- if $(M,\nu) \xrightarrow{t} (M',\nu')$ with $t \in T'$, then from the remark above, we first fire a sequence from $\overline{M}$ to empty all places $p_{t'}$, leading instantaneously to $(\overline{M}_1,\overline{\nu}_1)$, which is equivalent to (M,ν). Then transition t^- can be fired from $(\overline{M}_1,\overline{\nu}_1)$, immediately followed by t^+, leading to $(\overline{M}',\overline{\nu}')$, where all places p_t are empty again. Moreover, the transitions newly enabled by t^+ in $\overline{\mathcal{N}}$ are exactly those which were newly enabled by t in $\mathcal{N}$, so that $(M',\nu')\mathcal{R}(\overline{M}',\overline{\nu}')$.
- Conversely, suppose that a transition is fired from $(\overline{M},\overline{\nu})$ in $\overline{\mathcal{N}}$. If the transition is some t^+, then the new configuration $(\overline{M}_1,\overline{\nu}_1)$ is still equivalent to (M,ν) (as above), thus no move at all is necessary in $\mathcal{N}$.
  If $(\overline{M},\overline{\nu}) \xrightarrow{t^-} (\overline{M}',\overline{\nu}')$, then t can be fired from (M,ν) and the resulting marking is, (M',ν'), equivalent to $(\overline{M}',\overline{\nu}')$.
- if $(M,\nu) \xrightarrow{d} (M,\nu+d)$, for some delay d, then again we have to apply the emptying sequence from $(\overline{M},\overline{\nu})$, to reach a configuration $(\overline{M}_1,\overline{\nu}_1)$ still equivalent to (M,ν), where time can elapse. The relation between ν and $\overline{\nu}_1$ implies that this is possible, leading to $(\overline{M}_1,\overline{\nu}_1+d)$.
- Conversely, if $(\overline{M},\overline{\nu}) \xrightarrow{d} (\overline{M},\overline{\nu}+d)$, then all places p_t are empty in $\overline{M}$, so that the move $(M,\nu) \xrightarrow{d} (M,\nu+d)$ is also possible in $\mathcal{N}$.

The cases for a transition $t \in T \setminus T'$ are straightforward. Thus $\mathcal{R}$ is a bisimulation. Assuming that $\mathcal{N}$ is bounded, the boundedness of $\overline{\mathcal{N}}$ is mainly due to the following observation: if a place p_t is unbounded in $\overline{\mathcal{N}}$ then any input place of t is unbounded in $\mathcal{N}$. □

Proposition 2. *Let $\mathcal{N}$ be a time Petri net with atomic semantics. There exists a TPN $\overline{\mathcal{N}}$ with persistent atomic semantics which is weakly timed bisimilar to $\mathcal{N}$. The size of $\overline{\mathcal{N}}$ is linear w.r.t. the size of $\mathcal{N}$. Furthermore if $\mathcal{N}$ is bounded then $\overline{\mathcal{N}}$ is bounded.*

Proof. Here again, the construction is simple. Note that the only difference between the two semantics concerns the question wether a transition t can newly enable itself. With atomic semantics, this is the case as soon as t is enabled in the new marking while with persistent atomic semantics, this is never possible. In order to ensure that a transition t will be newly enabled if it is enabled in the new marking, we add an input place En_t^+ and an output place En_t^- to the transition, with an instantaneous loop b_t leading back to En_t^+, once the transition has been fired. The construction is represented in Figure 5, again from left to right.

We consider the equivalence relation $\mathcal{R}$ which contains all pairs $((M,\nu),(\overline{M},\overline{\nu}))$ such that:

- $M(p) = \overline{M}(p)$ for all places p in P, and
- for a transition $t \in En(M)$, $\nu(t) = \overline{\nu}(t)$ if t is enabled in $\overline{M}$ and 0 otherwise. Again the latter case corresponds in $\mathcal{N}$ to a newly enabled transition.

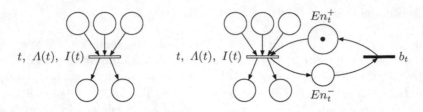

Fig. 5. From A to PA

Like in the previous proposition, the proof is mostly based on the fact that from any configuration $(\overline{M}, \overline{\nu})$, we can reach instantaneously a configuration $(\overline{M}_1, \overline{\nu}_1)$ such that $\overline{M}_1(En_t^+) = 1$ for all t, with the firing of a (possibly empty) sequence of transitions b_t, and again $(\overline{M}_1, \overline{\nu}_1)$ still equivalent to (M, ν). Furthermore the claim about boundedness is mainly due to the following invariants $\overline{M}(En_t^+) + \overline{M}(En_t^-) = 1$. □

3.2   Strict Inclusion

The next proposition shows that the expressive power of TPNs depends on the chosen semantics even in the bounded case.

Proposition 3. *There exists a bounded TPN $\mathcal{N}$ with persistent atomic semantics such that no TPN (even unbounded) with atomic semantics is bisimilar to $\mathcal{N}$.*

Proof. Consider the following bounded TPN with PA semantics composed by a single transition t labeled by ε: ⊏▭⊐ t, ε, $[0, 1[$

The (observable) behaviour of this net is simply to let time elapse without reaching 1. Suppose that there is a TPN $\mathcal{N}$ with atomic semantics bisimilar to this TPN and let d_{min} be the minimum of the non null upper bounds occuring in the intervals associated with the transitions of $\mathcal{N}$ and 0.5 (in fact any value less than 1 would be convenient).

There must be a sequence $(M_0, \nu_0) \xrightarrow{d_0 t_1 \dots t_k d_k} (M, \nu)$ with $\Sigma_{i=0}^{k} d_i = 1 - d_{min}/2$ and (M, ν) bisimilar to $(\emptyset, 1 - d_{min}/2)$.

From (M, ν), we fire or disable the transitions enabled at this configuration, which leads to a new configuration (M', ν') bisimilar to some $(\emptyset, 1 - \delta')$ with $0 < \delta' \leq d_{min}/2$. Now since (M', ν') is bimilar to $(\emptyset, 1 - \delta')$ there must be a sequence $(M', \nu') \xrightarrow{d'_0 t'_1 \dots t'_{k'} d'_{k'}}$ with $0 < \Sigma_{i=0}^{k'} d'_i < \delta'$.

Choose the first $d'_i > 0$ and let (M^*, ν^*) be the configuration reached before the duration d'_i. Since time may elapse in this state, all enabled transitions have a non null upper bound for their interval, hence these bounds are greater than or equal to d_{min}. Since the transitions have been enabled at or after configuration (M', ν'), we have $\forall t, \nu^*(t) \leq d_{min}/2 - \delta' < d_{min}/2$, thus $(M^*, \nu^*) \xrightarrow{d_{min}/2}$. But (M^*, ν^*) is bisimilar to $(\emptyset, 1 - \delta')$ which cannot let time elapse for a duration of $d_{min}/2$. This is a contradiction.

A similar proof could be developed with any interval $]a, b[$ or $[a, b[$ instead of $[0, 1]$. ☐

4 Equivalence Result for Bounded TPNs with Upper-Closed Intervals

Due to the strict inclusion established by proposition 3, we now restrict our study to bounded TPNs, with *upper-closed* intervals, *i.e.* with intervals $[a, b]$, $[a, \infty[$, $]a, b]$ or $]a, \infty[$.

Proposition 4. *Let $\mathcal{N}$ be a bounded TPN with upper-closed intervals and with persistent atomic semantics. There exists a bounded TPN $\overline{\mathcal{N}}$ with intermediate semantics which is weakly timed bisimilar to $\mathcal{N}$. The size of $\overline{\mathcal{N}}$ is linear w.r.t. the size of $\mathcal{N}$ and the logarithm of the bound.*

Proof. In this case, the construction of $\overline{\mathcal{N}}$ is more involved. Like above, we show how to simulate a transition t equipped with interval $[a, b]$, for $a \leq b$ (the other cases are similar). We first build a time subnet for t (Figure 6 below), to simulate time elapsing from the last time t was enabled, until reaching (and staying inside) interval $[a, b]$. The token is in place $start_t$ if the transition is enabled in the initial marking. The double arrow at the end indicates that the place end_t is both an input and an output place for the corresponding transition: time cannot progress. Clearly this part of the construction does not apply when the interval is not upper-closed.

Now, using the fact that the TPN is bounded, we consider its upper bound B and we associate with each place p a complementary place $\overline{p}$ such that for any reachable marking M, $M(\overline{p}) = B - M(p)$. Figure 7 represents a part of the subnet (on the right) for transition t (on the left), where $test_1$ is the beginning of the test step for what timing updates are required by the firing of t, and $Mutex$ ensures that the updates are done (instantaneously) before anything else, as explained further.

The remaining part of $\overline{\mathcal{N}}$ is devoted to these tests and updates for the other transitions from the original TPN, including t itself. Consider a given transition (say t_i), with again two input places p_1^i and p_2^i. The corresponding subnet consists of 4 modules, one for each case, depending on wether t_i can be fired or not before and after t. For this, two additional places are associated with t_i: E_{t_i}, which contains a token if t_i was enabled before the firing of t and NE_{t_i}

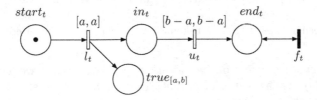

Fig. 6. Time subnet for interval $I(t) = [a, b]$ of transition t

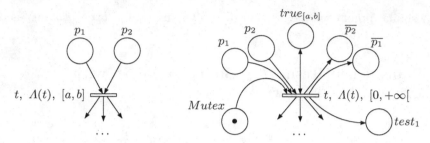

Fig. 7. From a transition in $\mathcal{N}$ to its translation in $\overline{\mathcal{N}}$

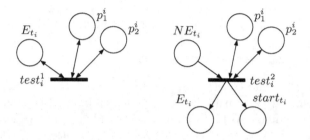

Fig. 8. Testing transition t_i: cases 1 and 2

its complementary place. If t_i is initially enabled then E_{t_i} is initially marked otherwise NE_{t_i} is marked. This group of 4 modules has a common input place $test_i$ and a common output place $test_{i+1}$, except for the last one where all outgoing transitions are linked to $Mutex$. These places, not shown in the figures, are introduced to obtain a sequential execution of the tests and updates.

Case 1: transition t_i is enabled both before and after firing t. To test this case, we use the simple module on the left of Figure 8, where E_{t_i} (test before t) and p_1^i and p_2^i (test after t) are input and output places.

Case 2: t_i is not enabled before but enabled after firing t. The module is very similar to the previous one and is on the right of Figure 8. Note that, in this case only, because of the PA semantics, there must be a reset on the valuation of the transition, which explains why the initial place $start_{t_i}$ of the time module for t_i is an output place.

Case 3: t_i is enabled neither before nor after firing t. To test this, we must find an input place of t_i, where the current number of tokens disable t_i. Here is the point where the boundedness hypothesis is required. In order to perform this test, we check whether $B - {}^\bullet t_i(p) + 1$ tokens can be removed from a complementary place $\overline{p}$.

Case 4: t_i is enabled before but not after firing t. In this case, we have a module (see Figure 10) similar to the one above, except that we must also test for all the different configurations of the time subnet corresponding to t_i, to disable the transitions by removing the tokens.

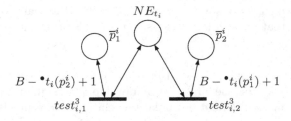

$$NE_{t_i}$$

$$\overline{p}_1^i \qquad \qquad \overline{p}_2^i$$

$$B - {}^\bullet t_i(p_2^i) + 1 \qquad\qquad B - {}^\bullet t_i(p_1^i) + 1$$

$$test_{i,1}^3 \qquad\qquad\qquad test_{i,2}^3$$

Fig. 9. Testing transition t_i: case 3

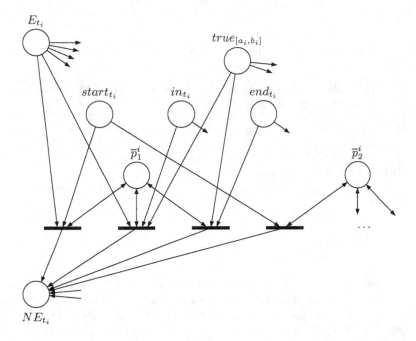

Fig. 10. Testing transition t_i: case 4 (names of transitions are omitted)

It can be seen in Figure 10 that there is a transition for each pair $(\overline{p}, state)$, where p is an input place of t_i and $state$ may be either the place $start_{t_i}$, the pair of places $(in_{t_i}, \, true_{[a_i,b_i]})$ or the pair $(end_{t_i}, \, true_{[a_i,b_i]})$. Like above, an edge from $\overline{p}$ to a transition must be labeled with $B - {}^\bullet t_i(p) + 1$ (which is omitted in the figure). Note that the number of states (here 3) depends on the kind of intervals but is bounded by a constant. Thus this construction is still linear w.r.t. the number of input arcs of t.

We consider the equivalence relation $\mathcal{R}$ containing all pairs $((M,\nu),(\overline{M},\overline{\nu}))$ such that

- M in $\mathcal{N}$ is obtained by projection: $M(p) = \overline{M}(p)$ for each place $p \in P$,
- for a transition t in T enabled by M: $\nu(t) = 0$ if the time subnet of t is empty, $\nu(t) = \overline{\nu}(l_t)$ if the place $start_t$ contains a token, $\nu(t) = a + \overline{\nu}(u_t)$

if the place in_t contains a token and $\nu(t) = b$ if the place end_t contains a token. Note that in both latter cases, $true_{[a,b]}$ also contains a token and the transition t can be fired in $\overline{\mathcal{N}}$.

Also note that if $\overline{M}(start_t) = 1$ and $\overline{\nu}(u_t) = a$, then by instantaneously firing u_t, transition t can also be fired. By a development similar to the previous ones, we can show that $\mathcal{R}$ is a bisimulation relation. More precisely, the proof is mainly based on emptying sequences from a configuration $(\overline{M}, \overline{\nu})$ of $\overline{\mathcal{N}}$: it is always possible to reach instantaneously a configuration $(\overline{M}_1, \overline{\nu}_1)$ such that the testing subnet is empty, with $(\overline{M}_1, \overline{\nu}_1)$ still equivalent to (M, ν). The details are omitted. $\qquad\qquad\square$

We conclude this section with the following table summarizing our results.

(Bounded) TPNs general intervals	I semantics	A semantics	PA semantics
I semantics		$\leq_W$	$<_W$
A semantics			$<_W$
Bounded TPNs upper-closed intervals	I semantics	A semantics	PA semantics
I semantics		$\approx_W$	$\approx_W$

5   Conclusion

Since the introduction of TPNs, numerous works have lead to verification algorithms, tool development and applications to real-time systems. In this paper, we investigated some questions relative to the expressiveness of three different semantics for TPNs. First, we presented some standard patterns of discrete event systems where the original semantics (i.e. the intermediate one) is not the most appropriate, thus showing that atomic and persistent atomics semantics could be interesting alternatives.

Then we undertook a theoretical analysis of the three semantics w.r.t. weak timed bisimilarity. We established a hierarchy between these semantics and proved that the PA semantics is strictly more expressive than the two other ones. Since the last result is due to non upper-closed intervals and is still valid for bounded nets, we focused our study on bounded nets with upper-closed intervals. In this last case, the three semantics are equivalent.

However, even in the restricted case we feel that PA semantics should be preferred to the other ones since the emulation of the other semantics by the PA semantics is natural whereas the reverse emulation is rather involved and yields a TPN whose readability is doubtful. Furthermore most verification techniques are based on the class graph construction which applies with the same complexity for these three semantics.

References

1. P. A. Abdulla and A. Nylén. Timed Petri nets and BQOs. In *ICATPN'01*, volume 2075 of *LNCS*, pages 53–72. Springer-Verlag, june 2001.
2. M. Ajmone Marsan and G. Balbo and G. Conte and S. Donatelli and G. Franceschinis. Modelling with Generalized Stochastic Petri Nets. Wiley Series in Parallel Computing, John Wiley and Sons, 1994, ISBN: 0-471-93059-8.
3. R. Alur and D. Dill. A theory of timed automata. *Theoretical Computer Science B*, 126:183–235, 1994.
4. T. Aura and J. Lilius. A causal semantics for time Petri nets. *Theoretical Computer Science*, 243(1–2):409–447, 2000.
5. B. Berthomieu and M. Diaz. Modeling and verification of time dependent systems using time Petri nets. *IEEE Transactions on Software Engineering*, 17(3):259–273, March 1991.
6. Bernard Berthomieu and Pierre-Olivier Ribet and François Vernadat. The tool TINA - Construction of Abstract State Spaces for Petri Nets and Time Petri Nets International Journal of Production Research, Vol.42, N°14, pp.2741-2756, 2004.
7. B. Berthomieu and F. Vernadat. State class constructions for branching analysis of time Petri nets. In *TACAS'2003*, volume 2619 of *LNCS*, pages 442–457, 2003.
8. Franck Cassez and Olivier H. Roux. Structural Translation of Time Petri Nets into Timed Automata. In Michael Huth, editor, *Workshop on Automated Verification of Critical Systems (AVoCS'04)*, Electronic Notes in Computer Science. Elsevier, August 2004.
9. D. de Frutos Escrig, V. Valero Ruiz, and O. Marroquín Alonso. Decidability of properties of timed-arc Petri nets. In *ICATPN'00*, Aarhus, Denmark, volume 1825 of *LNCS*, pages 187–206, june 2000.
10. M. Diaz and P. Senac. Time stream Petri nets: a model for timed multimedia information. In *ATPN'94*, volume 815 of *LNCS*, pages 219–238, 1994.
11. G. Gardey, D. Lime, and O. (H.) Roux. ROMÉO: A tool for Time Petri Nets Analysis, 2003. The tool can be freely downloaded from www.irccyn.ec-nantes.fr/irccyn/d/fr/equipes/TempsReel/logs.
12. W. Khansa, J.P. Denat, and S. Collart-Dutilleul. P-Time Petri Nets for manufacturing systems. In *WODES'96*, Scotland, pages 94–102, 1996.
13. J. Lilius. Efficient state space search for time Petri nets. *Electronic Notes in Theoretical Computer Science*, volume 18, 1999.
14. D. Lime and O. H. Roux. State class timed automaton of a time Petri net. In *PNPM'03*. IEEE Computer Society, September 2003.
15. P. M. Merlin. *A study of the recoverability of computing systems*. PhD thesis, University of California, Irvine, CA, 1974.
16. L. Popova. On time Petri nets. *Journal Information Processing and Cybernetics, EIK*, 27(4):227–244, 1991.
17. C. Ramchandani. *Analysis of asynchronous concurrent systems by timed Petri nets*. PhD thesis, Massachusetts Institute of Technology, Cambridge, MA, 1974.

Introducing Dynamic Properties with Past Temporal Operators in the B Refinement

Mouna Saad and Leila Jemni Ben Ayed

Faculté des Sciences de TUNIS,
Département des Sciences de l'Informatique
Fax. 0021671706698 – Tel. 00216706317
`mouna.saad@fst.rnu.tn, Leila.jemni@fsegt.rnu.tn`

Abstract. We are interested in specifying and verifying dynamic properties of reactive systems with the B method extended with propositional linear temporal logic PLTL. Commonly, specification of dynamic properties is done with pure future fragment of PLTL. However, the introduction of past operators enables the production of more natural formulation of a wide class of dynamic properties. In this paper, we show how the past fragment of PLTL, as well as the future fragment is preserved by the B refinement, and we present patterns of reformulation and the corresponding sufficient conditions to verify dynamic properties including past time operators by means of cooperation of theorem proving and model checking.

1 Introduction

To deal with reactive systems, Abrial [1] has proposed a variant of the B method: The B event based method [2]. It provides rigorous development formalism for reactive systems but its limitation relates to the type of properties concerned to express because only the invariants are considered which describes safety. Due to the fact that most properties of reactive systems are dynamic (liveness and temporal properties), several works have been interested in extending the B method [1] in order to express and verify such properties. For instance, in [3], Abrial and Mussat proposed an extension of the B method [2] to allow the description of dynamic properties with dynamic invariant and some modalities in the shape of linear temporal logic formulae(LTL) [18]. However, to verify such properties by means of theorem proving, the user must exhibit two decreasing functions, a variant and a loop invariant. These two functions are crucial to the automatisation of the proof strategy, but they aren't directly the concern of the specification, and in addition, they are quite difficult.

Another solution is to specify the dynamic properties with PLTL [15], and to use model checking technique for their verification. This solution offers the advantage of a possible and entire automatisation without requiring variant and loop invariant. Furthermore, its main inconveniences are related to its limitation to finite state systems in addition to the combinatorial explosion of the number of states to be checked. Two techniques have been proposed to avoid these drawbacks. The first one is modularity [11] [12], it uses the notion of refinement induced by the B method to

D.A. Peled and Y.-K. Tsay (Eds.): ATVA 2005, LNCS 3707, pp. 308–322, 2005.

model check properties in a modular way. The refinement of an abstract model by a concrete one induces the split of the concrete graph into subgraphs, and then the property is verified separately on each subgraph. The modular verification of a temporal property P consists, first, in computing the set of modules from abstract transition system, then verifying on each module if P is satisfied or not using the model checking technique, and finally, concluding under some conditions that P is satisfied if all the modules satisfy P. The second technique is reformulation [7, 8], it is based on refinement to use jointly proof and model checking. And because of most PLTL properties are preserved by refinement [8], the preservation of an abstract property P_1 that holds on an abstract system S_1 is used for proving that a property P_2 which refines P_1 holds on the system S_2 which refines the system S_1. The abstract property P_1 expressed in PLTL is verified with model checking technique because the abstract transition system S_1 has a small number of states. Then, after refinement, the reformulated property P_2 is verified with proof of some sufficient conditions associated to the reformulation pattern which is a couple of temporal operators of the abstract formula P_1 and the refined formula P_2. The temporal operators used in reformulation technique are limited to future tense operators and reformulation patterns proposed in [7] are couples of temporal operators ##' with #,#'∈ {O,U,◊}.

Our contribution in this paper consists in extending the reformulation technique developed for pure future PLTL with past temporal operators. It is well known that past time modalities do not increase expressiveness of PLTL [9]. This is why past operators have been viewed to be unnecessary for some time. However, many interesting dynamic properties are naturally formulated in a way that is not limited to the future evolution, but may refer to events in the past [13] and new results proved that LTL with past operators can be exponentially more succinct [14],[16]. For instance, to express that a grant may only occur if some request has been issued, we could write □ (grant⇒◆request), this property is not straightforward to express with future operators, but it may have a complicated equivalent pure future formula which is □¬ *grant*∨(¬*grant*) **U** request, expressing either there is no grant at all or there is no grant until the first request, when using translating methods [10].

Past temporal operators are being devoted increasing interest in requirement engineering and formal verification which could be automatic thanks to the NuSMV model checker [4], [17], [6].

To extend the reformulation technique to the past fragment of PLTL, firstly, we prove that temporal properties using PLTL past temporal operators are preserved by the B Refinement. Secondly, we propose some reformulation patterns to reformulate properties and we generate their sufficient conditions. The verification is then based on the verification with model checking technique of the abstract property and the verification with theorem proving technique of the sufficient conditions related to the past reformulation patterns used to reformulate properties. This paper is structured as follows. Section 2 recalls the steps of reformulation and some basic definitions. In section 3, we introduce the syntax and semantics of past temporal operators of PLTL, and we highlight the preservation of formulae of PLTL using past temporal operators by The B Refinement. In section 4, we give the past reformulation patterns that we have generated, we state reformulation patterns theorems and we give some proof. Finally we illustrate our approach through the example of robot cell.

2   Reformulation

Several works have been interested in extending the B method [1] in order to express and verify dynamic properties. Darlot and al [8] propose to specify the dynamic properties with PLTL, and to use model checking technique for their verification. This solution presents inconveniences related to its limitation to finite state systems in addition to the combinatorial explosion of the number of states to be checked. Reformulation [7] has been proposed to avoid these drawbacks. It is based on refinement to use jointly proof and model checking. And because of most PLTL properties are preserved by refinement [8], the preservation of an abstract property P_1 that holds on an abstract system S_1 is used for proving that a property P_2 which refines P_1 (by reformulation) holds on the system S_2 which refines the system S_1. The abstract property P_1 expressed in PLTL is verified with model checking technique because the abstract transition system S_1 has a small number of states. Then, after refinement, the reformulated property P_2 is verified with proof of some sufficient conditions associated to the reformulation pattern which is a couple of temporal operators of the abstract formula P_1 and the refined formula P_2. The temporal operators used in reformulation technique are limited to future tense operators and reformulation patterns proposed in [7] are couples of temporal operators ##' with $\#,\#' \in \{O, U, \Diamond\}$.

    In this section we give, at first, the steps of reformulation, then we give a set of basic definitions and a theorem [7]. We express the semantic of each B event system by a transition system. We will use, in the following, $s, s_0, s_1, s_2, \ldots$ which denotes states and V which is a set of variables $\{x1, \ldots, xn\}$ of type Dom(xi).

2.1   How to Reformulate Properties [7]

The B Refinement introduces some new details in the specification of abstract systems to get refined systems. Each PLTL property expressed on an abstract B event system should also be re expressed on the refined system. This process, similar to refinement of event systems, is called Reformulation when it concerns temporal properties. Each property is reformulated using a reformulation pattern which is a couple of temporal operators ##' of the abstract property P_1: $\Box(p_1 \Rightarrow \#q_1)$ and a reformulated property P_2 : $\Box(p_2 \Rightarrow \#'q_2)$ with $\#,\#' \in \{O, \Diamond, U\}$.

2.2   Reformulation Steps

The diagram in (Fig.1) shows different steps of the reformulation extended with past temporal operators. It consists on verifying that if a property P_1 holds on an abstract system TS_1, a property P_2 which refines P_1 (by reformulation) holds on the system TS_2 which refines the system S_1. Then P_1 is verified at each refinement step.

    1. The abstract property ϕ_1 is checked with model checker (as NuSMV) because the abstract system generally has a reduced number of states so there is no combinatorial explosion of states number.
    2. The abstract system TS_1 is refined by the system TS_2. The refinement is proved either with proof or model checking.

3. ϕ_1 is reformulated into ϕ_2, using one of the reformulation patterns.
4. ϕ_2 is verified by proof of the sufficient conditions corresponding to the used pattern.

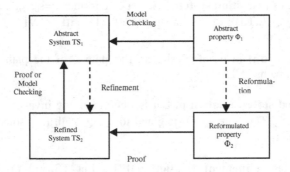

Fig. 1. Reformulation technique

In the following we give some basic definitions.

Definition1. Atomic propositions. The set APv $\overset{def}{=}$ {ap, ap_0, ap_1,...}is the set of atomic propositions over the set of variables V where ap is a formula $x_i=d_j$, with x_i $\in$ V and $d_j \in$ Dom(x_i).

Definition 2. State proposition. The set of state propositions over the set of variables V, written SPv $\overset{def}{=}$ {sp,sp_1,...}, is defined by:
  sp::= ap | sp$\vee$ sp| $\neg$ sp, where ap $\in$ APv.

Definition 3. Transition system. A labeled transition system, with set of variables V of a finite domain, is a 5-tuple TS = (Q,Q_0,L,T,l) where:
  -Q is a set of states;
  -Q_0 is set of initial states ($Q_0 \subseteq Q$) ;
  -L={a,a_1,...} is a set of transition labels which we call actions;
  -T$\in$ P(QxLxQ) is the transition relation;
  -l : Q $\rightarrow$P(SPv) is a function which associates to each state s$\in$ Q a decoration l(s) in the shape of state proposition giving the value of each variable as conjunctions

$\overset{n}{\underset{i=1}{\wedge}}$ ($x_i=d_j$), $d_j \in$ Dom(x_i).

We note $s_1 \overset{a}{\longrightarrow} s_2$ the transition (s_1,a,s_2).

Definition 4. A state satisfies a state proposition. Let $TS_1= (Q,Q_0,L,T,l)$ be a transition system over V. A state $s \in Q$ satisfies a state proposition $sp \in SPv$ (or sp holds on s, written $s \models sp$), iff $l(s) \Rightarrow sp$.

Definition 5. Path of transition system TS. Let us consider $\sigma=s_0,s_1,\ldots$ a sequence of states in $TS=(Q,Q_0,L,T,l)$. σ is a path of TS iff $\forall i.(i \geq 0 \Rightarrow \exists a.(a \in L \wedge (s_i \xrightarrow{\ a\ } s_{i+1} \in T)))$.

$\sigma(i)$ (written also (σ,i) in proof) designate the state s_i of the path σ and $\Sigma(TS)$ designate the set of paths of TS.

Definition 6. Glued states, relation μ. Let $I_{1,2}$ be the gluing invariant of transitions systems TS_1 and TS_2. The state $s_2 \in Q_2$ is glued to $s_1 \in Q_1$ with $I_{1,2}$, noted down $s_2 \mu s_1$, iff $(l_2(s_2) \wedge I_{1,2}) \Rightarrow l_1(s_1)$.

Definition 7. States refinement relation ρ [7] . Let $TS_1=(Q_1,Q_{01},L_1,T_1,l_1)$ and $TS_2=(Q_2,Q_{02},L_2,T_2,l_2)$ be two transition systems. Let $a \in L_1$. We consider the new transitions introduced by refinement process (those whose label is in $L_2 \backslash L_1$) as being non observable and they are called τ- transitions.

The relation $\rho \subseteq Q_2 x Q_1$ is the greatest binary relation included in μ and satisfying the following conditions:

1.Strict transition refinement: $(s_2 \rho s_1 \wedge s_2 \xrightarrow{\ a\ } s'_2 \in T_2) \Rightarrow \exists s'_1.(s_1 \xrightarrow{\ a\ } s'_1 \wedge s'_2 \rho s'_1)$.

2. *τ-Transitions refine skip:* $(s_2 \rho s_1 \wedge s_2 \xrightarrow{\ \tau\ } s'_2 \in T_2) \Rightarrow s'_2 \rho s_1$.

3. *Non introduction of deadlocks:* $(s_2 \rho s_1 \wedge s_2 \not\rightarrow_2) \Rightarrow (s_1 \not\rightarrow_1)$.

(We note $s \not\rightarrow_i$ when $\forall s', s''.(s \xrightarrow{\ a\ } s'') \in T_i \Rightarrow s \neq s'$)

4.Non τ-divergence: $\forall \sigma_2,k.(\sigma_2 \in \Sigma(TS_2) \wedge k \geq 0 \Rightarrow$

$$\exists a,k'.(a \in L_1 \wedge k' \geq k \wedge (\sigma_2,k'-1) \xrightarrow{\ a\ } (\sigma_2,k') \in T_2)).$$

5. *Preservation of the non determinism:*

$(s_1 \xrightarrow{\ a\ } s'_1 \wedge s_2 \rho s_1) \Rightarrow \exists s'_2,s''_2,s''_1.(s'_2 \rho s_1 \wedge s'_2 \xrightarrow{\ a\ }_2 s''_2 \in T_2 \wedge s_1 \xrightarrow{\ a\ } s''_1 \in T_1 \wedge s''_2 \rho s''_1)$

Each portion of path that contains τ-transitions must end by a transition labeled from L_1. That means that the new events should not take the control for ever in order to avoid the live locks. Besides that, τ-transitions shouldn't introduce deadlocks.

Definition 8. Refinement of TS [7]. The transition system $TS1=(Q_1,Q_{01},L_1,T_1,l_1)$ is refined by the transition system $TS_2=(Q_2,Q_{02},L_2,T_2,l_2)$ (written $TS_1 \subseteq_\rho TS_2$), iff $\forall s_2.(s_2 \in Q_{02} \Rightarrow \exists s_1 (s_1 \in Q_{01} \wedge s_2 \rho s_1))$.

Definition 9. Paths Refinement. Let TS_1 and TS_2 be two transition systems, $TS_1 \subseteq TS_2$, and σ_1 and σ_2 some respective paths of $\Sigma(TS_1)$ and $\Sigma(TS_2)$. σ_1 is refined by σ_2 (written $\sigma_1 \subseteq_\rho \sigma_2$) iff : $\forall i.(\sigma_2(i) \in Q_2 \Rightarrow \exists j.(\sigma_1(j) \in Q_1 \wedge \sigma_2(i) \rho \sigma_1(j)))$.

Lemma 1. Existence of an abstract path [7]: Let TS_1 and TS_2 be two transition systems such that $TS_1 \subseteq_p TS_2$, then $\forall\ s_2.(\ s_2 \in Q_2 \Rightarrow \exists s_1.(\ s_1 \in Q_1 \wedge s_2\ \rho\ s_1))$.

3   Refinement Preservation of PLTL Past Temporal Formulae

We present in this section semantics of past temporal operators, then we define the preservation validity of past temporal formulae and finally we prove their preservation by refinement.

3.1 Semantics of Past Temporal Operators (Definition 10)

Let σ be a sequence of execution, and ϕ, ψ two PLTL formulae. We define the PLTL past temporal operators at a state $i \geq 0$ of σ (written (σ, i) or $\sigma(i)$) as follows: We denote by $(\sigma, i) \models \phi$ the satisfaction of the formula ϕ in the state i of the sequence σ.

$(\sigma, i) \models \ominus \phi$ iff $i > 0 \wedge (\sigma, i-1) \models \phi$ (previous)

$(\sigma, i) \models \phi\, S\, \psi$ iff $\exists j.(j \leq i \wedge (\sigma, j) \models \psi$ and $\forall k.(i \geq k > j \Rightarrow (\sigma, k) \models \phi))$ (Since)

$(\sigma, i) \models \boxminus \phi$ iff $\forall j.(j \leq i \wedge (\sigma, j) \models \phi)$ (Always in the past)

$(\sigma, i) \models \Diamond \phi$ iff $\exists j.(j \leq i \wedge (\sigma, j) \models \phi)$ (Eventually in the past)

3.2 Preservation

We will show, in this section, how temporal properties are preserved through the refinement process. In fact, we will define the validity of past PLTL properties through the refinement process in order to reason with the abstract variables of abstract systems at refined levels.

Validity of state proposition through the gluing invariant [7] (Definition 11). Let TS_1 and TS_2 be two transition systems where TS_1 ((TS2 and I1,2 their gluing invariant. Let sp1 be a state proposition expressed with variables of TS1, and s2(Q2. s2 satisfies sp1 through I1,2 written $((s2, I1,2) \models_c sp1))$ iff $l2(s_2) \wedge I_{1,2} \Rightarrow sp_1$.

Validity of PLTL past temporal formulae by preservation (Definition 12). Let σ_2 be an execution path of TS_2 which refines TS_1 and $I_{1,2}$ their gluing invariant. Let ϕ and ψ be two temporal formulae expressing TS_1 properties. Past temporal formulae which are satisfied by preservation by σ_2 (written $((\sigma_2, j), I_{1,2}) \models_p \phi)$, are defined as following:

$((\sigma_2, j), I_{1,2}) \models_p sp,$ iff $((\sigma_2, j), I_{1,2}) \models_c sp$ and $sp \in SPv$

$((\sigma_2, j), I_{1,2}) \models_p \neg \phi,$ iff , it isn't true that $((\sigma_2, j), I_{1,2}) \models_p \phi,$

$((\sigma_2, j), I_{1,2}) \models_p \phi \vee \psi,$ iff $((\sigma_2, j), I_{1,2}) \models_p \phi,$ or $((\sigma_2, j), I_{1,2}) \models_p \psi$

$((\sigma_2, j), I_{1,2}) \models_p \ominus \phi,$ iff $\exists\, j'(0 \leq j' < j \wedge ((\sigma_2, j'), I_{1,2}) \models_p \phi)$

$((\sigma_2, j), I_{1,2}) \models_p \phi\, S\, \psi,$ iff $\exists\, j'.(0 \leq j' \leq j \wedge ((\sigma_2, j'), I_{1,2}) \models_p \psi$

$\wedge\ \forall j''.(j \geq j'' > j' \Rightarrow ((\sigma_2, j''), I_{1,2}) \models_p \phi))$

$((\sigma_2, j), I_{1,2}) \models_p \Diamond \phi,$ iff $\exists j'(0 \leq j' \leq j \wedge ((\sigma_2, j'),\ I_{1,2}) \models_p \phi)$

Satisfaction of PLTL past properties by TS (Definition 13). Given a PLTL past property ϕ, we say ϕ holds on TS (TS $\models \phi$) iff $\forall \sigma$ ($\sigma \in \Sigma(\text{TS}) \Rightarrow \sigma \models \phi$).

Refinement preservation of PLTL past formulae that hold on a path (Lemma 2).
Let ϕ be a PLTL past formula and σ_1 and σ_2 two paths of transition systems TS_1 and TS_2, where $\text{TS}_1 \subseteq_\rho \text{TS}_2$ and $I_{1,2}$ the gluing invariant of the transition systems, then
$\forall j,k(j\geq 0 \wedge k\geq 0 \Rightarrow (\sigma_2,k)\,\rho\,(\sigma_1,j) \wedge (\sigma_1,j) \models \phi \Rightarrow ((\sigma_2,k), I_{1,2}) \models_p \phi)$.

Asserting that if a formula ϕ holds on a state of the sequence σ_1, given that σ_2 refines σ_1, then ϕ modulo $I_{1,2}$ holds on a state of the sequence σ_2.

Proof: Consider the path σ_2 of TS_2 which refines a path σ_1 of TS_1, a, a',...,$a^{(n)}$ transition labels of TS_1 and τ the label of new transitions introduced by refinement, $\tau \in L_2 \backslash L_1$.

We will carry the proof inductively on the syntactic structure of formulae defined as: $\psi,\phi ::= \ominus \phi \mid \phi\,S\,\psi$, recall that this syntax is a basic set that allows to express PLTL past temporal formulae.

Let us prove that a $\ominus\phi$ formula is preserved by refinement if ϕ is preserved.

1. Let us consider a path $\sigma_1 = (\sigma_1,j\text{-}1) \xrightarrow{a} (\sigma_1,j) \wedge (\sigma_1,j) \models \ominus\phi,$: σ_2 refines σ_1, so:

1st case: $(\sigma_2,k\text{-}1) \xrightarrow{a} (\sigma_2,k) \in T_2$: then $(\sigma_2,k\text{-}1)\rho(\sigma_1,j\text{-}1)$, in addition $(\sigma_1,j) \models \ominus\phi$, that way $(\sigma_1,j\text{-}1) \models \phi$, and we have as hypothesis that ϕ is preserved so $((\sigma_2,k\text{-}1),I_{1,2}) \models_p \phi$. According to the first refinement clause, $(\sigma_2,k\text{-}1)\rho(\sigma_1,j\text{-}1) \wedge (\sigma_2,k\text{-}1)) \xrightarrow{a} (\sigma_2,k)$ $\Rightarrow \exists S'_1.((\sigma_1,j\text{-}1) \xrightarrow{a} S'_1 \in T_1$ $\wedge (\sigma_2,k)\rho S'_1)$ so, $S'_1 = (\sigma_1,j)$ (according to $\ominus\phi$ (definition 10)) and $(\sigma_2,k)\rho(\sigma_1,j)$, and we know that $((\sigma_2,k\text{-}1),I_{1,2}) \models_p\phi$, so, $((\sigma_2,k),I_{1,2}) \models_p\ominus\phi$ according to definition 12.	**2nd case:** $(\sigma_2,k'\text{-}1) \xrightarrow{\tau} (\sigma_2,k') \in T_2$ According to the clause 4 of refinement, we have a non τ-divergence, then $\exists a$, k so that $(a\in L_1 \wedge k>k' \wedge(\sigma_2,k') \xrightarrow{\tau} (\sigma_2,k'+1)$ $...\xrightarrow{\tau} (\sigma_2,k\text{-}1) \xrightarrow{a} (\sigma_2,k))$ According to the second clause of refinement we have: $(\sigma_2,k\text{-}1)\rho(\sigma_1,j\text{-}1)$. Then $(\sigma_2,k\text{-}1)\rho(\sigma_1,j\text{-}1)$ and $(\sigma_2,k\text{-}1) \xrightarrow{a} (\sigma_2,k)$, according to the clause 1 of refinement: $(\sigma_1,j\text{-}1) \xrightarrow{a} (\sigma_1,j)\in T_1$ and $(\sigma_2,k)\rho(\sigma_1,j)$, we also know that $(\sigma_1,j\text{-}1) \models\phi$ and that ϕ is preserved by refinement so, $((\sigma_2,k\text{-}1),I_{1,2}) \models_p \phi$. so, $((\sigma_2,k),I_{1,2}) \models_p \ominus\phi$.

As conclusion, $\ominus\phi$ is preserved by refinement.

2. Let us prove that $\phi\,S\,\psi$ formula is preserved by refinement, if ϕ and ψ are preserved.

We know that (hypothesis) $(\sigma_1,j) \models \phi S \psi$ which means that :

$$\exists j''. \ (j'' \leq j \wedge (\sigma_1,j'') \models \psi \qquad \text{(a)}$$
$$\wedge \ (\forall j'.(j \geq j' > j'' \ \Rightarrow (\sigma_1,j') \models \phi)) \qquad \text{(b)}.$$

1st case: Let $\sigma'_2 = (\sigma_2,k'') \xrightarrow{a} \ldots$
$\xrightarrow{a^{(n)}} (\sigma_2,k)$.

σ'_2 refines a finite part of the path σ'_1 and the states of the paths σ'_1 and σ'_2 are glued with ρ. We deduce that there a sequence of a-labeled transitions $a',\ldots,a^{(n)} \in L_1$ of σ_1, so that we have this finite path part :

$\sigma'_1 = (\sigma_1,j'') \xrightarrow{a} \ldots \xrightarrow{a^{(n)}} (\sigma_1,j)$.

(a): $\sigma'_2 \subseteq_\rho \sigma'_1$ so $(\sigma_2,k'')\rho \ (\sigma_1,j'')$
We have $(\sigma_1,j'') \models \psi$, and we know that (hypothesis) ψ is preserved by refinement, then $((\sigma_2,k''),I_{1,2}) \models_p \psi$.

(b): $\sigma'_2 \subseteq_\rho \sigma'_1$ so $(\sigma_2,k')\rho \ (\sigma_1,j') \ \forall j', k'.(k'' < k' \leq k \wedge j'' < j' \leq j)$
We know that $(\sigma_1,j') \models \phi$, and that ϕ is preserved by refinement, then $((\sigma_2,k'),I_{1,2}) \models_p \phi$
so we have $((\sigma_2,k),I_{1,2}) \models_p \phi S \psi$.

2nd case: Let $\sigma'_2 = (\sigma_2,k''') \xrightarrow{\tau} \ldots$
$\xrightarrow{a} (\sigma_2,k'')\ldots \xrightarrow{a^{(n)}} (\sigma_2,k)$.

σ'_2 refines a finite part of the path σ'_1 and the states of σ'_1 and σ'_2 are glued with ρ. We deduce that it exists a sequence of transitions of σ_1 having as labels $a, a',\ldots,a^{(n)} \in L_1$, so that we have the following finite part of path:

$\sigma'_1 = (\sigma_1,j'') \xrightarrow{a} \ldots \xrightarrow{a^{(n)}} (\sigma_1,j)$.

(a): $\sigma'_2 \subseteq_\rho \sigma'_1$ then $(\sigma_2,k''')\rho \ (\sigma_1,j'')$ and we know that $(\sigma_1,j'') \models \psi$, and that ψ is preserved by refinement, so $((\sigma_2,k'''),I_{1,2}) \models_p \psi$.

We have $(\sigma_2,k''') \xrightarrow{\tau} (\sigma_2,k'''+1)\ldots$
$\xrightarrow{\tau} (\sigma_2,k'')$,
and according to the second clause of refinement we have $(\sigma_2,k'')\rho \ (\sigma_1,j'')$,
We also know (hypothesis) that $(\sigma_1, j'') \models \psi$ and that ψ is preserved by refinement, so $((\sigma_2,k''), I_{1,2}) \models_p \psi)$.
(b): The same proof as *1st case (b)* of $\phi S \psi$.

As conclusion, $((\sigma_2,k),I_{1,2}) \models_p \phi S \psi$.

We give now, the theorem of preservation of a PLTL formula by refinement which is a generalization of the preservation of PLTL formulae on a path. In fact this theorem is stated in [7], and we have used Lemma 2 to extend it with past fragment of PLTL.

Preservation of PLTL formula by refinement (Theorem 3). Let ϕ be a PLTL formula, TS_1 and TS_2 two transition systems and $I_{1,2}$ their gluing invariant,
$$\text{if } TS_1 \subseteq_\rho TS_2 \text{ and } TS_1 \models \phi \text{ then } (TS_2, I_{1,2}) \models_p \phi.$$

4   Reformulation Patterns and Their Sufficient Conditions

In this section we give the theorem of sufficient conditions, then we state the reformulation patterns and their sets of sufficient conditions. For lack of space, we prove only some theorems.

All the reformulation patterns concerns temporal formulae in the shape of $\phi'_1=\square(p_1\Rightarrow\phi_1)$ reformulated into $\phi'_2=\square(p_2\Rightarrow\phi_2)$, with p_1 and p_2 two state propositions and ϕ_1 and ϕ_2 two PLTL formulae expressed respectively with variables of TS_1 and TS_2.

4.1   How Is the Preservation of PLTL Past Temporal Properties by Refinement Used?

Whenever an abstract property over the abstract system is proved correct and if this property is preserved by the refinement, it will remain correct over all the refined levels of the system. So when the property is verified once over the abstract system we don not need to verify it again if the system is refined. However, as we saw in definition 7, The B Refinement allows the introduction of new events, and then, the set of variables of the abstract level and the refined levels are not the same. But luckily, the variables of the abstract and the refined levels are linked together by the gluing invariant. This way an abstract property was proved to be satisfied by preservation on the refined levels (theorem 3). We will see how this result, added to some other sufficient conditions, makes the verification of refined (or reformulated) properties easier on refined systems.

4.2   What's a Past Reformulation Pattern?

A past reformulation pattern is a couple of temporal operators ##' of the abstract property P_1: $\square(p_1\Rightarrow\#q_1)$ and a reformulated property P_2: $\square(p_2\Rightarrow\#'q_2)$ with $\#,\#'\in\{\ominus, S,\ominus\}$ (definition10). The choice of the Reformulation pattern depends on the semantic required from the refinement. We have defined five patterns which are:$\ominus S$, $\ominus\diamondsuit,\diamondsuit\diamondsuit$, SS, $S\diamondsuit$.

4.3   What Are Sufficient Conditions and How Do We Use Them?

We have proved that the past temporal formulae of PLTL, as well as pure future formulae, are preserved by The B Refinement (section 3). So when a property is proved to be correct on one level "I" it remains correct on the next refined level "j", we just have to link variables of level "I" to ones of level "j" with a gluing invariant $I_{i,j}$. However, we also know that The B Refinement allows the introduction of new events, so the preservation of the temporal properties is not sufficient to prove reformulated properties due to the new details introduced. We have to verify by proof some other conditions in addition to preservation. These conditions are some sufficient conditions in the shape of simple propositional logical formulae which verification is automatic with theorem prover [7]. The sufficient conditions of each past reformulation pattern that we have established are given in the following theorems (5,6,7,8 and 9).

Theorem 4. Sufficient conditions [7]. Let TS_1 and TS_2 be two transition systems where $TS_1 \subseteq_\rho TS_2$ and $I_{1,2}$ their gluing invariant. Let p_1, p_2 be two state propositions, ϕ_1, ϕ_2 PLTL formulae expressed with respective variables of TS_1 and TS_2. Let $\phi'_1 = \square(p_1 \Rightarrow \phi_1)$ and $\phi'_2 = \square (p_2 \Rightarrow \phi_2)$. If $TS_1 \models \phi'_1$, $p_2 \wedge I_{1,2} \Rightarrow p_1$ and The sufficient conditions $CS_\phi(\phi_1, \phi_2)$ are satisfied , then $TS_2 \models \phi'_2$.

The set of conditions $CS_\phi(\phi_1, \phi_2)$. We call $CS_\phi(\phi_1, \phi_2)$ the set of conditions of the reformulation patterns used when refining ϕ_1 into ϕ_2, it states that if a state of the refined system satisfies ϕ_1 by preservation then this state satisfies the reformulated property ϕ_2.

$\forall \sigma_2, j.(\sigma_2 \in \Sigma(TS_2) \wedge j \geq 0 \Rightarrow (((\sigma_2, j) , I_{1,2}) \models_p \phi_1 \Rightarrow (\sigma_2, j) \models \phi_2))$ where ϕ_1 et ϕ_2 are expressed with future temporal operators and the past temporal operators « S » and «$\ominus$» (definition 10).

$\forall \sigma_2, j.(\sigma_2 \in \Sigma(TS_2) \wedge j > 0 \Rightarrow (((\sigma_2, j) , I_{1,2}) \models_p \phi_1 \Rightarrow (\sigma_2, j) \models \phi_2))$ in the case that the past temporal operator used in ϕ_1 or ϕ_2 is «$\ominus$»(the reformulation pattern is containing «$\ominus$» (definition 10)).

We will make explicit, in the following theorems, the set of conditions corresponding to each past reformulation pattern. The set CS_ϕ and the formula $p_2 \wedge I_{1,2} \Rightarrow p_1$ are called sufficient conditions.

Theorem 5. The pattern $\ominus S$. Let ϕ_1, ϕ_2 be two PLTL formulae that hold respectively on TS_1 and TS_2. $\phi_1 = \square(p_1 \Rightarrow \ominus q_1)$ and $\phi_2 = \square(p_2 \Rightarrow r_2 S q_2)$. If $TS_1 \models \phi_1$, $TS_1 \subseteq_\rho TS_2$, $I_{1,2}$ their gluing invariant, $p_2 \wedge I_{1,2} \Rightarrow p_1$, $p_1 \wedge I_{1,2} \Rightarrow r_2$ and $q_1 \wedge I_{1,2} \Rightarrow q_2$ then $TS_2 \models \phi_2$.

Proof: We have to prove that $\forall \sigma, j.(\sigma \in \Sigma(TS_2) \wedge j > 0 \Rightarrow (\sigma, j) \models r_2 S q_2)$, in other words, we must prove that the set of conditions $CS_\phi(\ominus q_1, r_2 S q_2) = \{p_1 \wedge I_{1,2} \Rightarrow r_2, q_1 \wedge I_{1,2} \Rightarrow q_2\}$ states that $\forall \sigma, j.(\sigma \in \Sigma(TS_2) \wedge j > 0 \Rightarrow (((\sigma, j), I_{1,2}) \models_p \ominus q_1 \Rightarrow (\sigma, j) \models r_2 S q_2))$, in order to use of the theorem of sufficient conditions.

$\forall \sigma, j.(\sigma \in \Sigma(TS_2) \wedge j > 0 \Rightarrow (\sigma, j) \models r_2 S q_2)$ means that (according to the semantic of Since): $\forall \sigma, j.(\sigma \in \Sigma(TS_2) \wedge j > 0 \Rightarrow \exists j''. (j'' \leq j \wedge (\sigma, j'') \models q_2)$ (a)

   $\wedge \forall j'.(j \geq j' > j'' \Rightarrow (\sigma, j') \models r_2)))$ (b)

Let us prove, first, that $\forall \sigma, j.(\sigma \in \Sigma(TS_2) \wedge j > 0 \Rightarrow \exists j''. (j'' \leq j \wedge (\sigma, j'') \models q_2))$.

We know that: $\forall \sigma, j.(\sigma \in \Sigma(TS_2) \wedge j > 0 \Rightarrow ((\sigma, j), I_{1,2}) \models_p \ominus q_1)$ (hypothesis: theorem 3)

This means, according to the semantic of the satisfaction by preservation of the operator $\ominus$, that $\forall \sigma, j.(\sigma \in \Sigma(TS_2) \wedge j > 0 \Rightarrow \exists j''.(j'' < j \wedge ((\sigma, j''), I_{1,2}) \models_p q_1))$

This is equivalent, according to the definition of $\models_p$, to

$\forall \sigma, j.(\sigma \in \Sigma(TS_2) \wedge j > 0 \Rightarrow \exists j''.(j'' < j \wedge l_2((\sigma, j'')) \wedge I_{1,2} \Rightarrow q_1))$

which implies when adding $I_{1,2}$ on the right of the implication:

$\forall \sigma, j.(\sigma \in \Sigma(TS_2) \wedge j > 0 \Rightarrow \exists j''.(j'' < j \wedge l_2((\sigma, j'')) \wedge I_{1,2} \Rightarrow q_1 \wedge I_{1,2}))$

We know too, according to the hypotheses, that $q_1 \wedge I_{1,2} \Rightarrow q_2$, so, given that the implication is transitive, we have:

$\forall\sigma, j.(\sigma\in\Sigma(TS_2)\wedge j>0\Rightarrow\exists\ j''.\ (j''<j\wedge l_2((\sigma,j'')))\wedge I_{1,2}\Rightarrow q_2))$
which implies that (because $I_{1,2}$ isn't needed to establish q_2):
$\forall\ \sigma, j.(\sigma\in\Sigma(TS_2)\wedge j>0\Rightarrow\exists\ j''.\ (j''<j\wedge\ (\sigma,j'')\models q_2))$

Let us prove, now, the maintaining part (b).

We know that transitions between j and $j'+1$ are τ-transitions. According to the clause 2 of refinement, we deduce that the states $(\sigma,j'+1)...(\sigma,j)$ refine a state (σ_1,k) of the abstract system where $(\sigma_1,k)\models p_1$, which implies that the states $(\sigma,j'+1)...(\sigma,j)$ satisfy p_1 by gluing :
$\forall\sigma,j.(\sigma\in\Sigma(TS_2)\wedge j>0\Rightarrow\exists\ j'.\ (j'\leq j\wedge(\sigma,j')\models q_2\wedge\forall\ j''.(j\geq j''>j'\Rightarrow l_2((\sigma,j''))\wedge I_{1,2}\Rightarrow p_1\ )))$
So we have, when adding $I_{1,2}$ on the right of the implication,
$\forall\sigma,j.(\sigma\in\Sigma(TS_2)\wedge j>0\Rightarrow\exists j'.(j'\leq j\wedge(\sigma,j')\models q_2\wedge\forall j''.(j\geq j''>j'\Rightarrow l_2((\sigma,j''))\wedge I_{1,2}\Rightarrow p_1\wedge I_{1,2})))$
but we have also $p_1\wedge I_{1,2}\Rightarrow r_2$, so the formula becomes
$\forall\ \sigma,j.(\sigma\in\Sigma(TS_2)\wedge j>0\Rightarrow\exists\ j'.\ (j'\leq j\wedge(\sigma,j')\models q_2\wedge\forall\ j''.(j\geq j''>j'\Rightarrow l_2((\sigma,j''))\wedge I_{1,2}\Rightarrow r_2)))$
and because $I_{1,2}$ is not needed to establish r_2, we have
$\forall\ \sigma,j.(\sigma\in\Sigma(TS_2)\wedge j>0\Rightarrow\exists\ j'.\ (j'\leq j\wedge(\sigma,j')\models q_2\wedge\ \forall\ j''.(j\geq j''>j'\Rightarrow (\sigma,j'')\models r_2\ ))).$

Theorem 6. The pattern $\ominus\Diamond$. Let ϕ_1, ϕ_2 be two PLTL formulae that hold respectively on TS_1 and TS_2. $\phi_1=\Box(p_1\Rightarrow\ominus q_1)$ and $\phi_2=\Box(p_2\Rightarrow\Diamond q_2)$. If $TS_1\models\phi_1$, $TS_1\subseteq_\rho TS_2$, $I_{1,2}$ their gluing invariant, $p_2\wedge I_{1,2}\Rightarrow p_1$, and $q_1\wedge I_{1,2}\Rightarrow q_2$ then $TS_2\models\phi_2$.

Theorem 7. The pattern $\Diamond\Diamond$. Let ϕ_1, ϕ_2 be two PLTL formulae that hold respectively on TS_1 and TS_2. $\phi_1=\Box(p_1\Rightarrow\Diamond q_1)$ and $\phi_2=\Box(p_2\Rightarrow\Diamond q_2)$. If $TS_1\models\phi_1$, $TS_1\subseteq_\rho TS_2$, $I_{1,2}$ their gluing invariant, $p_2\wedge I_{1,2}\Rightarrow p_1$, and $q_1\wedge I_{1,2}\Rightarrow q_2$ then $TS_2\models\phi_2$.

Theorem 8. The pattern SS. Let ϕ_1, ϕ_2 be two PLTL formulae that hold respectively on TS1 and TS2. $\phi_1=\Box(p_1\Rightarrow r_1 Sq_1)$ and $\phi_2=\Box(p_2\Rightarrow r_2 Sq_2)$. If $TS_1\models\phi_1$, $TS_1\subseteq_\rho TS_2$, $I_{1,2}$ their gluing invariant, $p_2\wedge I_{1,2}\Rightarrow p_1$, $r_1\wedge I_{1,2}\Rightarrow r_2$ and $q_1\wedge I_{1,2}\Rightarrow q_2$ then $TS_2\models\phi_2$.

Proof: Let us prove that the set of conditions $CS_\phi(r_1 Sq_1, r_2 Sq_2)=\{r_1\wedge I_{1,2}\Rightarrow r_2, q_1\wedge I_{1,2}\Rightarrow q_2\}$ states that $\forall\sigma,j.(\sigma\in\Sigma(TS_2)\wedge j\geq0\Rightarrow(((\sigma,j),I_{1,2})\models_p r_1 Sq_1\Rightarrow(\sigma,j)\models r_2 Sq_2))$ in order to use theorem 4.

According to the semantic of the satisfaction by preservation of the "since" operator we have $\forall\ \sigma, j.(\sigma\in\Sigma(TS_2)\wedge j\geq0\Rightarrow((\sigma,j),I_{1,2})\models_p r_1 Sq_1)$
This means that $\forall\ \sigma,j.(\sigma\in\Sigma(TS_2)\wedge j\geq0\Rightarrow\exists\ j'.\ (j'\leq j\wedge((\sigma,j'),I_{1,2})\models_p q_1$
$\wedge\ \forall\ j''.(j\geq j''>j'\Rightarrow (\sigma,j''),I_{1,2})\models_p r_1\ )))$
and we know also, that q_1 and r_1 are state propositions, so
$\forall\sigma,j.(\sigma\in\Sigma(TS_2)\wedge j\geq0\Rightarrow\exists j'.(j'\leq j\wedge((\sigma,j'),I_{1,2})\models_c q_1\wedge\forall j''.(j\geq j''>j'\Rightarrow((\sigma,j''),I_{1,2})\models_c r_1)))$
this implies that $\forall\ \sigma,j.(\sigma\in\Sigma(TS_2)\wedge\ j\geq0\Rightarrow\exists\ j'.(j'\leq j\wedge(l_2((\sigma,j'))\wedge I_{1,2})\Rightarrow q_1$
$\wedge\ \forall\ j''.(j\geq j''>j'\Rightarrow (l_2((\sigma,j''))\wedge I_{1,2})\Rightarrow r_1\ )))$
Adding $I_{1,2}$ on the right of the implication, we obtain
$\forall\sigma,j.(\sigma\in\Sigma(TS_2)\wedge j\geq0\Rightarrow\exists j'.(j'\leq j\wedge(l_2((\sigma,j'))\wedge I_{1,2})\Rightarrow q_1\wedge I_{1,2}\wedge\forall j''.(j\geq j''>j'\Rightarrow(l_2((\sigma,j''))\wedge I_{1,2})\Rightarrow r_1\wedge I_{1,2})))$
and we have, according to $CS_\phi(r_1 Sq_1,r_2 Sq_2)$: $r_1\wedge I_{1,2}\Rightarrow r_2$ and $q_1\wedge I_{1,2}\Rightarrow q_2$.

So, using the implication transitivity, the expression becomes
$\forall\sigma,j.(\sigma\in\Sigma(TS_2)\wedge j\geq 0\Rightarrow\exists j'.(j'\leq j\wedge(l_2((\sigma,j'))\wedge I_{1,2})\Rightarrow q_2$
$\wedge\forall j''.(j\geq j''>j'\Rightarrow(l_2((\sigma,j''))\wedge I_{1,2})\Rightarrow r_2)))$

We can omit $I_{1,2}$ from the left of the implication (because it is not needed to establish q_2 and r_2): $\forall\sigma,j.(\sigma\in\Sigma(TS_2)\wedge j\geq 0\Rightarrow\exists j'.(j'\leq j\wedge l_2((\sigma,j'))\Rightarrow q_2$
$$\wedge\forall j''.(j\geq j''>j'\Rightarrow l_2((\sigma,j''))\Rightarrow r_2)))$$
we have ,then, the semantic of "Since" operator
$$\forall\sigma,j.(\sigma\in\Sigma(TS_2)\wedge j\geq 0\Rightarrow((\sigma,j)\models r_2Sq_2)).$$

Theorem 9. The pattern $S\lozenge$. Let ϕ_1, ϕ_2 be two PLTL formulae that hold respectively on TS_1 and TS_2. $\phi_1=\Box(p_1\Rightarrow r_1Sq_1)$ and $\phi_2=\Box(p_2\Rightarrow\lozenge q_2)$. If $TS_1\models\phi_1$, $TS_1\subseteq_\rho TS_2$, $I_{1,2}$ their gluing invariant, $p_2\wedge I_{1,2}\Rightarrow p_1$ and $q_1\wedge I_{1,2}\Rightarrow q_2$ then $TS_2\models\phi_2$.

5 Example

We will present in this section the example of the robot cell used in [1] and adopted in [7] and [5].

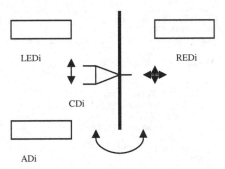

Fig. 2. Robot cell system

The robot cell (Fig .2) has to move some parts from the arrival device (ADi) to one of the exit devices called LEDi (left exit device) and REDi (right exit device) by means of a carrier device (CDi). The carrier device (CDi) can move horizontally, vertically and can pivot. It has two states, free (f) and busy (b).

Here, we show an abstract specification as well as a refined one called first refinement. We express the specification using B event system syntax. The variables corresponding to the abstract level are annotated with "1", whereas the variables corresponding to the refined level are a\nnoted with "2".

We give now, the theorem of preservation of a PLTL formula by refinement which is a generalization of the preservation of PLTL formulae on a path. In fact this theorem is stated in [7], and we have used Lemma 2 to extend it with past fragment of PLTL[12].

Abstract specification: In this level, we observe only the carrier device state. There are two events:

- Load: The carrier device takes a part then it becomes busy.
- Unload: The carrier device drops a part then it becomes free.

```
MACHINE ROBOT₁
SETS DEVICE_STATE= {f, b}
VARIABLES CD₁
INVARIANT CD₁ ∈ DEVICE_STATE
INTIALIZATION CD₁:=f
EVENTS
Load = SELECT CD₁=f THEN CD₁=b END;
Unload = SELECT CD₁=b THEN CD₁=f END;
END
```

The dynamic property that holds on this abstract model states that if the carrier device is busy, then, it was free at the previous state. It is expressed with the following past temporal formula : $\Box(\,CD_1=b \Rightarrow \ominus CD_1=f)$ (1).

Refined specification: In this level we consider left and right exit devices. The variable of the abstract and the refined level are linked together with the gluing invariant $I_{1,2} \overset{def}{=} CD_2=CD_1$.

We observe two new events:

- Levac: which sets the left exit device free.
- Revac: which sets the right exit device free.

```
MACHINE ROBOT₂ REFINES ROBOT₁
VARIABLES LED₂, RED₂, CD₂
INVARIANT  LED₂ ∈ DEVICE_STATE ∧LED₂ ∈ DEVICE_STATE∧
CD₂=CD₁
INTIALIZATION LED₂:=f|| RED₂:=f||CD₂:=f
EVENTS
/*Old Events*/
Load = SELECT CD₂=f THEN CD₂=b END;
Unload = SELECT (LED₂=f∨RED₂=f)∧CD₂=b
THEN IF LED₂=b THEN RED₂:=b
             ELSE IF RED₂=b THEN LED₂:=b
                        ELSE CHOICE LED₂:=b
                        OR RED₂:=b END
             END
      END
             || CD₂:=f
END;
/*New Events*/
Levac = SELECT LED₂=b THEN LED₂:=f END;
Revac = SELECT RED₂=b THEN RED₂:=f END;
END
```

This dynamic property expressed in (1) may be reformulated to hold on the refined level as follows: $\Box(\,CD_2=b \Rightarrow \diamondsuit CD_2=f)$(2) and it means that if the carrier device is busy, then, it was free at a previous state.

The reformulation of (1) into (2) follows the pattern $\ominus\diamondsuit$, so we have:

$p_1 \equiv CD_1 = b$, $q_1 \equiv CD_1 = f$, $p_2 \equiv CD_2 = b$, $q_2 \equiv CD_2 = f$.

The sufficient conditions corresponding to this pattern is:$\{p_2 \wedge I_{1,2} \Rightarrow p_1, q_1 \wedge I_{1,2} \Rightarrow q_2\}$.

- $p_2 \wedge I_{1,2} \Rightarrow p_1 : p_2 \equiv CD_2 = b$ and $I_{1,2} \overset{def}{=} CD_2 = CD_1$, so $p_1 = CD_1 = b$.
- $q_1 \wedge I_{1,2} \Rightarrow q_2 : q_1 \equiv CD_1 = f$ and $I_{1,2} \overset{def}{=} CD_2 = CD_1$, so $q_2 = CD_2 = f$.

Then the reformulated property is verified in the refinement level.

6   Conclusion and Perspectives

In this paper, we have extended the B method with PLTL past fragment as it was done with PLTL future fragment, and we have adapted the reformulation technique in order to verify the dynamic properties including past temporal operators. We have proved that temporal properties using PLTL past temporal operators are preserved by the B Refinement and we have generated some reformulation patterns and their sufficient conditions.

This extension allows us to formulate more natural properties that are not straightforward to express with future temporal operators and verify these properties over the refinement process. We have illustrated the extension results over an example of Robot cell system.

We propose as perspective to study another class of sufficient conditions that introduces the guards of events and may remedy the failure of proof based on sufficient conditions we have stated when it occurs. Another alternative is to study the extension of the modularity with past temporal operators.

References

1. Abrial, J.R.: The B Book. Cambridge University Press (1996).
2. Abrial, J.R.: Extending B without changing it (for developing distributed systems). In : Henri Habrias, editeur, Proc. of the 1-st Conference on the B method, Putting into Practice Methods and Tools for Information System Design, Nantes, France (1996) 169-190
3. Abrial, J.R., Mussat, L.: Introducing dynamic constraints in B. Second Conference on the B method. Lecture Note in Computer Science, *Vol. 1393,* Springer-Verlag, (1998) 83-128.
4. Benedetti, M., Cimatti, A.: Bounded Model Checking for Past LTL. TACAS (2003) 18-33.
5. Bellegarde, F., Darlot, C., Julliand, J., Kouchnarenko, O.: Reformulation : a way to combine dynamic properties and B refinement. FME 2001 ("Formal Methods Europe"), Lecture Notes in Computer Sciences, Vol. 2021. Springer Verlag, Berlin, Germany, (2001) 2-19.
6. Cimatti, A., Clarke, E.M., Giunchiglia, F., Roveri, M.: 17MV: a new Symbolic Model Verifier. In N. Halbwachs and D. Peled, editors. Eleventh Conference on Computer-Aided Verification (CAV'99). Lecture Notes in Computer Science, Vol. 1633. Springer Verlag, Trento Italy (1999) 495–499
7. Darlot, C. : Reformulation et Vérification de propriétés temporelles dans le cadre du raffinement de systèmes d'événements, Phd thesis, Université de Franche – Comté , (2002)
8. Darlot, C., Julliand, J., Kouchnarenko, O.: Refinement Preserves PLTL Properties. ZB 2003 – Turku.
9. Emerson, E. A., Temporel and modal logic. Handbook of Theoretical computer science, Vol. B. Elsevier Science Publisher. B.V., (1990).
10. Gabbay, D., The declarative past and imperative future. In H. Barringer, editor, Proceedings of the Colloquium on Temporal Logic and Specifications. Lecture Notes in Computer Science, Vol : 398. Springer-Verlag, (1989) 409-448
11. Julliand, J., Masson, P.-A., Mountassir, M.: Modular verification of dynamic properties for reactive systems. In Proc. of the 1-st Int. Workshop on Integrated Formal Methods (IFM'99). Springer Verlag, York, UK (1999) 89-108

12. Julliand, J., Masson, P.-A., Mountassir, H.: Vérification par model Checking modulaire des propriétés dynamiques introduites en B. *TSI*, Vol 20- n°7 (2001)

13. Lichtenstein, O., Pnueli, A., Zuck, L., The glory of the past. In R. Parikh, editor, Proceedings of the Conference on Logic of Programs. Lecture Note in Computer Science, Vol. 193. Springer Verlag, Brooklyn, NY (1985) 196-218

14. Laroussinie, F., Markey, N., Schnoebelen, Ph.: Temporal Logic with Forgettable Past. 17th Annual IEEE Symposium on Logic in Computer Science (LICS'02), Soc.Press, Copenhagen, Denmark (2002) 383-392

15. Manna, Z., Pnuelli, A.: The Temporal Logic of Reactive and Concurrent Systems Specification. Springer Verlag (1992)

16. Markey, N.: Past is for free: on the complexity of verifying linear temporal properties with past. In Proc. 9th Int. Workshop on Expressiveness in Concurrenc (EXPRESS'2002), Brno, Czech Republic. Electronic Notes in Theorie of Computer Science, Vol . 68. 2. Elsevier Science (2002)

17. http://17mv.irst.itc.it

18. Pnueli , A. : The temporal semantics of concurrent programs. Theoretical Computer Science, Vol 13 (1981) 45-60

19. Saad, M., Jemni Ben Ayed, L.: A way to Introduce Dynamic Properties with Past Temporal Operators in the B Refinement, accepted as poster in the international ACM/IEEE conference MEMOCODE 2004.

Approximate Reachability for Dead Code Elimination in Esterel*

Olivier Tardieu and Stephen A. Edwards

Department of Computer Science, Columbia University, New York
{tardieu,sedwards}@cs.columbia.edu

Abstract. Esterel is an imperative synchronous programming language for the design of reactive systems. Esterel* extends Esterel with a non-instantaneous jump instruction (compatible with concurrency, preemption, etc.) so as to enable powerful source-to-source program transformations, amenable to formal verification. In this work, we propose an approximate reachability algorithm for Esterel* and use its output to remove dead code. We prove the correctness of our techniques.

1 Introduction

Esterel [1,2,3] is a synchronous parallel programming language. Its syntax is imperative, fit for the design of reactive systems where discrete control aspects prevail. Sophisticated controllers may be described using sequential and parallel compositions of behaviors, suspension and preemption mechanisms, conditionals, loops, and synchronization through instantly broadcast signals. Both software [4,5] and hardware [6,7] synthesis are supported.

In this paper, we present an efficient, conservative reachability computation for Esterel* and use its output to direct a dead code elimination procedure. Esterel* [8,9,10] extends the language with a non-instantaneous jump statement that enables many compilation steps to be performed at the source level, making them easier to share across back ends.

We apply our dead code elimination procedure to cleaning up the output of structural transformations in optimizing compilers. Although in theory such transformations can be carefully engineered to avoid introducing dead code, doing so is generally very difficult. Instead, creating and proving a dead code elimination procedure for Esterel* as we do here frees us from this concern, and is a necessary first step toward a verified optimizing compiler. Previous attempts at the mathematical proof of an Esterel compiler [11,12] have been limited to simple, inefficient compilers.

Because the only known precise reachability algorithms for Esterel or Esterel* are exponential [13,14,15], we take a cheap, conservative approach that is, however, accurate enough to clean up most machine-generated code.

Source-level reachability analysis for Esterel is both challenging and rewarding. For example, Esterel's concurrent exception-handling mechanism demands any reachability algorithm track the relative priorities of exceptions, but this

D.A. Peled and Y.-K. Tsay (Eds.): ATVA 2005, LNCS 3707, pp. 323–337, 2005.
© Springer-Verlag Berlin Heidelberg 2005

is fairly easy to do because the needed information is explicit in the program source. The addition of the unstructured jump instruction to Esterel* further complicates an already complex issue.

Surprisingly, not every piece of code in an Esterel program that is never executed can be removed. In fact, the execution of an Esterel program relies on some preliminary probing, called causality analysis. As a result, a piece of code is truly irrelevant if and only if it is not only never executed but also never probed. Because of this distinction, previous work on dead code elimination for concurrent but not synchronous languages is largely irrelevant for Esterel.

Several such causality analyses have been proposed for Esterel by means of various formal semantics. For instance, in the so-called logical causality of the logical semantics [16], "present S then nothing end" and "nothing" are equivalent (strongly bisimilar). But, in the causality analysis of the constructive semantics [3], they are not, as the test may lead to a deadlock. However, with a maximal causality analysis [17], they would again be equivalent. In general, removing apparently useless code may turn a correct program w.r.t. the logical semantics into an incorrect one (cf. Section 2.3), or an incorrect program w.r.t. the constructive semantics into a correct one (by removing deadlock conditions).

Here, we take a conservative approach and build our analyses from an abstract semantics for Esterel* that safely approximates the logical, constructive, and deterministic semantics [18] of the language by simply ignoring signals. The correctness proofs for the dead code elimination, which we obtain for a particular choice of concrete semantics—a logical semantics—can be easily adapted to the other semantics. This also makes the analysis very efficient.

In Section 2, we describe the Esterel* language and its concrete and abstract semantics. In Section 3 we start with single-step reachability, which answers whether state s can be reached starting from state s_0 in one step of execution of the program p, and then apply a fixed-point iteration to answer whether state s can ever be reached during the execution of p (thus going beyond a purely structural analysis). Finally, in Section 4, we show how to match reachable states to the source code in order to eliminate dead code. We conclude in Section 5.

2   Esterel*

We consider Berry's kernel Esterel language [3] extended with the gotopause instruction of Tardieu [8]. We describe its syntax and main semantic features in Section 2.1 and provide a formal semantics for it in Section 2.2, from which we derive an abstract semantics in Section 2.3 that we use for reachability analysis.

2.1   Syntax and Intuitive Semantics

Fig. 1 is the grammar of our language. Non-terminals p and q denote programs, S signal names, ℓ positive integer labels, and d positive integer exit levels.

We denote $\mathcal{L}_p$ the set of labels of the pause instructions in p. Our definitions of the "present," ";," and "||" constructs insist these labels are pairwise distinct. In contrast, labels in gotopause instructions are unconstrained.

$p, q ::=$ **nothing**	Do nothing; terminate instantly
ℓ:**pause**	Suspend the execution for one instant
gotopause ℓ	Instantly branch to "ℓ:**pause**", which suspends the execution for one instant
signal S **in** p **end**	Declare signal S in p and execute p
emit S	Emit signal S and terminate instantly
present S **then** p **else** q **end**	Execute p if S is present; q otherwise
p ; q	Execute p followed by q if/when p terminates
$p \mathbin{\|\|} q$	Execute p in parallel with q
loop p **end**	Repeat p forever
try p **end**	Execute p, catching exits in p
exit d	Exit d enclosing "**try** ... **end**" blocks

Fig. 1. Syntax of Esterel*. In statements where both p and q appear, they must contain unique pause labels, i.e., $\mathcal{L}_p \cap \mathcal{L}_q = \emptyset$.

The infix ";" operator binds tighter than "$\|\|$". Brackets ([and]) may be used to group statements in arbitrary ways. In a **present** statement, **then** or **else** branches may be omitted. For example, "**present** S **then** p **end**" is short-hand for "**present** S **then** p **else nothing end**". Similarly, we may omit the label "ℓ:" of the instruction "ℓ:**pause**" in a program if there is no matching "**gotopause** ℓ" in this program.

Instants and reactions. An Esterel* program runs in steps called *reactions* in response to the *ticks* of a *global clock*. Each reaction takes one *instant*. Primitive constructs execute in the same instant except the **pause** and **gotopause** instructions. When the clock ticks, a reaction occurs, which computes the *output signals* and the *new state* of the program from the *input signals* and the *current state* of the program. It may either finish the execution instantly or delay part of it until the next instant because it reached at least one **pause** or **gotopause** instruction. In this case, the execution is resumed in the next tick of the clock from the locations of the **pause** instructions reached in the previous instant.

The program "**emit** A ; **pause** ; **emit** B ; **emit** C ; **pause** ; **emit** D" emits signal A in the first instant of its execution, then emits B and C in the second instant, finally emits D and terminates in the third instant. It takes three instants to complete, i.e., proceeds by three reactions. To the environment, signals B and C appear *simultaneously* since their emissions occur in the same instant.

Synchronous concurrency and preemption. One reaction of the parallel composition "$p \mathbin{\|\|} q$" is made of exactly one reaction of each non-terminated branch, until all branches terminate.

In sequential code, the "**exit** d" instruction jumps to the end of d enclosing "**try** ... **end**" blocks. When "**exit** d" executes in a group of parallel branches, it also terminates all the other branches. In Fig. 2a, A and D are emitted in the first instant, then B, E, and G in the second and final one. Neither C nor F is emitted. However, "**exit** 1" in the first branch does not prevent E from being emitted in the second one. This is *weak preemption*.

```
try                                              try
   emit A ; pause ; emit B ; exit 1 ; emit C       try
||                                                    try
   emit D ; pause ; emit E ; pause ; emit F              exit 1 || exit 2
end ;                                                 end ; emit A
emit G                                             end ; emit B
                                                 end
                (a)                                              (b)
```

Fig. 2. Concurrency and Preemption: Two Examples

When groups of statements running in parallel execute multiple `exit` instructions, priority is given to the branch with the highest exit level, i.e., the exit level of a group of parallel branches is the maximum executed level. Thus, the program in Fig. 2b only emits B.

Loops. The program "`loop emit S ; pause end`" emits S in each instant and never terminates. Combining `loop`, `try`, and `exit` constructs can produce loops that terminate after a finite number of iterations. Loop bodies may not be instantaneous [19]. For instance, "`loop emit S end`" is illegal since it suggests an unbounded amount of work in a reaction.

Signals. The instruction "`signal S in p end`" declares the *local* signal S in p. The free signals of a program are said to be *interface* signals for this program.

In an instant, a signal S is *emitted* if and only if one or more "emit S" statements are executed that instant. The *status* of S is either *present* or *absent*. A local signal is present iff it is emitted. An interface signal is present iff it is emitted or provided by the *environment*. If S is present in an instant then all "present S then p else q end" statements executed in this instant execute their then branches in that instant, otherwise they all execute their else branches.

The presence of a signal is therefore not persistent. For example, in program "`signal S in emit S ; pause ; present S then emit O end end`," signal S is emitted and thus present in the first instant of execution only, therefore O is not emitted by this statement, as S is absent at the time of the test.

Interface signals can interact with local signals. For example, in
```
signal S in
   present S then emit O end  ||  present I then emit S end
end,
```
signal I is present iff it is provided by the environment. Signal S is emitted, thus present, iff I is present. Signal O is emitted iff S is present. As a result, O is present iff I or O is provided by the environment. Only I and O may be observed by the environment as S cannot escape its scope of definition.

The instantaneous broadcast and instantaneous feedback implied by the *signal coherence law*, i.e., a local signal is present iff emitted, raise correctness issues. Broadly, there are three issues, as illustrated by the following examples:

1. In "`signal S in present S then emit S end end`," S could be absent or present. Such *non-deterministic* programs are illegal.

2. In "signal S in present S else emit S end end," S can neither be absent nor present. This program is illegal because it is *non-reactive*: it has no possible behavior.

3. Finally, signals can be self-reinforcing. Signal S can only be present in the program "signal S in present S then emit S else emit S end end" for instance. This program is said to be *logically correct*, being both reactive and deterministic. However, it is not *causal* (for the constructive causality of the constructive semantics), since the status of S has to be guessed before being confirmed. In summary, this program is legal w.r.t. a logical semantics, but not w.r.t. the constructive semantics.

Strengthening the signal coherence law to precisely define the semantics of such intricate examples is the central concern in choosing a causality analysis for Esterel. In this work, as mentioned before, we do not want to commit ourselves to a particular set of choices. As a result, we shall not only formalize a concrete semantics for the language (making such choices), but also an abstract semantics that conservatively approximates many possible concrete semantics.

Jumps. The gotopause instruction permits jumps in Esterel. The execution of the code following the target pause starts exactly one instant after the code preceding the gotopause instruction terminates. It makes it possible to specify state machines in a natural way and allows loops to be expressed differently. For instance, "1:pause ; emit S ; gotopause 1" emits S in each instant of execution starting from the second one. In fact, "loop emit S ; pause end" can be expanded into "try exit 1 ; 1:pause end ; emit S ; gotopause 1" using the pattern "try exit 1 ; ... end" to avoid a startup delay.

Just as "exit d" in "exit d || pause" has priority over the pause instruction, it preempts the jump in "exit d || gotopause ℓ".

We make no assumptions about the label in a gotopause instruction. A "gotopause ℓ" instruction may have no target if the program contains no corresponding "ℓ:pause" instruction. In such a case, the completion of the execution is delayed by one instant, but nothing takes place in its last instant. For example, the execution of "gotopause 1; emit S" takes two instants; S is not emitted in the second instant of execution.

Concurrent gotopause instructions may target arbitrary pause locations. In "[gotopause 1 || gotopause 2] ; [1:pause ; ... || 2:pause ; ...]" for instance, this is fine: in the second instant, the execution is resumed from the locations of the two pause instructions in parallel. In contrast, in the program "[gotopause 1 || gotopause 2] ; 1:pause ; ... ; 2:pause ; ...," resuming the execution from two locations in a sequence does not make sense. We say that this last program is not *well formed*, which we formalized earlier [10].

In this paper however, we have no need for such a correctness criterion. We decide that, in the last example and in similar cases, the execution will non-deterministically restart from either pause location. Importantly, giving such a peculiar semantics to non-well-formed programs (which are illegal anyway) does not make the analysis of well-formed program more costly or less precise, but simplifies the formalism.

$$\texttt{nothing} \xrightarrow[E]{\emptyset,0} \emptyset \qquad \text{(nothing)}$$

$$\ell\texttt{:pause} \xrightarrow[E]{\emptyset,1} \{\ell\} \qquad \text{(pause)}$$

$$\frac{S \in E}{\texttt{emit } S \xrightarrow[E]{\{S\},0} \emptyset} \qquad \text{(emit)}$$

$$\frac{\ell \in L_0}{\ell\texttt{:pause}/L_0 \xrightarrow[E]{\emptyset,0} \emptyset} \qquad \text{(resume)}$$

$$\texttt{gotopause } \ell \xrightarrow[E]{\emptyset,1} \{\ell\} \qquad \text{(goto)}$$

$$\texttt{exit } d \xrightarrow[E]{\emptyset,d+1} \emptyset \qquad \text{(exit)}$$

$$\frac{p\backslash X \xrightarrow[E]{O,k} L}{\texttt{try } p \texttt{ end}\backslash X \xrightarrow[E]{O,\downarrow k} L} \qquad \text{(try)}$$

$$\frac{p\backslash X \xrightarrow[E]{O,k} L \quad k \neq 0}{\texttt{loop } p \texttt{ end}/X \xrightarrow[E]{O,k} L} \qquad \text{(no-loop)}$$

$$\frac{p\backslash X \xrightarrow[E]{O,0} \emptyset \quad q \xrightarrow[E]{O',k} L}{p \texttt{ ; } q\backslash X \xrightarrow[E]{O\cup O',k} L} \qquad \text{(seq)}$$

$$\frac{p\backslash X \xrightarrow[E]{O,k} L \quad k \neq 0}{p \texttt{ ; } q\backslash X \xrightarrow[E]{O,k} L} \qquad \text{(seq-left)}$$

$$\frac{q/L_0 \xrightarrow[E]{O,k} L}{p \texttt{ ; } q/L_0 \xrightarrow[E]{O,k} L} \qquad \text{(seq-right)}$$

$$\frac{p\backslash X \xrightarrow[E\cup\{S\}]{O,k} L \quad S \in O}{\texttt{signal } S \texttt{ in } p \texttt{ end}\backslash X \xrightarrow[E]{O\backslash\{S\},k} L} \qquad \text{(signal+)}$$

$$\frac{p\backslash X \xrightarrow[E\backslash\{S\}]{O,k} L}{\texttt{signal } S \texttt{ in } p \texttt{ end}\backslash X \xrightarrow[E]{O,k} L} \qquad \text{(signal−)}$$

$$\frac{S \in E \quad p \xrightarrow[E]{O,k} L}{\texttt{present } S \texttt{ then } p \texttt{ else } q \texttt{ end} \xrightarrow[E]{O,k} L} \qquad \text{(present)}$$

$$\frac{S \notin E \quad q \xrightarrow[E]{O,k} L}{\texttt{present } S \texttt{ then } p \texttt{ else } q \texttt{ end} \xrightarrow[E]{O,k} L} \qquad \text{(absent)}$$

$$\frac{p/L_0 \xrightarrow[E]{O,k} L}{\texttt{present } S \texttt{ then } p \texttt{ else } q \texttt{ end}/L_0 \xrightarrow[E]{O,k} L} \qquad \text{(present-left)}$$

$$\frac{q/L_0 \xrightarrow[E]{O,k} L}{\texttt{present } S \texttt{ then } p \texttt{ else } q \texttt{ end}/L_0 \xrightarrow[E]{O,k} L} \qquad \text{(present-right)}$$

$$\frac{p/L_0 \xrightarrow[E]{O,0} \emptyset \quad p \xrightarrow[E]{O',k} L \quad k \neq 0}{\texttt{loop } p \texttt{ end}/L_0 \xrightarrow[E]{O\cup O',k} L} \qquad \text{(loop)}$$

$$\frac{p/L_0 \xrightarrow[E]{O,k} L \quad L_0 \cap \mathcal{L}_q = \emptyset}{p \texttt{ || } q/L_0 \xrightarrow[E]{O,k} L} \qquad \text{(par-left)}$$

$$\frac{q/L_0 \xrightarrow[E]{O,k} L \quad L_0 \cap \mathcal{L}_p = \emptyset}{p \texttt{ || } q/L_0 \xrightarrow[E]{O,k} L} \qquad \text{(par-right)}$$

$$\frac{p\backslash X \xrightarrow[E]{O,k} L \quad q\backslash X \xrightarrow[E]{O',l} L' \quad m = \max(k,l)}{p \texttt{ || } q\backslash X \xrightarrow[E]{O\cup O',m} \begin{cases} L \cup L' & \text{if } m = 1 \\ \emptyset & \text{if } m \neq 1 \end{cases}} \qquad \text{(par)}$$

Fig. 3. Logical State Semantics

2.2   Logical State Semantics

In Fig. 3, we specify the logical state semantics of Esterel* as a set of facts and deduction rules in a structural operational style [20]. Reactions of a program p are expressed via two kinds of labeled transitions:

$$p \xrightarrow[E]{O,k} L \qquad \text{for the first instant of execution}$$

$$p/L_0 \xrightarrow[E]{O,k} L \qquad \text{for subsequent instants of execution, } L_0 \text{ being the set of}$$
$\texttt{pause}$ locations (labels) the execution is resumed from.

corresponding to two classes of program *states* [7]: a unique *initial state*, simply written p; and many *intermediate states*, written p/L_0 for $L_0 \subseteq \mathbb{N}$. We denote $\mathcal{S}_p$ the set of all states of p and $p\backslash X$ a state of p of either class.

The set O lists the interface signals emitted by the reaction. The set E lists the interface signals assumed present at the time of the reaction. The set $L \subseteq \mathcal{L}(p)$ lists the labels of the $\texttt{pause}$ and $\texttt{gotopause}$ instructions *reached* by the reaction. The *completion code* $k \in \mathbb{N}$ encodes the status of the execution:

- $k = 0$ if the execution completes normally. L is empty.
- $k = 1$ if the reaction does not complete the execution of p. L is not empty.
- $k = 2, 3, \ldots$ if the execution terminates because of an `exit` instruction and $k - 1$ enclosing "`try ... end`" blocks must be exited. L is empty.

Technically, it is easier not to require L_0 in p/L_0 to be a subset of $\mathcal{L}(p)$. Nevertheless, we can identify the states p/L_0 and p/L_1 if $L_0 \cap \mathcal{L}_p = L_1 \cap \mathcal{L}_p$, thus only consider $2^{|\mathcal{L}_p|}$ intermediate states for the program p, thanks to:

Lemma 1. $p/L_0 \xrightarrow[E]{O,k} L$ iff $p/(L_0 \cap \mathcal{L}_p) \xrightarrow[E]{O,k} L$.

Proof. This and the following lemmas are established by induction on the structure of a program, or the structure of a proof tree of a reaction. For lack of space, we shall not include the proofs in the paper.

Rule (exit) defines the completion code of "`exit d`" as $d + 1$. In rule (try), if k is the completion code of p, then the completion code of "`try p end`" is:

$$\downarrow k = \begin{cases} 0 & \text{if } k = 0 \text{ or } k = 2 \quad \text{(normal termination or caught exception)} \\ 1 & \text{if } k = 1 \quad \text{(non-terminated execution)} \\ k - 1 & \text{if } k > 2 \quad \text{(uncaught exception)} \end{cases}$$

Rule (no-loop) applies when the control does not reach the end of the loop; otherwise rule (loop) does.

Rule (par) applies when a parallel statement is first reached—its execution starts—or restarted from both branches. Rules (par-left) and (par-right) apply when the parallel statement is resumed from one branch only, that is to say when the execution of the other branch has already completed.

As announced, if a state points to several locations in a sequence, the execution is non-deterministically resumed from one of them. For instance, respectively by rule (seq) and rule (seq-right),

$$\text{1:pause ; 2:pause}/\{1,2\} \xrightarrow[\emptyset]{\emptyset,1} \{2\} \quad \text{and} \quad \text{1:pause ; 2:pause}/\{1,2\} \xrightarrow[\emptyset]{\emptyset,0} \emptyset.$$

Rule (present) applies when a "`present S`" statement is reached with S present. Rule (absent) applies instead if S is absent. Rules (present-left) and (present-right) specify how the execution of the `present` statement is resumed (non-deterministically from either branch if both $L_0 \cap \mathcal{L}_p \neq \emptyset$ and $L_0 \cap \mathcal{L}_q \neq \emptyset$).

Rules (emit), (signal+), and (signal−) enforce the signal coherence law. We shall not discuss it further as we now abstract signals in this formal semantics.

2.3   Abstract Semantics

In "`signal S in present S then emit S else emit S end end`," S must be present. Therefore, "`else emit S`" is never executed. However, removing the else branch changes the behavior of the program, since S may be both absent and present in "`signal S in present S then emit S end end`". Because of signals, never executed code is not necessarily dead. Therefore, we choose to

$$\text{nothing} \xrightarrow{0} \emptyset \qquad \text{(nothing)}$$

$$\text{emit } S \xrightarrow{0} \emptyset \qquad \text{(emit)}$$

$$\ell\text{:pause} \xrightarrow{1} \{l\} \qquad \text{(pause)}$$

$$\frac{\ell \in L_0}{\ell\text{:pause}/L_0 \xrightarrow{0} \emptyset} \qquad \text{(resume)}$$

$$\text{gotopause } \ell \xrightarrow{1} \{l\} \qquad \text{(goto)}$$

$$\text{exit } d \xrightarrow{d+1} \emptyset \qquad \text{(exit)}$$

$$\frac{p\backslash X \xrightarrow{k} L}{\text{try } p \text{ end}\backslash X \xrightarrow{\downarrow k} L} \qquad \text{(try)}$$

$$\frac{p\backslash X \xrightarrow{0} \emptyset \quad q \xrightarrow{k} L}{p \text{ ; } q\backslash X \xrightarrow{k} L} \qquad \text{(seq)}$$

$$\frac{p\backslash X \xrightarrow{k} L \quad k \neq 0}{p \text{ ; } q\backslash X \xrightarrow{k} L} \qquad \text{(seq-left)}$$

$$\frac{q/L_0 \xrightarrow{k} L}{p \text{ ; } q/L_0 \xrightarrow{k} L} \qquad \text{(seq-right)}$$

$$\frac{p\backslash X \xrightarrow{k} L}{\text{signal } S \text{ in } p \text{ end}\backslash X \xrightarrow{k} L} \qquad \text{(signal)}$$

$$\frac{p\backslash X \xrightarrow{k} L}{\text{present } S \text{ then } p \text{ else } q \text{ end}\backslash X \xrightarrow{k} L} \qquad \text{(then)}$$

$$\frac{q\backslash X \xrightarrow{k} L}{\text{present } S \text{ then } p \text{ else } q \text{ end}\backslash X \xrightarrow{k} L} \qquad \text{(else)}$$

$$\frac{p/L_0 \xrightarrow{0} \emptyset \quad p \xrightarrow{k} L \quad k \neq 0}{\text{loop } p \text{ end}/L_0 \xrightarrow{k} L} \qquad \text{(loop)}$$

$$\frac{p\backslash X \xrightarrow{k} L \quad k \neq 0}{\text{loop } p \text{ end}\backslash X \xrightarrow{k} L} \qquad \text{(no-loop)}$$

$$\frac{p\backslash X \xrightarrow{k} L \quad q\backslash X \xrightarrow{l} L' \quad m = \max(k,l)}{p \text{ || } q\backslash X \xrightarrow{m} \begin{cases} L \cup L' & \text{if } m = 1 \\ \emptyset & \text{if } m \neq 1 \end{cases}} \qquad \text{(par)}$$

$$\frac{p/L_0 \xrightarrow{k} L \quad L_0 \cap \mathcal{L}_q = \emptyset}{p \text{ || } q/L_0 \xrightarrow{k} L} \qquad \text{(par-left)}$$

$$\frac{q/L_0 \xrightarrow{k} L \quad L_0 \cap \mathcal{L}_p = \emptyset}{p \text{ || } q/L_0 \xrightarrow{k} L} \qquad \text{(par-right)}$$

Fig. 4. Abstract Semantics

first abstract signals in the concrete semantics, then define dead code w.r.t. the resulting abstract semantics.

The abstract semantics is easily derived from the logical state semantics by making abstraction of signals. Its rules are gathered in Fig. 4. Rules (present) and (present-left) are merged into a unique (then) rule, (absent) and (present-right) into (else), and (signal+) and (signal−) into (signal).

It safely approximates the concrete semantics, i.e., preserves its reactions:

Lemma 2. If $p\backslash X \xrightarrow[E]{O,k} L$ then $p\backslash X \xrightarrow{k} L$.

Importantly, the abstract semantics also safely approximates other semantics such as the constructive semantics of Berry [3], dedicated to hardware synthesis.

3 Reachability Analysis

We say that a state p/L is *reachable in the execution of* p iff it may result of a chain of reactions starting from p. Exact reachability analysis is in general intractable, even w.r.t. the abstract semantics, as the number of states of a program may be exponential in its size. As a result, we choose to approximate the reachable states by means of reachable labels.

In "present S then 1:pause else 2:pause || 3:pause end" for example, we shall aim at computing the set of reachable labels $R = \{1,2,3\}$ rather than the more precise set of reachable states $S = \{p/\{1\}, p/\{2,3\}, p/\emptyset\}$. Of course, we want R to contain all the labels in S, i.e., $\bigsqcup S = \bigcup_{p/L_i \in S}\{L_i\}$, while

$$s(\texttt{nothing}) = \{0\}$$
$$s(\texttt{gotopause } \ell) = \{1_\ell\}$$
$$s(\texttt{signal } S \texttt{ in } p \texttt{ end}) = s(p)$$
$$s(\texttt{present } S \texttt{ then } p \texttt{ else } q \texttt{ end}) = s(p) \cup s(q)$$
$$s(\texttt{loop } p \texttt{ end}) = s(p) \setminus \{0\}$$

$$s(\texttt{emit } S) = \{0\}$$
$$s(\ell\texttt{:pause}) = \{1_\ell\}$$
$$s(\texttt{try } p \texttt{ end}) = \downarrow s(p)$$
$$s(\texttt{exit } d) = \{d{+}1\}$$
$$s(p \mathbin{||} q) = \max(s(p), s(q))$$

$$s(p \; ; \; q) = \begin{cases} s(p) & \text{if } 0 \notin s(p) \\ (s(p) \setminus \{0\}) \cup s(q) & \text{if } 0 \in s(p) \end{cases}$$

Fig. 5. Instantaneous Reachability from the Initial State

being as small as possible. In other words, we shall only consider sets of states of the form $\{p/L\}_{L \subseteq R}$ for $R \subseteq \mathbb{N}$.

While this choice leads to a less precise reachability analysis, it especially makes sense in the context of dead code elimination. In any case, the input of the dead code elimination algorithm (cf. Section 4) will be the list of alive **pause** instructions, that is to say R rather than S.

In Section 3.1, we first consider instantaneous reachability, i.e., reachability through a single reaction. We conclude for chains of reactions in Section 3.2.

3.1 Instantaneous Reachability

By definition,

- the intermediate state p/L is *instantly reachable from* $p \setminus X$ iff $\exists k : p \setminus X \xrightarrow{k} L$;
- the label ℓ is *instantly reachable from* $p \setminus X$ iff $\exists k, \exists L : p \setminus X \xrightarrow{k} L \wedge \ell \in L$.

We write $p \setminus X \Rightarrow p/L$ in the first case, $p \setminus X \Rightarrow \ell$ in the second. Importantly,

Lemma 3. *If* $p/L_0 \Rightarrow \ell$ *then* $\exists \ell_0 \in L_0 : p/\{\ell_0\} \Rightarrow \ell$.

Lemma 4. *If* $L_0 \subseteq R$ *and* $p/L_0 \Rightarrow p/L$ *then* $L \subseteq \bigcup_{\ell_0 \in R} \{\ell \in \mathcal{L}_p : p/\{\ell_0\} \Rightarrow \ell\}$.

Therefore, it makes sense to approximate a family $S = (p/L_i)_{i \in I}$ of intermediate states by the set of labels that appear in these states $R = \bigsqcup S = \bigcup_{i \in I} \{L_i\}$:

- $\bigsqcup \{p/L \in S_p : p \Rightarrow p/L\} = \{\ell \in \mathcal{L}_p : p \Rightarrow \ell\}$
- $\bigsqcup \left(\bigcup_{p/L_0 \in S} \{p/L \in S_p : p/L_0 \Rightarrow p/L\} \right) \subseteq \bigcup_{\ell_0 \in \bigsqcup S} \{\ell \in \mathcal{L}_p : p/\{\ell_0\} \Rightarrow \ell\}$

The set of labels instantly reachable from a family S of intermediate states can be safely approximated by the set of labels instantly reachable from the family of states $S' = (p/\{\ell_0\})_{\ell_0 \in \bigsqcup S}$, with the following trade-off:

- Because we replace the family S with up to $2^{|\mathcal{L}(p)|}$ states, by the family S' of at most $|\mathcal{L}(p)|$ states, the cost of the computation improves exponentially.
- Loss of precision may occur if $S \neq S'$. For instance, if p is the program "try 1:pause ; exit 1 || 2:pause ; 3:pause end," then the only instantly reachable state is $p/\{1, 2\}$. Because we approximate this state with the set of states $\{p/\emptyset, p/\{1\}, p/\{2\}, p/\{1, 2\}\}$, we end up computing that label 3 may be reachable in the execution of p (being instantly reachable from $p/\{2\}$), although it cannot be reached from $p/\{1, 2\}$.

$$d_R(\text{nothing}) = \emptyset$$
$$d_R(\text{gotopause } \ell) = \emptyset$$
$$d_R(\text{exit } d) = \emptyset$$
$$d_R(\text{signal } S \text{ in } p \text{ end}) = d_R(p)$$
$$d_R(\text{present } S \text{ then } p \text{ else } q \text{ end}) = d_R(p) \cup d_R(q)$$

$$d_R(\text{emit } S) = \emptyset$$
$$d_R(\ell{:}\text{pause}) = \begin{cases} \emptyset & \text{if } \ell \notin R \\ \{0\} & \text{if } \ell \in R \end{cases}$$
$$d_R(\text{try } p \text{ end}) = \downarrow d_R(p)$$
$$d_R(p \,\|\, q) = d_R(p) \cup d_R(q)$$

$$d_R(\text{loop } p \text{ end}) = \begin{cases} d_R(p) & \text{if } 0 \notin d_R(p) \\ (d_R(p) \cup s(p)) \setminus \{0\} & \text{if } 0 \in d_R(p) \end{cases}$$

$$d_R(p \,;\, q) = \begin{cases} d_R(p) \cup d_R(q) & \text{if } 0 \notin d_R(p) \\ (d_R(p) \setminus \{0\}) \cup s(q) \cup d_R(q) & \text{if } 0 \in d_R(p) \end{cases}$$

Fig. 6. Instantaneous Reachability from Intermediate States

Qualified completion codes. Denoting by "1_ℓ" a completion code 1 due to a pause or gotopause of label ℓ, we obtain the set of *qualified completion codes* $\mathcal{K} = \{0, 1_0, 1_1, \ldots, 2, 3, \ldots\}$. Formally, $\mathcal{K}$ is $(\mathbb{N} \setminus \{1\}) \cup \bigcup_{\ell \in \mathbb{N}} \{1_\ell\}$. Thanks to $\mathcal{K}$, we shall compute feasible completion codes and reachable labels simultaneously.

To recover regular completion codes from qualified completion codes, we define the projection $k \mapsto \hat{k}$ from $\mathcal{K}$ to $\mathbb{N}$ so that $\forall k \in \mathbb{N} \setminus \{1\} : \hat{k} = k$ and $\forall \ell \in \mathbb{N} : \hat{1_\ell} = 1$.

We equip $\mathcal{K}$ with the preorder "$\leq$" such that $k \leq l$ in $\mathcal{K}$ iff $\hat{k} \leq \hat{l}$ in $\mathbb{N}$. If $K, K' \subseteq \mathcal{K}$ then $\max(K, K')$ is $\{k \in K : \exists k' \in K', k' \leq k\} \cup \{k' \in K' : \exists k \in K, k \leq k'\}$. For instance, $\max(\{0, 1_4, 4, 6\}, \{1_1, 1_3, 3, 4\}) = \{1_1, 1_3, 1_4, 3, 4, 6\}$.

Finally, for $\ell \in \mathbb{N}$, we define $\downarrow 1_\ell = 1_\ell$.

We now compute the labels instantly reachable from p, then the labels instantly reachable from the set of states $\{p/L\}_{L \subseteq R}$ given the set of labels $R \subseteq \mathbb{N}$.

Initial state. Previously [19], we formalized a static analysis that computes the possible completion codes of reactions of the program p for a similar abstract semantics. We now extend this analysis so as to deal with gotopause instructions and obtain the labels instantly reachable from p at the same time.

Let $\mathcal{E}$ be the set of all Esterel* programs and $\mathcal{P}(\mathcal{K})$ be the powerset of $\mathcal{K}$. In Fig. 5, we specify the analysis function $s : \mathcal{E} \to \mathcal{P}(\mathcal{K})$ that overapproximates the set of qualified completion codes reachable from the initial state. It is easily derived from the rules of the abstract semantics for initial states. For instance, $s(\text{present } S \text{ then exit 7 end } \| \text{ 3:pause } \| \text{ gotopause 4}) = \{1_3, 1_4, 8\}$.

Lemma 5. $\exists L \subseteq \mathcal{L}_p : p \xrightarrow{k} L$ iff $\hat{k} \in s(p)$. Moreover, $p \Rightarrow \ell$ iff $1_\ell \in s(p)$.

Hence, the set of labels instantly reachable from p is:

Lemma 6. $\bigsqcup\{p/L \in \mathcal{S}_p : p \Rightarrow p/L\} = \{\ell \in \mathcal{L}_p : 1_\ell \in s(p)\}$.

Intermediate states. For $R \subseteq \mathbb{N}$, we define $d_R : \mathcal{E} \to \mathcal{P}(\mathcal{K})$ in Fig. 6 by now considering the rules applicable to intermediate states. Intuitively, $d_R(p)$ is meant to be the set of possible qualified completion codes of reactions of $p/\{\ell_0\}$ for $\ell_0 \in R$. If p is "1:pause ; 2:pause $\|$ 3:pause ; 4:pause ; exit 6" for instance, then $d_{\{1\}}(p) = \{1_2\}$, $d_{\{3,4\}}(p) = \{1_4, 7\}$, $d_{\{1,2,3,4\}}(p) = \{0, 1_2, 1_4, 7\}$.

Lemma 7. $\exists L \subseteq \mathcal{L}_p : p/\{\ell_0\} \xrightarrow{k} L$ iff $\hat{k} \in d_{\{\ell_0\}}(p)$. *Moreover,* $p/\{\ell_0\} \Rightarrow \ell$ iff $1_\ell \in d_{\{\ell_0\}}(p)$.

Lemma 8. *For all* R, R', $p : d_{R \cup R'}(p) = d_R(p) \cup d_{R'}(p)$.

Hence, the set of labels instantly reachable from the states $\{p/L_0\}_{L_0 \subseteq R}$ is:

Lemma 9. $\bigsqcup \left(\bigcup_{L_0 \subseteq R} \{p/L \in \mathcal{S}_p : p/L_0 \Rightarrow p/L\} \right) = \{\ell \in \mathcal{L}_p : 1_\ell \in d_R(p)\}$.

In Lemmas 6 and 9, we obtain equalities. Thus, this reachability analysis is exact w.r.t. the abstract semantics and for set of states of the form $\{p/L\}_{L \subseteq R}$.

3.2 Fixed Point

We define $\Delta_p : L_0 \mapsto \{\ell \in \mathcal{L}_p : 1_\ell \in s(p) \cup d_{L_0}(p)\}$. This function is monotonic over the complete lattice $\mathcal{P}(\mathcal{L}_p)$, therefore [21] it has a least fixed point $\mathcal{R}_p$. We already know that if $p \Rightarrow L$ then $L \subseteq \Delta_p(\emptyset)$ and if $p/L_0 \Rightarrow L$ then $L \subseteq \Delta_p(L_0)$. Therefore, $\mathcal{R}_p$ overapproximates the labels reachable in the execution of p, thus the reachable states.

Theorem 1. *If* $p \Rightarrow L_0$, $p/L_0 \Rightarrow L_1$, ..., $p/L_{n-1} \Rightarrow L_n$ *then* $L_n \subseteq \mathcal{R}_p$.

4 Dead Code Elimination

Checking program equivalence at the abstract level does not make sense since, for instance, "`nothing`" and "`emit S`" behave the same in the abstract semantics. For $R \subseteq \mathbb{N}$, we say that the programs p and q are:

- *initially equivalent* iff $\forall E, O, k, L : p \xrightarrow[E]{O,k} L \Leftrightarrow q \xrightarrow[E]{O,k} L$, and
- *R-equivalent* iff $\forall L_0 \subseteq R, \forall E, O, k, L : p/L_0 \xrightarrow[E]{O,k} L \Leftrightarrow q/L_0 \xrightarrow[E]{O,k} L$.

As with the definition of instantaneous reachability, these definitions give us the ability to derive program equivalence (a property of executions) from instantaneous equivalence properties (properties of reactions).

Lemma 10. *If* p *and* q *are initially equivalent and* $\mathcal{R}_p$-*equivalent then they are strongly bisimilar, that is to say behave the same in all contexts [22].*

Defining dead (unreachable) code can be managed at the abstract level. In the previous section, we defined instantly reachable labels, i.e., instantly reachable `pause` instructions. In fact, thanks to the structural definitions of s and d_R, we can extend the idea of instantaneous reachability to blocks of code:

- q in p is not *instantly reachable*, iff the computation of $s(p)$ does not involve the computation of $s(q)$.
- q in p is not *R-reachable*, iff $d_R(q)$ is empty and the computation of $d_R(p)$ does not involve the computation of $s(q)$.

Intuitively, q is not instantly reachable in p iff it is in sequence after a block of code r that cannot terminate instantly, that is to say $0 \notin s(r)$. Moreover, q is not R-reachable in p iff q does not contain any **pause** instruction with a label in R and q is not in sequence after a block of code that can terminate instantly if restarted from some **pause** instruction with a label in R.

In the sequel, we shall simplify programs so as to eliminate unreachable code while preserving program equivalence. Although our equivalence proofs depend on the semantics for which we define program equivalence, since our transformations only involve unreachable code, which we define at the abstract level, we claim that similar equivalence results hold for other concrete semantics, provided they share the same abstraction.

Simplifying "**try** p **|| exit 1 ;** q **end**" so as to preserve initial equivalence and R-equivalence for some set R requires to simplify p in the same way. Importantly, in Esterel*, q cannot be simply discarded because it can be reached through **gotopause** instructions. However, because of "**exit 1**," preserving R-equivalence for q is good enough. In other words, if p is "**emit S ; ...**" then "**emit S**" must be preserved. But, if q is, then "**emit S**" can be discarded.

To start with, we define the functions $\{sd_R\}_{R \subseteq \mathbb{N}}$ that gather the possible completion codes of the behaviors of the program p we want to reproduce:

$$
\begin{aligned}
sd_R : \mathbb{B} \times \mathcal{E} &\to \mathcal{K} \\
(0, p) &\mapsto d_R(p) \\
(1, p) &\mapsto d_R(p) \cup s(p)
\end{aligned}
$$

The Boolean b is 0 if only the behaviors of intermediates states (with labels in R) are relevant; b is 1 if, in addition, the initial behaviors of p are relevant.

In Fig. 7, we formalize code elimination as a family of R-equivalence-preserving functions $\{r_R : \mathbb{B} \times \mathcal{E} \to \mathcal{E}\}_{R \subseteq \mathbb{N}}$, which also preserve initial equivalence, if called with a Boolean parameter equal to 1. These functions are designed to delete as much code as possible while preserving the required equivalences.

As with the definition of d_R before, the structural definition of r_R makes sure that r_R is recursively applied to each block of the initial program, since any statement, whatever its position, can potentially be reached through jumps in Esterel*. However, not all statements can be reached "from the left," that is to say are in sequence after a statement that may terminate. The value of the Boolean parameter b in recursive calls is computed accordingly.

The simplifications implemented by r_R are the following:

- All **emit**, **exit**, and **gotopause** instructions are preserved iff left-reachable.
- A **pause** instruction is preserved if its label is in R or if it is left-reachable.
- The "**try ... end**" construct in "**try** p **end**" is preserved if the corresponding exception may occur. If removed, exception levels have to be adjusted accordingly: $\backslash p$ is obtained by decrementing all exit levels in p greater than the number of enclosing "**try ... end**" constructs in p, while replacing all **exit** instructions targeting the removed construct by **nothing**. For instance, $r_R(1, \text{try exit 1 || exit 2 end}) = r_R(1, \text{nothing || exit 1})$.

$$r_R(b, \texttt{nothing}) = \texttt{nothing}$$

$$r_R(b, \texttt{emit } S) = \begin{cases} \texttt{nothing} & \text{if } b = 0 \\ \texttt{emit } S & \text{if } b = 1 \end{cases}$$

$$r_R(b, \ell\texttt{:pause}) = \begin{cases} \texttt{nothing} & \text{if } (\ell \notin R) \wedge (b = 0) \\ \ell\texttt{:pause} & \text{if } (\ell \in R) \vee (b = 1) \end{cases}$$

$$r_R(b, \texttt{gotopause } \ell) = \begin{cases} \texttt{nothing} & \text{if } b = 0 \\ \texttt{gotopause } \ell & \text{if } b = 1 \end{cases}$$

$$r_R(b, \texttt{exit } d) = \begin{cases} \texttt{nothing} & \text{if } b = 0 \\ \texttt{exit } d & \text{if } b = 1 \end{cases}$$

$$r_R(b, \texttt{try } p \texttt{ end}) = \begin{cases} r_R(b, \searrow p) & \text{if } 2 \notin sd_R(b, p) \\ \texttt{try } r_R(b, p) \texttt{ end} & \text{if } 2 \in sd_R(b, p) \end{cases}$$

$$r_R(b, p \texttt{ ; } q) = \begin{cases} r_R(b, p)\boxed{;}\, r_R(0, q) & \text{if } 0 \notin sd_R(b, p) \\ r_R(b, p)\boxed{;}\, r_R(1, q) & \text{if } 0 \in sd_R(b, p) \end{cases}$$

$$r_R(b, \texttt{signal } S \texttt{ in } p \texttt{ end}) = \begin{cases} r_R(b, p) & \text{if } S \text{ does not occur in } r_R(b, p) \\ \texttt{signal } S \texttt{ in } r_R(b, p) \texttt{ end} & \text{if } S \text{ occurs in } r_R(b, p) \end{cases}$$

$$r_R(b, \substack{\texttt{present } S \texttt{ then } p \\ \texttt{else } q \texttt{ end}}) = \begin{cases} r_R(0, p \texttt{ ; try exit 1 ; } \nearrow q \texttt{ end}) & \text{if } b = 0 \\ \texttt{present } S \texttt{ then } r_R(1, p) \texttt{ else } r_R(1, q) \texttt{ end} & \text{if } b = 1 \end{cases}$$

$$r_R(b, \texttt{loop } p \texttt{ end}) = \begin{cases} r_R(b, p) & \text{if } 0 \notin sd_R(b, p) \\ \texttt{loop } r_R(1, p) \texttt{ end} & \text{if } 0 \in sd_R(b, p) \end{cases}$$

$$r_R(b, p \texttt{ || } q) = r_R(b, p) \boxed{||}\, r_R(b, q)$$

Fig. 7. Dead Code Elimination

- Depending on the possible termination of p in "p ; q," q is rewritten so as to preserve initial equivalence or not. Moreover, if p or q end up being nothing after simplification, it can be discarded as well as the ";" operator. We define: $p\boxed{;}\,\texttt{nothing} = p$, $\texttt{nothing}\boxed{;}\, q = q$, $p\boxed{;}\,q = p; q$ otherwise.
- Signal declarations are deleted if possible.
- A left-reachable "present S then p else q end" test is recursively simplified. A non-left-reachable test is first replaced by "p ; try exit 1 ; $\nearrow q$ end" to remove the test itself while preserving the branches, then simplified. Exception levels in q have to be adjusted: $\nearrow q$ is obtained by incrementing exit levels greater than the number of enclosing "try ... end" constructs in q. For example, $r_R(0, \texttt{present S then 1:pause ; emit 0 else 2:pause ; exit 3 end})$ is equal to $r_R(0, 1\texttt{:pause ; emit 0; try exit 1; 2:pause ; exit 4 end})$.
- A loop construct is deleted if its body never terminates. If it may terminate then initial equivalence must be preserved for the body, whatever b.
- The branches of a parallel are recursively rewritten. The parallel itself may be deleted if a branch reduces to nothing, hence the $\boxed{||}$ operator.

We establish initial equivalence and R-equivalence by structural induction:

Lemma 11. *Whatever R, $p \xrightarrow[E]{O, k} L \Leftrightarrow r_R(1, p) \xrightarrow[E]{O, k} L$.*

Lemma 12. *Whatever b, if $L_0 \subseteq R$ then $p/L_0 \xrightarrow[E]{O, k} L \Leftrightarrow r_R(b, p)/L_0 \xrightarrow[E]{O, k} L$.*

```
                              try
                                 exit 1;                         try
                                 try                                exit 1;
 loop                               present I then                 try
    try                                1:pause ; exit 1               1:pause;
      present I then                end;                              exit 1;
        1:pause;      loop          2:pause ; emit 0   dead code      2:pause;
        exit 1     expansion     end                 elimination     emit 0
      end;            ⟹       end;                      ⟹         end
      2:pause;                   try                               end;
      emit 0                        present I then                present I then
    end                              gotopause 1 ; exit 1            gotopause 1
 end                              end;                             end;
                                  gotopause 2 ; emit 0             gotopause 2
                               end
```

Fig. 8. Example

Theorem 2. p and $r_{\mathcal{R}_p}(1,p)$ behave the same (are strongly bisimilar).

This dead code elimination procedure is far from complete because of the approximations involved, yet it is already powerful, in particular w.r.t. machine-generated code. For instance, applying it after loop expansion [8] produces compact code, as illustrated in Fig. 8. While the expansion makes two copies of the loop body, the final code only contains one copy of "present I" and "emit 0".

$$\text{loop } p \text{ end} \overset{\substack{\text{loop}\\ \text{expansion}}}{\Longrightarrow} \text{try exit 1 ; } \nearrow p \text{ end ; } p[\ell:\text{pause} \mapsto \text{gotopause } \ell]$$

5   Conclusions

We have specified a static reachability analysis and an algorithm for dead code elimination in Esterel* programs. While we designed the reachability analysis with dead code elimination in mind, it can be used independently.

By abstracting signals from the analysis, we ensure it is applicable for many different semantics of the language. In addition, it makes it possible to safely dismantle states into their elementary components (locations of **pause** instructions), thus dramatically cutting the cost of the required fixed-point computation. Our analysis is exact and optimal with respect to this approximation.

In fact, apart from a single fixed-point computation, both the analysis and the transformation are obtained from structural traversals of the program source, resulting in simple correctness proofs.

We would like to extend this work in two directions. First, adopting either the logical or the constructive semantics of Esterel*, we shall consider synchronizations through signals, in addition to synchronizations through exceptions that we already take into account. Second, we plan to formalize and check our correctness proofs using a theorem prover, paving the way for embedding this work in a certified compiler for Esterel*.

References

1. Berry, G., Gonthier, G.: The Esterel synchronous programming language: Design, semantics, implementation. Science of Computer Programming **19** (1992) 87–152
2. Boussinot, F., de Simone, R.: The Esterel language. Another Look at Real Time Programming, Proceedings of the IEEE, Special Issue **79** (1991) 1293–1304
3. Berry, G.: The constructive semantics of pure Esterel, draft version 3. http://www-sop.inria.fr/esterel.org/ (1999)
4. Closse, E., Poize, M., Pulou, J., Vernier, P., Weil, D.: Saxo-rt: Interpreting Esterel semantic on a sequential execution structure. In: SLAP'02. Volume 65 of Electronic Notes in Theoretical Computer Science., Elsevier (2002)
5. Edwards, S.A., Kapadia, V., Halas, M.: Compiling Esterel into static discrete-event code. In: SLAP'04. Electronic Notes in Theoretical Computer Science, Elsevier (2004)
6. Berry, G.: Esterel on hardware. Philosophical Transactions of the Royal Society of London, Series A **19(2)** (1992) 87–152
7. Mignard, F.: Compilation du langage Esterel en systèmes d'équations booléennes. PhD thesis, Ecole des Mines de Paris (1994)
8. Tardieu, O.: Goto and concurrency: Introducing safe jumps in Esterel. In: SLAP'04. Electronic Notes in Theoretical Computer Science, Elsevier (2004)
9. Tardieu, O., de Simone, R.: Curing schizophrenia by program rewriting in Esterel. In: MEMOCODE'04. (2004)
10. Tardieu, O.: Loops in Esterel: from operational semantics to formally specified compilers. PhD thesis, Ecole des Mines de Paris (2004)
11. Schneider, K.: A verified hardware synthesis of Esterel programs. In: DIPES'00. (2001) 205–214
12. Schneider, K., Brandt, J., Schüele, T.: A verified compiler for synchronous programs with local declarations. In: SLAP'04. Electronic Notes in Theoretical Computer Science, Elsevier (2004)
13. Malik, S.: Analysis of cyclic combinational circuits. In: ICCAD'93. (1993) 618–625
14. Shiple, T., Berry, G., Touati, H.: Constructive analysis of cyclic circuits. In: Proc. International Design and Testing Conf (ITDC), Paris. (1996)
15. Namjoshi, K.S., Kurshan, R.P.: Efficient analysis of cyclic definitions. In: CAV'99. (1999) 394–405
16. Berry, G.: The semantics of pure Esterel. In Broy, M., ed.: Program Design Calculi. Volume 118 of Series F: Computer and System Sciences., NATO ASI Series (1993) 361–409
17. Schneider, K., Brandt, J., Schüele, T., Tuerk, T.: Maximal causality analysis. In: ACSD'05. (2005)
18. Tardieu, O.: A deterministic logical semantics for Esterel. In: SOS Workshop'04. Electronic Notes in Theoretical Computer Science, Elsevier (2004)
19. Tardieu, O., de Simone, R.: Instantaneous termination in pure Esterel. In: SAS'03. Volume 2694 of Lecture Notes in Computer Science., Springer (2003) 91–108
20. Plotkin, G.: A structural approach to operational semantics. Report DAIMI FN-19, Aarhus University, Denmark (1981)
21. Tarski, A.: A lattice-theoretical fixpoint theorem and its applications. Pacific Journal of Mathematics **5** (1955) 285–309
22. Park, D.: Concurrency and automata on infinite sequences. In: 5th GI Conference. Volume 104 of Lecture Notes in Computer Science., Springer (1981)

Synthesis of Interface Automata

Purandar Bhaduri

Department of Computer Science and Engineering,
Indian Institute of Technology Guwahati,
Guwahati 781039, India
pbhaduri@iitg.ernet.in

Abstract. We investigate the problem of synthesising an interface automaton R such that $P \parallel R \preceq Q$, for given deterministic interface automata P and Q. We show that a solution exists iff P and $Q^\perp$ are compatible, and the most general solution is given by $(P \parallel Q^\perp)^\perp$, where $P^\perp$ is the automaton P with inputs and outputs interchanged. We also characterise solutions in terms of winning input strategies in the automaton $(P \otimes Q^\perp)^\perp$, and the most general solution in terms of the most permissive winning strategy. We apply the synthesis problem for interfaces to the problem of synthesising converters for mismatched protocols.

1 Introduction

Interfaces play a central role in component based design and verification of systems. In this paper we study the problem of synthesising an interface R, which composed with a known interface P is a refinement of an interface Q. This is a central problem in component based top-down design of a system. The interface Q is an abstract interface, a high level specification of the component under development. The interface P is a known part of the implementation and we are required to find the most general (i.e., abstract) solution R satisfying the relation $P \parallel R \preceq Q$. Here $P \parallel Q$ is the composition of P and Q, and $P \preceq Q$ denotes 'P is a refinement of Q'. This problem has wide ranging applications from logic synthesis to the design of discrete controllers, and has been studied previously in [20, 21], where the composition is either the synchronous or parallel composition of languages, and refinement is inclusion. We study the problem in the setting of interface automata [6], where composition and refinement of interfaces are respectively the composition of interface automata and alternating refinement relations[2].

Interface automata are like ordinary automata, except for the distinction between input and output actions. The input actions of an interface automaton P are controlled by its environment. Therefore an input action labelling a transition is an *input assumption* (or constraint on P's environment). Dually, an output action of P is under P's control, and represents an an *output guarantee* of P. Note that unlike I/O automata [12], interface automata are *not* required to be input enabled. If an input action a is not enabled at a state s, it is an assumption on the automaton's environment that it will not provide a as an input in state s.

D.A. Peled and Y.-K. Tsay (Eds.): ATVA 2005, LNCS 3707, pp. 338–353, 2005.

When two interfaces P and Q are composed, the combined interface may contain incompatible states: states where one interface can generate an output that is not a legal input for the other. In the combined interface it is the environment's responsibility to ensure that such a state is unreachable [6]. This can be formalised as a two person game [6] which has the same flavour as the controller synthesis problem of Ramadge and Wonham [17]; in our setting the role of the controller is played by the environment. More formally, we follow de Alfaro [7] in modelling an interface as a game between two players, Output and Input. Player Output represents the system and its moves represent the outputs generated by the system. Player Input represents the environment; its moves represent the inputs the system receives from its environment. In general, the set of available moves of each player depends on the current state of the combined system. The interface is well-formed if the Input player has a winning strategy in the game, where the winning condition is to avoid all incompatible states. Clearly, the game aspect is relevant only when defining the composition of two interfaces.

Refinement of interfaces corresponds to weakening assumptions and strengthening guarantees. An interface P refines Q only if P can be used in any environment where Q can be. The usual notion of refinement is *simulation* or *trace containment* [12]. For interface automata, a more appropriate notion is that of *alternating simulation* [2], which is contravariant on inputs and covariant on outputs: if $P \preceq Q$ (P *refines* Q), P accepts more inputs (weaker input assumptions) and provides fewer outputs (stronger output guarantees). Thus alternating refinement preserves compatibility: if P and Q are compatible (i.e., $P \parallel Q$ is well-formed) and $P' \preceq P$, then so are P' and Q.

In this paper we show that a solution to $P \parallel R \preceq Q$ for R exists for deterministic interface automata iff P and $Q^\perp$ are compatible, and the most abstract (under alternating refinement) solution is given by $(P \parallel Q^\perp)^\perp$. Further, such an R can be constructed from the most permissive winning strategy for player Input in the combined game $(P \otimes Q^\perp)^\perp$. Here $P^\perp$ is the game P with the moves of the players Input and and Output interchanged, and $P \otimes Q$ is the combined game obtained from P and Q by synchronising on shared actions and interleaving the rest. We say a strategy π is more permissive than π' when, at every position in the game, the set of moves allowed by π includes those allowed by π'. The most permissive winning strategy is one that is least restrictive. This result ties up the relation between composition, refinement, synthesis and winning strategies, and should be seen as one more step towards a "uniform framework for the study of control, verification, component-based design, and implementation of open systems", based on games [7].

Note that the notation $P^\perp$ is borrowed from linear logic [8], where games play an important semantic role [3]. Using the notation of linear logic, the solution R to the synthesis problem can be written as $(P \otimes Q^\perp)^\perp = P^\perp \parr Q = P \multimap Q$, where $\otimes$, $\parr$ and $\multimap$ are respectively, the linear logic connectives 'With', 'Par' and linear implication. In our setting, the $\otimes$ connective of linear logic is parallel composition $\parallel$. The striking similarity of this solution with the language equation posed in

[20, 21] is intriguing. In their framework, the largest solution of the language equation $P \bullet R \subseteq Q$ for R is the language $\overline{P \bullet \overline{Q}}$ where $P \bullet Q$ is the synchronous (or parallel) composition of languages P and Q, and $\overline{P}$ is the complement of P. Clearly, there is a formal correspondence between $P \bullet Q$ and our $P \parallel Q$, between $\overline{P}$ and our $P^{\perp}$, and between language inclusion and alternating simulation.

We should also mention the formal resemblance of our work with Abramsky's Semantics of Interaction [1], based on the game semantics of linear logic. In particular, the strategy called *Application* (or *Modus Ponens*) in [1] is the solution to our synthesis problem in a different setting. The solution $R = P \multimap Q$ suggests that the problem of synthesis can be seen as the construction of a suitable morphism in an appropriate category of interface automata, along the lines of [13, 18]. However, we do not pursue this thread in this paper.

As a practical application we show how to apply interface synthesis to the protocol conversion problem for mismatched network protocols. The heterogeneity of existing networks often results in incompatible protocols trying to communicate with each other. The protocol conversion problem is, given two network protocols P_1 and P_2 which are mismatched, to come up with a converter C which mediates between the two protocols, such that the combined system conforms to an overall specification S. We show that a converter C, if it exists, can be obtained as the solution to $P \parallel C \preceq S$, where $P = P_1 \parallel P_2$ is the composition of the two protocols.

The controller synthesis problem and its solution as a winning strategy in a game has a long history, going back to Büchi and Landwebers' solution of Church's problem [4]. More recent applications of the idea in the synthesis of open systems occur in [13, 14, 16]. The control of discrete event systems [17] and the synthesis of converters for mismatched protocols [15] can be seen as applications of the same general principle. The present work extends the principle to the composition and refinement of interfaces.

2   Interface Automata

In this section we define interface automata and their composition and refinement. We follow the game formulation presented in [7]. Throughout this work we consider only *deterministic* interface automata.

Definition 1. *An* interface automaton P *is a tuple* $(S_P, S_P^0, \mathcal{A}_P^I, \mathcal{A}_P^O, \Gamma_P^I, \Gamma_P^O, \delta_P)$ *where:*

- S_P *is a finite set of* states.
- $S_P^0 \subseteq S_P$ *is the set of* initial states, *which has at most one element, denoted* s_P^0.
- $\mathcal{A}_P^I$ *and* $\mathcal{A}_P^O$ *are disjoint sets of* input *and* output *actions. The set* $\mathcal{A}_P = \mathcal{A}_P^I \cup \mathcal{A}_P^O$ *is the set of all* actions.
- $\Gamma_P^I : S_P \to 2^{\mathcal{A}_P^I}$ *is a map assigning to each state* $s \in S_P$ *a set (possibly empty) of* input moves. *Similarly,* $\Gamma_P^O : S_P \to 2^{\mathcal{A}_P^O}$ *assigns to each state*

$s \in S_P$ a set *(again, possibly empty) of* output moves. *The input and output moves at a state s correspond to actions that can be accepted and generated at s respectively. Denote by* $\Gamma_P(s) = \Gamma_P^I(s) \cup \Gamma_P^O(s)$ *the set of all actions at s.*

- $\delta_P : S_P \times \mathcal{A}_P \to S_P$ *is a transition function associating a target state* $\delta_P(s, a)$ *with each state* $s \in S_P$ *and action* $a \in \mathcal{A}_P$. *Note that the value* $\delta_P(s, a)$ *makes sense only when* $a \in \Gamma_P(s)$. *When* $a \notin \Gamma_P(s)$, *the value can be arbitrary.*

The interface automaton P is said to be *empty* when its set of initial states S_P^0 is empty. Empty interface automata arise when incompatible automata are composed.

Definition 2. *An* input strategy *for P is a map* $\pi^I : S_P^+ \to 2^{\mathcal{A}_P^I}$ *satisfying* $\pi^I(\sigma s) \subseteq \Gamma_P^I(s)$ *for all* $s \in S_P$ *and* $\sigma \in S_P^*$. *An output strategy* $\pi^O : S_P^+ \to 2^{\mathcal{A}_P^O}$ *is defined similarly. The set of input and output strategies of P are denoted by* Π_P^I *and* Π_P^O *respectively.*

An input and output strategy jointly determine a set of traces in S_P^+ as follows. At each step, if the input strategy proposes a set $\mathcal{B}^I$ of actions, and the output strategy proposes a set $\mathcal{B}^O$ of actions, an action from $\mathcal{B}^I \cup \mathcal{B}^O$ is chosen nondeterministically.

Definition 3. *Given a state* $s \in S_P$, *and input strategy* π^I *and an output strategy* π^O, *the set* $Outcomes(s, \pi^I, \pi^O) \subseteq S_P^+$ *of resulting plays is defined inductively as follows:*

- $s \in Outcomes_P(s, \pi^I, \pi^O)$;
- *if* $\sigma t \in Outcomes(s, \pi^I, \pi^O)$ *for* $\sigma \in S_P^+$ *and* $t \in S_P$, *then for all* $a \in \pi^I(\sigma t) \cup \pi^O(\sigma t)$ *the sequence* $\sigma t \delta_P(s, a) \in Outcomes_P(s, \pi^I, \pi^O)$.

A state $s \in S_P$ is said to be *reachable* in P, if there is a sequence of states $s_0, s_1, \ldots, s_n$ with $s_0 \in S_P^0$, $s_n = s$, and for all $0 \leq k < n$ there is $a_k \in \Gamma_P(s_k)$ such that $\delta_P(s_k, a_k) = s_{k+1}$. Reach$(P)$ denotes the set of reachable states of P

The refinement of interface automata is known as *alternating simulation*, the right notion of simulation between games [2]. Intuitively, an alternating simulation $\rho \subseteq S_P \times S_Q$ from P to Q is a relation for which $(s, t) \in \rho$ implies all input moves from t can be simulated by s and all output moves from s can be simulated by t.

Definition 4. *An* alternating simulation ρ *from P to Q is a relation* $\rho \subseteq S_P \times S_Q$ *such that, for all* $(s, t) \in \rho$ *and all* $a \in \Gamma_Q^I(t) \cup \Gamma_P^O(s)$, *the following conditions are satisfied:*

1. $\Gamma_Q^I(t) \subseteq \Gamma_P^I(s)$;
2. $\Gamma_P^O(s) \subseteq \Gamma_Q^O(t)$;
3. $(\delta_P(s, a), \delta_Q(t, a)) \in \rho$.

Refinement between interface automata is defined as the existence of an alternating simulation between the initial states.

Definition 5. *An interface automaton P refines an interface automaton Q, written $P \preceq Q$, if the following conditions are satisfied:*

1. $\mathcal{A}_Q^I \subseteq \mathcal{A}_P^I$;
2. $\mathcal{A}_P^O \subseteq \mathcal{A}_Q^O$;
3. *there is an alternating simulation ρ from P to Q, such that $(s^0, t^0) \in \rho$ for some $s^0 \in S_P^0$ and $t^0 \in S_Q^0$.*

We now define the parallel composition $P \parallel Q$ of interface automata P and Q in a series of steps.

Definition 6. P *and* Q *are* composable *if* $\mathcal{A}_P^O \cap \mathcal{A}_Q^O = \emptyset$.

We first define the *product automaton* $P \otimes Q$ of two composable interface automata P and Q, by synchronising their shared actions and interleaving all others. The set of shared actions of P and Q is defined by Shared$(P, Q) = \mathcal{A}_P \cap \mathcal{A}_Q$.

Definition 7. *The* product $P \otimes Q$ *of two composable interface automata P and Q is defined by*

- $S_{P \otimes Q} = S_P \times S_Q$;
- $S_{P \otimes Q}^0 = S_P^0 \times S_Q^0$;
- $\mathcal{A}_{P \otimes Q}^I = (\mathcal{A}_P^I \cup \mathcal{A}_Q^I) \backslash Comm(P, Q)$ *where* $Comm(P, Q) = (\mathcal{A}_P^O \cap \mathcal{A}_Q^I) \cup (\mathcal{A}_P^I \cap \mathcal{A}_Q^O)$ *is the set of* communication actions, *a subset of Shared(P, Q)*;
- $\mathcal{A}_{P \otimes Q}^O = \mathcal{A}_P^O \cup \mathcal{A}_Q^O$;
- $\Gamma_{P \otimes Q}^I((s, t)) = (\Gamma_P^I(s) \backslash \mathcal{A}_Q^O) \cup (\Gamma_Q^I(t)) \backslash \mathcal{A}_P^O)$ *for all* $(s, t) \in S_P \times S_Q$;
- $\Gamma_{P \otimes Q}^O((s, t)) = \Gamma_P^O(s) \cup \Gamma_Q^O(t)$, *for all* $(s, t) \in S_P \times S_Q$;
- *for all* $a \in \mathcal{A}_{P \otimes Q}$,

$$\delta_{P \otimes Q}((s, t), a) = \begin{cases} (\delta_P(s, a), \delta_Q(t, a)) & \text{if } a \in \mathcal{A}_P \cap \mathcal{A}_Q \\ (\delta_P(s, a), t) & \text{if } a \in \mathcal{A}_P \backslash \mathcal{A}_Q \\ (s, \delta_Q(t, a)) & \text{if } a \in \mathcal{A}_Q \backslash \mathcal{A}_P \end{cases}$$

Since interface automata need not be input enabled, there may be reachable states in $P \otimes Q$ where a communication action can be output by one of the automaton but cannot be accepted as input by the other. These states are called *locally incompatible*.

Definition 8. *The set Incomp(P, Q) of locally incompatible states of P and Q consists of all pairs $(s, t) \in S_P \times S_Q$ for which one of the following two conditions hold:*

1. $\exists a \in Comm(P, Q)$ *such that* $a \in \Gamma_P^O(s)$ *but* $a \notin \Gamma_Q^I(t)$,
2. $\exists a \in Comm(P, Q)$ *such that* $a \in \Gamma_Q^O(t)$ *but* $a \notin \Gamma_P^I(s)$.

A local incompatibility can be avoided if there is a helpful environment, which by providing the right sequence of inputs can steer the automaton away from such an undesirable state. The states from which Input can prevent the product $P \otimes Q$ from reaching a state in $\text{Incomp}(P, Q)$ are called *compatible*. In other words, the compatible states are those from which Input has a winning strategy. The calculation of winning strategy in such safety games, if one exists, by using the *controllable predecessors* of a set of states U and iterative refinement is standard [19].

Definition 9. *A state $s \in S_{P \otimes Q}$ is* compatible *if there is an input strategy $\pi^I \in \Pi^I_{P \otimes Q}$ such that, for all output strategies $\pi^O \in \Pi^O_{P \otimes Q}$, all $\sigma \subset \text{Outcomes}_{P \otimes Q}$ (s, π^I, π^O) and all incompatible states $w \in \text{Incomp}(P, Q)$, the state w does not appear in the sequence σ.*

The composition $P \parallel Q$ is obtained by restricting $P \otimes Q$ to the states that can be reached from the initial state under an input strategy that avoids all locally incompatible states. We call these states *backward compatible*. These are the states that are reachable from the initial state of $P \otimes Q$ by visiting only compatible states. Note that in [7] backward compatible states are called *usably reachable states*.

Definition 10. *A state $s \in S_{P \otimes Q}$ is* backward compatible *in $P \otimes Q$ if there is an input strategy $\pi^I \in \Pi^I_{P \otimes Q}$ such that:*

- *for all initial states $s_0 \in S^0_{P \otimes Q}$, all output strategies $\pi^O \in \Pi^O_{P \otimes Q}$, all outcomes $\sigma \in \text{Outcomes}_{P \otimes Q}(s_0, \pi^I, \pi^O)$ and all $w \in \text{Incomp}(P, Q)$, w does not occur in σ;*
- *there is an initial state $s_0 \in S^0_{P \otimes Q}$, an output strategy $\pi^O \in \Pi^O_{P \otimes Q}$, and an outcome $\sigma \in \text{Outcomes}_{P \otimes Q}(s_0, \pi^I, \pi^O)$ such that $s \in \sigma$.*

Definition 11. *The composition $P \parallel Q$ of two interface automata P and Q, with T the set of backward compatible states of the product $P \otimes Q$, is an interface automaton defined by:*

- $S_{P \parallel Q} = T$
- $S^0_{P \parallel Q} = S^0_{P \otimes Q} \cap T$
- $A^I_{P \parallel Q} = A^I_{P \otimes Q}$
- $A^O_{P \parallel Q} = A^O_{P \otimes Q}$
- $\Gamma^I_{P \parallel Q}(s) = \{a \in \Gamma^I_{P \otimes Q}(s) \mid \delta_{P \otimes Q}(s, a) \in T\}$ *for all $s \in T$*
- $\Gamma^O_{P \parallel Q}(s) = \Gamma^O_{P \otimes Q}(s)$ *for all $s \in T$*
- *for all $s \in T$, $a \in \Gamma_{P \parallel Q}(s)$,*

$$\delta_{P \parallel Q}(s, a) = \begin{cases} \delta_{P \otimes Q}(s, a) \text{ if } \delta_{P \otimes Q}(s, a) \in T \\ \text{arbitrary} \quad \text{otherwise} \end{cases}$$

Definition 12. *P and Q are said to be* compatible *if their composition is non-empty i.e., $s^0_{P \parallel Q} \neq \emptyset$. This is equivalent to $s^0_{P \otimes Q} \in T$, where T is the set of backward compatible states of $P \otimes Q$.*

Notation. We write $\text{Reach}^O(P)$ to denote the set of states of P that are reachable from the initial state s_P^0 by following only output actions.

We use the following lemma in our proof of Theorems 1 and 2 in Section 3. Since the best input strategy to avoid locally incompatible states is simply to generate no inputs to $P \otimes Q$ at any state, the set of compatible states in $P \otimes Q$ is simply the set of states from which $P \otimes Q$ cannot reach a state in $\text{Incomp}(P, Q)$ by a sequence of output actions.

Lemma 1. *P and Q are compatible iff the states in $\text{Reach}^O(P \otimes Q)$ are locally compatible, i.e., $\text{Reach}^O(P \otimes Q) \cap \text{Incomp}(P, Q) = \emptyset$.*

Proof. Suppose P and Q are compatible. Then $s_{P \otimes Q}^0$ is a backward compatible state in $P \otimes Q$. This implies there is an input strategy π^I for $P \otimes Q$ which avoids all locally incompatible states starting from $s_{P \otimes Q}^0$, no matter what the output strategy is. Now Output can always force $P \otimes Q$ to enter any state in $\text{Reach}^O(P \otimes Q)$. In other words, an output strategy π^O exists for which every state s in $\text{Reach}^O(P \otimes Q)$ appears in some sequence in $\text{Outcomes}_{P \otimes Q}(s_{P \otimes Q}^0, \pi^I, \pi^O)$. Since $s_{P \otimes Q}^0$ is a backward compatible in $P \otimes Q$, it follows that $\text{Reach}^O(P \otimes Q) \cap \text{Incomp}(P, Q) = \emptyset$. Conversely, suppose the states in $\text{Reach}^O(P \otimes Q)$ are locally compatible. This implies that any state in $\text{Incomp}(P, Q)$ can be reached, if at all, by following a sequence of actions which includes at least one input action. Then the input strategy which disables all such input actions avoids all locally incompatible states and so $s_{P \otimes Q}^0$ is backward compatible.   □

3   Synthesis of Interface Automata

Our goal is to find the most general solution R to $P \parallel R \preceq Q$ when it exists, and characterise the conditions under which it exists. By a most general solution we mean, a solution U, such that for any solution V, it is the case that $V \preceq U$. In this section we prove our main result, viz., the most general solution to $P \parallel R \preceq Q$ is give by $R = (P \parallel Q^\perp)^\perp$ and a solution exists iff P and $Q^\perp$ are compatible. Here $P^\perp$ is the same as P, except all the input actions in P become output actions in $P^\perp$ and similarly the output actions of P are the input actions of $P^\perp$.

Example 1. Figure 1 presents three examples to illustrate the synthesis idea with given interface automata P and Q. The construction of $Q^\perp$, $P \parallel Q^\perp$ and $R = (P \parallel Q^\perp)^\perp$ are shown in each case.

1. In Figure 1(a), the input actions are $\mathcal{A}_P^I = \mathcal{A}_Q^I = \{a, c\}$, and the output actions are $\mathcal{A}_P^O = \mathcal{A}_Q^O = \{b, d\}$. Note that in $P \parallel Q^\perp$, the transition labelled c? does not appear, as it is a shared action, and has to be present in both P and $Q^\perp$ to appear in their product. Note also, how b appears as an input action in the result $(P \parallel Q^\perp)^\perp$.
2. In Figure 1(b), the action sets are $\mathcal{A}_P^I = \{a\}$, $\mathcal{A}_P^O = \{b\}$, $\mathcal{A}_Q^I = \{a, c\}$ and $\mathcal{A}_Q^O = \{b, d\}$. In this case, the solution is essentially identical with Q,

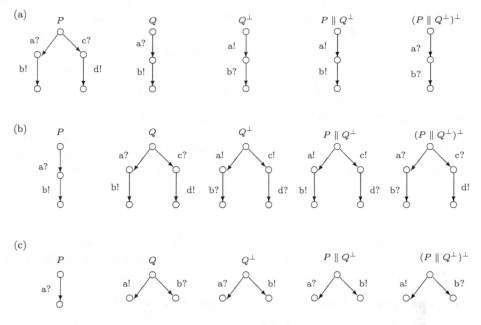

Fig. 1. Interface Automata Synthesis Examples

except for the polarity of action b. Note that there is already an alternating simulation between P and Q. The input transition labelled $b?$ appears in R because we assume $\mathcal{A}_P^O \subseteq \mathcal{A}_R^O$: in some sense, R can be thought of as a controller for P, and hence should be allowed to use all the output actions of P as input, in addition to driving the input actions of P. Note that if we changed the the input action set of P to be $\mathcal{A}_P^I = \mathcal{A}_Q^I = \{a, c\}$, then there would be no solution R, because P and $Q^\perp$ would not be compatible: in the initial state, $Q^\perp$ is ready to output a c, but P is not ready to accept it as input, even though c is a communication action between the two.

3. In Figure 1(c), the action sets are $\mathcal{A}_P^I = \{a\}$, $\mathcal{A}_P^O = \emptyset$, $\mathcal{A}_Q^I = \{b\}$ and $\mathcal{A}_Q^O = \{a\}$. In this example, an input of P appears as an output of Q. The result $(P \parallel Q^\perp)^\perp$ adds the input b and also converts a from an input to an output. In this case, R is identical to Q.

Note. Throughout this section we make the weak assumption that $\mathcal{A}_P^I \subseteq \mathcal{A}_Q^I \cup \mathcal{A}_Q^O$. This is to ensure that an environment E for which $Q \parallel E$ is a closed system (i.e., has no inputs) will also make $(P \parallel R) \parallel E$ a closed system. So any inputs to P will be provided by an output from the environment of Q or from R. In the latter case, such an input of P will be an output of Q. Further, we assume that the solution R satisfies $\mathcal{A}_P^O \subseteq \mathcal{A}_R^I$. This is to allow R to use the output actions of P as inputs in carrying out its control objectives. It is clear that any solution R will satisfy $\mathcal{A}_R^O \subseteq \mathcal{A}_Q^O \backslash \mathcal{A}_P^O$, and for the most general solution the two sets will be equal.

Notation. We write $p \xrightarrow{a} p'$ if $a \in \Gamma_P(p)$ and $\delta(p, a) = p'$ for states p, p' and action a in an interface automaton P. We call $p \xrightarrow{a} p'$ an *input transition* if a is an input action of P. An output transition is defined similarly.

First we prove a result about compatibility that is used in Theorem 1 below.

Lemma 2. *If P and $Q^{\perp}$ are compatible, then P and $(P \parallel Q^{\perp})^{\perp}$ are compatible.*

Proof. Suppose P and $Q^{\perp}$ are compatible, but P and $(P \parallel Q^{\perp})^{\perp}$ are not. By Lemma 1, this means there exists a state $(p, (p', q)) \in \text{Reach}^O(P \otimes (P \parallel Q^{\perp})^{\perp})$ which is in $\text{Incomp}(P, (P \parallel Q^{\perp})^{\perp})$. Since the interface automata we consider are deterministic, it must be the case that $p = p'$. This implies that there exists an $a \in \text{Comm}(P, (P \parallel Q^{\perp})^{\perp})$ such that either (a) $a \in \Gamma_P^O(p)$ and $a \notin \Gamma_{(P\parallel Q^{\perp})^{\perp}}^I(p, q) = \Gamma_{(P\parallel Q^{\perp})}^O(p, q) = \Gamma_P^O(p) \cup \Gamma_Q^I(q)$, which is impossible, or (b) $a \notin \Gamma_P^I(p)$ and $a \in \Gamma_{(P\parallel Q^{\perp})^{\perp}}^O(p, q)$ which implies $(p, q) \xrightarrow{a} (p', q')$ is an input transition in $P \parallel Q^{\perp}$ and $p \xrightarrow{a} p'$ is not an input transition in P. This is possible only if $a \in \mathcal{A}_Q^O$ but $a \notin \mathcal{A}_P^I$, which contradicts our assumption that $a \in \text{Comm}(P, (P \parallel Q^{\perp})^{\perp})$.   □

Theorem 1. *A solution R to $P \parallel R \preceq Q$ exists iff P and $Q^{\perp}$ are compatible.*

Proof. (If) Suppose P and $Q^{\perp}$ are compatible. By Lemma 2 so are P and $(P \parallel Q^{\perp})^{\perp}$. Take $R = (P \parallel Q^{\perp})^{\perp}$. We show that there exists an alternating simulation ρ between $P \parallel R$ and Q. Define the relation $\rho = \{((p, (p, q)), q) \mid (p, (p, q))$ is a state in $P \parallel R\}$. Since (s_P^0, s_Q^0) is the initial state of R, $(s_P^0, (s_P^0, s_Q^0))$ is the initial state of $P \parallel R$, and hence $((s_P^0, (s_P^0, s_Q^0)), s_Q^0)$ is in ρ. Now suppose $((p, (p, q)), q) \in \rho$ and $q \xrightarrow{a} q$ is an input transition in Q. It follows that $q \xrightarrow{a} q'$ is an output transition in $Q^{\perp}$. Therefore, $p \xrightarrow{a} p'$ is an input transition in P for some p', since (p, q), being in $P \parallel Q^{\perp}$, is backward compatible in $P \otimes Q^{\perp}$. Hence $(p, q) \xrightarrow{a} (p', q')$ is an output transition in $P \parallel Q^{\perp}$, and so an input transition in $(P \parallel Q^{\perp})^{\perp}$, whence $(p, (p, q)) \xrightarrow{a} (p', (p', q'))$ is an input transition in $P \parallel (P \parallel Q^{\perp})^{\perp}$ and by definition of ρ, $((p', (p', q')), q')$ is again in ρ. Similarly for the output side, suppose $((p, (p, q)), q) \in \rho$ and $(p, (p, q)) \xrightarrow{a} (p', (p'', q'))$ is an output transition in $P \parallel (P \parallel Q^{\perp})^{\perp}$. Since we consider only deterministic automata, $p' = p''$. Also, it must be the case that $a \in \text{Comm}(P, (P \parallel Q^{\perp})^{\perp})$, because an output action of P is an output action of $P \parallel Q^{\perp}$, and therefore an input action of $(P \parallel Q^{\perp})^{\perp}$. Suppose $p \xrightarrow{a} p'$ is an output transition in P, and because P and $Q^{\perp}$ are compatible, and (p, q) is backward compatible in $P \otimes Q^{\perp}$, $q \xrightarrow{a} q'$ is an input transition in $Q^{\perp}$, and hence an output transition in Q. On the other hand, if $p \xrightarrow{a} p'$ is an input transition in P, then since $(p, (p, q)) \xrightarrow{a} (p', (p', q'))$ is an output transition in $P \parallel (P \parallel Q^{\perp})^{\perp}$, $(p, q) \xrightarrow{a} (p', q')$ is an output transition in $(P \parallel Q^{\perp})^{\perp}$, and therefore an input transition in $(P \parallel Q^{\perp})$. From the assumption that $\mathcal{A}_P^I \subseteq \mathcal{A}_Q^I$ and by the definition of the product $P \otimes Q^{\perp}$ it follows that $q \xrightarrow{a} q'$ is an input transition of $Q^{\perp}$, and hence an output transition of Q. By the definition of ρ, $((p', (p', q')), q') \in \rho$, hence ρ is an alternating simulation as required.

(Only if) We show the contrapositive. Suppose P and $Q^\perp$ are not compatible. Then, by Lemma 1, there exists a state $(p, q) \in \text{Reach}^O(P, Q)$ which is incompatible, i.e., there is an a such that either (a) $a \in \Gamma_P^O(p)$ and $a \notin \Gamma_Q^O(q)$ or (b) $a \notin \Gamma_P^I(p)$ and $a \in \Gamma_Q^I(q)$. Both possibilities rule out the existence of an alternating simulation between $P \parallel R$ and Q for any R.

$\square$

Theorem 2. *When the condition stated in Theorem 1 is satisfied, the most general solution to $P \parallel R \preceq Q$ is $R = (P \parallel Q^\perp)^\perp$.*

Proof. In the proof of Theorem 1 (If part) we have already shown that $R = (P \parallel Q^\perp)^\perp$ is a solution. Suppose U is any solution to $P \parallel R \preceq Q$. We construct an alternating simulation ν from U to $(P \parallel Q)^\perp$ as follows. By assumption, there exists an alternating simulation ρ from $P \parallel U$ and Q. Define $\nu = \{(u, (p, q)) \mid ((p, u), q) \in \rho\}$. Clearly $(s_U^0, (s_P^0, s_Q^0)) \in \nu$, since $((s_P^0, s_U^0), s_Q^0) \in \rho$. Now suppose $(u, (p, q)) \in \nu$ and $u \xrightarrow{a} u'$ is an output transition in U. This implies $p \xrightarrow{a} p'$ is an input transition in P for some p', since by assumption $((p, u), q) \in \rho$ and therefore (p, u) is backward compatible in $P \otimes U$. Hence, $(p, u) \xrightarrow{a} (p', u')$ is an output transition in $P \parallel U$. It follows that $q \xrightarrow{a} q'$ is an output transition in Q for some q', with $((p', u'), q') \in \rho$, which is equivalent to $q \xrightarrow{a} q'$ is an input transition in $Q^\perp$. Therefore, $(p, q) \xrightarrow{a} (p', q')$ is an input transition in $P \parallel Q^\perp$, since (p, q) is backward compatible in $P \otimes Q^\perp$ by assumption. It follows that $(p, q) \xrightarrow{a} (p', q')$ is an output transition in $(P \parallel Q^\perp)^\perp$ and $(u', ((p', q')) \in \nu$ as required. Next suppose $(u, (p, q)) \in \nu$ and $(p, q) \xrightarrow{a} (p', q')$ is an input transition in $(P \parallel Q^\perp)^\perp$, which is the same as $(p, q) \xrightarrow{a} (p', q')$ is an output transition in $P \parallel Q^\perp$. This implies that either (a) $p \xrightarrow{a} p'$ is an input transition in P and $q \xrightarrow{a} q'$ is an input transition in Q or (b) $p \xrightarrow{a} p'$ is an output transition in P and $q \xrightarrow{a} q'$ is an output transition in Q. For the first case, by the existence of the alternating simulation ρ, $(p, u) \xrightarrow{a} (p', u')$ is an input transition in $P \parallel U$ for some state u' in U with $((p', u'), q') \in \rho$ and hence $(u', (p', q')) \in \nu$. For the second case, $u \xrightarrow{a} u'$ is an input transition in U for some u', since (p, u) is backward compatible in $P \otimes U$. Further $(u', (p', q')) \in \nu$, since $((p', u'), q') \in \rho$, and the conclusion follows.

$\square$

4   Winning Strategies and Synthesis

We now characterise the most general solution to $P \parallel R \preceq Q$ in terms of winning strategies. Specifically, we show that the most general solution corresponds to the *most permissive* winning strategy for Input in $P \otimes (P \parallel Q^\perp)^\perp$.

First we define winning strategies for Input and Output in games corresponding to the product $P \otimes Q$ of two interface automata P and Q. We also define a natural partial order $\sqsubseteq^I$ on input strategies, such that $\sigma_P^I \sqsubseteq^I \tau_P^I$ if the strategy τ_P^I generates more inputs than σ_P^I at every state of P. A similar order $\sqsubseteq^O$ is defined on output strategies. Since the orders are lattices, the *most permissive strategy* exists, as is given by the lattice join. We then show that the parallel composition $P \parallel Q$ can be extracted from the most permissive winning strategy for Input.

Definition 13. *Let P and Q be composable interface automata. A winning input strategy for $P \otimes Q$ is an input strategy π^I such that for all output strategies π^O, all initial states $s_0 \in S^0_{P \otimes Q}$, all $\sigma \in Outcomes_{P \otimes Q}(s_0, \pi^I, \pi^O)$, and all incompatible states $w \in Incomp(P, Q)$, the state w does not appear in the sequence σ. The definition of a winning output strategy is symmetric, where the winning condition is that a state in $Incomp(P, Q)$ must be reached in every run $\sigma \in Outcomes_{P \otimes Q}(s_0, \pi^I, \pi^O)$.*

We now define the order $\sqsubseteq$ on strategies. The idea is that an input strategy is higher in the order if it accepts more inputs. Dually an output strategy is higher in the order if it generates more outputs.

Definition 14. *The binary relation $\sqsubseteq^I$ on input strategies for P is defined by $\pi^I_0 \sqsubseteq \pi^I_1$ iff $\pi^I_0(\sigma) \subseteq \pi^I_1(\sigma)$ for all $\sigma \in S^+_P$. When $\pi^I_0 \sqsubseteq \pi^I_1$, we say π^I_1 is more permissive than π^I_0. Similarly, for output strategies, $\pi^O_0 \sqsubseteq^O \pi^O_1$ iff $\pi^O_0(\sigma) \subseteq \pi^O_1(\sigma)$ for all $\sigma \in S^+_P$.*

Clearly, the relations $\sqsubseteq^I$ and $\sqsubseteq^O$ are lattices, with top elements $\pi^I_T(\sigma s) = \Gamma^I_P(s)$ and $\pi^O_T(\sigma s) = \Gamma^O_P(s)$, and join and meet given by pointwise union and intersection. Note that the bottom elements are the empty strategies, which are allowed by the definition of strategies.

Corollary 1. *If there is a winning strategy for either player in a game then there is a most permissive winning strategy for that player.*

Proof. Simply take the join of the set of all winning strategies for the player. $\square$

Next we show how to extract an interface automaton $\pi^I(P \otimes Q)$ from an input strategy π^I for the game $P \otimes Q$, by cutting down some of its states and transitions.

Definition 15. *The interface automaton $\pi^I(P \otimes Q)$ defined by input strategy π^I for the game $P \otimes Q$ is defined as follows. Its set of input and output actions are the same as those of $P \otimes Q$. The set $S_{\pi^I(P \otimes Q)}$ contains those states of $P \otimes Q$ that are reached in some sequence in $Outcomes_{P \otimes Q}(s^0_{P \otimes Q}, \pi^I, \pi^O_T)$, where π^O_T is the top output strategy in the lattice of strategies (the one that produces the most output). The input moves of $\pi^I(P \otimes Q)$ are defined by $\Gamma^I(s) = \{a \mid a \in \Gamma^I_{P \otimes Q}$ such that $a \in \pi^I(\sigma s)$ for some $\sigma \in S^+_{\pi^I(P \otimes Q)}\}$. The input transitions of $\pi^I(P \otimes Q)$ are defined by $\delta(s, a) = \delta_{P \otimes Q}(s, a)$ when $a \in \Gamma^I(s)$ and an arbitrary element of $S_{\pi^I(P \otimes Q)}$ otherwise. The output moves and transitions are the straightforward restrictions of the output moves and transitions of $P \otimes Q$ to the set of states $S_{\pi^I(P \otimes Q)}$.*

The following proposition states that the parallel composition $P \parallel Q$ of interface automata P and Q is the interface automaton $\pi_w^I(P \otimes Q)$ defined by input strategy π_w^I for the game $P \otimes Q$, where π_w^I is the most permissive winning input strategy, if one exists.

Proposition 1. *For composable interface automata P and Q, $P \parallel Q$ can be obtained as $\pi_w^I(P \otimes Q)$ where π_w^I is the most permissive winning input strategy for $P \otimes Q$. If no winning input strategy exists then P and Q are incompatible.*

Proof. By Definition 13, if no winning input strategy exists, there exists an output strategy π^O such that an incompatible state appears in some sequence $\sigma \in \text{Outcomes}_{P \otimes Q}(s_{P \otimes Q}^0, \pi^I, \pi^O)$, for all input strategies π^I. From Definition 10, this implies that the set T of backward compatible states is empty, and hence by Definition 11 the composition $P \parallel Q$ is empty. Suppose there is a winning input strategy for $P \otimes Q$. We show that the set of states $S_{\pi_w^I(P \otimes Q)}$ is identical with the backward compatible states T of $P \otimes Q$, where π_w^I is the most permissive winning input strategy for $P \otimes Q$. Suppose $s \in S_{\pi_w^I(P \otimes Q)}$. Since π_w^I is a winning strategy, s satisfies the first clause in Definition 10 of backward compatibility. By Definition 15, s is reached in some play in $\text{Outcomes}_{P \otimes Q}(s_{P \otimes Q}^0, \pi_w^I, \pi^O)$ and therefore s satisfies the second clause as well. Now suppose s is a backward compatible state of $P \otimes Q$. By Definition 10 there exists a winning input strategy π^I and some output strategy π^O for $P \otimes Q$, for which s appears in some play $\sigma \in \text{Outcomes}_{P \otimes Q}(s_{P \otimes Q}^0, \pi^I, \pi^O)$. It follows that s appears in some play in $\text{Outcomes}_{P \otimes Q}(s_{P \otimes Q}^0, \pi_w^I, \pi^O)$, and by Definition 15, s is in $S_{\pi_w^I(P \otimes Q)}$. $\square$

Next we characterise solutions to $P \parallel R \preceq Q$ in terms of winning strategies for Input in $(P \otimes Q^\perp)^\perp$, and show that the most general solution arises from the most permissive strategy.

Theorem 3. *A solution to $P \parallel R \preceq Q$ exists iff a winning input strategy π exists for $(P \otimes Q^\perp)^\perp$. The most general solution to $P \parallel R \preceq Q$ is given by $\pi_w^I((P \otimes Q^\perp)^\perp)$, where π_w^I is the most permissive winning input strategy.*

Proof. From Theorems 1 and 2 it follows that a solution exists iff P and $Q^\perp$ are compatible, and in such a case $R = (P \parallel Q^\perp)^\perp$ is the most general solution. By Proposition 1, $(P \parallel Q^\perp)^\perp = \pi_w^I((P \otimes Q^\perp)^\perp)$ where π_w^I is the most permissive winning strategy for $(P \otimes Q^\perp)^\perp$. $\square$

5   Application: Network Protocol Conversion

In this section we describe an application of interface synthesis to the protocol conversion problem. In today's world global communication over heterogeneous networks of computers can often lead to protocol mismatches between communicating entities. The lack of a uniform global standard for communication protocols entails that protocol converters have to be built for mediating between incompatible protocols [5, 11]. We illustrate the use of interface synthesis to the protocol conversion problem through an example adapted from [10].

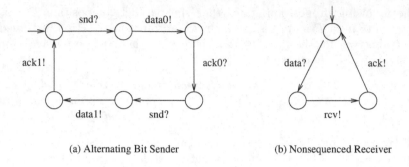

(a) Alternating Bit Sender   (b) Nonsequenced Receiver

Fig. 2. Two mismatched protocols

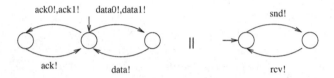

Fig. 3. Specification of Converter

Consider the two interface shown in Figure 2 representing two incompatible protocols. Figure 2(a) is a simplified version of a sender using the Alternating Bit Protocol (ABP), while the one in Figure 2(b) is a receiver using the Nonsequenced Protocol (NS). The ABP sender accepts data from the user (a higher level protocol) using the input action snd? and transmits it with label 0 using output action data0!. After receiving an acknowledgement with the correct label 0 via the input action ack0?, the sender is ready to accept the next piece of data from the user and transmit it with label 1. The protocol performs in a loop, alternating labels between 0 and 1. In this simplified version we ignore retransmissions due to timeouts and receipt of acknowledgements with wrong labels.

The NS receiver in Figure 2(b) is much simpler, which on receiving a data packet via input action data?, delivers it to the user via the output action rcv!, and sends an acknowledgement to the sender via ack!. Since the NS receiver does not use any labels for the data and acknowledgement packets there is a protocol mismatch between ABP and NS.

When we want the two protocols above to work together without causing any inconsistency by using a converter, we need to specify what the converter is allowed and not allowed to do. This idea was proposed in [15] in the setting of synchronous hardware-like protocols. We require that the system as a whole (the two protocols along with the converter) satisfies the interface described by Figure 3. This specification interface is obtained as the parallel composition of two interfaces. The one on the left specifies that the converter can send data packets and acknowledgements to the NS receiver and ABP sender, only after

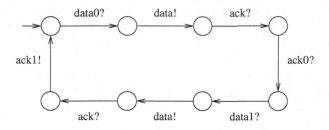

Fig. 4. Converter for the two protocols

receiving a data packet or acknowledgement from the other protocol. No data or acknowledgement can be sent speculatively, nor can packets be lost or duplicated. The interface on the right specifies the overall behaviour that the user expects from the system: the snd and rcv events will alternate strictly in any system run. Note that every action in Figure 3 is of type output.

The correct converter for the two protocols is shown is Figure 4. The converter can be obtained be as follows. Let P be the parallel composition of the two protocols which need conversion. Since we assume the two sets of actions to be disjoint, the composition is always well defined. The specification S for the converter relates the two actions sets by specifying temporal ordering of actions. For instance, in our example, the specification dictates that a data action can only follow a corresponding data0 or data1 action. The converter C is then the (most general) solution to $P \parallel C \preceq S$. Intuitively, the goal of the converter is to meet the specification, while satisfying the input assumptions of the two protocols. Moreover, the converter can control only the inputs to the protocols and not their outputs.

6   Conclusion

We have pointed out the connection between the most general solution to $P \parallel R \preceq Q$ and language equation solving [20, 21], protocol converter synthesis [5] and the semantics of interaction [1] in Section 1. This suggests an underlying algebraic framework for interface automata that is yet to be explored. Such a framework would have axioms and rules for combining interface automata using composition, alternating refinement and $(\_)^{\perp}$. This will simplify the kind of proofs we have presented in Section 3 and Section 4.

Tabuada [18] has shown the connection between control synthesis and the existence of certain alternating simulations and bisimulations between the specification and the system to be controlled. This was carried out using the span of open maps of Joyal et al [9]. It would be illuminating to see whether our synthesis problem can be cast in the same framework. To do this, we need to characterise the composition operation $P \parallel Q$ from the product $P \times Q$ in a suitable category of interface automata. Note that it is in the definition of composition that the interface automata formalism differs from the ones considered in [18].

In summary, our work should be seen as a first step towards a unified theory of component interfaces and their synthesis, with wide ranging applications across diverse domains.

Acknowledgements. We thank David Benson, Paddy Krishnan, Prahlad Sampath and S. Ramesh for their discussions and critical comments on earlier drafts of the paper.

References

1. S. Abramsky. Semantics of interaction: an introduction to game semantics. In *Proceedings of the 1996 CLiCS Summer School*, pages 1–31. Cambridge University Press, 1997.
2. R. Alur, T.A. Henzinger, O. Kupferman, and M.Y. Vardi. Alternating refinement relations. In *CONCUR 98: Concurrency Theory*, Lecture Notes in Computer Science 1466, pages 163–178. Springer-Verlag, 1998.
3. Andreas Blass. A game semantics for linear logic. *Annals of Pure and Applied Logic*, 56:183–220, 1992. Special Volume dedicated to the memory of John Myhill.
4. J.R. Büchi and L.H. Landweber. Solving sequential conditions by finite-state strategies. *Trans. Amer. Math. Soc.*, 138:295–311, 1969.
5. K. L. Calvert and S. S. Lam. Formal methods for protocol conversion. *IEEE Journal Selected Areas in Communications*, 8(1):127–142, January 1990.
6. L. de Alfaro and T.A. Henzinger. Interface automata. In *Proceedings of the Ninth Annual Symposium on Foundations of Software Engineering*, pages 109–120. ACM Press, 2001.
7. Luca de Alfaro. Game models for open systems. In *Proceedings of the International Symposium on Verification (Theory in Practice)*, volume 2772 of *Lecture Notes in Computer Science*. Springer-Verlag, 2003.
8. Jean-Yves Girard. Linear logic. *Theoretical Computer Science*, 50:1–102, 1987.
9. André Joyal, Mogens Nielsen, and Glynn Winskel. Bisimulation from open maps. *Information and Computation*, 127(2):164–185, June 1996.
10. Ratnesh Kumar, Sudhir Nelvagal, and Steven I. Marcus. A discrete event systems approach for protocol conversion. *Discrete Event Dynamic Systems*, 7(3):295–315, June 1997.
11. S. S. Lam. Protocol conversion. *IEEE Transactions on Software Engineering*, 14(3):353–362, March 1988.
12. Nancy A. Lynch and Mark R. Tuttle. Hierarchical correctness proofs for distributed algorithms. In *Proceedings of the Sixth Annual ACM Symposium on Principles of Distributed Computing*, pages 137–151, 10–12 August 1987.
13. P. Madhusudan and P. S. Thiagarajan. Controllers for discrete event systems via morphisms. In *CONCUR '98: Concurrency Theory, 9th International Conference*, volume 1466 of *Lecture Notes in Computer Science*, pages 18–33. Springer-Verlag, 1998.
14. Oded Maler, Amir Pnueli, and Joseph Sifakis. On the synthesis of discrete controllers for timed systems (an extended abstract). In *12th Annual Symposium on Theoretical Aspects of Computer Science*, volume 900 of *Lecture Notes in Computer Science*, pages 229–242, Munich, Germany, 2–4 March 1995. Springer.

15. Roberto Passerone, Luca de Alfaro, T.A. Henzinger, and Alberto L. Sangiovanni-Vincentelli. Convertibility verification and converter synthesis: Two faces of the same coin. In *ICCAD '02: Proceedings of the International Conference on Computer Aided Design*, pages 132–140. ACM, 2002.
16. A. Pnueli and R. Rosner. On the synthesis of a reactive module. In *POPL '89. Proceedings of the sixteenth annual ACM symposium on Principles of programming languages, January 11–13, 1989, Austin, TX*, pages 179–190, New York, NY, USA, 1989. ACM Press.
17. P. J. G. Ramadge and W. M. Wonham. The control of discrete event systems. *Proceedings of the IEEE; Special issue on Dynamics of Discrete Event Systems*, 77, 1:81–98, 1989.
18. Paulo Tabuada. Open maps, alternating simulations and control synthesis. In *CONCUR '04*, number 3170 in Lecture Notes in Computer Science, pages 466–480. Springer-Verlag, 2004.
19. Wolfgang Thomas. On the synthesis of strategies in infinite games. In *12th Annual Symposium on Theoretical Aspects of Computer Science*, volume 900 of *Lecture Notes in Computer Science*, pages 1–13, Munich, Germany, 2–4 March 1995. Springer.
20. Nina Yevtushenko, Tiziano Villa, Robert K. Brayton, Alex Petrenko, and Alberto Sangiovanni-Vincentelli. Solution of parallel language equations for logic synthesis. In *Proceedings of the 2001 International Conference on Computer-Aided Design (ICCAD-01)*, pages 103–111, Los Alamitos, CA, November 4–8 2001. IEEE Computer Society.
21. Nina Yevtushenko, Tiziano Villa, Robert K. Brayton, Alex Petrenko, and Alberto Sangiovanni-Vincentelli. Solution of synchronous language equations for logic synthesis. In *Proceedings of the 4th Conference on Computer-Aided Technologies in Applied Mathematics*, pages 132–137, September 2002.

Multi-valued Model Checking Games

Sharon Shoham and Orna Grumberg

Computer Science Department, Technion, Haifa, Israel
{sharonsh, orna}@cs.technion.ac.il

Abstract. This work extends the game-based framework of μ-calculus model checking to the *multi-valued* setting. In multi-valued model checking a formula is interpreted over a Kripke structure defined over a lattice. The value of the formula is also an element of the lattice. We define a new game for this problem and derive from it a *direct* model checking algorithm that handles the multi-valued structure without any reduction. We investigate the properties of the new game, both independently, and in comparison to the automata-based approach. We show that the usual resemblance between the two approaches does *not* hold in the multi-valued setting and show how it can be regained by changing the nature of the game.

1 Introduction

Model checking [8] is a successful approach for verifying whether a system model M satisfies a specification φ, written as a temporal logic formula. In multi-valued model checking the system is defined over a lattice $\mathcal{L}$. Both the labelling of states and the transitions of the system are interpreted as elements from the lattice. The meaning of a formula in the model is then also given by an element of the lattice.

Multi-valued model checking has many important applications within the verification framework. For example, 3-valued model checking, where the logic is based on the lattice L_3 (see Fig. 1), has been used to reason about abstract structures or structures with partial information [2,24,13]. In this context the value U is used to model *uncertainty*, with the meaning that the value can either be $\top$ or $\bot$. Recently, [1] has used a 6-valued logic as an extension of this approach for falsification of properties. Another useful lattice is the lattice $L_{2,2}$, with the values $\top\bot$ and $\bot\top$ representing *disagreement* (see Fig. 1). Model checking using this lattice (or its generalizations) has been used to handle inconsistent views of a system [11,17]. Temporal logic query checking [5,3,15] can also be reduced to multi-valued model checking, where the elements of the lattice are sets of propositional formulas.

One way of handling the multi-valued model checking problem is the *reduction* approach, where the problem is reduced to several traditional 2-valued problems [12,17,18,14,4] or 3-valued problems [19].

As opposed to the reduction approach, the *direct* approach checks the property on the multi-valued structure directly. It thus has the advantage of a more "on-the-fly" nature. Furthermore, a direct model checker can provide auxiliary information that explains its result. Such information can help analyzing the result. For example, in [24,13] the result of a direct model checking is used to suggest refinement of a 3-valued abstract structure. The same information cannot be retrieved from the model checking of two 2-valued structures [23].

D.A. Peled and Y.-K. Tsay (Eds.): ATVA 2005, LNCS 3707, pp. 354–369, 2005.

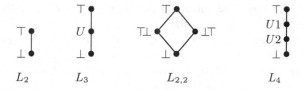

Fig. 1. Examples of Lattices

Several direct model checking algorithms for various multi-valued logics have been suggested in the literature. [2,24,13] studied the 3-valued case of CTL ([2,24]) and the μ-calculus ([13]). In [6] the logic LTL was considered over finite linear orders. The general multi-valued version of CTL was handled in [7]. Finally, an *almost* direct automata-based algorithm for the multi-valued μ-calculus was suggested in [4]. Their approach handled the multi-valued labelling directly, but still used a reduction to handle multi-valued transitions.

In this paper we suggest a *fully direct* model checking for the multi-valued μ-calculus, where both the multi-valued labelling and the multi-valued transitions are handled directly. The μ-calculus [20] is a powerful formalism for expressing properties of transition systems using fixpoint operators. It contains, for example, both CTL and LTL as its fragments. Our approach refers to its multi-valued semantics based on any finite distributive DeMorgan lattice.

We base our algorithm on the *game-theoretic* approach [25] and thus gain all of its advantages [24,13]. In the traditional game-based approach to model checking two players, the verifier (called ∃loise) and the refuter (called ∀belard), try to win a game. A formula φ is true in a model M iff the verifier has a winning strategy, meaning that the verifier can win any play, no matter what the refuter does.

We adapt this approach for the multi-valued case. In particular, we now talk about the *value* of the game. It turns out that in the multi-valued case there does *not* necessarily exist a *best* strategy for ∃loise. Instead, strategies may be incomparable and the value of the game is determined by their combination.

We suggest two definitions of a multi-valued game for the μ-calculus and prove their correctness. The proof turns out to be interesting in itself, as it uses similar techniques to those used in the reduction approach of [4]. This is in spite of the fact that our approach handles the multi-valued structure directly and uses no reductions.

When comparing our definitions to the work of [4], a surprising property is revealed. The direct algorithm of [4] is based on automata [21]. Usually, the game-based and the automata-based approaches to model checking have a strong resemblance [22]. Yet, in the multi-valued setting we find that our definition of the game is different in essence from the automata-based approach of [4]. We discuss this difference and suggest an alternative multi-valued game that regains the similarity to automata. More importantly, our resulting framework in fact generalizes the work of [4], as it handles directly not only the multi-valued labelling, but also the multi-valued transitions.

The game-based approach to model checking was already generalized to the 3-valued case [24,13]. However, it turns out that handling a general lattice, where there is more than one intermediate value and the elements are only partially ordered, is substantially more complex (see Section 7).

The rest of the paper is organized as follows. In Section 2 we give some background on lattice theory, multi-valued μ-calculus and model checking games. In Section 3 we provide our main definition of the multi-valued model checking game and prove its correctness. A model checking algorithm, based on the game, is then described in Section 4. In Section 5 we suggest an alternative definition for the game. We then discuss the relation to the automata-theoretic approach, which yields another definition of a multi-valued game, in Section 6. Finally, we compare the general multi-valued game to the much simpler 3-valued case in Section 7.

2   Preliminaries

Lattices. A *lattice* is a partially ordered set $(\mathcal{L}, \leq)$ where for each finite subset of elements there exists a unique *greatest lower bound* (*glb*) and *least upper bound* (*lub*). The glb is also called *meet* and is denoted by $x \wedge y$ or $\bigwedge A$ (for $x, y \in \mathcal{L}, A \subseteq \mathcal{L}$). The lub is also called *join* and is denoted $x \vee y$ or $\bigvee A$ (see Fig. 1 for examples).

Throughout this paper we refer to finite distributive DeMorgan lattices. Every finite lattice is *complete*, meaning that it has a greatest element, called *top*, denoted $\top$, and a least element, called *bottom*, denoted $\bot$. In a *distributive* lattice $x \wedge (y \vee z) = (x \wedge y) \vee (x \wedge z)$ and $x \vee (y \wedge z) = (x \vee y) \wedge (x \vee z)$ for all lattice elements x, y, z. In a *DeMorgan* lattice every element $x \in \mathcal{L}$ has a unique complement $\neg x \in \mathcal{L}$ such that $\neg\neg x = x$, DeMorgan's laws hold, and $x \leq y$ implies $\neg y \leq \neg x$ [1].

A *join-irreducible* element x of a distributive lattice $\mathcal{L}$ is an element $\neq \bot$ s.t. $x = y \vee z$ implies $x = y$ or $x = z$ for every $y, z \in \mathcal{L}$. We denote the set of join-irreducible elements of $\mathcal{L}$ by $\mathcal{J}(\mathcal{L})$. For example $\bot\top \in \mathcal{J}(L_{2,2})$, but $\top \notin \mathcal{J}(L_{2,2})$ (see Fig. 1).

μ-**calculus** [20]. Let $\mathcal{P}$ be a finite set of atomic propositions and $\mathcal{V}$ a set of propositional variables. We consider the logic μ-*calculus* in *negation normal form*, defined as follows:

$$\varphi ::= q \mid \neg q \mid Z \mid \varphi \vee \varphi \mid \varphi \wedge \varphi \mid \Diamond\varphi \mid \Box\varphi \mid \mu Z.\varphi \mid \nu Z.\varphi$$

where $q \in \mathcal{P}$ and $Z \in \mathcal{V}$. Let $\mathcal{L}_\mu$ denote the set of *closed* formulas generated by the above grammar, where the fixpoint quantifiers μ and ν are variable binders. We write η for either μ or ν. We assume that formulas are well-named, i.e. no variable is bound more than once in any formula. Thus, every variable Z *identifies* a unique subformula $fp(Z) = \eta Z.\psi$ of φ, where the set $Sub(\varphi)$ of *subformulas* of φ is defined as usual.

Semantics. The *concrete semantics* of a μ-calculus formula is given with respect to a Kripke structure. A (finite) Kripke structure is a tuple $\mathcal{M} = (\mathcal{S}, \mathcal{R}, \Theta)$, where $\mathcal{S}$ is a finite set of states, $\mathcal{R} \subseteq \mathcal{S} \times \mathcal{S}$ is a transition relation, which must be *total*, and $\Theta : \mathcal{S} \rightarrow 2^\mathcal{P}$ is a labelling function [8].

In this work we consider the multi-valued μ-calculus [4], where formulas are interpreted with respect to a Kripke structure defined over a lattice (also called χKripke structure). In a Kripke structure over a lattice $\mathcal{L}$, both the labelling and the transition relation have a multi-valued nature: Θ maps a state to a mapping from $\mathcal{P}$ to elements of

---

[1] Since we refer to temporal logic in negation normal form, negation can be defined arbitrarily. We chose to refer to DeMorgan lattices since they are most commonly used in this context.

$$\frac{s \vdash \varphi_0 \vee \varphi_1}{s \vdash \varphi_i} \; \exists : i \in \{0,1\} \qquad \frac{s \vdash \eta Z.\varphi}{s \vdash Z} \; \exists/\forall \qquad \frac{s \vdash \Diamond\varphi}{t \vdash \varphi} \; \exists : \mathcal{R}(s,t) \neq \bot$$

$$\frac{s \vdash \varphi_0 \wedge \varphi_1}{s \vdash \varphi_i} \; \forall : i \in \{0,1\} \qquad \frac{s \vdash Z}{s \vdash \varphi} \; \exists/\forall : \text{if } fp(Z) = \eta Z.\varphi \qquad \frac{s \vdash \Box\varphi}{t \vdash \varphi} \; \forall : \mathcal{R}(s,t) \neq \bot$$

Fig. 2. The 2-valued model checking game rules for $\mathcal{L}_\mu$

$\mathcal{L}$, that is $\Theta : \mathcal{S} \to (\mathcal{P} \to \mathcal{L})$. Furthermore, $\mathcal{R}$ maps pairs of states to lattice elements, that is $\mathcal{R} : \mathcal{S} \times \mathcal{S} \to \mathcal{L}$ (see Example 1). The totality requirement of $\mathcal{R}$ is now given by the requirement that for each $s \in \mathcal{S}$ there exists some state $s' \in \mathcal{S}$ with $\mathcal{R}(s,s') \neq \bot$.

The *semantics* $[\![\varphi]\!]_\rho^{\mathcal{M}}$ of a $\mathcal{L}_\mu$ formula φ w.r.t. a Kripke structure $\mathcal{M} = (\mathcal{S}, \mathcal{R}, \Theta)$ over a lattice $\mathcal{L}$ and an *environment* $\rho : \mathcal{V} \to (\mathcal{S} \to \mathcal{L})$, where ρ explains the meaning of free variables in φ, is a mapping from $\mathcal{S}$ to $\mathcal{L}$.

We assume $\mathcal{M}$ to be fixed and do not mention it explicitly anymore. With $\rho[Z \mapsto g]$ we denote the environment that maps Z to g and agrees with ρ on all other arguments. Later, when only closed formulas are considered, we will also drop the environment from the semantic brackets. In the following definition f is an element of $(\mathcal{S} \to \mathcal{L}) \to (\mathcal{S} \to \mathcal{L})$, defined by $\lambda g. [\![\varphi]\!]_{\rho[Z \mapsto g]}$ and νf, μf stand for the greatest and least fixpoints of f, which exist according to [26], since the functions in $\mathcal{S} \to \mathcal{L}$ form a complete lattice under pointwise ordering and the functional f is monotone w.r.t. this ordering.

$$
\begin{aligned}
[\![q]\!]_\rho \quad &:= \quad \lambda s.\Theta(s)(q) & [\![Z]\!]_\rho \quad &:= \rho(Z) \\
[\![\neg q]\!]_\rho \quad &:= \quad \lambda s.\neg\Theta(s)(q) & [\![\mu Z.\varphi]\!]_\rho &:= \mu f \\
[\![\varphi_1 \vee \varphi_2]\!]_\rho \quad &:= \quad \lambda s.[\![\varphi_1]\!]_\rho \vee [\![\varphi_2]\!]_\rho & [\![\nu Z.\varphi]\!]_\rho &:= \nu f \\
[\![\varphi_1 \wedge \varphi_2]\!]_\rho \quad &:= \quad \lambda s.[\![\varphi_1]\!]_\rho \wedge [\![\varphi_2]\!]_\rho & & \\
[\![\Diamond\varphi]\!]_\rho \quad &:= \quad \lambda s. \bigvee\{\mathcal{R}(s,s') \wedge [\![\varphi]\!]_\rho(s') \mid \mathcal{R}(s,s') \neq \bot\} & & \\
[\![\Box\varphi]\!]_\rho \quad &:= \quad \lambda s. \bigwedge\{\neg\mathcal{R}(s,s') \vee [\![\varphi]\!]_\rho(s') \mid \mathcal{R}(s,s') \neq \bot\} & &
\end{aligned}
$$

Given φ, $(\mathcal{M}, s)$ and $\mathcal{L}$, computing the value of $[\![\varphi]\!]^{\mathcal{M}}(s)$ is called the *multi-valued model checking problem*. A regular Kripke structure $\mathcal{M}$ can be viewed as a Kripke structure over lattice L_2 (see Fig. 1), by referring to the set of transitions and the set of atomic propositions that label a state by their characteristic functions. In this case we write $(M, s) \models \varphi$ for $[\![\varphi]\!]^{\mathcal{M}}(s) = \top$ and $(M, s) \not\models \varphi$ for $[\![\varphi]\!]^{\mathcal{M}}(s) = \bot$.

Model Checking Games. The *2-valued model checking game* $\Gamma_\mathcal{M}(s_0, \varphi_0)$ on a (regular) Kripke structure $\mathcal{M} = (\mathcal{S}, \mathcal{R}, \Theta)$ with $s_0 \in \mathcal{S}$ and a formula $\varphi_0 \in \mathcal{L}_\mu$ is played by players $\exists$loise (the prover) and $\forall$belard (the refuter) in order to determine the truth value of φ_0 in s_0, cf. [25]. Configurations are elements of $\mathcal{C} \subseteq \mathcal{S} \times Sub(\varphi_0)$, and written $t \vdash \psi$. Each *play* of $\Gamma_\mathcal{M}(s_0, \varphi_0)$ is a maximal sequence of configurations that starts with $s_0 \vdash \varphi_0$. The game rules are presented in Fig. 2. Each rule is marked by $\exists / \forall$ to indicate which player makes the move. A rule is applied when the player is in configuration C_i, which is of the form of the upper part of the rule. C_{i+1} is then the configuration in the lower part of the rule. The rules shown in the first and third columns present a choice which the player can make. Since no choice is possible when applying the rules in the second column, both players can apply them. If no rule can be applied the play terminates. This happens in *terminal* configurations of the form $t \vdash p$ or $t \vdash \neg p$.

Winning Criteria: Player $\exists$ *wins* a play $C_0, C_1, \ldots$ iff
1. the play terminates in $t \vdash q$ with $\Theta(t)(q) = \top$ or $t \vdash \neg q$ with $\Theta(t)(q) = \bot$, or
2. the outermost variable that occurs infinitely often is of type ν.
Player $\forall$ *wins* a play $C_0, C_1 \ldots$ iff
3. the play terminates in $t \vdash q$ with $\Theta(t)(q) = \bot$ or $t \vdash \neg q$ with $\Theta(t)(q) = \top$, or
4. the outermost variable that occurs infinitely often is of type μ.

A (memoryless) *strategy* for player Q is a partial function $\sigma : \mathcal{C} \to \mathcal{C}$, such that its domain is the set of configurations where player Q moves. Player Q plays a game according to a strategy σ if all his choices agree with σ. A strategy for player Q is called a *winning strategy* if player Q wins every play where he plays according to this strategy.

We have the following relation between the game and the semantics.

Theorem 1. *[25] For a regular Kripke structure* $\mathcal{M} = (\mathcal{S}, \mathcal{R}, \Theta)$, $s \in \mathcal{S}$, *and* $\varphi \in \mathcal{L}_\mu$:
(a) $\llbracket \varphi \rrbracket^{\mathcal{M}}(s) = \top$ *iff Player* $\exists$ *has a winning strategy for* $\Gamma_{\mathcal{M}}(s, \varphi)$,
(b) $\llbracket \varphi \rrbracket^{\mathcal{M}}(s) = \bot$ *iff Player* $\forall$ *has a winning strategy for* $\Gamma_{\mathcal{M}}(s, \varphi)$

3   A Multi-valued Game for the μ-Calculus

In this section we investigate the multi-valued model checking problem from the game-theoretic point of view. For the rest of the section let $\mathcal{M}$ be a Kripke structure over lattice $\mathcal{L}$, s_0 a state in $\mathcal{M}$ and φ_0 a μ-calculus formula. We suggest a *multi-valued* model checking game, $\Gamma_{\mathcal{M}}^m(s_0, \varphi_0)$, for evaluating φ_0 in state s_0 of $\mathcal{M}$.

The new game is still played by two players, $\exists$loise and $\forall$belard, and the moves of the players are defined as in the 2-valued game (see Fig. 2). In particular, in the rules of the third column the players can make a move along any transition whose value is not $\bot$. However, the concept of winning needs to be adapted. In fact, to capture the multi-valued nature of the problem, we no longer talk about *winning* a play versus *losing* it. Instead, we now associate with each play a *value* which is an element from the lattice.

In our definitions we take the point of view of $\exists$loise (we could dually describe the game from the point of view of $\forall$belard). Intuitively, we think of the value of a play as a measure for how close $\exists$loise is to winning; Winning of $\exists$loise in the 2-valued case now corresponds to the *top* value. Winning of $\forall$belard corresponds to the *bottom* value, but more values are possible. In these terms, the goal of the players is no longer to *win* the play. Instead, the goal of $\exists$loise is to maximize the resulting value, whereas the goal of $\forall$belard is to minimize this value.

Notation. We refer to the configurations of $\Gamma_{\mathcal{M}}^m(s_0, \varphi_0)$ as *nodes* in a *game graph*, divided to $\vee$-nodes, where $\exists$loise plays, versus $\wedge$-nodes, where $\forall$belard plays. Moves between configurations are *edges* in the graph. Each edge (move) has a value from the lattice: moves that use a transition of the model get its value. The rest get the $\top$ value. We abuse the notation of the transition relation and denote the value of an edge from n to n' by $\mathcal{R}(n, n')$. We refer to edges with values $\neq \top, \bot$ as *indefinite* edges.

Example 1. Consider the Kripke structure $\mathcal{M}$ of Fig. 3 over lattice $\mathcal{L}$, s.t. $x, y, z, w \in \mathcal{L}$. The labels of the transitions define their values. Unlabelled transitions have value $\top$. The states labelling denotes that $\Theta(s_0)(r) = z$, $\Theta(s_0)(h) = w$ and $\Theta(s_1)(q) = \Theta(s_2)(q) = \top$, where q, r, h are atomic propositions. Fig. 3 also shows the game-graph of $\Gamma_{\mathcal{M}}^m(s_0, \varphi_0)$, where $\varphi_0 = \Diamond q \wedge (r \vee h)$. Again, the edges are labelled by their values.

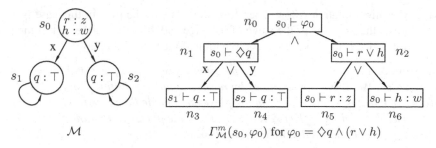

$$\mathcal{M}$$

$$\Gamma_{\mathcal{M}}^m(s_0, \varphi_0) \text{ for } \varphi_0 = \Diamond q \wedge (r \vee h)$$

Fig. 3. Example of a Multi-Valued Game

3.1 Plays and Their Values

A play in $\Gamma_{\mathcal{M}}^m(s_0, \varphi_0)$ is defined as before. To understand how we determine the value of a multi-valued play, consider again a 2-valued play. As explained above, if the winner is ∃loise, then in the multi-valued context we view its value as $\top$. Similarly, if the winner is ∀belard, then we view the value as $\bot$. However, in the multi-valued case we have two extensions, which introduce more values. First, the terminal nodes ($t \vdash q$, $t \vdash \neg q$) are no longer classified as winning or losing, but they have a value which results from the value of q in the state t. This affects the values of finite plays.

Furthermore, the moves are also multi-valued, due to the multi-valued nature of the model's transitions. The value that a player gains in the play also depends on the values of the transitions that were used. Intuitively, one can think of the moves of ∃loise as attempts at proving the formula and the moves of ∀belard as attempts at refuting it. In this context, the use of indefinite edges in the multi-valued case is interpreted as a weak attempt at proving or refuting (depending on the player).

Recall that we think of the value of the play as a measure for how close ∃loise is to winning. Therefore, when evaluating a play we take the point of view of ∃loise. Conceptually, we first give the play a *base* value, while ignoring the values of edges used. We then update the resulting value based on the edges.

Definition 1. *For a terminal node $n = t \vdash q$, we define $val(n)$ to be $\Theta(t)(q)$. For $n = t \vdash \neg q$ we define $val(n)$ to be $\neg\Theta(t)(q)$.*

Definition 2. *For a play p in the game, we define its* base *value, $base(p)$, as follows. If p is finite, $base(p) = val(n)$, where n is the terminal node in which p ends. If p is infinite, then $base(p) = \top$ if p is won by ∃loise in the 2-valued game. Otherwise $base(p) = \bot$.*

We update the base value by taking into consideration the values of the edges used by *both* players in the play. Intuitively, when ∃loise plays, she tries to show an evidence for truth. For her evidence to be "convincing", she needs to both continue to a position which is good for her, *and* also use an edge with a high value (which corresponds in a way to high certainty). Consequently, the value of the play is given by the *glb* of the value of the edge and the value of the rest of the play. On the other hand, when ∀belard plays, he tries to refute. When looking at the situation from the point of view of ∃loise, she succeeds in her goal better if ∀belard either reaches a position that is good for her, *or* if he uses an edge of low value (alternatively: high negated value), in which case the certainty of his refutation is low. Therefore, the value of the play in this case is given by the *lub* of the *negation* of the value of the edge and the value of the rest of the play. This intuition leads to a bottom-up computation of the value of a play.

Definition 3. *Let* $p = n_0, n_1, \ldots, n_k$ *be a finite prefix of a play, and let* $x \in \mathcal{L}$ *be a base value. We define* $update(p, x)$ *by reverse induction. Initially,* $val_k = x$. *Given* val_i, *we define* val_{i-1} *depending on the player that made the move from* n_{i-1} *to* n_i. *If it is* ∃*loise, then* $val_{i-1} = \mathcal{R}(n_{i-1}, n_i) \wedge val_i$. *If the player is* ∀*belard, then* $val_{i-1} = \neg\mathcal{R}(n_{i-1}, n_i) \vee val_i$. *Finally, we let* $update(p, x) = val_0$.

Note that edges with value $\top$ do not change the base value since $\top \wedge x = x$ and $\neg\top \vee x = x$ for all $x \in \mathcal{L}$ (since in a DeMorgan lattice $\neg\top = \bot$).

Definition 3 is directly applicable to defining the value of a finite play by taking x to be the base of p. Unfortunately, it is not suitable for infinite plays.

To handle infinite plays, we use the following key observations. We say that a prefix p_i of a play p is *total* if for each player, the set of values of edges used by the player in p_i is equal to the set of values used by the same player in p. Since the underlying lattice is finite, the set of values of edges used in the play by each player is finite. Thus, there always exists a *finite total* prefix of the (possibly infinite) play. Furthermore, it turns out that computing the value of the play by considering only such a (finite) prefix is sufficient, in the following sense. We define the value $val(p_i)$ of a prefix p_i of a play p similarly to the definition of the value of a finite play, except that the base value is set to the base value of the entire play p. That is, $val(p_i) = update(p_i, base(p))$. We now have the property that the value of *any* total prefix of p is the same.

Lemma 1. *Let* p_i, p_j *be two finite total prefixes of a play* p. *Then* $val(p_i) = val(p_j)$.

In other words, the play has a *limit* value. This property is surprising since the sequence of values of increasingly longer prefixes is not necessarily monotonic. Lemma 1 also implies that any finite total prefix of the play is a good representative for computing this value. We therefore define the value of a play as follows.

Definition 4. *For a play* p, $val(p) = update(p_i, base(p))$, *where* p_i *is the minimal total prefix of* p.

Example 2. Consider again the game described in Fig. 3. Terminal nodes in the game-graph are labelled by their values. One possible play in the game is $< n_0, n_1, n_3 >$. Its value is $\neg\top \vee (x \wedge \top) = x$. Another example is the play $< n_0, n_2, n_5 >$ whose value is $\neg\top \vee (\top \wedge z) = z$. More plays exist.

3.2   Strategies and Their Values

As always, to relate the game to model checking, we need to talk about strategies, rather than a single play. In the 2-valued game we talked about *winning* strategies and we were guaranteed that exactly one player had one. In the multi-valued case, we no longer talk about winning. Instead, we talk about the *gain* of each player in the game. We therefore need to replace the notion of winning strategies by strategies for gaining a value.

Consider again the 2-valued game. A winning strategy for ∃loise in the 2-valued game guarantees that every play, where ∃loise plays by the strategy is winning for

∃loise (or has value ⊤). On the other hand, a non-winning strategy for ∃loise is such that there exists a play where ∃loise plays by the strategy, but the play is winning for ∀belard (has value ⊥). Thus, we can say that a winning strategy for ∃loise ensures the value ⊤, whereas a non-winning strategy ensures only ⊥ (as it ensures a value ≥ ⊥, but not better than that). Furthermore, each strategy is either winning for ∃loise or non-winning. Thus, strategies are comparable, and there always exists a *best* strategy. The best strategy is a winning strategy if one exists, or a non-winning one otherwise.

When we move to the general multi-valued case, a strategy for ∃loise is defined as usual. However, unlike the usual case, here plays can have many values, which may be *incomparable* to one another. Given a strategy $\sigma_\exists$ for ∃loise, the value that will be achieved in practice depends on the choices of ∀belard. We want the value of $\sigma_\exists$ to be a *lower bound* on the set of all possible values that can be achieved in plays where ∃loise plays by $\sigma_\exists$, with the meaning that the strategy ensures a value which is greater or equal than its value. We choose the *greatest* possible lower bound, which characterizes the strategy as precisely as possible.

Definition 5. *For a strategy $\sigma_\exists$ for ∃loise, $val(\sigma_\exists) = \bigwedge\{val(p) \mid p$ is a play by $\sigma_\exists\}$.*

This definition implies that ∃loise can always achieve a value ≥ $val(\sigma_\exists)$ in any play where she plays by the strategy $\sigma_\exists$. Note that since $val(\sigma_\exists)$ is given by the glb of possibly incomparable values, it is possible that there does *not* exist a play with value $val(\sigma_\exists)$ by this strategy. Still, the strategy cannot ensure a strictly better (higher) value.

Similarly to the phenomenon of several values achieved by a single strategy, it may be the case that ∃loise has several different strategies, with incomparable values. ∃loise chooses which strategy to use. We therefore define the value that she achieves in the *game* to be the *least upper bound* on the values of all her strategies. It implies that ∀belard cannot enforce any value which is strictly lower than the value of the game.

Definition 6. *Let $\Gamma^m_{\mathcal{M}}(s_0, \varphi_0)$ be a multi-valued game. Then*

$$val(\Gamma^m_{\mathcal{M}}(s_0, \varphi_0)) = \bigvee\{\alpha \mid \exists loise \text{ has a strategy } \sigma_\exists \text{ with value } val(\sigma_\exists) = \alpha\}.$$

Note that in the general case, ∃loise does *not* necessarily have a *best* strategy that achieves the lub. However, if the lattice has a total order then such a best strategy exists.

Example 3. In the game of Fig. 3 ∃loise has two possible moves from n_1 and n_2 (the nodes where she moves). She thus has four possible (memoryless) strategies – one for each combination. Consider for example the strategy σ_1 in which ∃loise always proceeds to the left successor. The choice in n_0 is of ∀belard, therefore there are two possible plays by this strategy: $< n_0, n_1, n_3 >$ (when ∀belard chooses the left successor of n_0) and $< n_0, n_2, n_5 >$ (when ∀belard chooses the right successor of n_0) whose values are x and z respectively (see Example 2). Since the choice between the plays is of ∀belard, the value of the strategy is the glb of their values. That is, $val(\sigma_1) = x \wedge z$. This means that by σ_1, ∃loise can only ensure a value which is ≥ $x \wedge z$, where possibly $x \wedge z$ is strictly smaller than both x and z (see for example ⊥⊤ and ⊤⊥ in $L_{2,2}$).

Similarly, we get $val(\sigma_2) = x \wedge w$, $val(\sigma_3) = y \wedge z$ and $val(\sigma_4) = y \wedge w$. Since ∃loise chooses which strategy to use, the value of the game is then $val(\Gamma^m_{\mathcal{M}}(s_0, \varphi_0)) = val(\sigma_1) \vee val(\sigma_2) \vee val(\sigma_3) \vee val(\sigma_4) = (x \wedge z) \vee (x \wedge w) \vee (y \wedge z) \vee (y \wedge w)$. If all the latter values are incomparable, then ∃loise does *not* have a unique *best* strategy. By distributivity, $val(\Gamma_{\mathcal{M}}^m(s_0, \varphi_0)) = (x \wedge (z \vee w)) \vee (y \wedge (z \vee w)) = (x \vee y) \wedge (z \vee w)$. An inspection of the model shows that this is the value of $[\![\varphi_0]\!]^{\mathcal{M}}(s_0)$, which demonstrates the correctness of the game (see Theorem 2 in the following section).

Remark 1. One can think of the value of the game in the regular 2-valued case (from the point of view of ∃loise), as defined by the following formula

$$\exists \sigma_\exists \forall \sigma_\forall : val(outcome(\sigma_\exists, \sigma_\forall)) = \top$$

where $\sigma_\forall$ denotes a strategy for ∀belard and $outcome(\sigma_\exists, \sigma_\forall)$ is the unique play defined by the combination of $\sigma_\exists$ and $\sigma_\forall$. This formula describes the condition for a game to be won by ∃loise: it requires that ∃loise has a winning strategy $\sigma_\exists$, meaning that for each possible strategy $\sigma_\forall$ of ∀belard, the resulting play is winning for ∃loise (has value $\top$).

Similarly, in the multi-valued case, the definition of $val(\sigma_\exists)$ can be rephrased as $val(\sigma_\exists) = \bigwedge_{\sigma_\forall} \{val(outcome(\sigma_\exists, \sigma_\forall))\}$. This makes

$$val(\Gamma_{\mathcal{M}}^m(s_0, \varphi_0)) = \bigvee_{\sigma_\exists} \{\bigwedge_{\sigma_\forall} \{val(outcome(\sigma_\exists, \sigma_\forall))\}\}$$

That is, we replace the ∃ and ∀ quantifiers by the lub and glb operators respectively, since there are no longer *best* strategies for ∃loise and ∀belard. A similar phenomenon happens when considering probabilistic games [10], where it is possible that the limit probability in which ∃loise wins is 1, but there is no strategy that achieves probability 1. Instead, for every probability, as close to 1 as we want, there is a strategy that achieves it. There also, the ∃ and ∀ quantifiers are replaced by *supremum* and *infimum* respectively.

3.3 Correctness

Theorem 2. *Let $\mathcal{M}$ be a Kripke structure over lattice $\mathcal{L}$, s_0 a state in $\mathcal{M}$ and φ_0 a μ-calculus formula. Then $val(\Gamma_{\mathcal{M}}^m(s_0, \varphi_0)) = [\![\varphi_0]\!]^{\mathcal{M}}(s_0)$.*

To prove Theorem 2 we first give an alternative definition for $val(\Gamma_{\mathcal{M}}^m(s_0, \varphi_0))$, which mainly results from Birkhoff representation theorem for finite distributive lattices.

Lemma 2. $val(\Gamma_{\mathcal{M}}^m(s_0, \varphi_0)) = \bigvee\{\alpha \mid \exists loise \ has \ a \ strategy \ \sigma_\exists \ with \ val(\sigma_\exists) \geq \alpha\}$
$$= \bigvee\{\alpha \in \mathcal{J}(\mathcal{L}) \mid \exists loise \ has \ a \ strategy \ \sigma_\exists \ with \ val(\sigma_\exists) \geq \alpha\}$$

We now use similar techniques to those used in the reduction approach of [4]. There, the multi-valued model checking problem is reduced to several 2-valued model checking problems. First, to avoid a technical problem with negated atomic propositions, the formula is transformed to a formula with no negation symbols, by replacing each negated proposition $\neg q$ by a new atomic proposition q'. The labelling function Θ of $\mathcal{M}$ is extended to Θ' by setting $\Theta'(s)(q') = \neg\Theta(s)(q)$. Then, the Kripke structure $\mathcal{M}$ over $\mathcal{L}$ is reduced to several Kripke Modal Transition Systems (KMTSs).

Definition 7. *[16] A Kripke Modal Transition System (KMTS) is a tuple $\tilde{\mathcal{M}} = (\tilde{S}, R^+, R^-, \tilde{\Theta})$ with a must transition relation $R^+ \subseteq S \times S$ and a may transition relation $R^- \subseteq S \times S$. The labelling is given by $\tilde{\Theta} : \tilde{S} \to (\mathcal{P} \to L_3)$.*

Specifically, given an element $\alpha \in \mathcal{J}(\mathcal{L})$, a reduced KMTS $\mathcal{M}_\alpha$ is defined by setting

$$\Theta_\alpha(s)(q) = \Theta(s)(q) \geq \alpha$$
$$R_\alpha^+(s, s') = R(s, s') \geq \alpha$$
$$R_\alpha^-(s, s') = (\neg R(s, s')) \not\geq \alpha$$

Note that in this definition of the KMTS $\mathcal{M}_\alpha$ the value of $\Theta_\alpha(s)(q)$ is in fact defined over L_2. The formula is then interpreted over the KMTS $\mathcal{M}_\alpha$ w.r.t. a *2-valued* semantics, with the main difference being that

$$[\![\Diamond\varphi]\!]_\rho^{\mathcal{M}_\alpha} := \lambda s. \bigvee\{R_\alpha^+(s, s') \wedge [\![\varphi]\!]_\rho^{\mathcal{M}_\alpha}(s') \mid \text{all } s'\}$$
$$[\![\Box\varphi]\!]_\rho^{\mathcal{M}_\alpha} := \lambda s. \bigwedge\{\neg R_\alpha^-(s, s') \vee [\![\varphi]\!]_\rho^{\mathcal{M}_\alpha}(s') \mid \text{all } s'\}$$

It then holds that $(\mathcal{M}_\alpha, s_0) \models \varphi_0 \Leftrightarrow \alpha \leq [\![\varphi_0]\!]^{\mathcal{M}}(s_0)$ [4], and the following is implied.

Lemma 3. *[4]* $[\![\varphi_0]\!]^{\mathcal{M}}(s_0) = \bigvee\{\alpha \in \mathcal{J}(\mathcal{L}) \mid (\mathcal{M}_\alpha, s_0) \models \varphi_0\}$.

Now, to prove the correctness of our multi-valued game we combine Lemmas 2 and 3 with the following lemma. Together they imply $val(\Gamma_\mathcal{M}^m(s_0, \varphi_0)) = [\![\varphi_0]\!]^{\mathcal{M}}(s_0)$.

Lemma 4. $\bigvee\{\alpha \in \mathcal{J}(\mathcal{L}) \mid \exists \text{loise has a strategy } \sigma_\exists \text{ with } val(\sigma_\exists) \geq \alpha\} = \bigvee\{\alpha \in \mathcal{J}(\mathcal{L}) \mid (\mathcal{M}_\alpha, s_0) \models \varphi_0\}$.

Proof. We refer to the 2-valued game for KMTSs, defined in [23]. This game is similar to the 2-valued game for Kripke structures. The difference is that ∃loise uses only must-transitions, whereas ∀belard uses may-transitions. The winning conditions are as before, with the exception that a player can get stuck (if R^+ or R^- is not total), in which case he loses. Theorem 1 holds for this case as well. In our case this means that ∃loise has a winning strategy in the 2-valued game over $\mathcal{M}_\alpha$ iff $(\mathcal{M}_\alpha, s_0) \models \varphi_0$.

To prove Lemma 4 we show a 1-1 correspondence between strategies of ∃loise with value $\geq \alpha$ in the multi-valued game over $\mathcal{M}$ and winning strategies for ∃loise in the 2-valued game over $\mathcal{M}_\alpha$, for $\alpha \in \mathcal{J}(\mathcal{L})$. We use the following property of a distributive lattice $\mathcal{L}$. If $\alpha \in \mathcal{J}(\mathcal{L})$ and $y, z \in \mathcal{L}$, then $\alpha \leq y \vee z$ iff $\alpha \leq y$ or $\alpha \leq z$ [9].

Let σ be a strategy for ∃loise with $val(\sigma) \geq \alpha$. We show that the same strategy is winning in the 2-valued game. Consider a play played by σ in the 2-valued case. We show that ∃loise wins it. We know that in the multi-valued game its value is $\geq \alpha$.

First, if the play is infinite (in the 2-valued case) then the value y of each edge used by ∀belard is such that $\neg y \not\geq \alpha$ (otherwise it does not exist as a may-edge). Thus for the value of the play to be $\geq \alpha$, its base value has to be $\top$. This is because only edges of ∀belard can increase the value and by the previous property they cannot increase a base value of $\bot$ to be $\geq \alpha$, since α is join-irreducible. Since the base value is $\top$, we conclude that the play fulfills the winning criteria of ∃loise in the 2-valued game.

If the play is finite (in the 2-valued case), we first rule out the possibility that ∃loise is stuck. If ∃loise is stuck it means that the strategy defines for her to use an edge with value $y \not\geq \alpha$ (that does not exist as a must-edge in the 2-valued case). The same reasoning as before shows that for the value of the play to be $\geq \alpha$, there had to be an earlier edge of ∀belard with value y s.t. $\neg y \geq \alpha$, but such an edge does not exist as a may-edge in the 2-valued play, which leads to contradiction. Thus, either ∀belard gets stuck, in which case ∃loise wins, or the play ends in a terminal node of the form

$n = s \vdash q$. In the latter case, we again conclude by the same reasons that $val(n) \geq \alpha$, thus $\Theta(s)(q) \geq \alpha$ and in the KMTS $\mathcal{M}_\alpha$ this implies $\Theta_\alpha(s)(q) = \top$ and $\exists$loise wins.

For the other direction, let σ be a winning strategy for $\exists$loise in the 2-valued game. Once again, we show that the same strategy has a value $\geq \alpha$ in the multi-valued game, with the exception that if σ does not define a move from some configuration, we extend it arbitrarily. To prove that $val(\sigma) \geq \alpha$ we show that the value of every play where $\exists$loise plays by (the extended) σ in the multi-valued game has value $\geq \alpha$.

Consider such a play. First, if the same play exists in the 2-valued game, then it is winning for $\exists$loise, making its base value $\top$. Furthermore, all the edges used by $\exists$loise are must-edges, with values $\geq \alpha$. Since only edges of $\exists$loise can decrease the value of the play, this ensures that the value of the play is $\geq \alpha$.

If the play does not exist in the 2-valued game, it means that one of two possibilities occurred. The first is that $\forall$belard used an edge that does not exist as a may-edge in the 2-valued game, meaning that its value y fulfills $\neg y \geq \alpha$. But this immediately increases the value of the suffix of the play from that point to be $\geq \alpha$. By the same reasons as before the prefix of the play does not decrease the value below α, and thus it remains $\geq \alpha$. The second possibility is that $\exists$loise used an edge that does not exist in the 2-valued game. This could only happen if the play reached a configuration where σ was extended. This means that originally, in the 2-valued game, this configuration was not reachable by σ. But this implies that in order to reach it $\forall$belard made a move that was not possible in the 2-valued game, and we return to the first possibility.   □

4   Solving the Multi-valued Game

In this section we discuss how to solve the multi-valued model checking game. Given a game $\Gamma_\mathcal{M}^m(s_0, \varphi_0)$ our purpose is to compute its value. By Theorem 2 this gives us the result of the multi-valued model checking problem for $\mathcal{M}$, s_0 and φ_0. Since the game is defined directly on the multi-valued Kripke structure, we get a *direct* model checking algorithm for the multi-valued problem, that has all the advantages of the game-theoretic approach [24,13].

As usual, we solve the game by processing the game-graph and evaluating each node in it. The difference as opposed to the 2-valued case is that we need to propagate values from the lattice. We demonstrate this change for the *alternation-free* fragment of the μ-calculus, where no nesting of fixpoints is allowed.

We partition the game graph to *Maximal Strongly Connected Components* (MSCCs) and determine a (total) order on them, reflected by their numbers: $Q_1, \ldots, Q_k$. The order fulfills the rule that if $i < j$ then there are no edges from Q_i to Q_j. Such an order exists because the MSCCs of the game-graph form a *directed acyclic graph* (DAG).

The components are handled bottom-up. Consider a single Q_i. We label each node $n \in Q_i$ with a value, denoted $res(n)$, as follows. For a terminal node n, $res(n) = val(n)$. For an $\vee$-node n we set $res(n)$ to be $\bigvee\{\mathcal{R}(n, n') \wedge res(n') \mid \mathcal{R}(n, n') \neq \bot\}$. Similarly, if n is an $\wedge$-node then $res(n) = \bigwedge\{\neg\mathcal{R}(n, n') \vee res(n') \mid \mathcal{R}(n, n') \neq \bot\}$.

To handle Q_i's that form a non-trivial MSCC, we use the following observation: when dealing with the alternation-free μ-calculus, an infinite play has exactly one variable that occurs infinitely often [25]. Therefore, if Q_i is a non-trivial MSCC then it contains exactly one fixpoint variable Z. In this case we first label the nodes in Q_i with temporary values, $temp(n)$, that are updated iteratively. For nodes of the form $n_w = t \vdash Z$ we initialize $temp(n_w)$ to $\top$ if Z is of type ν, or to $\bot$ if Z is of type μ (the rest remain uninitialized). We then apply the previous rules until the temporary values do not change anymore. Finally, we set $res(n) = temp(n)$ for every node n in Q_i. Intuitively, this algorithm imitates the iterative computation of the fixpoint.

Several optimizations can be made on this computation. For example, consider an $\vee$-node n with a successor n' for which $res(n')$ is already computed. Furthermore, suppose that the values of edges leading to the rest of the successors of n have values $\leq \mathcal{R}(n, n') \wedge res(n')$. This means that the rest of the successors cannot increase the result of the lub over all successors of n and we can immediately set $res(n)$ to be $\mathcal{R}(n, n') \wedge res(n')$, regardless of whether or not the rest of its successors were handled. Such optimizations can spare us the need to process big subgraphs.

Theorem 3. *Let $\mathcal{M}$ be a Kripke structure over $\mathcal{L}$. Then for every state s_0 in $\mathcal{M}$ and every closed μ-calculus formula φ_0, we have that $val(\Gamma_{\mathcal{M}}^m(s_0, \varphi_0)) = res(s_0 \vdash \varphi_0)$. We conclude that $\llbracket \varphi_0 \rrbracket^{\mathcal{M}_0}(s_0) = res(s_0 \vdash \varphi_0)$.*

5   Avoiding Multi-valued Edges in the Game

Recall that the multi-valued edges used in the game posed a problem when we wanted to define the value of an infinite play. Our treatment of such plays relied on the finite nature of the lattice. In this section we suggest a different way of overcoming the problem. The new definition makes the value of a play much simpler to define.

The idea is to split each move along a multi-valued transition (of the model) into two moves: first the player who is supposed to play chooses a transition. Then, the opponent chooses whether he wants to examine the value of the transition or to continue in the play. If he chooses the value of the transition, the play ends with this value. This means that there are no longer multi-valued edges in the game. We only have multi-valued terminal nodes. That is, we reduce the multi-valued edges into more multi-valued terminal nodes. We emphasize that the reduction is performed in the game level, rather than the model level. The underlying Kripke structure still has multi-valued transitions.

Formally, given a Kripke structure $\mathcal{M}$ over lattice $\mathcal{L}$, a state s_0 and a μ-calculus formula φ_0, we define $\Gamma_{\mathcal{M}}^d(s_0, \varphi_0)$ (where d stands for *definite* edges) as follows. The configurations of the game are as before, with additional configurations of the form $(s, t) \vdash \Diamond\varphi$, $(s, t) \vdash \Box\varphi$, $(s, t) \vdash \top$ and $(s, t) \vdash \bot$ that act as intermediate configurations for the new rules. The rules are given by Fig. 2, where the rules in the third column are replaced by the rules in Fig. 4.

For example, in a configuration of the form $s \vdash \Diamond\varphi$, $\exists$loise chooses, as usual, a transition that is supposed to show evidence for $\Diamond\varphi$. Since it is a move of $\exists$loise, we have the meaning of the lub of all possibilities. However, the next move is a move of $\forall$belard, with the meaning of the glb between the two options. This means that for each possibility of $\exists$loise we examine the glb of both the value of the transition and the value of the rest of the play. Configurations of the form $s \vdash \Box\varphi$ are handled dually.

Configurations of the form $(s, t) \vdash \top$ and $(s, t) \vdash \bot$ are (new) terminal configurations. A configuration of the form $(s, t) \vdash \top$ is reached when $\forall$belard challenges the

$$\frac{s \vdash \Diamond\varphi}{(s,t) \vdash \Diamond\varphi} \; \exists : \; \mathcal{R}(s,t) \neq \bot \qquad \frac{(s,t) \vdash \Diamond\varphi}{(s,t) \vdash \top} \; \forall \qquad \frac{(s,t) \vdash \Diamond\varphi}{t \vdash \varphi} \; \forall$$

$$\frac{s \vdash \Box\varphi}{(s,t) \vdash \Box\varphi} \; \forall : \; \mathcal{R}(s,t) \neq \bot \qquad \frac{(s,t) \vdash \Box\varphi}{(s,t) \vdash \bot} \; \exists \qquad \frac{(s,t) \vdash \Box\varphi}{t \vdash \varphi} \; \exists$$

Fig. 4. New rules for $\Gamma^d_{\mathcal{M}}(s_0, \varphi_0)$

transition that ∃loise chose from $s \vdash \Diamond\varphi$. It expresses the fact that we are interested in the value of $\mathcal{R}(s,t)$ that determines the certainty in which ∃loise tries to prove the existential property. Dually, a configuration of the form $(s,t) \vdash \bot$ is reached when ∃loise challenges the transition that ∀belard chose from $s \vdash \Box\varphi$. In this case, we are interested in the value of $\neg\mathcal{R}(s,t)$, since from the point of view of ∃loise, her chances of proving are better as the value of $\mathcal{R}(s,t)$ used by ∀belard for refutation is lower (alternatively: $\neg\mathcal{R}(s,t)$ is higher). Following this intuition, we add the following definition.

Definition 8. *For a terminal node* $n = (s,t) \vdash \top$, *we define* $val(n)$ *to be* $\mathcal{R}(s,t)$. *For* $n = (s,t) \vdash \bot$ *we define* $val(n)$ *to be* $\neg\mathcal{R}(s,t)$.

Since there are no longer multi-valued edges in the game, the value of a play is now determined to be the base value, as defined earlier (see Definition 2) – no update is needed. The rest of the definitions of strategies, their values and the value of the game remain unchanged. Theorem 4 ensures that the correctness of the game is maintained.

Theorem 4. *Let* $\mathcal{M}$ *be a Kripke structure over lattice* $\mathcal{L}$, *with a state* s_0 *and let* φ_0 *be a μ-calculus formula. Then* $val(\Gamma^d_{\mathcal{M}}(s_0, \varphi_0)) = val(\Gamma^m_{\mathcal{M}}(s_0, \varphi_0))$.

6 Discussion: Games Versus Automata

In this paper we have investigated the multi-valued model checking problem from the game-theoretic point of view. In [4] the same problem was considered from the automata-theoretic point of view. There, model checking is performed by checking the nonemptiness of an automaton that represents the product of the model and the checked formula. In this section we discuss the essential difference between the two approaches in the multi-valued case.

It is well-known that the game-based and the automata-based approaches are closely related in the 2-valued setting: an accepting run corresponds to a winning strategy for ∃loise and vice versa [22]. Surprisingly, the same relation does *not* hold anymore in the multi-valued case. More specifically, in [4] *extended alternating automata (EAAs)* were used as the basis for model checking. To capture the multi-valued nature they referred to the *value* of an accepting run. They showed that there always exists an accepting run of the EAA with a *maximal* value. This maximal value defines the value of the emptiness of the automaton. In the multi-valued game, on the other hand, it is *not* necessarily the case that there exists a strategy of ∃loise with a maximal value. This clearly demonstrates the discrepancy between automata and games in the multi-valued setting.

It is possible to regain the relation to the automata-theoretic approach by defining the game differently. The alternative game is still played over the same game-graph, but the moves are different. Initially, ∃loise makes a statement with respect to the value of the initial node n_0, denoted $bet(n_0)$. In each node she proceeds by associating (possibly a subset) of its successors with a value in a consistent way based on the type of the node: in an $\vee$-node n the values have to fulfill the rule $bet(n) = \bigvee\{\mathcal{R}(n, n') \wedge bet(n') \mid \mathcal{R}(n, n') \neq \bot\}$. In an $\wedge$-node the values have to fulfill the rule $bet(n) = \bigwedge\{\neg\mathcal{R}(n, n') \vee bet(n') \mid \mathcal{R}(n, n') \neq \bot\}$. Once a bet is made on the value of a node it cannot be changed. The role of $\forall$belard is then to choose one successor n' for which $\exists$loise needs to continue and prove the value $bet(n')$. Intuitively, $\forall$belard will try to choose a successor for which the value is incorrect.

In this definition we return to talking about *winning* versus losing. Intuitively, $\exists$loise wins if she manages to proceed without contradictions. Formally, if $\exists$loise is stuck (meaning she cannot associate the successors of a node with values by the above rules) then $\forall$belard wins. If the play ends in a terminal node of the form $s \vdash q$ or $s \vdash \neg q$, then $\exists$loise wins iff the value she gave the node matches its real value ($\Theta(s)(q)$ or $\neg\Theta(s)(q)$ resp.). In an infinite play the winner is determined by the 2-valued winning conditions.

Note that here $\exists$loise moves in *both* types of nodes, which changes the basic nature of the game. However, we now have the desired property that the game is equivalent to the definition used in the context of EAA. It now holds that an accepting run of the automaton with value α corresponds to a winning strategy for $\exists$loise with an initial bet of value α, and vice versa. Thus, there exists a *maximum* value for which $\exists$loise has a winning strategy and this value is the multi-valued model checking result.

Our definition of the game is in fact more general than the automaton used in [4] as it handles the multi-valued transitions of the Kripke structure directly.

7   Comparison to the 3-Valued Game

One of the most useful applications of multi-valued model checking is the 3-valued case. In [24,13] the regular model checking game has been generalized to a 3-valued game over a KMTS (see Definition 7). A KMTS $\mathcal{M}$ can be viewed as a Kripke structure over lattice L_3 by giving the must transitions in R^+ value $\top$, the may transitions in $R^- \setminus R^+$ value U and the rest value $\bot$. In this section we compare the game of [13] to our general multi-valued game $\Gamma_{\mathcal{M}}^m(s, \varphi)$ and point out the main differences that make the 3-valued game much simpler.

When considering the 3-valued case, it is possible to give the indefinite value U an intuitive meaning of a *tie*. We can thus still talk about the notion of *winning* in a way that corresponds to the three possible values $\{\top, U, \bot\}$ in the logic (see L_3 in Fig. 1) [13]. This is unlike the multi-valued case where we need to talk about the general notion of a *value* of a play or a game. The correspondence between the value of the game and the formula is then given by a variant of Theorem 1, with an additional possibility [13]:

(c) $[\![\varphi]\!]^{\mathcal{M}}(s) = U$ iff no player has a winning strategy for $\Gamma_{\mathcal{M}}(s, \varphi)$

Another major difference arises from the fact that the lattice L_3 has a *total* order, meaning that all values are comparable. As a result, in the 3-valued case a strategy has a *precise* value (rather than a lower bound) and the same holds for the game. That is, strategies are comparable and there always exists a *best* strategy (either winning or non-winning) that determines the value of the game.

The combination of these differences results in another interesting property of the 3-valued game. As in the general multi-valued case, the result of the play in the 3-valued case also depends on the values of the edges that were used. However, in [13] this effect is captured by a *consistency* requirement that says that in order to win, the winner has to use only must edges (with value $\top$). The surprising part is that the opponent can use either type. Recall that in the general multi-valued case, on the other hand, we need to consider not only the edges that one player uses, but also those used by the opponent.

This results from the fact that in the 3-valued case only one intermediate result is possible. Furthermore, because of the total order on the elements of the lattice, a value cannot be achieved by a combination of values that are all different from it. Thus the values of the edges that the opponent uses in the 3-valued game cannot improve the result for the other player beyond a tie (or U). They are therefore irrelevant when we determine a *winner* in the play – recall that in the 3-valued case we are interested in the *winner* of the play. This is no longer the case in the multi-valued case, where we are interested in the (more general notion of a) *value* that each player achieves and this value can be achieved by a combination of several values, possibly incomparable ones.

References

1. T. Ball, O. Kupferman, and G. Yorsh. Abstraction for falsification. In *CAV*, 2005.
2. G. Bruns and P. Godefroid. Model checking partial state spaces with 3-valued temporal logics. In *Computer Aided Verification*, pages 274–287, 1999.
3. G. Bruns and P. Godefroid. Temporal logic query checking. In *LICS*. IEEE, 2001.
4. G. Bruns and P. Godefroid. Model checking with multi-valued logics. In *ICALP*, 2004.
5. W. Chan. Temporal-logic queries. In *CAV*, volume 1855 of *LNCS*, pages 450–463, 2000.
6. M. Chechik, B. Devereux, and A. Gurfinkel. Model-checking infinite state-space systems with fine-grained abstractions using spin. In *SPIN Workshop*, volume 2057 of *LNCS*, 2001.
7. M. Chechik, B. Devereux, A. Gurfinkel, and S. Easterbrook. Multi-valued symbolic model-checking. Technical Report CSRG-448, University of Toronto, April 2002.
8. E.M. Clarke, O. Grumberg, and D.A. Peled. *Model Checking*. MIT press, 1999.
9. B.A. Davey and H.A. Priestly. *Introduction to Lattices and Order*. Cambrifge University Press, 1990.
10. L. de Alfaro and R. Majumdar. Quantitative solution of omega-regular games. In *STOC'01*.
11. S.M. Easterbrook and M. Chechik. A framework for multi-valued reasoning over inconsistent viewpoints. In *ICSE*, pages 411–420, 2001.
12. P. Godefroid and R. Jagadeesan. Automatic abstraction using generalized model checking. In *CAV*, volume 2404 of *LNCS*, pages 137–150, 2002.
13. O. Grumberg, M. Lange, M. Leucker, and S. Shoham. Don't know in the μ-calculus. In *VMCAI*, 2005.
14. A. Gurfinkel and M. Chechik. Multi-valued model checking via classical model checking. In *CONCUR*, pages 263–277, 2003.
15. A. Gurfinkel, B. Devereux, and M. Chechik. Model exploration with temporal logic query checking. In *FSE*, pages 139–148. ACM, 2002.
16. M. Huth, R. Jagadeesan, and D. Schmidt. Modal transition systems: A foundation for three-valued program analysis. In *ESOP*, volume 2028, pages 155–169, 2001.
17. M. Huth and S. Pradhan. Lifting assertion and consistency checkers from single to multiple viewpoints. Technical Report 2002/11, Dept. of Computing, Imperial College, 2002.

18. B. Konikowska and W. Penczek. Reducing model checking from multi-valued CTL* to CTL*. In *CONCUR*, volume 2421 of *LNCS*, 2002.
19. B. Konikowska and W. Penczek. Model checking multi-valued modal mu-calculus: Revisited. In *Proc. of CS&P'04*, 2004.
20. D. Kozen. Results on the propositional μ-calculus. *TCS*, 27, 1983.
21. O. Kupferman, M.Y. Vardi, and P. Wolper. An automata-theoretic approach to branching-time model checking. *Journal of the ACM (JACM)*, 47(2):312–360, 2000.
22. M. Leucker. Model checking games for the alternation free mu-calculus and alternating automata. In *LPAR*, 1999.
23. S. Shoham. A game-based framework for CTL counterexamples and abstraction-refinement. Master's thesis, Dept. of Computer Science, Technion - Israel Institute of Technology, 2003.
24. S. Shoham and O. Grumberg. A game-based framework for CTL counterexamples and 3-valued abstraction-refinement. In *CAV*, volume 2725 of *LNCS*, pages 275–287, 2003.
25. C. Stirling. Local model checking games. In *CONCUR*, volume 962 of *LNCS*, 1995.
26. A. Tarski. A lattice-theoretical fixpoint theorem and its application. *Pacific J.Math.*, 5, 1955.

Model Checking Prioritized Timed Automata

Shang-Wei Lin, Pao-Ann Hsiung, Chun-Hsian Huang, and Yean-Ru Chen

Department of Computer Science and Information Engineering,
National Chung Cheng University, Chiayi, Taiwan−621, ROC
hpa@computer.org

Abstract. Priorities are often used to resolve conflicts in timed systems. However, priorities are not directly supported by state-of-art model checkers. Often, a designer has to either abstract the priorities leading to a high degree of non-determinism or model the priorities using existing primitives. In this work, it is shown how prioritized timed automata can make modelling prioritized timed systems easier through the support for priority specification and model checking. The verification of prioritized timed automata requires a subtraction operation to be performed on two clock zones, represented by DBMs, for which we propose an algorithm to generate the minimal number of zones partitioned. After the application of a series of DBM subtraction operations, the number of zones generated become large. We thus propose an algorithm to reduce the final number of zones partitioned by merging some of them. A typical bus arbitration example is used to illustrate the benefits of the proposed algorithms. Due to the support for prioritization and zone reduction, we observe that there is a 50% reduction in the number of modes and 44% reduction in the number of transitions.

Keywords: Prioritized timed automata, DBM subtraction, zone merging, zone reduction.

1 Introduction

Concurrency results in conflicts when resources are shared such as two or more processes trying to use the same processor or the same peripheral device in real-time embedded systems. To resolve such conflicts, scheduling, synchronization, and arbitration are some well-known solutions that have been popularly used in operating systems and in hardware designs. A common artifact of these solutions is the prioritization of contending parties. A low priority process is allowed to execute only when all processes with higher priorities are disabled.

System models used for design and verification such as timed automata, statecharts, and others allow non-determinisms which arise out of concurrency, interleaving, and information hiding. However, non-determinisms often result in unmanageably large state-spaces. Prioritization of transitions not only models real systems more accurately but also removes non-determinisms and thus reduces the size of state-spaces. Several modeling frameworks have been proposed for modeling and designing systems with priorities. However, their verification techniques are still very limited. All the above mentioned reasons have motivated us to model check timed systems with priorities.

D.A. Peled and Y.-K. Tsay (Eds.): ATVA 2005, LNCS 3707, pp. 370–384, 2005.

The target model for prioritization in this work will be timed automata (TA) [4], because it is widely used in most model checkers for real-time systems such as SGM [15,22], RED [21], UPPAAL [6], and Kronos [23]. In model checking timed automata with priorities, a subtraction operation between two clock zones, represented by *Difference Bound Matrices* (DBMs), is required. We have proposed an algorithm to perform the subtraction operation on two DBMs [14]. This algorithm generates the minimal number of zones partitioned. If there are multiple priorities in timed automata, a series of DBM subtraction operations are needed. After a series of DBM subtraction operations, the final number of zones partitioned may become very large resulting in a significant increase in state-space sizes. In this work, we propose another DBM subtraction operation that also generates the minimal number of zones partitioned. For handling the large number of zones generated after a series of DBM subtraction, we also propose a DBM merging algorithm to reduce the final number of zones partitioned by merging some of the zones.

The remaining portion is organized as follows. Section 2 describes previous work related to priority modeling and verification. Basic definitions used in our work are given in Section 3. Section 4 will formulate the solutions for solving the above described issues in prioritizing timed automata and then verifying them. Section 5 gives an example. The article is concluded and future research directions are given in Section 6.

2 Related Work

Several work of Joseph Sifakis [1,2,13,20,19] have focused on modeling timed systems with priorities. A solid theoretical basis has been laid by these work for modeling schedulers based on priorities. Several well-known scheduling methods such FIFO, rate-monotonic, earliest deadline first, least laxity first, priority ceiling protocol were modeled by priority rules. Deadlock-free controllers were also synthesized to meet safety properties expressed as priority rules [13]. A real-time process with arrival time, execution time, and period or deadline was formally modeled using different time urgencies such as *delayable* (must transit before the transition condition expires) and *eager* (must transit as soon as the transition condition holds) [2]. The compositionality of priorities was handled by priority choice operators [19]. In spite of these solid work on modeling and synthesis of schedulers for timed systems with priorities, little has been investigated on the verification of such systems.

Priorities have also been added to other modeling formalisms such as the work on a priority language for Timed CSP [16], in which some operators were refined into biased ones and several algebraic laws were given. Actions in process algebra have been prioritized by Cleaveland and Hennessy [11]. A prioritized version of ACP was proposed by Baeten et al. [5]. Camilleri proposed a prioritized version of CCS [17] with a left biased choice operator [8]. Priorities have not received as much focus in the model checking field as that in process algebra. The work here is an initial step in the verification direction. Some background on the model checking paradigm is given in the rest of this Section.

Model checking [9,10,18] is a technique for verifying finite state concurrent systems. One benefit of this restriction is that verification can be performed automatically.

The procedure normally uses an exhaustive search of the state space of a system to determine if some specification is true or not. Given sufficient resources, the procedure will always terminate with a *yes/no* answer. Moreover, it can be implemented by algorithms with reasonable efficiency, which can be run on moderate-sized machines. The process of model checking includes three parts: modeling, specification, and verification. *Modeling* is to convert a design into a formalism accepted by a model checking tool. Before verification, *specification*, which is usually given in some logical formalism, is necessary to state the properties that the design must satisfy. The *verification* is completely automated. However, in practice it often involves human assistance. One such manual activity is the analysis of the verification results. In case of a negative result, the user is often provided with an error trace. This can be used as a counterexample for the checked property and can help the designer in tracking down where the error occurred. In this case, analyzing the error trace may require a modification to the system and a re-application of the model checking algorithm.

When model checking is applied to real-time system verification, the model checker verifies if a system modeled by a set of concurrent *Timed Automata* (TA) satisfies a set of user-given specification properties expressed in the *Timed Computation Tree Logic* (TCTL). TA [3,4] is a timed extension of the conventional automata, which was proposed by Alur, Courcoubetis, and Dill in 1990 . TCTL [3] is a *timed* extension of the temporal logic called *Computation Tree Logic* (CTL) [9].

Our model checking procedures for prioritized timed automata are implemented in the *State-Graph Manipulators* (SGM) model checker [15,22], which is a high-level compositional model checker for real-time systems. Now, with the enhancement of prioritizations, SGM can also be used to model check real-time embedded systems such as *System-on-Chip* (SoC) architectures.

3   Preliminaries

Definition 1. Mode Predicate
Given a set C of clock variables and a set D of discrete variables, the syntax of a *mode predicate* η over C and D is defined as: $\eta := false \mid x \sim c \mid x - y \sim c \mid d \sim c \mid \eta_1 \wedge \eta_2 \mid \neg\beta_3$, where $x, y \in C$, $\sim \in \{\leq, <, =, \geq, >\}$, $c \in \mathcal{N}$, the set of non-negative integers, $d \in D$, η_1, η_2 are mode predicates, and β_3 is a discrete variable constraint. A mode predicate η can be expressed as a conjunction of a clock constraint ζ and a Boolean condition β on the discrete variables, that is, $\eta = \zeta \wedge \beta$.   □

Let $B(C, D)$ be the set of all mode predicates over C and D. We extend the conventional definition of TA by prioritizing some of the transitions in a TA, as defined in Definition 2.

Definition 2. Prioritized Timed Automaton
A *Prioritized Timed Automaton* (PTA) is a tuple $\mathcal{A}_i = (M_i, m_i^0, C_i, D_i, L_i, \chi_i, T_i, \lambda_i, \tau_i, \pi_i, \rho_i)$ such that:

- M_i is a finite set of modes,
- $m_i^0 \in M$ is the initial mode,

- C_i is a set of clock variables,
- D_i is a set of discrete variables,
- L_i is a set of synchronization labels, and $\epsilon \in L_i$ is a special label that represents asynchronous behavior (i.e. no need of synchronization),
- $\chi_i : M_i \mapsto B(C_i, D_i)$ is an *invariance* function that labels each mode with a condition true in that mode,
- $T_i \subseteq M_i \times M_i$ is a set of transitions,
- $\lambda_i : T_i \mapsto L_i$ associates a synchronization label with a transition,
- $\tau_i : T_i \mapsto B(C_i, D_i)$ defines the transition triggering conditions,
- $\pi_i : T_i \mapsto \mathcal{N}$ associates an integer priority with a transition, where a larger positive value implies higher priority and a zero value implies no prioritization, and
- $\rho_i : T_i \mapsto 2^{C_i \cup (D_i \times \mathcal{N})}$ is an *assignment* function that maps each transition to a set of assignments such as resetting some clock variables and setting some discrete variables to specific integer values. □

A system state space is represented by a *system state graph* as defined in Definition 3.

Definition 3.　Prioritized System State Graph

Given a system S with n components modelled by PTA $\mathcal{A}_i = (M_i, m_i^0, C_i, D_i, L_i, \chi_i, T_i, \lambda_i, \tau_i, \pi_i, \rho_i)$, $1 \leq i \leq n$, the system model is defined as a state graph represented by $\mathcal{A}_1 \times \ldots \times \mathcal{A}_n = \mathcal{A}_S = (M, m^0, C, D, L, \chi, T, \lambda, \tau, \pi, \rho)$, where:

- $M = M_1 \times M_2 \times \ldots \times M_n$ is a finite set of system modes, $m = m_1.m_2.\ldots.m_n \in M$,
- $m^0 = m_1^0.m_2^0.\ldots.m_n^0 \in M$ is the initial system mode,
- $C = \bigcup_i C_i$ is the union of all sets of clock variables in the system,
- $D = \bigcup_i D_i$ is the union of all sets of discrete variables in the system,
- $L = \bigcup_i L_i$ is the union of all sets of synchronization labels in the system,
- $\chi : M \mapsto B(\bigcup_i C_i, \bigcup_i D_i), \chi(m) = \wedge_i \chi_i(m_i)$, where $m = m_1.m_2.\ldots.m_n \in M$.
- $T \subseteq M \times M$ is a set of system transitions which consists of two types of transitions:
  - *Asynchronous transitions*: $\exists i, 1 \leq i \leq n, e_i \in T_i$ such that $e_i = e \in T$
  - *Synchronized transitions*: $\exists i, j, 1 \leq i \neq j \leq n, e_i \in T_i, e_j \in T_j$ such that $\lambda_i(e_i) = (l, in), \lambda_j(e_j) = (l, out), l \in L_i \cap L_j \neq \emptyset, e \in T$ is synchronization of e_i and e_j with conjuncted triggering conditions and union of all transitions assignments (defined later in this definition)
- $\lambda : T \mapsto L$ associates a synchronization label with a transition, which represents a blocking signal that was synchronized, except for $\epsilon \in L$, ϵ is a special label that represents asynchronous behavior (i.e. no need of synchronization),
- $\tau : T \mapsto B(\bigcup_i C_i, \bigcup_i D_i), \tau(e) = \tau_i(e_i)$ for an asynchronous transition and $\tau(e) = \tau_i(e_i) \wedge \tau_j(e_j)$ for a synchronous transition,
- $\pi : T \mapsto \mathcal{N}$, where $\pi(e) = \pi_i(e_i)$ for an asynchronous transition and $\pi(e) = \max\{\pi_i(e_i), \pi_j(e_j)\}$ for a synchronous transition, and
- $\rho : T \mapsto 2^{\bigcup_i C_i \cup (\bigcup_i D_i \times \mathcal{N})}, \rho(e) = \rho_i(e_i)$ for an asynchronous transition and $\rho(e) = \rho_i(e_i) \cup \rho_j(e_j)$ for a synchronous transition. □

In a mode predicate, there are Boolean and clock constraints. In most model checkers, the Boolean constraints are represented by *Binary Decision Diagrams* (BDD) [7] proposed by Bryant and the clock constraints are represented by *Difference Bound Matrices* (DBM) [12] proposed by Dill.

4   Model Checking Real-Time Embedded Systems

Our target problem is to model and verify real-time embedded systems with priority. A set of prioritized timed automata is used to model such a system and model checking is used to verify if the prioritized system state graph, obtained by merging the set of PTA, satisfies user-given TCTL properties. In this section, we will propose solutions to the issues that were introduced in Section 1. A precise definition of the semantics of prioritized timed automata will be given in Section 4.1. A major extension to the conventional semantics involves the negation of clock zones and its implementation using DBMs, which will be covered in Section 4.2.

4.1   Semantics of Prioritized Timed Automata

The syntax of priorities was given as non-negative integers associated with transitions such that a larger positive value implied higher priority, as defined in Definition 2. Besides an integer priority, a transition $t \in T_i$ also has a triggering condition $\tau_i(t) \in B(C_i, D_i)$, which, being a mode predicate (Definition 1), can be segregated into two parts, namely a clock constraint (or clock zone) $\zeta(t)$ and a Boolean condition $\beta(t)$ such that $\tau_i(t) = \zeta(t) \wedge \beta(t)$. Prioritization semantics require the negation of transition triggering conditions because a transition t can be executed only if all transitions t' with priorities higher than that of t cannot be executed, that is, they are disabled or their triggering conditions $\tau_i(t')$ do not hold. In other words, transition t can fire only when the following condition holds.

$$
\tau_i(t) \wedge \left(\bigwedge_{\pi_i(t') > \pi_i(t)} \neg \tau_i(t') \right), \tag{1}
$$

where transitions t and t' all originate from the same source mode.

Given a triggering condition $\tau_i(t) = \zeta(t) \wedge \beta(t)$, its negation is defined as follows.

$$
\begin{aligned}
\neg \tau_i(t) &= \overline{\zeta(t)} \vee \neg \beta(t) \\
\overline{\zeta(t)} &= x \sim' c, \quad \text{if } \zeta(t) = x \sim c, \\
&= x - y \sim c, \quad \text{if } \zeta(t) = x - y \sim c, \\
&= \overline{\zeta_1} \wedge \overline{\zeta_2}, \quad \text{if } \zeta(t) = \zeta_1 \wedge \zeta_2, \\
\neg \beta(t) &= d \sim' c, \quad \text{if } \beta(t) = d \sim c \\
&= \neg \beta_1 \vee \neg \beta_2, \quad \text{if } \beta(t) = \beta_1 \wedge \beta_2, \\
&= \beta_1, \quad \text{if } \beta(t) = \neg \beta_1,
\end{aligned} \tag{2}
$$

where $x, y \in C_i, d \in D_i, c \in \mathcal{N}, \sim' \in \{>, \geq, \neq, \leq, <\}$ corresponding respectively to $\sim \in \{\leq, <, =, >, \geq\}$, ζ_1, ζ_2 are clock constraints, and β_1, β_2 are Boolean conditions on discrete variables in D_i.

In the above definition for negation of a triggering condition in $B(C_i, D_i)$, the result of negation no longer belongs to the set $B(C_i, D_i)$, that is, the set of mode predicates is not closed under the negation operator. This is because all clock constraints, also called *clock zones*, in $B(C_i, D_i)$ are n-dimensional convex polyhedra for a system with n clocks. However, the result of negation may not be *convex*. This non-closure of negation has adverse effects on model checking because all operators on transition triggers and mode invariants need to guarantee closure so that the timed automata can be composed into state-graphs for model checking. Closure is also required to guarantee termination of the composition procedures for timed automata.

Conventional operators on clock zones such as *intersection, time elapse,* and *reset* all guarantee closure as their results are still clock zones (convex polyhedra). Nevertheless, the possibly non-convex polyhedron generated by negation can be converted into a set of convex polyhedra. In Section 4.2, we propose an algorithm for the optimal partitioning of non-convex polyhedra so that priorities can be modeled and verified for real-time embedded systems. Here, optimality means the least number of convex polyhedra is generated.

Returning to the condition for execution of a low priority transition t given in Equation (1), it can be expressed now more precisely as the following.

$$
\beta_i(t) \wedge \zeta_i(t) \wedge \left[\left(\bigwedge_{\pi_i(t') > \pi_i(t)} \neg\beta_i(t') \right) \vee \left(\bigwedge_{\pi_i(t') > \pi_i(t)} \overline{\zeta_i(t')} \right) \right] \tag{3}
$$

4.2   Optimal DBM Subtraction Algorithm

A *clock zone* is a clock constraint consisting of conjunctions of $x \sim c$ and $x - y \sim c$, where x, y are clock variables in C_i and $c \in \mathcal{N}$. A clock zone is also restricted to be a convex polyhedron. It is often implemented as a *Difference Bound Matrix* (DBM) [12], which is defined as follows.

Definition 4. Difference Bound Matrix (DBM)
Given a clock zone z that represents clock constraints on n clocks in $C_i = \{x_1, x_2, \ldots, x_n\}$, it can be implemented as a $(n+1) \times (n+1)$ matrix D, where the element $D(i, j) =\sim c, \sim \in \{<, \leq\}, c \in \mathcal{N}$, represents the constraint $x_i - x_j \sim c, 0 \leq i, j \leq n$. It is assumed $x_0 = 0$. $\square$

Geometrically, a clock zone over n clocks is an n-dimensional convex polyhedron. In the model checking of timed automata, three operations on clock zones are required, namely intersection, time elapse, and reset. The set of clock zones is closed under these three operations.

Definition 5. Unbounded and Bounded Element in DBM
Given a DBM D on n clocks, an element $D(i, j)$ of D is *unbounded* if $D(i, j) =''< \infty''$, where $i \neq j$; otherwise we call $D(i, j)$ *bounded*, where $i \neq j$. $\square$

Definition 6. Unrestricted DBM
Given a DBM D on n clocks, we call D *unrestricted*, if it satisfies the following: $D(i, j)$ is *unbounded* for all $0 \leq i, j \leq n$. $\square$

Definition 7. Complement Clock Constraint

Given a clock constraint $c_1 = x - y \sim c$ (or $x \sim c$), the *Complement Clock Constraint* $\bar{c}_1$ of c_1 is defined as : $\bar{c}_1 = x - y \sim' c$ (or $x \sim' c$), where $x, y \in C, c \in \mathcal{N}, \sim'$ $\in \{\leq, <, \neq, \geq, >\}$ corresponding respectively to $\sim \in \{>, \geq, =, <, \leq\}$. We can call that c_1 and $\bar{c}_1$ are *complement or $\bar{c}_1$ is complement to c_1*. $\qquad\square$

Definition 8. Reduced DBM

Given a DBM D on n clocks representing a clock zone z, D is *reduced* if D has the minimal number of *bounded* elements in all of the DBMs representing the same clock zone z. $\qquad\square$

In the verification of real-time embedded systems with priority, we need to subtract the clock zone representing the time a higher priority transition is enabled (trigger satisfied) from the clock zone representing the time a lower priority transition is enabled. We will call this the *subtraction* operator. In Section 4.1, for a given clock zone ζ, Equations (1, 2, 3) defined the negation of clock zones $\bar{\zeta}$. Using this negation, given two clock zones z_1 and z_2, we can calculate their difference as follows.

$$z_1 - z_2 = z_1 \cap \overline{z_2} \qquad (4)$$

where $\cap$ is the intersection operator between two zones.

As mentioned before in Section 4.1, $\overline{z_2}$ may not be a clock zone anymore as it may not be convex. We propose an algorithm here so that we can partition the possibly non-convex polyhedron $\overline{z_2}$ into a set of convex polyhedra. For ease of illustration, we will focus on the 2-dimensional case. It can be easily extended to n-dimensional zones, for any $n > 2$.

The optimal DBM subtraction algorithm, with $O(n^4)$ complexity for n clocks, is given in Algorithm 1 and described as follows. Given two clock zones represented by DBM z_1 and z_2, we can obtain the difference $z_1 - z_2$ by the following steps.

– Find $z_{intersect} = z_1 \cap z_2$ (Step 2)
– Reduce $z_{intersect}$ to obtain a DBM with minimal bounded elements so as to generate the minimal number of partitions (zones). (Step 3)
– Let z_{remain} record the remainder unpartitioned zone, which is initially assigned as z_1 (Step 4)
– For each non-diagonal and bounded element in the DBM $z_{intersect}$, we obtain a corresponding complement zone by reversing the relational operator. (Steps 5–7)
– For each complement zone, we find its intersection with z_{remain}, denoted as z_{tmp}, which is a zone. (Step 8)
– If z_{tmp} is not NULL, it means that we have subtracted a zone from z_{remain}. Then z_{tmp} is included into the set Z. (Step 10)
– After that, we have to recompute the remainder zone z_{remain}. (Step 11–13)

We can prove that a minimal number of partitions (zones) are generated after subtraction. Before we prove this, we give Theorem 1 as follows.

Theorem 1. *Given two DBMs namely z_1 and z_2, and $z_{intersect} = z_1 \cap z_2$, if the reduced DBM of $z_{intersect}$ has m unbounded elements, then $z_1 - z_2$ will generate at least m zones(DBMs).*

---

input : DBM: z_1, z_2
output: DBM*: Z //set of DBMs
DBM*: $z_{intersect}, z_{tmp}, z_{remain}$

$z_{intersect} \leftarrow z_2 \cap z_1$;
REDUCE($z_{intersect}$);

$z_{remain} \leftarrow z_1$;
for *each $z_{intersect}(i,j)$ and $i \neq j$ and $z_{intersect}(i,j)$ is bounded* **do**
    INIT(z_{tmp});   //set z_{tmp} *unrestricted*
    $z_{tmp}(i,j) \leftarrow \sim' c$;   //$z_{intersect}(i,j) = $ " $\sim c$",$\sim' \in \{>, \geq\}$ for $\sim \in \{\leq, <\}$,
        respectively
    $z_{tmp} \leftarrow z_{tmp} \cap z_{remain}$
    if $z_{tmp} \neq NULL$ **then**
        $Z \leftarrow Z \cup \{z_{tmp}\}$
        INIT(z_{tmp});   //set z_{tmp} *unrestricted*
        $z_{tmp}(i,j) \leftarrow \sim c$;   //$z_{intersect}(i,j) = $ " $\sim c$"
        $z_{remain} \leftarrow z_{remain} \cap z_{tmp}$;
    end
end
return Z

Algorithm 1: DBM Subtraction $z_1 - z_2$

Proof. Let $S = \{S_1, S_2, ..., S_n\}$ be the set of DBMs generated by $z_1 - z_2$, and $| S |$ is n. Let $\{c_1, c_2, ..., c_m\}$ be the m clock constraints corresponding to the m unbounded elements of $z_{intersect}$. Let $\{\overline{c}_1, \overline{c}_2, ..., \overline{c_m}\}$ be the m complement clock constraints with respect to $\{c_1, c_2, ..., c_m\}$. Because we want to subtract $z_{intersect}$ from z_1, therefore $\overline{c}_i \in S_j$, where $1 \leq i \leq m$, for some $j \in \{1, 2, ..., n\}$. Given every two element $\overline{c}_p$ and $\overline{c}_q \in \{\overline{c}_1, \overline{c}_2, ..., \overline{c}_m\}$, $\overline{c}_p$ and $\overline{c}_q$ will not belong to the same S_j for some $j \in \{1, 2, ..., n\}$, otherwise S_j will not be a zone (if so, S_j will not be a convex). So, $n \geq m$, that is, $z_1 - z_2$ will generate at least m zones (DBMs).

Theorem 2. *The number of zones generated by the DBM subtraction algorithm is minimal.*

Proof. Let z_1 and z_2 are two DBMs, and we want to do $z_1 - z_2$. Let $z_{intersect} = z_1 \cap z_2$. Let m be the number of bounded elements of the reduced DBM of $z_{intersect}$. By Theorem 1, we know that the number of zones generated by $z_1 - z_2$ is at least m. By Algorithm 1, we use each bound element of the reduced DBM of $z_{intersect}$ ⇒ the number of zones generated by Algorithm 1 is at most m. So, Algorithm 1 generates the minimal number of zones of $z_1 - z_2$.

Consider the example shown in Figure 1, we want to subtract the smaller zone from the bigger zone. Figure 2 shows the snap shots of Algorithm 1 operating on this example.

4.3 DBM Merging Algorithm

From Theorem 1 and Theorem 2, we know that we can obtain the minimal number of zones using Algorithm 1 when we want to subtract z_2 from z_1. Algorithm 1 operating on

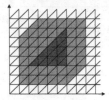

Fig. 1. An Example of DBM Subtraction

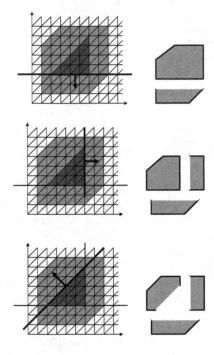

Fig. 2. Steps of DBM Subtraction

two zones is optimal, but if we want to do $z_1 - z_2 - z_3$, the number of zones generated may not be optimal. In other words, there may exist more than two zones which can be merged into a zone in the zone set after $z_1 - z_2 - z_3$.

In order to obtain the less number of zones after a series of zone subtraction operations, we propose an algorithm, which can help to determine whether given two zones z_1 and z_2 are mergeable. If not, the algorithm will return an unrestricted DBM. If yes, the algorithm will return a DBM representing $z_1 \cup z_2$. Note that all zones in the zone set S, after a series of subtraction operations, are disjoint. The input zones, say z_1 and z_2, of the algorithm have one restriction, which is that, z_1 cannot intersect with z_2. The DBM merging algorithm given in Algorithm 2 has $O(n^3)$ complexity and is described as follows. Given two clock zones represented by DBM z_1 and z_2 on n clocks, we can obtain the DBM z generated by merging z_1 and z_2 by the following steps.

- Reduce z_1 and z_2 (Steps 5–6)
- Set z unrestricted (Step 7)
- See if z_1 and z_2 are mergeable. If z_1 and z_2 are mergeable, then there exists a clock constraint $z_1(i,j)$, whose complement constraint is $z_2(j,i)$, for some $i,j \in \{1,2,...,n\}$. If there is no $z_1(i,j)$, whose complement constraint is the same as $z_2(i,j)$ for some $i,j \in \{1,2,...,n\}$, then z_1 and z_2 are not mergeable and the algorithm terminates. If yes, z_1 and z_2 are possibly mergeable. (Steps 8–17)
- If a pair of complement constraints is found in Steps 8–17 when $i = m$ and $j = n$, then $z(i,j)$ will be set as $z_2(i,j)$ and $z(j,i)$ will be set as $z_1(j,i)$. (Step 11–14)
- Besides the complement constraints found in Steps 8-17, if every corresponding bounded element pair $(z_1(i,j), z_2(i,j))$ is equal for all $i,j \in \{1,2,...,n\}$, then z_1 and z_2 are mergeable; otherwise, z_1 and z_2 are not mergeable. If z_1 and z_2 are mergeable,we can obtain $z(i,j)$ from bounded $z_1(i,j)$ or $z_2(i,j)$. (Step 22–38)

After illustrating how Algorithm 2 works on two zones, we will now show how to use Algorithm 2 to merge several zones generated by a series of zone subtraction operations on a zone. Theorem 3 tells us that given a zone set $Z = \{z_1, z_2, ..., z_n\}$, which consists of n clock zones, if $(z_1 \cup z_2 \cup ... \cup z_n)$ is a zone, then there exist two zones z_i and z_j which are mergeable for some $i,j \in \{1,2,...,n\}$, that is, there exists a merge sequence merging two zones at a time, which can merge $\{z_1, z_2, ..., z_n\}$ into Z.

We propose an algorithm which helps to merge a zone set $Z = \{z_1, z_2, ..., z_n\}$ into another zone set $Z' = \{z_1', z_2', ..., z_m'\}$, for $m \leq n$. This algorithm uses Algorithm 2 as a subroutine. The DBM set merging algorithm is given in Algorithm 3 and described as follows.

- Set Z' an empty set (Step 1)
- Merge $z_i \in Z$ with each other zone z_j , $i \neq j$, $i,j \in \{1,2,...,n\}$ and modify z_i into the output zone of DBM-Merge(z_i, z_j). (Step 3–9)
- Add z_i to Z' (Step 10)
- Do the above steps iteratively until every z_i has been considered. (Step 2–11)

Theorem 3. *Given a zone set* $Z = \{z_1, z_2, ..., z_n\}$ *and* $\mid Z \mid = n$. *If no pair of zones* z_i, $z_j \in Z$ *is mergeable, then* $(z_1 \cup z_2 \cup ... \cup z_n)$ *is not a zone.*

Proof. Let us prove this using a contradiction. We assume that $(z_1 \cup z_2 \cup ... \cup z_n)$ is a zone. Thus there must exist a zone $z_i \in Z$, such that $(z_1 \cup z_2 \cup ... \cup z_{i-1} \cup z_{i+1} \cup ... \cup z_n)$ is a zone for some $i \in \{1,2,...,n\}$, and of course z_i and $(z_1 \cup z_2 \cup ... \cup z_{i-1} \cup z_{i+1} \cup ... \cup z_n)$ are mergeable. Otherwise,$(z_1 \cup z_2 \cup ... \cup z_n)$ will not be a zone. Use the above property iteratively, we can obtain a zone Z' which consists of only two subzones z_p and z_q, such that $Z' = z_p \cup z_q$ for some $p,q \in \{1,2,...,n\}$, that is, z_p and z_q are mergeable. This contradicts the fact that no pair of zones z_i and $z_j \in Z$ is mergeable.

5   Application Example

In this section, we give a real example of bus arbitration. In a bus system, there are several masters and one arbiter attached to the bus. All masters on the bus will request the bus to do some data transfers, but the bus can only serve one master at a

```
   input  : DBM: z₁, z₂    //z₁ does not interset with z₂
   output: DBM: z     //the DBM generated by merging z₁ and z₂;If z₁ and z₂ cannot be
           merged, z will be unrestricted
 1 bool : mergable
 2 int : m, n;

 3 unMergable ← TRUE;
 4 m ← n ← 0;
 5 REDUCE(z₁);
 6 REDUCE(z₂);
 7 INIT(z)    //set z unrestricted
 8 for each z₁(i, j) and i ≠ j do
 9     if z₁(i, j) is complement to z₂(j, i) then
10         unMergable ← FALSE;
11         m ← i;
12         n ← j;
13         z(i, j) ← z₂(i, j);
14         z(j, i) ← z₁(j, i)
15         break;
16     end
17 end
18 if unMergable = TRUE then
19     return z;
20 end
21 else
22     for each z₁(i, j) and i ≠ j and i ≠ m, n and j ≠ m, n do
23         if z₁(i, j) ="< ∞" and z₂(i, j) ≠"< ∞" then
24             z(i, j) ← z₂(i, j);
25         end
26         else if z₁(i, j) ≠"< ∞" and z₂(i, j) ="< ∞" then
27             z(i, j) ← z₁(i, j);
28         end
29         else if z₁(i, j) ≠"< ∞" and z₂(i, j) ≠"< ∞" then
30             if z₁(i, j) = z₂(i, j) then
31                 z(i, j) ← z₁(i, j);
32             end
33             else
34                 unMergable ← TRUE;
35                 break;
36             end
37         end
38     end
39     if unMergable = TRUE then
40         INIT(z);    //set z unrestricted
41     end
42 end
43 return z
```

Algorithm 2: DBM Merging (z_1, z_2)

```
    input  : DBM: Z    //Z = {z₁, z₂, ..., zₙ}
    output : DBM: Z'    //Z' = {z'₁, z'₂, ..., z'ₘ}
 1  Z' ← ∅
 2  for each zᵢ ∈ Z do
 3      for each zⱼ ∈ Z  and  zⱼ ≠ zᵢ do
 4          z_tmp = DBM-Merge(zᵢ, zⱼ);
 5          if z_tmp ≠ unrestricted DBM then
 6              zᵢ ← z_tmp;
 7              Z = Z - {zⱼ};
 8          end
 9      end
10      Z' = Z' ∪ {zᵢ};
11  end
12  return Z
```

Algorithm 3: DBM Set Merging (Z)

time. In order to resolve conflicts, masters will usually be prioritized. When requests from masters arrive at the same time, the arbiter will decide which master can use the bus according the priorities of the masters. In our example, there are three masters and one arbiter attached to the bus system. The masters are modelled as in Figure 3.

Each of the three masters, namely Master A, Master B, and Master C, will request the bus when it wants to transfer data on the bus by entering the "requesting" state. It will stay in the "requesting" state until the arbiter grants its request. The priorities of Master A, Master B, and Master C are respectively 5, 3, and 2 where a higher value implies a higher priority.

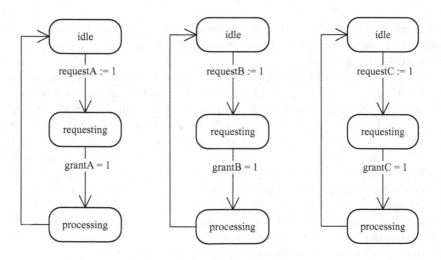

Fig. 3. PTA Model for Masters

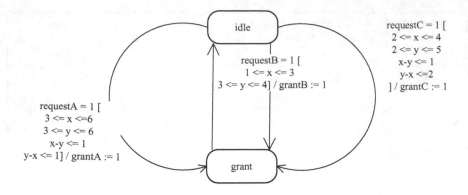

Fig. 4. PTA Model for Arbiter

Table 1. Prioritized Timed Automata of Arbiter

PTA	#Modes	#Trans
Without DBM Merging	2	7
With DBM Merging	2	5

Table 2. Verifying Bus-Arbitration Example (the whole state graph) With and Without DBM Merging

System State Graph	#Modes	#Trans	Mem (MB)	Time (sec)
Without DBM Merging	3,088	12,596	2.96	6.78
With DBM Merging	1,524	7,232	1.08	3.54
(reduction)	(50%)	(44%)	(64%)	(48%)

The arbiter is modelled as in Figure 4. If there is any request from the masters, it will decide which master can use the bus according their priorities and trigger conditions, and then enter the "grant" state.

The proposed DBM subtraction and merging algorithms were all implemented into the *State Graph Manipulators* (SGM) model checker [15,22] and applied to the bus arbitration example. Tables 1 and 2 show comparisons between applying and not applying the proposed DBM merging algorithm, for the arbiter alone and for the whole system graph, respectively. From Table 1, we can see that the arbiter PTA model illustrated in Fig. 4, which had 2 modes and 4 transitions, was transformed into a larger PTA model having 7 transitions when merging is not applied and having 5 transitions when merging is applied. This shows that merging significantly reduces the set of zones partitioned through a series of DBM subtraction. Further, it also shows that if priority is not supported, the user would have to model a larger PTA model. This increase in model size becomes significant with application complexity and will thus be a tedious task for a normal user. The burden of performing this tedious task is thus alleviated by our proposed methods.

The requirement for or the benefits of DBM merging after a series of DBM subtraction can be clearly observed from Table 2, which shows that there is a significant reduction in the number of modes (50%) and transitions (44%) after applying DBM merging. The computing resources are also reduced by a factor of 64% and 48% for memory space and CPU time, respectively.

6 Conclusions and Future work

In this work, we have proposed *Prioritized Timed Automata* to model timed systems with multiple priorities. We have also developed the semantics of Prioritized Timed Automata for model checking. Three algorithms were proposed for DBM subtraction and merging. The DBM subtraction algorithm generates the minimal number of partitioned zones. After a series of DBM subtraction operations, the number of zones partitioned may be mergeable. The DBM merging algorithm helps to reduce the final number of partitioned zones. The proposed algorithm when applied to a simple bus arbiter showed significant reductions in model size and computing resources. Future work will include reduction in the complexities of the proposed algorithms and their application to larger applications.

References

1. K. Altisen, G. Gössler, and J. Sifakis. A methodology for the construction of scheduled systems. In *Proceedings of the 6th International Symposium on Formal Techniques in Real-Time and Fault-Tolerant Systems (FTRTFT), Lecture Notes in Computer Science*, volume 1926, pages 106–120. Springer Verlag, September 2000.
2. K. Altisen, G. Gössler, and J. Sifakis. Scheduler modeling based on the controller synthesis paradigm. *Real-Time Systems*, 23:55–84, 2002.
3. R. Alur, C. Courcoubetis, and D.L. Dill. Model-checking for real-time systems. In *Proceedings of the 5th Annual Symposium on Logic in Computer Science*, pages 414–425. IEEE Computer Society Press, 1990.
4. R. Alur and D.L. Dill. A theory of timed automata. *Theoretical Computer Science*, 126(2):183–235, 1994.
5. J.C.M. Baeten, J.A. Bergstra, and J.W. Klop. Syntax and defining equations for an interrupt mechanism in process algebra. Technical Report CS-R8503, Centre for Mathematics and Computer Science, Amsterdam, The Netherlands, 1985.
6. J. Bengtsson, K. Larsen, F. Larsson, P. Pettersson, and Y. Wang. UPPAAL: a tool suite for automatic verification of real-time systems. In *Proceedings of Workshop on Verification and Control of Hybrid Systems III*, number 1066 in Lecture Notes in Computer Science, pages 232–243. Springer–Verlag, Oct 1996.
7. R.E. Bryant. Graph-based algorithms for Boolean function manipulation. *IEEE Transactions on Computers*, C-35(8):677–691, August 1986.
8. J. Camilleri. Introducing a priority operators to ccs. Technical Report 157, Cambridge, 1989.
9. E.M. Clarke and E.A. Emerson. Design and sythesis of synchronization skeletons using branching time temporal logic. In *Proceedings of the Logics of Programs Workshop*, volume 131 of *LNCS*, pages 52–71. Springer Verlag, 1981.
10. E.M. Clarke, O. Grumberg, and D.A. Peled. *Model Checking*. MIT Press, 1999.
11. R. Cleaveland and M. Hennessy. Priorities in process algebra. In *Proceedings of the 3rd Symposium on Logic in Computer Science*, Edinburgh, 1988.
12. David L. Dill. Timing assumptions and verification of finite-state concurrent systems. In *Proceedings of Workshop on Automatic Verification Methods for Finite State Systems*, volume 407 of *LNCS*, pages 197–212. Springer-Verlag, 1989.

13. G. Gössler and J. Sifakis. Priority systems. In *Proceedings of the 2nd International Symposium on Formal Methods for Components and Objects (FMCO), Lecture Notes in Computer Science*, volume 3188, pages 314–329. Springer Verlag, November 2003.

14. P.-A. Hsiung and S.-W. Lin. Model checking timed systems with priorities. In *Proceedings of the 11th IEEE International Conference on Embedded and Real-Time Computing Systems and Applications (RTCSA, Hong-Kong, China)*. IEEE Computer Society Press, August 2005. (accepted for publication).

15. P.-A. Hsiung and F. Wang. A state-graph manipulator tool for real-time system specification and verification. In *Proceedings of the 5th International Conference on Real-Time Computing Systems and Applications (RTCSA)*, October 1998.

16. G. Lowe. *Probabilities and Priorities in Timed CSP*. PhD thesis, St. Hugh's College, University of Oxford, Hilary Term, 1993.

17. R. Milner. *Communication and Concurrency*. Prentice Hall International, 1989.

18. J.-P. Queille and J. Sifakis. Specification and verification of concurrent systems in CESAR. In *Proceedings of the International Symposium on Programming*, volume 137 of *LNCS*, pages 337–351. Springer Verlag, 1982.

19. J. Sifakis. The compositional specification of timed systems. In *Proceedings of the 11th International Conference on Computer-Aided Verification (CAV), Lecture Notes in Computer Science*, volume 1633, pages 2–7. Springer Verlag, July 1999.

20. J. Sifakis. Modeling real-time systems — challenges and work directions. In *Proceedings of the 1st International Workshop on Embedded Software (EMSOFT), Lecture Notes in Computer Science*, volume 2211, pages 373–389. Springer Verlag, October 2001.

21. F. Wang. RED: Model-checker for timed automata with clock-restriction diagram. In *Proceedings of the Workshop on Real-Time Tools*, August 2001. Technical Report 2001-014, ISSN 1404-3203, Department of Information Technology, Uppsala University.

22. F. Wang and P.-A. Hsiung. Efficient and user-friendly verification. *IEEE Transactions on Computers*, 51(1):61–83, January 2002.

23. S. Yovine. Kronos: A verification tool for real-time systems. *International Journal of Software Tools for Technology Transfer*, 1(1/2):123–133, October 1997.

An MTBDD-Based Implementation of Forward Reachability for Probabilistic Timed Automata

Fuzhi Wang and Marta Kwiatkowska

School of Computer Science, University of Birmingham,
Birmingham B15 2TT, United Kingdom
{F.Wang, M.Z.Kwiatkowska}@cs.bham.ac.uk

Abstract. Multi-Terminal Binary Decision Diagrams (MTBDDs) have been successfully applied in symbolic model checking of probabilistic systems. In this paper we propose an encoding method for Probabilistic Timed Automata (PTA) based on MTBDDs. The timing information is encoded via placeholders stored in the MTBDDs that are independent of how the timing information is represented. Using the Colorado University Decision Diagrams (CUDD) package, an experimental model checker is implemented, which supports probabilistic reachability model checking via the forward algorithm. We use Difference Bound Matrices (DBMs) and Difference Decision Diagrams (DDDs) for representing timing information and present experimental results on three case studies. Our key contribution is a general placeholder encoding method for Probabilistic Timed Automata and an experimental MTBDD-based model checker which has been partly integrated with PRISM. This is the first symbolic implementation of the forward probabilistic reachability algorithm.

1 Introduction

Binary Decision Diagrams (BDDs) [7] are the main data structure used in symbolic model model checking. Their success relies on the ability of BDD-like data structures to compactly represent both sets of states and the transition relation between these states. BDDs, however, cannot represent quantitative information. Recently, Multi-Terminal Decision Diagrams (MTBDDs) [8] have been successfully applied in the verification of probabilistic systems [10,12], and various extensions, Difference Decision Diagrams (DDDs) [17], Clock Difference Diagrams (CDDs) [2] and Clock-Restriction Diagram (CRDs) [20], have been proposed for use in symbolic verification of real-time systems. However, no symbolic data structure exists for the verification of probabilistic real-time systems modelled as Probabilistic Timed Automata (PTA) [14], which contain both real-time clocks and probabilistic information. Probabilistic timed automata are a natural model for randomised distributed algorithms that use timing delays, and a number of models of such algorithms have been developed. The subclass of probabilistic timed automata with digital clocks [13] can be modelled and verified directly using the PRISM model checker [1]. For PTAs that do not comply with this restriction, currently two, non-symbolic, methods are supported: via the forward exploration algorithm of [14] using the KRONOS to PRISM connection

D.A. Peled and Y.-K. Tsay (Eds.): ATVA 2005, LNCS 3707, pp. 385–399, 2005.

[9], or forward/backward using the experimental implementation of [16]. Both these methods are based on a translation into the textual modelling language of PRISM, and are therefore rather involved.

In this paper, we investigate a fully symbolic implementation of model checking for probabilistic timed automata. We propose an MTBDD-based placeholder encoding method for representing probabilistic timed automata which is independent of the data structure used to represent timing information. The advantage of our proposal is that the method is general: firstly, other data structures for representing timing information could also be integrated with this encoding method; secondly, both forward and backward analysis can be supported. The main difficulty for the fully symbolic approach is that the state space is not known in advance, since the states are extracted dynamically via forward/backward exploration, in contrast to symbolic model checking for probabilistic systems where the size of the state space can be deduced from the syntactic model description. Using the CUDD package [19] an experimental tool has been implemented and partly integrated within PRISM. We report on the performance of our implementation of the forward probabilistic reachability algorithm on three case studies. This is the first fully symbolic implementation of the forward probabilistic reachability for probabilistic timed automata originally proposed in [14].

Related Work. The most commonly used data structure for representing timing information in real-time verification tools [6,3] is Difference Bound Matrices (DBMs) [4]. A number of BDD-like data structures, e.g. CDDs [2], DDDs [17] and CRDs [20], have been proposed for use in verifying real-time systems, but not yet extended to the probabilistic case. MTBDDs have been successfully applied in model checking of probabilistic systems, and also probabilistic timed automata and timed systems with digital clocks [12], but not in the case of the full class of PTAs. Recently, MTBDDs have also been applied to real-time systems [18]. Although the approach in [18] uses a single data structure (MTBDDs) to represent both timing and discrete information in order to leverage well-known techniques for BDDs or MTBDDs, it involves SAT-based analysis.

There are two, non-symbolic, methods for dense-time probabilistic timed automata: via the forward exploration algorithm implemented in [9], or forward/backward using the experimental implementation of [16]. The forward method is not guaranteed to produce exact reachability probabilities [14], but only requires simple operations; on the other hand, backward analysis can produce exact probabilities but at a cost of higher computational complexity. The method of [9], which combines KRONOS [6] and PRISM [1] to verify the IEEE-1394 Root Contention Protocol, requires three steps: firstly, a set of states reachable from the source state before the deadline is calculated using KRONOS [6]; secondly, the result is translated into a PRISM model description which is input into PRISM and, finally, probabilistic analysis is performed. This method is not efficient because it can generate large files that have to be parsed by PRISM. Our experimental implementation of [16] suffers from the same problem, as it performs a translation into the PRISM modelling language. In this paper we propose a general MTBDD-based encoding scheme that can deal with both forward and backward analysis in a single step, thus avoiding the expensive translation at the level of text.

2   The Symbolic Encoding Method

2.1   Syntax of Probabilistic Timed Automata

Let $\mathcal{R}$ be the *time domain* of the non-negative reals and $\mathcal{N}$ the natural numbers. We assume a given finite set $\mathcal{X}$ of *clocks*, variables $x \in \mathcal{X}$ that take values from the time domain $\mathcal{R}$. A point $\nu \in \mathcal{R}^{\mathcal{X}}$ is referred to as a *clock valuation*, with $0 \in \mathcal{R}^{\mathcal{X}}$ the valuation that assigns 0 to all clocks in $\mathcal{X}$. We use $\nu[X := d]$ to denote the clock valuation obtained from ν by resetting all of the clocks in $X \subseteq \mathcal{X}$ to d, where d is a natural number or zero with the value of the remaining clocks unaffected.

A *zone* of $\mathcal{X}$, written ζ, is a subset of the valuation space $\mathcal{R}^{\mathcal{X}}$ described by a conjunction of constraints. Formally, for a given set of clocks $\mathcal{X}$, a *zone* ζ is defined by the following syntax:

$$\zeta \ ::= \ x \sim c \mid x - y \sim c \mid \neg\zeta \mid \zeta \wedge \zeta$$

where $x, y \in \mathcal{X}$, $c \in \mathcal{N}$ and $\sim \in \{\leq, <, >, \geq\}$.

The set of zones of $\mathcal{X}$ is denoted by $Zones(\mathcal{X})$ for a given set of clocks $\mathcal{X}$.

Below we review the definition of probabilistic timed automata [14].

Definition 1. *A* probabilistic timed automaton (PTA) *is a tuple* $= (L, \mathcal{X}, \mathcal{L}, inv, prob)$ *where:*

- L *is a finite set of* locations;
- *the function* $inv : L \rightarrow Zones(\mathcal{X})$ *is the* invariant condition;
- *the finite set* $prob \subseteq L \times Zones(\mathcal{X}) \times Dist(2^{\mathcal{X}} \times L)$ *is the* probabilistic edge relation;
- $\mathcal{L} : L \rightarrow 2^{AP}$ *is a labelling function assigning atomic propositions to locations.*

A *state* of a probabilistic timed automaton is a pair (l, ν) where $l \in L$ and $\nu \in \mathcal{R}^{\mathcal{X}}$ are such that $\nu \lhd inv(l)$. The invariant condition describes the set of admissible states. Transitions are *probabilistic edges* $(l, g, p) \in prob$ where l is the source location, g is the enabling guard and p the probability distribution on target locations, together with the set of clocks to be reset as the edge is taken. It is more convenient to treat an *edge* of a PTA as a tuple $(n, l, inv(l), l', inv(l'), g, X, p)$ where n is the non-deterministic choice between simultaneously enabled distributions, coded as a natural number, such that $(l, g, p) \in prob$ and $p(X, l') > 0$. Such a tuple contains sufficient information for making a transition, and will be directly used in our encoding method.

2.2   Multi-Terminal Binary Decision Diagrams (MTBDDs)

MTBDDs [8] are an extension of BDDs [7] which allow one to represent functions over Boolean vectors that can take any value, not just 0 or 1. In other words, BDDs can have only two terminals, while MTBDDs can have more than two terminals. An MTBDD is a Directed Acyclic Graph (DAG) whose vertices, as for BDDs, are called nodes. There are two kinds of nodes in an MTBDD, non-terminal and terminal. Like in a BDD, a non-terminal node is labelled with a single variable and each non-terminal node has exactly two children. However, unlike BDDs, the terminal node which has no children is labelled by a real number. MTBDDs can be reduced to the canonical form by imposing an ordering of the variables. However, similarly to BDDs, the size of the MTBDDs is extremely sensitive to the ordering of its variables.

Probabilistic systems, for example, Markov Decision Processes (MDPs) that are induced from PTAs, are described in terms of probability matrices, and their analysis involves numerical computation such as solving a linear equation system or (as is the case with MDPs) a linear programming problem. MTBDDs can represent both probability vectors and matrices, and can therefore serve as a symbolic representation for probabilistic systems. Given a real-valued vector of length 2^n, an MTBDD encoding can be obtained by mapping to reals from vector's indices which are encoded into n Boolean variables. As far as numerical computation is concerned, MTBDDs support methods for implementing standard matrix operations, such as scalar multiplication, matrix addition and matrix multiplication.

2.3   Representations for Zones

DBMs. Difference Bound Matrices (DBMs) are data structures that can efficiently represent sets of adjacent regions (convex union of adjacent regions which is also called a zone). Non-convex zones are represented as lists of DBMs. A DBM is a square matrix whose elements represent bounds on the difference between two clock values. For a set of n clocks $\{x_1, \ldots, x_n\}$, and by using a special clock x_0 whose value is always zero, the constraints over these clocks can be encoded as a $(n+1) * (n+1)$ square matrix D whose indices range over the interval $[0..n]$ and whose elements belong to $\mathcal{N}_\infty \times \{<, \leq\}$, where $\mathcal{N}_\infty = \mathcal{N} \vee \{0, \infty\}$.

DDDs. Difference Decision Diagrams (DDDs) are designed for representing both convex and non-convex unions of zones, which are called Difference Constraint Expressions (DCE) in DDDs. DDDs are a BDD-like data-structure. Like a BDD, a difference decision diagram is also a DAG whose vertex set contains two terminals 0 and 1, and a set of non-terminal vertices, each with two children. A non-terminal vertex v corresponds to an integer- or real-valued difference constraint between two clocks. A path in a DDD is a finite sequence of edges, and it corresponds to a conjunction of difference constraints that is called a Difference Constraint System (DCS) in DDD. In contrast to BDDs, the same pair of clocks can appear more than once along a path in a DDD. A DCS corresponds to a DBM. DDDs contain DBMs as a special case. A path that ends with true or false is called a 1-path or 0-path respectively. A path p is feasible if and only if the corresponding DCS has a solution. If the Difference Constraint System has no solution, the path is infeasible. Unlike in BDDs, both 0- and 1-paths can be feasible or infeasible because the difference constraints can interact with each other along the path.

2.4   Encoding Probabilistic Timed Transitions

MTBDDs have been successfully applied for symbolic model checking of untimed probabilistic systems [1,12], and specifically Markov Decision Processes (MDPs) which arise as the representation of the PTAs. The method relies on encoding sets of states as BDDs and the (probabilistic) transition relation between these states using MTBDDs, which can be done compactly if there is sufficient regularity in the model. For finite untimed probabilistic systems the potential state space is known in advance of constructing the symbolic representation of the model, as it can be deduced from the syntactic model description. This fact is exploited when formulating heuristics that determine BDD variable ordering, a good choice of which is essential to guarantee a compact model representation. The difficulty with model checking of PTAs is that the size of the state space is unknown beforehand, and states (location-zone pairs) are generated dynamically through the process of exploration of the zone graph using timed predecessor or successor operations. The resulting symbolic representation has to be amenable to such dynamic manipulation of the state space which has the potential to destroy regularity. Although, if using the region graph, the size of the state space of a PTA can be established in advance of the model construction, such an approach is impractical due to the region graph being exponential in the number of clocks and the maximal constant appearing in the model.

In this section we propose an encoding method for probabilistic timed automata based on MTBDDs. Below we describe how to encode the *states* and *probabilistic edges*. In this paper we focus on application of our method to forward probabilistic reachability analysis. However, it is also suitable for backward analysis.

Firstly, let us consider how to encode the state space. Each state in the state space has the form of (l, ζ) where $l \in L$ is the discrete part and $\zeta \in Zones(\mathcal{X})$ is the zone. Our method is to use a Boolean vector to encode the discrete part of the pair and a separate Boolean vector for the zone part. The basic idea behind the Boolean encoding is that 2^n elements of a finite set could be encoded using n bits. For the discrete part, which is finite, the Boolean vector is further divided into several groups according the structure of the system, for example, the number of subcomponents and values of the non-clock variables following well-known heuristics established in [10,11].

The number of zones, unfortunately, could be infinite when forward analysis is used. The technique in [4] guarantees the termination of the forward reachability search, which means that a finite set of zones could be obtained. Since the set of zones is finite, informally, we use a one-to-one function to assign a unique index to each zone and similar logarithmic encoding is applied. The invariant and the guard appearing in the probabilistic transition are also zones, so a unique index value is assigned to each of them. In this paper we use a simple method for allocating indices; later, we discuss how this can be improved.

Next, let us consider the probabilistic transition relation. Each probabilistic edge has the form of the tuple $(n, l, inv(l), l', inv(l'), g, X, p)$, where n is (the encoding of) the non-deterministic choice, l and $inv(l)$ are the current location and its invariant, l' and $inv(l')$ are the next location and its invariant, g is the guard, X is the set of clocks to be reset and p is the probability value. The probability value is natively supported by MTBDDs. The number of non-deterministic choices in each state is finite and bounded. The maximum number of non-deterministic choices for all states is determined through parallel composition, and can therefore be encoded using the logarithmic encoding. It remains to encode the set X of clocks to be reset. There are a number of issues to consider when encoding the clock reset operation in the transition relation:

- Recall that each clock $x \in \mathcal{X}$ could be set to different values and not simply zero. If we encode each reset in the transition, this means we need two sets of Boolean BDD variables for it: one for the clock and the other for the value that the clock should be set to.
- The total number of clocks to be reset appearing in the transition could vary.

Thus, we opt for a simple approach: a Boolean vector is reserved in the transition for assigning a unique index value to each distinct set X and each set X is explicitly stored as a list.

Below we summarise the main issues that have to be addressed when applying our encoding method:

- Unlike in the case of non-probabilistic timed systems, in which the on-the-fly technique [5] could be applied to make search algorithms finish as early as possible, the forward probabilistic reachability search has to construct the whole reachable zone graph in order to obtain the probability value.
- The size of the state space and transitions between these states of the generated probabilistic system is uncertain before the forward/backward algorithm, which dynamically generates these states, terminates.

As a result, we cannot fix the size of the vector of Boolean variables needed to encode the zone part in advance. Instead, we pre-allocate the vector based on an estimate.

2.5   Implementation

Our proposed forward probabilistic reachability algorithm is given in Figure 1 in terms of MTBDD-based pseudo-code. Below we described the BDD and MTBDD operations needed for the algorithm. In the following, we assume M is an MTBDD, and $\underline{x}, \underline{y}, \underline{z}$ are the Boolean vectors which correspond to the MTBDD variables for row, column and non-deterministic choice in an MDP matrix.

- Operations $\times$ *and* $+$ are the MTBDD operations over the reals.
- Operations $\vee$, $\wedge$ *and* $\backslash$ are the BDD operations (and, or and difference) on sets.

- Function THRESHOLD(M, >, 0) returns the BDD by replacing each terminal node with 1 if and only if its value is greater than 0.
- Function THEREEXISTS($\underline{x}$, M) returns the MTBDD by deleting the nodes containing the Boolean vector $\underline{x}$.
- Function REPLACEVARS(M, $\underline{y}$, $\underline{x}$)) returns the MTBDD by replacing the Boolean vector $\underline{y}$ with $\underline{x}$.

The algorithm in Figure 1 is an MTBDD-based implementation of the algorithm of [14] with respect to our encoding. The algorithm $ModelCheckingPTA$ accepts three parameters: the probabilistic transition relation PS_{PTA}, which is an MTBDD-encoded representation of the syntax of the original probabilistic timed automaton, the initial set of states ϕ_{init} and the set of target states ϕ_{target}. Lines 1-4 deal with the initialisation: line 1 initialises the generated set of probabilistic transitions with the empty set, and lines 2-3 assign the initial set to both the front set and the reachable set. Lines 5-21 generate the finite-state graph, the edges of which are obtained in lines 8-11 by iterating timed and discrete successor operations. Each generated edge has the form of a tuple $(n, l, l', \zeta, \zeta', p)$, where n is the encoding of non-deterministic choice, (l, ζ) corresponds to current symbolic state, (l', ζ') is the next symbolic state in the generated transition, and p is the probability value. Line 6 constructs a temporary MTBDD with the information necessary for the timed and discrete successor operations by restricting to the front set: each path of the temporary MTBDD has the form of a tuple $(n, l, \zeta, inv(l), l', inv(l'), g, X, p)$, where l and l' are the current and next locations, $inv(l)$ and $inv(l')$ are the invariants associated with current and next location respectively, ζ is the current zone associated with current location, g is the guard, X is the set of clocks to be reset and p is the probability. Lines 12-19 extract the reachable states from the generated probabilistic transition set and check whether the fixed point is reached. Line 20 adds the set of newly generated edges to the old one. Finally, in line 22, model checking is performed on the resulting finite-state probabilistic system to obtain the maximum probability of reaching the set of target locations. Lines 9.1-9.3 give the MTBDD-based pseudo-code of the construction of a single probabilistic edge of the generated MDP. Line 9.1 obtains the next zone by using standard zone successor operation. Line 9.2 uses the technique in [4] to obtain the unique normal form of the next zone and adds it to the list of zones if it is a new one, and otherwise it returns the unique index to it in the list. Line 9.3 constructs and returns the probabilistic edge of the generated MDP.

Remark. For the forward reachability search, each zone obtained is convex, and can be stored as a single DBM. (A convex zone in DDDs can only have one path; this is also true for CRDs or CDDs.) The operation NORMALISE(ζ, k) (k-Normalization defined in [4]) to obtain the normal form of a zone ζ, where k is the maximal constant appearing in the model or the specification, is necessary to guarantee the termination of the forward reachability search. For DDDs, the zone can be first transformed into a DBM on which the k-Normalization can be applied, and then transformed back into a DDD. The case of CRDs and CDDs can be handled in a similar way.

$ModelCheckingPTA(\mathsf{PS}_{PTA}, \phi_{init}, \phi_{target})$
1. $\mathsf{PS}_{MDP} := \emptyset$
2. $\phi_{frontset} := \phi_{init}$
3. $\phi_{reach} := \phi_{init}$
4. $done := \mathbf{false}$
5. **while** $(done = \mathbf{false})$
6. $\mathsf{TmpPS} := \phi_{frontset} \times \mathsf{PS}_{PTA}$
7. $\mathsf{T} := \emptyset$
8.   **for each non-zero path** $of\,\mathsf{TmpPS}$
9.1. $\zeta' = ZoneSuccessor(l, inv(l), \zeta, l', inv(l'), g, X)$
9.2. $\zeta' = \textsc{AddZone}(\textsc{Normalise}(\zeta', k))$
9.3. $tr = n \times l \times \zeta \times l' \times \zeta' \times p$
10. $\mathsf{T} := \mathsf{T} + tr$
11.   **endfor**
12. $\mathsf{T}_{01} := \textsc{Threshold}(\mathsf{T}, >, 0)$
13. $\phi_{tmp} := \textsc{ThereExists}(\underline{z}, \mathsf{T}_{01})$
14. $\phi_{tmp} := \textsc{ThereExists}(\underline{x}, \phi_{tmp})$
15. $\phi_{tmp} := \textsc{ReplaceVars}(\phi_{tmp}, \underline{y}, \underline{x}))$
16. $\phi_{reach'} := \phi_{reach} \vee \phi_{tmp}$
17.   **if** $(\phi_{reach} = \phi'_{reach})$ **then** $done := \mathbf{true}$
18. $\phi_{frontset} := \phi_{reach'} \setminus \phi_{reach}$
19. $\phi_{reach} := \phi_{reach'}$
20. $\mathsf{PS}_{MDP} := \mathsf{PS}_{MDP} + \mathsf{T}$
21. **endwhile**
22. **return** $MaxProbReach(\phi_{init}, \phi_{reach}, \mathsf{PS}_{MDP})$

Fig. 1. The MTBDD version of the $ModelCheckingPTA$ algorithm

2.6 Backward Adaption

In this paper, we only present the application of our encoding method to forward analysis. However, it it also suitable for backward analysis. What is needed is a replacement of lines 9.1-9.3 with the corresponding backward step, and initialisation with the target set instead of the initial set.

3 Experimental Results

3.1 Tool Overview

Using the Colorado University Decision Diagrams (CUDD) package, a symbolic model checker has been implemented which supports forward probabilistic reachability model checking via the algorithm originally presented in [14]. This is the first symbolic implementation of the forward reachability algorithm.

Our tool takes as input a description of a system written in a probabilistic variant of the guarded commands language with real-time clocks (currently, the PRISM input language does not support real-time clocks). It first parses the PTA model from this description into an MTBDD, and then computes the set of probabilistically reachable states which comprise the model, which is an MDP over location-zone pairs [14]. The tool then performs model checking over this MDP in the standard way, and calculates the probability of reaching the target set to determine whether the specification is satisfied. In this tool, the model construction and reachability analysis are implemented using MTBDDs to represent both the discrete part of the state and the placeholder, reserved in the Boolean vector of the BDD variables, that represents the zone. The tool supports two kinds of representation of timing information: DBMs and DDDs.

The transition relation of the PTA model is encoded within MTBDDs. Unlike untimed probabilistic model checking, the MDP model is dynamically constructed via forward searching which involves timing operations, for example, the timed successor. The generated MDP differs from the original PTA in that it represents the dynamic behaviour of the PTA, which is computed via forward exploration and dynamically filled using the placeholders reserved in the BDD vector. Although the tool currently supports only forward analysis and two kinds of representation for timing information, our encoding method is general: firstly, other data structures for representing timing information could be integrated; secondly, backward reachability analysis is also suitable for this encoding.

3.2   Case Studies

We present experimental results based on three case studies: the IEEE 1394 FireWire root contention protocol, the IEEE 802.3 CSMA/CD (Carrier Sense, Multiple Access with Collision Detection) protocol and Milner's scheduler. The models for FireWire and CSMA/CD are the same as those used in [16]. The model for Milner's scheduler is that used in [17] with only one clock.

In the tables, "-" denotes that the data is not available. We omit the probability values since they all agree with those calculated previously by other methods.

The results obtained from verifying the abstract and the full models of Firewire root contention protocol [15] are shown in Table 1 and Table 2.

Table 1. Verification of the abstract model I_1^p with wire delay set to 360 ns

Deadline	States	Time(Explicit)			Time(Symbolic)			
					MTBDD/DDD		MTBDD/DBM	
		Forward	Construct.	M.C.	S.F.C.	M.C.	S.F.C.	M.C.
2000	64	0.26	0.14	0.01	0.06	0.01	0.07	0.01
2500	88	0.30	0.20	0.02	0.07	0.01	0.09	0.01
3000	88	0.28	0.20	0.02	0.08	0.01	0.09	0.01
3500	124	0.38	0.34	0.02	0.18	0.01	0.11	0.01
4000	162	0.41	0.61	0.02	0.20	0.01	0.13	0.01
4500	159	0.43	0.59	0.02	0.26	0.01	0.13	0.01
5000	208	0.51	0.96	0.026	0.29	0.01	0.16	0.01
5500	244	0.56	1.42	0.03	0.38	0.02	0.19	0.02
6000	253	0.58	1.42	0.03	0.42	0.02	0.19	0.02
7000	348	0.70	3.07	0.04	0.83	0.02	0.28	0.02
8000	438	0.80	4.67	0.05	0.98	0.03	0.35	0.03
9000	506	0.91	6.29	0.05	1.32	0.03	0.40	0.03
10000	609	1.12	10.34	0.06	1.85	0.04	0.56	0.04
20000	2124	3.20	117.37	0.13	17.77	0.19	0.56	0.04
30000	4546	10.87	615.42	0.30	76.80	0.39	2.29	0.18
40000	7851	27.20	1846.90	1.55	225.35	0.65	7.43	0.39
50000	12094	58.37	5017.27	2.77	534.15	1.00	18.54	0.65
60000	17231	103.09	-	-	1082.36	1.63	36.72	1.00
70000	23305	170.43	-	-	2492.07	2.42	66.43	1.65
80000	30251	273.99	-	-	4217.03	3.09	182.13	3.08
90000	38151	427.81	-	-	6753.72	3.95	276.52	3.97

Table 2. Verification of the full model $Impl^p$ with wire delay set to 360 ns

| Deadline | States | Time(Explicit) | | | Time(Symbolic) | | | |
| | | | | | MTBDD/DDD | | MTBDD/DBM | |
		Forward	Construct.	M.C.	S.F.C.	M.C.	S.F.C.	M.C.
2000	951	6.42	9.26	0.04	25.87	0.05	7.44	0.05
2500	1415	9.89	32.47	0.09	56.66	0.10	11.71	0.10
3000	1425	9.99	32.45	0.09	57.13	0.12	11.79	0.11
3500	2092	14.79	87.48	0.14	122.52	0.19	17.59	0.20
4000	2803	19.94	186.22	0.18	219.03	0.23	24.03	0.23
4500	2799	20.53	196.01	0.21	217.41	0.24	24.84	0.24
5000	3725	27.50	375.07	0.25	385.72	0.27	34.49	0.27
5500	4432	33.02	543.03	0.33	542.73	0.39	41.79	0.39
6000	4675	35.29	697.63	0.37	609.45	0.49	44.81	0.51
7000	6545	51.25	1403.52	0.52	1180.10	0.61	66.24	0.60
8000	8437	67.95	2523.33	0.71	1966.27	0.85	90.17	0.84
9000	9879	82.23	3925.66	0.86	2694.23	0.86	110.52	0.87
10000	11988	143.79	-	-	4662.95	1.47	135.65	1.39
20000	44335	543.16	-	-	-	-	947.65	5.37
30000	96592	1693.48	-	-	-	-	3607.68	12.42
40000	168514	4135.01	-	-	-	-	10112.92	22.84
50000	261131	-	-	-	-	-	23297.78	35.03
60000	373429	-	-	-	-	-	45553.48	54.89
70000	-	-	-	-	-	-	-	-
80000	-	-	-	-	-	-	-	-
90000	-	-	-	-	-	-	-	-

Table 3. Verification of the full CSMA/CD model (max, backoff=1)

| Deadline | States | Time(Explicit) | | | Time(Symbolic) | | | |
| | | | | | MTBDD/DDD | | MTBDD/DBM | |
		Forward	Construct.	M.C.	S.F.C.	M.C.	S.F.C.	M.C.
1000	6404	26.89	-	-	47.17	0.00	34.84	0.00
1200	9034	43.94	-	-	945.28	0.00	56.55	0.00
1400	11771	66.47	-	-	1611.72	0.01	82.79	0.01
1600	15329	100.45	-	-	2752.01	0.00	125.33	0.01
1800	19453	148.20	11021.07	0.79	4452.55	1.22	183.39	1.22
2000	23468	204.11	-	-	6517.29	2.76	255.06	2.66
2200	28516	281.92	-	-	9667.14	5.60	351.47	5.48
2400	34023	381.79	-	-	-	-	476.85	9.59
2600	39970	503.00	-	-	-	-	631.94	14.45
2800	45654	628.90	-	-	-	-	804.11	20.52
3000	52561	811.40	-	-	-	-	1028.94	27.25

The property verified is the minimum probability that, from the initial state, a leader (root) is chosen before the deadline is reached. Table 5 and Table 6 show the memory consumption. Table 3 and Table 4 include results for the CSMA/CD protocol when computing the maximum and minimum probability of both stations correctly delivering their packets by the deadline D. Table 7 and Table 8 show the memory consumption. Table 9 shows the result of verifying Milner's scheduler when computing the maximum probability of any two cyclers being in the critical section at the same time.

To evaluate our encoding method, we also implemented an explicit version of the data structure which stores explicitly the discrete part of the symbolic states.

Performance. In tables [1- 4], the term "Explicit" refers to the explicit version and "MTBDD/DDD" refers to the version which uses MTBDDs for encoding the discrete part and DDDs for timing information; "MTBDD/DBM" refers to the version which differs from the "MTBDD/DDD" by using DBMs instead of DDDs. However, in order to model check certain properties, the explicit version involves two steps: first, it generates the reachable states, and next it represents those as a model in the PRISM input language, which is then passed to PRISM to finish the verification process. On the other hand, in the "MTBDD/DDD" and

Table 4. Verification of the full CSMA/CD model (min, backoff=1)

Deadline	States	Time(Explicit)			Time(Symbolic)			
					MTBDD/DDD		MTBDD/DBM	
		Forward	Construct.	M.C.	S.F.C.	M.C.	S.F.C.	M.C.
1000	6408	26.86	934.96	0.26	471.32	0.32	34.53	0.32
1200	9038	44.14	2103.15	0.33	944.00	0.42	56.82	0.41
1400	11775	66.08	3567.70	0.41	1609.68	0.51	83.00	0.49
1600	15333	100.83	6106.86	0.51	2746.67	0.60	124.82	0.59
1800	19453	147.69	-	-	-	-	182.64	1.94
2000	23468	202.60	-	-	-	-	253.95	2.55
2200	28516	280.17	-	-	-	-	349.63	3.32
2400	34023	382.47	-	-	-	-	474.25	4.08
2600	39970	503.26	-	-	-	-	631.54	5.19
2800	45654	632.84	-	-	-	-	799.57	6.42
3000	52561	814.99	-	-	-	-	1027.52	7.68

Table 5. Memory consumption of the abstract model I_1^p with wire delay set to 360 ns

Deadline	Nodes (Explicit)	Nodes (Discrete)	Mem. (Zone)		
			DDD		DBM
			Peak	Estimated	
2000	218	255	49.52	5.47	1.27
2500	289	324	77.66	6.89	1.55
3000	289	325	91.38	7.85	1.69
3500	364	364	136.94	9.49	2.07
4000	481	503	220.61	12.47	2.64
4500	474	486	253.15	13.51	2.81
5000	580	552	356.84	16.02	3.34
5500	680	625	476.98	18.76	3.90
6000	701	656	555.90	20.40	4.22
7000	905	833	942.16	26.91	5.48
8000	1087	986	1365.55	32.54	6.61
9000	1219	1075	1951.06	39.29	7.88
10000	1401	1290	2759.18	46.87	9.42
20000	3143	2893	30232.26	157.91	31.18
30000	5171	4823	136341.71	336.74	66.27
40000	6892	7003	402995.33	579.55	113.98
50000	8980	8897	225775.35	890.07	174.97
60000	10792	11085	497021.90	1268.42	249.26
70000	12938	13557	666931.81	1712.98	336.59
80000	14810	18637	229405.34	2222.45	436.61
90000	-	18679	397636.89	2799.86	550.05

"MTBDD/DBM" versions, as they have already been partly integrated with PRISM, the overall checking process does not go through the PRISM input language: the tool constructs the target MDP models in MTBDDs and directly calls functions provided by PRISM.

Here we only consider the algorithm performance and the number of states obtained from the experiments. The leftmost column of these tables gives the different deadlines. The second column shows the number of symbolic states generated via the forward construction. The column "S.F.C." refers to the symbolic forward and construction. The column "M.C." refers to the computation time for model checking the given properties against the MDP model encoded as an MTBDD. The unit for all columns "Time" is seconds. Notice that there are three columns under the "Explicit" version: the first column represents the time taken to generate the reachable states and translate the model to the PRISM input language, while the second refers to model construction time by PRISM via explicit encoding.

The times for model checking are nearly same for the three versions. We comment on the time spent on constructing MDP models encoded as MTBDDs via forward analysis. Compared to the explicit implementation, the symbolic encoding version based on DBMs has a significant advantage: the time spent on

Table 6. Memory consumption of the full model $Impl^p$ with wire delay set to 360 ns

Deadline	Nodes (Explicit)	Nodes (discrete)	Mem. (Zone) DDD Peak	Mem. (Zone) DDD Estimated	Mem. (Zone) DBM
2000	1719	2489	46343.66	324.46	143.75
2500	2556	3616	93414.54	492.84	207.75
3000	2585	3718	94993.58	502.61	210.25
3500	3384	4927	184895.18	728.27	299.50
4000	4610	5834	318451.16	977.65	398.75
4500	4476	5735	322968.19	991.48	397.75
5000	5291	6695	546041.32	1311.11	525.25
5500	6003	8181	800000$^+$	1559.77	623.50
6000	6404	8220	800000$^+$	1653.37	657.75
7000	8449	10377	800000$^+$	2317.22	916.25
8000	9818	11865	800000$^+$	2983.175	1179.25
9000	11856	13735	800000$^+$	3519.195	1381.75
10000	-	15484	-	-	1673.50
20000	-	35157	-	-	6201.75
30000	-	56374	-	-	13534.50
40000	-	76978	-	-	23638.00
50000	-	99116	-	-	36661.75
60000	-	123220	-	-	52459.25
70000	-	-	-	-	-
80000	-	-	-	-	-
90000	-	-	-	-	-

Table 7. Memory consumption of the full model CSMA (max, backoff=1)

Deadline	Nodes (Explicit)	Nodes (discrete)	Mem. (Zone) DDD Peak	Mem. (Zone) DDD Estimated	Mem. (Zone) DBM
1000	-	10752	577832.75	1099.57	399.71
1200	-	13434	800000$^+$	1558.76	564.45
1400	-	15968	800000$^+$	2039.87	737.11
1600	-	19426	800000$^+$	2667.49	962.01
1800	16697	22903	800000$^+$	3397.76	1223.73
2000	19276	25962	800000$^+$	4108.15	1478.71
2200	22260	30181	800000$^+$	5005.77	1800.20
2400	-	33949	-	-	2151.37
2600	-	38187	-	-	2530.37
2800	-	41611	-	-	2894.82
3000	-	45527	-	-	3337.11

generating the MDP models is no longer a problem, since it took 110 seconds to perform both the forward construction and to generate the MDP in MTBDDs for the full model $Impl^p$ with deadline 9000 ns, whilst it took 3925 seconds to generate the MDP model alone with the same deadline with the explicit version.

For the abstract model, the DDD-based version performs as well as the DBM-based one. However, for the full model $Impl^p$, it is slower due to a large number of intermediate DDD nodes being generated, which forces the DDD run-time library to invoke garbage collection. The main reason is that DDDs have no canonical property.

Memory. With regard to memory usage, we need to consider two kinds of usage for each symbolic state: the memory for the discrete part and the zone part. In tables [5- 8], the unit for all columns under "Mem." is in kilo-Bytes and the unit for all columns under "Nodes" is the number of the nodes in the MTBDD where each node occupies 20 bytes.

Compared with the explicit version, both symbolic versions use more nodes. However, the chief contributor to the growth in the size of our symbolic data structures seems to be the fact that we do not exploit regularity in the zone

Table 8. Memory consumption of the full model CSMA (min, backoff=1)

Deadline	Nodes (Explicit)	Nodes (discrete)	Mem. (Zone)		
			DDD		DBM
			Peak	Estimated	
1000	7466	10868	578877.20	1100.67	400.10
1200	9753	13492	800000+	1559.85	564.84
1400	11383	16036	800000+	2040.96	737.50
1600	14227	19638	800000+	2668.59	962.40
1800	16714	23130	800000+	3397.76	1223.73
2000	19694	26331	-	-	1478.71
2200	-	30381	-	-	1800.20
2400	-	34271	-	-	2151.37
2600	-	38092	-	-	2530.37
2800	-	41681	-	-	2894.82
3000	-	45374	-	-	3337.11

representation because this first implementation allocates unique indices to zones in an arbitrary order which are then stored in the placeholders. The results of [9] show that such regularity exists and we have adapted this method and obtained preliminary results which will appear in the first author's coming thesis.

We note that the symbolic versions are performing the generation of the state space dynamically at the same time as calculating the encoding, while the explicit version does not start to encode the MTBDD until the whole state space is generated. We compare the memory usage on the zone part because those for the discrete part are the same for both symbolic versions. The memory consumption for DBMs is that actually used. For DDDs, we cannot give the actual memory consumption, and instead give both the estimated and peak time memory consumption. The column "Estimated" refers to an estimation of the memory consumption of all zones based on DDDs when reaching the fixed point. The column "Peak" refers to the highest value of memory consumption by DDDs when reaching the fixed point. The DBM-based representation uses less memory than the DDD-based representation. In practice, as shown in Table 6, the estimation of memory consumption for zones in DDDs is around 3-5 times as many as those in DBMs. However, compared with those by DBMs, the peak memory consumption of DDDs is huge, since DDDs use 1000 times more memory than DBMs for the full model $Impl^p$ with deadline 5000 ns. 800000^+ means garbage collection occurred (DDD run-time library configuration with 800M). We note, however, that since non-convex zones arise in backward exploration it is difficult to predict how the representations will behave in the latter case.

Scalability. In Table 9, the column "Prod. const." is the time spent on parallel composition to build the product model and the column "Encoding" the time on encoding the product model into MTBDDs. In the case study of Milner's

Table 9. Verification of the Milner's scheduler with only one clock

N	Symbolic/Time				Prob.
	Nodes (Discrete)	Prod. const.	Encoding	S.F.C	
4	1890	0.21	0.11	0.27	0.00
5	2981	0.35	0.30	0.63	0.00
6	4345	0.93	0.79	1.76	0.00
7	5989	3.50	2.42	5.22	0.00
8	7925	19.02	7.16	15.02	0.00
9	26276	113.56	19.18	40.14	0.00
10	143762	591.91	50.41	103.50	0.00
11	-	-	-	-	-

scheduler, which shows the scalability of our method and generates only five zones in total after the application of the forward algorithm, the result is not as good as those obtained with DDDs [17]. This is partly because the experimental nature of our implementation not only involves zone search but probability computation as well, and partly because the parallel composition of components is constructed explicitly and does not utilise the Kronecker approach [10] implemented in PRISM which is based on good heuristics for BDD variable ordering that can yield compact MTBDDs.

4   Conclusion

We have proposed an MTBDD-based placeholder encoding method for model checking of probabilistic timed automata and implemented an experimental tool using the CUDD package. The timing information is represented as either DBMs or DDDs. Our method allows one to use other data structures, for example, CRDs [20] or CDDs [2], for representing the timing information.

Future work will address the efficiency of the symbolic implementation presented in this paper, and in particular exploiting regularity in the zone graph, implementing Kronecker-based parallel composition of probabilistic timed automata, and augmenting PRISM with real-time clocks.

Acknowledgements. We would like to thank the authors of the DDD library for letting us use their DDD implementation. We would also like to thank Gethin Norman and David Parker for helpful discussion.

References

1. PRISM WebSite. http://www.cs.bham.ac.uk/~dxp/prism/.
2. G. Behrmann, K. G. Larsen, J. Pearson, C. Weise, and W. Yi. Efficient timed reachability analysis using clock difference diagrams. In *Proc. CAV '99*, pages 341–353, London, UK, 1999. Springer-Verlag.
3. J. Bengtsson, W. Griffioen, K. Kristoffersen, K. Larsen, F. Larsson, P. Pettersson, and W. Yi. Automated verification of an audio-control protocol using UPPAAL. *Journal of Logic and Algebraic Programming*, 52(3):163–181, 2002.
4. J. Bengtsson and W. Yi. Timed automata: Semantics, algorithms and tools. In *4th Advanced Course on Petri Nets*, volume 3098 of *LNCS*, pages 87–124. Springer, 2004.
5. A. Bouajjani, S. Tripakis, and S. Yovine. On-the-fly symbolic model checking for real-time systems. In *Proc. 18TH IEEE Real-Time Systems Symposium*, pages 25–34, Los Alamitos, 1997. IEEE CS Press.
6. M. Bozga, C. Daws, O. Maler, A. Olivero, S. Tripakis, and S. Yovine. Kronos: A model-checking tool for real-time systems. In *Proc. CAV '98*, pages 546–550, London, UK, 1998. Springer-Verlag.
7. R. E. Bryant. Graph-based algorithms for Boolean function manipulation. *IEEE Trans. Comput.*, C-35(8):677–691, Aug. 1986.

8. E. Clarke, M. Fujita, P. McGeer, K. McMillan, J. Yang, and X. Zhao. Multi-terminal binary decision diagrams: An efficient data structure for matrix representation. In *Proc. IWLS'93*, pages 1–15, 1993. Also available in *Formal Methods in System Design*, 10(2/3):149–169, 1997.
9. C. Daws, M. Kwiatkowska, and G. Norman. Automatic verification of the IEEE 1394 root contention protocol with KRONOS and PRISM. In *Proc. 7th FMICS'02*, volume 66.2 of *Electronic Notes in Theoretical Computer Science*. Elsevier, 2002.
10. L. de Alfaro, M. Kwiatkowska, G. Norman, D. Parker, and R. Segala. Symbolic model checking of concurrent probabilistic processes using MTBDDs and the Kronecker representation. In *Proc. 6th TACAS'00*, volume 1785 of *LNCS*, pages 395–410. Springer, 2000.
11. H. Hermanns, M. Kwiatkowska, G. Norman, D. Parker, and M. Siegle. On the use of MTBDDs for performability analysis and verification of stochastic systems. *Journal of Logic and Algebraic Programming*, 56(1-2):23–67, 2003.
12. M. Kwiatkowska, G. Norman, and D. Parker. Probabilistic symbolic model checking with PRISM: A hybrid approach. In *Proc. 8th TACAS'02*, volume 2280 of *LNCS*, pages 52–66. Springer, 2002.
13. M. Kwiatkowska, G. Norman, D. Parker, and J. Sproston. Performance analysis of probabilistic timed automata using digital clocks. In *Proc. FORMATS'03*, volume 2791 of *LNCS*, pages 105–120. Springer-Verlag, 2003.
14. M. Kwiatkowska, G. Norman, R. Segala, and J. Sproston. Automatic verification of real-time systems with discrete probability distributions. *Theoretical Computer Science*, 282:101–150, 2002.
15. M. Kwiatkowska, G. Norman, and J. Sproston. Probabilistic model checking of deadline properties in the IEEE 1394 FireWire root contention protocol. *Special Issue of Formal Aspects of Computing*, 14:295–318, 2003.
16. M. Kwiatkowska, G. Norman, J. Sproston, and F. Wang. Symbolic model checking for probabilistic timed automata. In *Joint Conference on FORMATS and FTRTFT*, volume 3253 of *LNCS*, pages 293–308. Springer, 2004.
17. J. Møller, J. Lichtenberg, H. R. Andersen, and H. Hulgaard. Fully symbolic model checking of timed systems using difference decision diagrams. In *Workshop on Symbolic Model Checking*, volume 23, The IT University of Copenhagen, Denmark, June 1999.
18. S. A. Seshia and R. E. Bryant. A boolean approach to unbounded, fully symbolic model checking of timed automata. Technical Report CMU-CS-03-117, Carnegie Mellon University, 2003.
19. F. Somenzi. CUDD: CU Decision Diagram Package Release, 1998.
20. F. Wang. Efficient verification of timed automata with BDD-like data-structures. In *Verification, model checking, and abstract interpretation*, volume 2575 of *LNCS*, pages 189–205. Springer, 2003.

An EFSM-Based Intrusion Detection System for Ad Hoc Networks

Jean-Marie Orset, Baptiste Alcalde, and Ana Cavalli

Institut National des Télécommunications, GET-INT, Evry, France
{jean-marie.orset, baptiste.alcalde, ana.cavalli}@int-evry.fr

Abstract. Mobile ad hoc networks offer very interesting perspectives in wireless communications due to their easy deployment and their growing performances. However, due to their inherent characteristics of open medium, very dynamic topology, lack of infrastructure and lack of centralized management authority, MANET present serious vulnerabilities to security attacks. In this paper, we propose an intrusion detection scheme based on extended finite state machines (EFSM). We provide a formal specification of the correct behavior of the routing protocol and by the means of a backward checking algorithm, detect run-time violations of the implementation. We choose the standard proactive routing protocol OLSR as a case study and show that our approach allows to detect several kinds of attacks as well as conformance anomalies.

1 Introduction

In the recent years, one could assist to a spectacular growth in the use of wireless equipments. The number of mobile devices such as PDAs, mobile phones, laptops, is also tremendously increasing. To ensure the connectivity between all these devices, ad hoc networks appear to be a promising solution. An ad hoc network is a collection of wireless mobile nodes which communicate together without the assistance of any fixed nor central infrastructure. Thus, participants must cooperate by acting as routers and forward messages to other nodes that are not within the same radio range. MANET can be used in scenarios where no infrastructure exists, or where the existing infrastructure does not meet application requirements for different reasons such as security, cost or quality. They also open new fields of applications in the domain of networking like battlefield operations, sensor networks, emergency rescues or roaming networking.

Beside their enticing capabilities, ad hoc networks suffer from a great weakness: due to their characteristics, they are much more vulnerable than wired networks. Indeed, they rely on a open medium and have a very dynamically changing topology. They trust others participants, can not rely on a fixed infrastructure to monitor the activity, to distribute keys or to manage security policies. As a result, MANET are vulnerable to many kinds of attacks like passive eavesdropping, usurpation, routing disruption or denials of service (DoS). Recently, many schemes have been proposed to secure the routing process in MANET. Most of them are preventive: they rely on cryptographic mechanisms

D.A. Peled and Y.-K. Tsay (Eds.): ATVA 2005, LNCS 3707, pp. 400–413, 2005.

for example, to authenticate participants within the network. Although they present interesting potentials, they are often inspired by the techniques used in traditional networks and are also not always well adapted to MANET (problem to exchange keys, high resource consumption, etc...). Furthermore, they only deal with *limited aspects of the protocols*. Thus, they do not allow to cope with all threats (e.g. corrupted node revealing the key, wrong messages flooding, non participation, etc...). Cryptographic mechanisms may help to identify the originators of an attack but if the attack is not detected, they remain useless. That is why one not only needs to prevent attacks but also to detect the incorrect behaviors in real time, in order to offer the network the opportunity to react efficiently. This is the role of an intrusion detection system (IDS).

Many intrusion detection schemes have been proposed in wired networks. However, the totally distributed context of MANET obliges to work out new approaches. In addition, experience shows that protocols are often subjects to design flaws which could further be exploited by an attacker to compromise the network. The contribution we bring in this paper is the definition and application of a specification-based approach (EFSM) to detect as well the anomalies in the implementation of the protocol as attacks against the routing operation. We chose the proactive ad hoc routing protocol OLSR as a case study. We thus manually abstract a correct behavior of an OLSR node according to the RFC [4]. Then, an algorithm analyzes all the messages exchanged locally by the nodes and test the conformance to the specification in real time. By the following, attacks are assimilated to violations of the specification. We illustrate that our approach allows to detect several kinds of attacks, without requiring to maintain an heavy scenario base on each nodes.

The remainder of the paper is organized as follows: section 2 describes related works on security and intrusion detection in ad hoc networks. section 3 presents the OLSR protocol as well as an overview of different attacks against ad hoc routing protocols. section 4 detailed our specification based approach and the passive testing algorithm used to perform the validation. Examples of application are described in section 3. Finally, we present the future work and conclude the paper in section 6.

2 Related Work

2.1 Cryptographic Schemes

In the recent years, most of the propositions to secure the routing process in MANET make use of cryptographic mechanisms. In [5] for example, the authors proposed the use of asymmetric cryptography to secure on-demand ad hoc network routing protocols. However, nodes in an ad hoc network may not have sufficient resources to verify asymmetric signatures. Thus, an attacker can trivially flood a victim with packets containing invalid signatures. Although those packets will be discarded, the verification will be prohibitively expensive for the victim.

As for the OLSR protocol, the main contribution comes from [1]. The authors proposed to rely on asymmetric cryptography to authenticate the originators of messages but also on timestamp to verify their freshness and counter replay attacks. In addition to the preceding drawbacks, there remains the problem of key certification. Since there is no fixed infrastructure in MANET, nodes can not rely on any certification authority to validate or revoke certificates.

The problem of these approaches is that even if the schemes are efficient and correctly implemented, they do not allow to cope with compromised nodes, nor authenticated nodes which deflect the normal operation of the routing process. Moreover, the secure protocol may itself contains flaws which could be further exploited by an attacker.

That is why many people propose to use intrusion detection schemes, as a complementary protection, to detect all malicious behaviors.

2.2   IDS in Ad Hoc Networks

One of the first worth proposals to develop IDS capabilities for MANET was described in [8]. This paper presented a set of rules that identify several well known attacks on MANET. Then, they developed a cluster-based detection approach in which a node is chosen to perform detection functions for all nodes within a cluster. Although interesting, the cluster based concept induces some security problems which need to be addressed.

One of the main drawback of all statistical based IDS is the high rate of false alarms. To circumvent that problem, others people choose to rely on specification based approaches to reduce the error margin in the detection of attacks.

2.3   Specification Based IDS

Some researchers [7] proposed recently a solution based on an FSM-based specification to detect vulnerabilities in the AODV protocol. They used an FSM to specify an AODV correct behavior and distributed networks monitor to detect run-time violations on the specification. In addition to the fact that FSMs constitute a too limited tool to manage the complexity of an ad hoc routing protocol, some of the assumptions are too strong so that security aspects of the architecture are not clearly addressed. Finally, in [3], the authors propose to extend the preceding solution on several aspects. Firstly, they rely on EFSA to specify the behavior of the AODV protocol. Then, they propose to use specification-based and statistical approaches complementarily, in order to detect attacks that do not directly violate the specification.

3   Attacks in Ad Hoc Networks

3.1   The Optimized Link State Routing Protocol

The OLSR protocol is a link-state proactive protocol, based on the Open Shortest Path First (OSPF) protocol and designed specifically for mobile ad-hoc networks. OLSR manages to diffuse routing information through an efficient flooding technique. The key innovation of this protocol is the concept of Multi Point Relays

(MPRs). A node's multipoint relay is a subset of its neighbors whose combined radio range covers all nodes two hops away. In order for a node to determine its minimum multipoint relay set based on its two-hop topology, periodic broadcasts are required. Similar to conventional link-state protocols the link information updates are propagated throughout the network. However in OLSR, when a node has to forward a link update it only forwards it to its MPR set of nodes. Finally, the distribution of topological information is realized with the use of periodic topology control messages and as a result, each node knowing a partial graph of the topology of the network that is further used to calculate the optimal routes. OLSR is mostly preferred when the ad hoc network consists of a large number of nodes and has a high density. One of the main advantages of the OLSR protocol is that it does not make any assumption concerning the underlying link layer, allowing it to be used in a variety of configurations.

3.2 Vulnerabilities

Currently, OLSR does not specify any special security measures. As a proactive routing protocol, OLSR makes a target for various attacks. In OLSR, each node is injecting topological information into the network through the transmission of *HELLO* messages and, for some nodes, *TC* messages. If some nodes (malicious or malfunctioning) inject invalid control traffic, network integrity may be compromised. Here are examples of situations that may occur due to lack of data integrity functionality.

Identity usurpation. By sending false *HELLO* messages, a node may pretend to be another node. Then, the target node identifies the originator address as from one of its neighbor. This may result in creating conflicting routes to the node with the corresponding address, errors in the routing tables, link loss, etc...

Insertion of false control messages. A node broadcasts a wrong *HELLO* message claiming symmetrical links to non-neighbor nodes or to non-present nodes. As a consequence, the node may be selected as an MPR and the traffic between other nodes will be routed by itself. It can then discards all the traffic or just the control messages (*Hello*, *TC*) to disturb the routing operation.

Alteration of control messages. A node may listen to the *TC* messages from neighbors, add non existing nodes with symmetrical connectivity and replay the packet by spoofing the originator. Then, the target node is designed as an MPR whereas it is unable to reach the nodes. In the same manner, a node may also include non-existing links (i.e. links to non-neighbor nodes) in a *TC* message. That may yield routing loops and conflicting routes in the network.

Another alteration attack which has a great impact consists for an attacker, to forward a TC message with a sequence number increased from x to $x + i$. By the following, the receiver will stop to analyze and forwards packets from the originator with sequence number lower than $x + i$.

As we can see, OLSR present several serious vulnerabilities which could lead to paralyze the communications within the network. All the cited attacks hijack the normal operation of the protocol and can not always be prevented by classic authentication schemes. Indeed, such schemes only allow to verify the origin of messages but not their relevance. By formally specifying the normal operation of OLSR, we are able to detect many anomalies and intrusions on the protocol since each one will be detected in real-time, as a violation of the specification. Moreover, it is very difficult in MANET to establish a clear difference between a malicious behavior and normal operations in some circumstances (battery sparing, presence of obstacles, very dynamic topology, etc...). By using a formal specification, we allow to decrease consequently the margin of error in the detection of attackers.

4   Description of the IDS

4.1   Motivation and Assumptions

Intrusion detection techniques used in traditional (wired) networks can not be applied directly to ad hoc networks. In wired architectures, the monitoring is generally realized on routers or hubs. In ad hoc networks, there is no infrastructure nor single management entity, making it difficult to perform any kind of centralized management or control. Hence, the intrusion detection has to be distributed to all nodes within the network. We also achieve the distribution of the intrusion detection mechanism by implementing a Local Intrusion Detection System (LIDS) on each node. A potential drawback of this approach could reside in the difficulty to correlate the traces of the different nodes. Indeed, if one states that every node is an omnipotent observer that can see and monitor all the traffic inside the network, one has to rely on strong assumptions such as a global synchronization of nodes (to order the different traces) and a strong authentication mechanism to ensure the integrity of the traces exchanged by the different nodes. However in our approach, such complex mechanisms are not required since one only needs to analyse the informations exchanged between nodes of the same neighborhood. Indeed, the use of MPR relays in OLSR allows to divide the network in different subsets. Thus, each node only needs to know the messages locally, inside the MPR sets.

Considering the specification, our algorithm allows to detect errors in an exhaustive manner. Thus, we are able to detect violations which correspond to conformance errors as well as violations which directly result from a security attack. To characterize more precisely the real nature of the detected violation (attack or error in the implementation itself) one may use a complementary intrusion detection scheme based on attack signatures. Accordingly, each time an anomaly is raised, an algorithm is applied to check if this corresponds to the pattern of any well-known attack. In that case, our approach is similar to misuse detection schemes since it allows to efficiently detect instances of known attacks. On the other hand, if the anomaly does not corresponds to any attack pattern, it may either imply that one identified a new attack, either that one raised an error in the implementation itself, what anyhow characterizes a potential flaw in the routing protocol. Afterward, this analysis has to be performed by an expert of this domain or by a dedicated algorithm. This is out of the scope of this paper.

What is important to keep in mind is that our approach allows to detect truly innovative errors, compared to signature based schemes which are only able to detect well known attacks. Another significant advantage is that there is no false positive since one only considers the normal behavior described in the specification. Thus, whatever the anomaly the algorithm raised, one can always be sure it corresponds to a potential flaw.

4.2 Extended Finite State Machine

We chose to rely on the EFSM formalism because it suits very well to the analysis of flows and allows to put constraints on the variables of the transitions.

Definition 1. *An Extended Finite State Machine M is a 6-tuple $M = < S, s_0, I, O, \vec{x}, T >$ where S is a finite set of states, s_0 is the initial state, I is a finite set of input symbols (eventually with parameters), O is a finite set of output symbols (eventually with parameters), $\vec{x}$ is a vector denoting a finite set of variables, and T is a finite set of transitions. A transition t is a 6-tuple $t = < s_i, s_f, i, o, P, A >$ where s_i and s_f are the initial and final state of the transition, i and o are the input and the output, P is the predicate (a boolean expression), and A is the ordered set (sequence) of actions.*

We manually derived the EFSM directly from the IETF specification [4]. The verification process consists to map the traces of I/O events (messages received and sent) recorded on each node, with the specification. To compare the traces with the EFSM, we chose an approach based on backward tracking [2].

Another consequent advantage brought by the backward testing approach is that it allows to consider that the traces can start at any moment of the implementation execution, not only the initial state.

Given a trace from the implementation, our algorithm will detect three types of errors:

- **the output errors:** when the output of a transition in the implementation differs from the output of the corresponding transition in the specification.
- **the transfer errors:** when the ending state of a transition in the implementation differs from the ending state of the corresponding transition in the specification.
- **the mixed errors:** a mix between the two errors defined above.

4.3 Overview of the Backward Checking Approach

The Backward Checking algorithm is an approach of passive testing on EFSMs derived from the testing by determination of variables intervals. We consider that we have a system under test on which we place an observation point. We suppose that this observation point records the event traces respecting their causal order. We assume that finding the order of these events is a well studied and resolved problem.

The Backward Checking algorithm (cf. [2]) is composed of two main phases. First, it follows a given event trace backward to find the possible initial configurations at the beginning of the trace.

Secondly, it starts from these configurations and explore backward, every possible path of the specification with help of pruning operation and a transition choice strategy, to reduce as much as possible the search.

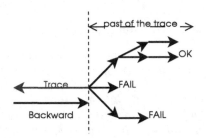

Fig. 1. Overview of Backward Checking

In the trace. During the first phase, if an inconsistency is detected it means that the event trace is not correct and that an error has been detected. If at the end of the event trace analysis no inconsistency has been found, it means the studied trace is possible with the obtained initial configuration. Then, the second phase is launched, i.e. the exploration of the past of this trace.

In the past of the trace. In the second phase, we try to confirm the intervals in which the variables are defined according to the initial configurations. The algorithm finishes with a positive answer (trace is valid) at the first confirmed configuration, i.e. the first configuration in which every determinant variables has been confirmed, or with a negative answer (invalid trace) if every branch of the exploration tree leads to an inconsistency. One can say that this algorithm is optimal in the way that it will be fast to say that there is no error, but slower to say that there is one. This fact is coherent with reality because we suppose that an error in an event trace is an exceptional behavior.

The different branches of the exploration tree are the possible successions of transitions, taken in a backward manner from the initial configurations resulting from the first phase.

4.4 OLSR Extended Finite State Machine

For the sake of simplicity, we decided not to specify all the functionalities of OLSR. For example, we consider that each node has only one interface and also that it can only claims one link to a same node. Since OLSR is a link state routing protocol, we decided to model the behavior of every node according to its state and its connectivity with its neighbors. Indeed, OLSR makes difference between links depending if they are asymmetric or bidirectional and also between nodes, depending if they are normal nodes or multipoint relays - what implies they have a priori, a better connectivity. Our EFSM only represents the interactions between two nodes. This implies there is a unique EFSM for each link between two nodes. We reuse the notation of [3], i.e. we use the abbreviation *obs* and *cur* to specify respectively the destination and the local node (*obs* stands for **obs**erved node and *cur* for **cur**rent node). The events which correspond to a received packet are noted with a '?' while those with a '!' relate sent packets. The typical notation is also *"address - type of event - type of message - fields"*.

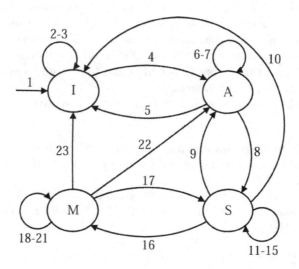

Fig. 2. OLSR Extended Finite State Machine (see Appendix for details)

The goal of the first transition is to initialize all the timers and variables. OLSR is a proactive protocol, so it needs to periodically send control messages though the network to keep the link states updated. This is represented on the figure by the timers *HelloTimer* and *UpdateTimer* which respectively time the *Hello* message sending and the the link state updating. Normally, a node should update its link state as soon as it receives a *Hello* message. However, we needed two timers here, to specify the behavior of a node when he receives no message (its connectivity may decrease). Thus, in the *Initial* state, the node uses the first timer to perform its neighbor discovery. Since it has none actually, it sends an empty *Hello*. It remains in the same state if it has received no message after the specified second timeout.

By receiving a message from another participant, the node immediately goes on the second state *Asymmetrical*, which means it has heard another node but can not yet claim a symmetrical link with it. We also record the address of the heard node in a list of asymmetrical neighbors to further verify if one can rightfully pass in the next state. From that state, a node may:

- receive no message and return in the preceding state after the timeout
- receive another *Hello* message from the same node and remain in that state
- receive an *Hello* message from a node

If the sending node has recorded it as an asymmetrical one (use of the constant *ASYM*), one can pass in the **Symmetrical** state. But this is only plausible if the current node previously sent an empty *Hello* message, what can be verified by the mean of the variable *SentHello*, which must be set to *true*. This precaution allows to avoid that malicious nodes claim non-existent links. The sending node could also have directly recorded it as a symmetrical neighbor (use of constant *SYM*). In that case, that node must have been recorded previously in the asymmetrical list(*AsymList*).

Once it reaches the symmetrical state a node has to advertise its neighbors. Hence, it may:

- send a Hello message to claim a symmetrical link with the observed node
- advertise that it chose the observed node as one of its MPR nodes (by using the constant *MPR*)
- send data to one of its MPR, to be forwarded
- receive **Topology Control** messages (only if the sender has been previously chosen as a MPR)

As for the receiving, if the node only receives empty *Hello* after a certain time (it is not seen anymore), it goes back in the asymmetrical state, since it can still listen nodes. If it is claimed by the observed node as an asymmetrical or a symmetrical node, it stays in its state. Finally, the node can be chosen as a MPR (the constant *MPR* is used). If so, it records the address of the sender in its MPR selectors list (*MprSelList*).

When a node finally reaches the MPR state, he has to keep on advertising periodically its MPR selectors. From now, it has also the responsibility to forward data from selectors. To do that, it just has to ensure that the message really comes from one of its MPR selectors, what can be easily verified by examining the list *MprSelList*. The second function of MPR nodes is to generate the link state messages. The representation we choose allows easily to verify that this kind of message can only be sent by an MPR node, as specified in [4]. Finally, depending on the received messages, the node will eventually reach another state. If it keeps on being claimed as a MPR node by the same neighbor, it stays in that state. If it is claimed only as a symmetrical node, it will become again a simple symmetrical neighbor, regarding the sender. As for the preceding state, if it receives message in which it can find its own address, it goes back to the asymmetrical state. Finally, if after the timer expires it has not received any message, it goes back to the initial state. In both cases, the lists are flushed and the timer are reset.

One has to note that there is an EFSM for each connection between two participants. Thus, a node could be in the *MPR* state regarding one node and be in a *SYM* or *ASYM* state with relation to another one.

5 Detecting Attacks

To test the effectiveness of our approach, we applied our violation detection algorithm to the traces corresponding to the two attacks described in section 3.

5.1 Hello Message Insertion

Let us recall that in this scheme, an attacker advertised a non-existent symmetrical link to its neighbors, thus perturbing their routing table calculation process. According to our notation (see Appendix), the corresponding trace is also:

```
HelloTimerOut / cur!Hello()
UpdateTimerOut
obs?Hello()
UpdateTimer
obs?Hello(cur) with cur=SYM
```

Here is how our algorithm proceeds to verify the trace: starting from the last event, it determines which could be the corresponding transitions. By examining the different possible transitions, one observes that this event can match the transitions 8, 15 and 17, which respectively start from the states A, S and M. These are the only transitions which correspond to the reception of a *Hello* message claiming a symmetrical link. Here, we have also three state possibilities with the following parameters:

State: A; Parameters: cur=SYM, obs∈AsymList
State: S; Parameters: cur=SYM
State: M; Parameters: cur=SYM, obs∈MprList

At that time, the algorithm shifts on the preceding event (*UpdateTimer*) and searches within the EFSM, all the transitions containing that event, which can lead to the states A, S or M. By looking into the list of all transitions, one can immediately verify that there is none which satisfy the requirements. The algorithm also raises a transfer error violation, that reveals the trace does not corresponds to the specification. From this anomaly, one may bring out two conclusions. Either we consider the implementation is correct and thus, there is a security attack in the network, either one considers that the implementation needs to be validated and we also exhibit a conformance error.

5.2   MPR Usurpation

Let us now consider the second attack in which an attacker sends Topology
Control messages without having been elected as a MPR. A corresponding trace
would have the pattern:

```
cur!Hello(obs) with obs=MPR
cur!Hello(obs) with obs=SYM
obs!TC(cur) with cur=MPRSEL
```

This is an example of trace where a node keeps on claiming to be a MPR
node after having been demoted as a simple symmetrical one. The current node
elects the observed one as a MPR (and may perform some transitions). Then,
it demotes the observed node (after having recalculated its routing table for
example) but keeps on receiving TC messages from it.

The process is then the same than for the previous attack. The algorithm
searched for a transition which corresponds to the emission of a TC message
with the variable 'cur' set to '$MPRSEL$'. It appears that this event match the
transition 14. This transition leads to state with the predicate $obs \in MprList$. So
now, the algorithm shifts to the previous event ($cur!Hello(obs)$ with $obs=SYM$)
and searches backward all the transitions that contained it, which also reach
the state A. By checking all the possible transitions in the EFSM, it appears
that only the transition 11 matches. Nevertheless, the transition 11 has, as an
effect, to remove the address of the observed node from the $MprList$ of the
current node. That is in total opposition with the predicate of the transition
14. The algorithm also raises this time, an output error and discloses a new
anomaly. Again, it can result from a dysfunction in the observed node or a willful
security attack.

Note that this scheme is quite similar to the case where a node falsely ad-
vertises symmetrical links through the TC messages. Both anomalies will be
identically detected.

Thus, it appears that our approach allows to detect several kinds of typical
attacks on the OLSR protocol. These attacks are not taken into account in the
original specification of the protocol and could constitute a serious risk if one is
not able to detect them.

6   Conclusions and Further Work

We proposed a specification based approach that rely on the use of extended
finite state machines to detect attacks on the OLSR protocol. The use of EFSM
makes possible to analyze in depth, the messages exchanged between nodes. We
applied a backward checking algorithm to detect violations on the specification.
This approach brings a significant benefit on the quickness of the verification
process, what is crucial in the context of run-time verification. We then, applied
our algorithm to detect flaws on the OLSR protocol and showed that it makes
it possible do detect several kinds of anomalies.

We plan to integrate this approach and this algorithm in a complete IDS infrastructure. We also envisage to use in a complementary way, a signature analysis tool to detect attacks that can not yet be easily detected by a specification-based approach(e.g. DoS. attacks).

References

1. Cédric Adjih, Thomas Clausen, Philippe Jacquet, Anis Laouiti, Paul Mühlethaler, and Daniele Raffo. Securing the olsr protocol. In *Proceedings of IFIP Med-Hoc-Ned*, pages 125–134, 2003.
2. B. Alcalde, A. Cavalli, D. Chen, D. Khuu, and D. Lee. Network protocol system passive testing for fault management - a backward checking approach. In *Formal Techniques for Networks and Distributed Systems - FORTE 2004*, pages 150–166, Madrid, Spain, september 27-30 2004. Springer.
3. Yi an Huang and Wenke Lee. Attack analysis and detection for ad hoc routing protocols. In *Proceedings of the 7th International Symposium on Recent Advances in Intrusion Detection (RAID'04)*, 2004.
4. Thomas Clausen and Phillipe Jacquet. *IETF RFC 3626: Optimized Link State Routing Protocol (OLSR)*. The Internet Society http://www.ietf.org/rfc/rfc3626.txt, 2003.
5. B. Dahill, B. Levine, E. Royer, and C. Shields. A secure routing protocol for ad hoc networks, 2001.
6. Yih-Chun Hu, Adrian Perrig, and David B. Johnson. Ariadne: A secure on-demand routing protocol for ad hoc networks. In *Proceedings of the Eighth Annual International Conference on Mobile Computing and Networking MobiCom 2002*, pages 12–23, 2002.
7. Chin-Yang Tseng, Poornima Balasubramanyam, Calvin Ko, Rattapon Limprasitti-porn, Jeff Rowe, and Karl Levitt. A specification-based intrusion detection system for aodv. In *SASN '03: Proceedings of the 1st ACM workshop on Security of ad hoc and sensor networks*, pages 125–134, New York, NY, USA, 2003. ACM Press.
8. Yongguang Zhang, Wenke Lee, and Yi-An Huang. Intrusion detection techniques for mobile wireless networks. *Wirel. Netw.*, 9(5):545–556, 2003.

Appendix

Here are the different transitions corresponding to the EFSM of the figure 4.4. P are used to denote predicates while A stand for actions. Uppercase variables denote constants and are used to specify the nature of a node depending if it is asymmetrical, symmetrical, a MPR node or a MPR selector.

1. A: reset SentHello, HelloTimer, UpdateTimer, TcTimer; clear AsymList, MprSelList, MprList

2. HelloTimerOut / cur!Hello()
   A: set SentHello=true; set HelloTimer

3. UpdateTimerOut
   A: reset UpdateTimer ; set SentHello=false

4. obs?Hello()
   A: reset UpdateTimer ; Add(obs,AsymList)

5. UpdateTimerOut
   A: reset UpdateTimer; Remove(obs,AsymList)

6. HelloTimerOut / cur!Hello(obs)
   A: set obs=ASYM; reset HelloTimer

7. obs?Hello()
   A: reset UpdateTimer

8. obs?Hello(cur)
   P: (cur=ASYM AND SentHello=true) OR (cur=SYM AND obs∈AsymList)
   A: reset UpdateTimer

9. obs?Hello()
   A: reset UpdateTimer; reset SentHello; remove (obs,MprList)

10. UpdateTimerOut
    A: reset UpdateTimer; Remove(obs,AsymList); reset SentHello;
                                                            remove(obs,MprList)

11. HelloTimerOut / cur!Hello(obs)
    A: set obs=SYM; reset HelloTimer; remove(obs,MprList)

12. HelloTimerOut / cur!Hello(obs)
    A: set obs=MPR; reset HelloTimer; add(obs,MprList)

13. cur!Data()
    P: obs∈MprList

14. obs?TC(cur)
    P: cur=MPRSEL AND obs∈MprList

15. obs?Hello(cur)
    P: cur=SYM OR cur=ASYM
    A: reset UpdateTimer

16. obs?Hello(cur)
    P: cur=MPR
    A: Add(obs,MprSelList); reset UpdateTimer; reset TcTimer

17. obs?Hello(cur)
    P: cur=SYM OR cur=ASYM
    A: reset UpdateTimer; Remove(obs,MprSelList)

18. HelloTimerOut / cur!Hello(obs)
    A: set obs=MPRSEL; reset HelloTimer

19. TcTimerOut / cur!TC(obs=MPRSEL)
    A: reset TcTimer

20. obs?Data() / cur!Data()
    P: obs∈MprSelList

21. obs?Hello(cur)
    P: obs∈MprSelList AND cur=MPR
    A: reset UpdateTimer

22. obs?Hello()
    A: reset UpdateTimer; clear MprSelList

23. UpdateTimerOut
    A: reset updateTimer; clear AsymList; clear MprSelList; reset SentHello

Modeling and Verification of a Telecommunication Application Using Live Sequence Charts and the Play-Engine Tool*

Pierre Combes[1], David Harel[2], and Hillel Kugler[3]

[1] France Telecom Research and Development, Paris, France
Pierre.Combes@francetelecom.com
[2] The Weizmann Institute of Science, Rehovot, Israel
dharel@weizmann.ac.il
[3] New York University, New York, NY, USA
kugler@cs.nyu.edu

Abstract. We apply the language of live sequence charts (LSCs) and the Play-Engine tool to a real-world complex telecommunication service. The service, called **Depannage**, allows a user to make a phone call and ask for help from a doctor, the fire brigade, a car maintenance service, etc. This kind of service is built on top of an embedded platform, using both new and existing service components. The complexity of such applications stems from their distributed architecture, the various time constraints they entail, and the fact the underlying systems are rapidly evolving, introducing new components, protocols and associated hardware constraints, all of which must be taken into account. We present the results of our work on the specification, animation and formal verification of the Depannage service, and draw some initial conclusions as to an appropriate methodology for using a scenario-based approach in the telecommunication domain. The complete specification of the Depannage application in LSCs and some animations showing simulation and verification results are made available as supplementary material. [1]

1 Introduction

The challenging complexity of telecommunication systems, together with a high demand for rapid deployment, encourages development of innovative techniques in order to design and deploy new applications in a quick and secure manner [2]. In the telecommunication domain, components play a crucial role. The majority of these components is embedded in a large and complex architecture which involves hard and soft real-time constraints and requirements. Moreover, non-functional requirements, in particular time dependent properties, also play an important role. A telecommunication application is always built from a set of

---

* This research was supported by the European Commission project OMEGA (IST-2001-33522).

[1] http://cs.nyu.edu/~kugler/Depannage/

D.A. Peled and Y.-K. Tsay (Eds.): ATVA 2005, LNCS 3707, pp. 414–428, 2005.
© Springer-Verlag Berlin Heidelberg 2005

embedded service components, and in the emerging architecture a challenge is providing a ubiquitous environment for telecommunication users. This means that the telecommunication applications should be provided in several contexts with a high level of quality of service, and always in a comprehensive way to the end-users. Nowadays, due to openness of the telecommunication architecture, a multiplicity of services and service features could be provided by several teams or companies, and must be dynamically added and updated. The consistent use of components and service features is becoming more critical in order to ensure that undesired behaviors do not occur [11]. The time seems ripe to go from ad-hoc techniques for component composition toward more integrated and formal ones. Such techniques should be based on the use of formal languages for design and verification. The languages and design models should be readable in order to facilitate the communication between telecommunication engineers and specialists in formal verification. A comprehensive animation tool is also very important in order to enhance the understanding of the model, and in order to show verification results to engineers and clients [4]. A proposed approach should enable quick and secure telecommunication service creation, answering questions like how to build an architecture based on a set of components (reused or/and shared by several services) in such a way that we can guarantee providing complete applications respecting quality of service and safety requirements.

2   Live Sequence Charts and the Play-Engine

Understanding system and software behavior by looking at various "stories" or scenarios seems a promising approach, and it has focused intensive research efforts in the last few years. One of the most widely used languages for specifying scenario-based requirements is that of message sequence charts (MSCs), adopted long ago by the ITU [15], or its UML variant, sequence diagrams [14]. Sequence charts (whether MSCs or their UML variant) possess a rather weak partial-order semantics that does not make it possible to capture many kinds of behavioral requirements of a system. To address this, while remaining within the general spirit of scenario-based visual formalisms, a broad extension of MSCs has been proposed, called live sequence charts (LSCs) [6]. Among other things, LSCs distinguish between behaviors that must happen in the system (universal) from those that may happen (existential). A universal chart contains a *prechart*, which specifies the scenario which, if successfully executed, forces the system to satisfy the scenario given in the actual chart body. Existential charts specify sample interactions between the system and its environment, and must be satisfied by at least one system run. They thus do not force the application to behave in a certain way in all cases, but rather state that there is at least one set of circumstances under which a certain behavior occurs. The distinction between mandatory (hot) and provisional (cold) applies also to other LSC constructs, e.g., conditions and locations, thus creating a rich and powerful language, which among many other things can express forbidden behavior ("anti-scenarios").

In [9,10] a methodology for specifying and validating requirements, termed the "play-in/play-out approach", is described, as well as a supporting tool called the Play-Engine. According to this approach, requirements are captured by the user playing in scenarios using a graphical interface of the system to be developed or using an object model diagram. The user "plays" the GUI by clicking buttons, rotating knobs and sending messages (calling functions) to objects in an intuitive manner. By similarly playing the GUI, the user describes the desired reactions of the system and the conditions that may, must or may not hold. As this is being done, the supporting tool, the Play-Engine, constructs a formal version of the requirements in the form of LSCs. Note that it is not always necessary to spend much time designing a fancy graphical interface. In many cases, it is enough to use a standard object model diagram. The Play-Engine tool, supports class diagrams and allows to work with internal objects that are not reflected in the GUI.

Play-out is a complementary idea to play-in, which, rather surprisingly, makes it possible to execute the requirements directly. In play-out, the user simply plays the GUI application as he/she would have done when executing a system model, or the final system implementation, but limiting him/herself to "end-user" and external environment actions only. While doing this, the Play-Engine keeps track of the actions and causes other actions and events to occur as dictated by the universal charts in the specification. Here too, the engine interacts with the GUI application and uses it to reflect the system state at any given moment. This process of the user operating the GUI application and the Play-Engine causing it to react according to the specification has the effect of working with an executable model, but with no intra-object model having to be built or synthesized.

Smart play-out [7] is a powerful technique for executing scenario-based requirements using verification methods. It can be used for driving the execution of the system, or for checking if a given existential chart can be satisfied without violating any of the universal charts. Smart play-out is integrated in the Play-Engine tool and allows developers to apply formal verification methods at early design stages in a user-friendly manner.

3   Components and System Architecture

3.1   The Telecommunication Application

We apply LSCs and the Play-Engine to a telecommunication service called Depannage, provided by France Telecom. The Depannage service allows a user to make a phone call and ask for the help of a doctor, fire brigade, car maintenance, etc. The service invocation software first asks for authentication of the calling user, and then searches for the calling location. Once the calling location is found, the software searches in a data base for numbers of potential service providers corresponding to the Depannage society members in the vicinity of the caller. Once various numbers are found, the service tries to connect the caller to one of the potential called numbers (in a sequential or parallel way). In any case the caller should be connected to a secretary or to a vocal box. In parallel a second logic will make periodic location requests to the Depannage society members in order to record their latest locations in the data base. The Depannage service is implemented as a layered application consisting of several components. Each layer or component is described by a group of scenarios; the connection between layers is very clean and precise. The objects in each layer communicate only among themselves and with the objects in the adjacent layers. This architecture enables applying methodological approaches to break down the complexity of the system.

3.2   Components and Composites

A telecommunication system is based on a set of components — reusable software units specified by their interfaces. The specification of these interfaces should be given by the signatures of the required and provided methods and signals, and by the description of the dynamic behaviors. Components should be reusable, thus they should be specified independently of any embedding system.

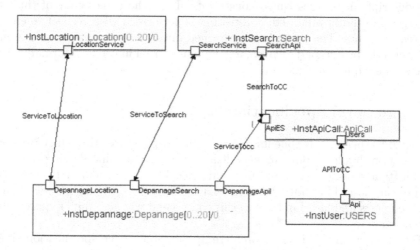

Fig. 1. The architecture of the Depannage application

A composite structure will be specified as a white box by the set of embedded components and the connections between these components [14]. Such structural design could use hierarchical composition. The top-level of the composite structure will correspond to the complete system provided to the client, in our case the telecommunication service Depannage.

Fig. 1 shows a partial view of the complete application (using UML composite structure diagram), the main components involved and the communication between these components using ports and connectors.

4   Overall View of a Design Methodology Based on Verification

A classical problem in telecommunication is that of "feature interaction" [11]. Telecommunication infrastructure and applications are in a continuous evolution, new services and service features are developed and deployed in the network along with existing ones. They are developed by several teams in parallel, in order to satisfy new customer requirements. The feature interaction problem occurs when the introduction of a new service (feature) causes the new system to violate an existing service requirement. This is a critical problem in telecommunication — involving significant loss of time and money during testing and operation phases. It can be properly solved only by identifying the problems during the design and modeling phases.

To address these issues we present a methodology that supports an incremental paradigm for specifying and developing telecommunication applications. First, we describe a high level specification of the service and component behavior, including the behavior of the communication between these components. This description includes timed constraints. Then the consistency of this high level specification is validated, and testing is performed with respect to end-to-end requirements. The analysis is performed initially by simulation and animation methods. In a second step, smart play-out is used in order to formally verify some of the requirements.

5   High Level Specification

The wish to specify components in a reusable way requires that the component specification should be done independently of any embedding architecture. Such specification should correspond in a universal LSC to an abstract view of the component, describing how the component will react to events coming from its provided ports and how (and when) this component will act on its required ports (execution flows).

For the system — i.e., the complete application — the specification should be enhanced by universal LSCs describing the communications between these components. Such LSCs could include time constraints and delays on the communication. The end-to-end requirements are expressed by existential LSCs and will be validated during the simulation/animation of the model.

In this paper, we will focus our presentation on the **Search** component, the **Users** component and the communication between these components. A detailed description of the entire model is available online at [5].

5.1   Search Component

This component has two ports, **SearchService** for communicating with the application that will use it and **SearchApi** in order to communicate with platform components and indirectly with the users and the environment.

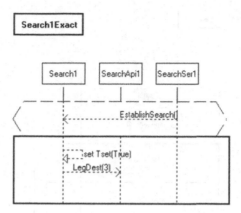

Fig. 2. First LSC for Search Component - Concrete

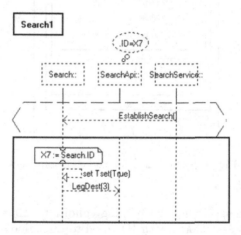

Fig. 3. First LSC for Search Component - Symbolic

The universal chart **Search1Exact**, appearing in Fig. 2, requires that whenever **SearchSer1** sends the **EstablishSearch** method to **Search1**, as specified in the prechart, the **Search1** port sets the value of **Tset** to **TRUE** and then sends the **LegDest(3)** method to **SearchApi1**.

In order to specify this requirement in a generic way, so it will hold for all other instantiations of the classes **SearchService**, **Search** and **SearchApi**, we use symbolic instances [12] as shown in the chart **Search1** in Fig. 3. Whenever an instance of class **SearchService** sends the **EstablishSearch** method to an instance of class **Search**, the **Search** instance sets the value of **Tset** to **TRUE** and then sends the **LegDest(3)** method to a **searchApi** instance which has an ID that is identical to the ID of the **Search** instance. This is done by storing the **Search** ID using an assignment to variable **X7**, and in the ellipse above the

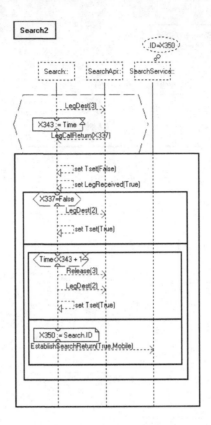

Fig. 4. Second LSC for Search Component

SearchApi instance specifying the binding condition .ID = x7, meaning that an instance of class SearchApi with ID equal to the value stored in X7 will be bound to this chart, and then later the LegDest(3) method will be sent to it.

The universal chart Search2, appearing in Fig. 4 specifies a behavioral requirement that is relevant when the SearchApi gets information on the LegCallReturn and forwards it to the Search port. The prechart of Fig. 4 contains a scenario and not a single message as in Fig. 3. The chart will be activated if an instance of class Search sends the LegDest(3) method to a searchApi instance, and this searchApi instance sends the LegCallReturn message back to the Search instance.

Another LSC feature introduced in Fig. 4 is the If-Then-Else construct used to specify conditional behavior. In the main chart, if the parameter of LegCallReturn is FALSE (the parameter is stored in variable X337) then Search sends LegDest(2) to the SearchApi instance and sets the value of Tset to TRUE. Otherwise, the other part of the subchart is taken, which involves a nested If-Then-Else construct. Here we branch according to the time that has elapsed since the LegDest(3) message was sent. If this time is less than 1 time unit

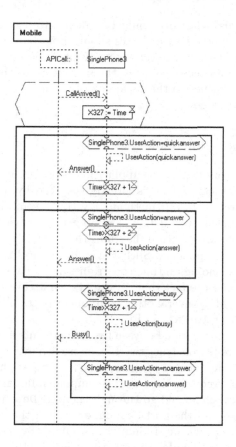

Fig. 5. The Mobile Phone

`Search` sends `LegDest(2)` and sets the value of `Tset` to `TRUE` as before. This corresponds to a situation in the system where a very quick answer by the mobile phone means that we will be connected to its vocal box, a situation which should be avoided in the Depannage service. If the time that has elapsed since the `LegDest(3)` message was sent is greater than or equal to 1 time unit the message `EstablishSearchReturn(TRUE, Mobile)` is sent to the appropriate `SearchService` instance, corresponding to continuing the process of connecting to the mobile phone.

5.2   The Users

We model only a simple view of the user behavior, focusing for a fixed phone on three possible states, corresponding to user actions : `busy`, `answer` with a delay, or `noanswer`. The specification of a mobile phone, shown in Fig. 5 introduces an additional state `quickanswer`. In reality, if a mobile phone is reachable but in a disconnected state, the communication will quickly be connected to the vocal box of the phone. This behavior should be taken into account carefully while designing the service. Some service logics should not connect the calling party to a vocal box. In the Depannage service we want to be connected to a person which is available or to a secretary or in the worst case to the vocal box of the depannage company, but not to the vocal box of the mobile phone of one of the Depannage service providers.

5.3   The Communication View

Developing a new telecommunication application is performed by taking existing components (each such component is already specified by a set of LSCs), and connecting them together. In our methodology this assembly of components is also done by specifying universal LSCs defining the connection between components. Following the architecture diagram, these LSCs will specify the communications between components. Such LSCs for connector behaviors may be simple or complex, depending on time constraints and delays, on the parallelism of thread execution, and the fact that, in the system architecture, a component port could be connected to several other component ports (for example the port ApiES of the component ApiCall in Fig. 1).

To specify the communication between two components following an architectural diagram, we have to construct two LSCs for each event. Consider the connection between the components Depannage and Search. We have to express that the event EstablishSearch required by the component Depannage and provided by the component Search should go through the port DepannageSearch of the component Depannage and the port SearchService of the component Search. This is described in the charts DepToSearch1 and DepToSearch2 in Fig. 6(a),(b). Similar LSCs are also specified for the return event EstablishSearchReturn in Fig. 7(a),(b).

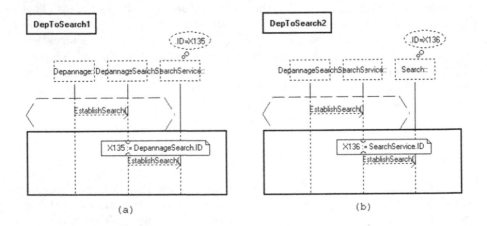

(a)   (b)

Fig. 6. Connectors between components Depannage and Search

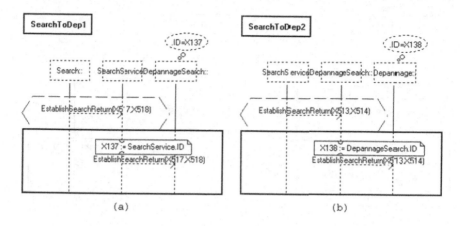

Fig. 7. Connectors between components Search and Depannage

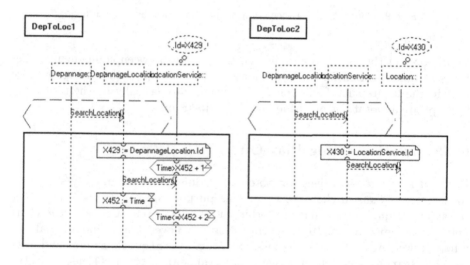

Fig. 8. Connectors between components Depannage and Location

The connection between the components `Depannage` and `Location` is described in Figs. 8, 9. In these LSCs we also introduce time delay on the communication. The LSC `DepToLoc1` of Fig. 8 specifies that the method `SearchLocation` will take between 1 and 2 time units. The method `SearchLocation` is an asynchronous method, designated by the open arrow, in contrast to the closed arrows for synchronous methods. This time constraint is specified by storing the time in variable `x452` immediately after sending `SearchLocation` and adding the two hot conditions requiring `Time > x452 + 1` and `Time <= x452 + 2`. A similar requirement that the method `SearchLocationReturn` will take between 1 and 2 time units is specified in Fig. 9.

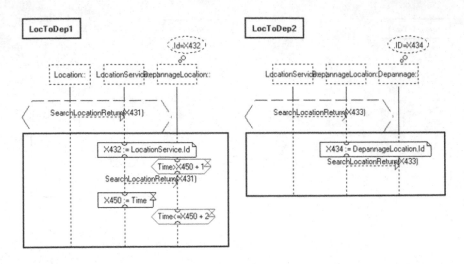

Fig. 9. Connectors between components Location and Depannage

In some of the cases, describing the connection between components using LSCs is quite straightforward, as shown in the examples above. We propose that in the future such LSCs could be derived automatically by the tool using appropriate annotations on the architecture diagram.

6   Simulation Using Play-Out

Play-out allows a convenient way to debug requirements at an early stage and to detect problems in the design. For this purpose we can use anti-scenarios, behavioral requirements that are forbidden in the system. Consider the chart NoQuickAnswer2 in Fig. 10. It specifies that whenever SinglePhone3 makes a quick answer by sending the self message UserAction(quickAnswer) and after that DepSearch1 sends the message EstablishSearch Return(True, Mobile) to Depannage1, then the condition FALSE specified in the main chart must hold — which can never occur — implying that this sequence of messages specified in the prechart corresponding to a connection to the vocal box of a mobile phone must never occur.

In play-out mode, if this chart participates in the execution, the prechart will be traced and if it is completed the user will get a message that the system has aborted due to the violation of a hot condition, as shown in Fig. 11. In this case the violation was caused by a time delay in the APICall which is triggered by setting the property CondTime of this object to TRUE. In general, once a violation is detected it indicates a problem in the specification or the design of the service and should be looked into carefully to identify and fix the cause of the violation.

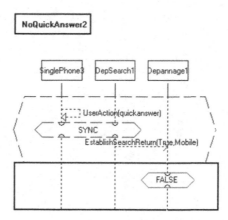

Fig. 10. A forbidden scenario - No connection to the vocal box of a mobile phone

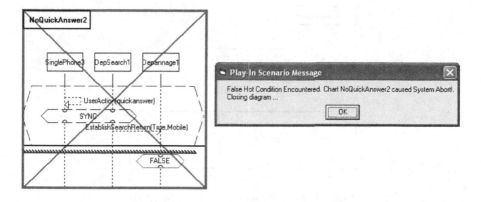

Fig. 11. Violation of a forbidden scenario during play-out

7   Verification Using Smart Play-Out

Smart play-out [7] uses verification methods, mainly model-checking, to execute and analyze LSCs. There are various modes in which smart play-out can work. In one of the modes smart play-out functions as an enhanced play-out mechanism, helping the execution to avoid deadlocks and violations. Thus, in this mode smart play-out utilizes verification techniques to run programs, rather than to verify them. In another mode, smart play-out is given an existential chart and asked if it can be satisfied without violating any of the universal charts. If it manages to satisfy the existential chart the satisfying run is played out, providing full information on the execution and reflecting the behavior in the GUI.

In the Depannage application we mainly used existential charts for specifying scenarios that should not occur, and then asked smart play-out if they can be

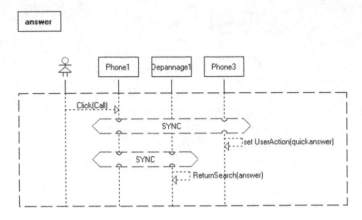

Fig. 12. An existential chart implying connection to the vocal box of a mobile phone

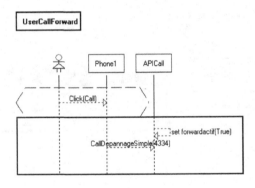

Fig. 13. A new feature of forwarding calls

satisfied. If the existential chart was satisfied, this means we have discovered an error in our specification model, and the execution can provide insights on what went wrong. A cleaner way would have been to specify these scenarios as anti-scenarios, as shown in Fig. 10. An enhancement to smart play-out is currently being developed to support this work-flow.

Consider the existential chart shown in Fig. 12. It describes a scenario that implies a user (on **Phone1**) being connected to the vocal box of a mobile phone (**Phone3**), an undesired behavior since then the user does not get a personal response to his request as is desired for the Depannage service. Smart play-out proves given the universal charts in the model that this scenario cannot be satisfied.

We then added a new feature to our telecommunication model, forwarding calls, shown in Fig. 13, applied smart play-out, and it found a way to satisfy the chart of Fig. 12. The interaction of the new feature of the forwarding calls

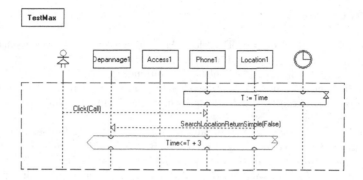

Fig. 14. Timing Requirements

allowed an erroneous situation in which a user is connected to a vocal box. A short animation of this behavior is shown in [5].

The current version of smart play-out is still restricted in terms of the language features it supports. Thus to use it some restrictions should be made on the model: no symbolic-instances, and only one parameter for each signal. We are currently working on lifting these restrictions. We have also abstracted and simplified the model to avoid the well known state-explosion problem. In a similar manner we have verified also timed properties of the application, as specified in Fig. 14. The entire model and the reduced versions are all available in [5].

8 Related Work and Future Directions

Scenario-based specification is very helpful in early stages of development [1], and is used widely by engineers. A considerable amount of experience has been gained from it being integrated into the MSC ITU standard [13] and the UML [14]. The latest versions of the UML recognized the importance of scenario-based requirements, and UML 2.0 sequence diagrams have been significantly enhanced in expressive capabilities, inspired in part by the LSCs of [6]. In [8], we report on the methodological experience gained by using LSCs and the Play-Engine in several industrial case studies. (We briefly mention the Depannage application too.)

Performance requirements — the number of requests that a system can manage — are very important in telecommunication applications but are not considered in this work. Simulation techniques based on queuing theory can be used for such performance evaluation. These techniques are, in many tools, based on the description of dynamic behavior as execution flows between components and machines. Thus, LSCs seem to be a suitable language for integrating performance evaluation and formal verification [3].

References

1. R. Alur, G.J. Holzmann, and D. Peled. An analyzer for message sequence charts. *Software Concepts and Tools*, 17(2):70–77, 1996.
2. R. Castanet, A. Cavalli, P. Combes, P. Laurencot, M. MacKaya, A. Mederreg, W. Monin, and F. Zaidi. A multi-service and multi-protocol validation platform-experimentation results. In *TestCom*, volume 2978 of *Lect. Notes in Comp. Sci.*, pages 17–32. Springer-Verlag, 2004.
3. P. Combes, F. Dubois, W. Monin, and D. Vincent. Looking for better integration of design and performance engineering. In R. Reed, editor, *SDL Forum*, volume 2708 of *Lect. Notes in Comp. Sci.*, pages 1–17. Springer-Verlag, 2003.
4. P. Combes, F. Dubois, and B. Renard. An Open Animation Tool: Application to Telecommunications Systems. *Computer Networks*, 40(5):599–620, December 2002.
5. P. Combes, D. Harel, and H. Kugler. Supplementary material on the depannage application. http://cs.nyu.edu/~kugler/Depannage/.
6. W. Damm and D. Harel. LSCs: Breathing life into message sequence charts. *Formal Methods in System Design*, 19(1):45–80, 2001. Preliminary version appeared in Proc. 3rd IFIP Int. Conf. on Formal Methods for Open Object-Based Distributed Systems (FMOODS'99).
7. D. Harel, H. Kugler, R. Marelly, and A. Pnueli. Smart play-out of behavioral requirements. In *Proc. 4th Intl. Conference on Formal Methods in Computer-Aided Design (FMCAD'02), Portland, Oregon*, volume 2517 of *Lect. Notes in Comp. Sci.*, pages 378–398, 2002. Also available as Tech. Report MCS02-08, The Weizmann Institute of Science.
8. D. Harel, H. Kugler, and G. Weiss. Some Methodological Observations Resulting from Experience Using LSCs and the Play-In/Play-Out Approach. In *Proc. Scenarios: Models, Algorithms and Tools*, volume 3466 of *Lect. Notes in Comp. Sci.* Springer-Verlag, 2005.
9. D. Harel and R. Marelly. *Come, Let's Play: Scenario-Based Programming Using LSCs and the Play-Engine.* Springer-Verlag, 2003.
10. D. Harel and R. Marelly. Specifying and Executing Behavioral Requirements: The Play In/Play-Out Approach. *Software and System Modeling (SoSyM)*, 2(2):82–107, 2003.
11. L. Logrippo and D. Amyot. *Feature Interactions in Telecommunications and Software Systems VII.* IOS Press, 2003.
12. R. Marelly, D. Harel, and H. Kugler. Multiple instances and symbolic variables in executable sequence charts. In *Proc. 17th Ann. ACM Conf. on Object-Oriented Programming, Systems, Languages and Applications (OOPSLA'02)*, pages 83–100, Seattle, WA, 2002.
13. ITU-TS Recommendation Z.120 (11/99): MSC 2000. ITU-TS, Geneva, 1999.
14. UML. Documentation of the unified modeling language (UML). Available from the Object Management Group (OMG), http://www.omg.org.
15. Z.120 ITU-TS Recommendation Z.120: Message Sequence Chart (MSC). ITU-TS, Geneva, 1996.

Formal Construction and Verification of Home Service Robots: A Case Study

Moonzoo Kim and Kyo Chul Kang

CSE Dept. Pohang University of Science and Technology,
Pohang, South Korea
{moonzoo,kck}@postech.ac.kr

Abstract. Home service robots have attracted much attentions to anticipate improved quality of human life. Considering that malfunctions of home service robots can directly threat the safety of human users, the assurance of robot's safe operation is a crucial prerequisite for the wide deployment of home service robots. Current practice of robot development, however, often fails to satisfy this requirement. Robot developers tend to concentrate on technical components only and fail to consider how these components will integrate to create the service. This practice frequently causes *feature interaction problems*. Furthermore, reactive nature of the robot applications adds to further complexity. Traditional testing is unsuccessful with this setting due to the difficulty of testing embedded systems and uncertainty caused by sensor devices. These situations make *formal construction and verification* essential to ensure safe operation of home service robots.

In this paper, we present our experience of formally constructing and verifying the core of Samsung Home Robot (SHR) with the use of Esterel. First, we reverse-engineered SHR to identify and analyze the core of SHR. Then, we re-implemented the core part in Esterel and verified SHR to satisfy safety properties regarding stopping behaviors through model checking. Through the verification, we detected and solved a feature interaction problem which caused the robot to ignore a stop command.

1 Introduction

With the advances of robotics, computer science, and other related areas, home service robots have received a strong academic and industrial attention. It is because home service robots can increase a quality of human life in a wide range of application areas. Thus, those leading companies such as Sony [3], Honda [2], and Samsung have invested a great deal of efforts in developing home service robots. Home service robots utilize various technology-intensive components such as vision recognizer, speech processors, and actuators to offer services. Thus, robot applications should coordinate these components in harmony. Robot developers, however, tend to focus on technical components at an early stage of product development without any consideration of how they will integrate these components to provide services. In addition, these components are developed by

D.A. Peled and Y.-K. Tsay (Eds.): ATVA 2005, LNCS 3707, pp. 429–443, 2005.

separated teams, which makes integration of these components more difficult. As a result, robot products often suffer from feature interaction problems [9,17]. Furthermore, reactive nature of home service robots adds further complexity to robot applications. Therefore, it is a highly challenging task to develop robot applications satisfying stringent temporal and safety requirements.

Due to high complexity of robot applications, testing and debugging often takes more than a half of total development time but still fails to provide satisfying result. Thus, the necessity of *formal validation and verification (V&V)* has been recognized in robotics areas [11,18]. Also, robot domain specific V&V frameworks such as ORCAAD [7] and MAESTRO [8] have been developed. In robot industry, however, a practice of applying formal methods is not very popular because robot industry does not have enough field experiences with formal methods yet. In addition, the gap between a formal model and a real implementation discourages developers from adopting formal methods as well. Therefore, we need to apply a *unified formal framework* supporting both *construction* and *verification* of robots. Furthermore, for practicality, we should aim to apply formal methods to the *core* of relatively a small size with an acceptable development overhead, rather than to the whole applications [12].

In this paper, we describe our experience of formally constructing and verifying Samsung Home Robot (SHR) with Samsung Advanced Institute of Technology (SAIT). First, we reverse-engineered SHR application that SAIT had developed. Based on the extracted architectural information, we re-engineered SHR application while identifying the core of the application. Then, we re-implemented the core in Esterel [6] and verified that SHR satisfied safety properties regarding stopping behaviors through model checking. Through the verification, we detected and solved a feature interaction problem which caused the robot not to stop when a user commanded the robot to stop. [1]

Section 2 describes background of SHR. Section 3 overviews the Esterel framework. Section 4 illustrates the previous SHR application and re-engineered one. Section 5 shows the verification results about stopping behaviors of SHR. Finally, Section 6 concludes with the summary of this paper.

2   Background of SHR100

Sect. 2.1 gives an overview of the SHR project and Sect. 2.2 explains the services which SHR provides. Sect. 2.3 describes statistics on the SHR application code.

2.1   SHR Project

We have developed three versions of SHR - SHR00, SHR50, and SHR100. The development of SHR00 started in 2002 by four separate teams of SAIT consisting

---

[1] We used the Esterel framework for this project mainly because we can verify an Esterel program by model checking and generate a C code from the verified Esterel program. This unified framework is suitable for industrial projects, which require a reliable working code as a final result with minimal overhead.

of thirteen people working on speech recognition, vision recognition, simultaneous localization and mapping (SLAM), and actuator control. SHR50 as well as SHR00, however, often experienced unstable behaviors such as missing user's commands and showed stuttered movement even though each part worked successfully before the integration (this kind of failure is not uncommon in robotics field [9]). After ten months into the new development of SHR100, for higher reliability, SAIT requested POSTECH to re-engineer SHR100 supporting "call and come" and "user following" services (see Sect. 2.2). With this request, POSTECH re-engineered an existing implementation for six months. The overview of the SHR100 components is illustrated in Fig. 1.

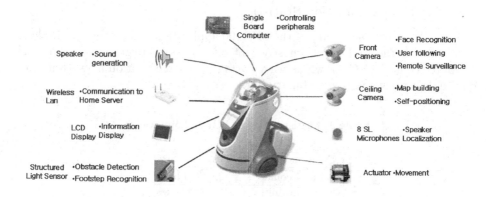

Fig. 1. HW Components of SHR100

2.2   Services of SHR100

Some of the primary services of SHR100 are described as follows.

– Call and Come (CC)
  There are two commands: namely "come" and "stop". Once a "come" command is recognized, the robot tries to detect the direction of sound source by comparing the strength of sound captured via microphones. Then, the robot rotates to the direction of sound source and tries to recognize user's face by analyzing images captured through the front camera. If the caller's face is detected, the robot moves forward until it reaches within one meter from the user. A "Stop" command makes the robot stop. CC is *preemptible*, i.e., while CC is executed, newly recognized command makes the robot ignore the previous command and allow to proceed the new one.
– User Following (UF)
  This service is triggered right after CC is completed. Once UF is triggered, the robot constantly checks vision data and data from the structured light sensor which is used to locate the user. The robot tracks down the user within the distance of one meter range. If the robot misses a user, the robot

notifies the user by speaking "I lost you" and UF ends. Similar to CC, UF is a preemptible service.

- Tele-presence (TP)
  A remote user can control a robot by using a PDA. In addition, the robot can send images obtained from the front camera to the PDA for surveillance purpose through a home server.
- Security Monitoring (SM)
  The robot patrols around a house using the map generated by SLAM component for surveillance. When accidents are detected, the robot reports to the user.

2.3   SHR100 Application Statistics

The rough statistic summary of the SHR100 application is described in Table 1. Some parts of the application (mostly controller parts) were given to POSTECH as source code in C/C++ while other parts (mostly recognition algorithms and device drivers) were given as binary libraries.

Table 1. Statistics on the SHR100 application

Components	# of files	Size
Call and come	29	4000 lines
User following	43	9000 lines
Others	43	3600 lines
Libraries	39	38 MB

3   The Esterel Framework

In this section, we briefly describe the Esterel language and its toolset.

3.1   The Esterel Language

Esterel [6] is a language for programming reactive systems that wait for a set of inputs, and react to these inputs by computing and producing outputs. Since Esterel is based on the "synchrony hypothesis", every reaction to a set of inputs should be instantaneous. In practice, this means that a system should react to input signals before input signals of the next cycle arrive. Synchrony hypothesis considerably simplifies the specifications of reactive systems. Furthermore, many application areas satisfy this hypothesis.

A program written in Esterel specifies the components (called modules) running in parallel. Modules communicate with each other and the outside world through input/output signals, which are broadcasted and may carry values of arbitrary types. Thus, the interaction between components can be clearly described. Furthermore, Esterel provides reactive/preemptive operators which are useful for developing robot applications. An Esterel program has its semantics as a finite state Mealy machine whose transitions are labeled with pairs of input and output signals (see Fig 6).

3.2 The Esterel Toolset

Esterel toolset consists of the following three components. [2]

- Esterel compiler `esterel`
- graphical simulator `xes`
- model checker `xeve`

`esterel` compiles an Esterel program into various formats including the C language. Using `esterel`, once a developer has proved the correctness of an Esterel program through model checking, one can generate correct C code without a manual conversion. This WYPIWYE (What You Prove Is What You Execute) principle is a strong advantage of Esterel over other formal modeling languages. In addition, an Esterel program can be seamlessly integrated with existing C/C++ codes through well-defined APIs. Furthermore, generated C code is platform neutral so that a developer can port an Esterel program into different OS/HW platforms (e.g. Linux or VxWorks) without a difficulty.

`xes` supports interactive simulation as well as guided simulation. With a given Esterel program, a user can execute the program by symbolically selecting input signals to emit and advancing its ticks (time instants). `xes` is also used to examine the execution trace of a counter example generated from `xeve`.

`xeve` minimizes and analyzes a finite state machine generated from an Esterel program. Basic verification process of `xeve` is to check the presence of output signals with given configuration of input signals by model checking. A simple property such as "if a user does not give a command to a robot, the robot must not move" (see Sect. 5.2) can be checked in this way. More complex property can be checked by building an observer module which emits a violation signal when the property is violated (see Sect. 5.3). [15] proved that safety properties described in temporal logic could be translated into observer modules in Esterel.

4   Re-engineering of SHR100

In this section, we describe both previous SHR100 implementation (Sect. 4.1) and re-engineered SHR100 implementation (Sect. 4.2).

4.1   Previous SHR100 Implementation

SHR100 was implemented in a service-oriented way because each service feature such as CC and UF, had been developed separately. Consequently, operations

---

[2] A commercial Esterel studio [1] provides an integrated development environment including a visual language editor.

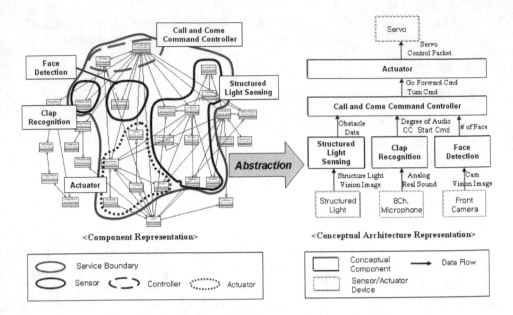

Fig. 2. Previous architecture of SHR100 regarding the CC service

of a service were dispersed among components, which does not clarify component architecture design. In addition, there existed redundant computational components because some computational components (e.g. vision) were used by different services. Therefore, developers experienced difficulty in identifying the interactions among the components of its original implementation, which often caused feature interaction problems. In order to improve reliability, we needed to clarify the previous SHR100 architecture first. Otherwise, it would be difficult to identify and analyze the core. Also, re-writing the core of SHR100 in Esterel would be messy because the new core should cooperate with existing C/C++ components.

Fig. 2 illustrates the recovery of a conceptual architecture from the object relationship diagram of CC through abstraction. The left part of Fig. 2 describes CC service unit and its constituent operational units. Using functional cohesion as a criterion, we classified operational units into three categories - *sensor (input)*, *controller (coordination)*, and *actuator (output)*. Then, we identified five operational units -"Face Detection", "Clap Recognition", "SL Sensing", "CC Command Controller", and "Actuator". After a data flow analysis, these units are configured into the conceptual architecture depicted in the right part of Fig. 2. We found out that "CC Command Controller" unit, which consists of CCallComeDlg and CPlanner classes, serves as the core of CC service by receiving data from the sensor units and making decisions to the actuator unit. Also, we found that the core was executed fast enough to satisfy the synchrony hypothesis required by the Esterel framework (see Sect. 3.1).

Through the re-engineering process, several bugs in the original implementation were found. For example, a main control function of the CC service is void CCallComeDlg ::processState() as in Fig. 3. processState() is called periodically once in every 100 milliseconds. Given a command, CC executes the command through multiple sequential steps. Each step is represented by a corresponding case statement block and is identified by the value of m_order declared at line 2. At the end of each case statement block, m_order is updated to determine the next step. After one step is executed, processState() is terminated and is called again after 100 milliseconds. If a new command is given between these two adjacent invocations, a previous command is ignored and the new command is processed.

```
01:class CCallComeDlg {
02:    int m_order;
03:    ...
04:    void processState() {
05:        ...
06:        switch(m_order) {
07:            case 0: STOP();
08:                    m_order++;
09:                    break;
10:            case 1: ROTATE();
11:                    m_order++;
12:                    break;
13:            case 2: static int nCount = 0;
14:                    if (abs(m_bef0-cur0)==0) nCount++;
15:                        else nCount = 0;
16:                    if (nCount > 2) m_order++;
17:                    break;
18:            ...
19:            case 9: CC_DONE();
20:                    m_order = -1;
21:                    break;
22:}    }    }
```

Fig. 3. A main control procedure for the CC service in C++

This pattern of reactive programming is a straight-forward way to allow preemption in C++, and is found frequently in robot applications. This pattern of reactive programming is, however, error-prone. For example, at line 16, nCount is used to test *twice* whether SHR100 stops its rotation or not. However, testing may happen only once because nCount is declared as a *static* local variable at line 13 and can be greater than two all the time without re-initialization. This error decreases the accuracy of user recognition due to blurred images captured while the robot does not stop its rotation completely. As a number of possible cases increase by adding more features, the complexity of C/C++ code increases rapidly so that developers can hardly manage and debug the program. Note that Esterel prevents such errors by handling a preemptive event e with preemption operator every e do *statements* end every (see line 11 to line 24 in Fig. 5).

4.2   New SHR100 Implementation

The architecture model in Fig. 2 is not adequate for multiple services; it does not provide the coordination of multiple service controllers (e.g. CC controller and UF controller) to handle interaction among services. Furthermore, the complexity of interactions among services grows exponentially within the previous architecture due to spaghetti-like communications among the components. Therefore, based on the extracted conceptual architectures, we re-designed the architecture of SHR100 concerning with handling issues such as priorities among services or global system modes (for more details on the re-engineering process of SHR100, see [14]). We separated *control plane* containing control components from *data plane* containing computational components. Firstly, we could easily identify four separate control components (CC, UF, TP, and SM) which specify their own behaviors for corresponding services. In addition, we defined Mode Manager to control global behaviors (e.g. initialization and interaction policy) of the robot by receiving all up-stream events from the computational components and managing control components. Each of these control components was implemented as a separate Esterel module. [3] Secondly, after data flow analysis, we could come up with five computational components - SLAM, Navigation, User Interface, Vision Manager, and Audio Manager. Fig. 4 describes the new software architecture.

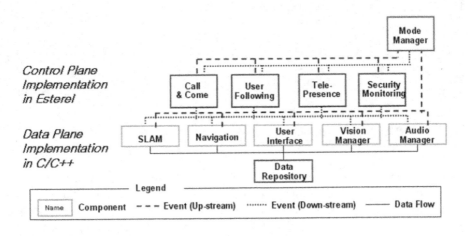

Fig. 4. New SHR100 architecture

---

[3] The size of the Esterel program is around 200 lines. A generated C code from the Esterel program is around 1700 lines. Memory usage and execution speed of the new implementation does not show observable difference from the previous one.

Fig. 5 is a skeleton of the re-implemented CC service in Esterel. A module control_plane (line 1 to line 5) represents a whole control application including the Mode Manager mm, the CC service cc, the UF service uf, and so on (see line 4). Communication among those modules is implemented by using input/output signals declared at line 2 and line 3 (note that the output signals in Fig. 5 invoke the C functions of the same names shown in Fig. 3). COME_CMD and STOP_CMD are input signals corresponding to the "come" and "stop" commands. A "come" command is handled from line 14 to line 18 and a "stop" command is handled from line 19 to line 21. A task of rotating SHR100 toward the user and detecting the user is implemented as a submodule rot_det and is executed at line 16.

```
01:module control_plane:  % Control software
02:    input COME_CMD, STOP_CMD, ...
03:    output STOP, ROTATE, GO, CC_DONE, UF_DONE,...
04:    run mm || run cc || run uf || run tp || run sm ...
05:end module
06:
07:module cc:        % Call and Come service
08:    input COME_CMD, STOP_CMD;
09:    output STOP,ROTATE,GO,CC_DONE,...
10:    signal Reset in
11:        every immediate [COME_CMD or STOP_CMD] do
12:            weak abort
13:                present
14:                case COME_CMD do    % come command
15:                    emit STOP; pause;
16:                    run rot_det;
17:                    ...
18:                    emit CC_DONE;pause;
19:                case STOP_CMD do    % stop command
20:                    emit STOP;
21:                    emit CC_DONE;pause;
22:                end present;
23:            when Reset;
24:        end every
25:    end signal
26:end module
27:...
```

Fig. 5. Skeleton Esterel code for the CC service

As we have seen, the new implementation defines components concretely using modules/submodules. In addition to this, the new implementation makes interaction visible among the components by using explicit communication mechanisms such as input/output signals. These features assign responsibility for the behaviors to these components clearly and it helps to analyze feature interaction problems.

5   Formal Verification of SHR100 Movement

There are various safety properties to assure SHR100's correct operation. In this project, we concentrate on the most critical safety properties, which are about movements that may cause crash with any obstacles (e.g. furniture or users). There can be many causes for collision such as obstacle recognition failure, HW failure to signal actuator, etc. We focused on, however, discrete SW controller which we re-wrote in Esterel. *Stopping behavior* of SHR100 is the first target to verify. Considering that SHR100 can move upto 2 m/s (=7.2 km/h), these properties should be checked carefully for user's safety.

In this section, we describe safety properties P_1, P_2, and P_3 regarding stopping behavior of SHR100. We describe the most primitive safety property P_1 first, then incrementally refine P_1 into P_2 and P_3. Sect. 5.1 describes verification preliminary for SHR100. Sect. 5.2 and Sect. 5.3 illustrate verification of SHR100 running the CC service only. Sect. 5.4 describes verification of SHR100 running CC and UF concurrently. Sect. 5.5 summarizes the verification results. [4]

5.1   Verification Preliminary for SHR100

We used the `xeve` model checker [4] to verify safety properties. First, `xeve` performs bisimulation minimization on FSM which is generated from an Esterel program. Then, a user selects input signals as "always present", "always absent", or "having any value". In addition, a user can specify exclusion relation among input signals (e.g. `COME_CMD` and `STOP_CMD` cannot present at the same time). Finally, the user selects an output signal to check if it can be emitted with given configuration of input signals. Simple properties (e.g. P_1 in Sect. 5.2) can be checked easily in this way. More complex properties (e.g. P_2 in Sect. 5.3 and P_3 in Sect. 5.4) can be checked by building an observer which emits a violation signal when given properties are violated.

Basically, safety properties on stopping behavior can be described using bounded-response formula [5] in temporal logic [16]

$$\Box(C_{stop} \rightarrow \Diamond_d stop)$$

where C_{stop} and *stop* stand for `STOP_CMD` and `STOP` signals in the Esterel implementation. The actual safety properties for robot application, however, are more complex. First, when `STOP` is emitted, `GO` or `ROTATE` must *not* be emitted without any new command. In other words, we also need to check signals *nullifying* `STOP` such as `GO` and `ROTATE`. In addition, we have to check whether output signals are emitted arbitrarily regardless of input signals. For example, if a user does *not* give a command to the robot, the robot must *not* move at all. We could describe a safety property in temporal logic and then translate the property into an Esterel observer following the guideline of [15]. This generates, however, a unnecessarily complex observer. Thus, we developed an observer directly in Esterel without describing and translating a temporal logic property.

---

[4] Preliminary verification results are from [13].

5.2   Verification of the CC Service Without an Observer

First, we checked the CC service without other services. Consider the following property P_1.

> P_1 : If a user does not give a command to the robot, the robot must not move.

Although P_1 looks obvious, this requirement is important to ensure a safe operation of the robot. Violation of P_1 may lead the robot to move autonomously without a user's command and as a result, it can cause damage to house appliances or accidently hurt a man. Furthermore, guaranteeing satisfaction of P_1 is a difficult task without model checking because a developer has to find out all the possible test cases [10].

There are only two output signals to make the robot move - GO and ROTATE. We checked if the CC service satisfied P_1 by setting COME_CMD and STOP_CMD as "always absent" and selecting GO as an output signal to check. Then, xeve showed that GO is *never* emitted by the robot. In the same way, xeve showed that ROTATE is never emitted, either. Thus, we concluded that the CC service satisfied P_1.

Slightly refined property P_1' can be described as follows.

> P_1' : If a user does not give a "come" command, but may give a "stop" command to the robot, the robot does not move.

We can verify that the CC service satisfies P_1' too.

Using a FSM visualization tool atg, we could explore the FSM of the new SHR100 implementation written in Esterel. This FSM exploration helps understand global behavior of SHR100. For example, Fig. 6 depicts the behavior of the CC service. Each transition is labeled with a pair of input/output signals. A present input signal has a prefix ? and an input signal which is not present has a prefix #. A present output signal has a prefix !. An initial state (a doubly circled state at the top left corner) of the CC service has only two outgoing transitions.

- a self transition α :#CM.#ST + #CM.?ST.!STOP.!CC_DONE [5]
- a transition β (going to a lower state) :?CM.!STOP

The first half of α transition (#CM.#ST) indicates that SHR100 does not move without any command, which corresponds to the verification result on P_1. The second half of α transition means that "stop" commands alone do not make the robot move, which corresponds to the verification result on P_1'. Once a "come" command is given, SHR100 takes β transition and traverses the FSM.

---

[5] To increase readability of Fig. 6, we use shorthand notations CM and ST for COME_CMD and STOP_CMD respectively.

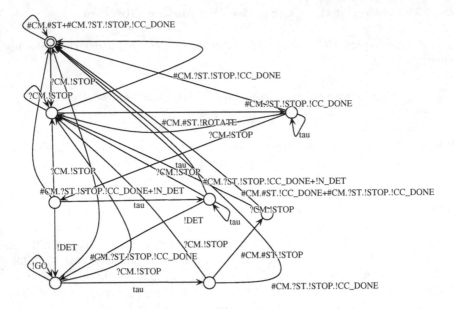

Fig. 6. A FSM for the CC service

5.3 Verification of the CC Service Using an Observer

Consider the property P_2 as below.

> P_2 : *If a user gives a "stop" command, the robot stops and does not move without any new command.*

To verify P_2, we built an observer as in Fig. 7. We incorporated observer with the cc module in parallel. observer emits STOP_VIOLATION at line 9 and line 13 if P_2 is violated. If a "stop" command is given (line 5) and the robot stops immediately (line 6), then observer keeps its watch if the robot rotates or moves forward (line 7 to line 11) unless any new command is given by the user. We verified that STOP_VIOLATION is never emitted.

5.4 Verification of the Concurrent CC and UF Services

We checked if the control software which consists of the CC and UF services satisfied P_1 and P_1'. We showed that the control software satisfied P_1, but surprisingly not P_1'. The verification result on P_1' claimed that ROTATE and GO could be possibly emitted when COME_CMD was absent and STOP_CMD might be given. In general, verification result from xeve is sound but *not* complete because a FSM is generated from an Esterel program without evaluating expressions. [6] Therefore, a user has to check whether a violation is a real one or a false alarm.

---

[6] xeve ignores external C functions as well because the expressions containing return values of external C functions are ignored anyway.

```
01:module observer: % Observer for detecting safety violation
02:     input STOP_CMD, COME_CMD, ROTATE, STOP, GO;
03:     output STOP_VIOLATION;
04:     weak abort
05:         every immediate STOP_CMD do
06:               present STOP then
07:               loop
08:                    present [ROTATE or GO]
09:                    then emit STOP_VIOLATION;
10:                    end present;pause;
11:               end loop;
12:               end present
13:               emit STOP_VIOLATION;
14:         end every
15:     when COME_CMD;
16:end module
```

Fig. 7. An observer for detecting violation of P_2

Through simulations displaying interactions between the CC and UF components, we could figure out that UF made the robot rotate and move forward when a "stop" command was given; the violation was a real one. This violation occurred because UF was triggered by CC_DONE which was emitted by CC when a "come" command or a "stop" command was successfully processed (see Sect. 2.2 and line 18/line 21 of Fig. 5). UF should have been triggered only after a "come" command was processed, not after a "stop" command was processed. Thus, we refined CC_DONE into CC_COME_DONE and CC_STOP_DONE. Then, we modified the UF implementation so that only CC_COME_DONE could invoke UF. After this modification, the concurrent CC and UF services satisfied P_1'.

SAIT had not find this feature interaction problem previously. During UF service, SHR100 does not move unless it succeeds to detect the user. While the user was testing SHR100, he did not intend to be detected by the robot when he gave a "stop" command because he expected the robot to stop, not to start UF service. Thus, the user was usually outside the vision area of SHR100 when he gave a "stop" command. In addition, due to uncertainty of the vision recognizer (e.g. low accuracy in a dark room or with strong light), SHR100 often misses the user. When the robot fails to detect the user, it should report to the user by synthetic voice. It happened, however, that voice synthesis sometimes did not work when running with other components. Therefore, without thorough testing, SAIT simply thought that SHR100 stopped accordingly to a given "stop" command and missed the problem.

We checked if P_2 was satisfied by the revised control software running CC and UF concurrently. We used **observer** in Fig. 7 without modification and verified that the control software satisfied P_2.

Furthermore, we refined P_2 into P_3 by adding a real-time constraint.

P_3 : *If a user gives a "stop" command, the robot stops within one second and does not move without any new command.*

P_3 is more general than P_2 because the robot may not stop immediately with a given "stop" command but within one second due to an urgent situation such as collision avoidance. Temporal property can be encoded in an observer by using the fact that the CC service is invoked every 100 milliseconds (see Sect. 4.2). We verified that the CC and UF services satisfied P_3 after modifying the observer to check this temporal property.

5.5   Experimental Results of the Verification

We used a WindowsXP machine with Pentium IV 2.8C and 1GB memory for the verification. Verification of each property of P_1, P_1', P_2, and P_3 generated around 100 states and took less than ten seconds and 128 MB memory, which was not burdensome to developers. Notice that what we had verified here was a *real implementation*, not an abstract model. We replaced the legacy C/C++ implementation of control software loaded on SHR100 with the Esterel program. After replacing the control software, SHR100 operated successfully with high reliability obtained by formal V&V.

As we have seen through Sect. 5.2 to Sect. 5.4, defining safety properties takes considerable effort. We believe, however, that such effort can reduce an overall development and its field operation costs by increasing the reliability of applications.

6   Conclusion

We have reported our experience of formally developing and verifying a home service robot SHR100. Our task to develop a robot with high reliability was a challenging target due to its own reactive nature and its complexity caused by coordinating diverse components together. The gist of our approach is to re-engineer a robot application to formally develop and verify *the core* for increased reliability. Through the re-engineering process, we found and fixed several subtle bugs which would be uncovered otherwise. In addition, we could demonstate that formal V&V was useful to identify feature interaction problems which were hard to detect through traditional testing. Furthermore, the new SHR100 implementation re-written in Esterel became compact and easy to analyze due to its clear component definitions and explicit communication mechanisms.

References

1. Esterel technology. http://www.esterel-technologies.com.
2. Honda asimo home page. http://asimo.honda.com/.

3. Sony qrio home page. http://www.sony.net/SonyInfo/QRIO/top_nf.html.
4. A.Bouali. Xeve: an esterel verification environment. Technical report, INRIA, 2000.
5. R. Alur and T. Henzinger. Time for logic. *ACM SIGACT News*, 22(3), 1991.
6. G. Berry. The foundations of esterel. *Proof, Language and Interaction: Essays in Honour of Robin Milner*, 2000.
7. J. Borrelly, E. Coste-Maniére, B. Espiau, K. Kapellos, R. Pissard-Gibollet, D. Simon, and N. Turro. The orccad architecture. *International Journal of Robotics Research*, 17(4):338–359, 1998.
8. E. Coste-Maniére and N. Turro. The maestro language and its environment : Specification, validation and control of robotic missions. *Proceedings of the 10th IEEE/RSJ International Conference on Intelligent Robots and Systems*, 1997.
9. A. C. Domínguez-Brito, D. Hernández-Sosa, J. Isern-González, and J. Cabrera-Gámez. Integrating robotics software. *IEEE International Conference on Robotics and Automation*, 2004.
10. E.M.Clarke, O.Grumberg, and D.A.Peled. *Model Checking*. MIT Press, January 2000.
11. B. Espiau, K. Kapellos, and M. Jourdan. Formal verification in robotics: Why and how? *International Symposium on Robotics Research*, Oct 1995.
12. G.H. Holzmann and M.H. Smith. Automating software feature verification. *Bell Labs Technical Journal*, 5(2):72–87, 2000.
13. M. Kim, K. Kang, and H. Lee. Formal verification of robot movements - a case study on home service robot shr100. *International Conference on Robotics and Automation*, 2005.
14. M. Kim, J. Lee, K. Kang, Y. Hong, and S. Bang. Re-engineering software architecture of home service robots: A case study. *International Conference on Software Engineering*, 2005.
15. L. J. Jagadeesan, C. Puchol, and J. E. Von Olnhausen. Safety property verification of Esterel programs and applications to telecommunications software. In P. Wolper, editor, *Proceedings of the 7th International Conference On Computer Aided Verification*, pages 127–140, Liege, Belgium, 1995.
16. Z. Manna and A. Pnueli. *The Temporal Logic of Reactive and Concurrent Systems: Specification*. Springer-Verlag, New York, 1992.
17. R.T. Pack, D. Mitchell Wilkes, and K. Kawamura. A software architecture for integrated service robot development. *IEEE Internationall Conference on Systems, Man and Cybernetics*, 1997.
18. L.E. Pinzon, H.-M. Hanisch, M.A. Jafari, and T. Boucher. A comparative study of synthesis methods for discrete event controllers. *Formal Methods in System Design*, 15(2):123–267, 1999.

Model Checking Real Time Java
Using Java PathFinder

Gary Lindstrom[1], Peter C. Mehlitz[2], and Willem Visser[2]

[1] University of Utah
[2] NASA Ames Research Center

Abstract. The *Real Time Specification for Java* (RTSJ) is an augmentation of Java for real time applications of various degrees of hardness. The central features of RTSJ are real time threads; user defined schedulers; asynchronous events, handlers, and control transfers; a priority inheritance based default scheduler; non-heap memory areas such as *immortal* and *scoped*, and non-heap real time threads whose execution is not impeded by garbage collection. The Robust Software Systems group at NASA Ames Research Center has JAVA PATHFINDER (JPF) under development, a Java model checker. JPF at its core is a state exploring JVM which can examine alternative paths in a Java program (e.g., via backtracking) by trying all nondeterministic choices, including thread scheduling order. This paper describes our implementation of an RTSJ profile (subset) in JPF, including requirements, design decisions, and current implementation status. Two examples are analyzed: jobs on a multiprogramming operating system, and a complex resource contention example involving autonomous vehicles crossing an intersection. The utility of JPF in finding logic and timing errors is illustrated, and the remaining challenges in supporting all of RTSJ are assessed.

1 Overview

The possibility of using Real Time Specification for Java (RTSJ) [fJEG] software on future missions is under consideration at NASA, for all the familiar reasons: standardized (i.e., platform independent) semantics, a rich and vigorous marketplace of implementations and tools, and the overall software engineering advantages of Java as a type safe object-oriented programming language. RTSJ is not based on any Java core language extensions; rather, all its capabilities are conveyed by new classes with special semantics, albeit with some refinement of semantics for existing Java classes. This design decision in effect strikes a bargain: less run time predictability, in exchange for language stability. An alternative choice might have been to enhance the declarative content of the language in the interest of stronger compile time program validation, as was done for example with exceptions in Java.

The dual consequence of this design decision is inadequacy of static analysis for RTSJ software verification and validation, and a corresponding vital need for techniques performing dynamic analysis, e.g., model checking. In particular,

D.A. Peled and Y.-K. Tsay (Eds.): ATVA 2005, LNCS 3707, pp. 444–456, 2005.

many of the dynamic features of RTSJ are beyond the scope of current worst-case execution time (WCET) analysis techniques. While RTSJ programmers can in principle restrict themselves to an RTSJ subset amendable to WCET analysis, this would significantly reduce the appeal and advantages of using RTSJ over existing real time languages. We report here on an application of the JAVA PATHFINDER model checker (JPF) [VHB+03, JPFa] to RTSJ programs, focusing on the latter's dynamic, time quantified behavior, with the goal of developing a tool capable of validating RTSJ applications, ideally to the level of mission deployability. Our approach emphasizes the central issue of temporal correctness (e.g., threads meeting deadlines) under nondeterministic choices; correctness of memory usages and asynchronous control flow are reserved for future work. Thus we are focusing on *classical* correctness issues in real time software, rather than issues related to specialized JVM behavior.

Our approach uses discrete event simulation (DES) as a basis for modeling time. Real time threads are modeled as ordinary Java threads, constrained to run one at a time, i.e., as *coroutine*'s. Their interactions, e.g., through CPU scheduling, are modeled by resource contention techniques familiar to DES programming (a summary of DES concepts is given in §3). This permits execution of programs within our RTSJ profile on any Java implementation.

However, two important capabilities are provided by analyzing (running) RTSJ programs under JPF: (a) execution cost logging at the bytecode level, and (b) alternative execution path exploration via nondeterministic choice selection. Point (a) permits closing an important causality loop impossible on an ordinary JVM:

$$thread\ execution\ cost \rightarrow deadline\ misses \rightarrow miss\ events \rightarrow$$
$$event\ handlers \rightarrow additional\ thread\ execution\ cost$$

Analyzing such loops is a critical requirement in the validation and verification of complex RTSJ applications, and is well beyond the capability of current static analyzers.

2   RTSJ Under JPF: Requirements and Objectives

The first question is clearly *what does it mean to model check an RTSJ program?* The starting point is to view the RTSJ program as just another Java program (albeit with a class library with special semantics), and simply execute it using the model checking vigilance of JPF. This is fine, except that this presumes the availability of an RTSJ enabled JVM within JPF, which we do not have.

Unlike a simple Java program, in which the notion of time generally plays an insignificant role, time in RTSJ programs plays a major correctness role, e.g., in quantifying real time deadlines. Moreover, an RTSJ program (the *embedded* program) must be exercised within an implementation of its environment (the *embedding* program). In our view, specifying, constructing and verifying such environments are often tasks of difficulty equal to or greater than that of the embedded system. An example is a flight control system, where a fully accurate embedding system must model all the dynamics of the aircraft, as is done in a flight simulator. Hence ensuring that embedding code is correct is as important (or more so) than ensuring that the embedded code is correct.

We adopted the following goals for model checking RTSJ under JPF:

1. Make no changes to the JPF implementation – clearly, a major software engineering win if achievable.
2. Implement the embedding code in Java, and model check the entire combined system – a major validation win if possible.
3. Deal with time through DES modeling – a familiar and well understood technology.
4. Implement all RTSJ thread interactions (e.g., priority based scheduling with priority inversion avoidance via priority inheritance) through resource contention techniques traditional to DES.
5. Exploit the run time cost accounting capabilities of JPF to detect deadline misses by real time threads, and to take appropriate actions, e.g., invoking overrun handlers in the embedded code.
6. Finally, utilize the path coverage capabilities of JPF to locate bugs involving nondeterminacy and race conditions, notably nondeterministic choice points in the embedding code providing greater test coverage.

3   Step 1: RTSJ in a Simulation Environment

The first step in model checking RTSJ is to implement a profile of RTSJ as a set of conventional Java classes. This we have done to a first level of realism – several features have yet to be implemented, as discussed in §10. The classes in our implementation include RealtimeThread, PriorityScheduler, AsyncEvent, AsyncEventHandler, OneShotTimer, PeriodicTimer and RelativeTime.

The fundamental concepts of DES (as developed in the Simula system of the 1970's [BDMN73]) can be summarized as follows:

– Individual *processes* (the traditional terminology – henceforth we will use *thread*) are conceptually concurrent, but in fact execute in an interleaved fashion as coroutines, as mentioned above.
– A thread may be *executing*, *activated*, or *passivated*.
  • An *executing* thread is the one currently running as a coroutine;
  • An *activated* thread is not executing, but is scheduled to do so in the future at a time indicated its event notice on the simulation's event list.
  • A *passivated* thread is neither executing nor active; such threads are typically waiting for some condition to become true, such as being granted a resource.
– Scheduling operations on threads include *activate* (schedule), *passivate*, and *hold*, which is a compound operation comprising activation at a later scheduled time time, and passivation.

- The main thread controls the overall simulation by repeatedly dequeueing from the event list the event notice with the earliest event time, advancing the simulation clock to the time in that event notice, and notifying the associated thread to run – until the event list becomes empty, or a global shutdown operation is invoked.

Since RealtimeThread's are constrained to run as coroutines, the JVM scheduler has only one scheduling choice possible, and DES event based scheduling is used in an *outboard* manner to orchestrate thread interleaving. As mentioned in §2, all RealtimeThread interactions are achieved by contention for Resource objects, e.g., a *CPU*. The upshot is that no changes are necessary to the schedulers of the underlying JVM or JPF to implement scheduling policies such as priority inheritance with FIFO ordering within priorities, as required by the default RTSJ scheduler. Since Java's real time clock is replaced by the simulation clock, all RTSJ executions in this implementation are deterministic (repeatable), even if they use pseudo random methods to draw numbers from probability distributions (assuming fixed seeds) or offer the option of pseudo randomly selecting orders of events scheduled at identical times.

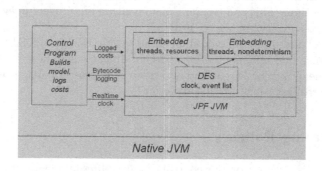

Fig. 1. RTSJ architecture under JPF

4   Step 2: Combining RTSJ and JPF

Embedded code written in our RTSJ profile, together with its embedding test code using DES facilities including simulated time, comprise an ordinary Java program that can be run under any Java implementation (without accurate run time modeling, however). The next step is to run the combined program under JPF, with the following additional benefits:

- *Nondeterministic state exploration*, including all orderings of equal priority events scheduled for the same instant, and choice points in the embedding code, and
- *Cost accounting*, with overrun detection and invocation of appropriate handlers, as described below.

Our adaptation of JPF is being done in two stages. The first stage exploits two customization features already available in JPF: its JVM *listener interface* [JPFb], and its *Model Java Interface* (MJI) [JPFc] (both features are utilized in the *Control Program* box in Fig. 1).

JVM listener interface: Logging run time (albeit idealized) for Java code under JPF can be done using JPF's JVM listener interface, which invokes control program listener methods on various occurrences, including the execution of each byte code instruction. We use a very simple accounting technique here, whereby each byte code is assigned a fixed run time in a look up table. By this technique the execution time (summed byte code costs) from the start to the end of a RealtimeThread can be accumulated. Similarly, this interface is used to detect execution path backtracking by the JPF JVM, so that path specific accounting data structures can be correspondingly backtracked.

Model Java interface: The MJI interface permits Java code executing under JPF's specialized JVM to access the underlying JVM for access to native facilities. This turns out to be crucial in arranging that run time cost logging, which executes *outside* the JPF JVM, is accessible to the RTSJ application code, which executes *within* the JPF JVM. For example, suppose an AsyncEventHandler invocation has a run time in excess of its stipulated limit, as observed through an MJI native method. This can trigger the invocation of an *overrun event handler*, which must execute within the JPF JVM.

The second and more difficult stage of adapting JPF for RTSJ concerns features that must be implemented by JVM modifications. These features, which include non-heap memory areas and non-heap real time threads, as well as asynchronous control transfers, are discussed in §7.1.

5   Scheduling Policies

We now give more details on our control of scheduling by means of resource contention policies. We illustrate our approach by discussion of five representative policies: *FIFO, priority, priority inheritance, priority ceiling,* and *preemption.* The first two are naive policies inviting priority inversion; the third is obligatory in RTSJ's default scheduler; the fourth is an explicit option, and the RTSJ specification is silent on the fifth.

1) *FIFO:* This simplistic policy guarantees fairness, but ignores thread priority.

2) *Priority:* Here threads waiting for a resource are selected by (fixed) priority first, and then by FIFO within equal priorities. This policy, as well as FIFO above, provides no defense against priority inversion.

3) *Priority inheritance* (PI): This well known policy works by increasing the priority of the thread possessing a PI resource to equal the maximum priority of any thread waiting for that resource (its *dynamic priority*). There are two perhaps unobvious consequences of this policy:

1. Since a thread may possess multiple resources, its dynamic priority is based on the maximum priority of any thread waiting for any of the resources it possesses, and
2. The priorities involved are of course dynamic priorities, so an attempted seize of a resource held by a thread waiting for another resource can cause cascaded priority inheritance effects (and conversely for release's).

4) *Priority ceiling* (PC): A PC resource has a fixed priority (its *ceiling priority*) which is used to temporarily elevate the priority of any thread possessing it. If a thread has a dynamic priority greater than the resource's ceiling priority, an attempt to seize the resource causes a PriorityCeilingException to be thrown (the absence of which is an important verification condition).

5) *Preemption*: A resource managed under this policy does not change a thread's priority when seized. A thread seizing a resource of this kind only waits if the resource is currently held, and the thread's priority is less than or equal to the priority of the thread holding the resource. If the thread's priority is greater that that of the thread holding the resource, it *steals* the resource.

Modeling the first four policies is straightforward DES programming. Preemption is a bit trickier, because possession periods (e.g., modeling computational activity by a thread using a CPU resource) can be prematurely ended when the resource is stolen by a higher priority thread. This can be implemented by wrapping such hold method calls in loops that sum actual hold times, and re-exert hold invocations until the stipulated hold time is attained. All five policy implementations easily generalize to multiprocessing systems by managing pools of CPU resources.

6   Applications

We now discuss application of our RTSJ implementation in JPF to two example programs. The first is a simple model of a multiprogramming operating system (OS), while the second is a complex resource contention example involving autonomous cars crossing an intersection. The utility of JPF in finding logic and timing errors in each is illustrated.

6.1   Multiprogramming Operating System

This example models a simple multiprogramming computer system, where jobs (as RealtimeThread's) contend for a CPU, which is a resource of one of the five types discussed in §5. Of these, *preemption* is the most interesting, because (i) it guarantees absence of priority inversion, (ii) it is pervasive in modern operating systems, (iii) its behavior on realistic job mixes defies static analysis, and consequently (iv) real time OS's typically do not employ it, despite the appeal of (i).

A fixed job mix was analyzed using our RTSJ implementation in JFP, using CPU's of each of our five resource types. The results are given in Fig. 2. In

CPU	Job1 (6)	Job2 (5)	Job3 (4)	Job4 (3)	Time
FIFO	3681 / 72% / 6.0	3780 / 73% / 5.0	3879 / 74% / 4.0	3979 / 74% / 3.0	3979
Priority	1891 / 46% / 6.0	1990 / 49% / 5.0	3880 / 74% / 4.0	3979 / 74% / 3.0	3979
PC (6)	1891 / 46% / 6.0	1990 / 49% / 5.2	3880 / 74% / 4.5	3979 / 74% / 3.7	3979
PI	1891 / 46% / 6.0	1990 / 49% / 5.2	3880 / 74% / 4.0	3979 / 74% / 3.2	3979
Preempt	1004 / 0% / 6.0	2008 / 49% / 5.0	3012 / 66% / 4.0	4015 / 74% / 3.0	4015

Fig. 2. Multiprogramming results, by resource type. The parenthesized number in for each job indicates its priority. Columns for each job indicate its duration in simulated milliseconds, followed by its percentage wait time and average priority. *Time* is the completion time of the entire job mix, in simulated milliseconds.

this scenario, there are four jobs that are identical in behavior (10 compute / wait cycles), with identical wait times between cycles. They are all started at time zero. This simple *stress test* keeps the CPU 99% busy independent of its resource type (the simulation ends after the last job terminates). The following observations can be made of the results in Fig. 2:

- The *FIFO* CPU gives the most fair service to the four jobs – because it ignores priority.
- The *Priority*, *Priority Ceiling*, and *Priority Inheritance* CPUs deliver identical service, because the priority of a job only affects its competitive position when more than one job is waiting for the CPU, which does not occur in this simple scenario (an example of priority improving service is given in §6.2).
- Jobs under the *Preemptable* CPU finish strictly according to priority. However, the overall completion time is slightly longer, due to the additional scheduling overhead.

When run under JPF with nondeterminism turned on, there are 4! = 24 choices for activation order at time zero for the four jobs (the statistically rare case of events scheduled at exactly the same time does not occur after simulation start). Priority inversion was detected in all 24 paths under *FIFO* and *Priority* CPUs, and on no paths under *Priority Ceiling (6)*, *Priority Inheritance*, and *Preemptable* CPUs.

6.2   Intersection Crossing

The example in §6.1 emphasizes the effect of role of resource types in thread scheduling. Our second application is a more complex example, illustrating more advanced features of our RTSJ implementation in JPF. This models autonomous cars transiting an intersection, where the cars (real time threads) can drive straight through, turn right, or turn left. Cars are given priorities chosen from 1 to 8.

The intersection is modeled by four sectors (*NW*, *NE*, *SW*, *SE*), each of which is a resource. For a car driving north, turning right requires possession

Sector type	Car 0 (5/N/S)	Car 1 (2/S/L)	Car 2 (8/E/L)
FIFO	33 / 0%	183 / 18%	49 / 21%
Priority	33 / 0%	183 / 18%	49 / 21%
PC(8)	25 / 0%	63 / 40%	45 / 15%
PI	30 / 0%	180 / 16%	46 / 17%

Fig. 3. Intersection results using four sector resource types. (5/N/S) indicates that *Car 0* has priority 5, is heading north, and going straight, etc. *Car 0* and *Car 1* start at time 0; *Car 2* has a start delay of 5 seconds. The figures in each column are completion time in seconds, and percentage wait time.

of sector *SE*; driving straight requires *SE* and *NE* (granted simultaneously, to avoid deadlock; *SE* is released half way through), and turning left involves (i) seizing *SE* and *NE* together; (ii) releasing *SE*, (iii) seizing *NW*, (iv) releasing *NE* and *NW*. The net effect is a model of an uncontrolled intersection of two lane roads, where cars follow the common conventions that a car can drive straight through if the car on its left (if any) is not driving straight through or turning left, the car on its right (if any) is not driving either straight, left or right, and the opposing car (if any) is not turning left.

These rules are complex but deadlock free, which as been confirmed (for specific scenarios) by exhaustive search using JPF on initial event scheduling orders. By comparison, deadlocks caused by the naive policy of seizing all of *SE*, *NE*, and *NW* for a northbound car making a left turn (and correspondingly for cars heading in other directions) were quickly located by JPF.

Car speed is governed by car priority, in the following manner. The time required by a car to transit a sector is $t = 100 \ sec/p$, where p is the car's priority. At the extremes, $p = 1$ yields a sector transit time of 100 seconds, and $p = 8$ yields 12.5 seconds. Experiments were run using four resource types for sectors: *FIFO*, *priority*, *priority ceiling* 8, and *priority inheritance*. There are ready intuitions for each of these cases: *FIFO* is round robin, *priority* is fastest vehicle first, *priority ceiling* is a minimum sector speed, and *priority inheritance* is when one sees an ambulance rapidly approaching, and speeds up accordingly. The *preemption* case is physically impossible!

Sample results are shown in Fig. 3. Note that all cars benefit from higher priority under *priority ceiling*, and marginally so under *priority inheritance*.

The utility of run time cost logging under JPF was demonstrated by giving each car a maximum lifetime (its *release deadline* in RTSJ's vocabulary). If the deadline is set uniformly at 75 seconds, under *priority inheritance* the RTSJ *miss handler* for *Car 1* is invoked, but not for *Cars 0* or *Car 2*.

The above analysis can be accomplished under both native Java and JPF, since it is based solely on simulated time. By contrast, analysis of *miss handler* behavior in RTSJ programs can only be exercised under JPF, where a listener method in our control program records each byte code execution in the subject program. To demonstrate this capability, an onboard computer was postulated for each car (its *autonomous* controller), and a *cycle soaker* method was invoked during passage through each sector (arbitrarily set at 100,000 double divides, with 100 nanosecond cost per byte code; a total of 1,400,024 DDIV's are observed in the deterministic case). If a cost limit of 350 milliseconds is imposed, under *priority inheritance Car 0* terminates without handler invocation, *Car 2* terminates with cost overrun handler invocation, and *Car 1* terminates with both handlers invoked.

7   Critique of JPF

This application breaks new ground for JAVA PATHFINDER in its focus on quantified time as a program correctness issue. Much as been learned about its flexibility in supporting this new and unanticipated correctness dimension, as well as the limits of our approach that implements RTSJ without making any modifications to JPF.

7.1   Features Not Easily Implemented Under This Approach

In §4 we indicated two areas pose more difficult challenges, which we believe can only be implemented by JVM modification:

- ScopedMemoryArea's and NoHeapRealtimeThread's, which deal with non garbage collected MemoryArea's, and
- Asynchronous transfers of control (ATC), e.g., threads that implement the Interruptible interface and methods that throw AsynchronouslyInterruptedException.

While it may be possible in principle to implement at least the first these features using per-bytecode analysis in a JPF listener method, the overhead of this approach is likely to be prohibitive.

7.2   Opportunities for Application of Other JPF Features

This project thus far has used only basic JAVA PATHFINDER features. Several advanced features of JPF offer attractive opportunities for increased utility in verifying RTSJ programs.

Heuristic search: The default program path exploration strategy is depth first search, using backtracking. Other strategies, such as bounded breadth-first search, can selectively search longer paths due to elimination of the backtrack stack [GV04]. Several criteria for preferring paths in RTSJ programs with higher error potential are evident, such as favoring states with threads whose extrapolated completion time is beyond their stipulated deadlines.

State abstraction: By default JPF saves all previously encountered program states and performs precise equality checks to detect re-encountered states. This policy has several consequences, including (i) significant space overhead, and (ii) inability to recognize states that insignificantly vary from previously seen states.

In particular, the extremely fine representation of time in RTSJ (to nanosecond precision), exacerbates (ii). To illustrate, consider state abstraction methods focusing on the core data structure of our system, the scheduled event list. Opportunities for abstraction here include *fuzz* on scheduled event times, e.g., equality to resolution of say 100 nanoseconds, or even ignoring event times altogether, and considering two event lists to be equal if they reference the same real time threads positioned at the same execution point (say, method and byte code address).

Symbolic execution: JPF interfaces to a constraint system that can solve equations involving linear inequalities [SKV03]. This presents the possibility of asserting constraints on scheduled event times.

- For example, it could be asserted that event e_1 should run at time $t_0 + t(e_2)$, where $t(e)$ is the scheduled time of an event e, and $t(e_2)$ is not yet known, i.e., is symbolic. When $t(e_2)$ becomes bound, e_1 would be scheduled at a concrete time.
- Now suppose two scheduled events e_1 and e_2 have symbolic event times $t(e_1)$ and $t(e_2)$, and the event list is otherwise empty. We then have two options to pursue nondeterministically: (a) e_1 runs next, $t(e_1) \leq t(e_2)$ is asserted, and the simulation clock is set (symbolically) to $t(e_1)$, or (b) symmetrically, e_2 runs next, $t(e_2) \leq t(e_1)$ is asserted, and the simulation clock is set to $t(e_2)$.

Fault driven automatic test case generation: The execution driven symbolic constraint refinement technique just sketched can be the basis for finding necessary and sufficient conditions that lead to specific faults [VPK04]. For example, suppose the real time code is modeling the performance of an aircraft pre-landing checklist. There have been published accident scenarios where a mandatory aircraft response, e.g., completion of landing gear deployment, did not occur in time to ensure the safety of the next step in the checklist, and the pilot under time pressure (the ground is approaching) inappropriately proceeded [Deg04]. Conditions revealing such flaws in real time checklist procedures might be determined by symbolic execution in this manner.

8 Performance

We now present performance figures for our RTSJ profile implementation in JPF. All performance figures are taken from executions in the Eclipse Java IDE with a heap size of one gigabyte on a Pentium 2 laptop with 768MB of RAM.

Our system can be run in five modes: native Java with deterministic or pseudo random choice selection, or JPF with deterministic, pseudo random, or nondeterministic choice selection. We have tested our system in all five modes on the applications presented in §6. Run time figures for the multiprocessing operating system example in § 6.1 under deterministic mode are 120ms for native Java vs. 6,257ms under JPF (the pseudo random mode numbers are analogous). These absolute numbers are not important; instead, their relative magnitudes are more informative. Two observations emerge: (a) the native Java implementation is quite fast, and (b) the JPF implementation is slower by a factor of about 50 – but it must be remembered that under JPF an interpretive JVM (written in Java) is being employed, cost logging presents a linear execution time overhead, and state saving is performed to support exploration of alternative execution paths (not exploited in the deterministic and pseudo random cases).

CPU type	Run time
FIFO	79.4 sec
Priority	80.9 sec
PC(6)	91.6 sec
PI	99.6 sec
Preemptable	106.2 sec

Fig. 4. Run times for the multiprogramming example under JPF nondeterministic search (backtracking over 24 paths)

To illustrate the cost of JPF state exploration, the CPU example was run under nondeterminism, exploring the $4! = 24$ choices for activation order at time zero for the four jobs discussed in § 6.1 Results are shown in Fig. 4.

9   Related Work

Model checking of timed automata representations has become very popular ([BLR05]; see [BY04] for a good overview) for the analysis of real time systems. Our approach differs in that we are analyzing systems with complex transitions but simple explicit timing information, whereas in the timed automata approach is typically applied to analyze systems with complex timing, but simple transitions (e.g., between abstract states in given time intervals). By contrast we are performing genuine program execution (not abstracted, or symbolic). The notion of applying timed automata style reasoning is appealing, but represents a major new line of research, due to the complex transitions in our program executions, e.g. memory allocation, exception handling, etc.). Our emphasis at present is checking program safety properties including scheduling errors such as priority inversion, as well as classic Java errors such as uncaught exceptions and assertion violations.

It has been reported that more than 3000 people have used the RTSJ reference implementation or a commercial RTSJ-compliant JVM to create application prototypes [Loc04]. Tools are available to benchmark RTSJ implementations [CS02].

Model checking is a vigorously evolving research area. Bandera [Ban], Bogor [DHHR05], and the work of Bart Jacobs et al. on *JavaCard* verification [JMR04] are examples of model checking applied to Java programs. A closely related area is run time verification of Java systems [KKLS01]. Capability for dealing with time in model checkers has also been evolving rapidly, often through monitoring of event sequences with respect to assertions in linear time logic (LTL) [Hav]. RTSJ itself is drawing critical and insightful analysis, such as the work on Ravenscar [Bur, Wel04].

Finally, the advent of the Java Platform Debugger Architecture (JPDA) offers the potential of greatly improved flexibility and performance for our dual JVM implementation strategy. However, major research issues are presented by implementing state saving and backtracking under this approach. Moreover, the challenges of implementing the RTSJ features missing in our system, e.g., memory varieties and ATC, would still be present — unless an RTSJ compliant JVM could be obtained that supports JDPA, which seems unlikely.

10   Status and Continuing Work

Our implementation of RTSJ within a DES environment is operational, including RealtimeThread's, AsyncEvent's and AsyncEventHandler's, cost overrun handlers, binding of external happenings to events, simulated and real time Clock's, and various timers, e.g., OneShotTimer and PeriodicTimer, and PhysicalMemoryArea's. API documentation including designation of individual classes and methods not implemented is publicly available [Lin]. Continuing work includes:

1. Maximizing the RTSJ profile we can implement without JVM modification,
2. Development of a more realistic, calibrated execution cost model, taking into account effects of garbage collection, JIT compilation, class loading, etc.,
3. Development of more challenging test cases, with assessment of the scalability of RTSJ under JPF,
4. Extending JPF's JVM (written Java) to include the remaining crucial RTSJ features summarized in § 7.1 (probably using Ravenscar's profile as a guide), and
5. Perhaps most importantly, exploiting advanced JPF features to increase the scale of RTSJ systems that can be analyzed, through techniques as discussed in § 7.2.

Acknowledgements

Michael R. Lowry conceived this project and is providing the resources. The critical comments of Robert E. Filman are gratefully acknowledged.

References

[Ban]   http://bandera.projects.cis.ksu.edu/.
[BDMN73]   G. M. Birtwistle, O.-J. Dahl, B Myhrhaug, and K. Nygaard. *Simula BEGIN*. Auerbach/Studentliteratur, Philadelphia, 1973.
[BLR05]   Gerd Behrmann, Kim G. Larsen, and Jacob I. Rasmussen. Optimal scheduling using priced timed automata. *ACM SIGMETRICS Performance Evaluation Review*, 32(4):34–40, March 2005.

[Bur]   Alan Burns. The Ravenscar profile. http://polaris.dit.upm.es/~ork/
               documents/RP_spec.pdf.
[BY04]   Johan Bengtsson and Wang Yi. Timed automata: Semantics, algorithms
               and tools. In W. Reisig and G. Rozenberg, editors, *Lecture Notes on
               Concurrency and Petri Nets*. Springer-Verlag, 2004. LNCS 3098.
[CS02]   Angelo Corsaro and Douglas C. Schmidt. Evaluating Real-Time Java
               features and performance for real-time embedded systems. In *Proc. 8th
               Real-Time and Embedded Technology and Applications Symposium*. IEEE
               Computer Society, September 24-27, 2002.
[Deg04]   Asaf Degani. *Taming HAL: Designing Interfaces Beyond 2001*. Palgrave
               Macmillan, 2004.
[DHHR05]   Matthew B. Dwyer, John Hatcliff, Matthew Hoosier, and Robby. Build-
               ing your own model checker using the Bogor extensible model checking
               framework. In *In Proc. 17th Conference on Computer-Aided Verification
               (CAV 2005)*, 2005.
[fJEG]   The Real-Time for Java^{TM} Expert Group. https://rtsj.dev.java.net.
[GV04]   A. Groce and W. Visser. Heuristics for model checking Java programs.
               International Journal on Software Tools for Technology Transfer, 2004.
[Hav]   Klaus Havelund. Eagle Flier, a rule-based runtime verification framework.
               http://yangtze.cs.uiuc.edu/~ksen/eagle/.
[JMR04]   B. Jacobs, C. Marche, and N. Rauch. Formal verification of a commercial
               smart card applet with multiple tools. In C. Rattray, S. Maharaj, and
               C. Shankland, editors, *Algebraic Methodology and Software Technology
               (AMAST'04)*, pages 21–22. Springer LNCS 3116 2004.
[JPFa]   http://javapathfinder.sourceforge.net/.
[JPFb]   http://ase.arc.nasa.gov/jpf/Listeners.html.
[JPFc]   MJI – the Model Java Interface, http://ase.arc.nasa.gov/jpf/MJI.html.
[KKLS01]   Moonjoo Kim, Sampath Kannan, Insup Lee, and Oleg Sokolsky. Java-
               MaC: a run-time assurance tool for Java. In *First International Workshop
               on Run-time Verification*. Paris, France, July 23, 2001. Electronic Notes
               in Theoretical Computer Science, vol. 55 No. 2.
[Lin]   Gary Lindstrom. RTSJ-JPF API. http://www.cs.utah.edu/~gary/RTSJ/
               doc/.
[Loc04]   C. Douglass Locke. Real-Time Java moving into the mainstream. *RTC
               Journal*, January 2004.
[SKV03]   C. S. Parareanu S. Khurshid and W. Visser. Generalized symbolic exe-
               cution for model checking and testing. In *Proceedings of TACAS*, April
               2003.
[VHB$^+$03]   W. Visser, K. Havelund, G. Brat, S. Park, and F. Lerda. Model checking
               programs. *Automated Software Engineering Journal*, 10(2), April 2003.
[VPK04]   Willem Visser, Corina S. Pasareanu, and Sarfraz Khurshid. Test input
               generation with Java PathFinder. In *Proceedings of ISSTA*, July 2004.
[Wel04]   Andy Wellings. *Concurrent and Real-Time Programming in Java*. John
               Wiley & Sons, Ltd., Chichester, West Sussex, England, 2004.

Using Parametric Automata for the Verification of the Stop-and-Wait Class of Protocols*

Guy Edward Gallasch and Jonathan Billington

Computer Systems Engineering Centre, University of South Australia,
Mawson Lakes Campus, SA 5095, Australia
guy.gallasch@postgrads.unisa.edu.au
jonathan.billington@unisa.edu.au

Abstract. The Stop-and-Wait protocol (SWP) has two (unbounded) parameters: the maximum sequence number (MaxSeqNo) and the maximum number of retransmissions (MaxRetrans). Our aim is to verify this protocol for all possible values of these parameters. Model checking such a system requires considering an infinite family of state spaces (reachability graphs). We firstly show that the size of these state spaces is linear in MaxSeqNo and quartic in MaxRetrans. This leads us to develop a symbolic representation for the reachability graphs which can be viewed as a symbolic Finite State Automaton (FSA). We apply automata reduction techniques directly to the symbolic FSA to obtain a language equivalent FSA representing the sequences of externally visible events. This FSA is independent of the parameters. We confirm that this is language equivalent to the Stop-and-Wait service of alternating send and receive events. The results are significant as we have: 1. a novel algebraic representation of the infinite set of reachability graphs and their related FSAs of our SWP model; and 2. verified conformance of the SWP to its service, for *all* values of the unbounded MaxSeqNo parameter.

Keywords: Stop and Wait Protocols, Symbolic Reachability Graphs, Symbolic Automata, Coloured Petri Nets, Language Equivalence, Parametric Verification.

1 Introduction

Stop-and-Wait is an elementary form of flow control [22,23] used by communication protocols to prevent buffer overflow in the receiver. After sending a message, the sender must stop and wait for an acknowledgement from the receiver before it can send the next message. When the Stop-and-Wait Protocol (SWP) operates over noisy channels, acknowledgements are also used for transmission error recovery. In this case, a checksum is used to detect transmission errors in the message or acknowledgement. If an error is detected, the message (or acknowledgement) is discarded. A timeout/retransmission scheme, such as Automatic

---

* Partially supported by Australian Research Council (ARC) Discovery Grant DP0559927 and Linkage International Grant LX04544639, and the French-Australian Science and Technology programme FR040062.

D.A. Peled and Y.-K. Tsay (Eds.): ATVA 2005, LNCS 3707, pp. 457–473, 2005.

Repeat ReQuest [23], is used to recover from this loss. Sequence numbers are used to detect (and then discard) duplicates of previous messages.

The Stop-and-Wait mechanism forms the basis of many practical data transfer protocols, such as the Internet's Transmission Control Protocol (TCP) [21]. An understanding of how these mechanisms work and how they may fail is essential for the verification of more complex protocols like TCP. These protocols have a number of parameters, such as the maximum sequence number (MaxSeqNo) or the maximum number of retransmissions (MaxRetrans). The value of these parameters may vary depending on the application (e.g. TCP has a 32 bit sequence number, whereas others may use a 3 bit sequence number). It is thus of interest to verify these protocols for all values of these parameters.

Petri nets have proven to be a suitable formal method for protocol verification [4, 5, 13, 14, 16, 17, 20, 27]. A Coloured Petri net (CPN) [15, 18] model of the SWP, parameterised by MaxSeqNo and MaxRetrans, was developed and analysed in [6, 7, 8] following the *protocol verification methodology* presented in [8]. Because the model parameters are unbounded there is an infinite set of CPN models to verify. One of the properties of interest is conformance of the SWP to the Stop-and-Wait *service* of alternating send and receive events using *language equivalence*. However, using our methodology, we were only able to verify conformance using automated *language analysis* [11] for small parameter values due to the state explosion problem [25]. Thus we were motivated to find a way to verify the SWP for any finite (but unbounded) value of the parameters.

Related work on parametric verification considers only the MaxRetrans parameter. Abdulla et al [1] consider a single infinite OG, rather than an infinite set of finite OGs, for unbounded retransmissions, with MaxSeqNo = 1, corresponding to the Alternating Bit Protocol (ABP). It also analyses a variant of the ABP called the Bounded Retransmission Protocol, modelled with a nondeterministic value of MaxRetrans (subtly different from modelling an explicit parameter value as we do). A restricted class of regular expressions is used in TReX (Tool for Reachability Analysis of Complex Systems) [24] to represent the content of the unbounded lossy ordered channels and trace equivalence [25] is used to verify the protocols against their respective services. Another tool for symbolic analysis is FAST (Fast Acceleration of Symbolic Transition Systems) [10]. Systems are represented using automata extended with unbounded integer variables (*counter systems*) [2]. The symbolic results obtained using TReX and our initial investigations modelling the SWP using FAST [9] were successful when MaxRetrans was a parameter, but were only successful for small values of MaxSeqNo. In [26] a variant of the ABP using limited retransmission (with an arbitrary MaxRetrans) and operating over channels with a capacity of one message only, was verified using Valmari's Chaos-Free-Failures-Divergences (CFFD) equivalence. In contrast, our model operates over unbounded lossy ordered channels (similar to [1]), explicitly considers any maximum sequence number (not just the alternating bit) and uses language equivalence.

In this paper we obtain a symbolic expression for the infinite set of OGs over the MaxSeqNo parameter. On identifying final states, this expression becomes a symbolic Finite State Automaton (FSA). This FSA embodies the *protocol language* (the set of all sequences of user-observable events called *service primitives*) for each value of MaxSeqNo. We verify that the SWP conforms to the Stop-and-Wait service for all values of this parameter, by applying automata reduction techniques directly to the symbolic FSA and comparing the result with the *service language* of alternating send and receive events.

The contribution of this paper is threefold. Firstly, we present formulae for the size of the symbolic OG, in terms of our two parameters. Secondly, we derive an algebraic expression that represents the family of OGs of the SWP CPN model for *any* MaxSeqNo > 0, for the base case of MaxRetrans = 0, and prove it correct by induction. Thirdly, in this case, we verify that the SWP conforms to its service of alternating send and receive events for *any* MaxSeqNo > 0 by applying FSA reduction techniques directly to the corresponding symbolic FSA. These results extend our work [7, 8] and complement the symbolic verification work in [1] and [9] by verifying the SWP for every value of MaxSeqNo > 0 (with MaxRetrans = 0.) The authors are not aware of any previous attempts to verify a parameterised model of the class of Stop-and-Wait protocols by obtaining an explicit algebraic representation for the family of OGs over the MaxSeqNo parameter. A more detailed description of this work can be found in [12].

The rest of this paper is organised as follows. Section 2 presents our parametric Stop-and-Wait CPN model. Formulae for the size of the symbolic OG are given in Section 3 which then derives the symbolic OG for the case when MaxRetrans = 0. In Section 4 we obtain the symbolic FSA (representing an infinite family of protocol languages) directly from the symbolic OG. By applying reduction techniques we obtain the corresponding minimal deterministic FSA, and verify the SWP against its service for all values of MaxSeqNo. Conclusions and future work are presented in Section 5. Familiarity with basic CPN concepts and terminology is assumed. For a thorough introduction to CPNs the reader is referred to [15, 18].

2   The Stop-and-Wait Protocol CPN Model

The SWP is modelled using Coloured Petri nets [15, 18] as shown in Figs. 1 and 2. The two parameters MaxRetrans and MaxSeqNo can be seen at the top of Fig. 2. The model is divided into three parts: Sender, Network and Receiver.

The Sender comprises three places and four transitions. Place sender_state models the two states of the sender (ready or waiting for an acknowledgement) and is given an initial marking of s_ready. The send_seq_no place stores the sender sequence number and the retrans_counter place records the number of retransmissions of an unacknowledged message. Transition send_mess writes the sequence number (as the message) to the message channel and changes the sender state to wait_ack. Message content is not modelled as it does not influence the operation of the protocol. Retransmission of the currently unacknowledged message is modelled by transition timeout_retrans. The guard ensures that retransmission can only occur at most MaxRetrans times (rc < MaxRetrans). Transition receive_ack

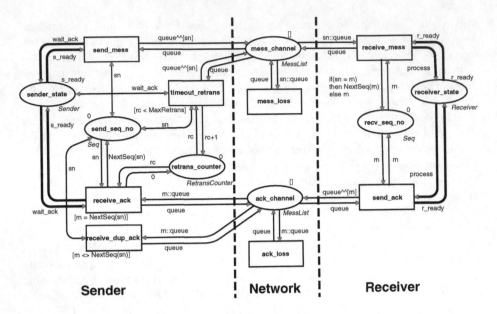

Fig. 1. A CPN of the Stop-and-Wait Protocol operating over an in-order medium

```
val MaxRetrans = 0;
val MaxSeqNo = 1;

color Sender = with s_ready | wait_ack;
color Receiver = with r_ready | process;
color Seq = int with 0..MaxSeqNo;
color RetransCounter = int with 0..MaxRetrans;
color Message = Seq;
color MessList = list Message;

var sn,rn : Seq;
var rc    : RetransCounter;
var queue : MessList;

fun NextSeq(n) = if(n = MaxSeqNo) then 0 else n+1;
```

Fig. 2. Declarations of the CPN shown in Fig. 1

processes expected acknowledgements by returning the sender to the ready state, resetting the retransmission counter and incrementing (modulo MaxSeqNo+1) the sender sequence number. Duplicate acknowledgements are discarded by the receive_dup_ack transition.

The network is modelled as an in-order bidirectional channel. The channel places mess_channel and ack_channel contain single lists and all arcs incident on these places have inscriptions written to manipulate these lists as FIFO queues.

(The operator ^^ concatenates two lists while :: concatenates an element to the head of a list.) Transitions mess_loss and ack_loss model loss, both in the network (buffer overflow in a router) and by discarding messages and acknowledgements with transmission errors (checksum failures).

The receiver has two states (r_ready, process) modelled by the token in receiver_state (initially r_ready). The recv_seq_no place stores the sequence number of the next expected message (initially 0). When an expected message is received (transition receive_mess with sn=rn) the receiver sequence number is incremented using modulo arithmetic (NextSeq), otherwise the message is discarded as a duplicate and the receiver sequence number remains unchanged (sn≠rn). Once an acknowledgement is sent containing the receiver sequence number (transition send_ack) the receiver returns to the ready state.

3   An Algebraic Formula for the Infinite Set of SWP CPN OGs

From empirical data gathered from examination of the OG of the SWP CPN for small parameter values, we derive a formula for the number of nodes and arcs in the OG over both parameters. Based on the intuition gained from this examination of the OG for small values of MaxSeqNo, we then derive an algebraic formula for the OG when MaxRetrans = 0 and prove it to be correct.

3.1   Size of the Occurrence Graph

Evidence of a regular structure to the occurrence graphs comes in the form of the size of the OGs. OGs have been generated for a large range of parameter values ($1 \leq$ MaxSeqNo ≤ 1023 and $0 \leq$ MaxRetrans ≤ 4) and the results reported in [7]. Due to length considerations we do not reproduce these results here. However we discovered that the number of nodes and arcs in the OGs is factorable in the two parameters. The number of nodes and arcs grows linearly with MaxSeqNo for a fixed MaxRetrans and quartically in MaxRetrans for a fixed MaxSeqNo. For example, the number of nodes and arcs grows by 6 for each increment of MaxSeqNo when MaxRetrans = 0. We have established formulas for the size of the OG in the two parameters using standard techniques for fitting polynomials to data.

Conjecture 1. For the Stop-and-Wait CPN of Figs. 1 and 2, the number of nodes in the occurrence graph is given by

$$|V| = ((\text{MaxSeqNo} + 1)/3)(\text{MaxRetrans}^4 + 13\text{MaxRetrans}^3 +$$
$$41\text{MaxRetrans}^2 + 47\text{MaxRetrans} + 18)$$

and the number of arcs is given by

$$|A| = \begin{cases} 6(\mathsf{MaxSeqNo} + 1) & \text{for MaxRetrans} = 0, \\ ((\mathsf{MaxSeqNo} + 1)/6)(10\mathsf{MaxRetrans}^4 \\ + 115\mathsf{MaxRetrans}^3 + 266\mathsf{MaxRetrans}^2 & \text{for MaxRetrans} > 0. \\ + 167\mathsf{MaxRetrans} + 24) \end{cases}$$

3.2   An Algebraic Formula for the OG

Figure 3 (a) shows the occurrence graph of our SWP CPN for the base case of MaxRetrans=0 and MaxSeqNo=1. Each state is annotated with an integer pair representing the sender sequence number and receiver sequence number in that state. Each arc is labelled with a description of the corresponding action from the model. The main loop represents the behaviour of the SWP when no messages or acknowledgements are lost. As there are no retransmissions the dead markings arise when either a message or an acknowledgement is lost.

Figure 3 (b) shows the OG when MaxSeqNo=2. The regular structure of the OGs begins to emerge. For each sequence number, there are 6 markings generated that can be partitioned into two sets of three. The first set of three contains markings where the sender and receiver sequence numbers are identical. The second set of three contains markings where the receiver sequence number is one greater (modulo MaxSeqNo+1) than the sender sequence number. This pattern continues for the OGs generated when MaxSeqNo=3,4 etc.

Based on this intuition, let us now formally define the parametric OG of our SWP CPN with MaxRetrans = 0, based on definitions in [16].

Definition 1. *For $n \in \mathbb{N}^+$ (the positive integers), CPN_n is defined as the Stop-and-Wait Protocol CPN of Figs. 1 and 2 with MaxSeqNo=n and MaxRetrans=0. The occurrence graph of CPN_n, with initial marking M_0 and a set of binding elements BE, is a labelled directed graph $OG_n = (V_n, A_n)$ where*

1. *$V_n = [M_0\rangle$ is the set of reachable markings of CPN_n; and*
2. *$A_n = \{(M, b, M') \in V_n \times BE \times V_n \mid M[b\rangle M'\}$ is the set of labelled directed arcs, where $M[b\rangle M'$ denotes that the marking of CPN_n changes from M to M' on the occurrence of binding element $b \in BE$.*

Let $V^n_{(\mathsf{ssn},\mathsf{rsn})} \subset V_n$ denote the subset of nodes in OG_n with sender sequence number ssn = $M(\mathsf{send\_seq\_no})$ (the value of the token in place send_seq_no) and receiver sequence number rsn = $M(\mathsf{recv\_seq\_no})$. We refer to 'the message with sequence number i' as 'message i' for brevity. For each message sent with sequence number $i \in \{0, 1, \ldots, n\}$ we have a set of 6 markings comprising $V^n_{(i,i)} \cup V^n_{(i,i\oplus_n 1)}$, where $\oplus_n$ is modulo $(n + 1)$ addition. The 3 nodes in $V^n_{(i,i)}$ represent: 1. the sender has received an acknowledgement (or it is the initial marking) and message i is ready to be sent; 2. message i has been sent; and 3. message i has been lost. The 3 nodes in $V^n_{(i,i\oplus_n 1)}$ represent: 1. message i has been received; 2. the

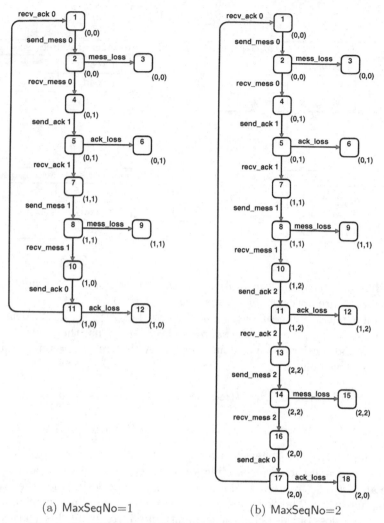

(a) MaxSeqNo=1   (b) MaxSeqNo=2

Fig. 3. The OGs of our SWP CPN when MaxSeqNo=1 and 2

acknowledgement for this message has been sent; and 3. the acknowledgement for this message has been lost. We define this formally for $0 \leq i \leq n$:

$$V_{(i,i)}^n = \{M \in V_n | M(\text{recv\_seq\_no}) = M(\text{send\_seq\_no}) = i\}, \text{ and}$$

$$V_{(i,i\oplus_n 1)}^n = \{M \in V_n | (M(\text{recv\_seq\_no}) = M(\text{send\_seq\_no}) \oplus_n 1 = i \oplus_n 1)\}$$

These markings are given in Tables 1 and 2. The first column shows the marking name. The subscript of a marking (ssn, rsn) is the sender and receiver sequence number for that marking and the superscripts correspond to the maximum sequence number (n) and the 'type' of marking just described. The remaining columns of these tables show the markings of each place in the SWP CPN of Fig. 1. Note that retrans_counter always has a value of 0 (one '0' token)

Table 1. $V_{(i,i)}^n$ for $0 \le i \le n$

Node	sender_state	send_seq_no	mess_ch.	ack_ch.	receiver_state	recv_seq_no
$M_{(i,i)}^{(n,1)}$	s_ready	i	[]	[]	r_ready	i
$M_{(i,i)}^{(n,2)}$	wait_ack	i	$[i]$	[]	r_ready	i
$M_{(i,i)}^{(n,3)}$	wait_ack	i	[]	[]	r_ready	i

Table 2. $V_{(i,i\oplus_n 1)}^n$ for $0 \le i \le n$

Node	sender_state	send_seq_no	mess_ch.	ack_ch.	receiver_state	recv_seq_no
$M_{(i,i\oplus_n 1)}^{(n,1)}$	wait_ack	i	[]	[]	process	$i \oplus_n 1$
$M_{(i,i\oplus_n 1)}^{(n,2)}$	wait_ack	i	[]	$[i \oplus_n 1]$	r_ready	$i \oplus_n 1$
$M_{(i,i\oplus_n 1)}^{(n,3)}$	wait_ack	i	[]	[]	r_ready	$i \oplus_n 1$

and is thus omitted from the tables, and that transitions receive_dup_ack and timeout_retrans are never enabled when MaxRetrans=0.

A similar partitioning of the arcs is defined. Let $A_{(\mathsf{ssn},\mathsf{rsn})}^n \subset A_n$ denote the subset of arcs in OG_n in which the *source* node of the arc has the sender sequence number ssn and receiver sequence number rsn. As before, rsn = ssn or ssn $\oplus_n 1$. For $0 \le i \le n$ we define:

$$A_{(i,i)}^n = \{(M, b, M') \in A_n | M(\mathsf{recv\_seq\_no}) = M(\mathsf{send\_seq\_no}) = i\}, \text{ and}$$

$$A_{(i,i\oplus_n 1)}^n = \{(M, b, M') \in A_n | (M(\mathsf{recv\_seq\_no}) = M(\mathsf{send\_seq\_no}) \oplus_n 1 = i \oplus_n 1)\}$$

Partitioning the arcs in this way means that $A_{(\mathsf{ssn},\mathsf{rsn})}^n$ contains all the outgoing arcs of the nodes in the corresponding set $V_{(\mathsf{ssn},\mathsf{rsn})}^n$, for a given ssn and rsn.

The arcs in $A_{(i,i)}^n$ represent: 1. sending message i; 2. losing message i; and 3. receiving message i. The arcs in $A_{(i,i\oplus_n 1)}^n$ represent: 1. sending an acknowledgement $i \oplus_n 1$; 2. loss of this acknowledgement; and 3. receiving this acknowledgement. These arcs are given in Tables 3 and 4. The subscripts and superscripts have the same meaning as for the nodes. The binding element refers to the transition of the CPN model that occurs, with the specific binding of values to variables for that transition.

Next we state the theorem for our parametric OG.

Theorem 1. *For $n \in \mathbb{N}^+$, $OG_n = (V_n, A_n)$ where*

$$V_n = \bigcup_{0 \le i \le n} (V_{(i,i)}^n \cup V_{(i,i\oplus_n 1)}^n), \quad A_n = \bigcup_{0 \le i \le n} (A_{(i,i)}^n \cup A_{(i,i\oplus_n 1)}^n)$$

Proof. We prove Theorem 1 by induction over MaxSeqNo (n). The proof draws inspiration from [19] for recursively defining a service OG. We prove the induction step in two parts. Firstly we prove that all but the last 3 nodes in OG_k

Table 3. $A_{(i,i)}^n$ for $0 \leq i \leq n$

Name	Source node	Binding Element	Dest. Node
$a_{(i,i)}^{(n,1)}$	$M_{(i,i)}^{(n,1)}$	send_mess<sn=i, queue=[]>	$M_{(i,i)}^{(n,2)}$
$a_{(i,i)}^{(n,2)}$	$M_{(i,i)}^{(n,2)}$	mess_loss<sn=i, queue=[]>	$M_{(i,i)}^{(n,3)}$
$a_{(i,i)}^{(n,3)}$	$M_{(i,i)}^{(n,2)}$	receive_mess<sn=i, rn=i, queue=[]>	$M_{(i,i\oplus_n 1)}^{(n,1)}$

Table 4. $A_{(i,i\oplus_n 1)}^n$ for $0 \leq i \leq n$

Name	Source node	Binding Element	Dest. Node
$a_{(i,i\oplus_n 1)}^{(n,1)}$	$M_{(i,i\oplus_n 1)}^{(n,1)}$	send_ack<rn=i$\oplus_n$1, queue=[]>	$M_{(i,i\oplus_n 1)}^{(n,2)}$
$a_{(i,i\oplus_n 1)}^{(n,2)}$	$M_{(i,i\oplus_n 1)}^{(n,2)}$	ack_loss<rn=i$\oplus_n$1, queue=[]>	$M_{(i,i\oplus_n 1)}^{(n,3)}$
$a_{(i,i\oplus_n 1)}^{(n,3)}$	$M_{(i,i\oplus_n 1)}^{(n,2)}$	receive_ack<sn=i, rn=i$\oplus_n$1, rc=0, queue=[]>	$M_{(i\oplus_n 1,i\oplus_n 1)}^{(n,1)}$

$(V_{(k,0)}^k)$ are identical to the nodes in OG_{k+1}, and similarly for the arcs. Then, using reachability analysis, we generate the last 9 nodes and 10 arcs of OG_{k+1}.

Basis. We assume that Design/CPN can correctly generate the OG of CPN_1. The generated OG matches that defined in Tables 1 to 4 for $n=1$.

Induction. We assume Theorem 1 is true for $n=k$ and then prove it holds for $n=k+1$. The following lemma states that the behaviour of the CPN is unchanged for $n=k$ and $n=k+1$ up to the point where sequence numbers wrap.

Lemma 1. *For CPN_k and OG_k as given in Definition 1, the subgraph of OG_k corresponding to $(V_k \setminus V_{(k,0)}^k, A_k \setminus (A_{(k,0)}^k \cup \{a_{(k,k)}^{(k,3)}\}))$ is invariant on increasing MaxSeqNo from k to $k+1$, where $V_{(k,0)}^k$ and $A_{(k,0)}^k$ are defined in Tables 2 and 4 respectively by substituting $i=k$, and $a_{(k,k)}^{(k,3)}$ is the third arc in Table 3 with $i=k$.*

Proof. By examining the CPN model, the only way the value of MaxSeqNo affects the model is through the NextSeq function. Further, an increase in MaxSeqNo only affects behaviour at the point at which sequence numbers wrap, i.e. in CPN_k, NextSeq$(k) = 0$, but in CPN_{k+1}, NextSeq$(k) = k + 1$.

Because NextSeq behaves identically up to the point where wrapping occurs in OG_k, we conclude that the behaviour of the CPN, (thus the OG) is unchanged for all values of sender and receiver sequence number up to the point where wrapping occurs, i.e. for the subset of nodes $\bigcup_{0\leq i<k}(V_{(i,i)}^k \cup V_{(i,i+1)}^k)\cup V_{(k,k)}^k \subseteq V_k$. The arc $a_{(k,k)}^{(k,3)}$ where receive_mess occurs from $M_{(k,k)}^{(k,2)} \in V_{(k,k)}^k$ causes the receiver sequence number to wrap to 0, so the markings in $V_{(k,0)}^k$ are no longer reachable when n is increased from k to $k+1$. The subset of arcs that remains unaffected is given by $\bigcup_{0\leq i<k}(A_{(i,i)}^k \cup A_{(i,i+1)}^k)\cup A_{(k,k)}^k \setminus \{a_{(k,k)}^{(k,3)}\} \subseteq A_k$. The remaining arcs $(A_{(k,0)}^k \cup \{a_{(k,k)}^{(k,3)}\})$ can no longer occur as either their source or destination nodes (or both) are no longer reachable when MaxSeqNo equals $k + 1$. $\square$

We have determined that the set of nodes $V_k \setminus V_{(k,0)}^k$ from OG_k is unaffected by an increase in MaxSeqNo to $k+1$. This implies $V_{(i,i)}^{k+1} = V_{(i,i)}^k$ for $0 \le i \le k$ and $V_{(i,i+1)}^{k+1} = V_{(i,i+1)}^k$ for $0 \le i \le k-1$. Similarly for arcs, we know that $A_{(i,i)}^{k+1} = A_{(i,i)}^k$ and $A_{(i,i+1)}^{k+1} = A_{(i,i+1)}^k$ for $0 \le i \le k - 1$ but $A_{(k,k)}^{k+1} \neq A_{(k,k)}^k$ solely because the destination node of $a_{(k,k)}^{(k,3)} \in A_{(k,k)}^k$ is not reachable in OG_{k+1}. When invoking the induction step we can assume that the nodes and arcs remaining invariant in V_{k+1} and A_{k+1} are correct. Having determined the subset of nodes and arcs in OG_k that are the same in OG_{k+1} we now determine the set of additional reachable markings and arcs:

Lemma 2. *The set of additional reachable markings of CPN_{k+1} with respect to CPN_k is given by $V_{(k,k+1)}^{k+1} \cup V_{(k+1,k+1)}^{k+1} \cup V_{(k+1,0)}^{k+1}$.*

Lemma 3. *The set of additional arcs in OG_{k+1} with respect to OG_k is given by $A_{(k,k+1)}^{k+1} \cup A_{(k+1,k+1)}^{k+1} \cup A_{(k+1,0)}^{k+1} \cup \{a_{(k,k)}^{(k+1,3)}\}$.*

Proof. From Lemma 1, the behaviour of CPN_{k+1} is the same as CPN_k up until the point where sequence numbers wrap. The occurrence of receive_mess<sn=k, rn=k, queue=[]> in $M_{(k,k)}^{(k+1,2)}$ leads to a new marking, $M_{(k,k+1)}^{(k+1,1)}$ in which the receiver sequence number is $k + 1$ (not 0). The only transition enabled in $M_{(k,k+1)}^{(k+1,1)}$ is send_ack with binding <rn=k+1, queue=[]>. Occurrence of this leads to the marking $M_{(k,k+1)}^{(k+1,2)}$. From here, either the acknowledgement just sent may be lost through occurrence of ack_loss<rn=k+1, queue=[]> leading to the dead marking $M_{(k,k+1)}^{(k+1,3)}$, or the acknowledgement will be received and the sender sequence number incremented through occurrence of receive_ack<sn=k, rn=k+1, rc=0, queue=[]>, leading to the marking $M_{(k+1,k+1)}^{(k+1,1)}$.

From $M_{(k+1,k+1)}^{(k+1,1)}$ the only possible action is send_mess<sn=k+1, queue=[]> leading to $M_{(k+1,k+1)}^{(k+1,2)}$. Transitions mess_loss and receive_mess are enabled in this marking. Occurrence of mess_loss<sn=k+1, queue=[]> leads to the dead marking $M_{(k+1,k+1)}^{(k+1,3)}$. Occurrence of receive_mess<sn=k+1, rn=k+1, queue=[]> leads to marking $M_{(k+1,0)}^{(k+1,1)}$. From this marking the only possible action is send_ack< rn=0, queue=[]> leading to the marking $M_{(k+1,0)}^{(k+1,2)}$. The acknowledgement just sent may be lost (ack_loss<rn=0, queue=[]>) leading to the dead marking $M_{(k+1,0)}^{(k+1,3)}$, or the acknowledgement may be received by the sender (receive_ack<sn =k+1, rn=0, rc=0, queue=[]>) leading back to the initial marking, $M_{(0,0)}^{(k+1,1)}$.

From Tables 1 and 2 defining the sets of nodes, the 9 nodes generated above correspond to $V_{(k,k+1)}^{k+1} \cup V_{(k+1,k+1)}^{k+1} \cup V_{(k+1,0)}^{k+1}$, obtained by substituting k and $k+1$ for i in Table 2 and $k+1$ for i in Table 1. The 10 new arcs correspond to $A_{(k,k+1)}^{k+1} \cup A_{(k+1,k+1)}^{k+1} \cup A_{(k+1,0)}^{k+1} \cup \{a_{(k,k)}^{(k+1,3)}\}$, obtained in a similar way.   □

From Lemmas 1, 2 and 3 it follows that $V_{k+1} = \bigcup_{0 \le i \le k+1}(V_{(i,i)}^{k+1} \cup V_{(i,i\oplus_n 1)}^{k+1})$ and $A_{k+1} = \bigcup_{0 \le i \le k+1}(A_{(i,i)}^{k+1} \cup A_{(i,i\oplus_n 1)}^{k+1})$. Thus the induction holds and the theorem is proved. $\qquad\square$

4   An Algebraic Formula for the Protocol Language

In this paper we are interested in checking conformance to the SWP service. The service is not concerned with internal protocol actions (acknowledgements, retransmissions, sequence numbers) so we define the *service primitives* of the Stop-and-Wait service as $SP = \{\text{send}, \text{receive}\}$. We define the SWP *service language* over a lossy medium as $(\text{send}, \text{receive})^* \text{send}^\dagger$ where $a^\dagger$ represents 0 or 1 occurrences of a. This indicates that the last send may not be followed by a receive if the last message that was sent is lost, i.e. the system will halt.

The protocol language comprises all sequences of service primitives exhibited by the protocol. Obtaining an expression for the protocol language from the symbolic OG of Theorem 1 will enable us to verify symbolically the conformance of the SWP to its service for *all* values of MaxSeqNo > 0. We state this in the following theorem, which is proved in the following subsections. For a more detailed version of the proof, please see [12].

Theorem 2. *The Stop-and-Wait protocol, as specified by CPN_n in Definition 1, conforms to the Stop-and-Wait service of alternating send and receive events, i.e.* $(\text{send}, \text{receive})^* \text{send}^\dagger$, *for all values of MaxSeqNo > 0.*

4.1   Mapping from the Algebraic OG to an Algebraic FSA

By interpreting the OG as a symbolic Finite State Automaton (FSA) and relabelling binding elements as either service primitives or epsilon (empty) moves, we show how standard algorithms [3] for the reduction of (non-symbolic) FSAs can be applied to the symbolic FSA to obtain the minimal deterministic FSA which embodies the protocol language (of send and receive events).

Any finite OG can be interpreted as a FSA simply by defining a set of halt states and an initial state. In our case, we also want to relabel the arcs from binding elements to service primitives, or ϵ. We begin by defining the necessary mappings to relabel the markings with integers and relabel the arcs with service primitives (or ϵ):

Definition 2. *Let $I : [M_0\rangle \to \mathbb{N}^+$ be an injection, mapping from the reachable markings of CPN_n with initial marking M_0 into the set of positive integers. Let $Prim : BE'_n \to SP \cup \{\epsilon\}$ be a mapping from the set of binding elements of CPN_n to either a service primitive name or to ϵ, where*

- $BE'_n \subseteq BE_n$ *is the set of binding elements that occur in CPN_n; and*
- $SP = \{\text{send}, \text{receive}\}$.

To relabel markings $M_{(i,j)}^{(n,t)}$ in OG_n with an integer we define the injection I as $I(M_{(i,j)}^{(n,t)}) = 6i + t$ when $j = i$ and $3(2i + 1) + t$ when $j = i \oplus_n 1$, where $1 \leq t \leq 3$ corresponds to the 'types' of markings described in Section 3 and $0 \leq i \leq n$. We do not simplify the node label $3(2i + 1) + t$ to $6i + (3 + t)$ as the type t of the marking would no longer be readily evident from the node label.

The mapping $Prim$ maps all occurrences of send_mess to the primitive send and only those occurrences of receive_mess corresponding to acceptance of a new message (sn = rn) to the primitive receive. All other transition occurrences, including occurrences of receive_mess corresponding to detection and discarding of a duplicate (sn ≠ rn), are mapped to ϵ.

We define the initial state of the FSA as the equivalent initial marking of the CPN, i.e. $I(M_0) = I(M_{(0,0)}^{(n,1)}) = 1$. As we have an arbitrary number of messages to send, we define a legitimate halt state as any state in which 0 or more messages have been sent and successfully acknowledged, so that both the sender and receiver are in their ready states and there are no messages or acknowledgements in the channel. These states correspond to the markings $I(M_{(i,i)}^{(n,1)})$ for all $0 \leq i \leq n$. We also include the dead markings of OG_n in the set of halt states, i.e. $I(M_{(i,i)}^{(n,3)})$ and $I(M_{(i,i\oplus_n 1)}^{(n,3)})$ for all $0 \leq i \leq n$ as they represent expected halt states of the protocol when operating over a lossy medium.

We are now ready to define the algebraic FSA associated with OG_n:

Definition 3. *The FSA associated with OG_n of CPN_n, with initial marking M_0, is $FSA_{OG_n} = (V_{FSA}^n, SP, A_{FSA}^n, v_0, F_{FSA}^n)$ where*

- $V_{FSA}^n = \{I(M)|M \in V_n\}$ *is the set of nodes;*
- $SP = \{$send, receive$\}$ *is the set of service primitive names of interest (the alphabet of the FSA);*
- $A_{FSA}^n = \{I(M), Prim(b), I(M')|(M, b, M') \in A_n\}$ *is the set of transitions labelled by service primitives or epsilons for internal events (the transition relation of the FSA);*
- $v_0 = I(M_0) = I(M_{(0,0)}^{(n,1)}) = 1$ *is the initial state of the FSA as defined above, corresponding to the initial marking of CPN_n; and*
- $F_{FSA}^n \subseteq V_{FSA}^n$ *is the set of final states defined above as* $\bigcup_{0 \leq i \leq n}\{I(M_{(i,i)}^{(n,1)}), I(M_{(i,i)}^{(n,3)}), I(M_{(i,i\oplus_n 1)}^{(n,3)})\}$.

Table 5 summarises FSA_{OG_n} obtained by applying the mappings from Definition 2 to the algebraic expressions for the OG. Figure 4 gives a graphical representation of Table 5. Note that the relabelling of arcs has led to nondeterminism.

4.2 Removing Empty Cycles

The first step in determinising a FSA using standard algorithms [3] is the removal of empty cycles. In our case, there are no empty cycles:

Proposition 1. *FSA_{OG_n}, given by Table 5, contains no empty cycles.*

Table 5. FSA_{OG_n} where $0 \leq i \leq n$

Source node	Arc Label	Dest. node	Dest. = Halt?
$6i + 1$	send	$6i + 2$	false
$6i + 2$	ϵ	$6i + 3$	true
$6i + 2$	receive	$3(2i + 1) + 1$	false
$3(2i + 1) + 1$	ϵ	$3(2i + 1) + 2$	false
$3(2i + 1) + 2$	ϵ	$3(2i + 1) + 3$	true
$3(2i + 1) + 2$	ϵ	$6(i \oplus_n 1) + 1$	true

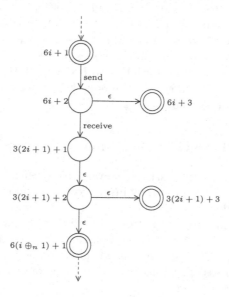

Fig. 4. The fragment of FSA_{OG_n} corresponding to any given $i, 0 \leq i \leq n$

Proof. There is only one cycle in FSA_{OG_n} and it is not an empty cycle. This can be verified if we evaluate the source and destination nodes of all arcs for all values $0 \leq i \leq n$. For any given value of i, the graphical representation given by Fig. 4 contains no cycles. The last node in the ith segment becomes the first node in the $(i \oplus_n 1)^{th}$ segment. For all values of i up to $n - 1$, no arcs lead back to previously seen nodes. However, the last node in the nth segment (i.e. when $i = n$) is node $(6(n \oplus_n 1) + 1) = 1$, the initial node. Therefore the only arc to return to an already seen node (and thus close a cycle) is the last arc in the nth segment, thus there is only one cycle. This cycle contains non-ϵ primitives (one send and receive for each segment) and thus it is not an empty cycle.   □

4.3   Removing Empty Moves

The next step is removal of empty moves from the algebraic FSA. Removing the empty moves to deadlocked nodes of type $t = 3$ (nodes $6i + 3$ and $3(2i + 1) + 3$, $0 \leq i \leq n$) involves deleting the arcs leading to these nodes and flagging the

Table 6. FSA_{OG_n} after removal of ϵ moves and deletion of inaccessible states, where rows 2 and 3 are evaluated for $0 \leq i \leq n$

Source node	Arc Label	Dest. node	Dest. = Halt?
1	send	2	true
$6i + 2$	receive	$3(2i + 1) + 1$	true
$3(2i + 1) + 1$	send	$6(i \oplus_n 1) + 2$	true

source nodes of these arcs (nodes $6i + 2$ and $3(2i + 1) + 2$) as halt states. This causes the nodes $6i + 3$ and $3(2i + 1) + 3$ to become inaccessible. Removal of the remaining empty moves between nodes $3(2i+1)+1, 3(2i+1)+2$ and $6(i \oplus_n 1)+1$ is done in a similar way, resulting in the nodes $3(2i + 1) + 2$ and $6(i \oplus_n 1) + 1$ becoming inaccessible from the initial state (except for the initial state itself, $6(n \oplus_n 1) + 1 = 1$). Table 6 shows the symbolic FSA after removal of all ϵ-moves and deletion of all inaccessible states.

4.4   Determinisation and Minimisation

After the removal of empty moves, the algebraic FSA given by Table 6 is once again deterministic, which can be proved by inspection as all nodes accept exactly one service primitive and have exactly one successor. However the FSA is not minimal.

To obtain a minimal representation [3] we begin by partitioning the states into two subsets, based on halt-state status. Both subsets are further divided if states within each subset are *distinguishable* [3] based on the input symbols that they accept. The process of refining the partitioning of states continues until no more refinements can be made.

From Table 6 it can be seen that all states are halt states, so we begin with all states placed in the same subset, i.e. $\{1, 6i + 2, 3(2i + 1) + 1 \mid 0 \leq i \leq n\}$. States are now divided based on the input symbols they accept, either send or receive, giving us the two subsets $\{1, 3(2i + 1) + 1 \mid 0 \leq i \leq n\}$ and $\{6i + 2 \mid 0 \leq i \leq n\}$. These subsets cannot be further refined, as all states in the first subset accept send leading to a state from the second subset, and vice versa for the states in the second subset accepting receive. To construct the minimum FSA we choose the representative '1' to represent the first subset in the minimal FSA and the representative '2' (when $i = 0$) to represent the second subset. Both are halt states and '1' is the initial state. send and receive arcs are defined accordingly. The resulting minimised deterministic FSA is given in Table 7.

Table 7. The minimised deterministic FSA_{OG_n} representing the protocol language of CPN_n

Source node	Arc Label	Dest. node	Dest. = Halt?
1	send	2	true
2	receive	1	true

This minimised deterministic FSA represents the protocol language for *all* values of MaxSeqNo. We have gone from an algebraic representation of an infinite number of FSAs to a single minimised deterministic representation. Because both states are halt states this FSA verifies that the SWP does indeed satisfy the Stop-and-Wait service of (send, receive)*send†, for all values of MaxSeqNo, and thus Theorem 2 is proved.

5   Conclusions and Future Work

We have proved a theorem which gives an algebraic expression for the infinite family of OGs of a parameterised CPN model of the class of Stop-and-Wait protocols, for the simplest case when there are no retransmissions. Additionally, we have presented for the first time, formulas for the size of the OG as a function of MaxRetrans and MaxSeqNo. Both the number of nodes and the number of arcs are linear in MaxSeqNo and quartic in MaxRetrans. From the algebraic expression we have obtained a symbolic FSA representing the protocol language. We demonstrated how to apply (non-symbolic) reduction techniques directly to the symbolic FSA to obtain a simple automaton for the protocol language and confirmed that it is language equivalent to the Stop-and-Wait service. We believe this is the first time such a result has been obtained by directly constructing an algebraic expression for the family of occurrence graphs of a CPN model of the class of Stop-and-Wait protocols. This is important as it eliminates reachability analyses for each value of the (unbounded) parameter and provides a general result.

The results in this paper extend those in [8] to any value of MaxSeqNo (MaxRetrans = 0) rather than just the small values of the parameters that could be handled by automatic tools [11]. The next step is to generalise this result for any value of MaxRetrans.

Our ultimate goal is to use these symbolic expressions representing an infinite set of occurrence graphs for more complete protocol verification. For example, deadlocked states can be identified from Tables 3 and 4 as those that never appear as source nodes (the states superscripted by the type '3') caused by message or acknowledgement loss. Further, from Tables 1 and 2 we can determine upper bounds on the channel content by examining the length of the queues (the message and acknowledgement channels are bounded by 1).

In the future, we would like to prove properties of the Stop-and-Wait class of protocols over reordering channels, corresponding to their use over the Internet. Establishing an algebraic expression for the occurrence graphs over both parameters and following the same procedure used here for the MaxSeqNo parameter seems promising and is the subject of current investigations. We would then like to use this result to verify such properties as absence of deadlocks and the stop and wait service, and to determine channel bounds for arbitrary parameter values.

Acknowledgement. The authors are grateful to their colleague, Lin Liu, for her inspiration for the proof of Theorem 1 and technical discussions regarding the symbolic minimisation procedure.

References

1. P. Aziz Abdulla, A. Collomb-Annichini, A. Bouajjani, and B. Jonsson. Using Forward Reachability Analysis for Verification of Lossy Channel Systems. *Formal Methods in System Design*, 25(1):39–65, 2004.
2. S. Bardin, A. Finkel, and J. Leroux. FASTer Acceleration of Counter Automata in Practice. In *Proceedings of TACAS'2004*, volume 2988 of *Lecture Notes in Computer Science*, pages 576–590. Springer, 2004.
3. W.A. Barrett and J.D. Couch. *Compiler Construction: Theory and Practice*. Science Research Associates, 1979.
4. J. Billington. Formal specification of protocols: Protocol Engineering. In *Encyclopedia of Microcomputers*, volume 7, pages 299–314. Marcel Dekker, New York, 1991.
5. J. Billington, M. Diaz, and G. Rozenberg, editors. *Application of Petri Nets to Communication Networks*, volume 1605 of *Lecture Notes in Computer Science*. Springer-Verlag, 1999.
6. J. Billington and G. E. Gallasch. How Stop and Wait Protocols Can Fail Over The Internet. In *Proceedings of FORTE'03*, volume 2767 of *Lecture Notes in Computer Science*, pages 209–223. Springer-Verlag, 2003. (invited paper).
7. J. Billington and G. E. Gallasch. An Investigation of the Properties of Stop-and-Wait Protocols over Channels which can Re-order messages. Technical Report CSEC-15, Computer Systems Engineering Centre Report Series, University of South Australia, May 2004.
8. J. Billington, G. E. Gallasch, and B. Han. A Coloured Petri Net Approach to Protocol Verification. In *Lectures on Concurrency and Petri Nets, Advances in Petri Nets*, volume 3098 of *Lecture Notes in Computer Science*, pages 210–290. Springer-Verlag, 2004.
9. J. Billington, G.E. Gallasch, and L. Petrucci. Transforming Coloured Petri Nets to Counter Systems for Parametric Verification: A Stop-and-Wait Protocol Case Study. In *Proceedings of 2nd International Workshop on Model-Based Methodologies for Pervasive and Embedded Software (MOMPES'05), Rennes, France*, TUCS General Publication, No. 39, pages 37–55, May 2005.
10. FAST - Fast Acceleration of Symbolic Transition systems. http://www.lsv.ens-cachan.fr/fast/.
11. FSM Library, AT&T Research Labs. http://www.research.att.com/sw/tools/fsm/.
12. G. E. Gallasch and J. Billington. Towards the Parametric Verification of the Class of Stop-and-Wait Protocols over Ordered Channels. Technical Report CSEC-21, Computer Systems Engineering Centre Report Series, University of South Australia, March 2005, revised June 2005.
13. S. Gordon. *Verification of the WAP Transaction Layer using Coloured Petri Nets*. PhD thesis, Institute for Telecommunications Research and Computer Systems Engineering Centre, School of Electrical and Information Engineering, University of South Australia, Adelaide, Australia, November 2001.
14. B. Han. *Formal Specification of the TCP Service and Verification of TCP Connection Management*. PhD thesis, Computer Systems Engineering Centre, School of Electrical and Information Engineering, University of South Australia, Adelaide, Australia, December 2004.
15. K. Jensen. *Coloured Petri Nets: Basic Concepts, Analysis Methods and Practical Use. Vol. 1, Basic Concepts*. Springer-Verlag, 2nd edition, 1997.

16. K. Jensen. *Coloured Petri Nets: Basic Concepts, Analysis Methods and Practical Use. Vol. 2, Analysis Methods.* Springer-Verlag, 2nd edition, 1997.
17. K. Jensen. *Coloured Petri Nets: Basic Concepts, Analysis Methods and Practical Use. Vol. 3, Practical Use.* Springer-Verlag, 1997.
18. L.M. Kristensen, S. Christensen, and K. Jensen. The Practitioner's Guide to Coloured Petri Nets. *International Journal on Software Tools for Technology Transfer*, 2(2):98–132, 1998.
19. L. Liu and J. Billington. Tackling the Infinite State Space of a Multimedia Control Protocol Service Specification. In *Proceedings of ICATPN'02*, volume 2360 of *Lecture Notes in Computer Science*, pages 273–293. Springer-Verlag, 2002.
20. C. Ouyang. *Formal Specification and Verification of the Internet Open Trading Protocol using Coloured Petri Nets.* PhD thesis, Computer Systems Engineering Centre, School of Electrical and Information Engineering, University of South Australia, Adelaide, Australia, June 2004.
21. J. Postel. Transmission Control Protocol. RFC 793, September 1981.
22. W. Stallings. *Data and Computer Communications.* Prentice Hall, 6th edition, 2000.
23. A. Tanenbaum. *Computer Networks.* Prentice Hall, 4th edition, 2003.
24. The TReX Tool. http://www.liafa.jussieu.fr/~sighirea/trex/.
25. A. Valmari. The State Explosion Problem. In *Lectures on Petri Nets I: Basic Models*, volume 1491 of *Lecture Notes in Computer Science*, pages 429–528. Springer-Verlag, 1998.
26. A. Valmari and I. Kokkarinen. Unbounded Verification Results by Finite-State Compositional Techniques: 10^{any} States and Beyond. In *Proceedings of International Conference on Application of Concurrency to System Design*, pages 75–85. IEEE Computer Society, March 1998.
27. M. E. Villapol. *Modelling and Analysis of the Resource Reservation Protocol.* PhD thesis, Institute for Telecommunications Research and Computer Systems Engineering Centre, School of Electrical and Information Engineering, University of South Australia, Adelaide, Australia, November 2003.

Flat Acceleration in Symbolic Model Checking*

Sébastien Bardin[1], Alain Finkel[1], Jérôme Leroux[2], and Philippe Schnoebelen[1]

[1] LSV: ENS de Cachan & CNRS UMR 8643,
61, av. Pdt. Wilson, 94235 Cachan Cedex, France
{bardin, finkel, phs}@lsv.ens-cachan.fr
[2] IRISA, Vertecs project, INRIA,
Campus de Beaulieu, 35042 Rennes Cedex, France
jleroux@irisa.fr

Abstract. Symbolic model checking provides partially effective verification procedures that can handle systems with an infinite state space. So-called "acceleration techniques" enhance the convergence of fixpoint computations by computing the transitive closure of some transitions. In this paper we develop a new framework for symbolic model checking with accelerations. We also propose and analyze new symbolic algorithms using accelerations to compute reachability sets.

Keywords: verification of infinite-state systems, symbolic model checking, acceleration.

1 Introduction

Context. The development of model checking techniques [19] for infinite-state systems is now an active field of research. These techniques allow considering models like pushdown systems [13], channel systems [1,14], counter systems [8,31,38], and many other versatile families of models. Such models are very expressive and often lead to undecidable verification problems. This did not deter several research teams from developing powerful innovative model checkers for infinite-state systems. For example, tools for checking reachability properties of counter systems are ALV [6], BRAIN [37], LASH [33], TREX [3], and our own FAST [8]. For infinite-state systems, model checking must be "symbolic" since one manipulates (symbolic representations of) potentially infinite sets of configurations. The most popular symbolic representations are based on regular languages: these are quite expressive and automata-theoretical data structures provide efficient algorithms performing set-theoretical operations as well as pre- and post-image computations. With these ingredients, it becomes possible to launch a fixpoint computation for forward or backward reachability sets, as exemplified in [32].

The problem of convergence. When dealing with infinite-state systems, a naive fixpoint computation procedure for reachability sets, in the style of Procedure 1 (section 3.2), has very little chance to terminate: convergence in a finite number of steps can only occur if the system under study is uniformly bounded (see section 3.2). To make fixpoint

---

* This work was supported by the ACI Sécurité & Informatique (project Persée) funded by the French Ministry of Research.

D.A. Peled and Y.-K. Tsay (Eds.): ATVA 2005, LNCS 3707, pp. 474–488, 2005.

computations converge more frequently, so-called *"acceleration techniques"* have been developed. These techniques can compute subsets of the reachability set that are not uniformly bounded. This can be done, for example, by replacing a control loop `"x:=x+1; y:=y-1"` by its transitive closure `"k:=random_int(); x:=x+k; y:=y-k"`. Currently, many different acceleration techniques for different families of systems exist [1,2,12,14,26,38]. Some of them have been implemented [3,8,33] and promising case-studies have been reported [1,2,3,8,9]. Acceleration shares some similarities with the widening techniques used in abstract interpretation [22] but also exhibits some clear differences: acceleration aims at exact computation for some given control structures, while widening mostly ignores control structures and usually trades exactness for termination.

A field in need of foundations. The existing acceleration results usually amount to a (sometimes difficult) theorem stating that the transitive closure of an action, or of a sequence of actions, can be effectively computed. The difficulty of these results usually lies in finding the precise conditions on the action and on the set of initial states that yield effectiveness. How to use acceleration results is not really known: the theorems and algorithms for computing reachability sets with acceleration methods do not exist in general! With some tools, e.g., LASH, the user has to choose which loops to accelerate and how to mix the outcomes with more standard symbolic computation; in other cases, e.g., with TREX, some default strategy is implemented outside of any theoretical framework and without discussions about its efficiency or completeness.

Our contributions. (1) We propose the first theoretical framework for symbolic model checking with acceleration. We distinguish three natural levels for accelerations (*"loop"*, *"flat"*, and *"global"*), depending on which sequences of transitions can be computed: transitive closure of cycles (resp. of length 1) for flat (resp. loop) acceleration; or any regular set of sequences for global acceleration. These levels can account for most acceleration results on specific systems (pushdown systems, channel systems, counter systems, . . .). For each level we give a symbolic algorithm with acceleration computing reachability sets and we characterize the conditions necessary for its termination.

Flat acceleration is the most interesting level. As a matter of fact, loop acceleration is not sufficient for many of the example systems we have analyzed with our tool FAST. Furthermore, the majority of existing acceleration results stated at the loop acceleration level may be extended to the level of flat acceleration. At the other end of the spectrum, global acceleration is always sufficient but it occurs very rarely in practice and is essentially restricted to particular subclasses (e.g., pushdown systems, reversal-bounded counter systems [31] or particular subclasses of Petri nets).

(2) We develop new concepts for the algorithmic study of flat acceleration. The notions of *flattenings* and of *flattable systems* provide the required bridge between flat acceleration and the effective computation of the reachability set.

We propose new symbolic procedures and analyze them rigorously. We show Procedure REACH2 terminates iff it is applied to a flattable (rather than flat) system, which is the first completeness result on symbolic model checking with acceleration. We remark that most of the case studies we analyzed in earlier works with FAST are flattable but not flat, underlining the relevance of this concept.

(3) Procedure REACH2 is schematic and it can be specialized in several ways. We propose one such specialization, REACH3, geared towards the efficient search of all flattenings of a nonflat system, without compromising completeness.

It appears that a key issue with REACH3 is the reduction of the number of circuits the procedure has to consider. FAST implements specific algorithms for counter systems that reduce exponentially the number of considered circuits and we show how to generalize these ideas to other families of systems. It is these algorithms that make FAST succeed in verifying several examples (see section 6) for which tools like LASH and ALV, based on similar technology but restricted heuristics, do not terminate. More generally, the comparisons in section 6 suggest that flat acceleration greatly enhances termination of symbolic reachability set computation, and is fully justified in practice.

Outline. We define the systems under study in section 2, and the symbolic frameworks in section 3. Section 4 introduces the three levels of accelerations and defines flattable systems. Section 5 provides our procedure for flattable systems, and gives several algorithmic and/or heuristic refinements. Section 6 compares several existing tools through the new framework. All omitted proofs can be found in the full version of this paper.

2   Systems and Interpretations

Notations. A *(binary) relation* r on some set X is any subset of $X \times X$. We write $x \, r \, x'$ when $(x, x') \in r$ and denote by $r(x)$ the set $\{x' \in X \mid x \, r \, x'\}$. For $Y \subseteq X$, $r(Y)$ is $\bigcup_{x \in Y} r(x)$. Given $r_1, r_2 \subseteq X \times X$, the *compound relation* $r_1 \bullet r_2$ contains all pairs (x, z) s.t. $x \, r_1 \, y$ and $y \, r_2 \, z$ for some $y \in X$. Note that, in $r_1 \bullet r_2$, relation r_1 is applied first. For $i \in \mathbb{N}$, r^i is defined inductively by $r^0 = Id_X$ and $r^{i+1} = r \bullet r^i$, where Id_X is the *identity* on X. $r^* = \bigcup_{i \in \mathbb{N}} r^i$ is the *reflexive and transitive closure* of r.

Here, a *system* is a finite state control graph extended with a finite number of variables that range over arbitrary domains and are modified by actions when a transition is fired. Specific families of systems have been widely studied (see section 2.1). Formally:

Definition 2.1 (Uninterpreted system). *An* uninterpreted system S *is a tuple* S $= (Q, \Sigma, T)$, *where* Q *is a finite set of* locations, Σ *is a (possibly infinite) set of formulae called* actions, $T \subseteq Q \times \Sigma \times Q$ *is a finite set of* transitions.

Given a *uninterpreted system* S $= (Q, \Sigma, T)$, the *source, target* and *action* mappings $\alpha : T \to Q$, $\beta : T \to Q$ and $l : T \to \Sigma$ are defined as follows: for any transition $t = (q, \sigma, q') \in T$, $\alpha(t) = q$, $\beta(t) = q'$, $l(t) = \sigma$.

Definition 2.2 (Interpretation). *Given a (possibly infinite) set of formulae Σ and a set D, an* interpretation I *of* Σ, *shortly an* interpretation, *is a tuple* $I = (\Sigma, D, \llbracket \cdot \rrbracket)$ *such that* $\llbracket \cdot \rrbracket : \Sigma \to 2^{D \times D}$ *maps formulae to relations on D.*

Definition 2.3 (System). *An interpreted system S (shortly a system) is a pair* (S, I) *of an uninterpreted system* S $= (Q, \Sigma, T)$ *and an interpretation* $I = (\Sigma, D, \llbracket \cdot \rrbracket)$ *of* Σ, *shortly written* $S = (Q, \Sigma, T, D, \llbracket \cdot \rrbracket)$.

Fig. 1 displays S_0, a simple uninterpreted system, in graphical notation.

In this example the actions may be assignments that can be guarded by Boolean expressions, but we will not specify it more precisely. A possible interpretation for a_1 ,a_2 and a_3 (the actions appearing in S_0) assumes that the domain D is $\mathbb{Z}^{\{x,y\}}$, or equivalently $\mathbb{Z}^2$, i.e., we decide that x and y range over integers. We then interpret the actions in the obvious way. For example $[\![a_2]\!] = \{((x,y),(x',y')) \mid x \neq y \wedge y' = y + x \wedge x' = x\}$. This turns S_0 into an interpreted system S_0.

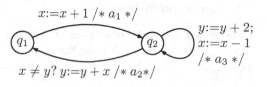

Fig. 1. S_0, a simple uninterpreted system

Behaviour. The *set of configurations* $\mathcal{C}_S$ of S is $Q \times D$, and each transition $t \in T$ is interpreted as a relation $\xrightarrow{t} \subseteq \mathcal{C}_S \times \mathcal{C}_S$ defined by: $(q, \mathsf{x}) \xrightarrow{t} (q', \mathsf{x}')$ if $q = \alpha(t), q' = \beta(t)$ and $(\mathsf{x}, \mathsf{x}') \in [\![l(t)]\!]$. This definition extends to sequences $\pi \in T^*$ of transitions. Let ε denote the *empty word*. Then $\xrightarrow{\varepsilon} = Id_{\mathcal{C}_S}$ and $\xrightarrow{t \cdot \pi} = \xrightarrow{t} \bullet \xrightarrow{\pi}$. We also define $\xrightarrow{\mathcal{L}}$ for *any language* $\mathcal{L} \subseteq T^*$ by $\xrightarrow{\mathcal{L}} = \bigcup_{\pi \in \mathcal{L}} \xrightarrow{\pi}$. Similarly $[\![\cdot]\!]$ is extended to any language $\mathcal{L} \subseteq \Sigma^*$. In the following we omit the S subscript whenever this causes no ambiguities.

Reachability problems. We are interested in checking *safety properties*, which can be expressed in terms of reachability using standard techniques. For any $X \subseteq \mathcal{C}_S$ and any $\mathcal{L} \subseteq T^*$, we define $\mathrm{post}_S(\mathcal{L}, X) = \{x' \in \mathcal{C}_S \mid \exists x \in X; (x, x') \in \xrightarrow{\mathcal{L}}\}$. The set $\mathrm{post}(T, X)$ of all configurations reachable in one step from X is denoted by $\mathrm{post}(X)$. The set $\mathrm{post}(T^*, X)$ of all configurations reachable from X is *the reachability set of X*, denoted by $\mathrm{post}^*(X)$.

In practice, we usually ask whether $\mathrm{post}^*(X_0) \subseteq P$, for X_0 a set of initial configurations, and P a set of "safe" configurations. We focus here on the reachability set computation which is the key issue. Since $\mathrm{post}^*(X_0)$ is not recursive in general, the best we can hope for are partially correct procedures, with no guarantees of termination, but that are efficient on interesting subclasses of systems, and in practical case-studies.

Backward computation. One may also rely on *backward reachability* and check if, for a set P of "bad" configurations, $\mathrm{pre}^*(P) \cap X_0$ is empty (with obvious definition for pre). Since, for our level of abstraction, adaptation to backward computation is straightforward, we consider only forward computation. However it is worth remembering that, depending on the case at hand, one of the approaches may be more adapted than the other. Along the paper specific results for backward computation are pointed out.

Transition relation computation. A third approach is to compute *the reachability relation* $\xrightarrow{T^*}$ once and for all (e.g., [21,25]). Then $\mathrm{post}^*(X_0) = \xrightarrow{T^*} (X_0)$. Our framework extends smoothly in this direction but, since it requires additional notations, we postpone this until the full version of this work.

2.1 Families of Systems

Definition 2.4 (Family of systems). *Given an interpretation* $I = (\Sigma, D, [\![\cdot]\!])$, *the family of systems built on* I *(shortly the family of systems) denoted by* $\mathcal{F}(I)$ *is the class of all systems* $S = (Q, \Sigma, T, D, [\![\cdot]\!])$ *using* I *to interpret actions.*

Well known models can be obtained by instantiating Definition 2.4:

Minsky machines: are obtained by defining $D = \mathbb{N}^{Var}$ where $Var = \{x_1, x_2, \ldots\}$ is a set of variables, and Σ as the set of increments "$x_i := x_i + 1$", guarded decrements "$x_i > 0?\ x_i := x_i - 1$" and 0-tests "$x_i = 0?$" with the obvious interpretation.

Counter systems [18,34]: are obtained by considering the same domain, or a variant $D = \mathbb{Z}^{Var}$, and all actions definable in Presburger arithmetic. Many restrictions exist, e.g., linear systems where actions are linear transformations with guards expressed in Presburger [26,38], reversal-counter systems [31], many extensions of VASS (or Petri nets) and so on.

Pushdown systems: the domain is $D = \Gamma^*$, the set of all words on some stack alphabet Γ. Actions add or remove letters on or from the top of the stack.

Channel systems [17]: consider the domain is $D = (\Gamma^*)^C$ where C is a set of fifo channels, and Γ is some alphabet of messages. Actions add messages at one end of the channels and consume them at the other end.

Timed automata [5]: consider the domain $D = \mathbb{R}_+^{Var}$. Here some actions are guarded by simple linear (in)equalities and they can only reset clocks. Other actions, left implicit in the standard presentation, account for time elapsing.

Hybrid systems [4]: extend timed automata in that the real-valued variables do not increase uniformly when time elapses. Rather they each increase according to their own rate (as given by the current location).

3 A Symbolic Framework for Symbolic Model Checking

In practice model checking procedures use symbolic representations (called here *regions*) to manipulate sets of configurations. The definition below follows directly from ideas expressed for example in [15,32,22].[1]

Definition 3.1 (Symbolic framework). *A symbolic framework is a tuple* $SF = (\Sigma, D, [\![\cdot]\!]_1, L, [\![\cdot]\!]_2)$ *where* $I = (\Sigma, D, [\![\cdot]\!]_1)$ *is an interpretation,* L *is a set of formulae called* regions, $[\![\cdot]\!]_2 : L \to 2^D$ *is a region concretization, and such that there exists a decidable relation* $\sqsubseteq$ *and recursive functions* $\sqcup$, POST *satisfying:*

1. *there exists an element* $\bot \in L$ *such that* $[\![\bot]\!]_2 = \emptyset$,
2. $\sqsubseteq\ \subseteq L \times L$ *is such that for all* $x_1, x_2 \in L$, $x_1 \sqsubseteq x_2$ *iff* $[\![x_1]\!]_2 \subseteq [\![x_2]\!]_2$,
3. $\sqcup : L \times L \to L$ *is such that* $\forall x_1, x_2 \in L$, $[\![x_1 \sqcup x_2]\!]_2 = [\![x_1]\!]_2 \cup [\![x_2]\!]_2$,
4. POST $: \Sigma \times L \to L$ *is such that* $\forall a \in \Sigma, \forall x \in L$, $[\![\text{POST}(a, x)]\!]_2 = [\![a]\!]_1 ([\![x]\!]_2)$.

---

[1] Some weakened versions of the symbolic framework are sometimes considered. A *weak inclusion* ensures only that $x_1 \sqsubseteq x_2$ implies $[\![x_1]\!] \subseteq [\![x_2]\!]$ while a *weak union* satisfies $[\![x_1]\!] \cup [\![x_2]\!] \subseteq [\![x_1 \sqcup x_2]\!]$ (typical widening in abstract interpretation [22]). In the following, we do not consider weakened framework.

Notation. Usually given an interpretation $I = (\Sigma, D, [\![\cdot]\!]_1)$ and a set of regions L, $[\![\cdot]\!]_2$ is understood. Thus in the following, we write $[\![\cdot]\!]$ for both $[\![\cdot]\!]_1$ and $[\![\cdot]\!]_2$, and we denote symbolic frameworks as $SF = (I, L)$. In the rest of the paper, we fix an arbitrary symbolic framework $SF = (I, L)$. When referring to a system S, if nothing is specified we assume that $S \in \mathcal{F}(I)$.

Well-known symbolic frameworks for some of the families listed in section 2.1 are:

Regular languages: have been used for representing sets of configurations of push-down systems [13], distributed protocols over rings of arbitrary size [32], and channel systems [36]. Restricted sets of regular languages are sometimes used for better algorithmic efficiency: languages closed by the subword relation [1] or closed by semi-commutations [16].

(finite union of) Convex polyhedra [4]: are conjunctions of linear inequalities defining subsets of $\mathbb{R}_+^{Var}$, relevant in the analysis of hybrid systems.

Number Decision Diagrams [18,26]: are automata recognizing subsets of $\mathbb{Z}^{Var}$ and have been used in the analysis of counter systems.

Real Vector Automata [11]: are Büchi automata recognizing subsets of $\mathbb{R}_+^{Var}$ and have been used in the analysis of linear hybrid systems.

Difference Bounds Matrices [5]: are a canonical representations for convex subsets of $\mathbb{R}_+^{Var}$ defined by simple diagonal and orthogonal constraints that appear in timed automata.

Covering Sharing Trees [24]: are a compact representation for upward-closed subsets of $\mathbb{N}^{Var}$. These sets appear naturally in the backward analysis of broadcast protocols [26] and several monotonic extensions of Petri nets.

Given a system S with a set of locations Q, and $X \subseteq \mathcal{C}_S$, post$^*(X)$ is of the form $\bigcup_{q \in Q}\{q\} \times D_q$ where the D_q are subsets of D. Assuming an implicit ordering on locations $q_1, \ldots, q_{|Q|}$, we work on tuples of regions in $L^{|Q|}$. We extend $[\![\cdot]\!]$ to $L^{|Q|}$ by $[\![(x_1, \ldots, x_{|Q|})]\!] = \bigcup_{i=1}^{|Q|}\{q_i\} \times [\![x_i]\!]$. Extensions of $\sqsubseteq$ and $\sqcup$ are component-based. POST is extended into POST $: T \times L \to L$ by: POST$((q_i, a, q_j), (x_1, \ldots, x_{|Q|}))$ is equal to $(x'_1, \ldots, x'_{|Q|})$ such that $x'_p = \bot$ if $p \neq j$, POST(a, x_i) otherwise. POST is then extended to sequence of transition in the obvious way. We define POST $: L^{|Q|} \to L^{|Q|}$ by POST$(x) = \bigsqcup_{t \in T}$ POST(t, x).

3.1 Limits of the Symbolic Approach

A subset of configurations $X \subseteq \mathcal{C}_S$ is *L-definable* if there exists $x \in L^{|Q|}$ such that $[\![x]\!] = X$. Obviously, computing post$^*(X)$ using regions is feasible only if post$^*(X)$ is *L*-definable and the question "is post$^*([\![x]\!])$ *L*-definable?" is undecidable in general.

Furthermore, *L*-definability of post$^*(X)$ is not a sufficient condition for its computability. We say below that post* (or any other function) is *effectively L-definable* if there exists a recursive function $g : L^{|Q|} \to L^{|Q|}$ such that $\forall x \in L^{|Q|}$, post$^*([\![x]\!]) = [\![g(x)]\!]$. (We often abuse terminology and write that "post$^*([\![x]\!])$", instead of post*, "is effectively *L*-definable"). It can well be the case that post$^*([\![x]\!])$ is *L*-definable but not effectively so (e.g., the family of lossy channel systems and the framework defined by simple regular expressions).

3.2 Standard Symbolic Model Checking Procedure

REACH1 (Procedure 1) is the standard symbolic procedure for reachability sets. It is only guaranteed to terminate on L-uniformly bounded systems.

```
procedure REACH1(x₀)
parameter: S
input: x₀ ∈ L^|Q|
 1:  x ← x₀
 2:  while POST(x) ⋢ x do
 3:      x ← POST(x) ⊔ x
 4:  end while
 5:  return x
```

Procedure 1: Standard symbolic model checking algorithm (forward version)

Definition 3.2 (L**-uniformly bounded**). *A system S is L-uniformly bounded if for all* $x \in L^{|Q|}$, *there exists $n_x \in \mathbb{N}$ such that, for all $c_1 \in Q \times [\![x]\!]$ and $c_2 \in Q \times D$, if $c_2 \in \mathsf{post}^*(\{c_1\})$ then $c_2 \in \bigcup_{i \le n_x} \mathsf{post}^i(\{c_1\})$.*

Theorem 3.3. *Given a symbolic framework $SF = (I, L)$ and a system $S \in \mathcal{F}(I)$*
1. when REACH1 terminates, $[\![\text{REACH1}(x_0)]\!] = \mathsf{post}^*([\![x_0]\!])$ (partial correctness);
2. REACH1 terminates on any input iff S is L-uniformly bounded (termination).

Remark 3.4. Termination for L-uniformly bounded systems does not hold if $\sqsubseteq$ or $\sqcup$ are weak.

In practice systems are rarely L-uniformly bounded and Procedure 1 seldom terminates. A notable exception are the well-structured transition systems with upward-closed sets as regions [28,27]. They are *L-backward* uniformly bounded so that a backward version of Procedure 1 always terminates.

4 Flat Acceleration for Flattable Systems

4.1 Acceleration Techniques

In order to improve the convergence of the previous procedure, *acceleration techniques* consist in computing the transitive closure of some transitions.

Definition 4.1 (Acceleration). *A symbolic framework $SF = (I, L)$ supports*
1. loop acceleration if there exists a recursive function POST_STAR : $\Sigma \times L \to L$ s.t.
   $\forall a \in \Sigma, \forall x \in L, [\![\text{POST\_STAR}(a, x)]\!] = [\![a^*]\!]([\![x]\!])$;

2. flat acceleration *if there exists a recursive function* POST_STAR : $\Sigma^* \times L \to L$ *s.t.*
   $\forall \pi \in \Sigma^*, \forall \mathbf{x} \in L$, $[\![\text{POST\_STAR}(\pi, \mathbf{x})]\!] = [\![\pi^*]\!] ([\![\mathbf{x}]\!])$;

3. global acceleration *if there exists a recursive function* POST_STAR : $RegExp(\Sigma) \times L \to L$ *s.t. for any regular expression* e *over* Σ, *for any* $\mathbf{x} \in L$, $[\![\text{POST\_STAR}(e, \mathbf{x})]\!] = [\![e]\!] ([\![\mathbf{x}]\!])$.

We often write that "S", rather than (I, L), "supports loop acceleration, or flat, ..."

Consider S_0 from Fig. 1 and let $A \subseteq D$. Loop acceleration only concerns action a_3, and comes down to computing $[\![a_3^*]\!] (A) = \{(x', y') \in \mathbb{Z}^2 | \exists(x, y) \in A; \exists k \in \mathbb{N}; x' = x - k \wedge y' = y + 2 \cdot k\}$. Flat acceleration requires computability of $[\![(a_1 \cdot a_2)^*]\!] (A)$, $[\![(a_1 \cdot a_3 \cdot a_2)^*]\!] (A)$, $[\![(a_1 \cdot a_3 \cdot a_3 \cdot a_2)^*]\!] (A)$, $[\![(a_3 \cdot a_2 \cdot a_1)^*]\!] (A)$ and so on. Global acceleration requires the computation of more complex interleaving of actions, like $[\![(a_1 \cdot a_3^* \cdot a_2)^*]\!] (A)$.

Definition 4.1 applies to symbolic frameworks and hence uses sequences of actions. However, in practice, POST_STAR is used with sequences of transitions. Let us illustrate this in the case of flat acceleration: Consider a sequence $\pi = (q_1, a_1, q_2) \cdot (q_3, a_2, q_4) \cdot (q_5, a_3, q_6)$ of transitions. There are two cases. If the sequence is *invalid* (i.e., $q_2 \neq q_3$ or $q_4 \neq q_5$) then the associated relation is empty and POST_STAR$(\pi, (q, \mathbf{x}))$ is $(q, \mathbf{x})$. If the sequence is *valid*, then the sequence is equivalent to $(q_1, a_1 \cdot a_2 \cdot a_3, q_6)$. If the sequence is not a cycle ($q_1 \neq q_6$) it can be fired at most once and POST_STAR$(\pi, (q_1, \mathbf{x}))$ is $(q_6, \text{POST}(a_1 \cdot a_2 \cdot a_3, \mathbf{x})) + (q_1, \mathbf{x})$. If the sequence is a cycle (i.e., $q_1 = q_6$) then POST_STAR$(\pi, (q, \mathbf{x}))$ is $(q_1, \text{POST\_STAR}(a_1 \cdot a_2 \cdot a_3, \mathbf{x}))$ if $q = q_1$, and $(q, \mathbf{x})$ otherwise. Finally POST_STAR is extended to $L^{|Q|}$ in the obvious way. The extension for global acceleration considers the intersections of the regular language e with the regular languages of transitions from a location q to another location q'.

Example 4.2. **Loop acceleration.** Minsky machines support loop acceleration in frameworks where formulae in L define *upward-closed sets* or *semi-linear sets*. But upward-closed sets (for example) are not expressive enough to support flat acceleration.
Flat acceleration. Counter systems (with finite monoid) equipped with Presburger formulae supports flat acceleration [26, theorem 2]. Other examples are channel systems with cqdd [14, theorem 5.1], non-counting channel systems with slre [27, theorem 5.2] or qdd[12, theorem 6], lossy channel systems with sre [1, corollary 6.5]. Restricted counter systems used by TREX equipped with arithmetics almost supports flat acceleration [2, lemma 5.1]: their POST_STAR is not recursive.
Global acceleration. Reversal-counter systems [31], 2-dim VASS [34], lossy VASS and other subclasses of VASS with Presburger formulae [35], pushdown systems with regular languages or semi-commutative rewriting systems with APC languages [16], support global acceleration.

Obviously "global $\Rightarrow$ flat $\Rightarrow$ loop". Loop acceleration is often easy to obtain, but rarely sufficient in fixpoint computations. Flat acceleration is more flexible, but often requires good compositional properties of Σ and more complex methods for POST_STAR. Global acceleration is a very strong property that ensures post* is effectively L-definable. Clearly most interesting families of systems do not support global acceleration since they are Turing powerful. Then for our purpose, flat acceleration is likely to be the best compromise. The rest of the paper will focus on flat acceleration.

4.2   Restricted Linear Regular Expressions

Flat acceleration allows to compute the effect of more general expressions than iterations of sequences of actions. Given an alphabet A, a *restricted linear regular expression* (rlre) over A is a regular expression ρ of the form $u_1^* \ldots u_n^*$ where, for all i, $u_i \in A^*$. This is closely related to semi-linear regular expressions [27,30].

Proposition 4.3. *Let S support flat acceleration. Then for any* rlre *ρ over T and for any* $x_0 \in L^{|Q|}$, $\mathrm{post}(\rho, [\![x_0]\!])$ *is effectively L-definable.*

4.3   Flat Systems and Flattenings

In general, flat acceleration does not ensure computability of the reachability set. However it does in some cases, for example with *"flat"* systems, that have *no nested loops*. Consider the system on the right: its reachability

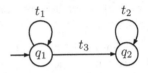

set can be computed by iterating first t_1, then firing t_3, and finally iterating t_2.

Definition 4.4   (Flat system [20,27,30]). *An uninterpreted system* $S = (\Sigma, Q, T)$ *is* flat *if for any location q, there exists at most one elementary cycle containing q. A system* $S = (\Sigma, Q, T, D, [\![\cdot]\!])$ *is* flat *if* $S = (\Sigma, Q, T)$ *is flat.*

In Fig. 1, S_0 is not flat because its two elementary cycles both visit q_2.

Proposition 4.5. *If S is a flat system supporting flat acceleration, then* $\mathrm{post}_S^*([\![x]\!])$ *is effectively L-definable.*

Not all systems of interest are flat, and a possible method for dealing with a non-flat system S is to find an equivalent flat system, called a *flattening* of S.

Definition 4.6   (Flattening). *A system* $S' = (Q', \Sigma, T', D, [\![\cdot]\!])$ *is a flattening of a system* $S = (Q, \Sigma, T, D, [\![\cdot]\!])$ *if (1) S' is flat, and (2) there exists a mapping* $z : Q' \to Q$, *called* folding, *such that* $\forall (q_1', w, q_2') \in T'$, $(z(q_1'), w, z(q_2')) \in T$.

Flattening is a form of partial unfolding. The following figure shows a system (left) and one of its flattenings (right).

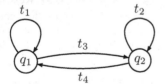
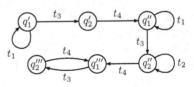

Assume S' is a flattening of some S. The z folding extends to configurations of S' by $z((q', x)) = (z(q'), x)$. Extension of z to $X \subseteq \mathcal{C}_{S'}$ is defined by:

$$z\left(\bigcup_{q' \in Q'} \{q'\} \times D_{q'} \right) = \bigcup_{q \in Q} \{q\} \times \left(\bigcup_{q' \in z^{-1}(q)} D_{q'} \right).$$

This gives an effective extension of z to L-definable subsets of $\mathcal{C}_{S'}$. Given $X' \subseteq \mathcal{C}_{S'}$, Definition 4.6 ensures that $z(\mathrm{post}_{S'}^*(X')) \subseteq \mathrm{post}_S^*(z(X'))$ and that for any language $\mathcal{L} \subseteq T^*$, $z(\mathrm{post}_{S'}(\mathcal{L}, [\![x']\!])) = \mathrm{post}_S(z(\mathcal{L}), z([\![x']\!]))$.

Definition 4.7 (*L*-**flattable**). *A system* $S = (Q, \Sigma, T, D, [\![\cdot]\!])$ *is* L-*flattable iff for any* $\mathbf{x} \in L^{|Q|}$, *there exists a flattening* $S' = (Q', \Sigma, T', D, [\![\cdot]\!])$ *of* S *and a* $\mathbf{x}' \in L^{|Q'|}$ *such that* $z([\![\mathbf{x}']\!]) = [\![\mathbf{x}]\!]$ *and* $z(\text{post}^*_{S'}([\![\mathbf{x}']\!])) = \text{post}^*_S(z([\![\mathbf{x}']\!]))$.

Prop. 4.5 extends to flattable systems:

Theorem 4.8. *If* S *is a* L-*flattable system supporting flat acceleration, then* $\text{post}^*_S([\![\mathbf{x}]\!])$ *is effectively* L-*definable.*

A natural question is whether L-flattable systems are common or rare. It appears that many systems with L-definable reachability sets are flattable. For example 2-dim VASS [34], timed automata [21], k-reversal counter machines, lossy VASS and other subclasses of VASS [35] and all L-uniformly bounded systems (see section 3) are L-flattable. Clearly, there is no equivalence in general: lossy channel systems have L-definable reachability sets but are not flattable. Interesting open questions are whether well-known subclasses with L-definable reachability sets (like Presburger definable VASS) are L-flattable or not.

We conclude by noting that L-flattability is undecidable in general, even when restricting to 2-counter systems:

Theorem 4.9. *Assuming the symbolic framework of 2-counter systems and Presburger formulae, the question of whether a 2-counter system* S *is* L-*flattable is undecidable.*

5 Computing Reachability Set Using Flat Acceleration

The previous characterization leads to a complete procedure for flattable systems: (1) enumerate all flattenings S' of S; (2) for each S', compute its reachability set X; (3) check whether $z(X)$ is closed by post in S.

However flattenings are not easy to handle and this motivates the following alternative characterization based on rlre's.

Theorem 5.1. *A system* $S = (Q, \Sigma, T, D, [\![\cdot]\!])$ *is* L-*flattable iff for all* $\mathbf{x} \in L^{|Q|}$, *there exists a rlre* ρ *over* T *such that* $\text{post}^*([\![\mathbf{x}]\!]) = \text{post}(\rho, [\![\mathbf{x}]\!])$.

Hence reachability set computation for flattable systems reduces to exploring the set of rlre over T, which can be achieved by increasing a sequence of rlre: see Procedure 2. Observe that REACH2 must choose *"fairly"*. Here this means that, in a nonterminating execution of the procedure, each $w \in T^*$ is selected infinitely often. Many simple schemes ensuring such a fair choice are possible.

Theorem 5.2. *Given a symbolic framework* $SF = (I, L)$ *and a system* $S \in \mathcal{F}(I)$
1. when REACH2 *terminates,* $[\![\text{REACH2}(\mathbf{x}_0)]\!] = \text{post}^*([\![\mathbf{x}_0]\!])$ *(partial correctness);*
2. REACH2 *terminates on any input iff* S *is* L-*flattable (termination).*

Remark 5.3. Termination for L-flattable systems does not hold if the symbolic framework provides only a weak inclusion (or if POST_STAR returns an over-approximation).

```
procedure REACH2(x₀)
parameter: S
input: x₀ ∈ L^|Q|
 1: x ← x₀
 2: while POST(x) ⊈ x do
 3:     Choose fairly w ∈ T*
 4:     x ← POST_STAR(w, x)
 5: end while
 6: return x
```

Procedure 2: Computing reachability sets with flat acceleration

5.1   Faster Enumeration of Flattenings

A major practical issue with REACH2 is to implement **Choose** so that we converge quickly to the fixpoint. For this purpose the following heuristic proved very efficient in FAST: one picks a bound $k \in \mathbb{N}$ and restricts **Choose** to sequences $w \in T^{\leq k}$, i.e., of length at most k. This method, called k-flattable, is eventually stopped by a **Watchdog** if it does not terminate. Then k is incremented and k-flattable is launched again.

This leads to Procedure REACH3 below. For "fairness" we require that **Watchdog** fires infinitely often, but only after **Choose** picked each $w \in T^{\leq k}$ at least once.

```
procedure REACH3(x₀)
parameter: S
input: x₀ ∈ L^|Q|
 1: x ← x₀ ; k ← 0
 2: k ← k + 1
 3: start
 4:     while POST(x) ⊈ x do          /* k-flattable */
 5:         Choose fairly w ∈ T^{≤k}
 6:         x ← POST_STAR(w, x)
 7:     end while                      /* end k-flattable */
 8: with
 9:     when Watchdog stops goto 2
10: return x
```

Procedure 3: Flat acceleration and circuit length increasing

Theorem 5.4. *Given a symbolic framework $SF = (I, L)$ and a system $S \in \mathcal{F}(I)$*
1. when REACH3 terminates, $[\![REACH3(x_0)]\!] = \text{post}^*([\![x_0]\!])$ (partial correctness);
2. REACH3 terminates for any input iff S is L-flattable (termination).

Technical issues. When implementing REACH3 one faces (at least) two practical problems. First the *size* [2] of the region x computed so far may be explosive. Then **Watchdog**

---

[2] Each set of regions has its own natural measure for size, depending on data structures and implementation.

needs some criterion. Below we describe the implementation choices made in FAST on these two issues, believing that these solutions may adapt to other domains. Let us point out that these choices do not respect exactly the specification for REACH3 since fairness is not ensured, and FAST should be improved in this way.

Choose: In general there is no direct relationship between the size of a region x and the "size" of its concretization $[\![x]\!]$. Intermediate regions may be much larger than the final region for post*($[\![x_0]\!]$). To avoid such large regions, **Choose** selects a next $w \in T^{\leq k}$ such that $|\text{POST\_STAR}(w, x)| < |x|$. If there is no such w then the size of the current x is allowed to increase and the next w is picked. In practice, this enumeration works well (while a cyclic enumeration of $T^{\leq k}$ almost always runs out of memory).

Watchdog: FAST's criterion is simply a fixed (but user-modifiable) limit on the number of iterations in **k-flattable** for any given value of k. This cannot be fair but it works well in practice since, once a k large enough is considered, the fixpoint is usually found within a few iterations.

5.2 Reduction of the Number of Cycles

A remaining issue in REACH3 is that the cardinal of $T^{\leq k}$ grows exponentially with k. We introduce the notion of reduction to compact the number of relevant transitions.

Definition 5.5 (k-Reduction). *Given an interpretation* $I = (\Sigma, D, [\![\cdot]\!])$, *a k-reduction r maps each system* $S = (Q, \Sigma, T, D, [\![\cdot]\!]) \in \mathcal{F}(I)$ *to a system* $S' = (Q, \Sigma, T', D, [\![\cdot]\!]) \in \mathcal{F}(I)$ *such that: (1)* $\forall t' \in T', \xrightarrow{t'} \subseteq \xrightarrow{T^*}$, *(2)* $\forall w \in T^{\leq k}, \exists \rho \in rlre(T'). \xrightarrow{w^*} \subseteq \xrightarrow{\rho}$, *(3)* $|T'| \leq |T^{\leq k}|$.

Hence a k-reduction replaces T by a new set T' that can stand for $T^{\leq k}$ but is smaller. In particular, if S is L-flattable, then $r(S)$ is too, and they both have the same reachability set. Obvious (and naive) k-reductions are the removals of identity loops. More useful generic reductions are *conjugation reduction*: only keep one sequence of transitions among each conjugacy class (e.g., keep $t_1 \cdot t_2 \cdot t_3$ but remove $t_2 \cdot t_3 \cdot t_1$ and $t_3 \cdot t_1 \cdot t_2$) and *commuting reduction*: if t_1 and t_2 commute, i.e., if $\xrightarrow{t_1 t_2} = \xrightarrow{t_2 t_1}$, then remove both $t_1 \cdot t_2$ and $t_2 \cdot t_1$ (works since $\xrightarrow{(t_1 \cdot t_2)^*} = \xrightarrow{t_1^* t_2^*}$).

Proposition 5.6. *Conjugation reduction and commuting reduction are k-reductions. Conjugation reduction satisfies* $|T'| = \mathcal{O}(\frac{|T^k|}{k})$.

Beyond these generic reductions, it is worth developing reductions dedicated to a specific interpretation. For linear counter systems with a finite monoid, [26] presents a reduction where $|T'|$ remains polynomial in k (while $|T^{\leq k}|$ is exponential). This appears to be a key reason for FAST's performances.

Here are reduction results for the swimming pool protocol (a VASS with 7 transitions and 6 variables studied in [29]). Computing the reachability set requires considering cycles of length $k = 4$. In the table $V_k \subseteq T^{\leq k}$ is the set of *valid sequences* in $T^{\leq k}$. T' (resp. T'') is from the system after the reduction of [26] (resp. further combined with commuting reduction).

k	$|V_k|$	$|T'|$	$|T''|$
1	7	7	7
2	36	21	16
3	156	56	28
4	**578**	**126**	**47**
5	1890	252	86

6   Conclusion: Flat Acceleration in Practice

6.1   Tools Comparison

Our framework is useful when comparing ALV, FAST, LASH and TREX, four symbolic model checkers that can perform reachability analysis on counter systems (see section 2.1). We restrict this comparison to the exact forward computation of $post^*(\llbracket x_0 \rrbracket)$. ALV [6]

	ALV	FAST	LASH	TREX
system	full	linear		restricted
regions	Presburger formula			arith. undec. $\sqsubseteq$
acceleration	no	flat	loop	$\approx$ flat
termination	UB	F	1F	kF (oracle $\sqsubseteq$)

handles full counter systems. Regions are Presburger formulae. The heuristic used is similar to REACH1. Both FAST [8] and LASH [33] handle linear counter systems with Presburger formulae: flat acceleration is supported for functions whose monoid is finite, but while FAST really takes advantage of full flat acceleration (Procedure REACH3), the heuristics in LASH are restricted to loop acceleration (Procedure REACH2 where w is chosen in $T^{\leq 1}$ instead of T^*). TREX [3] handles restricted counter systems. Regions are arithmetic formulae (hence $\sqsubseteq$ is not recursive). A partially recursive flat acceleration procedure is available. The heuristic is REACH2 restricted to $T^{\leq k}$ for a user-defined k. See [23] for an in-depth comparison of FAST and TREX. UB, F and kF stands for L-uniformly bounded, L-flattable and L-flattable with length k (UB $\subseteq$ 1F $\subseteq$ kF $\subseteq$ F).

Procedure comparison on case studies. The following table compares how ALV, FAST and LASH behave in practice. "Yes" means termination within 1200 seconds on a Pentium III 933 MHz with 512 Mb. k is the length of cycles FAST considered in Procedure REACH3. All case studies are infinite-state systems, taken from FAST's web site [8]. Experimental results show strong relationship with the acceleration framework: flat acceleration (FAST) has the better termination results, loop acceleration ($k =$

System	ALV	LASH	FAST	k
TTP	no	yes	yes	1
prod/cons (2)	no	yes	yes	1
prod/cons (N)	no	no	yes	2
lift control, N	no	no	yes	2
train	no	no	yes	2
consistency	no	no	yes	3
CSM, N	no	no	yes	2
swimming pool	no	no	yes	4
PNCSA	no	no	no	?
IncDec	no	no	no	?
BigJAVA	no	no	no	?

1) is not always sufficient, while simple iteration (ALV) is not sufficient on these complex examples (results are consistent with [10]). These experiments clearly suggest that **flat acceleration greatly enhances termination and is fully justified in practice, at least for counter systems.**

6.2   Tool Design

The flat acceleration framework provides guidelines for designing new techniques and tools. FAST supports completely this framework. Complex case studies have been conducted [8,9]. The following table shows performances of FAST on a significant pool of counter systems collected on the web sites of tools like ALV, BABYLON [7], BRAIN, LASH and TREX, and ranging from tricky academic puzzles (swimming pool) to complex industrial protocols (TTP). (More examples are given in the full version of this paper.) They all are infinite-state and are thus beyond the scope of traditional model checking techniques and tools. Furthermore, most of these systems also go beyond

System	var	$\|T\|$	sec.	Mb	k
CSM	13	13	45.57	6.31	2
FMS	22	20	157.48	8.02	2
Multipoll	17	20	22.96	5.13	1
Kanban	16	16	10.43	6.54	1
swimming pool	9	6	111	29.06	4
last i.-first s.	17	10	1.89	2.74	1
PC Java(2)	18	14	13.27	3.81	1
PC Java(N)	18	14	723.27	12.46	2
Central server	13	8	20.82	6.83	2
Consistency	12	8	275	7.35	3
M.E.S.I.	4	4	0.42	2.44	1
M.O.E.S.I.	4	5	0.56	2.49	1

System	var	$\|T\|$	sec.	Mb	k
Synapse	3	3	0.30	2.23	1
Illinois	4	6	0.97	2.64	1
Berkeley	4	3	0.49	2.75	1
Firefly	4	8	0.86	2.59	1
Dragon	5	8	1.42	2.72	1
Futurebus+	9	10	2.19	3.38	1
lift - N	4	5	4.56	2.90	3
barber m4	8	12	1.92	2.68	1
ticket 2i	6	6	0.88	2.54	1
ticket 3i	8	9	3.77	3.08	1
TTP	10	17	1186.24	73.24	1

VASS or Petri nets, so that methods like covering trees or backward computation do not apply. The results are for forward computation of the reachability set, on an Intel Pentium 933 Mhz with 512 Mb. Comparing them with other complex case studies analyzed with ALV, LASH, and TREX [3,6,10,33] confirms that flat acceleration is a powerful technique for handling infinite-state systems.

References

1. P. A. Abdulla, A. Collomb-Annichini, A. Bouajjani, and B. Jonsson. Using forward reachability analysis for verification of lossy channel systems. *FMSD*, 25(1):39–65, 2004.
2. A. Annichini, E. Asarin, and A. Bouajjani. Symbolic techniques for parametric reasoning about counter and clock systems. In *Proc. CAV'00*, LNCS 1855, pages 419–434, 2000.
3. A. Annichini, A. Bouajjani, and M. Sighireanu. TReX: A tool for reachability analysis of complex systems. In *Proc. CAV'01*, LNCS 2102, pages 368–372, 2001.
4. R. Alur, C. Courcoubetis, N. Halbwachs, T. A. Henzinger, Pei-Hsin Ho, X. Nicollin, A. Olivero, J. Sifakis, and S. Yovine. The algorithmic analysis of hybrid systems. *TCS*, 138(1):3–34, 1995.
5. R. Alur and D. L. Dill. A theory of timed automata. *TCS*, 126(2):183–235, 1994.
6. ALV. www.cs.ucsb.edu/~bultan/composite/.
7. BABYLON. www.ulb.ac.be/di/ssd/lvbegin/CST/.
8. S. Bardin, A. Finkel, J. Leroux, and L. Petrucci. FAST: Fast Acceleration of Symbolic Transition systems. In *Proc. CAV'03*, LNCS 2725, pages 118–121, 2003
9. S. Bardin, A. Finkel and J. Leroux. FASTer acceleration of counter automata. In *Proc. TACAS'04*, LNCS 2988, pages 576–590, 2004.
10. C. Bartzis and T. Bultan. Widening arithmetic automata. In *Proc. CAV'04*, LNCS 3114, pages 321–333, 2004.
11. B. Boigelot, L. Bronne, and S. Rassart. Improved reachability analysis method for strongly linear hybrid systems. In *Proc. CAV'97*, LNCS 1254, pages 167–178, 1997.
12. B. Boigelot, P. Godefroid, B. Willems, and P. Wolper. The power of QDDs. In *Proc. SAS'97*, LNCS 1302, pages 172–186, 1997.
13. A. Bouajjani, J. Esparza, A. Finkel, O. Maler, P. Rossmanith, B. Willems, and P. Wolper. An efficient automata approach to some problems on context-free grammars. *IPL*, 74(5–6):221–227, 2000.

14. A Bouajjani and P. Habermehl. Symbolic reachability analysis of FIFO-channel systems with nonregular sets of configurations. *TCS*, 221(1–2):211–250, 1999.
15. A. Bouajjani, B. Jonsson, M. Nilsson and T. Touili. Regular Model Checking. *Proc. CAV'00*, LNCS 1855, pages 403–418, 2000.
16. A. Bouajjani, A. Muscholl, and T. Touili. Permutation rewriting and algorithmic verification. In *Proc. LICS'01*, pages 399–408, 2001.
17. D. Brand and P. Zafiropulo. On communicating finite-state machines. *JACM*, 30(2):323–342, 1983.
18. T. Bultan, R. Gerber, and W. Pugh. Symbolic model-checking of infinite state systems using Presburger arithmetic. In *Proc. CAV'97*, LNCS 1254, pages 400–411, 1997.
19. E. M. Clarke, O. Grumberg, and D. A. Peled. *Model Checking*. MIT Press, 1999.
20. H. Comon and Y. Jurski. Multiple counters automata, safety analysis, and Presburger arithmetic. In *Proc. CAV'98*, LNCS 1427, pages 268–279, 1998.
21. H. Comon and Y. Jurski. Timed automata and the theory of real numbers. In *Proc. CONCUR'99*, LNCS 1664, pages 242–257, 1999.
22. P. Cousot. Abstract interpretation. *ACM Comp. Surv.*, 28(2):324–328, 1996.
23. Ch. Darlot, A. Finkel, and L. Van Begin. About Fast and TReX accelerations. In *Proc. AVoCS'04*, ENTCS 128(6), pages 87–103, 2005.
24. G. Delzanno, J.-F. Raskin, and L. Van Begin. Covering sharing trees: a compact data structure for parameterized verification. *JSTTT*, 5(2–3):268–297, 2004.
25. J. Esparza. Petri nets, commutative context-free grammars, and basic parallel processes. *Fund. Informaticae*, 31(1):13–25, 1997.
26. A. Finkel and J. Leroux. How to compose Presburger-accelerations: Applications to broadcast protocols. In *Proc. FSTTCS'02*, LNCS 2556, pages 145–156, 2002.
27. A. Finkel, S. Purushothaman Iyer, and G. Sutre. Well-abstracted transition systems: Application to FIFO automata. *Inf. & Comp.*, 181(1):1–31, 2003.
28. A. Finkel and Ph. Schnoebelen. Well-structured transition systems everywhere! *TCS*, 256(1–2):63–92, 2001.
29. L. Fribourg and H. Olsén. Proving Safety Properties of Infinite State Systems by Compilation into Presburger Arithmetic, In *Proc. CONCUR'97*, LNCS 1243, pages 213–227, 1997.
30. L. Fribourg. Petri nets, flat languages and linear arithmetic. In M. Alpuente, editor, *Proc. WFLP'00*, pages 344–365, 2000.
31. O. H. Ibarra, Jianwen Su, Zhe Dang, T. Bultan, and R. A. Kemmerer. Counter machines and verification problems. *TCS*, 289(1):165–189, 2002.
32. Y. Kesten, O. Maler, M. Marcus, A. Pnueli, and E. Shahar. Symbolic model checking with rich assertional languages. *TCS*, 256(1–2):93–112, 2001.
33. LASH. www.montefiore.ulg.ac.be/~boigelot/research/lash/.
34. J. Leroux and G. Sutre. On flatness for 2-dimensional vector addition systems with states. In *Proc. CONCUR'04*, LNCS 3170, pages 402–416, 2004.
35. J. Leroux and G. Sutre. Flat counter automata almost everywhere! In *Proc. ATVA'05*, this volume.
36. J. K. Pachl. Protocol description and analysis based on a state transition model with channel expressions. In *Proc. PSTV '87*, pages 207–219, 1987.
37. T. Rybina and A. Voronkov. Brain: Backward reachability analysis with integers. In *Proc. AMAST'02*, LNCS 2422, pages 489–494, 2002.
38. P. Wolper and B. Boigelot. Verifying systems with infinite but regular state spaces. In *Proc. CAV'98*, LNCS 1427, pages 88–97, 1998.

Flat Counter Automata Almost Everywhere!*

Jérôme Leroux[1] and Grégoire Sutre[2]

[1] IRISA, Vertecs Project, Campus de Beaulieu, Rennes, France
jleroux@irisa.fr
[2] LaBRI, CNRS UMR 5800, Domaine Universitaire, Talence, France
sutre@labri.fr

Abstract. This paper argues that flatness appears as a central notion in the verification of counter automata. A counter automaton is called flat when its control graph can be "replaced", equivalently w.r.t. reachability, by another one with no nested loops. From a practical view point, we show that flatness is a necessary and sufficient condition for termination of accelerated symbolic model checking, a generic semi-algorithmic technique implemented in successful tools like FAST, LASH or TREX. From a theoretical view point, we prove that many known semilinear subclasses of counter automata are flat: reversal bounded counter machines, lossy vector addition systems with states, reversible Petri nets, persistent and conflict-free Petri nets, etc. Hence, for these subclasses, the semilinear reachability set can be computed using a *uniform* accelerated symbolic procedure (whereas previous algorithms were specifically designed for each subclass).

1 Introduction

Petri nets and *counter automata* are widely used formalisms to model concurrent distributed systems. Basically, a counter automaton is a finite-state automaton extended with counters that hold nonnegative integer values. Operations on counters can be defined by formulas in Presburger arithmetic. As the counters are unbounded, counter automata are naturally *infinite-state* systems.

Various formalisms have been proposed to model desired properties on systems. In this work, we only consider *safety* properties: these properties (of the original system) may often be expressed by *reachability properties* on the model.

Reachability properties are algorithmically checkable for *finite-state* systems (and efficient implementations exist). However, the situation is more complex for *infinite-state* systems: the reachability problem is undecidable even for restricted classes of systems, such as Minsky machines [Min67].

Dedicated algorithms for counter automata. Many specialized algorithms have been designed to solve verification problems for various classes of counter automata. The reachability problem for Petri nets has been proved decidable [May84, Kos82]. The binary reachability relation is effectively semilinear for reversible Petri nets [Tai68] and for BPP-nets [Esp97], and the reachability set post* is effectively semilinear for cyclic Petri

---

* This work was supported by the French Ministry of Research (Project PERSÉE of the ACI Sécurité et Informatique).

D.A. Peled and Y.-K. Tsay (Eds.): ATVA 2005, LNCS 3707, pp. 489–503, 2005.
© Springer-Verlag Berlin Heidelberg 2005

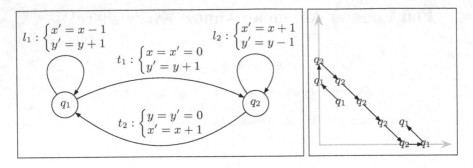

Fig. 1. A non-flat counter automaton

nets [AK77], for persistent Petri nets [LR78, May81] and for regular Petri nets [VVN81]. The reachability sets post* and pre* are effectively semilinear for reversal-bounded counter machines [Iba78], for lossy VASS [BM99] and for 2-dimensional VASS [HP79]. It was later shown that post* / pre* are still effectively semilinear for various extensions of 2-dim VASS [FS00b, FS00a]. However, these methods suffer from serious drawbacks: (1) they cannot be easily extended or combined, (2) from an implementation perspective, a dedicated tool would be needed for each specialized algorithm, and (3) in practice, counter automata rarely belong entirely to one of these semilinear classes. Thus, generic symbolic model-checking techniques for general (undecidable) classes have been recently developped and implemented.

Accelerated symbolic model-checking.   Verification of reachability properties usually proceeds through an iterative fixpoint computation of the *forward reachability set* post* (resp. *backward reachability set* pre*), starting from the initial states (resp. from the error states). When the state space is infinite, finite *symbolic representations* for sets of states are required. To help termination of this fixpoint computation, so-called *acceleration* techniques (or *meta-transitions*) are applied [BW94, BGWW97, BH99, FIS03, FL02]. Basically, acceleration consists in computing in one step the effect of iterating a given loop (of the control flow graph). Accelerated symbolic model checkers such as LASH [Las], TREX [ABS01], and FAST [BFLP03] implement this approach.

Even though it behaves well in practice, accelerated symbolic model-checking is only a *semi*-algorithm: it does not provide any guarantee of termination. For instance, iteration of loops is not sufficient to compute the whole semilinear reachability set of the counter automata depicted in figure 1, with initial state $(q_1, (0, 0))$ (see Examples 2.4 and 4.5). Thus, we would like to combine the best of both approaches, by integrating, for each known semilinear class, the dedicated algorithm's technology into improved acceleration techniques that would ensure termination of the generic accelerated semi-algorithm for this class. A first step towards this objective consists in characterizing the classes for which the generic accelerated semi-algorithm fials to terminate.

Our contribution.   In this work, we investigate termination of accelerated symbolic model-checking for known semilinear classes of counter automata. A natural notion in this framework is *flatness* [FO97, CJ98]: a counter automaton S is called *flat*[1] when its control graph can be "replaced", equivalently w.r.t. reachability, by another one with no nested loops. We show that (global) flatness is a necessary and sufficient condition for termination of (binary) reachability set computations by acceleration-based semi-algorithms. In particular, we get that accelerated symbolic model checkers terminate on a given system iff this system is flat (and a suitable search strategy is used).

We then turn our attention to the analysis of flatness for known semilinear classes of counter automata. We show that most of the known semilinear classes of counter automata (in particular the ones cited above) are flat. Our main technical contributions are the proofs of flatness for the following classes: reversal-bounded counter machines, reversible Petri nets and conflict-free Petri nets. In particular, we obtain that the binary reachability relation is effectively semilinear of conflict-free Petri nets. We also show that cyclic Petri nets, persistent Petri nets, regular Petri nets and Lossy / Inserting counter machines are flat, and we recall that BPP-nets and 2-dim VASS are flat. As flatness implies effective semilinearity of the forward / binary reachability set, our results give new "uniform" proofs that these classes are semilinear. In particular, we obtain a simpler semilinearity proofs for reversal-bounded counter machines and reversible Petri nets.

It is also remarkable that accelerated symbolic model checkers designed to analyse counter automata, such as LASH and FAST, terminate on all these classes. From a practical viewpoint, our approach has several benefits: (1) we can apply a *generic* algorithm, which was designed for a much larger class of (undecidable) systems, and (2) the — forward, backward and binary — reachability sets can be computed using the same generic algorithm.

Outline. The paper is organized as follows. Section 2 presents general counter automata. We introduce the notion of flatness in Section 3 and we show that flatness is a necessary and sufficient condition for termination of accelerated symbolic model-checking. In the last two sections, we show that many known semilinear restricted classes of counter automata are flat: Section 4 deals with classes of counter machines, and Section 5 deals with classes of Petri nets.

Proofs. Some proofs had to be omitted due to space constraints. A self-contained long version of this paper (with detailed proofs for all results) can be obtained from the authors.

2   General Counter Automata

This section is devoted to the presentation of general counter automata. We will consider in section 4 a more effective subclass of counter automa based on guarded commands. We first give basic definitions and notations that will be used throughout the paper.

---

[1] Our notion of flatness is actually more general than in [CJ98]: there, a system is called flat when it contains no nested loops.

2.1 Numbers, Vectors, Relations

Let $\mathbb{Z}$ (resp. $\mathbb{N}$, $\mathbb{Z}^-$, $\mathbb{Q}$, $\mathbb{Q}_+$) denotes the set of *integers* (resp. *nonnegative integers, nonpositive integers, rational numbers, nonnegative rational numbers*). We denote by $\leq$ the *usual total order on* $\mathbb{Q}$. Given $k, l \in \mathbb{N}$, we write $[k \mathinner{..} l]$ (resp. $[k \mathinner{..} \infty[$) for the *interval of integers* $\{i \in \mathbb{N} \;/\; k \leq i \leq l\}$ (resp. $\{i \in \mathbb{N} \;/\; k \leq i\}$). We write $|X|$ the *cardinal* of any finite set X.

Given a set X and $n \in \mathbb{N}$, we write X^n for the set of n-dim *vectors* x of elements in X. For any index $i \in [1 \mathinner{..} n]$, we denote by $\mathsf{x}[i]$ the ith *component* of an n-dim vector x.

We now focus on n-dim vectors of (integer or rational) numbers. We write 0 for the *all zero vector*: $0[i] = 0$ for all $i \in [1 \mathinner{..} n]$. We also denote by $\leq$ the *usual partial order on* $\mathbb{Q}^n$, defined by $\mathsf{x} \leq \mathsf{y}$ if for all $i \in [1 \mathinner{..} n]$ we have $\mathsf{x}[i] \leq \mathsf{y}[i]$.

Operations on n-dim vectors are componentwise extensions of their scalar counterpart (e.g. for $\mathsf{x}, \mathsf{x}' \in \mathbb{Q}^n$, $\mathsf{x} + \mathsf{x}'$ is the vector $\mathsf{y} \in \mathbb{Q}^n$ defined by $\mathsf{y}[i] = \mathsf{x}[i] + \mathsf{x}'[i]$ for all $i \in [1 \mathinner{..} n]$). For $\alpha \in \mathbb{Q}$ and $\mathsf{x} \in \mathbb{Q}^n$, $\alpha \mathsf{x}$ is the vector $\mathsf{y} \in \mathbb{Q}^n$ defined by $\mathsf{y}[i] = \alpha \mathsf{x}[i]$ for all $i \in [1 \mathinner{..} n]$.

These operations are classically extended on sets of n-dim vectors (e.g. for $P, P' \subseteq \mathbb{Q}^n$, $P + P' = \{\mathsf{p} + \mathsf{p}' \;/\; \mathsf{p} \in P, \mathsf{p}' \in P'\}$). Moreover, in an operation involving sets of n-dim vectors, we shortly write x for the singleton $\{\mathsf{x}\}$ (e.g. for $P \subseteq \mathbb{Q}^n$ and $\mathsf{x} \in \mathbb{Q}^n$, we write $\mathsf{x} + P$ for $\{\mathsf{x}\} + P$).

A *binary relation* R on some set X is any subset of $X \times X$. We shortly write $x \, R \, x'$ whenever $(x, x') \in R$. Given a set Y, we denote by $R[Y]$ the *relational image* of Y by R, defined by $R[Y] = \{x \in X \;/\; \exists y \in Y, y \, R \, x\}$. The *inverse* of a binary relation R on X is the binary relation R^{-1} on X defined by $x \, R^{-1} \, x'$ iff $x' \, R \, x$. We say R is *symmetric* if $R = R^{-1}$. Given two binary relations R_1, R_2 on X, the *composed binary relation* $R_1 \cdot R_2$ on X is defined by $x \, (R_1 \cdot R_2) \, x'$ if we have $x \, R_1 \, y$ and $y \, R_2 \, x'$ for some $y \in X$. We denote by R^* the *reflexive and transitive closure* of R. The *identity relation on* X is the binary relation $Id_X = \{(x, x) \;/\; x \in X\}$. In the rest of the paper, we will only consider binary relations, and they will shortly be called *relations*.

2.2 Presburger Arithmetic and Semilinear Sets

Presburger arithmetic (the first order additive theory over the integers $\langle \mathbb{Z}, +, \leq \rangle$) is a decidable logic used in a large range of applications. As described in [Lat04], this logic is central in many areas including integer programming problems, compiler optimization techniques, program analysis tools and model-checking.

Presburger-definable subsets of $\mathbb{Z}^n$ may also be represented in terms of *semilinear sets* [GS66]. For any subset $P \subseteq \mathbb{Z}^n$, we denote by P^* the set of all (finite) linear combinations of vectors in P:

$$P^* = \left\{ \textstyle\sum_{i=0}^{k} c_i \, \mathsf{p}_i \;/\; k, c_0, \ldots, c_k \in \mathbb{N} \text{ and } \mathsf{p}_0, \ldots, \mathsf{p}_k \in P \right\}$$

A subset $S \subseteq \mathbb{Z}^n$ is said to be a *linear set* if $S = (\mathsf{x} + P^*)$ for some $\mathsf{x} \in \mathbb{Z}^n$ and for some finite subset $P \subseteq \mathbb{Z}^n$; moreover x is called the *basis* and vectors in P are called *periods.* A *semilinear set* is any finite union of linear sets. Let us recall that semilinear sets are precisely the subsets of $\mathbb{Z}^n$ that are definable in Presburger arithmetic [GS66].

Observe that any finite non empty set Q can be "encoded" using a bijection η from Q to $[1 .. |Q|]$. Thus, these semilinearity notions and Presburger-definability notions naturally carry[2] over subsets of $Q \times \mathbb{Z}^n$ and over relations on $Q \times \mathbb{Z}^n$.

2.3   Counter Automata

Definition 2.1. *A n-dim counter automaton $\mathcal{S}$ (counter automaton for short), is defined as a tuple $\mathcal{S} = (Q, T, \alpha, \beta, (G_t)_{t \in T})$, where Q is a finite non empty set of locations, T is a finite non empty set of transitions, $\alpha : T \to Q$ and $\beta : T \to Q$ are the source and target mappings, and $(G_t)_{t \in T}$ is a family of binary relations on $\mathbb{N}^n$ called flow guards.*

An n-dim counter automaton is basically a finite graph whose edges are labeled by relations over n-dim vector of integers. Each component $i \in [1 .. n]$ corresponds to a counter ranging over $\mathbb{N}$. Operationally, control flows from one location to another along transitions, and counters simultaneously change values according to the transition's flow guard.

Formally, let $\mathcal{S} = (Q, T, \alpha, \beta, (G_t)_{t \in T})$ be a n-dim counter automaton. The *set of configuration* $\mathcal{C}_\mathcal{S}$ of $\mathcal{S}$ is $Q \times \mathbb{N}^n$, and the semantics of each transition $t \in T$ is given by the *action reachability relation* $\mathcal{R}_\mathcal{S}(t)$ over $\mathcal{C}_\mathcal{S}$ defined by:

$$(q, \mathsf{x}) \; \mathcal{R}_\mathcal{S}(t) \; (q', \mathsf{x}') \qquad \text{if} \qquad q = \alpha(t) \text{ and } q' = \beta(t) \text{ and } \mathsf{x} \, G_t \, \mathsf{x}'$$

Definition 2.2. *An initialized n-dim counter automaton $(\mathcal{S}, I)$ is a tuple such that $\mathcal{S}$ is an n-dim counter automaton and $I \subseteq \mathcal{C}_\mathcal{S}$.*

We write T^+ for the set of all *non empty words* $t_0 \cdots t_k$ with $t_i \in T$, and ε denotes the *empty word*. The set $T^+ \cup \{\varepsilon\}$ of all *words* π over T is denoted by T^*. For any word $\pi \in T^*$ and for any $t \in T$, we let $|\pi|_t$ denote the number of occurences of t in π. Flow guards and transition reachability relations are naturally extended to words:

$$\begin{cases} G_\varepsilon = Id_{\mathbb{N}^n} \\ G_{\pi \cdot t} = G_\pi \cdot G_t \end{cases} \qquad \begin{cases} \mathcal{R}_\mathcal{S}(\varepsilon) = Id_{\mathcal{C}_\mathcal{S}} \\ \mathcal{R}_\mathcal{S}(\pi \cdot t) = \mathcal{R}_\mathcal{S}(\pi) \cdot \mathcal{R}_\mathcal{S}(t) \end{cases}$$

A *language* over T is any subset L of T^*. We also extend flow guards and reachability relations to languages : $G_L = \bigcup_{\pi \in L} G_\pi$ and $\mathcal{R}_\mathcal{S}(L) = \bigcup_{\pi \in L} \mathcal{R}_\mathcal{S}(\pi)$. For any language $L \subseteq T^*$ and for any set of configurations $I \subseteq \mathcal{C}_\mathcal{S}$, we respectively denote by $\mathsf{post}_\mathcal{S}(L, I)$ and by $\mathsf{pre}_\mathcal{S}(L, I)$ the set of *successor* configurations $(\mathcal{R}_\mathcal{S}(L))[I]$ and the set of *predecessor* configurations $(\mathcal{R}_\mathcal{S}(L))^{-1}[I]$.

Definition 2.3. *Given a counter automaton $\mathcal{S}$, the one-step reachability relation of $\mathcal{S}$ is the relation $\mathcal{R}_\mathcal{S}(T)$, shortly written $\mathcal{R}_\mathcal{S}$. The global reachability relation of $\mathcal{S}$ is the relation $\mathcal{R}_\mathcal{S}(T^*)$, shortly written $\mathcal{R}_\mathcal{S}^*$. Given a subset $I \subseteq \mathcal{C}_\mathcal{S}$, the sets $\mathsf{post}_\mathcal{S}(T^*, I)$, shortly written $\mathsf{post}_\mathcal{S}^*(I)$, and $\mathsf{pre}_\mathcal{S}(T^*, I)$, shortly written $\mathsf{pre}_\mathcal{S}^*(I)$, are respectively called the forward reachability set of $(\mathcal{S}, I)$ and the backward reachability set of $(\mathcal{S}, I)$.*

---

[2] Obviously, the extension of these notions does not depend on the "encoding" η.

Remark that the global reachability relation is the reflexive and transitive closure of the one-step reachability relation. A *reachability subrelation* is any relation $R \subseteq \mathcal{R}_{\mathcal{S}}^*$. For the reader familiar with transition systems, the operational semantics of $\mathcal{S}$ can be viewed as the infinite-state transition system $(\mathcal{C}_{\mathcal{S}}, \mathcal{R}_{\mathcal{S}})$.

The *inverse counter automaton* $\mathcal{S}^{-1}$ of a counter automaton $\mathcal{S}$ is obtained from $\mathcal{S}$ by replacing the flow guards G_t with their inverse G_t^{-1}. As $\mathrm{pre}_{\mathcal{S}}(L, I) = \mathrm{post}_{\mathcal{S}^{-1}}(L, I)$ for every $L \subseteq T^*$ and $I \subseteq \mathcal{C}_{\mathcal{S}}$, we restrict our attention (without loss of generality) to the *global reachability relation* and the *forward reachability set* (shortly called *reachability set* from now on).

Consider two locations q and q' in a system $\mathcal{S}$. A word $\pi \in T^*$ is called a *path from q to q'* if either (1) $\pi = \varepsilon$ and $q = q'$, or (2) $\pi = t_0 \cdots t_k$ with $k \in \mathbb{N}$ and satisfies: $q = \alpha(t_0)$, $q' = \beta(t_k)$ and $\beta(t_{i-1}) = \alpha(t_i)$ for every $i \in [1 \mathinner{..} k]$. A path from q to q is called a *loop on q*, or shortly a *loop*. We denote by $\Pi_{\mathcal{S}}(q, q')$ the set of all paths from q to q' in $\mathcal{S}$. The set $\bigcup_{q, q' \in Q} \Pi_{\mathcal{S}}(q, q')$ of all *paths* in $\mathcal{S}$ is written $\Pi_{\mathcal{S}}$. A *trace* of an initialized counter automaton $(\mathcal{S}, I)$ is any word $\pi \in T^*$ such that $\mathrm{post}(\pi, I) \neq \emptyset$. Note that every trace is a path, but the converse is not true.

Notation. In the following, we will simply write $\mathcal{R}$ (resp. post, Π, C) instead of $\mathcal{R}_{\mathcal{S}}$ (resp. $\mathrm{post}_{\mathcal{S}}$, $\Pi_{\mathcal{S}}$, $\mathcal{C}_{\mathcal{S}}$), when the underlying counter automaton is unambiguous. We will also sometimes write $\rightarrow$ (resp. $\xrightarrow{\sigma}$, $\xrightarrow{L}$, $\xrightarrow{*}$) instead of $\mathcal{R}$ (resp. $\mathcal{R}(\sigma)$, $\mathcal{R}(L)$, $\mathcal{R}^*$).

Example 2.4. Consider the 2-dim counter automaton $\mathcal{E}$ depicted in figure 1. Counters are denoted by x and y and flow guards are given by predicates over x, y, x', and y' (with an implicit conjunction between equalities). Intuitively, the loop l_1 on location q_1 transfers the contents of the first counter into the second counter, while the loop l_2 on location q_2 does the converse. *Intermediate locations* along $(q_1, (1, 2)) \xrightarrow{l_1 t_1 l_2^4 t_2 l_1} (q_1, (4, 1))$ are also depicted above. This counter automaton exhibits a simple global reachability relation, since it is readily seen that $(q_1, (x, y)) \xrightarrow{*} (q_1, (x', y'))$ if and only if: $(x' + y') - (x + y)$ is even, and $x' + y' = x + y$ implies $x' \leq x$. Relation $(q_2, (x, y)) \xrightarrow{*} (q_2, (x', y'))$ is similar, and thus we obtain, by composition with relations $\mathcal{R}_{\mathcal{E}}(t_1)$ and $\mathcal{R}_{\mathcal{E}}(t_2)$, that $\mathcal{E}$ has a semilinear global reachability relation. □

3   Flatness as a Criterion for Acceleration Completeness

We now investigate termination of accelerated symbolic reachability computations on counter automata. An important concept used in this paper is that of *semilinear path scheme (SLPS)* [LS04].

Definition 3.1. *[LS04] A linear path scheme (LPS for short) for a counter automaton $\mathcal{S}$ is any language $\rho \subseteq \Pi_{\mathcal{S}}$ of the form $\rho = \sigma_0 \theta_1^* \sigma_1 \cdots \theta_k^* \sigma_k$ where $\sigma_0, \theta_1, \sigma_1, \ldots, \theta_k, \sigma_k$ are words. A semilinear regular path scheme (SLPS for short) is any finite union of LPS.*

Definition 3.2. *A counter automaton $\mathcal{S}$ (resp. initialized counter automaton $(\mathcal{S}, I)$) is called* globally flat *(resp.* flat*) if there exists an SLPS ρ for $\mathcal{S}$ satisfying $\mathcal{R}^* = \mathcal{R}(\rho)$ (resp. $\mathrm{post}^*(I) = \mathrm{post}(\rho, I)$).*

This *flatness* condition may seem to be a very restrictive property. However, we will later prove that most of the known semilinear classes of counter automata are in fact flat. The following lemma follows from Lemma 4.1 in [LS04], and it will be crucial to prove flatness for several classes of counter automata. Observe that this lemma is not a (direct) consequence of Parikh's Theorem, since we require the SLPS ρ to be a subset of the considered regular language L. Recall that, assuming a linear order $T = \{t_1, \ldots, t_m\}$ on T, the *Parikh map* Ψ is the total mapping from T^* to $\mathbb{N}^m$ defined by $\Psi(\pi) = (|\pi|_{t_1}, \ldots, |\pi|_{t_m})$.

Lemma 3.3. *Given a counter automaton* $\mathcal{S}$, *for any regular language* $L \subseteq \Pi$, *there exists an SLPS* $\rho \subseteq L$ *such that* $\Psi(\rho) = \Psi(L)$.

Accelerated symbolic model-checking consists in the usual iterative fixpoint computation, accelerated with the computation of (the effect of) some loops. In order to cope with the many variants, we analyze termination for generic versions of these accelerated reachability computations. Thus, the semi-algorithms presented below cannot be directly implemented. Effectivity issues will be discussed in Remark 3.5.

Semi-Algorithm `Accel-`$\mathcal{R}^*(\mathcal{S})$	**Semi-Algorithm** `Accel-post`$^*(\mathcal{S}, I)$
Input:	**Input:**
A counter automaton $\mathcal{S}$.	An initialized counter automaton $(\mathcal{S}, I)$.
Output:	**Output:**
The global reachability relation $\mathcal{R}_\mathcal{S}^*$.	The reachability set $\text{post}_\mathcal{S}^*(I)$.
let $R \leftarrow Id_{\mathcal{C}_\mathcal{S}}$	let $X \leftarrow I$
repeat forever	repeat forever
select one of the following tasks:	select one of the following tasks:
• if $\mathcal{R}(T) \cdot R \subseteq R$ return R	• if $\text{post}(T, X) \subseteq X$ return X
• select $\pi \in T^*$ and $R', R'' \subseteq R$	• select $\pi \in T^*$ and $X' \subseteq X$
let $R \leftarrow R \cup (R' \cdot \mathcal{R}(\pi^*) \cdot R'')$	let $X \leftarrow X \cup \text{post}(\pi^*, X')$
• select $t \in T$ and $R', R'' \subseteq R$	• select $t \in T$ and $X' \subseteq X$
let $R \leftarrow R \cup (R' \cdot \mathcal{R}(t) \cdot R'')$	let $X \leftarrow X \cup \text{post}(t, X')$

Theorem 3.4. *Given any counter automaton* $\mathcal{S}$ *and any subset* $I \subseteq \mathcal{C}_\mathcal{S}$, *we have:*

i) *for every terminating execution of* `Accel-`$\mathcal{R}^*(\mathcal{S})$ *(resp.* `Accel-post`$^*(\mathcal{S}, I)$*), the returned value* `ret` *satisfies:* `ret` $= \mathcal{R}_\mathcal{S}^*$ *(resp.* `ret` $= \text{post}_\mathcal{S}^*(I)$*).*

ii) *there exists a terminating execution of* `Accel-`$\mathcal{R}^*(\mathcal{S})$ *(resp.* `Accel-post`$^*(\mathcal{S}, I)$*) iff* $\mathcal{S}$ *is globally flat (resp.* $(\mathcal{S}, I)$ *is flat).*

Remark 3.5. In order to implement these two semi-algorithms, a symbolic representation for sets of (pairs of) configurations is required. Semilinear sets are usually used since (1) they are expressive enough to express most practical flow guards, and (2) they enjoy nice decidability and closure properties. Moreover, effective acceleration results [FL02, CJ98, Boi03] can be used in order to perform the second task of the algorithm (for some classes of semilinear flow guards).

Remark 3.6. Model-checkers FAST, LASH and TREX implement "deterministic refinements" of the semi-algorithms `Accel-post`* and `Accel-`$\mathcal{R}^*$. FAST takes as input an initialized counter automaton in the form of a *finite-linear system*, where flow guards are given by partial integral affine transformations with semilinear definition domains. The heuristics implemented in FAST ensure termination for all flat finite-linear system [FL02].

4   Flat Counter Machines

In the remaining of this paper, we focus on a restricted class of counter automata, called counter machines, where flow guards are restricted semilinear relations given by guarded commands. Counter machines form a fairly large class of counter automata, as it contains for instance Petri nets and Minsky machines. We will show, in this section and in the next section, that many known semilinear subclasses of counter machines are flat.

First, we introduce some new notations that will be used subsequently. Recall that a *minimal element* of a subset $X \subseteq \mathbb{Q}^n$ is any $m \in X$ such that for every $x \in X$, if $x \leq m$ then $x = m$. We denote by $\mathrm{Min}(X)$ the *set of minimal elements* of X. It is well known that any subset of $\mathbb{N}^n$ has finitely many minimal elements [Dic13].

For every $i \in [1 .. n]$, we denote $\mathbf{e}_i$ the ith *basis vector* of $\mathbb{N}^n$ defined by: $\mathbf{e}_i[j] = 1$ if $j = i$ and $\mathbf{e}_i[j] = 0$ otherwise. The set $\{=, \geq\}^n$ will be considered as an alphabet, and every symbol $\# \in \{=, \geq\}^n$ will also denote the partial order on $\mathbb{Q}^n$ defined by: $x \# y$ if $x[i] \#[i] y[i]$ for all $i \in [1 .. n]$.

4.1   Counter Machines

Flow guards of counter machines belong to a basic subclass of semilinear relations, called guarded commands, which we now present. An *n-dim guarded command* is any relation over $\mathbb{N}^n$ that may be written as $\{(x, x') \in \mathbb{N}^{2n} \ / \ x \# \mu \text{ and } x' = x + \delta\}$ for some $\# \in \{=, \geq\}^n$, $\mu \in \mathbb{N}^n$, and $\delta \in \mathbb{Z}^n$ such that $\mu + \delta \geq 0$.

Remark 4.1. The class of n-dim guarded commands is the closure under composition of three kinds of basic relations:

- *increment* of a counter $i \in [1 .. n]$: $\{(x, x') \in \mathbb{N}^{2n} \ / \ x' = x + \mathbf{e}_i\}$
- *decrement* of a counter $i \in [1 .. n]$: $\{(x, x') \in \mathbb{N}^{2n} \ / \ x' = x - \mathbf{e}_i\}$
-     *0-test* of a counter $i \in [1 .. n]$: $\{(x, x') \in \mathbb{N}^{2n} \ / \ x[i] = 0 \text{ and } x' = x\}$

Definition 4.2. *An n-dim counter machine (counter machine for short) is an 8-tuple* $\mathcal{S} = (Q, T, \alpha, \beta, (G_t)_{t \in T}, \#, \mu, \delta)$, *where* $(Q, T, \alpha, \beta, (G_t)_{t \in T})$ *is a counter automaton, and where* $\# : T \rightarrow \{=, \geq\}^n$, $\mu : T \rightarrow \mathbb{N}^n$ *and* $\delta : T \rightarrow \mathbb{Z}^n$ *are three transition labelings satisfying:* $\mu(t) + \delta(t) \geq 0$ *and* $G_t = \{(x, x') \ / \ x \#(t) \mu(t) \text{ and } x' = x + \delta(t)\}$ *for every* $t \in T$.

Transition labelings $\#$, μ and δ will be called *condition labeling*, *min labeling* and *displacement labeling* respectively. We extend the displacement labeling δ to words in the obvious way: $\delta(\varepsilon) = 0$ and $\delta(\pi \cdot t) = \delta(\pi) + \delta(t)$.

When $\#(t) \in \{\geq\}^n$ for every transition $t \in T$, we say that the counter machine $\mathcal{S}$ is *test-free*. The class of test-free counter machines is equivalent to the class of *vector addition systems with states* [HP79].

Obviously, any counter machine may be viewed as a counter automaton. In the following, we will identify a counter machine with its corresponding counter automaton. Observe that for any configurations (q, x) and (q', x') of a counter machine $\mathcal{S}$, and for any word $\pi \in T^*$, we have: $(q, x) \xrightarrow{\pi} (q', x')$ implies $x' = x + \delta(\pi)$.

The following *acceleration theorem* for counter machines, which was actually proved for larger classes of counter automata, shows that the reachability subrelation "along" any SLPS is effectively semilinear. As a direct consequence of this theorem (see for instance [LS04]), we obtain that flatness (resp. global flatness) implies effective semilinearity of the reachability set (resp. of the global reachability relation).

Theorem 4.3 ([CJ98, FL02, Boi03]). *For any SLPS ρ in a counter machine $\mathcal{S}$, the reachability subrelation $\mathcal{R}_\mathcal{S}(\rho)$ is effectively semilinear.*

Corollary 4.4. *The global reachability relation $\mathcal{R}_\mathcal{S}^*$ (resp. reachability set $\mathrm{post}_\mathcal{S}^*(I)$) of any globally flat counter machine $\mathcal{S}$ (resp. flat initialized counter machine $(\mathcal{S}, I)$) is effectively semilinear.*

Our example counter automaton $\mathcal{E}$, which actually is a counter machine, shows that the converse of this corollary does not hold (see also Remark 4.11).

Example 4.5. Recall that the counter automaton $\mathcal{E}$ introduced in Example 2.4 has a semilinear global reachability relation. In particular the reachability set $\mathrm{post}_\mathcal{E}^*(I)$ is semilinear for any semilinear set $I \subseteq \mathcal{C}_\mathcal{E}$. However, $(\mathcal{E}, (q_1, (0, 0)))$ is not flat. Intuitively, any loop $\theta \in T^*$ is either in $l_1^*, l_2^*, l_1^* t_1 T^* t_2 l_1^*$, or in $l_2^* t_2 T^* t_1 l_2^*$. In each case, we can verify that $\mathrm{post}_\mathcal{E}(\theta^*, I)$ is finite for any finite $I \subseteq \mathcal{C}_\mathcal{E}$. An induction over the length of an SLPS ρ, proves that $\mathrm{post}_\mathcal{E}(\theta^*, I)$ is finite for any finite $I \subseteq \mathcal{C}_\mathcal{E}$ and for any SLPS ρ. As the reachability set $\mathrm{post}_\mathcal{E}^*(\{(q_1, (0,0))\}) = \{(q_1, (x, y)) \ / \ x + y \in 2\mathbb{N}\} \cup \{(q_2, (x, y)) \ / \ x + y - 1 \in 2\mathbb{N}\}$ is infinite we deduce that $(\mathcal{E}, (q_1, (0, 0)))$ is not flat.

Remark 4.6. Unfortunately, flatness is undecidable for counter machines. Indeed, the boundedness problem (is $\mathrm{post}_\mathcal{S}^*(\{(q, x_0)\})$ finite?), which is known to be undecidable for 2-dim counter machines, is reducible to the flatness problem as follows: (1) if $(\mathcal{S}, I)$ is flat, then we can compute a semilinear description $\mathrm{post}_\mathcal{S}^*(I)$ and decide whether $\mathrm{post}_\mathcal{S}^*(I)$ is finite ; (2) if $(\mathcal{S}, I)$ is not flat, then $\mathrm{post}_\mathcal{S}^*(\{(q, x_0)\})$ is necessarily infinite.

4.2 Reversal-Bounded Counter Machines

We focus in this subsection on reversal-bounded counter machines. Intuitively, an initialized counter machine $(\mathcal{S}, I)$ will be called reversal-bounded when there exists $r \in \mathbb{N}$ such that every counter in every run of $\mathcal{S}$ from I makes at most r reversals (alternations between nondecreasing and nonincreasing modes) [Iba78]. The definition will be made precise with the use letter morphisms.

Consider a finite set T of transitions and a displacement labeling $\delta : T \to \mathbb{Z}^n$. For every $i \in [1 \mathinner{..} n]$, we define the morphism $\varphi_i^\delta : T^* \to \{+, -\}^*$ by: $\varphi_i^\delta(t) = +$ if $\delta(t)[i] > 0$, $\varphi_i^\delta(t) = -$ if $\delta(t)[i] < 0$, and $\varphi_i^\delta(t) = \varepsilon$ if $\delta(t)[i] = 0$.

Definition 4.7. *An* initialized counter machine $(\mathcal{S}, I)$, *with transition set T and displacement labeling δ, is called* reversal-bounded *if there exists $r \in \mathbb{N}$ such that $\varphi_i^\delta(\pi) \in (\{+\}^* \cup \{-\}^*)^r$ for every $i \in [1 \mathinner{..} n]$ and every trace π of $\mathcal{S}$ from I. A counter machine $\mathcal{S}$ is called* globally reversal-bounded *if $(\mathcal{S}, C_{\mathcal{S}})$ is reversal-bounded.*

Recall that the global reachability relation (resp. reachability set) of any reversal-bounded counter machine (resp. initialized counter machine) is effectively semilinear [Iba78]. We show that these two classes are flat. Note that these results do not follow from the effective semilinearity proof given in [Iba78] which uses Parikh's Theorem and manipulations on semilinear sets.

Proposition 4.8. *Every reversal-bounded initialized counter machine is flat. Every globally reversal-bounded counter machine is globally flat.*

4.3   Lossy/Inserting Counter Machines

Let us now focus on lossy/inserting counter machines. An n-dim counter machine will be called lossy (resp. inserting) when for every location q and for every counter $i \in [1 \mathinner{..} n]$, there is a loop[3] on q whose flow guard is the decrement (resp. increment) of counter i. Formally:

Definition 4.9. *A counter machine $\mathcal{S}$, with location set Q and transition set T, is called* lossy *(resp.* inserting*) if for every $q \in Q$ and for every $i \in [1 \mathinner{..} n]$, there exists a loop π on q such that $G_\pi = \{(\mathsf{x}, \mathsf{x}') \in \mathbb{N}^{2n} \mid \mathsf{x}' = \mathsf{x} - \mathbf{e}_i\}$ (resp. $G_\pi = \{(\mathsf{x}, \mathsf{x}') \in \mathbb{N}^{2n} \mid \mathsf{x}' = \mathsf{x} + \mathbf{e}_i\}$).*

Observe that the inverse of any lossy (resp. inserting) counter machine is an inserting (resp. lossy) counter machine. The reachability set of any initialized lossy (resp. inserting) counter machine is obviously semilinear since it is downward (resp. upward) closed (w.r.t. the usual partial order on configurations of counter automata). Moreover, it is effectively semilinear for any initialized lossy test-free counter machine and for any initialized inserting counter machine [BM99]. We show that these two classes are flat.

Proposition 4.10. *Every initialized lossy test-free counter machine is flat. Every initialized inserting counter machine is flat.*

The previous proposition cannot be extended to global flatness, since there exists a 3-dim lossy test-free counter machine having a non semilinear (and hence non flat) global reachability relation [LS04]. Moreover, the test-freeness condition cannot be relaxed for lossy counter machines, since the semilinear reachability set is not in general constructible for initialized lossy counter machines [DJS99, BM99]. The following remark shows that the test-freeness condition cannot be removed even in dimension 2.

---

[3] We use an explicit representation of losses and insertions. Our flatness results given in Proposition 4.10 also hold when losses and insertions are "hardcoded" in the semantics.

Remark 4.11. Recall that every initialized 2-dim lossy counter machine has an effectively semilinear reachability set [FS00a]. Still, there are initialized 2-dim lossy counter machines that are not flat. Consider for instance our example counter machine $(\mathcal{E}, \{(q_1, (1, 0))\})$, which is not flat according to Example 2.4, augmented with loss loops on each location: the resulting 2-dim lossy counter machine obviously remains non flat.

4.4 Test-Free 2-Dim Counter Machines

We briefly recall in this section known results on test-free 2-dim counter machines. The reachability set of any initialized test-free 2-dim counter machine is effectively semilinear [HP79]. Moreover, the global reachability relation is also effectively semilinear for this class [LS04]. The proof of this second result actually used flatness-based proof techniques:

Proposition 4.12 ([LS04]). *Every test-free 2-dim counter machine is globally flat.*

5 Flat Petri Nets

We now restrict our attention to a well-known and extensively studied subclass of counter machines: Petri nets. Usually, a Petri net is given by a directed graph whose nodes are either places or transitions. We give an equivalent definition in terms of counter machines.

Definition 5.1. *An n-dim Petri net (Petri net for short) is any test-free n-dim counter machine whose location set is a singleton.*

As the set Q of locations in a Petri net is a singleton, we unambiguously denote any configuration (q, x) by x.

5.1 Cyclic and Reversible Petri Nets

We focus in this subsection on two subclasses of Petri nets: *cyclic Petri nets* [AK77] and *reversible Petri nets* [Tai68]. Intuitively, an initialized Petri net will be called cyclic if its reachability set is a strongly connected component ; and a Petri net will be called reversible if every transition has an inverse.

Definition 5.2. *An initialized Petri net* $(\mathcal{S}, I)$ *is called* cyclic *if* $I \subseteq \mathsf{post}^*(X)$ *for every* $X \subseteq \mathsf{post}^*(I)$. *A Petri net* $\mathcal{S}$ *is called* globally cyclic *if* $(\mathcal{S}, \mathsf{x}_0)$ *is cyclic for every* $\mathsf{x}_0 \in \mathcal{C}_{\mathcal{S}}$.

Definition 5.3. *A Petri net with transition set* T *is called* reversible *if for every* $t \in T$, *there exists* $t' \in T$ *such that* $\mathcal{R}(t') = \mathcal{R}(t)^{-1}$.

Observe that a Petri net is globally cyclic iff its global reachability relation is symmetric iff for every transition t, there exists a path π such that $\mathcal{R}(\pi) = \mathcal{R}(t)^{-1}$. Thus, every reversible Petri net is globally cyclic. It is well-known that the global reachability relation (resp. reachability set) of any reversible Petri net (resp. cyclic initialized Petri net) is effectively semilinear [AK77, Tai68, BF97]. We show that these three classes are flat.

Proposition 5.4. *Every cyclic initialized Petri net is flat. Every globally cyclic Petri net is globally flat.*

Remark 5.5. Recall that global flatness implies effective semilinearity of the global reachability relation. Hence, combined with the short proof given in [Hir94] that every congruence on $\mathbb{N}^n$ is semilinear, the previous proposition gives an easy proof of effective semilinearity of $\mathcal{R}^*$ for reversible petri nets. The first proof (and only proof, to our knowledge) of this result is presented in [Tai68] and it is very difficult to read.

5.2   Regular Petri Nets

We now turn our attention to the class of regular Petri nets [VVN81]. Recall that the trace set of an initialized Petri net $(\mathcal{S}, I)$ is the set of all paths $\pi \in T^*$ such that $\mathrm{post}(\pi, I) \neq \emptyset$.

Definition 5.6. *An initialized Petri net is called* regular *if its trace set is a regular language.*

A *singly-initialized Petri net* is any initialized Petri net $(\mathcal{S}, I)$ where I is a singleton. It follows from Parikh's Theorem that the reachability set of any regular singly-initialized Petri net is effectively semilinear [VVN81]. We deduce from Lemma 3.3, which is a variant of Parikh's Theorem, that this class is actually flat.

Proposition 5.7. *Every regular singly-initialized Petri net is flat.*

5.3   Persistent and Conflict-Free Petri Nets

Persistent and Conflict-free Petri nets are among the first subclasses of Petri nets introduced in the literature. Intuitively, a Petri net is conflict-free if every "enabled" transition remains enabled until it is taken. For persistent Petri nets, this condition only has to hold for reachable configurations.

Definition 5.8. *An initialized Petri net $(\mathcal{S}, I)$ is called* persistent *if for any transitions t_1, t_2 with $t_1 \neq t_2$, and for any $x, x_1, x_2 \in \mathrm{post}_\mathcal{S}^*(I)$ such that $x \xrightarrow{t_1} x_1$ and $x \xrightarrow{t_2} x_2$, there exists $x' \in \mathrm{post}_\mathcal{S}^*(I)$ such that $x \xrightarrow{t_1 t_2} x'$.*

Definition 5.9. *A Petri net $\mathcal{S}$ is called* conflict-free *if $(\mathcal{S}, \mathcal{C}_\mathcal{S})$ is persistent.*

Semilinearity of the reachability set for singly-initialized persistent Petri nets was first proved in [LR78] in a non-constructive way, and a constructive proof was later presented in [May81]. It turns out that flatness, and hence effective semilinearity, can actually be deduced from the first proof. Let us first recall two lemmas from [LR78]: a weaker version of Lemma 3.1 and Lemma 4.3.

Lemma 5.10. *Given any singly-initialized persistent Petri net $(\mathcal{S}, \{x_0\})$, for any two traces σ_1 and σ_2 with $\Psi(\sigma_1) \leq \Psi(\sigma_2)$, there exists a path σ' such that $\sigma_1 \sigma'$ is a trace and $\Psi(\sigma_2) = \Psi(\sigma_1) + \Psi(\sigma')$.*

Lemma 5.11. *For any singly-initialized persistent Petri net* $(\mathcal{S}, \{x_0\})$, *there exists a finite set* F *of paths* $\pi \in T^+$ *with* $\delta(\pi) \geq 0$ *such that for every* $x_0 \xrightarrow{*} x \xrightarrow{*} x'$, *if* $x \leq x'$ *then there exists* $\pi_1, \ldots, \pi_k \in F$ *such that* $x \xrightarrow{\pi_1 \cdots \pi_k} x'$.

Following the proof given in [LR78] that singly-initialized persistent Petri nets have semilinear reachability sets, we deduce the following theorem.

Theorem 5.12. *Every semilinearly-initialized persistent Petri net is flat.*

Corollary 5.13. *Every conflict-free Petri net is globally flat.*

Remark 5.14. Recall that global flatness implies effective semilinearity of the global reachability relation. Hence, the we obtain that the global reachability relation is effectively semilinear for conflict-free Petri nets.

5.4   BPP-Nets

We briefly recall in this section known results on BPP-nets. An n-dim Petri net, with transition set T and min labeling μ, is called a *BPP-net* if for every $t \in T$, $\mu(t) = \mathbf{e}_i$ for some $i \in [1 .. n]$.

Let us recall that the global reachability relation is effectively semilinear for BPP-nets [Esp97, FO97]. The proof of this result given in [FO97] actually uses flatness-based proof techniques:

Proposition 5.15 ([FO97]). *Every BPP-net is globally flat.*

References

[ABS01]   A. Annichini, A. Bouajjani, and M. Sighireanu. TReX: A tool for reachability analysis of complex systems. In *Proc. 13th Int. Conf. Computer Aided Verification (CAV'2001), Paris, France, July 2001*, volume 2102 of *Lecture Notes in Computer Science*, pages 368–372. Springer, 2001.

[AK77]   T. Araki and T. Kasami. Decidable problems on the strong connectivity of Petri net reachability sets. *Theoretical Computer Science*, 4(1):99–119, 1977.

[BF97]   Z. Bouziane and A. Finkel. Cyclic petri net reachability sets are semi-linear effectively constructible. In *Proc. 2nd Int. Workshop on Verification of Infinite State Systems (INFINITY'97), Bologna, Italy, July 1997*, volume 9 of *Electronic Notes in Theor. Comp. Sci.* Elsevier, 1997.

[BFLP03]   S. Bardin, A. Finkel, J. Leroux, and L. Petrucci. FAST: Fast Acceleration of Symbolic Transition systems. In *Proc. 15th Int. Conf. Computer Aided Verification (CAV'2003), Boulder, CO, USA, July 2003*, volume 2725 of *Lecture Notes in Computer Science*, pages 118–121. Springer, 2003.

[BGWW97]   B. Boigelot, P. Godefroid, B. Willems, and P. Wolper. The power of QDDs. In *Proc. Static Analysis 4th Int. Symp. (SAS'97), Paris, France, Sep. 1997*, volume 1302 of *Lecture Notes in Computer Science*, pages 172–186. Springer, 1997.

[BH99]   A. Bouajjani and P. Habermehl. Symbolic reachability analysis of FIFO-channel systems with nonregular sets of configurations. *Theoretical Computer Science*, 221(1–2):211–250, 1999.

[BM99]   A. Bouajjani and R. Mayr. Model checking lossy vector addition systems. In *Proc. 16th Ann. Symp. Theoretical Aspects of Computer Science (STACS'99), Trier, Germany, Mar. 1999*, volume 1563 of *Lecture Notes in Computer Science*, pages 323–333. Springer, 1999.

[Boi03]   B. Boigelot. On iterating linear transformations over recognizable sets of integers. *Theoretical Computer Science*, 309(2):413–468, 2003.

[BW94]   B. Boigelot and P. Wolper. Symbolic verification with periodic sets. In *Proc. 6th Int. Conf. Computer Aided Verification (CAV'94), Stanford, CA, USA, June 1994*, volume 818 of *Lecture Notes in Computer Science*, pages 55–67. Springer, 1994.

[CJ98]   H. Comon and Y. Jurski. Multiple counters automata, safety analysis and Presburger arithmetic. In *Proc. 10th Int. Conf. Computer Aided Verification (CAV'98), Vancouver, BC, Canada, June-July 1998*, volume 1427 of *Lecture Notes in Computer Science*, pages 268–279. Springer, 1998.

[Dic13]   L. E. Dickson. Finiteness of the odd perfect and primitive abundant numbers with r distinct prime factors. *Amer. Journal Math.*, 35:413–422, 1913.

[DJS99]   C. Dufourd, P. Jančar, and Ph. Schnoebelen. Boundedness of Reset P/T nets. In *Proc. 26th Int. Coll. Automata, Languages, and Programming (ICALP'99), Prague, Czech Republic, July 1999*, volume 1644 of *Lecture Notes in Computer Science*, pages 301–310. Springer, 1999.

[Esp97]   J. Esparza. Petri nets, commutative context-free grammars, and basic parallel processes. *Fundamenta Informaticae*, 31(1):13–25, 1997.

[FIS03]   A. Finkel, S. P. Iyer, and G. Sutre. Well-abstracted transition systems: Application to FIFO automata. *Information and Computation*, 181(1):1–31, 2003.

[FL02]   A. Finkel and J. Leroux. How to compose Presburger-accelerations: Applications to broadcast protocols. In *Proc. 22nd Conf. Found. of Software Technology and Theor. Comp. Sci. (FST&TCS'2002), Kanpur, India, Dec. 2002*, volume 2556 of *Lecture Notes in Computer Science*, pages 145–156. Springer, 2002.

[FO97]   L. Fribourg and H. Olsén. A decompositional approach for computing least fixed-points of Datalog programs with Z-counters. *Constraints*, 2(3/4):305–335, 1997.

[FS00a]   A. Finkel and G. Sutre. An algorithm constructing the semilinear $post^*$ for 2-dim reset/transfer vass. In *Proc. 25th Int. Symp. Math. Found. Comp. Sci. (MFCS'2000), Bratislava, Slovakia, Aug. 2000*, volume 1893 of *Lecture Notes in Computer Science*, pages 353–362. Springer, 2000.

[FS00b]   A. Finkel and G. Sutre. Decidability of reachability problems for classes of two counters automata. In *Proc. 17th Ann. Symp. Theoretical Aspects of Computer Science (STACS'2000), Lille, France, Feb. 2000*, volume 1770 of *Lecture Notes in Computer Science*, pages 346–357. Springer, 2000.

[GS66]   S. Ginsburg and E. H. Spanier. Semigroups, Presburger formulas and languages. *Pacific J. Math.*, 16(2):285–296, 1966.

[Hir94]   Y. Hirshfeld. Congruences in commutative semigroups. Research report ECS-LFCS-94-291, Laboratory for Foundations of Computer Science, University of Edinburgh, UK, 1994.

[HP79]   J. E. Hopcroft and J.-J. Pansiot. On the reachability problem for 5-dimensional vector addition systems. *Theoretical Computer Science*, 8(2):135–159, 1979.

[Iba78]   O.H. Ibarra. Reversal-bounded multicounter machines and their decision problems. *Journal of the ACM*, 25(1):116–133, 1978.

[Kos82]   S. R. Kosaraju. Decidability of reachability in vector addition systems. In *Proc. 14th ACM Symp. Theory of Computing (STOC'82), San Francisco, CA, May 1982*, pages 267–281, 1982.

[Las]   LASH homepage. http://www.montefiore.ulg.ac.be/~boigelot/research/lash/.

[Lat04]   L. Latour. From automata to formulas: Convex integer polyhedra. In *Proc. 19th Annual IEEE Symposium on Logic in Computer Science (LICS'04), Turku, Finland July 2004*, pages 120–129. IEEE Comp. Soc. Press, 2004.

[LR78]   L.H. Landweber and E.L. Robertson. Properties of conflict-free and persistent petri nets. *Journal of the ACM*, 25(3):352–364, 1978.

[LS04]   J. Leroux and G. Sutre. On flatness for 2-dimensional vector addition systems with states. In *Proc. 15th Int. Conf. Concurrency Theory (CONCUR'04), London, UK, Aug.-Sep. 2004*, volume 3170 of *Lecture Notes in Computer Science*, pages 402–416. Springer, 2004.

[May81]   E. W. Mayr. Persistence of vector replacement systems is decidable. *Acta Informatica*, 15:309–318, 1981.

[May84]   E. W. Mayr. An algorithm for the general Petri net reachability problem. *SIAM J. Comput.*, 13(3):441–460, 1984.

[Min67]   M. L. Minsky. *Computation: Finite and Infinite Machines*. Prentice Hall, London, 1 edition, 1967.

[Tai68]   M.A. Taiclin. Algorithmic problems for commutative semigroups. *Soviet Math. Doklady*, 9(1):201–204, 1968.

[VVN81]   R. Valk and G. Vidal-Naquet. Petri nets and regular languages. *Journal of Computer and System Sciences*, 23(3):299–325, 1981.

Author Index

Lecture Notes in Computer Science

For information about Vols. 1–3629

please contact your bookseller or Springer

Vol. 3677: J. Dittmann, S. Katzenbeisser, A. Uhl (Eds.), Communications and Multimedia Security. XIII, 360 pages. 2005.

Vol. 3676: R. Glück, M. Lowry (Eds.), Generative Programming and Component Engineering. XI, 448 pages. 2005.

Vol. 3675: Y. Luo (Ed.), Cooperative Design, Visualization, and Engineering. XI, 264 pages. 2005.

Vol. 3674: W. Jonker, M. Petković (Eds.), Secure Data Management. X, 241 pages. 2005.

Vol. 3673: S. Bandini, S. Manzoni (Eds.), AI*IA 2005: Advances in Artificial Intelligence. XIV, 614 pages. 2005. (Subseries LNAI).

Vol. 3672: C. Hankin, I. Siveroni (Eds.), Static Analysis. X, 369 pages. 2005.

Vol. 3671: S. Bressan, S. Ceri, E. Hunt, Z.G. Ives, Z. Bellahsène, M. Rys, R. Unland (Eds.), Database and XML Technologies. X, 239 pages. 2005.

Vol. 3670: M. Bravetti, L. Kloul, G. Zavattaro (Eds.), Formal Techniques for Computer Systems and Business Processes. XIII, 349 pages. 2005.

Vol. 3669: G.S. Brodal, S. Leonardi (Eds.), Algorithms – ESA 2005. XVIII, 901 pages. 2005.

Vol. 3668: M. Gabbrielli, G. Gupta (Eds.), Logic Programming. XIV, 454 pages. 2005.

Vol. 3666: B.D. Martino, D. Kranzlmüller, J. Dongarra (Eds.), Recent Advances in Parallel Virtual Machine and Message Passing Interface. XVII, 546 pages. 2005.

Vol. 3665: K. S. Candan, A. Celentano (Eds.), Advances in Multimedia Information Systems. X, 221 pages. 2005.

Vol. 3664: C. Türker, M. Agosti, H.-J. Schek (Eds.), Peer-to-Peer, Grid, and Service-Orientation in Digital Library Architectures. X, 261 pages. 2005.

Vol. 3663: W.G. Kropatsch, R. Sablatnig, A. Hanbury (Eds.), Pattern Recognition. XIV, 512 pages. 2005.

Vol. 3662: C. Baral, G. Greco, N. Leone, G. Terracina (Eds.), Logic Programming and Nonmonotonic Reasoning. XIII, 454 pages. 2005. (Subseries LNAI).

Vol. 3661: T. Panayiotopoulos, J. Gratch, R. Aylett, D. Ballin, P. Olivier, T. Rist (Eds.), Intelligent Virtual Agents. XIII, 506 pages. 2005. (Subseries LNAI).

Vol. 3660: M. Beigl, S. Intille, J. Rekimoto, H. Tokuda (Eds.), UbiComp 2005: Ubiquitous Computing. XVII, 394 pages. 2005.

Vol. 3659: J.R. Rao, B. Sunar (Eds.), Cryptographic Hardware and Embedded Systems – CHES 2005. XIV, 458 pages. 2005.

Vol. 3658: V. Matoušek, P. Mautner, T. Pavelka (Eds.), Text, Speech and Dialogue. XV, 460 pages. 2005. (Subseries LNAI).

Vol. 3657: F.S. de Boer, M.M. Bonsangue, S. Graf, W.-P. de Roever (Eds.), Formal Methods for Components and Objects. VIII, 325 pages. 2005.

Vol. 3656: M. Kamel, A. Campilho (Eds.), Image Analysis and Recognition. XXIV, 1279 pages. 2005.

Vol. 3655: A. Aldini, R. Gorrieri, F. Martinelli (Eds.), Foundations of Security Analysis and Design III. VII, 273 pages. 2005.

Vol. 3654: S. Jajodia, D. Wijesekera (Eds.), Data and Applications Security XIX. X, 353 pages. 2005.

Vol. 3653: M. Abadi, L. de Alfaro (Eds.), CONCUR 2005 – Concurrency Theory. XIV, 578 pages. 2005.

Vol. 3652: A. Rauber, S. Christodoulakis, A M. Tjoa (Eds.), Research and Advanced Technology for Digital Libraries. XVIII, 545 pages. 2005.

Vol. 3651: R. Dale, K.-F. Wong, J. Su, O.Y. Kwong (Eds.), Natural Language Processing – IJCNLP 2005. XXI, 1031 pages. 2005.

Vol. 3650: J. Zhou, J. Lopez, R.H. Deng, F. Bao (Eds.), Information Security. XII, 516 pages. 2005.

Vol. 3649: W.M. P. van der Aalst, B. Benatallah, F. Casati, F. Curbera (Eds.), Business Process Management. XII, 472 pages. 2005.

Vol. 3648: J.C. Cunha, P.D. Medeiros (Eds.), Euro-Par 2005 Parallel Processing. XXXVI, 1299 pages. 2005.

Vol. 3646: A. F. Famili, J.N. Kok, J.M. Peña, A. Siebes, A. Feelders (Eds.), Advances in Intelligent Data Analysis VI. XIV, 522 pages. 2005.

Vol. 3645: D.-S. Huang, X.-P. Zhang, G.-B. Huang (Eds.), Advances in Intelligent Computing, Part II. XIII, 1010 pages. 2005.

Vol. 3644: D.-S. Huang, X.-P. Zhang, G.-B. Huang (Eds.), Advances in Intelligent Computing, Part I. XXVII, 1101 pages. 2005.

Vol. 3643: R. Moreno Díaz, F. Pichler, A. Quesada Arencibia (Eds.), Computer Aided Systems Theory – EURO-CAST 2005. XIV, 629 pages. 2005.

Vol. 3642: D. Ślezak, J. Yao, J.F. Peters, W. Ziarko, X. Hu (Eds.), Rough Sets, Fuzzy Sets, Data Mining, and Granular Computing, Part II. XXIII, 738 pages. 2005. (Subseries LNAI).

Vol. 3641: D. Ślezak, G. Wang, M. Szczuka, I. Düntsch, Y. Yao (Eds.), Rough Sets, Fuzzy Sets, Data Mining, and Granular Computing, Part I. XXIV, 742 pages. 2005. (Subseries LNAI).

Vol. 3639: P. Godefroid (Ed.), Model Checking Software. XI, 289 pages. 2005.

Vol. 3638: A. Butz, B. Fisher, A. Krüger, P. Olivier (Eds.), Smart Graphics. XI, 269 pages. 2005.

Vol. 3637: J. M. Moreno, J. Madrenas, J. Cosp (Eds.), Evolvable Systems: From Biology to Hardware. XI, 227 pages. 2005.

Vol. 3636: M.J. Blesa, C. Blum, A. Roli, M. Sampels (Eds.), Hybrid Metaheuristics. XII, 155 pages. 2005.

Vol. 3634: L. Ong (Ed.), Computer Science Logic. XI, 567 pages. 2005.

Vol. 3633: C. Bauzer Medeiros, M. Egenhofer, E. Bertino (Eds.), Advances in Spatial and Temporal Databases. XIII, 433 pages. 2005.

Vol. 3632: R. Nieuwenhuis (Ed.), Automated Deduction – CADE-20. XIII, 459 pages. 2005. (Subseries LNAI).

Vol. 3631: J. Eder, H.-M. Haav, A. Kalja, J. Penjam (Eds.), Advances in Databases and Information Systems. XIII, 393 pages. 2005.

Vol. 3630: M.S. Capcarrere, A.A. Freitas, P.J. Bentley, C.G. Johnson, J. Timmis (Eds.), Advances in Artificial Life. XIX, 949 pages. 2005. (Subseries LNAI).